UNIX Made Easy

Unix and Linux Basics & Beyond

Third Edition

JOHN MUSTER

McGraw-Hill Osborne

New York / Chicago / San Francisco
Lisbon / London / Madrid / Mexico City / Milan
New Delhi / San Juan / Seoul / Singapore / Sydney / Toronto

McGraw-Hill/Osborne
2600 Tenth Street
Berkeley, California 94710
U.S.A.

To arrange bulk purchase discounts for sales promotions, premiums, or fund-raisers, please contact **McGraw-Hill**/Osborne at the above address. For information on translations or book distributors outside the U.S.A., please see the International Contact Information page immediately following the index of this book.

UNIX Made Easy: UNIX and Linux Basics & Beyond, Third Edition

234567890 DOC DOC 019876543

ISBN 0-07-219314-X

Publisher.
Brandon A. Nordin

Vice President & Associate Publisher
Scott Rogers

Acquisitions Editor
Francis Kelly

Project Editor
LeeAnn Pickrell

Acquisitions Coordinator
Emma Acker

MLA Project Director
Nate Hinerman

MLA Illustrator
Issac Chellin

MLA Technical Reviewer
Marcelo Carvalho

Technical Editor
Narender Reddy

Copy Editor
Jan Jue

Proofreader
Susie Elkind

Indexer
Karin Arrigoni

Computer Designers
Mickey Galicia, Lauren McCarthy

Illustrators
Lyssa Wald, George T. Charbak

Series Design
Peter F. Hancik

Cover design
Jeff Weeks

This book was composed with Corel VENTURA™ Publisher.

If you want to become a skilled UNIX/Linux professional and are willing to work carefully through the following exercises, this book was written for you in the hope that you enjoy successfully teaching yourself UNIX/Linux.

John Muster
Berkeley, CA 2002

About the Author

Students consistently report that John Muster obviously loves teaching. Helping students learn is at the center of his work. He facilitates learning—in the classroom, in the Teacher Education Seminar, in the books and media he develops, and in the programs he supports. His scientific work began in astronomy and now focuses on how people learn complex skills or content, and how to develop materials, exercises, events, problems, and ways of guiding students that support their growth and success. John Muster teaches and conducts educational development at the educational center of Silicon Valley and the University of California's Extension Division, where he was given the Honored Teacher Award. In addition to teaching and multimedia development, he consults and teaches for clients in industry, government, and universities across the globe. His undergraduate and graduate education took place at Otterbein College, The Ohio State University, and the University of California, Berkeley.

Contents

Part II
Programming in the Shell with Power Utilities

Acknowledgments

For more than 20 years I have thoroughly enjoyed writing, teaching UNIX/Linux, listening to students' questions and suggestions, solving problems, consulting, revising the chapters, teaching, revising…. The evolution of these exercises was possible because I have had the good fortune to be engaged with committed students at the University of California and at corporate education facilities around the world. Thank you for your challenges, comments, and ideas.

Nate Hinerman demonstrated that a remarkably competent project director could facilitate teamwork, mutual support, and unexpected productivity. Isaac Chellin brought gifted artistic talent, cutting-edge technical skills, and a cooperative design approach to the development of both the illustrations and the related web pages. Marcelo Carvalho was tireless in his testing, evaluating, and checking of the materials.

From my earliest days, I have enjoyed watching the lights go on as people make sense out of what they are studying. Through the years of physics and computer science education I have enjoyed interacting with committed colleagues who have shared that same joy—and have affected how this book works. Thank you Phil Barnhart, Lelia Braucher, Catherine Cavette, Marjorie Conrad, John Coulter, Lillian Frank, Peter Kindfield, John Laubach, Albert Levy, Mama McKinney, Mel Mayfield, James Miller, Walter Mitchell, Catherine M. Muster, John T. Muster, Nate Hinerman, Bob Place, Siggy Selquist, Lyle Strand, and David Waas.

In the last analysis, it's the relationships. Catherine, Cassy, extended family, dear friends: thank you for the support, encouragement, and affection.

About This Book

If you want to know general facts about Mount Everest, get a good reference book or encyclopedia. If you want to really experience Mount Everest, find a good guide, an experienced Sherpa to lead you through all the right steps to the summit.

This book is a Sherpa, not a reference text. Although command summaries and tables are included, this book is fundamentally a guide designed to help people really learn the skills needed to master the UNIX/Linux environment. Through carefully developed, hands-on interactions with a UNIX/Linux system, you are guided through a grand, stimulating journey from the absolutely basic system features to a rich mastery of the details employed by experts.

If you are looking for a quick reference text, put this book back on the shelf. There are many good reference texts available. This book stands alone. It is a learning guide. It is a Sherpa.

Introduction

Teach Yourself with UNIX Made Easy

The title of this book is not the ultimate oxymoron. Learning UNIX can be reasonably easy—if you approach it the same way you learned to ride a bicycle. Remember how your parents set up the overhead projector in the living room and showed you 50 minutes worth of slides in rapid succession, explaining the intricacies of micro-human bicycle propulsion? No, and you did not learn how to ride your bike by reading the manual either.

You got on your bike. Someone steadied it and at the precise moment that it was needed, gave you the specific, appropriate information that supported your mastering the needed skills: turn the handlebars this way; to stop, just start peddling backwards; lean into the curve; avoid that rock...

The same is true as you master UNIX/Linux skills using *UNIX Made Easy*.

Get on to a UNIX system. Start at the beginning of the first chapter and start peddling. The key is to actually do each exercise on a live UNIX/Linux system so you can see how it responds and exactly what you must do to get results. As you work through the chapters of this book, you enter commands, read about what is happening, and enter more commands. Instructions in the chapters guide you carefully from the most tentative, initial steps; to exploring the essential features; to mastery of basic and advanced user and programming skills.

Each step is specified; the implications are discussed as you investigate each feature.

This book can be your UNIX tutor—your Sherpa—as you climb and teach yourself UNIX.

If you're an experienced user, start at the beginning and quickly pass through a topic if you have done it several times before. Create all files as instructed because they are needed in later exercises. Wade in until you are in deep enough to swim, then carefully do each exercise. Most people, unless they are very experienced, find new skills even in the first chapters.

After the basic skills are mastered, you explore more complex features built on the basics. You carefully construct your knowledge of UNIX, adding each piece as it is appropriate.

When you are asked to enter a command, the instruction step is numbered.

Explanations generally *follow* the keyboard exercise. If results are puzzling, read on.

UNIX is a collection of powerful programs, the foundation for modern operating systems, the ultimate user-hostile interface, a Tinkertoy for adults, a fascinating and enjoyable programming environment...

Log on and let us guide you as you have fun and teach yourself UNIX/Linux.

Mastering Essential UNIX/Linux

1

Accessing the System Using Graphical Desktops

S K I L L S   C H E C K

Before beginning this chapter, you should

- Have access to a UNIX or Linux system
- Have the login name and password for your account
- Be able to use a keyboard

O B J E C T I V E S

After completing this chapter, you will be able to

- Log onto a UNIX/Linux system
- Exit from a session

If you have the graphical interface available after you log in, you will also be able to:

- Identify and use the default desktop icons
- Start a terminal window
- Choose programs and manage desktop operations from the Task bar
- Access the Internet from the graphical user interface (GUI) desktop

The goals for this first chapter are to provide guidance so that you can log onto your account on the system, access a character-based terminal or terminal window, navigate through the major features of the graphical desktop if you have access to one, and log off the system. The exploration of the standard features of Linux/UNIX begins with Chapter 2, "Touring the Features of UNIX/Linux," where you will take a complete tour of the essentials. Chapter 3, "Editing with the Visual Editor," will explore nearly all aspects of the visual editor; in Chapter 4, "Using Basic UNIX Utilities," you employ powerful utilities or programs, and so on. But first, we will examine the essential skills of logging on, accessing a terminal, using the graphical desktop, and logging off.

1.1 Establishing Communication with UNIX/Linux

This initial section guides you through the steps needed to establish communication with a UNIX/Linux system: *logging on.* Because many system administrators modify the login process to fit local needs, the steps listed here may not exactly match your situation. If you run into trouble, first make certain you entered the information correctly, then locate an accomplished user to show you how to get onto the system. Once you are logged on, the differences among systems largely melt away.

Obtaining What You Need to Log On

The UNIX computing environment is designed to serve many users at the same time. When the system's administrator adds a user to a system, an *account* associated with a *login* name is created. Usually, an initial *password* is also added. To gain access to the system, a user must specify the correct account (login name) and provide the appropriate password. If the user enters either a login or password that does not match what is recorded in the system files, access is denied.

If you are on a stand-alone system and were given the information to log on using an account named *root*, you need to create a regular user account.

> **C A U T I O N :** The account named **root** is the account used to administer the system. Because this account carries substantial authority over system events and operations, you can hurt/destroy a system by issuing the wrong commands. It is unwise to use the root account except for specific tasks, and then only very carefully.

Creating a User Account as Superuser

If you have a regular user login and password, with a name other than *root*, skip this section and go on to the next.

If you have access to the superuser *root* account and were *not* given a regular user account name and password, then you must use the *root* account to create a regular user account for yourself. Be careful out there.

Depending on the version of Linux you are running, steps in creating a new user account may vary. In fact, they may very widely. If the following steps do not work, consult the user manual that came with your system for the correct procedures.

1. Log in as *root* on your Linux system and provide the correct password.
2. At the # prompt, enter the following, using whatever lowercase *login-name* you want to call your account:

   In most Red Hat environments:

   > **adduser** *login-name*

   In most SuSE environments:

   > **useradd -m** *login-name*

   For instance, **adduser** *cassy* creates a user account named *cassy* in Red Hat. And, **useradd -m** *cassy* does the same in SuSE environments.

   The next command will add a password for the new account.

   You must enter the command **passwd** followed by a space and then the *login-name* of the new account you just created. It is critically important to properly include your account name.
3. Enter:

   > **passwd** *login-name*

   For instance, **passwd** *cassy* starts the process of adding a password to the *cassy* account.

4. Enter a new password for your account that includes a number and is not based on a word.

5. When asked, enter the password again.

   If the two passwords you enter do not match, the program will announce that it failed, and you will either be given a chance to try again, or you will have to start over with the **passwd** *login-name* command.

   Congratulations! You have created a new account on your Linux system.

6. Log out of the root account by typing:

   exit

7. Log on as the regular user *login-name* that you just created by completing the steps in the next section.

Logging Onto the System

For security reasons, entry to Linux/UNIX is granted when a user provides a *login-name* and password that match an established user on the system.

Identifying the User Account

You are greeted with the login banner. It appears either in a graphical box in the center of the screen or in plain type at the top-left of the screen:

```
login:
```

1. Identify yourself by specifying the name of your account, your *login*. On most systems, the login must be entered in lowercase letters.

2. After entering the exact account information, press ENTER.

Providing the Password

Whether or not you entered the login correctly, most installations require a password, and the following prompt for password is displayed:

```
Password:
```

1. Enter your password exactly as you created it, or as it was provided to you.

   For security reasons, as you type your password, it is not displayed on the screen. Usually there is no confirmation that you are entering anything.

2. When you have entered your password, press ENTER.

If you provided a corresponding set of login and password entries, you are moved on to the next step. However, if either the login or password you supplied was incorrect, an error message appears, such as:

```
Login incorrect
```

Following are some common mistakes made when entering either the login or password that result in an incorrect login:

- Users confuse the numeral *1* and the letter *l* ("el"), or confuse the numeral *0* (zero) and the letter *O* ("oh").
- Users make simple typing mistakes.
- Users employ the BACKSPACE to correct an error. (Although many modern systems permit making corrections, many others do not.)
- Users type in uppercase letters.
- The information is wrong.

3. If you think you made an error in typing, reenter the login and password.
4. If your error was that you used uppercase to type something, the computer is now treating your terminal as a teletype device, old machines that only used uppercase letters. When UNIX starts communicating only in CAPS, most ordinary terminals display a backslash (\) in front of the uppercase letters. If that is the case, you can end the login program and start over.
5. Hold down the CTRL key and press D once.

   This terminates the login program. Another instance of the program immediately starts up, displaying a new login banner so you can start over.

Beginning a New Session

When you log onto the system, you have started a *session*. At this point, you are logged on and either:

- You are presented with a full graphical environment, probably complete with a menu bar at the top, some icons on the screen, and a control bar at the bottom.

Or:

- You are given a character-based terminal window with a prompt such as $ or % or *SystemName* $.

Linux and UNIX provide both environments. The remaining exercises in the following chapters explore how the system works by issuing commands in a terminal. As you will soon see, if you are in the graphical world, you can start a terminal window that works just as well as a character-based terminal.

The graphical desktop is great fun and provides some powerful tools. Much of this first chapter is an exploration of the graphical desktop's functionality.

If you are presented with a terminal window at login, often you can still start the graphical environment.

Starting a Graphical Windows Environment from a Terminal

If you log onto your system and a terminal window is started without a graphical environment, you can probably start the needed programs.

1. At a command prompt of the terminal window, you need to do one of the following:

   In UNIX environments, enter:

   > **xinit &**

   Or in Linux, enter:

   > **startx**

   The **xinit** command starts the fundamental graphics program, known as an X Window, which will run any one of several graphical desktop applications. It may read a configuration file and start other programs; it may allow you to specify which you would like to run.

   The **startx** command also starts the fundamental programs, and it then launches your account's default windowing system.

> **N O T E :** If neither command works, you probably do not have access to the graphical environment. Skip forward to the section "Starting Additional Linux Terminal Sessions," complete that section, and then go on to Chapter 2.

Launching the Desktop Environment

After you have started an X Window session using the **xinit** command, you may get a very plain screen. If so, you should choose which graphical interface you want to execute. Usually, several are available. If one of the following is not successful, ask another user or the system administrator.

1. Enter:

   gnome &

   If you receive an error message when you type **gnome &**, you may not have this particular graphical interface. If so, enter:

   kde &

   This command tells the X window system to run the Komon Desktop Environment (KDE).

   Or enter:

   mwm &

   which starts the Motif Window Manager.

   Or enter:

   blackbox &

   Blackbox is a very efficient, relatively small desktop program.

Starting Additional Linux Terminal Sessions

We can have multiple active sessions at the same time. For example, in UNIX we can log on from several terminals connected to the same system. These different sessions all belong to you, but are independent of one another. In Linux or UNIX, you can have many active sessions on the same machine. In Linux, one monitor and keyboard can be used for multiple login sessions.

Once you are logged onto your Linux machine, in graphical or terminal mode, you can access other virtual terminals.

1. Press:

   CTRL-ALT-F2

   (While holding down the CTRL key and the ALT key, press the F2 key.)
   A new logon screen appears.
2. Log on again at this prompt.

   You are given a new shell prompt.
3. Type the following:

   who

and press ENTER.

By entering the command **who**, you are requesting that the **who** program be executed. The **who** program lists current users and you are listed twice. You are logged on through the initial terminal and again through a virtual terminal, *F2*.

4. Press:

   CTRL-ALT-F3

   A new logon prompt appears again.

5. Log on again.

Exiting a Virtual Terminal

1. Enter:

   exit

   The **exit** command ends the login session in this virtual terminal; it does not log you off of others.

In Linux environments, we can press CTRL-ALT-F2, CTRL-ALT-F3, CTRL-ALT-F4, through CTRL-ALT-F7 (sometimes CTRL-ALT-F8) and create seven (sometimes eight) independent sessions on the same computer. If you log into a terminal window, it is probably terminal *F1*.

Locating the Graphical Virtual Terminal

If you log on and are placed in the graphical environment, it is using virtual terminal *F7* or *F8*. You can toggle back and forth between active sessions by using the CTRL-ALT-F3 command.

1. Press:

   CTRL-ALT-F7

   If you started a graphical desktop, this is where it is usually located, although it may be at F8.

2. If you logged on into a terminal, return to it, probably with:

   CTRL-ALT-F1

Ending a Terminal Login Session

If you do not have access to a graphical environment, the remainder of this chapter is of little value. Fortunately, the rest of the book explores the system by issuing commands to a terminal or terminal window rather than employing the graphical windows. If you do not have the graphical programs, you should log out and start Chapter 2.

To end a nongraphical session, for example, a session at CTRL-ALT-F2, you must be at the CTRL-ALT-F2 terminal and then type the following at the command-line prompt:

exit

or

logout

1. If you are logged on through a graphical environment, return there. Enter:
   CTRL-ALT-F7   (OR CTRL-ALT-F8)

1.2 Exploring the Graphical Desktop Environment

There are many graphical user interfaces available for UNIX and Linux. Two of the most popular are GNOME (GNU Network Object Model Environment) and KDE (Komon Desktop Environment). At least one of these two graphical desktops is available in nearly every Linux version. They can also be downloaded for free from **www.gnome.org** and **www.kde.org**.

The following exercises introduce you to the major features of gnome and KDE. Because there are many variations among the various GUIs, providing exact step sequences that will work in the wide variety of GUI environments is impossible. This exploration of the major desktop environments describes the central features. You will probably need to explore a bit to locate some of the applications.

Your GUI probably appears similar to the desktop shown in Figure 1-1.

The GUI interface usually consists of four parts: a desktop, which covers most of the screen; various icons sprinkled about the area; a Task bar or Dashboard at the bottom; and possibly a bar of menus at the top.

Navigating the Task Bar

The Task bar usually appears by default at the bottom of the desktop. In the GNOME interface, various buttons, such as *Main Menu, Terminal Emulator, Help,*

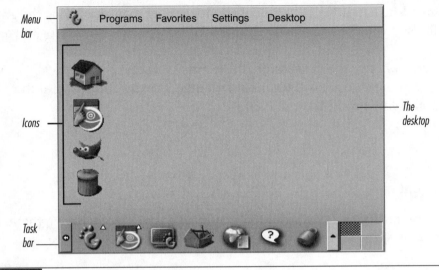

FIGURE 1-1 gnome desktop

and so on, allow you to access applications, including a web browser. The KDE interface includes many of the same buttons, such as *Terminal Emulator, Help,* and a web browser, as well as some differently named buttons that have similar types of functionality as GNOME offers, such as *Start Application.* In any GUI environment, the Task bar contains a staggering variety of configurable settings and features.

Accessing Applications Through the Main Menu

Depending on which desktop you are using, the appearance of your Task bar, the names of the particular buttons, and the locations where configurable settings are stored may differ from those discussed here. Yet, the essential features are the same.

Usually on the left end of the Task bar is a button labeled something like *Main menu* (GNOME) or *Start Application* (KDE).

1. Locate and click the button on the Task bar:

    If you are using gnome:

      Main Menu

    If you are using KDE:

      Start Application

    These buttons produce pop-up menus that provide access to various programs, utilities, settings, applets, and other system menus.

2. In the menu, try to locate the calculator. You might try looking under:

> **Office | Calculation**

or

> **System Menus | Office | Calculation**

Explore various menus until you find the calculator. When you locate it:

3. Click one time on the menu option to start the calculator.

4. Continue to explore the menu's options by locating your system *Games*.

The *Main Menu/Start Application* generally organizes nearly every critical system function on your machine. Most of these options you can manipulate. However, you must be logged on as the super user ***root*** to configure administrative features.

Starting a Terminal Emulator

Another important feature on the Task bar is the *Terminal Emulator*. If you move your mouse slowly over and then stop on the buttons on the Task bar, the names of the buttons will appear as small pop-up windows.

1. Locate and click the following button on the Task bar:

> *Terminal Emulator*

The Terminal Emulator looks like a terminal. It starts a new terminal window.

2. Move the newly created window to a different part on the desktop by clicking the top of the window frame and using the mouse to drag it to your desired location.

You can move this window anywhere on the desktop, as well as reshape the size of it using the handles located on the sides and corners of the window.

This window can also be minimized to rest in the center of the Task bar by clicking the minimize button at the top right.

3. To end this terminal session, type the following at the command prompt:

> **exit**

You can create multiple terminal windows using the *Terminal Emulator*.

Obtaining Help

The Help browser is an interface to the various forms of documentation on your computer as well as the Internet.

1. Locate and click the following button on the Task bar:

   Help

   Scan the information provided and get acquainted with the Help resources available to you.

2. When you are finished reading these *Help* descriptions, close this window by clicking the x in the upper corner of the *Help* window.

Connecting to a Web Browser

There is almost always a web browser included on the Task bar. Occasionally, it is on the desktop in the form of an icon (or in both places). Probably Netscape, Galeon, or Mozilla is available.

1. Locate the browser on the Task bar and click its button.

   You can customize the various adjustable browser settings by using the *File, Edit, View,* and *Search* drop-down lists on the Menu bar. Using the window handles, you can also reshape your window or minimize it to rest on the Task bar.

2. To close your browser window, click the x in the upper corner of your browser window.

Customizing the Desktop

The desktop is the aesthetic centerpiece of the graphical environment. It's here that icons sit and application windows reside when running.

1. Move the mouse to an area on the desktop where no window or icon is resting.

2. With the mouse, right-click the desktop.

   A menu appears.

3. Select *Change Desktop Background* or *Configure Desktop* (or maybe *Configure Background*) from the pop-up menu.

   Here you can choose your desktop theme, color, and wallpaper. You can also select a default word processing editor and configure peripheral devices such as your mouse. In addition, you can select a screen saver. There are many options pertaining to your GUI settings that can be determined here. Explore them.

4. When you are finished reviewing the menu options, close the window by clicking the x in the upper corner.

Starting Programs with Icons

There are various types of desktop icons you might see (by default), and all of these can be customized or removed altogether. Certain old favorites include a trash disposal icon, a web browser, and maybe an icon for your home directory.

1. Explore your desktop icons by clicking on each one to verify its effect.
2. Click the Trash icon.

   Inside the Trash will be items awaiting deletion. Their presence in the Trash does not have to be final. You can restore a particular item by dragging it back onto the desktop.
3. To permanently delete a file from the system, open Trash and select:

   File | Empty Trash

   The Trash is taken out, and all items that were in the Trash are now gone.

Employing Alternate Desktops

In the Task bar are usually four clustered buttons labeled *1 2 3 4.*

1. Click one of them.

   An alternate desktop is displayed. The four desktops are like having four places to work, all in the same login session. You can start terminals in one desktop, run other applications in a second, and so forth.
2. Move among the desktops by clicking various numbers at the Task bar and customize the background color of each.

Using the Menu Bar

The Menu bar is at the top of your desktop. Not all graphical interfaces include Menu bars because they do not possess any functionality that is not found elsewhere. Rather, the Menu bar functions like a quick reference location for frequently used applications, configurations, and even your favorite web sites.

1. Locate and click *Programs* on the Menu bar.

   A list of topics such as *Applications, Utilities, Development, Games, Graphics, Internet, Multimedia,* and various other headings appears on a drop-down menu. These are exactly the same topics found in the Task bar listed under *Main Menu.*

2. Try to locate the settings for your CD player. Usually, this is listed under the Menu topic *Multimedia.*

3. Locate and click *Favorites* on the Menu bar.

   If you have saved any pages as Favorites in your browser, they will appear for quick reference.

Exiting the Session from the Desktop

You can exit your desktop session in a variety of ways.

1. Locate and click the button on the Task bar:

   If you are using gnome:

   > *Main Menu*

   If you are using KDE:

   > *Start Application*

   You may choose to simply select *Lock Screen,* which keeps alive your current session, but requires anyone wanting to use this computer first to provide the current user's password in order to "unlock" the screen.

2. To exit your session, choose *Logout* from the pop-menu.

You might also try to log out from your system by using the Menu bar, or by right-clicking the desktop and then selecting *Logout* from those pop-up menus.

■ Conclusion

The graphical environment in Linux/UNIX is a powerful, feature-rich windows desktop that is used to access applications and programs. A major component is the *terminal window,* which, though it runs in the graphical environment, is still a character-based terminal. We will use the terminal to explore UNIX and Linux in detail throughout the following chapters.

Touring the Features of UNIX/Linux

2

Before beginning this chapter, you should

- Have an account on a working UNIX system
- Be able to access a terminal window

OBJECTIVES

After completing this chapter, you will be able to

- Create and manage files
- Copy, sort, move, remove, and print files
- Change the access permissions for a file
- Communicate with other users on the system
- Collect data about users, the system, and its files using standard UNIX programs
- Properly communicate basic instructions to the UNIX command interpreter
- Have the output of a program saved in a file
- Connect the output from one program to the input of another
- Move to specific standard directories and then return to your home directory
- Identify instances of running programs
- Create and execute a basic shell script
- Identify and make changes to a file's permissions
- Obtain information from the online manual pages
- Modify your computing environment
- Change your password

One way to visit a major city for the first time is to begin by going to the top of one of its highest buildings. From that lofty perch, you can easily identify the major features and see how streets are laid out. You can then consult a map or guidebook that provides basic facts about the city's major landmarks. Next, you can get information about how to use the public transportation system and briefly visit the major features of the city. A quick tour of the highlights like that would show you how the major systems work and would give you a foundation for more in-depth investigations of the most interesting parts of the city.

This chapter takes you on a guided, "hands-on" whirlwind tour of a UNIX/ Linux system. You will master fundamental skills that will enable you to get around the system, use essential tools, identify the major features, and take advantage of the system's underlying design structures through direct interaction with a functioning system.

After you finish this introductory tour, the book's remaining chapters guide your further exploration of the individual features. Hundreds of thousands of people have carefully worked through the exercises that follow and have read the associated explanations, teaching themselves to be proficient users of the UNIX system and its major features.

UNIX/Linux is a collection of user and system programs, called an *operating system*, that runs on equipment of essentially any size made by nearly all such manufacturers. The UNIX operating system was initially developed by a group of young inventive scientists at Bell Laboratories. The code was then licensed to the University of California at Berkeley, where significant additional development in programs and networking took place. Several UNIX system manufacturers added new features or modified the operating system to meet their particular needs. In recent years, Linus Torvalds and a host of Internet accomplices wrote Linux, an open-source UNIX-like operating system that also works on a wide range of hardware platforms. As a result, UNIX is not simply a "single" operating system. Rather, the term *UNIX* includes many slightly different flavors of the same general operating system.

From the user's perspective, the various flavors essentially have no impact because nearly all commands work the same in the most recent versions of UNIX and Linux.

This chapter examines all the fundamental aspects of UNIX/Linux:

- Running programs
- Communicating directions to the command interpreter
- Managing files
- Moving around the directory structures
- Locating resources
- Altering access permissions
- Tailoring the environment
- Examining the way UNIX/Linux functions

2.1 Running Programs in UNIX

UNIX/Linux is not a single program, but consists of many individual programs that users run or have executed. This first section examines how to execute programs.

1. Log on by entering your login name at the login prompt, followed by your password.

Meeting the Shell

Once you have successfully logged on, you may receive some informational messages, the screen may clear, one or more windows may be displayed, and a mouse may or may not be active.

Starting a Terminal Window

If you are using a graphical workstation and there is no terminal window displayed with a shell prompt on the screen, you need to start a terminal window.

In the first chapter, which toured the desktop, you started a terminal or shell window using three methods:

- Clicking the terminal icon on the dashboard
- Selecting a terminal from the menu of applications
- Choosing a terminal from the main window mouse menus

In this chapter, we will interact through a terminal.

1. Start a terminal window by using any method.

   At this point, you are using either a nongraphical terminal or a graphical terminal window. A prompt is displayed by the shell to inform you that you can start issuing commands. The prompt may be customized for your site, or it may be one of the default prompts, such as

   $

   or

   %

   The prompt is displayed on your screen by a program called the *shell*. Soon you will give the shell instructions, also known as *commands*. The shell reads your instructions and interprets them to the remainder of the system. On most systems, the shell is automatically started when you log on.

Issuing a Command to the Shell

After you've successfully logged on, the shell displays its prompt on the screen, which is the shell command interpreter's way of asking what you want to do next. The cursor is at the shell prompt.

1. Enter the following command:

   date

   and press ENTER.

When you press ENTER, the command line you typed is sent to the shell, which interprets your instructions and executes whatever programs you specify.

In this case, the **date** program runs. Its output, which includes the current day, date, and time, is displayed on your screen.

Though you may not be ready to exit, it is useful to know how to quit.

Logging Out

In the previous chapter, you learned how to log out from the graphical desktop. If you are in a terminal rather than a graphical environment, exiting the login terminal logs you off the system. In a graphical environment, exiting the terminal just ends the terminal window, not the session.

Logging Off the System from a Terminal

If you are in a nongraphical terminal environment, you can easily log out.

1. Enter:

   exit

   and press ENTER.

   This usually logs you off the system.

2. If **exit** does not work, type one of these commands:

   logout

   and press ENTER.

   or

   CTRL-D

   That is, hold down the CTRL key while you press the lowercase D key once.

   You have now logged off your system. If you are in a graphical environment, you have simply killed your terminal window.

3. Log back onto your system if you logged out. If you are in a graphical environment, start a terminal window.

Determining Who Is on the System

In a multiuser environment, it is often useful to find out whether a colleague is logged on.

1. At the shell prompt, type the following lowercase command:

   who

   and press ENTER.

   A list of users currently logged on is displayed.

The command line you just entered instructs the shell to execute a program or utility named **who**. The **who** utility determines who is currently logged on and formats a display of information concerning those logged-on users. In this instance, that data, the *output* of the **who** program, is sent to your screen.

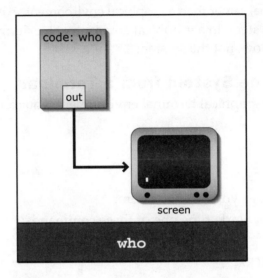

The output that **who** generates is in the following form. The data in your output contains information about users currently on your system.

```
anna      tty4     Apr 24 17:58
kyle      tty6     Apr 24 14:11
marty     pts4     Apr 23 21:13    (purdy.muster.com)
cassy     pts3     Apr 23 14:31    (thamzin.muster.com)
```

Identifying the Fields in the Output of who

Each line in the output of **who** contains data about one of the users who is currently logged on. Each line consists of several *fields* separated by one or more spaces. For instance, the components of the entry for *cassy* are as follows.

Each terminal or monitor is attached to the computer through a wire connected to a *port*—a physical location on the back of the computer. Each port has a designation that usually begins with the letters *tty* and a number. A terminal connected through a network uses an electronic or pseudo port named *pts*. When you issue the **who** command, the shell executes the **who** utility, which searches specific system files to determine the login name, port, and time each user logged on. The **who** utility then formats the information and outputs it. In this case, the output comes to your screen.

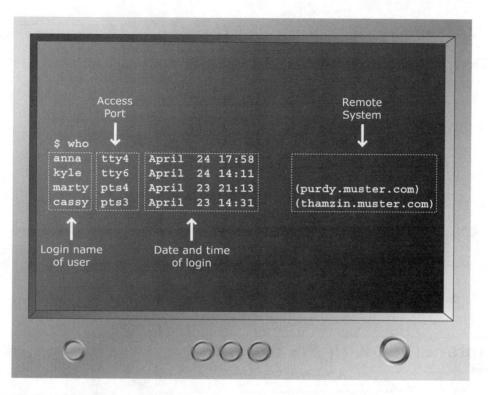

After **who** has completed its work, it exits and tells the shell that all went well. The shell then displays a new prompt, indicating that it is ready for your next instruction.

Obtaining Calendar and System Information

Many programs on UNIX are time dependent. For example, you just used **who** to determine the date and time when current users logged on.

The system monitors and can provide the current date and time information.

1. Enter:

   date

   and press ENTER. The output of **date** is displayed on your screen.

2. To see the current month's calendar, enter:

   cal

   and press ENTER.

Listing Files and Clearing the Screen

Depending on how your account is set up and whether you have used it before, you may or may not have files in your home directory. We can list the contents.

1. Enter:

   ls

   ENTER

   The **list** utility lists the contents of the current directory's standard files. If you have files, their names are displayed.

   Another useful command instructs the shell to clear the screen.

2. Enter:

   clear

   The data on the screen is cleared, and the prompt is displayed at the top of the screen or window.

Interacting with the System

The procedure you just followed is the way we work:

- After we log on or start a terminal window, the shell displays a prompt indicating that it is ready to receive instructions.
- We enter a command and press ENTER.
- Usually the shell starts a new environment called a *child process* for executing the code of a utility.
- The shell then tells the new process to execute the requested utility, such as **date**, **cal**, or **ls**.
- The process executes the utility's code.
- When the end of the code is reached, the process tells your shell that it is finished and dies.
- Upon receiving the exit code, the shell displays another prompt and waits for your next instruction.

The interaction cycle is depicted in Figure 2-1.

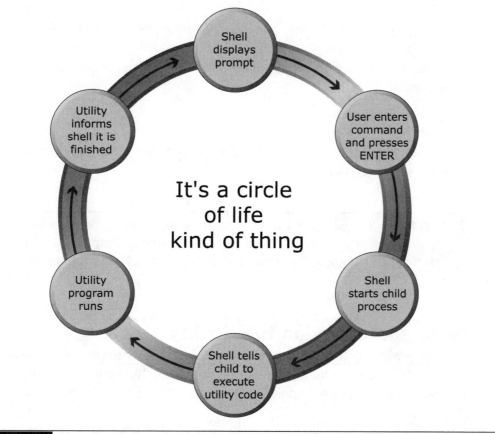

FIGURE 2-1   How the shell works

Making Corrections While Entering a Command Line

In this exercise, you will make an error entering the **date** command and correct it.

1. Type the following four letters, but do *not* press ENTER:

   dzte

2. Try using the BACKSPACE key to move the cursor back.

   Beware that on many machines, pressing BACKSPACE does not move the cursor back.

3. Enter the command correctly:

   date

4. Press ENTER.

5. Whether or not the BACKSPACE key worked in step 2, again enter:

   dzte

6. Try backing up and retyping to correct the error, using each of the following:

   DELETE

   CTRL-H

At least one of these keys works to move the cursor back and erase whatever you type.

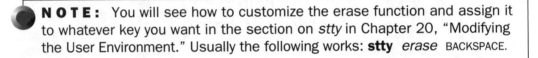

> **N O T E :** You will see how to customize the erase function and assign it to whatever key you want in the section on *stty* in Chapter 20, "Modifying the User Environment." Usually the following works: **stty** *erase* BACKSPACE.

Passing Information to a Utility

Included in most distributions of UNIX and Linux is a program that provides a 12-month calendar for whatever year you choose. In this exercise, you will display a calendar and learn how to pass information to a utility in a shell command.

1. At the prompt, enter the following two commands:

   cal
   ENTER
   cal*99*
   ENTER

The shell reports that the command **cal***99* is not found. We know from previous experience that **cal** is a legitimate utility, but **cal***99* is not.

The problem is, shells communicate like humans.

   Thissentenceishardtoparsebecausetherearenospaces!

Or, if you prefer,

   This sentence is hard to parse because there are no spaces!

In human communication, spaces are used to identify each string of characters that forms a word. Likewise, for the shell, we need to provide spaces to identify each word or token.

2. Include a space between the **cal** utility and the information we want to pass to **cal**, called its *argument*:

> **cal** *99*
>
> ENTER

The output displayed on your screen clearly cannot be for the year 1999. Dec 31 is not a Friday on this calendar, and we know the great party on Dec 31, 1999, was held on a Friday evening. Providing **cal** with the argument 99 is instruction to output the calendar for the year 99 A.D. We asked for 99, and we got 99.

3. Obtain the calendar for the year *1999*:

> **cal** *1999*
>
> ENTER

S U M M A R Y : In the commands you have used so far, you entered just the name of the utility to be executed and the shell runs it. When we enter a command followed by other information, such as **cal** *99*, we are telling the shell (1) to run the utility and (2) to pass to the utility the specific information that comes after the command—in this case, the number of the year you want displayed. Information passed to a utility is called an *argument.* Arguments affect how utilities run.

Passing Arguments to cal

1. Examine the calendar for the year 1752 by entering the following command:

> **cal** *1752*
>
> ENTER

This command instructs the shell to run the **cal** utility and to pass **cal** the argument *1752*, which **cal** interprets as the year to display.

2. Look at September 1752.

The old Julian calendar defined the year as 365.2500 days long and added a leap-year day every four years to keep the calendar coordinated with the solar year. Unfortunately, the solar year is actually 365.2422 days long, so adding a leap-year day every four years added too many days. In 1582, the Gregorian calendar reduced the number of leap-year days by declaring centuries to be leap years only if they are divisible by 400. They also threw out 10 days to bring the equinox back to March 21. In 1752, Great Britain finally adopted the Gregorian calendar. Because in the intervening 170 years the calendar had gotten farther out of sync, the number of extra leap-year days was higher; they had to toss out 12 days to match the Gregorian calendar used in the rest of the North Atlantic.

3. Obtain the calendar for the current year.

   The **cal** utility can interpret two arguments.

4. Obtain only a month by entering:

   cal *9 1752*

   The calendar for September 1752 is displayed.

   When two arguments are given, **cal** interprets the first as a month and the second as the year.

5. Provide **cal** with the correct two arguments to see the month in which you were born.

6. Check on the century leap-year days with:

   cal *2 1700*
   cal *2 1800*
   cal *2 1900*
   cal *2 2000*
   cal *2 2300*
   cal *2 2400*

   After 1752, only centuries divisible by 400 are leap years. However, more important for our present study, we must include spaces between a utility and its first argument and between subsequent arguments.

   Many utilities accept arguments.

7. Enter:

   ls */*

   This command is instruction to the shell to start the **ls** utility and give it one argument, the slash, which **ls** interprets as the root directory at the top of the file system. The files and directories listed at *root* are displayed.

   On UNIX/Linux systems, information is retained in files—system program files, user-created files, as well as other types of files. The files and directories listed in the *root* directory are essential to the system's operations.

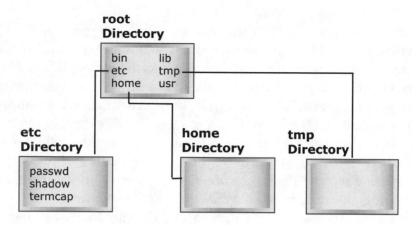

8. Enter:

   ls */etc*

   In this case, the argument passed to **ls** is */etc*, so **ls** outputs the names of the files listed in the */etc* directory, which is in *root*.

   UNIX and Linux contain a complete dictionary.

9. Enter:

   look *psycho*

   This command instructs the shell to run **look** and give it the argument *psycho.* The **look** utility interprets the argument *psycho* as the first part of a word, then outputs all words in the dictionary that begin with *psycho.*

2.2 How UNIX Does Its Work

Because UNIX is a multitasking system, it runs many programs at once. Each time you execute a utility, the system allocates memory, locates the needed code, and gives the request CPU attention—a child *process* is under way. Any time you ask for a utility to be executed, you are requesting a process to be started to run the code of the utility.

Examining the Components of a Shell Command

In the last few exercises, you asked for and were given information. The shell puts a prompt on the screen. You say what you want done by entering the name of a program to run, possibly with an argument. Then you press ENTER. The shell starts a new process that runs the program. The results generated by the program are displayed on the screen. Where does the information come from? Why is it displayed on the screen? Why isn't it placed in a file or on a neighbor's screen?

When people first use UNIX or Linux, they sometimes get the impression that it is the shell that figures out who is logged on, the date, or the ingredients of the calendar, and all we have to do is ask. Actually, the shell knows nothing about these matters. When you enter the command **date** and press ENTER, you are instructing the shell *to run the **date** program or utility*. This program is a separate program from the shell. What the shell *does* know is how to start a new process; where utilities such as **cal**, **who**, and **date** are located on the system; and how to get those instructions executed in the new process.

After you press ENTER to indicate the end of the command line you want executed, the shell starts a new process. The shell passes the new process any arguments included after the utility name on the command line. The shell locates the code for the utility and finally has the process execute it. After we instruct the shell to execute the **date** utility, the child process follows the code in **date**. It checks the system clock and formats the display output. The utility sends the results out its output "door." By default, the output door of a utility is connected to your display screen unless, as you will see, you request that the shell connect it to a file or even to another utility.

Listing Processes

1. Obtain a listing of your current processes by entering the following command:

   ps

   The output is a list of the processes currently associated with your login, along with some information about each process. For instance, the TT or TTY field is the *tty* number or port where the process is attached. The PID is the ID number of the process, and so forth. You will probably have at least two processes running—the shell and the **ps** command—and maybe several others. (Some systems do not list the **ps** among the current processes, but most do.) Each process is a program you are running on the system. After **ps** has completed its work of figuring out what processes are running, it displays its output and dies.

When you run a program, a new process is executed.

2. Enter the following:

    ps

If the **ps** is listed among your processes, you can see the process identification number is different each time you run the program.

Listing Systemwide Processes

The **ps** command you entered in the preceding exercise gave you the status of *your* processes. You can also display the processes running on the entire system, including those of all the users currently logged on and system processes.

1. Type each of the following commands:

    ps -aux
    ps -ef

One or both commands should result in a long display of processes, probably running off the screen. You will soon be able to tame this list.

This output of **ps** includes more information than most users really want. It's a list of the process status of every process currently running on the entire system, along with a plethora of information on each process. Many of these are system processes that keep all the services like printing and the network alive. This information is very useful to system administrators and other people supervising the UNIX environment, especially when they are troubleshooting problems on the system. And it is interesting to the rest of us, too.

Identifying the Current Directory

Because UNIX is a multiuser system, each user is given a separate workspace or *home directory* to do his or her work. When you log on, you are attached to your home directory. Because every user is in his or her home directory, we don't step on each other.

We can identify our current location.

1. Enter:

    pwd

The output is something like:

/home/cassy

or

/export/home/cassy

This information is the path from the top of the file system called **root** (and identified as /) to your current directory; in this case, your home directory.

For instance, the */home/cassy* data says that in **root** is a directory named *home,* and in *home* is a directory named *cassy*. The last directory listed in a path is your current directory.

2.3 Giving Instructions to the Shell

So far, you have entered the names of programs and included arguments for those arguments. New processes are started and the programs are executed. The shell's job is to do what you request. However, the shell does much more than start processes, pass arguments, and execute programs.

Redirecting Output from a Utility to a File

When you tell the shell to execute the **who** utility, the code for **who** runs and outputs a listing of current users. The process running the **who** utility locates the needed information and formats the report. The default output destination for the formatted results of running the **who** utility is your screen.

You can instruct the shell to *redirect* the output of a utility away from your screen to a file.

1. Look at your current directory contents:

   ls

2. Type the following shell command line that includes the > symbol:

   who > *users_on*

Nothing appears on the screen except the next shell prompt. There is no confirmation or acknowledgment that your command was successful. In UNIX/Linux, silence usually means success.

You just told the shell to create a new file and connect it to the output of the process that is running the **who** utility.

3. Confirm the file exists by entering:

ls

There are three components of this command line. The shell interprets each one.

who	Instruction to start a new process that will run the code for the **who** utility.
>	Instructs the shell to create a new file and connect the output of the process to that file.
users_on	Filename assigned to the new file that receives output of **who**.

The process runs the **who** utility and writes its output to a new file. The output is said to be *redirected* away from your screen to the new file.

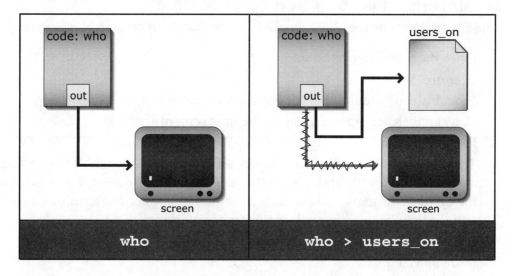

4. Create a file in your account of the calendar of the year 1752. Enter:

cal *1752* **>** *lost-days*

A child process is started, is given the argument *1752*, and its output is connected to the new file *lost-days*. Once that "plumbing" is done, the shell tells the child process to run the **cal** utility code. To **cal**, the argument *1752* is a year. When **cal** is finished, it writes to output, which in this case is connected to the *lost-days* file.

5. Create a new file called *today* with the output of **date**:

date **>** *today*

This command instructs the shell to start a child process, create a new file named *today*, connect the output of the process to the file, and have the process run the code for **date**.

6. Create a file called *birth* with the month of your birth as contents.

7. Confirm the files exist with:

> **ls**

Examining the Contents of Files

The UNIX system includes several utilities that display the contents of files on the screen. Each utility handles the task differently.

Displaying a File One Screen at a Time

One way to examine the contents of a file is to display it one screen at a time.

1. Enter the following command:

> **more** *lost-days*

Probably only the first part of the file *lost-days* is output to the screen.

You can instruct **more** to display the next screenful of text.

2. Press SPACEBAR.

The next page of the file is displayed. After **more** reaches the end of a file, it automatically quits, and the shell again displays a prompt. There is a long file on most systems that contains information about how terminals behave and that can be used to explore how **more** works.

3. Enter:

more */etc/termcap*

The **more** utility displays the beginning of the *termcap* file.

4. Move through the file with:

> SPACEBAR
> SPACEBAR

5. Quit **more** with:

> **q**

The **more** utility dies and a shell prompt is displayed.

Counting Elements in a File

It is often useful to count the lines, words, or characters in a file.

1. Enter the following command:

> **wc** *lost-days*

This command line instructs the shell to run the **wc** utility and pass it one argument: *lost-days*. The **wc** utility interprets the argument as a file to read and examine. After counting the elements of the *lost-days* file, the word count utility outputs its results in a display similar to the following:

```
35     452     1989  lost-days
```

This output consists of the number of lines (35), words (452), and characters (1989) in the file, followed by the name of the file that **wc** read.

Counting Only Lines

Like most UNIX utilities, the **wc** utility offers options that instruct **wc** to run in different ways. We can tell **wc** to limit the count just to lines, words, or characters, or any combination thereof.

1. For example, enter the **wc** command with the option **-l** (minus lowercase el):

> **wc -l** *lost-days*

The **wc** utility interprets the argument **-l** as an option to count the lines in *lost-days*. The counts of total characters and words in the file are not output. Most command options or flags are arguments that begin with a minus sign and are listed after the command name. We specify which optional form of the command we want by entering a **-flag**, such as the **-l** you just used.

2. Enter:

> **wc -l** *users_on*
> **wc -l** *today*

In each of these command lines, two arguments are passed to **wc**: the **-l** option and a filename.

The **-l** option instructs **wc** to output only the number of lines it reads from the file. The minus sign in the argument tells **wc** that the l is an option, not a file to read as data.

3. Use **wc** to count the elements of some other files:

> **wc** */etc/passwd*
> **wc -l** */etc/passwd*
> **wc** */etc/termcap*
> **wc -l** */etc/termcap*

Creating and Listing Files in Your Current Directory

In the preceding exercise, you created new files. You own them and you have access to them. The files are listed in your home directory.

1. List the names of the files in your current (home) directory. Type the command,

ls

and press ENTER.

With this command line, you are asking the shell to locate and run the **ls** utility. When **ls** runs, it obtains the names of the files listed in your current directory and outputs a formatted display of those filenames. Because you did not ask the shell to redirect the output of **ls** anywhere else, it is displayed on your screen. After the **ls** utility completes its work, the program exits and notifies the shell. The shell then provides another prompt to see what you want to do next.

Essentially, any utility's output can be redirected to a file that **ls** lists.

2. Enter:

ls > *myfiles1*
more *myfiles1*
ls
cal *2003* > *2003*
ls
more *2003*
q
ps > *myprocesses*
ls
more *myprocesses*

S U M M A R Y : When a utility generates output, it is displayed on the screen, unless you tell the shell to redirect the output elsewhere. The general form **utility** > *filename* redirects the output of the utility to a file.

Appending Output to the End of a File

In the previous exercises, you told the shell to connect the output of utilities to new files. We can also tell the shell to append data to the end of an existing file.

Try the following:

1. **date** > *thismonth*
2. **more** *thismonth*
3. **cal** >> *thismonth*
4. **more** *thismonth*
5. **date** >> *thismonth*
6. **more** *thismonth*

The > redirection special character instructs the shell to connect the output of the previous utility to a file. In contrast, the >> double redirect is instruction to *append* the output of the utility to the end of an existing file.

7. Add more text to *lost-days*:

   cal *2002* >> *lost-days*
   more *lost-days*

Redirecting Output to Another Utility

When you run a utility, the output by default is displayed on your terminal. The output of **ls** comes to the screen. You have directed the output of a utility to a file using the > redirect.

1. Enter the following:

   ls
   ls > *ls.out*
   more *ls.out*
   wc *ls.out*

The output of **ls** comes to the screen if we do not redirect it. The **ls** > *ls.out* command is instruction to the shell to redirect output of **ls** to a file named *ls.out*. With **wc** we can count the number of lines, words, and characters in the new *ls.out* file.

We can also redirect the output of **ls** directly to another utility.

2. Enter:

   ls | wc

(The | key is usually near the ENTER key. It may be a solid or broken vertical bar.)

The output of **wc** is displayed on the screen. This command line instructs the shell to start two processes, connect the output of the first process to the input of the second process, and then run **ls** in the first process and **wc** in the second.

The output of **ls** does not come to the screen, and it is not redirected to a file. It is redirected to the input of the second process running the **wc** utility. Then **wc** counts the number of lines, words, and characters in its input, the output of **ls**. Finally, **wc** outputs the results to your screen.

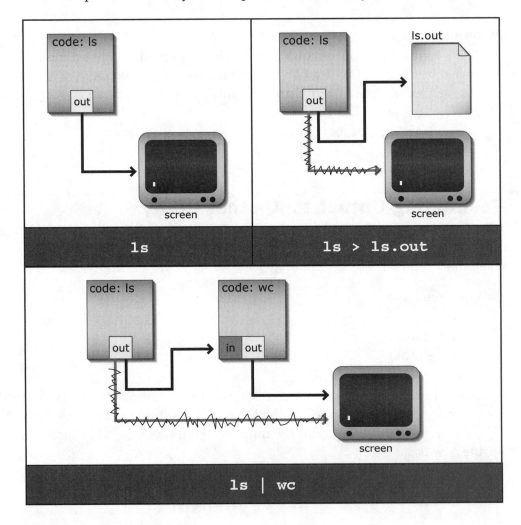

3. Enter:

    cal *1752* | **wc**

The output of **cal** is redirected to **wc**, which counts the elements.

The | is instruction to the shell to connect the output of the utility on the left to the input of the utility on the right.

4. Enter:

> **ps -ef | more**

or

> **ps -aux | more**

The output of **ps** is redirected to the input of **more**.

5. Quit **more**:

> **q**

The output of **ps -ef** or **ps -aux** is a long list of all process information, and this list more than fills the screen. By passing its output to **more**, we can control the display.

6. Enter:

> **who | wc -l**

The output of the initial utility is redirected to the input of the second utility.

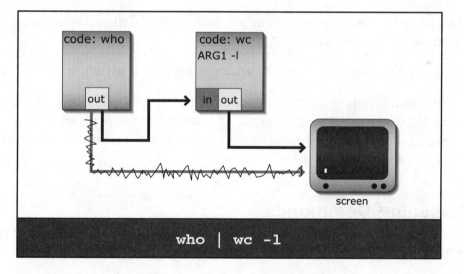

Determining the Role of Tokens on Command Lines

Thus far, you entered many commands such as:

> **who**
> **date**
> **who** > *users_on*

In all of these command lines, the utility is the first token.

The shell is programmed to read the initial character string token as a program to run or action to take.

Utilities are also located on command lines after pipes (|). You have entered commands such as:

who | wc
ps -ef | more

The shell interprets the token after a pipe as the name of the utility that should receive as input the output of the previous utility.

Consider the following. What must each token be?

_____ ____ ____ | ____ ____ | ____ > ____

The location on the command line determines how the shell interprets each token. The first token must be a utility, and the tokens following pipes also must be utilities. The token following the redirect must be the file that receives the output from the last utility.

All other tokens must be arguments to the utility that precedes them. Hence, the line is interpreted as:

utility *argument argument* | **utility** *argument* | **utility** > *file*

The first utility is given two arguments. The output from the first utility is connected to the input of the second. The second utility is given one argument; its output is passed to the input of the third utility. The output from the third utility is connected to the file.

Reissuing Commands

On modern shells, we can tell the shell to repeat a command. The way to request a replay of a particular command depends on which shell you are using.

1. Type the command:
    date
2. Try to reissue this command by entering:
    !!

If **date** runs again, you're using the C shell, a *tcsh* shell, or a *bash* shell.

3. If the **!!** did not work, enter:

   date

   r

   If the **date** utility is executed a second time in response to the **r** command, you are communicating with a Korn shell, *ksh*.

> **N O T E :** If neither works, you are probably in an *sh* shell. You can start a more modern shell by entering *csh* or *ksh* or *bash*.

4. Enter:

   cal *2003*

   The calendar for the year 2003 is displayed.

5. Repeat the calendar display by entering:

   !!

   or

   r

   The **!!** and **r** commands tell the appropriate shells to reexecute your last command line.

Running Utilities Again by Number and Name

The shell keeps track of commands you issue.

1. Enter:

   history

   A list of the commands you have executed is displayed, with a number next to each command. (If not, enter **set** *history = 100* to start it.)

   We can instruct the shell to rerun an earlier command based on its number or based on its name.

2. Enter the following (watch the spaces):

   !d (csh, tcsh, or bash)

   or

   r *d* (ksh)

   The last command that began with the letter **d** is executed.

3. Try:

> *!ca*

or

> **r** *ca*

The last command that began with *ca*, probably **cal**, is executed again.

4. Examine the **history** list:

> *!h*

or

> **r** *h*

5. Identify a command on the history list, and use its number as the ## in the following command. (If the **date** command is listed as number 27, then the command to issue would be !27 in the tcsh.)

> **!##**

or

> **r** ##

The command of number ## is reexecuted.

Using Nicknames for Commands

The korn, bash, and C shells allow us to assign alternate names to commands.

1. In the csh and tcsh shells, enter:

> **alias** *DIR* **ls**
> **alias** *now* **date**
> **alias** *h* **history**

2. In the bash and ksh shells, enter:

> **alias** *DIR=***ls**
> **alias** *now=***date**
> **alias** *h=***history**

3. Try each:

> *DIR*
> *now*
> *h*

The shell also lists all current aliases.

4. Enter:

> **alias**

When you log out, the shell dies and takes the memory of the aliases with it. Later, you will examine how to use startup files to tell each new shell how you want it to behave.

■ Review 1

Answers are listed at the end of the chapter.

1. What utility produces a list of currently logged on users?

   _____

2. When you enter the command **cal** *2004,* what are you asking the shell to do and what is the result?

   _____

3. What command tells the shell to repeat the last command?

   _____

4. What command results in the creation of a new file named *myfile* that contains a list of the names of the files in your current directory?

   _____

5. What command line outputs just the number of files in the current directory?

   _____

6. What command results in creation of a new file named *friend-bday* that contains the month and year of a friend's birth?

   _____

7. What command results in adding today's date and time to the end of the *friend-bday* file?

   _____

8. How can we tell the tcsh or csh shells that when we enter *cl* we want the shell to run the **clear** command?

   _____

9. How can we tell the bash or ksh shells that when we enter *cl* we want the shell to run the clear command?

_____

10. How can we request a display of the filenames listed in the current directory?

_____

11. What command lists the processes you currently have running?

_____

12. Where an object is located on a command line tells the shell a great deal about the object (utility, file, argument, redirection). If we enter a command line of the following form to the shell, how does the shell interpret each object?

____ ____ ____ | ____ > ____

13. What do each of the following accomplish?

    echo *file1 file2*
    more *file1 file2*
    wc *file1 file2*
    !w
    r *12*

_____

_____

_____

_____

_____

14. How does the shell interpret the following, and what results?

    look *psy* | **wc -w** > *psy*

_____

_____

_____

2.4 Using Utilities to Examine and Manage Files

In UNIX, specific utilities are used to list, copy, rename, move, and remove files. This section examines how to use the file management utilities.

Effectively Moving Through a File with more

Files contain data. Users need to see all of, see part of, and carefully examine files. The **more** utility that you met briefly in a previous exercise is an effective tool for examining the contents of files.

1. Have **more** display the long *termcap* file:

   more */etc/termcap*

   The top of the file of terminal specification information is displayed on the screen.

2. Move a few screens into the file by pressing:

   SPACEBAR
   SPACEBAR
   ENTER
   ENTER

   The SPACEBAR tells **more** to advance one screen; the ENTER key tells **more** to advance one line.

Finding a String of Characters

If we give **more** a target string of characters, **more** will go to the first page containing the target string and display that page.

1. Enter:

   /sun

   The first page containing the string *sun* is displayed.

2. Move on through the file's instances of the target by pressing a series of:

   n
   n
   n

3. Move forward a few pages:

   SPACEBAR
   SPACEBAR

4. Instruct the **more** utility to move backward a screen at a time:

>   **b**
>   **b**
>   **b**
>   **q**

Each **b** command is instruction to move backward one screenful through the file.

The **more** utility displays files one screen at a time and waits for input from users:

SPACEBAR	Advance one screen.
ENTER	Advance one line.
b	Go back toward the top of the file one screen.
/xxx	Go forward to the first *xxx* and display the page.
q	Quit **more**.

Displaying a Few Lines from a File

At times, it is helpful to view part of a file to examine the contents or to confirm particular data.

1. Examine *lost-days* with:

>   **head** *lost-days*

The **head** utility reads the first ten lines of file(s) named as arguments; in this case, the file *lost-days*. You can pass a number as an argument to the **head** utility to specify the number of lines to read and output.

2. Enter the following:

>   **head** *-6 /etc/passwd*
>   **head** *-6 lost-days*

The first six lines of the file are displayed. (Several are blank lines in *lost-days*.)

3. Use **head** to list the first eight lines of two of your files:

>   **head** *-8 lost-days users_on*

The first eight lines of the two filenames listed as arguments to **head** are displayed.

On many systems, you can also view the last lines from a file.

4. Enter:

> **tail** *lost-days*
> **tail** *-6 /etc/passwd*
> **tail** *-1 users_on* (number one, not the lowercase letter el)

Displaying All of a File

The **more** utility displays files one screenful at a time. Another utility displays files without interruption.

1. Enter the following:

> **cat** *lost-days*

The whole file *lost-days* is displayed with the initial part of the file scrolling off the top of the screen.

2. Try the following:

> **cat** *today*

The shell starts a child process, passes it one argument, *today*, and tells the process to run the code for **cat**. The **cat** utility interprets the *today* argument as a file to open and writes each line to output, which is connected to your terminal. When a file is short, the **cat** utility is a quick way to display the file's contents.

Just like other utilities, the output of **cat** can be redirected.

3. Enter the following variation on the last command:

> **cat** *today* > *today2*

The following table examines what this command instructs the shell to do.

COMMAND COMPONENT	INSTRUCTION TO THE SHELL
cat	Start a new process to run the **cat** utility.
today	Pass the argument *today* to the child process.
> *today2*	Redirect the output of the process to a new file, created by the shell, named *today2*.

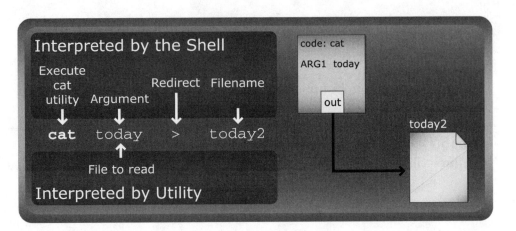

After starting the process, passing the argument, and redirecting the output, the shell tells the process to execute the **cat** utility. Once **cat** is executed, **cat** simply reads from the file *today* and writes to its output, which the shell connected to the new file *today2*.

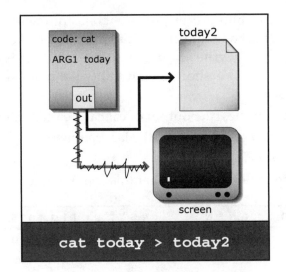

4. Confirm the existence of the new file by listing the contents of your current directory:

   ls
   more *today2*
   cat *today2*

Because the **cat** utility reads each line from the file *today* and writes to output, the new file *today2* is a copy of the *today* file.

Copying Files

You have thus far created several files by instructing the shell to redirect the output of utilities such as **who, date**, and **cal** to new files. The files you create are listed in your home directory, a workspace on the hard drive provided to you. The files and directories you create are accessible from this, your home directory.

You can also create new files by copying existing files.

1. Enter:

    ls

2. To make a copy of *users_on* and give it the name *users_on_2*, type:

    cp *users_on users_on_2*

3. Obtain a listing of the files in your current directory:

    ls

    The new *users_on_2* file is listed among your other files.

4. Examine the contents of *users_on_2* by entering:

    more *users_on_2*

    The **cp** utility interprets the first argument as an existing file and the second as the name to give a copy of the first. The file *users_on_2* is an exact copy of *users_on*. Each file is a separate entity; either one can be modified or removed without affecting the other.

5. Create a copy of *thismonth* and name it *junk* by typing the following:

    cp *thismonth junk*

6. Create three other copies of files by entering:

    cp *junk junk2*
    ls
    cp *lost-days lost-2*
    ls
    cp *lost-days lost-3*

7. Confirm that the new files are created, by entering:

    ls

When we give the **cp** command two arguments, it interprets the first as the name of an existing file and the second as the name to assign the copy.

Copying a File onto an Existing File

This next exercise will not work properly if someone has set up your account with **cp** aliased to **cp -i**, a topic examined shortly.

1. Check to see if **cp** is aliased:

   alias

2. If **cp** is listed as having an alias, enter the following:

   unalias cp

3. Examine the contents of *lost-3* and *junk2*:

   more *lost-3*
   more *junk2*

   The calendar for 1752 and 2002 is seen in *lost-3*. The file *junk2* contains the date, the calendar, followed by the date again.

4. With **cp** in its normal mode, try copying a file into an existing file:

   cp *junk2 lost-3*
   more *lost-3*
   more *junk2*

The contents of *lost-3* are overwritten by *junk2*. If you copy a file onto an existing file, **cp** overwrites the file.

Overwriting with Confirmation

1. Instruct the shell to use its inquire option:

   cp -i *junk2 lost-3*

   The file *lost-3* already exists. **cp** interprets the **-i** option as instruction to inquire if you want to overwrite the existing file *lost-3*.

2. Keep *lost-3* as it is. Enter:

   n

 S U M M A R Y : When you want to copy an existing file, use the **cp** command with two arguments:

cp *oldfile newfile*

The **cp** utility reads its first argument, *oldfile*, as the name of an existing file, and the second argument, *newfile*, as the name of a file to create as an exact copy of the first. To protect against overwriting an existing file with **cp**, use the **-i** option.

Renaming Files

When you create a file, you give it a name. Each file's name is listed in its directory, and the name is used to identify and access the file. Filenames are not permanent. We can change them.

1. Examine the contents of your file named *lost-3*:

    more *lost-3*

2. Change the name of the file *lost-3* by typing the following command:

    mv *lost-3 phon*

3. List the files in your current directory:

    ls

    There is no file named *lost-3* in the output of **ls**, but *phon* is present.

4. Display the contents of the new *phon* file using **more**:

    more *phon*

    It is the same file, with a new name.

 SUMMARY: When you use the **mv** utility to change the name of a file, you enter **mv** along with two additional arguments on the same line with the command. The first argument is the current name of the target file; the second argument is the new name you want to assign to the file. The command is in the format

mv *file newfile*

The **mv** utility changes the name of *file* to *newfile*. Although the utility name implies that it **mov**es the file, in this instance it just changes the name of the file in the current directory. Later, you will use the same **mv** utility to move files from one directory to another.

Removing Files

When you decide a file is no longer needed, you can delete or **rem**ove it from your account.

1. Enter the following command to remove the *users_on_2* file:

    ls
    rm *users_on_2*

If **rm** inquires as to whether you really want to remove the file, enter **n**. Then enter:

> **unalias rm**

Go back and do step 1 again.

2. Confirm that the file is removed:

> **ls**

The **rm** *filename* command is instruction to the shell to run the **rm** utility and to pass **rm** one additional piece of information, the filename argument.

Removing Files with Confirmation

There is a "silence" about UNIX/Linux systems that often disturbs people. For example, when you instruct **rm** to remove a file, all you get in response is the next shell prompt. The **rm** utility does not beep, buzz, or even send a message of acknowledgment. It silently does as requested and quits. The shell then prompts you for your next instruction.

If you would like the opportunity to confirm your request to have a file removed before **rm** actually destroys it, you must tell **rm** to prompt you.

A few steps back you created a file named *junk*.

1. Request removal of *junk* with the command:

> **rm -i** *junk*

and press ENTER.
The **rm** command first displays a message asking if you really want *junk* removed.

2. Tell **rm** not to remove the file:

> **n**
> ENTER

3. Confirm that you still have too much *junk* with:

> **ls**

When you enter the command **rm -i** *junk*, you instruct the shell to run the **rm** utility and to pass to **rm** two arguments: **-i** and *junk*. The **-i** is an argument that **rm** interprets as an option. The **-i** option to **rm** is the instruction to ask for confirmation before removing any filenames listed as other arguments. With the **-i** option, **rm** asks you if you really want to remove the *junk* file.

4. Again request removal of the *junk* file with:

> **rm -i** *junk*

5. This time, instruct **rm** to go ahead and discard *junk* by answering the inquiry with:

    y

6. Confirm that *junk* has been removed by entering:

    ls

Removing Several Files at Once

The **rm** command accepts multiple filenames as arguments.

1. Use **cp** to create a new file called *uson2*:

    cp *users_on uson2*

2. Create two more files by entering the following commands:

    date > *today3*
    ls > *file-list*

3. Confirm that the files are created by checking the contents of your directory:

    ls

4. Remove all three files at once with:

    rm *uson2 today3 file-list*

5. Confirm that the files are removed by entering:

    ls

    The **rm** command line is instruction to the shell to run the **rm** utility and to pass it three arguments, the names of three files. The **rm** utility interprets all arguments (that are not options) as files to remove.

6. Attempt to remove a nonexistent file to see the error message.

    rm *xyz*

   The child process ran **rm**. Unable to locate the file, **rm** sends an error out the "error door," which is connected to your terminal.

 SUMMARY: When you issue the **rm** command, you provide the name(s) of the file(s) you want removed as argument(s) after **rm** on the command line. The **rm** utility interprets its arguments as the names of files to be removed. To be asked if you really want the file removed, include the **–i** option as an argument.

Deciphering Utility Error Messages

When the shell or a utility is not prepared to interpret a portion of a command you enter, it sends an error message to your screen.

1. Enter the following command that tells the shell to run a utility that is not available:

   Copy (capital C)

   The shell looks but cannot find **Copy**. In this case, the shell sends you the error message.

2. Enter:

   cat *xyZ*

   The **cat** utility is started and passed the argument *xyZ*. Because **cat** interprets *xyZ* as a file to read, it looks for the file. Not finding the file, **cat** sends an error message to your screen telling you that the file does not exist. The shell did not check to see if the files existed. The shell did not interpret *xyZ* as a filename. It just passed the character string *xyZ* as an argument to the utility. Unable to find the file, the utility complained.

3. Instruct the shell to run **cp** and pass it three arguments:

   cp *users_on phon total*

   The **cp** utility informs you about its *usage.*

   The message says that to use **cp**, you can use the options listed in the brackets. You must either give it two arguments or, if you want files copied into a directory, you can list several filenames, providing the last argument is the directory in which you want the copies placed. This topic is explored in Chapter 5, "Using Multiple Utilities in Scripts."

   The **cp** utility found three arguments, determined the last was not a directory, and so complained.

4. Try:

   mv *abc def ghi*

   The **mv** utility functions in the same way.

5. Enter:

   cat *users_on xyZ > junk3*
   more *junk3*

   The **cat** utility interprets its arguments as files to read. Unable to find *xyZ*, **cat** complains, but reads the other file and writes its contents to the file *junk3*.

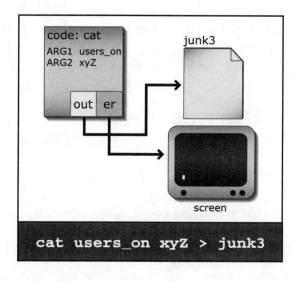

```
cat users_on xyZ > junk3
```

2.5 Employing the UNIX Toolbox of Utilities

The UNIX operating system user programs, or utilities, that you've examined thus far have located system information and output it to the display, or they removed, renamed, and manipulated user files. Each utility program is a tool that performs a set of very specific tasks. This section examines utilities that read input from files, modify the data that they read, and send the output to your screen, to a file, to the printer, or to another utility.

Listing the Contents of the Directory

We have used **ls** to output the filenames listed in the current directory. Options to **ls** provide more information.

1. List the files in the current directory including permissions and other file information:

   ls -l

   If a filename begins with a period, **ls** assumes it is a housekeeping file and does not list it when you ask for a listing of filenames.

2. Enter:

   ls -a

The output is all files in the current directory including the dot or hidden files associated with your account. The files such as *.profile*, *.login*, *.cshrc*, and so on, are files read by shells and other programs when they are started.

Counting the Elements of a File

You have used **wc** to count the number of lines, words, and characters in a file.

1. Enter the command:

    wc *users_on*

    The output from the **wc** (word count, not water closet) utility consists of four fields:

    ```
    2       12      102       users_on
    ```

    The meaning of each field in the output of the **wc** utility is

Number of Lines	Number of Words	Number of Characters	File
2	12	102	users_on

    In addition to counting the elements of files, **wc** can be used to count the words, lines, and characters in the output of previous utilities in a command line.

2. Enter this command:

    who | wc

    The **who** utility outputs one line of information for each current user. The | is instruction to connect the output from **who** to the input of **wc**, which counts the elements. The **wc** utility then tosses the information that comes from **who** and just outputs its count totals.

    You have used the –l option with **wc**, and there are others.

3. Try each of the following options to **wc**:

Lines only	**wc** -l *users_on*
Words only	**wc** -w *users_on*
Characters only	**wc** -c *users_on*

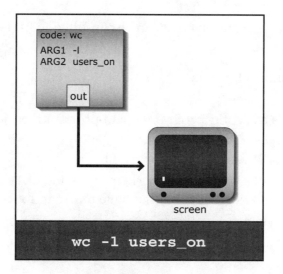

Combining the wc Utility Options

More than one option can be used at the same time.

1. For example, enter the following commands:

   wc -c -l *users_on*
   wc -lc *users_on*
   wc -cl *users_on*

Both the line count and the character count options are passed as arguments to **wc**, and the results are displayed. It makes no difference what order the arguments are entered, nor whether the options are separate arguments or combined.

> **SUMMARY:** The **wc** utility reads from its input or a file; counts the number of characters, words, and lines; and then outputs one, two, or all three totals, depending on the options provided.

Obtaining Information About Utilities

Throughout these exercises, we introduce new utilities and explore how the utilities work. Later chapters investigate them more completely. UNIX systems usually have an online manual that can be consulted to list options and learn more about each utility.

1. To find out more about one of the utilities, enter:

    man wc

    The display is a cryptic, programmer-to-programmer description of the utility.

2. Press SPACEBAR to see the next page of the manual.

    If pressing SPACEBAR does not work, try pressing ENTER. In one of the first few pages, the various options that have meaning to **wc** are listed.

3. Enter **b** to locate the **-c** option.

4. To quit the **man** display, enter:

    q

5. Check on the **ls** utility:

    man ls

    q

Sorting Lines in a File

Many files contain data concerning users or individuals. We have briefly looked at */etc/passwd* (the *password file*), which contains one line of information (a *record*) for each user. Every time a new user is added to the system, a new line is added (usually to the bottom of the file). As a result, the password file is not in sorted order. In the following exercise, you will sort some of the lines from the password file. To make visual examination easier, start by creating a file consisting of the first few lines of the file.

1. Create a file containing the first 20 lines of the password file on your machine by entering:

    head -20 */etc/passwd* **>** *mypasswd*

2. Examine the file by entering:

    cat *mypasswd*

3. Sort the lines in the *mypasswd* file by entering:

    sort *mypasswd*
    cat *mypasswd*

The **sort** utility reads the file *mypasswd* into memory and rearranges the lines into a sorted order. Output is displayed on the screen. The *mypasswd* file itself is not modified; rather, its data is read, sorted, and written to your screen.

Sorting and Counting Multiple Files

1. Review the contents of two of your files by entering the following commands:

   cat *mypasswd*
   cat *users_on*

   Use **sort** to sort the lines from the two files you just examined.

2. Enter:

   sort *mypasswd users_on* | **more**

   The contents of both files are read and sorted together. The output is a sorted version of all lines from both files.

3. Try:

   sort *users_on lost-days* | **more**

   In the **sort** order, lines beginning with numbers precede lines beginning with uppercase letters, which precede lines that begin with lowercase letters. Unless instructed otherwise, the **sort** utility sorts in ASCII order. (ASCII is an acronym for the American Standard Code for Information Interchange.)

4. On most systems, you can examine the ASCII order by entering this command:

   man ascii

   In ASCII order, most nonalphanumeric characters are first, then numbers, followed by uppercase characters, more nonalphanumeric characters, and then lowercase characters. The **sort** utility follows that order.

5. Enter:

   sort *mypasswd users_on* | **more**
   wc *mypasswd users_on*
   more *mypasswd users_on*

   Examine the output. The **sort** utility reads both files (*users_on* and *mypasswd*) and sorts all the lines that it reads from both files. The resulting output is the lines from *mypasswd* and *users_on*, merged together and sorted. The files are not sorted individually. Neither the original *users_on* nor *mypasswd* file is changed.

Unlike **sort**, the **wc** utility counts each file individually. It outputs the stats for each file and produces a total.

Reversing the Sorted Order

To sort a file in reverse ASCII order, you must specify an option to the utility on the command line, instructing it to work in a particular way.

1. Type the following command:

   sort *users_on mypasswd* | **more**
   sort -r *users_on mypasswd* | **more**

   Compare the output to that of the previous **sort**. In this case, you instructed the shell to run the **sort** utility and to pass it three arguments: the **-r** option and the two filename arguments. The **-r** "reverse option" is one of several options to the **sort** utility that instruct **sort** to change the way it functions.

2. Look at the other **sort** options with:

   man sort

3. When you have seen enough, enter:

   q

Visiting Echo Point

When we pass an argument to a utility, that utility's code determines how the argument is interpreted.

1. Enter:

   ls

   Among your files is a file named *2003*.

2. Enter:

   wc *2003*
   cat *2003*
   cal *2003*
   rm *2003*
   ls

   The same argument is passed to four different utilities with four different results. The **wc** utility interprets the argument *2003* as the name of a file to read and count lines, words, and characters. To **cat**, *2003* is a file to read and output. To **cal**, *2003* is a calendar year to calculate and display. To **rm**, *2003* is a file to remove from the directory.

3. Enter:

   echo *2003*

   To **echo**, *2003* is simply a character string argument to be read and written to output, which by default is to your screen.

4. Enter:

   echo *who date ls cat*

   The shell interprets the command line as instruction to run **echo** and pass it four arguments consisting of strings of characters: *who, date, ls,* and *cat*. The command is of the form:

   util *arg arg arg arg*

   These are not utilities to be run; they are just character strings to **echo** that **echo** reads and writes to output.

   Instruct the shell to redirect the output of **echo**.

5. Enter:

   echo *A B C D > e1*
   more *e1*

   This command line tells the shell to:

   - Start a child process.

   - Pass four arguments to the process.

   - Redirect the output of the process to a new file *e1*.

   - Have the process execute the **echo** code.

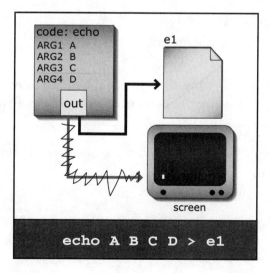

When **echo** is executed, it reads the four arguments and writes them to output that the shell has redirected to the new file *e1*.

Creating Combination Files

People often place related data in several different files, such as individual chapters of a book. At times, the data that is in several files needs to be brought together.

1. Type the following:

   date > *c1*
   echo *'hello, this is echo'* > *c2*
   cal > *c3*
   cat *c1 c2 c3*

   This command line instructs the shell to run the **cat** utility and to pass it three arguments. To the **cat** utility, each argument is interpreted as the name of a file to be opened, read, and written to output. The **cat** utility reads each of the lines of the first file and writes them to output (the screen by default). After **cat** reads and writes all the lines from the first file, it opens the next file and reads and writes all the lines in it. This process continues until **cat** reaches the end of the last file. The resulting output is a concatenation of the three files displayed on the screen.

   In step 1, the output of the **cat** utility is displayed on the screen. You can also tell the shell to redirect the output of **cat** to a file.

2. Enter the following:

   cat *c3 c2 c1* > *total*

3. Examine the *total* file by entering:

   more *total*

   The *total* file consists of the contents of the file *c3* followed by the contents of the file *c2* followed by the lines from *c1*. All lines read by **cat** are written to the new file *total*.

   When you look at the output, *total*, there is no way to tell where one file ends and another begins.

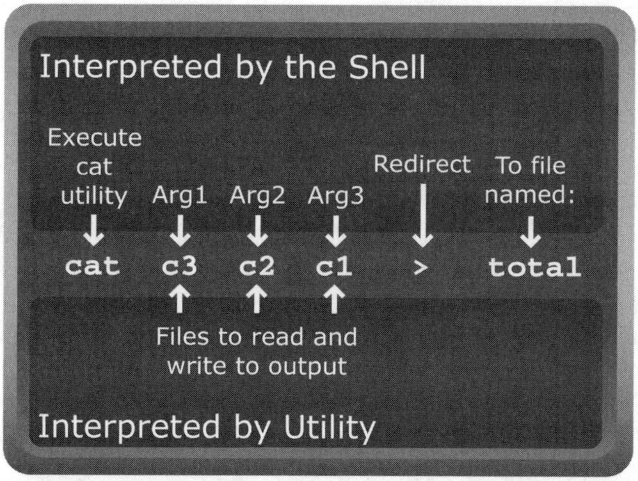

This command line instructs the shell to start a new process, pass three arguments (*c3*, *c2*, and *c1*) to it, and then redirect the process' output to a new file *total*. Lastly, the shell instructs the process to run the **cat** program. Once started, **cat** interprets all of its arguments as names of files to locate, open, and read. Every line **cat** reads is written to output, which is connected to the file *total*.

Locating Specific Lines in a File

It is often useful to locate the lines in a file that contain a word or string of characters.

1. Reexamine the file total:

    cat *total*

2. Select lines that contain a target string:

    grep *is total*

    Every line containing the string *is* from the file *total* is selected and output. The file *users_on* contains a record for each user who was logged on when you created the file.

3. Type the following command, replacing *yourlogin* with your actual login name:

    grep *yourlogin users_on*

    The **grep** utility selects and outputs a line in the file *users_on* only if it contains the string of characters that is *yourlogin*.

4. Now look for all lines in the file *letc/passwd* that contain the string *root*. Enter:

    grep *root letc/passwd*

This command line asks the shell to run the **grep** utility and pass it two arguments. Many utilities, including **sort** and **rm**, interpret all arguments as files to be acted on. They **sort** or remove them all. Not **grep**. To the **grep** utility, the first argument is the *target string,* and all *other* arguments are files to be opened and searched. In this case, **grep** looks through the file *letc/passwd* for lines that contain the target string *root* and selects those lines that match. It outputs only the matched lines. The original file is not affected.

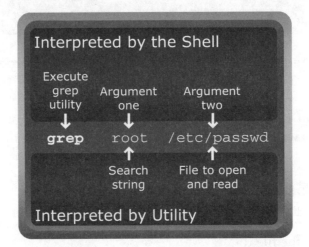

5. Look in several files for lines that contain the string *is*:

    grep *is c1 c2 c3 total*

grep interprets the string *is* as the target search string and the other arguments as files to open and search. The filename and matching lines are output.

Printing a File

At this point in the chapter, you have created several files and examined them on the screen. An essential feature is printing files on paper.

The UNIX commands to send a file to a printer for printing are system dependent. To print a file, try each of the following commands.

1. Enter:

    lp *lost-days*

    or

    lpr *lost-days*

    The system may respond to one of these commands with an error message that the command is not found. Use whichever one works.

    You may get an error message about a lack of a destination printer. If so, you will need to ask a colleague or your system administrator for the name of a printer available to you.

2. If you need to use the printer name, type one of the following commands. The *dest* part of the argument refers to the name of the destination printer that you are selecting to print your file. Type in the printer name you obtained from your system administrator.

    lp -d*dest* *lost-days*

    or

    lpr -P*dest* *lost-days*

    There is no space between the option and the destination printer name.

    If you have several printers available, the **-P** option with **lpr** and the **-d** option with **lp** allow you to specify which printer to use.

N O T E : In these chapters, we will use the default form of the command, **lpr**. If you need to specify a printer or you use **lp**, include the appropriate **-P** or **-d** option with the correct command.

---

3. Try printing several files from your account, replacing *f1, f2,* and *f3* with names of three of your own files:

    lpr *f1 f2 f3*

The **lp** and **lpr** utilities manage the printer. They accept multiple filenames as command-line arguments and print all files named.

SUMMARY: You get work done in UNIX by interacting with the shell. The first word or token on a command line is a utility you want the shell to execute. Utilities are used to change filenames, remove files, copy files, display the contents of files, and obtain information from the system. The output of a utility is displayed on the screen unless you instruct the shell to redirect it to a file. The behavior of a utility can be modified by including arguments after the utility name on the command line. Thus far, options and filenames have been given as arguments to utilities.

2.6 Managing Input and Output

We have directed the output of utilities to your terminal and redirected output to files and other utilities. Now we tell the shell where to connect input and output.

Specifying a File as Input

When you want to designate a specific input source, there are two ways to get a file opened and read as input by a utility.

1. Enter the following command:

   sort *mypasswd*

   Here the shell is instructed to run the **sort** utility and pass it one argument, *mypasswd*. To the **sort** utility, the argument *mypasswd* is interpreted as a file to open and read as input. **sort** reads *mypasswd,* sorts the contents, and outputs the data by default on the workstation screen.

   Because **sort** has an argument, it interprets it as a file and does not read from input. Only when there is no filename argument does **sort** read from input.

2. Enter:

   who | sort

   In this case, **sort** does not have an argument, so it reads from its input door, which the shell connected to the output of **who**.

3. Enter the following:

   sort < *mypasswd*

The results are the same as the **sort** *mypasswd* command. A sorted version of the file *mypasswd* is displayed on the screen. The < in this command is instruction to the *shell* to open the file *mypasswd* and connect it to the *input* of **sort**. No argument is passed to **sort**, so **sort** does not open a file. In the command line in step 1, the shell passes the filename as an argument to **sort**. In this step, the shell opens the file itself and connects the file to the input to **sort**.

4. You can also connect files to the input of other utilities. For example, type:

   cat < *mypasswd*

   In this case, you are instructing the shell to connect the file *mypasswd* to the *input* of **cat**. Because no output destination is specified, the output is by default connected to your monitor. Thus, the file *mypasswd* is read by **cat** and displayed on the workstation screen.

The redirection symbol is an important feature because several utilities cannot open files, so we must instruct the shell to do it.

COMMAND	INTERPRETATION
utility > *filename*	Shell connects output of utility to *filename*.
utility < *filename*	Shell connects *filename* to input of utility.
utility1 | **utility2**	Shell connects output of **utility1** to input of **utility2**.

Employing Default Input/Output Connections

Utilities receive input, do a task, and write output. Some utilities (**date, who, ls**) get their information from system files. Others, like **sort** and **wc**, open and read the contents of files. In this tour of the system, you have been using the > redirection symbol to specify where utilities are to write their output. For instance, when you enter **who** > *file1*, the output of **who** is connected to *file1*. If you do not redirect the output, the utility writes to your screen.

When you issue a command like **who** \| **sort**, you are instructing the shell to connect the output of **who** to the input of **sort**. You are specifying that the output of one utility be connected to the input of another.

Listing Misspelled Words from a File

Many UNIX systems contain a spellcheck program that examines files for misspelled words. On some systems, the **spell** program only reads from input. It cannot open files.

1. Examine *users_on* for misspelled words with the following command:

    spell < *users_on* (or: **ispell -l** < *users_on*)

All strings in the file that **spell** does not find in the online dictionary are viewed as misspelled words in the file and are displayed on the screen. In this case, the shell opens the file *users_on* and connects it to the input of **spell**. The output is not redirected, so the output is displayed on the screen.

Determining Where Utilities Read Input

1. You have specified files as arguments. Enter the following command:

    sort *total*

The character string *total* is given to **sort** as an argument. The **sort** program interprets *total* as a file to open and read. The output is a sorted version of the file *total*.

If no input is specified for a utility, and no filename argument is provided, where does it read for input?

The Default Input Source

1. Enter the following command, which does not specify a file to read nor does it receive input from another utility:

    sort

The cursor moves to a new line. No shell prompt is displayed.

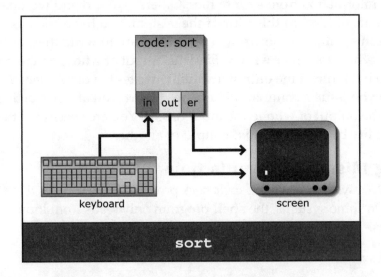

2. Enter the following lines:

```
hello
DDD
2
Hello
110
good-bye
```

3. Press ENTER to enter a blank line, and then press ENTER again.

4. On a line by itself, press CTRL-D.

A sorted version of the lines you just entered is displayed on the screen. The CTRL-D is the *end-of-file* (EOF) character. It indicates to the utility that there is no more input and that the utility can do its thing and then quit. The utility **sort** reads the lines you enter, sorts them, and outputs the results to your display.

When a new process is first started, the default input is the terminal keyboard, with output and error messages connected to the terminal. Because no filename arguments were specified in the preceding command, the **sort** utility read its input from the default input source, your keyboard. You entered lines of text and then the end of file, CTRL-D. Then **sort** wrote the results as output to your screen.

5. Try the following:

wc

6. Enter several lines, then press CTRL-D on a new line.

The output is a **w**ord **c**ount of whatever text you entered.

7. For another example of the default input source, enter the following:

sort > *sort-test*

8. Enter several lines of text as you did in step 2.

9. When you are finished, press ENTER to put the cursor on a line by itself.

10. Press CTRL-D.

11. Examine the contents of the new file:

more *sort-test*

In this command line, you instructed the shell to connect the output of **sort** to the new file *sort-test,* but you did not specify any input for **sort**. By default, input is connected to the keyboard if it is not redirected to another source. The **sort** utility read what you entered as input and wrote its output. Because you instructed the shell to connect the output of **sort** to the new file *sort-test* when **sort** wrote its output, it went to the new file.

Creating a Text File with cat

You will usually create text files using an editor such as the visual editor, **vi**. However, you can quickly create small text files without first mastering an editor, by using one of several other utilities. You will become familiar with the **vi** editor in Chapter 3, "Editing with the Visual Editor."

1. Type the following:

    cat > *first_file*

    and press ENTER.

    The cursor returns to the beginning of the next line. The shell does not display a new prompt. This command line instructs the shell to start the **cat** utility and to connect its output to the new file *first_file*. There is no request to redirect the input, so input is still connected to the default—your keyboard. You are no longer in communication with the shell; what you now type is read by the **cat** utility, which simply writes to output whatever it reads from input.

2. Type the following lines:

    This is a line of text in the first_file.

    Press ENTER and then type:

    This is another.

    The **cat** utility reads your input and writes it to its output, which the shell connected to a new file named *first_file*.

3. To inform the **cat** utility that you have finished adding text, press ENTER to advance to a new line and then press:

    CTRL-D

    This CTRL-D (end-of-file or EOF character) tells **cat** there is no additional input. The **cat** utility dies, and the shell displays another prompt.

4. From the shell, obtain a listing of your files using:

    ls

    The file *first_file* is listed.

5. Examine the contents of *first_file* by typing:

    more *first_file*

    The *first_file* file consists only of the text you typed. No additional data about the file, such as the file's name or your name, is added to the file by the system. The file contains just the text you typed. The file's name is kept in the directory. The information about a file is in a system storage unit associated with your file.

6. Create another text file with another **cat** command:

    cat > *second_file*

7. Add some text, and return to the shell with CTRL-D.

8. Obtain a listing of the files in your current directory with:

    ls

9. Examine the contents of *second_file* with:

    more *second_file*

    The file consists of the lines you entered as input to **cat**.

The **cat** utility takes its name from the word "con**cat**enate" because if given several filenames as arguments, it reads all files and splices them together. The command **cat** > *filename* instructs the shell to connect the output from **cat** to the file *filename* and to execute the **cat** utility. By default, the keyboard is connected to the input of **cat**. Whatever you type is read by **cat** from your keyboard and written to output, connected to the file. The **cat** utility is not very complicated; it simply reads input and writes output, making no modifications.

Managing Input and Output with Redirection: A Summary

The role and effect of file input and output redirection symbols are summarized in Table 2-1.

COMMAND	INPUT	OUTPUT	EFFECT
sort	Keyboard	Display screen	The **sort** utility receives no arguments, so it opens no file. Instead, **sort** reads from input. Whatever is entered at the keyboard is read by **sort**, sorted, and output to the screen.
sort > *file1*	Keyboard	*file1*	Keyboard input is sorted, and output is connected to *file1*.

TABLE 2-1   Passing Arguments and Opening Files

COMMAND	INPUT	OUTPUT	EFFECT
sort < *file2*	*file2*	Display screen	*file2* is opened by the shell and connected to the input of **sort**. When **sort** runs, it reads from input (*file2*) and the output is displayed on the screen.
sort *file1*	*file1*	Display screen	*file1* is passed as an argument to **sort**, which opens it and reads its contents. Contents of *file1* are sorted and written to output, connected to the screen.
sort < *file1* > *file2*	*file1*	*file2*	The shell connects *file1* to input and *file2* to output of **sort**. When **sort** runs, it reads from input, sorts the lines, and writes to output. The lines from the file *file1* are sorted and the output placed in *file2*.
sort *file1* > *file2*	*file1*	*file2*	The shell passes *file1* as an argument to **sort** and connects the output of **sort** to the file *file2*. The **sort** utility opens *file1* and sorts the lines; the output goes to *file2*.

TABLE 2-1   Passing Arguments and Opening Files *(continued)*

The two methods for opening files are needed because, as you will soon see, some utilities read all arguments as instructions and cannot open files.

Communicating with Other Users

Several UNIX utilities allow you to communicate with other users on your system or on the network.

Writing a Message to Another User

Often, workstations attached to your system are located great distances apart. A utility provides a means of communication among the workstations. If you want to contact another user who is logged on, you can send messages to that workstation. This exercise is most useful if you and a colleague are using terminals that are adjacent so you can see what happens on each screen. If that is not possible, use your own login and communicate to your own screen.

1. Start the message-sending process by typing the following command, using the login of your colleague for *other_login* or your own login if you are writing to your own screen.

    write *other_login*

    The **write** utility sends a message to the screen that *other_login* is using, informing them that you are sending a message. Your keyboard is the input to **write**.

2. Type a line or two of text.

3. When you have finished, conclude the **write** session by returning to a new line and pressing:

    CTRL-D

    When you want to use **write** to communicate with another user, use the **who** command to find a colleague who is logged on, and note his or her login. A user's login name is the first field in the **who** output.

    When you are using **write** and you receive the message

```
Permission Denied
```

it means the user you want to **write** to has turned off permission for others to write to his or her terminal.

If you receive the message

```
write:  other_login logged in more than once ... writing to
terminal
```

then *other_login* is logged onto at least two terminals or windows.

4. You can verify this by using the **who** utility:

    who

    In the output, note that for each instance that *other_login* is logged on, there is a unique terminal named in the second column.

    The **write** utility connects to the first instance of *other_login* listed in **who**.

5. You may override this default behavior by giving **write** a second argument:

    write *other_login other_terminal*

    where *other_terminal* is the specific terminal on which *other_login* is listed in **who**. This command line instructs **write** to connect to the terminal port where *other_login* is located.

6. You control whether people can write to your screen. To allow others to write to your display, enter the following:

mesg *y*

To deny access to others, enter:

mesg *n*

Writing (Sending) a File to Another User's Screen

You can also use the **write** utility to send files rather than keyboard input to another user's screen.

1. Type the following command:

write *other_login* < *first_file*

The input to write is, by default, your keyboard. The < *first_file* portion of this command line instructs the shell to connect the file *first_file* to the input of **write** (to redirect the input for **write** away from your keyboard and connect it to the file). The **write** utility reads *first_file* instead of your keyboard and displays what it reads on the terminal that *other_login* is using. The **write** utility cannot open files. It needs the shell's help; the < tells the shell to connect the file to a utility's input, not output.

> **SUMMARY:** Some utilities read existing files as input and act on the data. They can be used to accomplish many tasks, including display, print, sort, search for a character string, and count the elements of a file or the output of another utility. Output from a utility can be redirected to another utility, a file, or, if not redirected elsewhere, the default output is displayed on the screen.

2.7 Employing Special Characters in Command Lines

When communicating with the shell, the only tool is the keyboard. The characters available on the keyboard and words or tokens created by combining those characters constitute the entire language we can use to communicate with the shell. Many characters have special meaning to the shell, such as the redirect > symbol. The shell interprets the > as instruction to connect the output of the previous utility to a file named right after the redirect. Likewise, the | is instruction to connect the output of one utility to the input of another utility. This section introduces other special characters used in shell commands.

Accessing Shell Variables

We use variables in life all the time. We fill out forms such as:

Last name: _____

First name: _____

All of us, except Cher, have values in our memories for the **Last name** and **First name** variables.

We can use specific characters to indicate which tokens in a sentence are variables. For example, consider:

I am $fname $lname. I live in $city. I was born in $birthplace

When I read the previous line, I read:

I am John Muster. I live in Berkeley. I was born in Canton, Ohio

To me, the value of the *fname* variable is John.

Everyone reads the line differently because everyone has different *values* for the variables that are identified with dollar signs. In this case, we interpret the **$** to mean, "Find the value of the variable that has the following name and replace (the dollar sign and variable name) with the variable's value."

1. Ask the shell to evaluate a variable and pass its value to **echo** by entering:

   echo $USER

   If there is no *USER* variable, try:

   echo $LOGNAME

   The **$** character has the same special meaning to the shell described earlier. It tells the shell to "locate the variable whose name follows, and replace this string with the variable's value." In the command you just entered, *USER* is the variable that the shell evaluates, because it is preceded with a **$**. After replacing the variable and **$** with its value, your actual login name, the shell passes your name as an argument to **echo**. Then **echo** reads the argument and writes it to your screen. The important distinction here is that the shell passes your login name, not *$USER*, to **echo**.

Let's see how having the shell evaluate *$USER* and replacing the variable with its value can be very useful.

2. Enter:

who | grep *$USER*

The shell replaces the *$USER* with your login ID and then passes that value to **grep** as its first argument. To **grep**, the first argument is its search string. The line from the output of **who** that contains your login ID is selected by **grep** and output to your screen.

Have the shell evaluate some other variables.

3. Enter:

echo my shell is *$SHELL* and my home is *$HOME*

In this case, two variables are evaluated by the shell. The resulting values are passed to **echo** as arguments. The **echo** utility reads all its arguments and writes them to output. By default, the output is connected to your monitor. The value of the first variable, *SHELL*, is the shell that is started up for you at login; the other variable, *HOME*, is where your home directory is located on the system. These variables and their values were obtained by your shell when you logged on. Your colleagues have their own variable values. The shell and all other programs you run are given these variables and these values.

We can count the number of times you are logged on:

who | grep *$USER* | wc -l

Exploring Environment Variables

The shell program that interprets your commands is started as a process when you log on. Several pieces of information are given to your particular shell so that your computing environment is appropriate. We can obtain a listing of those environmental variables.

1. From the shell, type the following:

env

or

printenv

The output is a listing of some of the variables that are currently set for your shell. Among the many lines displayed, you should find something like the following.

For C shell users:

```
USER      forbes
SHELL     /bin/csh
HOME      /users1/programmers/forbes
PATH      /usr/ucb:/bin:/usr/bin:/usr/local:/lurnix/bin:/usr/new:.
```

For Korn shell users:

```
HOME=/usr/home/nate
LOGNAME=nate
PATH=/usr/ucb:/bin:/usr/bin:/usr/local:/lurnix/bin:/usr/new:.
SHELL=/bin/ksh
```

- The *user* or *USER* or *LOGNAME* variable is your account name that you entered when you logged on.
- The *shell* or *SHELL* line indicates which of several shell programs is started at login to interpret the commands that you enter: *csh* is the C shell, *sh* is the Bourne shell, *ksh* is the Korn shell, *bash* is the bash shell, and *tcsh* is the tcsh shell. They all handle basic commands in essentially the same way, and for now it makes little difference which is running.
- The *home* or *HOME* variable is the location of your workspace or home directory.

The *path* or *PATH* variable lists the directories where the shell looks to find UNIX utilities you request.

The subject of local and environment variables is explored in some detail in Chapter 8, "Specifying Command-Line Instructions to the Shell."

Replacing a Wildcard with All Filenames in a Directory

Another special character to the shell is the filename wildcard.

1. If you list several filenames after the **wc** utility on the command line, the **wc** utility examines all of the files. Enter this command:

    wc *total lost-days*

    The number of elements in each file is counted and output.

2. To have **wc** examine all files whose names begin with the letter u, enter:

wc $u*$

The shell interprets the $u*$ as instruction to replace the string $u*$ on the command line with the names of all files in the current directory that start with the letter u and have zero or more additional characters following the u in their names. The shell then runs the **wc** utility, passing it all the arguments that it generated—the names of all files in the directory that were matched.

3. Confirm that it is the shell that is expanding (replacing the string with) the * into filenames by entering:

echo $u*$

The shell replaces the string $u*$ with the filenames in the current directory that begin with the letter u. Those names are passed as arguments, this time to **echo**, which writes the arguments to output.

4. You can also have the shell list *all* files in your current directory as arguments to a command by typing:

echo *

The shell replaces the asterisk with the names of all the files in your directory and then executes **echo**, passing all the filenames it generated as arguments. The **echo** utility reads its arguments (the filenames) and writes them to output, which in this case is your screen.

5. Do a word count of all the elements of all the files in your directory by entering:

wc *

The shell replaces the * with the names of all files in the current directory and passes all the names as arguments to **wc**. The **wc** utility examines all files listed as arguments and displays output like this:

```
 8    39    190    junk
 9    29    175    mypasswd
 8    39    190    phon
 1     5     22    today
12    59    310    total
14    80    220    users_on
52   251   1107    total
```

The output from **wc** is a list of information pertaining to all input files, followed by a total of these counts.

> **N O T E :** If you created a file named *total*, it is listed in alphabetical order among the other files. The "total" at the end of the **wc** output is the sum of the statistics for all files examined by the utility.

6. You can also have the shell pass all filenames as arguments to the **grep** utility. The **grep** utility searches for the target string in all the files in your directory. Type the following:

   grep *is* *
   grep *$USER* *

   These command lines tell the shell to replace the asterisk with all the filenames listed in your current directory. The first argument passed to **grep** is a string of characters that **grep** interprets as the *target*. The remaining arguments **grep** sees as the names of *files*. The **grep** utility then searches each line in all files listed as arguments for the target string of characters and outputs the lines that contain a match.

Instructing the Shell Not to Interpret Special Characters

You have seen how the characters *, !, and $ have special meaning to the shell. Sometimes it is necessary to instruct the shell to not interpret special characters and to treat them as ordinary characters instead.

1. Enter the following:

   echo *

   In response to this command, the shell does not expand the asterisk to match filenames, but passes it as a one-character argument to **echo**, uninterpreted. The **echo** utility reads the asterisk argument and outputs it, in this case, to your screen. When a special character is preceded by a backslash, the shell interprets that character as ordinary (lacking any special meaning). To **echo**, the * is just an *.

2. Enter the following:

   echo \$HOME

The **$** is *not* interpreted as instruction to evaluate the *HOME* variable. Because it is preceded by a backslash, it is just an ordinary dollar sign, the string *$HOME* is passed to the **echo** utility as an argument.

In the previous commands, the arguments the shell gave to **echo** after it interpreted the * and \$ did not include the backslash. When the shell interprets *, it reads the \ as a specific instruction—don't ascribe special meaning to the character that immediately follows. The only character that gets passed is the one character that follows the \ character. The \ is not passed to **echo** because it has meaning to the shell and is interpreted by the shell.

3. Try the following:

   echo \$USER * $USER

   The output is *$USER *** and your login name. The last *$USER* is interpreted because there is no backslash in front of the **$** telling the shell not to interpret it.

   Use **echo** to place interpreted and not interpreted variables into a file.

4. Enter:

   echo *var1* **$USER** > *test-interp*
   echo *var2* **\$USER** >> *test-interp*
   more *test-interp*

   The shell interprets the **$** in *$USER* in the *var1* line, but does not interpret the **$** in the *var2* line. Note the second line in *test-interp* is:

   var2 $USER

   The backslash is not passed by the shell to **echo**.
   Have **grep** look for strings in the *test-interp* file:

   grep **$USER** *test-interp*

   The shell interprets the variable *$USER* and passes the value of your login name to **grep** as the first argument. Then **grep** interprets the first argument (your login name) as the search string. The line with your login name is selected and output:

   grep **\$USER** *test-interp*

   The shell interprets the backslash as instruction to *not* interpret the very next character, the **$**, so the string *$USER* is passed to **grep** as the first argument. The **grep** utility searches for the actual string *$USER* in the file.
   The same is true with the filename expansion wildcard * character.

5. Enter:

> **echo** *u**
> **echo** *u**
> **wc** *u**
> **wc** *u**

The shell interprets the *u** as instruction to replace the characters *u** with all the filenames in the current directory that start with the letter *u*, and then pass the words as arguments. **echo** reads the arguments and writes them to output. **wc** interprets the arguments as filenames and counts the elements of each named file. The shell interprets *u** as a *u* and an uninterpreted ***. The argument to **echo** is *u**, which it displays. To **wc**, the *u** is the name of a file, a file that it cannot locate.

Not Interpreting the ENTER

When you press ENTER at the end of a command line, you are signaling the end of the command. The shell interprets the ENTER as a special character, one that indicates the end of the command to be interpreted, and starts processing.

1. Enter the following command:

> **who > **

and press ENTER.
The backslash instructs the shell to not interpret the character that immediately follows. Hence, the ENTER is not to be interpreted as the end of the command. At this point, the shell has not been told to process the command line, because no real ENTER has been received.
It waits for more input. In fact, what you have entered so far is not a complete command. The shell needs to redirect the output of **who** to a file, but the filename is not included.

2. Enter the filename:

> *users2*

and press ENTER again.
This time, the ENTER is not preceded by a backslash. The shell interprets it as a real ENTER, so the command, which now happens to span two input lines, is processed.

3. Confirm that the new file is created by entering:

> **ls**
> **more** *users2*

When you want a command line to span more than one input line, precede the first line's ENTER with a backslash character to instruct the shell to not interpret the ENTER's special meaning.

Not Interpreting Several Characters in a String

The backslash is interpreted by the shell as instruction to not interpret the special meaning of the single character that follows.

You can turn interpretation off for more than one character.

1. Enter:

    echo '$USER * $USER'
    echo '$HOME $USER'
    echo $USER '$HOME $USER' $USER

The output is the literal string of characters entered. When inside single quotes, the * and $ are seen just as characters, so the shell does not expand the * to match filenames. The *$HOME* and *$USER* are not evaluated for the variable values. The arguments passed to **echo** are just the uninterpreted character strings. The first single quote tells the shell to turn off interpretation of special characters. The second turns interpretation back on again. Because the special characters are inside the single quotes where interpretation is off, they are not interpreted.

Creating Multiple Token Arguments

Because we can tell the shell to not interpret special characters inside single quotes, we can tell the shell to not interpret spaces.

Examining Arguments to echo

1. Pass several arguments to **echo** with several spaces between them:

    echo *AA   BB   CC   DD*

    The shell interprets one or more spaces as separating the utility and its arguments. When **echo** reads its arguments, it outputs a single space between them.

2. Tell the shell to not interpret the spaces:

    echo *'AA   BB   CC   DD'*

A single argument consisting of the line as it was entered is passed to **echo**, which outputs the argument, spaces and all.

Creating Complex Aliases

In an earlier exercise we created simple aliases such as:

    alias *DIR* **ls**   **(csh, tcsh)**

 or

    alias *DIR*=**ls**   **(ksh and bash)**

1. Try the following, which on most shells does not work:

    alias *xxx* **ls -l**

 or

    alias *xxx*=**ls -l**

Most shells expect a single token as the alias and complain if they find more than one. We can use the single quotes to tell the shell to not interpret the spaces.

2. Enter:

In the C, csh and tcsh shells:

    alias ll 'ls -l'
    alias *me-on* **'who | grep $USER | wc'**
    alias *on* **'who | sort'**
    alias *rm* **'rm −i'**
    rm *test-interp*
    alias *mv* **'mv −i'**
    mv *junk2 junk3*

In the ksh shell:

    alias ll='ls -l'
    alias *me-on* **='who | grep $USER | wc'**
    alias *on*=**'who | sort'**
    alias *rm*=**'rm -i'**
    rm *test-interp*
    alias *mv*=**'mv −i'**
    mv *junk2 junk3*

Passing Complex Arguments

One of the most useful functions of modern computers is database management. The UNIX operating system provides several utilities that are used with database information.

1. Type the following command:

   who | awk '{print $1}'

   The **awk** utility extracts the first field from each line of the output of **who**. The output of **awk** is displayed on the screen.

2. Change the command line to instruct **awk** to select the second field. Enter:

   who | awk '{print $2}'

   This table describes the pieces of the command line:

COMMAND	INTERPRETATION
who	Instruction to the shell to run the **who** utility.
|	Instruction to the shell to connect the output of **who** to the input of the next utility, **awk**.
awk	Instruction to the shell to run the **awk** utility.
' '	Instruction to the shell to not interpret any special character between the single quotes, but to pass the enclosed characters as-is to **awk** as an argument.
{print $2}	The quoted string that is passed to **awk**. This instruction is interpreted by **awk** as "For every line of input, print out only the **2**nd field."

3. Enter:

   awk '{print $2, $1}' *lost-days*

   Notice the output is the second field, a space, and then the first field of all records (lines) in the file *lost-days*.

   The **awk** utility can be used to select and print specific fields, make calculations, and locate records by the value of specific fields. You will use it more extensively in Chapters 4, "Using Basic UNIX Utilities," and 17, "Data Manipulation with awk."

Communicating with Processes

Control characters send important signals to processes.

Signaling the End of File

We have used the control character CTRL-D to end input.

1. Enter:

   wc

2. Add a few words and then press ENTER.

3. On the new line, press:

   CTRL-D

The CTRL-D is the end-of-file marker. When we are entering text from the keyboard to the input of a utility, we signal the end of our input by pressing CTRL-D. The **wc** utility counts the lines, words, and characters in whatever text that you entered before pressing CTRL-D. The **wc** utility then displayed the results and quits. Every file has a CTRL-D (EOF) character at the end to indicate where to stop reading.

Telling a Process to Quit

There are other important control characters.

1. Start **wc** again without input or arguments:

   wc

2. Enter some text and then press:

   CTRL-C

   The **wc** program stops, and a shell prompt is displayed. No output from **wc** is displayed. The CTRL-C is the interrupt signal, which kills the process. The end-of-file CTRL-D says, "End of input, do whatever you do now," but the CTRL-C says, "Stop, put toys away, process nothing more, be gone."

3. Enter:

   sleep *30*

   You did not put the process in the background; no new shell prompt is displayed.

4. Try to end the sleep with:

   CTRL-D

   Because you are not providing input to sleep, the EOF, CTRL-D has no meaning.

5. Kill the process with:

   CTRL-C

   The interrupt signal reaches the process and it dies.

Backgrounding a Process

Many of the processes running on the system are not associated with a particular user, but are important elements of the operating system. These processes are running *in the background* and are invisible to most users. This section examines running processes in the background.

1. Type the following command:

   sleep *6*

   The shell runs **sleep** and gives it the number *6* as an argument. While **sleep** is counting to *6*, the shell waits. No new prompt is presented until **sleep** is finished.

2. Enter:

   sleep *60* **&**

   This command line tells the shell to run the **sleep** command in the background. The ampersand (**&**) at the end tells the shell to execute the whole command line, but instead of waiting until **sleep** is finished, the shell is to return a new shell prompt so that you can continue working.

3. Obtain a list of current programs by entering:

   ps

   The **sleep** process is running. When you execute this command, a number is displayed. This is the process ID number of the **ps** utility as it is executed. When the process is finished, a message is sent to the screen.

   This feature allows you to run time-consuming programs in the background while you continue work in the foreground. Obviously, with a command process that runs quickly, backgrounding isn't so crucial; but there are times when it will save you time and work.

Programming with Utilities

Thus far in these examples, communication with the shell has been interactive. We enter a command line; the shell reads whatever we enter from the keyboard and processes it. The shell will also read a file of instructions.

Creating a File of Commands

Until we examine the visual editor in the next chapter, we can use **cat** to read whatever we type and write it to a file.

1. Enter:

   cat > *commands-file*

2. Enter the following lines, pressing ENTER after each:

   echo *Hi $USER*
   date
   cal
   sleep *2*
   ps
   echo *Bye $USER*

3. Conclude the input by pressing ENTER and then:

   CTRL-D

4. Make sure the file contents are as just prescribed:

   more *commands-file*

If there is a mistake, remove the file and re-create it. There is no simple way to modify a file without an editor.

Instructing the Shell to Read a File

We can tell the current shell to read a file and execute each line in the file.

1. Enter in the **csh** or **tcsh**:

   source *commands-file*

   In the **ksh** or **bash** or **sh**:

   . *commands-file*

   The commands that are the contents of the file are executed one after the other.

Both the **source** and dot (.) commands instruct the current shell to read the file named as an argument and to execute every line in the file as though we just typed it in from the keyboard.

2.8 Modifying the User Environment

One of the strengths of the UNIX operating system is its flexibility. The system allows you to customize a variety of programs to your liking.

Instructing the Shell to Not Overwrite Files

Thus far, you have used the > symbol to instruct the shell to connect the output of a utility to a new file. What happens when you redirect output to an existing file depends on the shell you are using and the value of a variable named *noclobber*. You make the decision whether files are overwritten by the shell.

1. To make sure that *noclobber* is *off* for the following demonstration, enter the following commands.

   In the C shell or tcsh shell:

   unset *noclobber*

   In the Korn or bash shell:

   set +o *noclobber*

2. Create a new file and examine its contents by entering:

   ls > *test-list*
   cat *test-list*

3. Instruct the shell to put the output of **date** into the same file and examine the file:

   date > *test-list*
   cat *test-list*

   The original contents of the file have been *replaced* by the output of **date**.

   When we tell the shell to redirect the output of a utility to a file, the shell creates the file *if it does not exist*. If there is a file by that name, the current contents are *deleted* to make room for the new output.

4. Instruct the shell to not clobber files when redirecting output.

   In the C shells:

   set *noclobber*

   In the Korn or bash shell:

   set -o *noclobber*

5. Attempt to redirect output from another utility to the file:

   ls > *test-list*

   An error message is displayed in the Korn and C shells. The Bourne shell overwrites files with redirection and has no *noclobber* feature.

6. To see whether shell variables like *noclobber* are on or off, try the following.

   In the **csh** or **tcsh** shell:

   set

The list of variables currently set is displayed.

In the **ksh** or **bash** shell:

    set -o

A list of shell operational variables is displayed.

	Turn noclobber On	Turn noclobber Off
C, tcsh	**set** *noclobber*	**unset** *noclobber*
Korn, bash	**set -o** *noclobber*	**set +o** *noclobber*

Avoiding Accidental Logout

If you accidentally enter a CTRL-D to your login shell, you may be logged out. The end-of-file character says, "no more input; exit," so the shell exits.

1. Start a child process by entering:

    csh

2. List your processes:

    ps

The child **csh** is listed.

3. Issue an end-of-file to your shell:

    CTRL-D

4. List your processes again:

    ps

The **csh** is gone. The CTRL-D instructs it to exit.

5. Try the same thing with a Korn shell:

    ksh
    date
    ps
    CTRL-D

6. You can tell the shells to ignore end-of-file characters with the following command.

In the **csh** or **tcsh** shells:

    set *ignoreeof*

In the **ksh** and **bash** shells:

    set -o *ignoreeof*

7. Now press CTRL-D.

You receive a message telling you to use **exit** or **logout**, not to use CTRL-D.

You will soon customize your account to have *ignoreeof* and *noclobber* set at all times. For now, enter each after you log on to protect yourself from accidental overwrite and accidental logout.

Changing Your Password

One of the most important ways to customize your account is to choose a secure but memorable password. This is not only convenient, but necessary for maintaining security of everyone's data on the computer.

Before you begin the process of changing your password, decide on an appropriate new one. There are several words to avoid when choosing a password because they are easily guessed. Do *not* use:

- Your login ID
- Any first or last name
- Your address
- A word listed in a dictionary in any language
- Obscenities
- Pop culture words

It is best to include both upper- and lowercase letters, and at least one numeral or other character as well.

With all these considerations, you may find it difficult to create a secure password that can be remembered. One way to formulate a memorable yet difficult password is to use the first letters of every word in a sentence that has meaning. For example, if you enjoy the work of a particular author, your password might be:

```
MfaiMT60
```

This looks difficult to remember. It *is* extremely difficult to crack—but it's easy to recall because it stands for

My **f**avorite **a**uthor **is** Mark Twain,
and I am **60** years old

or

```
OwaiS19
```

which stands for

Our wedding anniversary is Sept 19.

When you have decided on a new password and are ready to change your current password, take the following steps:

1. Determine from a colleague or system administrator if your system is running the Network Information Service (NIS).

2. Once you have decided on a new password, type whichever of the following commands is appropriate. (If you are not sure whether you are on an NIS site, try the **yppasswd** command first. If you get an error message, try **passwd**.)

3. If your system is running NIS, type:

    yppasswd

    Otherwise, enter:

    passwd

    You are prompted for your *current* password. To protect you, the program will not continue unless you identify yourself by correctly providing the current password.

4. Type your *current* password and press ENTER.

    You are now prompted for a *new* password.

5. Type your new password and press ENTER.

    The program asks you to repeat the new password to make certain that you type it correctly and can remember it.

    Type your new password again and press ENTER.

6. When the shell prompt returns with no error messages, your password has been changed. It might even confirm that all went well.

The **passwd** utility accomplishes tasks you cannot do. It actually changes a system file that you are not permitted to alter. Because you have that power when running the **passwd** utility, it grills you extensively to be sure you are legitimate and that you can remember your new password.

Changing the Prompt

Throughout the chapter, we have talked about the shell prompt. There are some standard shell prompts, shown next. The prompt your shell displays, like much of your user environment, can be modified.

PROMPT	SHELL
$	Bourne and Korn shells
%	C shells
#	Any shell as **root**

1. Look at the current variables:

   set

   If the list includes a variable named *prompt*, you are interacting with a **csh** or **tcsh** shell. If the output of **set** includes a *PS1* variable, you are in a **ksh** or **bash** shell.

2. If you are using a C or tcsh shell, type the following command:

   set *prompt*='*myname*'

   where *myname* is whatever you want the prompt to be.

3. If you are using the Bourne or Korn shell, type the following:

   PS1='*myname*'

Your prompt is now reset. This "personalized" prompt remains set until you log out. Later you will learn more about setting up your computer environment, and you will have the opportunity to permanently customize various aspects of your workspace, such as the shell prompts and how the shell behaves.

2.9 Examining the File System

Files are listed in directories. When we create a new directory, its name is listed in the current directory. Your home directory is listed in some directory, which is listed in some other directory…. The whole collection is the file system.

Determining Your Location in the File System

When you log onto the system, your shell is started, and you are placed in your home directory.

1. To get a listing of where your home directory is located, type the command:

   pwd

   The **pwd** utility displays your **p**resent **w**orking **d**irectory. The output looks something like this:

   ```
   /home/your_login
   ```

This is the *full path* from the top of the file system to your present working directory. Your home directory on the right is listed in a parent directory, which in turn is listed in the one above it, and so on to the topmost directory, *root*, symbolized by \.

2. Obtain a listing of the files in your current (home) directory with the usual command:

   ls

The output is a listing of files that you have created. Their names are written in your home directory.

Viewing the File System from the Top

The top of the UNIX directory system is generally referred to as *root*, or sometimes "slash," because it is symbolized by the forward slash character.

1. Obtain a listing of the files and directories in the *root* directory with the following command:

   ls /

This command tells the shell to run the **ls** utility and pass it the **/** argument. The **ls** utility reads the names of the files in the **/** directory and displays that list on the screen. The output is a listing of some of the system directories, including *dev*, *tmp*, *bin*, and *usr*. The listing also contains the first directory after *root* (**/**) that is in the path to your home when you type **pwd** from your home directory.

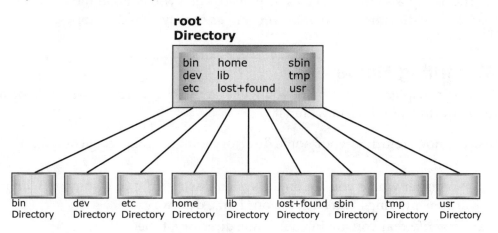

2. Check to see what your present working directory is by entering:

pwd

Your current directory is not changed, even though you generated a listing of the contents of the *root* directory. The current directory is still your home directory. The **ls** utility allows you to obtain listings of other directories without actually changing directories.

Changing Directories

When you need to, you can change directories.

1. To change from your present working directory to *root*, type the following command:

cd /

The command **cd** is instruction to change directory.

2. Confirm that your current directory is now the **root** directory by typing:

pwd

The output is not terribly descriptive:

/

Your current directory is *root*, which is at the top of the UNIX file system.

3. Display a list of the files and directories in the *root* directory by entering:

ls

The listing is the same as was displayed when you entered the **ls /** command earlier. The directories *dev*, *tmp*, *bin*, and *usr* are system directories.

Returning Home

In a later chapter on directories, you will examine the directory system in detail, and how to move around within it.

1. For now, return to your home directory with the following command:

cd

No matter where you are on the system, issuing the **cd** command with no argument brings you back to your home directory.

2. To verify that you are in your home directory, type:

pwd

Creating a Directory

You are in your home directory. As a user, you can create directories.

1. Make a subdirectory in your home directory by entering:

   mkdir *Private*

2. Confirm that the directory exists with:

   ls -F

   Among your files now is a listing for the new directory, *Private.* On most systems it is listed first, not because it is a directory, but because its name begins with a capital letter.

3. Create another directory:

   mkdir *Kitchen*
   ls -F

   This time the directory is not listed first, but it does have a / after its name. The **-F** option to **ls** is instruction to put a / after all directory names and a * after executable files. If you use uppercase letters for directories, they are listed at the top of the **ls** output on most systems. However, using **ls -F** also makes them obvious.

4. Change directories into *Private* by entering:

   cd *Private*

   Because *Private* is a subdirectory of your home directory, you can change to *Private* from your home directory by using **cd** with one argument, *Private.*

5. Confirm your location:

   pwd

6. Ask for a listing of files:

   ls

   There are no files in your new *Private* directory. The files you created earlier are listed in your home directory, not in this subdirectory.

7. Create a new file in the *Private* directory by entering:

   cat > *secrets*

8. Enter a line or two of text, and quit by going to a new line and pressing CTRL-D.

9. Once you are back at the shell, list the contents of the directory:

   ls

10. To return to your home directory, enter the usual:

    cd

11. From your home directory, list the contents of the *Private* directory by entering:

    ls *Private*

Directories are used in UNIX as they are in other computing systems—as places to store files that go together. For now, do all your work associated with this book in your home directory.

Copying a File into a Subdirectory

You are in your home directory.

1. List your files and copy one into the *Private* directory:

    ls
    cp *users_on Private*
    ls *Private*

If the last argument to **cp** is a directory, **cp** copies files (the other arguments) to the directory.

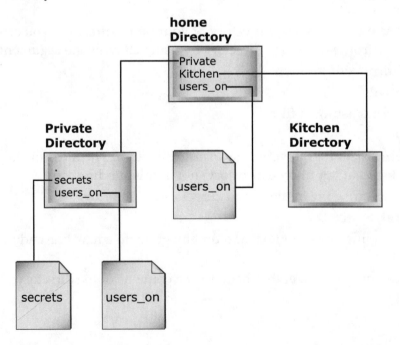

2.10 Examining the Components of a Functioning System

We have been examining the system utilities, processes, shell interactions, and parts of the file system. How do they all work?

Examining the Toolboxes That Contain the Utilities

Throughout this chapter, you have been issuing commands that call for the shell to execute a utility.

1. Enter the following misspelled command:

    datte

    The error message is:

    ```
    Command Not Found
    ```

    Where is the shell looking that it reports "Not Found"? We ask our five-year-old to go upstairs and get a book that is either on the desk or the nightstand. She leaves and returns with the book. It must have been on the desk or on the nightstand. Had it been on the bed with large red arrows pointing at it, she would have returned with the error message:

    ```
    Book Not Found
    ```

    Just like the shell.

2. Ask the shell to display the value of the PATH variable:

    echo $PATH

    The variable PATH is something like:

    ```
    /bin:/usr/bin:/usr/local/bin:/usr/bin/x11:/usr/hosts
    ```

    This variable consists of a series of directories separated by colons. These are the "desk" or "nightstand" places the shell checks for a utility when you ask for one to be executed. The shell looks first in the directory listed on the left, then the next, and so on.

    The */bin* directory contains some of the utilities available on the system in the form of binary files.

3. Obtain a listing of the utilities in */bin*. (Note: The / is important; do not omit it.)

    ls */bin*

The **ls** utility outputs a list of the files in the directory */bin*. You may recognize some of these files—they are utilities you have already used, including **cat**, **rm**, and **ls**. These are some of the executable programs that you access when you type a command. As you saw when you examined your *PATH*, the */bin* directory is not the only directory that contains executable code. The list of directories (PATH) that your shell examines can be modified to include other directories. See Chapter 20, "Modifying the User Environment."

Determining Where a Utility Is Located

The shell looks for utilities and reports on their location.

   1. Enter:

      which who
      which xterm
      which ls
      which set

If you ask for the location of a utility that you know exists and the shell reports it cannot be found, that program, like **set**, is built into the shell itself. The shell cannot find it in the path because it already contains the code.

Examining the Elements of the Password File

Many system files are consulted by utilities as they perform their jobs. When you log on, a program called *login* asks for your password and starts your shell. Your shell gets information like *USER* and *HOME* so it can access the needed information about your account.

   Your user ID number, probably your password, and other information about you reside in a file called */etc/passwd*. This file is read whenever you or any other user logs on.

   1. Type the following command:

      more */etc/passwd*

   If it is a very long file, press SPACEBAR to page through the file.
   If on a large network, try:

      ypcat passwd | more

   2. Locate the entry for your account.

3. Press **q** to stop and return to the shell.

4. Now examine your own personal entry in the *letc/passwd* file. Type the following commands:

> **grep $USER /etc/passwd**

or

> **ypcat passwd | grep $USER**

In these versions, you are asking the shell to evaluate the variable *USER* and pass its value to **grep** as the search target. The **grep** utility then selects the line that matches your login name in the file.

The records in the *letc/passwd* file consist of seven fields separated by colons. The general format is as follows:

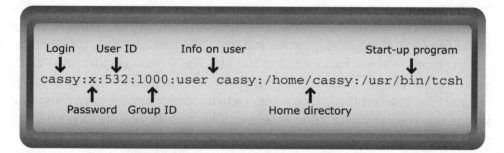

The fields of the password file are described in the following table:

FIELD	INFORMATION
login	The login or name for your account.
password	Your encrypted password. (May be an *x* if the passwords are kept in a secure **/etc/shadow** file. May be a *.)
uid	Your user ID, the unique number that is assigned to your account.
gid	Your group ID. Each user must be a member of at least one group. Every user who has the same number in this field as you have is in your group. You can share files with group members using permissions.
misc	The Miscellaneous field need not be filled. It contains information about the user.
home	Your home directory. This is your current directory when you first log on.
Start-up program	The program that is started when you log on—usually a shell such as the tcsh (/bin/tcsh) or the Korn shell (/bin/ksh), but it does not have to be a shell. It can be anything, including a data entry program or a menu for accessing your accounts at a bank.

Modifying the Permission on Files

As the owner of a file, you determine who has permission to read the contents of the file or to change the contents of the file. If it is a command file, you can specify who can execute it.

1. To view the permissions of the *users_on* file, type the following command:

    ls -l *users_on*

    The output resembles the following:

    ```
    rw-rw-r--  1  cassy       453 Jul 18 11:17 users_on
    ```

The **-l** option is interpreted by **ls** as instruction to provide a long listing of information about the file. The first field in the output, which consists of ten character places, shows the permissions currently set for that file. In a later chapter you will explore setting file permissions in much more depth. For now, however, look at the permissions field. In this example, the first **r** and **w** indicate that *you* have permission to **read** and **write** to the file. The second **rw** indicates that other users who have been assigned to your group have read and write permissions for your file. The last three characters indicate the permission granted to all other users who are not in your group; in this case, they get **read** permissions.

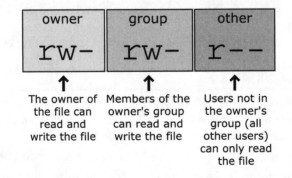

The owner of the file can read and write the file

Members of the owner's group can read and write the file

Users not in the owner's group (all other users) can only read the file

Denying and Adding Read Permission on a File

You can change the permission on a file to make the file inaccessible to all users. (Because you own it, you can still change its permissions again at any time.) No user can read or copy your file if you don't grant read permission.

1. Type the following command to remove read permission from the file *users_on*:

    chmod -r *users_on*

2. Examine the permissions field for *users_on* by typing:

    ls -l

    Notice that although the previous permissions were read and write for you and your group, the new permissions only include a **w**. You removed read permission.

3. Verify the state of the file's permissions by trying to display the file with the following command:

    cat *users_on*

    You immediately receive an error message saying that you do not have permission to read the file. Even though you own the file, if you deny yourself read, you can't read it. But you still own it. You can change the permissions again.

4. Return the read permission to the file with the following command:

    chmod +r *users_on*

    The **chmod** command is used to **ch**ange the **mode** of a file.

   In Chapter 9, "Setting File and Directory Permissions," you will examine what each permission—**r**, **w**, and **x**—controls for files and directories, as well as how to specifically set the permissions for owner, group, and other users.

Programming with UNIX Tools

You can use UNIX to program in a variety of formats and languages. The UNIX operating system gives programmers a number of programming tools that either are packaged with the system or that can be added.

Creating a Shell Script

One of the most basic and useful program tools is the shell itself. You have been using the shell as an interactive command interpreter. It is also a powerful programming environment.

1. Type the following command to create a new file:

    cat > *new_script*

2. Type the following lines:

    echo *Your files are*
    ls

>   **echo** *today is*
>   **date**

Press ENTER to move the cursor to a new line and press CTRL-D.

At this point, the file *new_script* contains a series of shell commands.

3. Examine the file to be certain it is correct:

>   **cat** *new_script*

If there are errors, remove the file *new_script* and return to step 1 to create it again.

4. Try to run the script by entering its name:

>   *new_script*

It does not run.

5. Display the permissions of the file by entering:

>   **ls -l** *new_script*

The permissions indicate that the file is not *executable.* To run the script by simply calling its name, you must grant yourself execute permission.

6. Type the following command to make *new_script* executable:

>   **chmod +x** *new_script*

7. To see the new permissions, enter:

>   **ls -l**

You now have execute permission, as well as read and write permissions for the file.

8. Execute the new script by typing its name:

>   *new_script*

All the commands that you typed into the file are executed, and their output is sent to the screen.

9. If you receive an error message such as:

```
Command not found
```

type the following:

>   *./new_script*

This command line tells the shell exactly where to find the shell script, *new_script*, in your current directory known as "dot."

S U M M A R Y : The steps to create and use a shell script are:

1. Create a file of shell commands.
2. Make the file executable with **chmod**.
3. Execute the file by entering the script name.

When you execute a script, the shell that is reading the script follows those instructions. It executes each line of the script as though it were a line you entered at the keyboard. All utilities in the script are executed.

In an earlier exercise, you told your current shell to read the script and execute the contents of the file with the **source** command. In this case, we issue the script name, which your current shell interprets as instruction to start a child process to read the script. Read permission is enough when you source a script. Execute is needed if you start a child shell to execute it. You will create many scripts in later chapters.

■ Review 2

1. What is the effect of each of the following commands?

   a. lpr *file1 file2*

   _____

   b. sort *file1 file2*

   _____

   c. wc *file1 file2*

   _____

   d. grep *file1 file2*

   _____

   e. who | **sort** > *abc*

   _____

   f. mv *file1 file2*

   _____

   g. cat *file1 file2 file3*

   _____

2. What option to **rm**, **cp**, and **mv** instructs them to get confirmation from the user before deleting or overwriting files?

_____

3. What command results in a reverse sorting of all lines in the *letclpasswd* file that contain a zero somewhere on the line?

_____

4. What do each of the following mean to **more**?
   a. /dec

   _____

   b. b

   _____

5. What will be in the file *file1* as a result of each of the following?
   cp *users_on file1*

   _____

   echo *file1* **>>** *file1*

   _____

   grep *file1* * **>** *file1*

   _____

6. How do each of the following commands work? What results?
   a. **spell** *file1*

   _____

   b. **spell** < *file1*

   _____

   c. **cat** *file1* | **spell**

   _____

7. When you enter the following command, what happens and why?
   cat > *dog*

   _____

8. What results from the following commands?

   a. who | grep $USER

_____

   b. grep \\$HOME *file1*

_____

   c. echo u* >> *file1*

_____

   d. echo 'u*' >> *file1*

_____

   e. alias

_____

   f. ps

_____

   g. . *fileA*

_____

   h. set noclobber

_____

   i. set -o

_____

   j. chmod +x *file2*

_____

9. How can we instruct the **ksh** to interpret **cp** as **cp -i** when we enter it?

_____

10. What command instructs **awk** to output just the time that each user logged on?

_____

11. How can we change the prompt to be *Next?* in both families of shells (C shells and Korn shells)?

_____

12. How can we make sure we are in the home directory, then make a subdirectory in our home directory named *Danny*, then change to the *Danny* directory and confirm our location?

_____

13. What is the output of the command **echo $PATH**

_____

14. What data is in each field in the *passwd* file?

_____: _____: _____: _____: _____: _____: _____

15. What command instructs the shell to not accept CTRL-D as a signal to log off?

_____

■ Conclusion

UNIX is a multiuser, multitasking operating system. It includes numerous utilities that can be linked together for efficiency. UNIX is a complex, powerful, and occasionally unusual operating system. In this chapter, you have been introduced to the fundamental commands and concepts. The skills you mastered in this chapter are the basis for more extensive investigations of the same topics in later chapters. Be sure to read through the Command Summary to remind yourself what each command does.

■ Answers to Review 1

1. who
2. It is a request that the shell start a new process, run the **cal** utility, and pass an argument to *2004*. The **cal** utility interprets the argument as a year. A 12-month calendar for the year 2004 is formatted and output. The output is displayed on the screen.
3. In the C and **bash** shells:

    !!

In the Korn shell:

   r

4. **ls** > *myfile*

5. **ls | wc -l** or **ls | wc -w**

6. **cal** *month year* > *friend-bday*

7. **date** >> *friend-bday*

8. **alias** *cl* **clear**

9. **alias** *cl*=**clear**

10. **ls**

11. **ps**

12. **util** *arg arg* | **util** > *file*

13. **echo** *file1 file2*

   The strings *file1* and *file2* are displayed on the screen.

      more *file1 file2*

   The files *file1* and *file2* are displayed on the screen, one screen at a time.

      wc *file1 file2*

   The number of lines, words, and characters in the files *file1* and *file2* and the totals for both files are displayed.

      !w

   In the csh or tcsh, rerun the last command that started with a **w**.

      r *12*

   In the ksh or bash, rerun command number *12* in the current history list.

14. The **look** utility finds all words in the dictionary beginning with the *psy* character string. The output from **look** is connected to **wc**'s input so **wc** counts just words (**-w**) and writes that count to its output which is connected to the file *psy*.

OBJECT	SHELL INTERPRETATION
look	Utility to execute.
psy	Argument to pass to **look**, which **look** interprets as the beginning of words to locate in the dictionary.
|	Pipe redirects output from previous utility to input of next utility.
wc	Second utility to execute.
-w	Argument to give to **wc**, which **wc** interprets as instruction to count only words.

OBJECT	SHELL INTERPRETATION
>	Redirection connects the output from the previous utility to the file that follows.
psy	Name of file where shell connects output from **wc**.

■ Answers to Review 2

1. The answers are as follows:
   a. Prints *file1* and *file2*
   b. Creates a sorted output consisting of the lines from *file1* and *file2*, merged together in ASCII order. The output is displayed on the screen.
   c. The output of **wc** displayed on the screen is the number of lines, words, and characters in *file1*, and *file2*, and a total of the elements of both.
   d. The output of **grep** displayed on the screen is every line in *file2* that contains the string of characters *file1*.
   e. The output of **who** is passed to **sort**, which sorts the lines. The output of **sort** is redirected to a new file *abc*.
   f. Renames *file1* as *file2*, and if *file2* exists, overwrites it.
   g. Reads each file and outputs all lines concatenated.

2. **-i**

3. **grep** *0* **/etc/passwd | sort -r**

4. */dec*

   Go to the next page that contains the string *dec*.

   > **b**

   Move one screen back toward the top of the file.

5.   **cp** *users_on file1*

   The contents of *users_on* is written to the file *file1*.

      echo *file1 >> file1*

   The character string *file1* is appended to the end of the file *file1*.

      grep *file1 * > file1*

   The shell replaces the * with the name of all files in the current directory. Hence, **grep** is given several arguments. The string *file1* is the target search string which **grep** looks for in all of the files in the current directory. **grep** searches the contents of all files for lines containing the string *file1* and outputs lines that match. **grep**'s output then is written to a file named *file1*.

6. On most systems, all three result in a spellcheck of the file named *file1*. The difference is which program opens the file.

a. **spell** *file1*

Here **spell** is given an argument and so it interprets that argument as a file to open, read, and locate words not in the dictionary.

b. **spell** < *file1*

In this version, the shell opens the file named *file1* and connects it to the input of the process that will run **spell**. After execution, **spell** has no filename arguments so **spell** reads from input where it finds the file quietly waiting.

c. cat *file1* | spell

In this version, the shell starts two processes and connects the output from the first to the input of the second. The string *file1* is passed to **cat** as an argument, which **cat** interprets as a file to open, read, and write all lines to its output, connected to the input of **spell**. Again, **spell** has no arguments, and it so reads from input—the output of **cat**.

7. The shell starts a child process and redirects its output to a file named *dog*. Input is not redirected and instead is connected to the terminal's keyboard. The shell instructs the process to execute the code for **cat**. When **cat** starts, it finds no arguments, so it reads from default input, which is the keyboard. Whatever the user types until a CTRL-D is entered is read and written to the file *dog*.

8. The answers are as follows:

a. The shell starts two processes and connects the output from the first to the input of the second. The shell interprets the value of the variable **USER** and passes its value to the second process as an argument. The shell instructs the first process to run **who** and the second to run **grep**. The output of **who** is passed to **grep**, which looks for all lines containing the user's login name.

b. The shell interprets the backslash as instruction to not interpret the $ that follows, so the shell passes two arguments to **grep**: *$HOME* and *file1*. To **grep** the target string is *$HOME* and the file to search is *file1*.

    c. The shell replaces the **u*** with all filenames starting with a **u** in the current directory then passes those names as arguments to the process running **echo**. The shell connects the output of **echo** to the end of the file *file1*.

    d. The shell interprets this command line exactly like the previous line, except the shell does not expand the **u*** to be filenames because it is in single quotes. The shell passes the string **u*** uninterpreted to **echo** which sees it as an argument, reads it and writes it to the end of the file *file1*.

    e. Since **alias** has no arguments, **alias** lists the current aliases.

    f. Runs **ps** which lists current processes.

    g. Instruction to the ksh or bash to read the file *fileA* and interpret all lines in it as command lines to execute.

    h. In the csh and tcsh, sets the variable **noclobber** which is instruction to not overwrite files using > redirection.

    i. Instruction to the ksh and bash to list all **-o** variables that determine how the shell behaves.

    j. Instruction to the shell to run the **chmod** utility and pass it two arguments: **+x** and the filename *file2*. **chmod** adds execute to user, group, and other.

9. alias *cp*='cp -i'

10. **who | awk '{print $5)'**

11. ksh, bash: **PS1='***Next? *** '**
    tcsh, csh: **set prompt='***Next? *** '**
    It is important to have a space after the prompt when you enter commands.

12.   **cd**
    mkdir *Danny*
      cd *Danny*
      pwd

13. The value of the **PATH** variable lists directories on the system that the current shell examines to locate utilities requested by the user.

14. username: passwd or x : Userid : groupid : info : home : startup program

15. C shell: set *ignoreeof*
    or
    Korn shell: **set -o** *ignoreeof*

COMMAND SUMMARY

Logging On and Off

exit Kills the current shell. (See also **logout**.)

logout Informs the shell you want to end the login session.

passwd Changes user's password.

Working with Directories

cd *Dir* Changes the working directory to *Dir*.

cd Changes directory to home directory.

ls Lists the contents of the current directory.

ls -l Outputs a long listing of the contents of the current directory with one file or directory per line.

mkdir Dir Creates a directory *Dir*.

pwd Displays the full pathname of the current directory.

File Displaying Utilities

cat *file1 file2* Concatenates *file1* and *file2*. (Outputs *file1* then *file2*.)

grep *word filename* Searches for lines containing a particular *word* (or pattern) in *filename*.

head *filename* Displays first ten lines of *filename*.

wc *filename* Counts the lines, words, and characters in *filename*.

Database Utilities

awk '{print $x}' *file* Prints the *x*th field of *file*.

paste *file1 file2* Combines *file1* and *file2,* line by line.

File Management Utilities

cp *file1 file2* Copies *file1* to *file2*.

mv *file1 file2*   Renames *file1* as *file2*.

rm *filename*   Deletes *filename*.

rm -i *filename*   Same as **rm** *filename,* but asks the user to confirm the deletion.

Data Producing and Examining Utilities

tty   Displays the path and filename for the current terminal.

grep *word filename*   Searches for lines containing a particular *word* (or pattern) in *filename*.

sort *filename*   Displays the lines in *filename* in sorted order.

spell *filename*   Checks the spelling in *filename*.

who   Displays a list of users currently logged on.

Printing

lp *filename*   Prints *filename* on the line printer.

lpr *filename*   Prints *filename* on the line printer.

Communication Utilities

write *otherlogin*   Writes a message to another user's workstation.

Redirection of Input and Output

utility < *filename*   Makes *filename* the input for **utility**.

utility > *filename*   Sends the output of **utility** to *filename*.

utility1 | utility2   Makes the output of **utility1** the input of **utility2**.

File Permissions

chmod -r *filename*   Removes permission to read *filename*.

chmod +r *filename*   Gives permission to read *filename*.

chmod +x *filename*   Grants execute permission on the file.

chmod -x *filename*   Removes execute permission on the file.

Shell Programming

set   Lists the variables that are set for your shell and their values. In C shell, lists local variables. In Korn shell, lists local and environment variables.

env   Lists environment variables.

printenv   Lists environment variables.

$*var*   Evaluates a variable, *var*.

*   Expands to match filenames.

****   Interprets next character as ordinary character without special meaning.

'   '   Interprets all characters between the single quotes as ordinary characters.

scriptname   Executes the commands in the file **scriptname**.

History

!!   In the C shell, reexecutes the last shell command.

r   In the Korn shell, reexecutes the last shell command.

Working with Aliases

alias   Lists your aliases and their values.

alias *string* 'command'   In the C shell, accepts *string* as equivalent of *command*.

alias *string*='command'   In the Korn shell, accepts *string* as equivalent of *command*.

Setting the User Environment

set *prompt* = "*string*"   In the C and **tsch** shells, makes *string* the new prompt.

PS1="*string*"   In the Bourne, **bash**, or Korn shell, makes *string* the new prompt.

Process Monitoring

ps   Displays current processes for this login session.

Additional Utilities

date   Outputs system date and time.

cal   Displays calendar of current month. **cal** *2002* displays the calendar year *2002*.

clear   Clears the terminal screen.

look *keyword*   Outputs all words in the dictionary that begin with *keyword*.

history   Displays a listing of your previously executed commands.

more   Displays output one screen at a time.

tail   The last lines of a file are displayed.

unalias *name*   Removes previously created alias *name*.

man   Displays useful information about a utility, and provides basic instruction on how to use it.

echo   Reads arguments and writes them to output.

mesg   Controls write access to your terminal. (y or n)

which *utility-name*   Reports the location of *utility-name*.

ypcat   Reads network database files the way that cat reads local files.

Editing with the Visual Editor

3

O B J E C T I V E S

After completing this chapter, you will be able to use **vi** to

- Create and access files
- Quickly find specific text in a document
- Add lines, words, and characters to files
- Move the cursor to particular words or lines in a file
- Delete characters, lines, and blocks of text
- Change characters, lines, and blocks of text
- Cut and paste lines of text
- Undo changes
- Properly move between the editor modes
- Make global changes
- Customize the editing environment
- Use the visual editor startup control file

When writing text or computer programs, you create files, insert new lines, rearrange lines, modify content, and make other necessary changes. Computer text editors were developed to accomplish these tasks. The UNIX **v**isual editor, **vi**, is a powerful, fast, command-driven screen editor. You give all your instructions to the editor by entering combinations of keystrokes. The **vi** visual editor is available on all UNIX systems and is an essential UNIX tool. By using the **vi** editor, you can create text as well as make specific and global changes to text—precisely and, with practice, easily.

In this chapter, you will use the visual editor to access files, move to various locations in the text, and make content editing changes within the file, such as replacing text, deleting lines, reading in other files, and rearranging portions of files. Copies of a document in varying stages of development can be saved and printed.

3.1 Introducing the Visual Editor

In the 1970s, people edited files on UNIX with the line editor by issuing cumbersome commands. There was no way to move the cursor to a particular word and make a correction. Instead, to correct the spelling of a word in the 14th line, you had to issue a command such as *14/s/misteak/mistake/*. A graduate student at the University of California at Berkeley, Bill Joy, wrote the **vi** visual editor to allow movement of the cursor to specific locations in a file for editing. An old editing program, **vi** is not a word processor and does not support many of the features available in today's word processing programs. There is no mouse, no pull-down menu, and no page formatting. However, the **vi** editor is present in every UNIX environment, uses few computing resources, includes many tools that make editing efficient, and once its commands are learned, is actually quite fast.

Two major versions of the editor are widely available. Standard UNIX releases include **vi**, and Linux provides **vim**, which includes some **vim**provements. The same command, **vi**, usually accesses **vim** in Linux.

It's not easy to master **vi**'s two modes—*command* mode and *append/insert* mode—nor to keep track of the many commands you enter from the keyboard. Once mastered, **vi** is an essential tool in UNIX for three reasons:

- It is provided as part of all standard UNIX releases, so it is available everywhere.

- Once you can use the basic commands, **vi** is a fast and effective editor.
- Although **vi** uses few computing resources, it possesses advanced features not available on other editors. The visual editor is actually the editor of choice for advanced users and programmers.

In this first section, you will tour **vi**'s features and learn the basic commands. In later sections, you will explore in depth the many ways to move around, delete, add, change, and manipulate blocks of text.

We suggest you:

1. Complete the quick tour in the first section, and then start using **vi** with that limited set of commands.
2. Work through the remainder of the chapter.
3. Do not attempt to remember all the commands at first. Master a reasonable collection, and then expand with time.
4. Return to the "Command Summary" at the end of this chapter and reread it often, selecting commands to include in your repertoire.
5. When you want to reinforce the commands, redo the chapter. It takes much less time the second go-round.

3.2 Working in an Existing File with vi

Files are central to the UNIX computing environment. Business letters, college theses, program code, program output, data, e-mail, and data records are all stored as files. The visual editor is used to create new files and edit existing files. Even though a file is created using another utility such as **who**, it can still be identified by its name and accessed by **vi**.

The visual editor, however, is built in a way opposite to most other editing environments. When you start a letter with a typewriter or a PC word processor, the one thing you can do right away is type in or add text to the file. Not so with **vi**. When you start editing a file with **vi**, the one thing you *can't* do is add text. You can move around in the file and delete words, lines, and characters, but you cannot add text to the file without first issuing an "I want to add text" command.

For that reason, it is easiest to learn to use **vi** by starting with an existing file.

Creating a Practice File

Begin by creating a practice file that you will edit throughout this chapter.

1. Log onto your user account (not as root).

2. One of the many ways to create a file in UNIX is with the **cat** utility. Start the process of creating a new file by typing:

    cat > *practice*

3. Press ENTER.

4. Type in the following lines. When you make mistakes, don't try to fix them. In later exercises, you can use **vi** to correct those errors. Be sure to include the blank lines.

    This practice file will be used
    several times in this course.

    Although I am creating this file with the cat command,
    later I will be editing it with the visual editor.

    a b c d
    2 3 4 5
    2 3 4 5
    A B C D
    E F G H

    (This is not making too much sense.)
    Hello, I will be sure to add several more
    lines of text before quitting:

    To tell the **cat** utility that you are through typing text, do the following:

5. Get to a new line by pressing ENTER.

6. Tell **cat** there is no more input by pressing CTRL-D.

    The **cat** program ends and a shell prompt is displayed.

7. Add more text to the file by entering the following command lines. Be sure to use the double redirection to add to the file.

    head */etc/passwd* >> *practice*
    cal *1752* >> *practice*

3.3 Touring the Visual Editor

Before examining the visual editor commands in detail, this section takes you on a quick tour of the editor's features. You will master some fundamental commands and examine the structure of the editor.

You have just used the command **cat** > *filename* to create a new file. The *filename* you assign to a file (such as *practice*) becomes the identification label used by UNIX to locate the file when you want to work on it.

1. To start editing your new *practice* file using the **vi**sual editor, enter the command:

   vi *practice*

   and press ENTER.

This command line instructs the shell to start the **vi** program and to give it one argument, *practice.*

At this stage, the editor is running; it interprets the argument *practice* as a file, which it opens and displays on your screen. The cursor appears on the first line of the file. You are no longer talking to the shell. Instead, you are in the *command* mode of the visual editor, where you can do several things to the file: move around, delete text, copy and paste text, and move to the *append* mode, where you add text to the file or make changes in the text. It is also from command mode that you will later quit the editor and return to the shell.

Moving Around in the File

When editing a file, you often need to correct the spelling of a word, remove specific lines of text, or insert additional code at different locations in the file. To accomplish edits, you must inform **vi** exactly where you want to add text, or which specific character, word, or line you want to change. There is no mouse. To communicate with **vi**, you move the screen cursor to the appropriate location in the text before you start an editing operation.

> **NOTE:** In these first exercises, you will move around and delete text. If you suddenly are adding characters to the file, you have pressed a key that moved you to append mode. Press ESC to return to command mode and continue the exercises.

Moving One Character or Line at a Time

A fundamental way to move the cursor through a file is with the *direction keys*.

1. Press **j** one time.

   The cursor moves down one line. If the cursor does not move, press ESC and then try again.

   Most workstations include arrow keys that also instruct the editor to move the cursor on the screen.

2. Press the ↓ one time.

   If the cursor moves down to the second line, the arrow keys work in **vi** on your system.

   When you telnet into a location, the arrow keys may not work. In that case, use the **h**, **j**, **k**, and **l** direction keys.

3. Move around the file using each of the four arrow keys.

4. Move the cursor left, down, up, and right through the text using the **h**, **j**, **k**, and **l** direction keys.

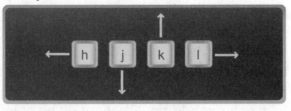

5. Move your cursor to a blank space, whether between words or accidentally placed at the end of a line.

   Spaces are characters.

6. Try to move the cursor beyond the text—to the right and left, above the first line, and below the last line.

   When you attempt to go beyond the existing text, the cursor does not move, and the workstation either flashes or beeps.

Moving Efficiently to a Specific Target

Thus far, you have been moving around the file character by character and line by line. There are several faster and more explicit ways to move the cursor.

An efficient way to move the cursor to a specific word in the text is with the forward search command.

1. To move the cursor forward to the first word *be* in the file, enter:

   /be

   and press ENTER.

   As you type the slash character **/** and each letter of the target word *be*, they appear in the lower-left corner of the screen. The characters are *not* entered into your file. The editor is just displaying your forward search command as you type it.

   After you press ENTER, the cursor moves forward to the specified word (*be*) in the text. If this doesn't happen, press ESC and try again. If there is no *be* in your file, try */a* instead.

2. Try the following:

   /me followed by ENTER
   /Sep followed by ENTER
   /7 followed by ENTER

3. Use the forward search command to locate another word, such as *text*.

After you enter a search command and press ENTER, the cursor moves to the target text, and you are still in command mode.

Finding Other Instances of the Target

If a string of characters appears more than once in your file, the forward search command moves the cursor to the first instance of the character or characters after the cursor. You can go on to others.

1. Search for the word *will* in your *practice* file:

   /will

2. Once you've located the first occurrence of the word, locate the next occurrence by entering:

   n

3. Keep typing **n**ext.

   When the editor reaches the end of the file, it loops back to the beginning of the file and continues the search.

4. Move the cursor to the next colon by entering:

   /:

5. To move to others, press:

> n
> n
> n

S U M M A R Y : You must be in command mode to search for text characters. When you enter /*targetstring* and press ENTER, the cursor moves forward through the text to the next occurrence of "*targetstring*." When the editor reaches the end of the file, it goes back to the beginning and searches forward until it either locates the target or returns to your previous location. To go to the next occurrence, use the **n** command.

Quitting the Editor

At this point, you are editing the file *practice* with **vi**. A single command instructs the editor to write the file back to the hard drive and quit the editor program.

1. Enter:

> **:wq**

The shell prompt is displayed.

2. Confirm you are again communicating with the shell:

> **date**
> **ls**

3. Return to editing by entering:

> **vi** *practice*

Conceptualizing the Visual Editor in Command Mode

As each series of **vi** commands is introduced in this chapter, a conceptual map is included to assist you in learning and reviewing the commands. Figure 3-1 is the conceptual map of **vi**'s command mode.

1. In Figure 3-1, locate the box marked **Shell**, with the **$** prompt. Notice the arrow labeled **who** that leads from the shell to the box describing what the **who** command does. When **who** completes its task, you are returned to the shell.

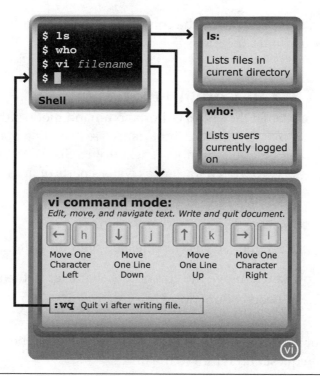

$ ls
$ who
$ vi *filename*
$

Shell

ls:

Lists files in
current directory

who:

Lists users
currently logged
on

vi command mode:
Edit, move, and navigate text. Write and quit document.

| ← | h | ↓ | j | ↑ | k | → | l |

Move One
Character
Left

Move
One Line
Down

Move
One Line
Up

Move One
Character
Right

:wq   Quit vi after writing file.

FIGURE 3-1   Conceptual map: The command mode of *vi*

2. Find the arrow leading down from the shell, labeled **vi** *filename.* When you used the **vi** command earlier, you entered *practice* as the *filename.*

   According to the conceptual map, when you are in the shell and type the command **vi** *filename*, you leave the shell and move into **vi**'s command mode. In command mode, you can move around, examine, and delete text from the file.

   The command **vi** *filename* is an instruction to the shell to start **vi**. Then **vi** opens the file and puts you in command mode.

   At this point, you are in **vi**. The shell is no longer interpreting the commands you type—the visual editor is.

   When you press a direction key, the editor moves the cursor and then waits for your next command. You can type one cursor movement command after another without ever leaving command mode.

3. Find the arrows and direction key commands in Figure 3-1. These commands do not move you into another mode and do not require the use of the

ENTER key. When you issue the commands, they take effect immediately, moving you around the file.

Deleting Text in Command Mode

So far, you have been in the visual editor's command mode moving around the file by issuing commands. Another important class of editing operations, available only from command mode, is removing text from a file. With **vi** you can remove one or more lines, words, or characters as well as parts of lines or whole sections of text.

Removing Whole Lines

One or more lines in a file can easily be deleted with the editor.

1. Use an arrow key to move the cursor to a character in the middle of a line.
2. Type the **drop-d**ead command:

    dd

    You do not need to press ENTER. As soon as you type the second **d**, **vi** does what you request and removes the line.
3. Move to another line and delete it.

   Blank lines, as well as text lines, can be deleted with the **dd** command.
   The **dd** command tells the editor to delete the current line; you are still in command mode.

Deleting Individual Characters

You can also delete a single character from a file.

1. Move your cursor to any character, such as the *H* in the word *Hello*.
2. Delete the character under the cursor by entering a lowercase:

    x

    The **x** (x-out) command deletes only the single character under the cursor. It is the "delete one character at a time" command.
3. Move to different locations in the file and delete individual characters.

    Spaces between words on a line are characters just like letters or numbers.
4. Use the **x** to delete a space from the file.

   See Figure 3-2, in which both navigating and deleting are summarized.

Shell starts vi and passes
it the argument *filename*

$ vi *filename*

Shell

vi opens file

vi command mode:
Edit, move, and navigate text. Write and quit document.

← ↓ ↑ → -Move cursor left, down, up, and right.

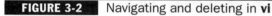 / *word* -Move cursor to next instance of *word*.

x -Delete one character under the cursor.

d d -Delete the line.

:wq Quit vi after writing file.

(vi)

FIGURE 3-2   Navigating and deleting in **vi**

Undoing Text Changes

1. Delete a line of text by entering:

   dd

2. To bring back the line you just removed, type the following:

   u

   The undo goes back one change.

3. Delete a character with **x**.

4. Bring it back with:

   u

   After you make an alteration to the file, you can undo the change.

Adding Text to the File

Thus far, you have been moving around and deleting text from the file, but you have not yet added any text. There are several ways to add text, including adding new text on either side of the cursor, opening a line below the cursor, opening a line above the cursor, adding to the end of the line...

At this point, you will examine how to add text after the cursor and in a line below the cursor.

Appending Text to the Right of the Cursor

You have been instructing the editor to move the cursor around the file by issuing specific commands in command mode. Pressing the keys on the keyboard does not add text to the file. To add text, you must tell the editor to leave command mode and put you in *append* or *insert* mode.

You are presently in the command mode, where the keys are used to issue position-change and delete commands, not to enter text.

1. Move the cursor to any line on the screen, and delete the line by typing:

   dd

   The **dd** tells the editor to *delete one line* when you are in the **vi** command mode.

2. Enter the command mode request to undo the deletion:

   u

3. Use the → or the l key to move the cursor to the end of the first line in the file.

4. In command mode, type the following command one time:

   a

   Notice that the **a** is not displayed on the screen.

5. Now type a **dd** again. The **dd** appears on the screen and is added to the file; nothing gets deleted because you are in append mode.

   The **a** command tells **vi** to start adding everything you type to the file, placing the new text in the file starting on the right of the present cursor location.

6. Now that you are in append mode, press ENTER and type the following:

   I am now adding more text.
   Therefore I must be in append mode.
   The a command moves me into append mode.
   Whatever I type is added to the file.

Examine the conceptual map in Figure 3-3. Note that the **a** command takes you out of command mode and puts you into append or insert mode. Whatever you type no longer is interpreted as a delete or move-around command; instead **vi** reads what you type and enters it into the file starting at the right of the cursor.

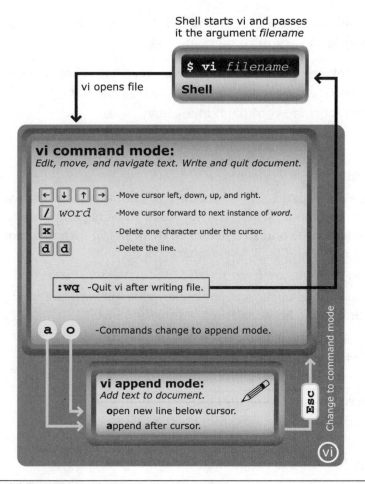

Shell starts vi and passes
it the argument *filename*

$ **vi** *filename*
Shell

vi opens file

vi command mode:
Edit, move, and navigate text. Write and quit document.

← ↓ ↑ → -Move cursor left, down, up, and right.

/ *word* -Move cursor forward to next instance of *word*.

x -Delete one character under the cursor.

d d -Delete the line.

:wq -Quit vi after writing file.

a o -Commands change to append mode.

vi append mode:
Add text to document.
open new line below cursor.
append after cursor.

Esc

Change to command mode

vi

FIGURE 3-3 Adding text in *vi*

Leaving Append Mode and Returning to Command Mode

In the last exercise, you moved the cursor around with specific commands while in command mode, and then you typed the **a** command. In command mode, the keyboard is used to enter editing commands, such as **h**, **j**, **k**, **l**, and **dd**. Those keys are not text to be added; rather, they are commands to the editor. The **a** tells the editor to leave **vi**'s command mode and enter append mode. In append mode, the editor reads whatever you type and adds it to the file at the cursor location. You then add text.

As long as you are in append mode, every key you type continues to be appended to the text; you do not return to command mode. When you have finished typing text, you need a way to instruct the **vi** editor to move you out of append mode and back into command mode.

1. Take a look at Figure 3-3. Find the command that appears on the arrow that moves you from append mode back to command mode.

2. Press the return to command mode key:

   ESC

   Nothing appears to be different on the screen.

3. Enter **dd**.

   A line is deleted; **dd** is now a command, not text to be added. You are again in command mode, where the keyboard is for issuing commands to move around in the file and to delete text. By pressing ESC, you move out of append mode and back to command mode.

4. Confirm that you are in command mode; press ESC a second time.

   If a beep sounds or the screen flashes, **vi** is telling you that it cannot move to command mode because you are already there.

5. Use the arrow keys to go to the end of a word on the screen.

6. Tell **vi** you want to enter text after the word by entering:

   a

7. Add several words of text to the file.

8. When you have finished adding text, press:

   ESC

   You are returned to command mode.

9. Move to another location in the file, and again go through the cycle of moving to append mode, adding text, and returning to command mode.

Opening a Line Below the Cursor

The editor also adds a line between two existing lines.

1. Make sure you are in command mode and then move the cursor to any location on a line near the middle of your screen. Type the **o**pen command (lowercase):

   o

   The **o** command opens a new blank line below the cursor line and before the next line in your file. You are again in append mode.

2. Add text such as this:

   *There is more than one way to move from
   command mode to append!
   Each one starts adding text in a different place
   with respect to the cursor.*

3. Return to command mode by pressing ESC.

NOTE: The ESC key is an essential component of the visual editor. Whenever you are in doubt about where you are in **vi**—command or append mode—press ESC. In append mode, ESC moves you to command mode. In command mode, ESC produces a beep or flash, indicating that you are already in command mode. In either case, after you press ESC, you are certain to be in command mode. From this point, you can decide what you want to do.

Ending an Editing Session

When ending an editing session, two issues must be addressed: saving changes to your file and quitting the editor.

Saving the File and Quitting the Editor

To save the modified file and quit the editor, you must be in command mode. Make certain you are in command mode.

1. Press ESC.

   You have been editing a copy of your *practice* file.

2. To write the changes back to the original file and quit, enter:

   :wq

   and press ENTER.

   The file is **written** (saved) and the editor **quits**. You are back communicating with the shell. See Figure 3-4.

   Issue a shell command such as **date**.

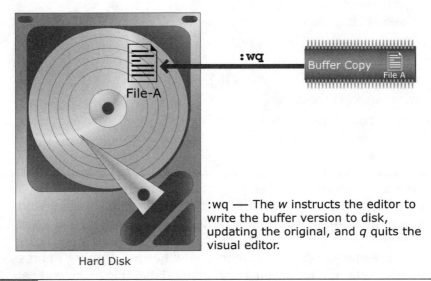

:wq — The *w* instructs the editor to
write the buffer version to disk,
updating the original, and *q* quits the
visual editor.

Hard Disk

FIGURE 3-4   Saving a file and quitting the editor

Quitting Without Saving

In this exercise, you will make changes to a file and then quit without saving
the changes.

1. Start editing practice with:
      vi *practice*
2. From command mode, open a line and go into append by entering:
      o
3. Add the following line:
      this line added to practice xxxx
4. Press ESC and return to command mode.
5. This time, attempt to quit the editor by entering:
      :q
   The editor informs you that you have not decided the fate of the changes
   you made to the file.
   ```
   No write since last change.
   ```
6. Tell the editor to quit without writing:
      :q!
7. Examine the file
      head *practice*

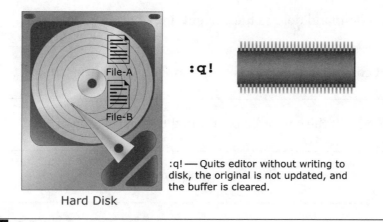

:q! — Quits editor without writing to disk, the original is not updated, and the buffer is cleared.

Hard Disk

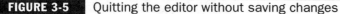

FIGURE 3-5   Quitting the editor without saving changes

The line you added to the file was not saved, the file was not saved, and the file is as it was before your last editing. See Figure 3-5.

Review 1

Examine the conceptual map in Figure 3-2, and then answer the following questions. The answers are given at the end of the chapter.

1. What command allows you to move the cursor one character to the left?

2. What command allows you to move the cursor one line up?

3. What mode must you be in to move around a file?

4. What mode must you be in to issue the **dd** command?

5. What command takes the cursor forward to the word *Admin*?

6. What command takes the cursor forward to the next occurrence of the word *Admin*?

7. What command deletes the current line of text?

_____

8. What command deletes a single character under the cursor?

_____

9. Where must the cursor be positioned to delete a line of text?

_____

10. What command reverses the change you made?

_____

11. What command do you type to add text to the right of the cursor?

_____

12. What command opens a line below the cursor?

_____

13. What mode must you be in to enter text into the file?

_____

14. What command tells the editor to take you back to command mode from append mode?

_____

15. What command do you type to leave **vi** without saving the changes to a file?

_____

16. What command instructs **vi** to save changes and return you to the shell?

_____

17. What mode must you be in to save the changes you made into the file?

_____

3.4 Quickly Moving Around in a File

In the tour you just completed, you mastered enough of the editor to survive. Now the goal is to become proficient.

In the **vi** tour you just completed, you moved around the file, deleted text, and added text using just a few commands. The following sections of this chapter look in detail at moving around, deleting, adding, and changing text as well as modifying the editing environment.

Although you can edit files using the limited set of commands introduced thus far, the commands that populate the remainder of the chapter, once mastered, will greatly increase your speed and power.

Augmenting the Direction Keys

You have been moving through the file one character or one line at a time. You can go faster than this. The number keys (1 through 9) located at the top of your keyboard or in the keypad to the right can be used as part of the direction key commands. Try the following:

1. Begin editing the *practice* file again by entering:

    vi *practice*

2. To have the cursor move four spaces down, type:

    4

    and then press either ↓ or **j** without pressing ENTER.

    By preceding the direction key or arrow with a *4*, you instruct **vi** to move the cursor down four lines.

3. Move around the screen using augmented direction commands such as these:

    2 ↑
    6 →
    3 ←
    4 ↓
    3 **j**
    2 **h**
    3 **k**
    3 **l**

4. Many workstations will repeat an operation if you press the key and hold it down. Press and hold down a direction key now to see how it works on your workstation.

The arrow keys or the **h, j, k,** and **l** direction keys—either alone or in conjunction with number keys—allow you to move the cursor to any character in the file. As you will see, there are more efficient ways to move the cursor long distances.

Locating Characters, Not Words

You have seen how the forward search command finds the string of characters that you specify. This command is used to locate *character strings*, not words.

1. For instance, enter:

/it

The *it* in the following words are located: with, editing, it, editor, and quitting.

You can also use the power of the forward search command to locate a string of several words. For instance:

2. Look at your screen and locate two words on a line such as *several times.* Try the following command to search for these two words:

/several times

The blank space characters can be included in a search string.

3. Move the cursor to some other locations in the file, using the forward search feature of the editor.

Searching in Both Directions

You can also instruct the editor to search backward through the text to the previous instance of the target word or character string.

1. Place your cursor in the middle of the file, using a command such as:

5 ↓or

5 j

2. Search forward through the file for the next letter *e* by entering:

/e

3. Search backward through the file by entering:

> *?e*

The cursor goes to the previous *e*.

4. Continue the search by pressing each of the following:

> **n**
>
> **n**
>
> **N**
>
> **n**
>
> **N**

The lowercase **n** takes you to the next instance of the target in the current direction. The uppercase **N** reverses the search direction.

S U M M A R Y : The **/** is used to instruct the editor to search forward for a target string; the **?** is used to search backward. Regardless of which direction you are searching, you can move to the next occurrence of the word in the same direction using the **n** command and reverse the search direction with a capital **N**.

Moving the Cursor in Word Increments

So far, you have used the **h**, **j**, **k**, and **l** keys or the arrow keys to move the cursor individual characters or lines. You can also move the cursor through the text a word at a time, either forward or backward.

Moving Forward and Backward Word by Word

1. In the file *practice,* use the **/** command to position the cursor to any word in one of the first few lines of text.

2. Type the following lowercase command:

> **w**

The cursor advances to the beginning of the next word. You do not use the **/** search command, and you do not press ENTER. You are in command mode, and the **w** simply instructs the editor to move ahead one word.

3. Type the **w** command several more times.

Each time you do, the cursor advances forward to the *beginning* of the next word.

The visual editor can also move the cursor to the **e**nd of a word and **b**ackward to previous words.

4. Enter each of the following commands and observe the results:

> **w**
> **w**
> **w**
> **e**
> **b**

(Could this be the origin of the *world wide web*?)

Moving Multiple Words

1. All of these cursor-moving commands can be augmented to move through several words at a time. Try the following:

> **3b**
> **2e**
> **3w**
> **4b**

Figure 3-6 summarizes these commands.

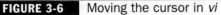

FIGURE 3-6   Moving the cursor in *vi*

Specifying Locations on the Current Line

You can move the cursor to specific places on the current line.

Moving to the End or Beginning of a Line

1. Move the cursor to the beginning of a line that has lots of text.
   Then enter:

   $

   ^

   $

   0 (zero)

The dollar sign ($) instructs the editor to move the cursor to the end of the current line. Both the caret (^) and the zero (0) move the cursor to the beginning of the line.

Moving to a Specific Character or Numbered Character

You can also move the cursor to any character on the line, no matter where it is.

1. Move the cursor to the beginning of a line such as the one starting with *Each*:

   /Each

   Select a character on the line such as the *x* in *text* and enter the following:

   fx

   where the *x* is any target character on the current line.

   The cursor moves to the first *x* on the line.
2. Press ENTER until you are on another line with a lot of text.
3. Move the cursor one word by entering:

   w

   To use the **f** command, you do not have to be at the beginning of the line.
4. Move the cursor forward to a specified character by replacing the *y* in the following command with your selected character:

   f*y*

   The **f** command takes one argument and that argument is placed immediately next to the **f**. The target character argument must be a character to the right of the cursor on the current line. The cursor moves to the selected character.
5. Move the cursor back to the beginning of the line:

   ^

6. Tell the editor to go to the 15th character position by entering:

     15 |

7. Move to the second character on the line:

     2 |

Figure 3-7 summarizes these commands.

Going to Lines Using their Numbers

Every line in a file is numbered starting with line 1.

1. Request that the editor display the line numbers by entering the command:

     :set number
     ENTER

   The colon and ENTER are essential.

2. Tell the editor to go to specific lines in the file by entering:

     5G
     G
     1G
     :8
     ENTER
     :15
     ENTER
     :$
     ENTER
     –
     +

   The editor interprets a command such as **5G** as instruction to move the cursor to the fifth line. Likewise *:8* is instruction to move the cursor to line 8. Although the $ alone is seen as instruction to move the cursor to the end of the current line, the command :$ means go to the last line of the file.

   All commands that start with : must be concluded with an ENTER. The other vi commands are executed as soon as you type them.

3. Instruct the editor to turn off the numbers with:

     :set *nonumber*

4. You can now have the line numbers by entering:

     :set *number*

   or turn them off using **:set** *nonumber* as you wish.

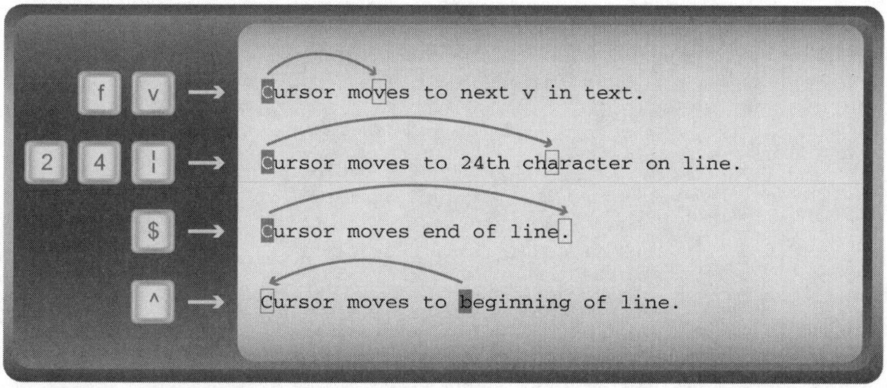

FIGURE 3-7 Moving the cursor in **vi**

Moving to Locations on the Current Screen Display

In the previous exercises, you moved the cursor to lines specified by the line number in the file. The following exercise instructs the editor to move the cursor to lines that happen to be at locations on the display, such as the topmost line on the screen.

1. Enter:

    M
    L

2. Press the ↓ or ↑ to bring new text into the display.
3. Try the screen location commands again:

    L
    M
    H

The cursor moves to whatever line is currently at specific locations on the display. See Figure 3-8.

L	Positions cursor at lowest line displayed on the screen
M	Positions cursor at line near midpoint of the screen
H	Positions cursor at highest line on the screen

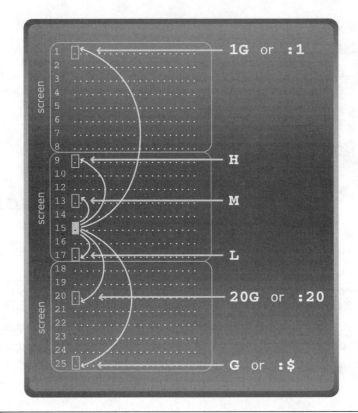

FIGURE 3-8 Moving the cursor by line address and location display

Returning to the Last Cursor Position

Often while editing, you need to move to a distant location in the file to check on some specific concern or perform an editing task, and once the task is completed, you need to return to the initial location and continue editing there.

1. Before you move the cursor, mentally note the line number where the cursor is currently located.

2. Then reposition the cursor to some distant line that you need to see. For example, move the cursor to line 11 by typing the command:

    11G

3. At this location, add a line of text:

    o

4. Return to command mode:

    ESC

5. In command mode, type two single quotation marks (*not* double quotation marks):

    ' '

    You just entered the secret passage. The two single quotation marks instruct the editor to return you to your previous line in a file, no matter where it is, and even though you have made changes to the file at the new location.

Adjusting the Screen's Display of Text

The cursor movement commands like */word* or **17G** relocate the cursor to a new character, word, or line in the file, and the screen display follows along. These commands are line and text oriented, not display oriented. The screen display is determined by the cursor location. You can also move the display forward or backward in the file, forcing the cursor to follow along.

1. From command mode, press:

    CTRL-F

    This time the screen moves forward to the next half-screen of text, and the cursor comes along for the ride. The commands described in the following table are used to adjust the workstation's screen display and to move forward or backward to a different block or section of text, regardless of its context. There are two commands for moving in each direction.

2. Read through these display adjustment commands.

3. Try each several times.

DISPLAY ADJUSTMENT COMMAND	FUNCTION
CTRL-D	Scrolls down one screen of text in the file
CTRL-U	Scrolls up one screen of text in the file
CTRL-F	Displays the next half-screen of text in a file
CTRL-B	Displays the previous half-screen of text in a file

See the graphical view of display adjustment commands in Figure 3-9.

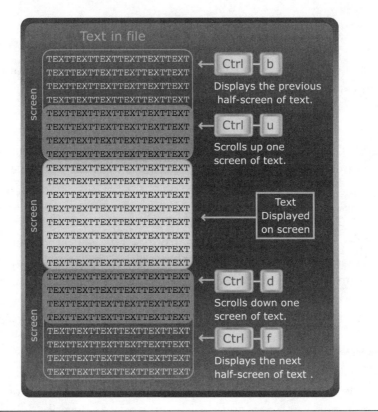

FIGURE 3-9   Adjusting the display

Changing the Display and Moving the Cursor— A Summary

The commands in this section of the chapter examine two kinds of "move around the file" functions:

- *Cursor-positioning commands* move the cursor to a particular designated position in your file. When the cursor moves, the screen display has to compensate.

- *Display-adjusting commands* move the screen display forward or backward in the file relative to the cursor's current position and display a new section of text. The cursor has to follow along.

Moving the Cursor to Specific Targets, Display Follows

The square in the center (over the letter *c* in *certain*) is the cursor. To move the cursor to the top left (to the *T* in *This*), you type the uppercase command **H**. In this figure, the arrows connecting the cursor to the various destinations have the command key printed next to them.

Figure 3-10 lists commands you use to move the cursor without leaving command mode. Practice each command again several times, making sure to note the position of the cursor before and after you perform each command.

■ Review 2

1. What command moves the cursor down three lines?

   _____

2. What mode must you be in to move around the screen using the direction keys?

   _____

3. What command moves the cursor to the right seven characters?

   _____

Cursor Positioning Command	Function
0 (zero)	Moves cursor to the beginning of the current line.
^	Moves cursor to the beginning of the current line.
$	Moves cursor to the end of the line.
nnG	Moves cursor to line nn, where nn is the line number.
G	Moves cursor to the beginning of the last line in your file.
-	Moves the cursor to the beginning of the prior line.
+	Positions cursor at the beginning of the next line.
nn|	Positions cursor at column nn of current line, where nn is the column number.
/abc	Moves cursor to the next occurrence of string abc in text.
L	Positions cursor at lowest line displayed on the screen.
M	Positions cursor at line near midpoint of the screen.
H	Positions cursor at highest line on the screen.
fx	Moves cursor forward on the line to next x, where x is a specified character.
n	Moves to the next pattern identified in a previously issued /word or ?word.
' '	Returns cursor to the last line cursor was located on.
b	Moves the cursor to the beginning of the previous word.
w	Moves cursor to the beginning of the next word.
e	Moves cursor to the end of the current word.
h	Moves cursor left one character.
j	Moves cursor down one character.
k	Moves cursor up one character.
l	Moves cursor right one character.

FIGURE 3-10   Cursor positioning commands

4. What command locates the words *wonderful heroes*?

_____

5. What command searches backward through the file for the string *time*?

_____

6. What command takes the cursor to the next instance of the target string in the current direction?

_____

7. What command takes the cursor to the next instance of the target string in the reverse direction?

_____

8. What command moves the cursor to the beginning of the next word?

_____

9. What command moves the cursor backward to the beginning of the current or the previous word?

_____

10. What command moves the cursor to the beginning of the current line?

_____

11. What command moves the cursor to the end of the current line?

_____

12. What command moves the cursor forward to the first instance of the character _t_?

_____

13. What command moves the cursor to the eighth character position regardless of the current cursor position?

_____

14. What command requests that the **vi** editor display the line number at the beginning of each line?

_____

15. What command requests that the **vi** editor turn off the line number display?

_____

16. What command takes the cursor to the beginning of the 15th line of the file?

_____

17. What command takes the cursor to the beginning of the last line of the file?

_____

18. What command takes the cursor to the beginning of the first line of the file?

_____

19. What command do you type to leave **vi** without saving the changes to the file?

_____

20. What command positions the cursor at the lowest line displayed on the screen?

_____

21. Assume you are on a line of text, and enter /*target*. The cursor then moves to the line containing the string *target*. How can you tell the editor to return to the original line?

_____

22. What command scrolls the text down one screen of text in the file?

_____

23. What command displays the previous half-screen of text in a file?

_____

3.5 Deleting Text from a File

In the tour of the editor, you deleted lines with **dd** and single characters with **x**. Essentially, any portions of a file can be specified and deleted.

Deleting Several Lines

Like the direction keys, the **dd** command can be prefaced with a number to delete more than one line at the same time.

1. Move to the top of your file and issue the command:

    2dd

    The cursor line and the one following it are deleted.

2. Undo the deletion:

    u

3. Move to another location and issue:

    4dd

4. Use the **G** key to go to the last line in your file.

5. Type the command:

    3dd

    In this case, nothing is deleted, because you are requesting **vi** to remove more lines than are available to delete.

Deleting Multiple Characters

In the tour of **vi**, you deleted individual characters using the **x** command.

1. Move to the beginning of a line containing text and enter:

    x
    w
    5x
    w
    10x
    u

    An **x** deletes the character beneath the cursor. Augment the **x** with a number, and delete that number of characters.

Deleting One or Several Words

In addition to deleting lines and parts of lines, the editor lets you delete words.

1. Move your cursor to the beginning of a line containing many words.

2. Type the following **vi** commands, and observe the results:

   w
   dw
   3dw

   The **dw** command deletes words and can be modified or augmented with a number, just like most **vi** commands.

3. Place the cursor in the middle of a long word and type:

   dw

   This time the editor removes all characters from the cursor *to and including* the next space. To remove the whole word, place the cursor on the first letter as you did in step 1.

4. Place the cursor on the (character.

5. Request deletion of two words with:

   2dw

   Note that **vi** treats the (as a word and deletes it. The same is true for other characters that are not numbers or letters (*nonalphanumeric*).

6. Position the cursor on the beginning of one of the last two words near the end of any line of text.

7. Type the delete-four-words command:

   4dw

   The last two words on the current line and the first two words on the next line are deleted. The editor accepts arguments that affect words on more than one line. In some versions of **vi**, the **w** will not span ends of the line if there is a space at the end of the line.

Deleting the Remainder of a Line

The visual editor does not limit you to deletion of whole lines.

1. Move the cursor to the middle of a long line in the *practice* file, and type the following uppercase command:

   D

   This uppercase **D** is instruction to **D**elete the remainder of the line, starting with the character under the cursor.

2. Move to the middle of another line and delete the remainder with:

   D

Deleting All Text to a Character on a Line

Previously, you moved the cursor to a selected character on a line by issuing *f?* where *?* was the character on the line you wanted to be the new cursor location.

1. Select a line of text in your file, and place the cursor at the beginning of the line. Identify a character on the line to the right of the cursor such as an *e* in a word like *the*.

2. Enter:

    f*e*

    where *e* is the target character.

    The cursor moves to the first instance of the target character you selected.

3. Move the cursor back to the beginning of the line by entering:

    ^

4. Now enter:

    df*e*

    Again replace the *e* with the letter you chose on the line.

    The text from the cursor to the selected character is deleted.

5. Bring the text back with **undo**:

    u

6. Go to another long line in the text.

7. Move right one word:

    w

8. Select a character on the current line to the right of the cursor and use it in place of the *?* in the following:

    df*?*

Deleting Lines Using Line Number Addresses

In the editor tour, you moved the cursor to specific lines. You can also enter commands such as *6G* or *51G* or *G* to move to line 6, line 51, or the end of a file. In the section on moving about a file, you moved the cursor to specific lines using the editor line commands like *:6* or *:51* or *:$*, which tell the editor to move the cursor to lines 6, 51, or the end of the file.

Once a line is addressed, you can take other actions.

1. Enter:

    :5d

    The fifth line is identified and deleted.

2. Undo the deletion by entering:

    u

3. Delete another line using the line address and the delete command; then undo the deletion:

    :15d

    u

    There are numerous ways to delete blocks of text in your file.

4. Delete the first eight lines of your file and then undo the deletion:

    1G

    8dd

    u

5. Or, regardless of the location of the cursor, you can type:

    15G

    :1, 8d

    u

    This command instructs the editor to find lines 1 through 8 and delete them. See the graphical description of deleting text with the colons in Figure 3-11.

6. Delete a block range of lines:

    :4, 9d

7. Undo the removal:

    u

8. Empty the file:

    :1, $d

9. Quickly undo the deleting of all lines:

    u

The commands that employ the line addresses, like *:4, 9d*, begin with a colon and require an ENTER to be started. Command mode instructions such as **u** or **4dd** are not preceded with a colon and occur automatically without pressing

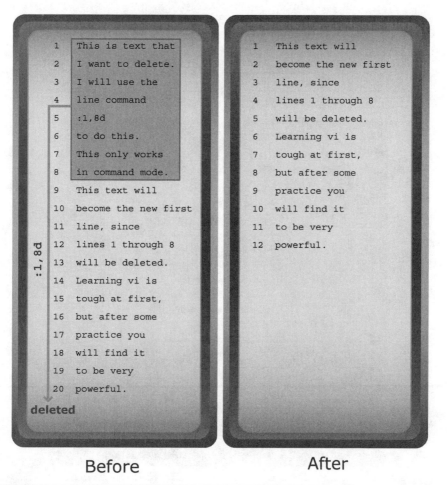

Before   After

FIGURE 3-11 Using numbers to delete text

ENTER. The following table and Figure 3-12 summarize the delete commands you have just used:

OBJECT TO DELETE	COMMAND
Character	**x**
Word	**dw**
Line	**dd**
Remainder of line	**D**
To a character *y* on the line	**df***y*

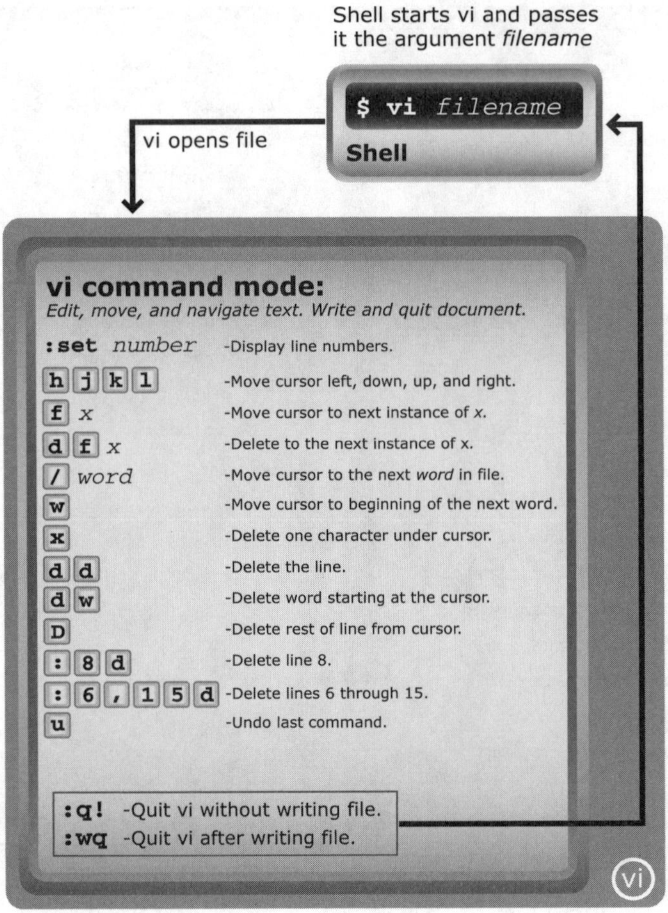

Shell starts vi and passes
it the argument *filename*

```
$ vi filename
Shell
```

vi opens file

vi command mode:
Edit, move, and navigate text. Write and quit document.

`:set number`	-Display line numbers.
`h` `j` `k` `l`	-Move cursor left, down, up, and right.
`f` *x*	-Move cursor to next instance of *x*.
`d` `f` *x*	-Delete to the next instance of x.
`/` *word*	-Move cursor to the next *word* in file.
`w`	-Move cursor to beginning of the next word.
`x`	-Delete one character under cursor.
`d` `d`	-Delete the line.
`d` `w`	-Delete word starting at the cursor.
`D`	-Delete rest of line from cursor.
`:` `8` `d`	-Delete line 8.
`:` `6` `,` `1` `5` `d`	-Delete lines 6 through 15.
`u`	-Undo last command.

`:q!`	-Quit vi without writing file.
`:wq`	-Quit vi after writing file.

(vi)

FIGURE 3-12   Navigating and deleting text in *vi*

3.6 Adding Text to a File

When you tell the editor you want to start adding text, the command you enter is determined by where that text is to be added to the file, relative to your cursor.

Inserting Text to the Left of the Cursor

You have seen how the **a** command adds text *to the right of the cursor.* Another command is used to insert text *to the left of the cursor.*

1. In command mode, move the cursor to the beginning of a word of text on the screen.

2. Type the insert command:

    i

3. Type the following text, and note that the existing text moves to the right as you type:

    The difference between the
    i and a commands does not seem to be very
    obvious.

4. Return to command mode by pressing:

    ESC

Comparing the a and i Commands

Both the **a** and **i** commands instruct the editor to add text at the cursor position. This next exercise demonstrates the difference between the two commands.

1. Place the cursor at the beginning of a line that already has some text.

2. Now type the *right of cursor* **a**ppend command.

    a

3. Enter four spaces.

    The first character in the line, the one the cursor was over when you entered the **a** command, remains at the beginning of the line. The added spaces are appended to the right of the cursor location, after the first character on the line.

4. Press ESC to return to command mode.

5. Press ENTER to put the cursor at the beginning of the next line of the file that has some text.

6. Type the *left of cursor* insert command:

    i

7. Again type in four spaces.

    The text is added to the left of the cursor at the beginning of the line.

8. Try both the **a** and **i** commands with the cursor in various locations—at the beginning, middle, and end of a word; on both sides of a period; and at the end of a line.

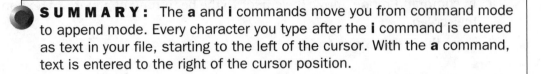

SUMMARY: The **a** and **i** commands move you from command mode to append mode. Every character you type after the **i** command is entered as text in your file, starting to the left of the cursor. With the **a** command, text is entered to the right of the cursor position.

Opening a Line Above the Cursor

In addition to opening lines below the cursor with lowercase **o**, you can open a new line above the cursor with uppercase **O**.

1. Move the cursor to any location in any line.

2. Enter:

    O

    The **O** command opens a line above the line where the cursor resides and places you in append/insert mode.

3. Add some text, such as this:

    It is essential to be able to place
    text above the current line,
    especially when I want to enter text
    before the first line in a file.

4. Tell the editor to return to command mode by pressing:

    ESC

5. Move to the first line in your file:

    1G

6. Enter the appropriate command to add some text above the first line:

    O

7. Add some text.

    As with the other commands that put you in append/insert mode, you can continue typing as many lines as you wish. You are not limited to that one line.

8. Tell **vi** to return to command mode by pressing ESC.

9. Save the file as it is now written and return to the shell by typing:

    :wq

Summarizing the Cursor Append Commands

You have now added (appended) text on all four sides of the cursor. The commands used for these tasks are summarized in the following table:

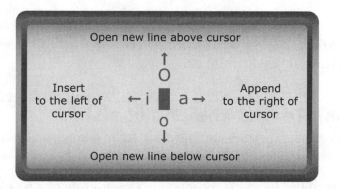

APPEND MODE COMMAND	ACTION
i	Inserts to the left of the cursor
a	Appends to the right of the cursor
O	Opens a line above the cursor
o	Opens a line below the cursor

Inserting Text at the Beginning of a Line

Often when you need to add text to the beginning or end of the line, the cursor may be located at a word in the middle of the line. Rather than overwork the arrow keys, you can issue specific text-adding commands that move the cursor directly to the end of a line.

1. Return to editing the file *practice* by entering:

    vi *practice*

    Move the cursor to the middle of any line of text in your file, and type the uppercase command:

    I

    The cursor moves to the beginning of the line. You are now in append mode, and anything you type is Inserted before the first character of the original line.

2. Add some text, such as this:

    I was in the middle of a line,
    now I am adding text to the beginning.

3. Leave append mode and return to command mode by pressing:

    ESC

The **I** command instructs the editor to move the cursor to the beginning of the line and to change to append mode. Every character you type is Inserted as additional text until you press ESC.

Appending Text at the End of a Line

No matter where the cursor is initially located on a line, you can instruct the editor to start adding text to the end of the line.

1. In command mode, move the cursor to the middle of a text line, and type the uppercase command:

    A

    The cursor moves to the end of the line, and you are now in append mode.

2. Add some text, such as the following:

    Adding text to the end of a line
    is easy with the A command.

3. Return to command mode with ESC.

4. Save and quit:

    :wq

SUMMARY: All append commands move you into append mode until ESC is pressed. The various append commands differ only in where text is added to the file, relative to the cursor. The following illustration illustrates where on the line the text is added with each command.

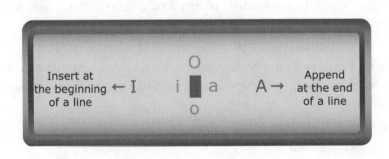

The commands used thus far are summarized in Figure 3-13. As you examine this figure, pay particular attention to the modes, which commands are executed in each mode, and how to change from one mode to another.

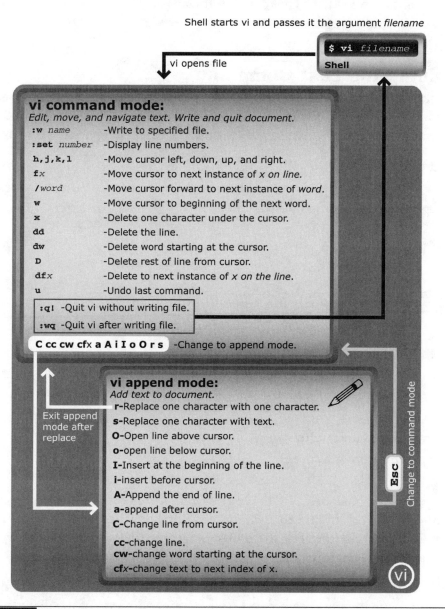

Shell starts vi and passes it the argument *filename*

`$ vi filename`
Shell

vi opens file

vi command mode:
Edit, move, and navigate text. Write and quit document.

`:w` *name*	-Write to specified file.
`:set` *number*	-Display line numbers.
`h,j,k,l`	-Move cursor left, down, up, and right.
`f`*x*	-Move cursor to next instance of *x* on line.
`/`*word*	-Move cursor forward to next instance of *word*.
`w`	-Move cursor to beginning of the next word.
`x`	-Delete one character under the cursor.
`dd`	-Delete the line.
`dw`	-Delete word starting at the cursor.
`D`	-Delete rest of line from cursor.
`df`*x*	-Delete to next instance of *x* on the line.
`u`	-Undo last command.

`:q!` -Quit vi without writing file.
`:wq` -Quit vi after writing file.

`C cc cw cf`x `a A i I o O r s` -Change to append mode.

vi append mode:
Add text to document.

Exit append mode after replace

r-Replace one character with one character.
s-Replace one character with text.
O-Open line above cursor.
o-open line below cursor.
I-Insert at the beginning of the line.
i-insert before cursor.
A-Append the end of line.
a-append after cursor.
C-Change line from cursor.

cc-change line.
cw-change word starting at the cursor.
cfx-change text to next index of x.

Esc Change to command mode

FIGURE 3-13 Commands Summary for Append and Command Modes

3.7 Undoing and Repeating Editing Commands

Two powerful features of the visual editor are its *undo* and *repeat* functions. What they do is determined by what command was last typed. Thus far, you used the undo command to restore lines that you removed.

Undoing the Last Command

Mistakez happen. Words are misspelled; lines are accidentally deleted; text is added that is no improvement. An essential tool for humans is the **u**ndo command, which undoes (rescinds) the most recent text-changing command.

1. Start editing *practice* with:

   vi *practice*

2. Open a new line and add some text:

   o

3. When you are finished, press:

   ESC

4. Place your cursor on the first line in the file. Type:

   dd
   2dd
   3dd

   You are still in command mode; one, then two, then three lines are removed.

5. Type the **u**ndo command:

   u

   The deleted lines return.

6. Move the cursor to the end of the file:

   G

7. Type **u** again. Depending on your system's version of **vi**, either it undoes another text-changing command, bringing back the deleted lines, or typing **u** a second time rescinds the undo. Either the lines again disappear, or the lines you deleted earlier reappear.

   The **u**ndo command affects only the previous text-changing command. You can only issue the **u**ndo command from command mode of the visual editor. However, you can move the cursor without affecting the **u** command.

Multiple Undos Using vim

If you are on Linux or another system using **vim**, the open source **vi** from the Free Software Foundation, you can continue to **u**ndo changes, one at a time.

1. Enter the following:

   dd
   dw
   dd
   dd
   dd
   u
   u
   u
   u
   u

   You deleted lines and a word. When you entered the *u*'s, each undid a previous editing change. Any change or text addition can be undone.

Undoing All Editing Changes on a Line

There is a second Undo command that undoes any number of changes that you've made to the current line where the cursor is.

1. Select a line of your text, and delete one word from the line:

   dw

2. Without leaving the line, move the cursor to another word, and **x** out some characters with:

   x

3. Move to the end of the line and add a word:

   $
   a

4. Press ESC to return to command mode.

5. Go to the beginning of a line and delete a word:

   dw

6. Without moving the cursor off the line, type the lowercase command:

   u

   One change is undone.

7. While still on the line, enter:

  U

  The line returns to its original state. All changes are reversed. The line returns to its condition before you made any changes.

8. Repeat steps 1 and 2.

9. After you make the changes, move the cursor to another line.

10. Enter the **U** command. The **U** command fails. You changed another line before entering **U**.

Following is a summary of the undo commands:

UNDO COMMAND	ACTION
u (lowercase)	**u**ndoes the effect of the last text change command given, even if you have moved from the line
U (uppercase)	**U**ndoes the effect of all changes made to the current line, provided that you have not made a change on another line

Repeating the Last Text-Changing Command

Users often need to make the same editing change to several locations in a file. For instance, suppose you need to add the text *This is an addition* to the end of different lines.

1. Select a line in the file, and move the cursor to any location in the line.

2. Type the command to add text to the end of a line:

  A

  The cursor moves to the end of the line; you are now in append mode.

3. Add text such as:

  This is an addition

4. Without making any other text changes, return to command mode by pressing:

  ESC

5. Press ENTER to move to the next line.

6. From command mode, type one single period to repeat your last **A** command. Yes, just a single period is the repeat command.

The last text-changing command is repeated; the addition is made to the current line.

7. Press ENTER and make the same addition to another line using the period command.

8. Delete a word.

9. Move the cursor to another word.

10. Press the period key to delete the second word.

The period is the visual editor's "Play it again, Sam" command. It instructs the editor to repeat whatever text-changing command was just accomplished.

3.8 Avoiding Confusion Between the Shell and the vi Editor

So far, you have issued commands to the shell and to the visual editor, in both command mode and append mode. Each command interpreter acts on your commands in a different way.

Giving Instructions to the Shell

1. Exit the editing session by entering:

   :wq

   You are back communicating with the shell.

2. From the shell, type:

   who

   A listing of users currently logged on appears on your screen. To the shell, the three characters **w h o** are interpreted as "Locate and execute the utility named **who**." The **who** utility determines who is logged on and formats a report that is output, in this case, to your screen.

3. Leave the shell, and call up the editor to work on the file *practice* that you have been using in this chapter by entering:

   vi *practice*

You are now in command mode of the visual editor, editing a file.

Giving the Same Instruction to the Command Mode

1. Place the cursor at the beginning of a word in the text, and type the following three characters:

    w

    h

    o

As you can see, the characters **w h o** have a very different meaning in the visual editor command mode:

- The **w** says move to the right one word.
- The **h** says move the cursor back one space.
- The **o** says open a line below the current line and enter append mode.

You are now in the append mode of the editor.

Instructing the Append Mode

1. To complete the comparison, type the same three characters again.

    This time, in append mode, the effect of typing **w h o** is that three letters are added to the file.

2. Press ESC to return to command mode.

3. Quit the editor by entering:

    :wq

Comparing the Command Interpreters

The distinction between the two modes within the **vi** editor is a critical one. Whenever you leave the shell and enter the **vi** editor, you *always* enter command mode. A set of specific commands is understood and acted upon by **vi** in this mode. Keystrokes result in movement of the cursor, deletion of text, shifting into append mode, or leaving **vi** to return to the shell.

When you give an append command (such as **a** or **o**), the editor starts treating every character you type as input to the file. One way to describe that difference is to say that **a** or **o** is an instruction to change from command mode to append mode. Once in append mode, virtually every character you type is put in the file as text and displayed on the screen. You remain in append mode until you press ESC.

Pressing ESC is the only way to return to command mode, regardless of which command you used to enter append mode. The ESC key is always the way back to command mode.

On Linux **vim**, you can use the arrow keys to move the cursor around while in append mode. A common error on many systems is to try to move the cursor while you are in append mode instead of command mode. If you do this, on most systems a series of control characters (^K^H) appears on the screen. The ^K or ^H type characters are the control characters associated with the arrow keys. Because you are in append mode, **vi** is happily adding the characters you type to your file. In this case, the added characters are the control characters. Should this happen, you need to press ESC and use the **x** command to delete the unwanted characters.

3.9 Creating New Files with the Visual Editor

Thus far, you have been moving the cursor around, deleting text, and adding text to an existing file. The visual editor is also used to create new files.

Invoking the Editor and Adding Text

Begin the process of creating a new file by typing:

vi *scrp1*

The screen clears, a column of tildes lines up on the left of the screen, and you are placed in **vi**'s command mode. There is no text; a clean slate awaits your wisdom. But you cannot add text yet, because whenever you start the editor, you are in command mode.

1. Type the following command to go into append mode:

   a

2. Add the following lines of text:
   echo *Hello* **$USER**
   cal
   date

Adding to a Line

1. Tell the editor you want to stop adding text and return to the command mode:

   ESC

2. While in command mode, use arrow keys to move the cursor to the beginning of the line containing the text:

   cal

3. Instruct the editor to add text at the end of the line:

   A

4. Add a space and the current year using four digits.

5. Press ESC.

6. Write the file, leave the editor, and return to the shell with the usual command:

   :wq

7. Obtain a listing of the files in your directory by entering:

   ls

The new file is listed among the contents in your current directory.

> **N O T E:** The editor acts the same whether you are creating a new file or editing an old one. The command to create a new file is exactly the same command you type to edit an existing file: **vi** *filename*. In both cases, you supply the filename.

One of two things happens when you type the **vi** *filename* command:

- If the *filename* you enter already exists in your directory, **vi** makes a buffer copy of that file for you to edit.

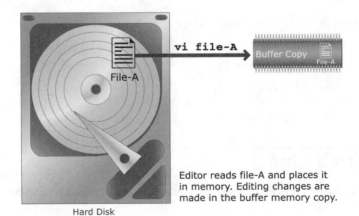

Editor reads file-A and places it in memory. Editing changes are made in the buffer memory copy.

Hard Disk

- If the *filename* you supply does not exist, the editor starts editing a memory buffer using the new *filename*.
- When you enter **:wq**, the buffer is written to the disk and given *filename* as its name.

Executing a Script

1. Make the file you just created executable by entering:

   chmod +x *scrp1*

2. Execute the script:

   scrp1

   All the commands in the script are executed, and the output is displayed on the screen.

   In this exercise, you used the **vi**sual editor to create a new file.

Failing to Enter Command Mode

One of the most common errors people make with the **vi**sual editor is to enter **vi** *filename* and then to start entering text without first leaving command mode and entering append mode.

Follow these steps exactly to see what happens:

1. Start the editor:

   vi *practice*

2. Go to the last line:

   G

3. Enter:

   15

4. Then enter:

   a

5. Enter the following text:

   September 2004

6. Press ENTER.

7. Leave append mode with:

   ESC

The line *September 2004* is entered into your file 15 times, because that is what was requested.

Often people start to edit a file and, while in command mode, enter text like *15 September 2004*. They enter the *15*, realize they are still in command mode, enter **a** and continue entering text. Because the 15 was entered before the **a**, the editor interpreted the 15 as the number of times to **add** the following text.

When starting to edit a new file, enter **a** or **i** immediately. You enter append/insert mode. Type away.

■ Review 3

1. What command deletes the current line plus seven more?

   _____

2. What command deletes five characters starting with the character under the cursor?

   _____

3. What command deletes all characters from the cursor to and including the next space?

   _____

4. The cursor is near the middle of a word. How do you delete two words forward including the current one the cursor is on?

   _____

5. What happens when you are in the command mode and enter **2j3dw**?

   _____

6. What command deletes the remainder of the line, starting with the character under the cursor?

   _____

7. What command deletes all characters on the line, starting with the character under the cursor to the first character *H* on the line?

   _____

8. What command deletes the 15th line when the cursor is on another line?

   _____

9. What command deletes lines 2 through 33 regardless of the location of the cursor?

   _____

10. What command deletes all the lines when you are in the file?

    _____

11. What command do you type to add text to the left of the cursor?

    _____

12. What command do you type to add text to the right of the cursor?

    _____

13. What command opens a line above the cursor?

    _____

14. What happens when you type in the word *open* in command mode?

    _____

15. What command do you type to add text to the end of the current line?

    _____

16. What command do you type to insert text at the beginning of the current line?

    _____

17. What happens when you type in the word *Impact* in command mode?

    _____

18. What command do you type to undo any number of changes that you've made to the current line?

    _____

3.10 Making Text Changes

Thus far, you have added and deleted text. To effectively edit, you must be able to make character, word, and line substitutions.

Replacing One Character with Another

You can remove one character and replace it with a single character.

1. While in command mode, move the cursor to any word you want, using the forward search command:

   /word

2. Replace the first letter of this word by typing the command:

   r

   and then following the **r** with any *replacement character* such as:

   M

3. Try another example. Place the cursor at the first *o* in the word *too*.

4. Type the **r** command, followed by the letter *w*.
   The first *o* in *too* is replaced by a *w*. The word *too* becomes *two*.

   The command **r** instructs the editor to replace the character located under the cursor with the very next character that you type. The character is replaced, and you are returned to command mode.

Breaking Up a Long Line

One important use of the replace character command is to break one long line into two lines. When a line is too long, you need to place your cursor in the middle and press ENTER, making it two lines.

1. Move the cursor to the space between two words in the middle of a long line.

2. Type the replace command (**r**) and then press ENTER.

   You are replacing the space character between the two words with a new-line character by pressing ENTER. As a result, the second part of the long line moves to a new line. This works because when you press ENTER, it enters a special character that indicates a new line. You are left in command mode.

Joining Two Lines of Text

At times you will need to join two lines together.

1. Select two short adjacent lines in your file, and position the cursor anywhere on the first line.
2. Type the uppercase command:

   J

   The two lines are now Joined.
3. Move to another line and join it with the one that follows.

Typing Over Text Character by Character

The **r** command instructs the editor to replace the single character under the cursor with whatever single character is typed next. At times it is convenient to replace a whole string of text character by character. Using the **r** command for this is cumbersome.

1. Make sure you are in command mode, and type the uppercase command:

   R
2. Start typing.

   You are now in "typeover mode." Each letter you type replaces the single letter under the cursor as it moves down the line.
3. After you have replaced some text with the typeover command, **R**, return to command mode with ESC.

Replacing a Single Letter with Many Characters

You have used the **r** command to replace a single character with one other character. Often an author or programmer needs to remove one character and then substitute several characters or even pages for the deleted character.

1. With the cursor positioned over any character in the file, type this lowercase command:

   s

   The dollar sign ($) may appear on the character, or the character may just disappear.

2. Add text such as this:

> *Is it true that I am now in append mode?*
> *I must be, text that I am entering*
> *is going onto the screen,*
> *and, I expect, into the file.*

3. Press ESC to return to command mode.

4. Select another character in the text, and replace it with a different character by using the **r** command.

5. Choose another letter in the file, and use the **s** command to remove it and substitute an entire sentence for it.

Both the **r** and **s** commands add text replacing a single character in a file. Because the amount of text entered can vary in length, the **s** command must be followed by an ESC when you have finished typing text. This is not the case with the **r** command, because the extent of the replacement is always known—one character.

> **S U M M A R Y :** The **r** command replaces one character with a single new character and then returns you automatically to command mode. You are not left in append mode, and you do not use the ESC key.
>
> In contrast, the **s** command substitutes the character under the cursor with whatever text you type until you press ESC. The **s** command allows you to substitute as many characters as you wish for the one removed character. You move from command mode to append mode and stay there until you use the ESC key to return to command mode.
>
> Likewise, after the **R** command is entered, the editor replaces each character the cursor passes over with only one character, but you must press ESC to quit replacing text.

Substituting Several Words for One Word

It is also possible to change one word in your text into another word or into a multitude of other words.

1. Using the / command, place your cursor on a word in the middle of the file.
2. Type the change word command:

   cw

   The dollar sign ($) may appear at the end of the word, indicating the end of the text that is being replaced, or the word may disappear.
3. Add text such as this:

   XXX This is text entered
   after a cw command XXX
4. When you are finished, leave append mode by pressing ESC.

Typing the **cw** command tells the editor to remove one word and put you in append mode. Everything you type is entered into the file until you press ESC.

Substituting Lines

The **s** and **cw** commands allow you to substitute text for a single character and for specific words, respectively. You can also substitute entire lines in your file.

1. Place the cursor anywhere on a line.
2. To substitute new text for the line, type the following lowercase command:

   cc

   The text on the line is removed, and the cursor is at the beginning. You are in append mode.
3. Add text such as this:

   And this is a new line of text!
   Well, actually two, taking the place of one.

   With the change line **cc** command, whatever you type is entered into the file in place of the current line. Your replacement for the one line is not limited to only one line. You can append any number of lines at this point. The **cc** command deletes the text from the current line and moves you from command mode to append mode.
4. You remain in append mode, adding text.
5. Return to command mode by entering ESC.

Changing the Remainder of a Line

You can change text from the cursor to the end of the current line, replacing it with new text.

1. Move the cursor to the middle of a line of text.
2. Type the uppercase command:

   C

   The dollar sign appears at the end of the line, indicating the last character that is removed to make way for new text, or the remainder of the line is removed. Either way you are in append mode.
3. Add a couple of lines of text.
4. Return to command mode:

   ESC

   The **C** command puts you in append mode and lets you **C**hange the part of the line from the cursor position to the end of the line. The characters from the left margin up to, but not including, the cursor remain unchanged. Whatever text you type until you press ESC is substituted for the remainder of the line.

Changing All Text to a Specific Character on a Line

In earlier sections, you moved the cursor to a particular character, like *e*, by entering the **f***e* command. Likewise, you deleted up until a specific character with the **d**f*e* command.

1. Move the cursor to the beginning of a long line.
2. Select a character on the line, such as *e*.
3. Enter:

   cf*e*

   where *e* is the character you selected on the line.
4. Enter some text.
   The text from the cursor to the selected character is removed, and you are in append mode entering replacement text.
5. Write the changes by entering:

   ESC

   :w

The delete and substitute commands are summarized in the following table:

ACTION	CHARACTER	WORD	LINE	REMAINDER OF LINE	TEXT TO CHARACTER Y ON A LINE
Delete	x	dw	dd	D	df*y*
Substitute	s	cw	cc	C	cf*y*

3.11 Making Global Changes

So far, you have used the colon commands to copy, move, and remove blocks of text. You can also use the colon commands to search for a word and substitute a different word.

Searching for the First Occurrence of a Word

The substitute, a colon command, is used to substitute one regular expression for another in a file.

1. Move the cursor to a line containing the word *creating*. (If the word *creating* does not appear in the file, add it to the end of a line, and keep the cursor on that line.)

2. Change the word *creating* to *producing*, by entering:

   :s*/creating/producing/*

   The first instance of the word *creating* is changed to *producing*.

The substitute command requires two words separated by slashes. The action performed by the **s** command is to check the addressed line(s) for the pattern on the left (the *target pattern*) and, if it is found, substitute the expression on the right (the *replacement pattern*) for the target pattern. Thus, this command told **vi** to find the word *creating* on the current line and substitute the word *producing*.

If **vi** cannot find the target pattern you specify, an error message is displayed.

Searching for the First Occurrence of a Word on All Lines

An extension of the **s** colon command instructs the editor to act on *all* lines in the file.

1. Add the following lines to your file:

   betty 2001 2003 2002
   alan 2003 2004
   betty 2002 2002 2002
   bob 2002 2003
   margot 2002 2003 2003

2. Leave append mode:

   ESC

3. To implement a change, enter the command:

   :1,$ s/2002/ xxxxxx /

   This command instructs the editor to check all of the addressed lines through the last, looking for the string *2002* and, on lines where this string is found, to substitute the pattern string *xxxxxx* for the first instance of *2002* on each line.

4. Undo the changes by entering the **u** command.

Searching on All Selected Lines

You can select lines containing a specified word or string of characters and replace the occurrence of some other pattern on the line.

Previously, you substituted a new pattern for an old one on all lines using this command:

:1,$ s/pattern1/pattern2/

1. To select lines based on the presence of a target and make a substitution using another target, enter:

   :g */betty/s/2002/A2003B/*

   This instruction asks **vi** to select all lines containing the word *betty*, then locate instances of the string *2002*, and then substitute *A2003B* for the first occurrences of that string on each line.

2. Undo the changes by entering the **u** command.

3.12 Searching for the Line Target

In the previous exercises, you provided a line target; then for selected lines, a search target was specified.

1. You can also make changes to the target you specify for selecting lines:

   :g */2003/s//1776/*

The target *2003* is used to select lines and then is used as the target for substitution, because no substitution target is specified between the first two slashes after the **s**.

Here the **//** in the substitute command receives the last word matched—in this case, *2003*. This instruction has the same result as the following:

    :1,$ s/2003/1776/

If no substitution target is specified, the line target is assumed.

The main difference between the two commands is execution time. The command using a **g** and default target takes longer to execute on larger files than the shortcut and is only presented here because it is often used.

  2. Undo the changes.

Searching for Multiple Occurrences on All Lines

You may have noticed that the substitute command only works on the first occurrence of a pattern on an addressed line. If a line has more than one instance of the target pattern, only the first is affected. You can also have this command work on all occurrences of a pattern within a line.

  1. Enter the command

    *:1,$ s/2002/1776/***g**

This command instructs the editor, as shown in the following table:

COMMAND	INTERPRETATION
1,$	Go from line 1 to the last line in the file...
s	and make **s**ubstitutions...
2002	replacing the string *2002*...
1776	with the string *1776*...
*/***g**	**g**lobally in the file.

The **g** at the end of the substitute command is called a *flag*. It works differently from the **g** at the beginning of the command line, which is the default address for all lines in the file (*1,$*). The **g** flag, global, instructs the substitute command to perform the replacement on all occurrences of the target pattern within the addressed line(s).

3.13 Moving and Copying Text

Often the expedient task is to move or copy lines, words, or blocks of text.

Copying and Pasting Text

With the **vi** editor, you can move and copy blocks of text.

1. If you are not already editing the *practice* file, start by entering:

   vi *practice*

2. Move the cursor to a line part way down the screen.

3. Type the lowercase command:

   yy

   Although it appears that nothing has happened, the **vi** editor has "**yy**anked" and made a copy of this line and is holding the copy in memory. The line that was copied is not deleted or otherwise affected by the **yy**ank command.

4. Move the cursor to a different location in your text. Type the lowercase command:

   p

   The line that was yanked is now put or pasted as a new line in the new location below the cursor line.

5. The yank feature is most useful for copying blocks of text. For instance, to yank seven lines of text, beginning with the cursor line, type:

   7yy

6. Move the cursor to a line where you want the yanked lines to be put, such as the end of the file:

   G

7. Now **p**ut the seven yanked lines after the cursor:

   p

   A copy of the seven yanked lines of text now appears inserted as seven new lines below the current cursor location.

Putting Lines in Several Places

When you yank lines of text, you are not limited to putting them in only one place.

1. Move to a new location.

2. Now **put** the seven lines of text there:

   p

3. Move the cursor to another location, and **put** the lines of text there, too.

The yanked lines of text have now been copied and pasted in three locations.

Determining Placement of Put Lines

Thus far, the lines have been put below the cursor line.

1. Yank the current single line by entering:

   yy

2. Move to the first line in the file:

   1G

3. Type the lowercase command:

   p

4. Return to line 1 in the file:

   1G

5. Enter an uppercase command:

   P

Uppercase **P** instructs the editor to put the yanked text on the line *above* the cursor location, and lowercase **p** puts the copied text on the line *below* the cursor location.

Deleting and Putting Lines

The **yy**ank command makes a copy to be placed elsewhere and is the forerunner of copy and paste. The delete commands can also be combined with **put** commands to cut and paste.

1. Select a line to move somewhere else in your file.
2. Position the cursor on any character on the line to be moved and type:

   dd

3. Move the cursor to the end of the file.
4. Put the line:

   p

   The line was "cut" and "pasted" at the end of the file.

Figure 3-14 illustrates deleting text, holding text in the buffer, and placing text.

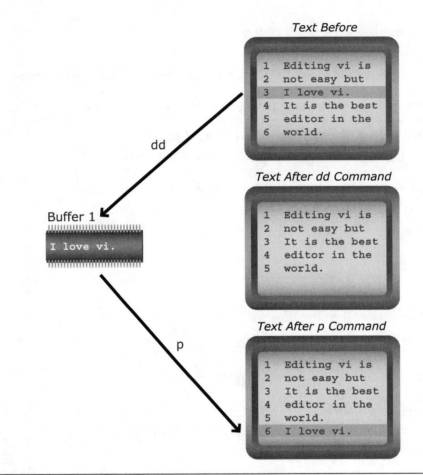

FIGURE 3-14 Deleting and placing text using a buffer

Copying and Moving Words and Characters

The yank command can be used to yank one or more words instead of lines.

1. Move your cursor to the beginning of a word in the file.
2. While in command mode, enter:

   yw
3. Move to the space between two other words in the file.
4. Enter:

   p

   The yanked word is put at the new location.

5. This time delete a word with:

   dw

6. Again move to the space between two words and enter:

   p

   The deleted word is placed at a new location.

   The lowercase **put** command combined with the **x** command can be used to quickly transpose characters in your text.

7. Move the cursor to the first letter of any word in your text and type:

   x

8. Now type:

   p

   Notice that the two characters are transposed.

Copying and Moving Part of a Line

As **df**x deletes from the cursor to the x on the current line, and **cf**x changes the text to the x, you can also yank a part of a line.

1. Select any character (x) on the current line and enter:

   yfx

   where x is the character you chose.

2. Move the cursor to the end of the line and put the yanked text:

   p

   The copy-paste feature on modern editors is like the yank-put feature of **vi**.

3. Move back to the beginning of the line:

   ^

4. Delete from the cursor to any character (x) on the line:

   dfx

5. Move to the end of line 1 and put the deleted text:

   1G

   $

   p

6. Move the cursor to the middle of a line of text and enter:

   d$

   u

   d^

The objects end of line and beginning of line can also be operated on.

Examining Objects and Operators

You have issued a variety of commands like **dd**, **dw**, **yy**, **yw**, **cc**, **cw**, and so on. Examine the following table:

OBJECT	DELETE	CHANGE	YANK
Whole line	**dd**	**cc**	**yy**
Rest of line	D or **d$**	C or **c$**	**y$**
To a character *x* on the line	**df***x*	**cf***x*	**yf***x*
Word	**dw**	**cw**	**yw**
Character	**x**	**s**	**yl**

The operator for **delete** is **c**, for **change** is **c**, and for **yank** is **y**. If you want to operate on the whole line, enter the operator twice: **dd**, **cc**, and **yy**. For delete and change, you can specify the remainder of the line by capitalizing the operator. For all three operators, the **$** can be used as the object end of line. If the object you want to affect is the text between the cursor and a character *x*, place the operator before the **f***x*, such as the **df***x*, **cf***x*, and **yf***x* commands. The object word (*w*) is affected by the operators delete (**dw**), change (**cw**), and yank (**yw**).

The character object only fits the pattern partially. We can **x** out a single character, **s**ubstitute for a single character, and **yl** yank the character under the cursor.

1. Try each of the commands in this table one more time, keeping the operator/object model in mind.
2. With your cursor on line 1 in the file, enter the following operator-object commands:

   d3G
   u
   d10|
   u
   d3w
   u
   d8h
   u

Many of the commands in this chapter can be summarized in this way. Figure 3-15 lists the three operators (**d**, **c**, and **y**) in column one, many of the objects in column two, and their meaning in column three.

3. Try these objects with each of the operators.

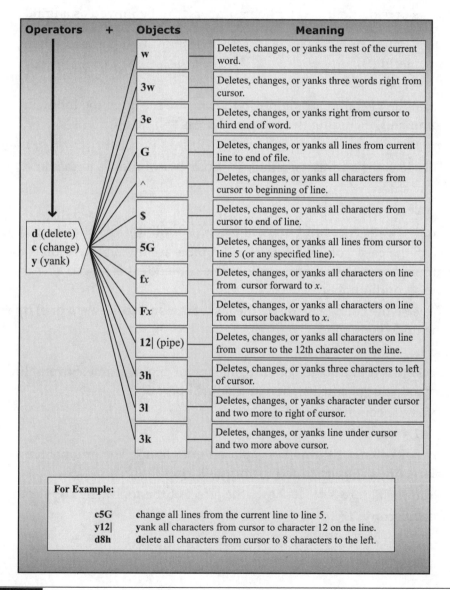

Operators	+	Objects	Meaning
		w	Deletes, changes, or yanks the rest of the current word.
		3w	Deletes, changes, or yanks three words right from cursor.
		3e	Deletes, changes, or yanks right from cursor to third end of word.
		G	Deletes, changes, or yanks all lines from current line to end of file.
		^	Deletes, changes, or yanks all characters from cursor to beginning of line.
d (delete)		**$**	Deletes, changes, or yanks all characters from cursor to end of line.
c (change)		**5G**	Deletes, changes, or yanks all lines from cursor to line 5 (or any specified line).
y (yank)		**f**x	Deletes, changes, or yanks all characters on line from cursor forward to x.
		Fx	Deletes, changes, or yanks all characters on line from cursor backward to x.
		12| (pipe)	Deletes, changes, or yanks all characters on line from cursor to the 12th character on the line.
		3h	Deletes, changes, or yanks three characters to left of cursor.
		3l	Deletes, changes, or yanks character under cursor and two more to right of cursor.
		3k	Deletes, changes, or yanks line under cursor and two more above cursor.

For Example:

    c5G   change all lines from the current line to line 5.
    y12| yank all characters from cursor to character 12 on the line.
    d8h   delete all characters from cursor to 8 characters to the left.

FIGURE 3-15 The delete, change, and yank commands

Copying Blocks of Text

The visual editor offers several commands for copying a single line or many lines of text from one place to another in a file. The following line address commands perform many of the same functions you learned previously (yank and paste), but are easier to use when you are working with more than a few lines.

Blocks of text, identified by line numbers, can be moved as a unit.

1. Display line numbers on your screen, if they are not already there, by entering:

   :set *number*

2. From the **vi** command mode, in the *practice* file, type the following command, including the colon and press ENTER:

   :10

   The *:10* is the address of a line, 10. Your cursor moves to that line.

3. Now enter:

   :2 **copy 4**

   Press ENTER. A copy of line 2 is placed after line 4 in your file.

   With the copy command, the first number following the colon is the line number of the text that is copied. The copied text is placed *after* the line at the second number.

4. Reverse the change made by the last command (copying a line) by entering the undo command:

   u

5. You are not limited to copying one line of text at a time. Several lines can be copied to a specific location in a single operation.

   Type the command:

   :1,4 **copy 7**

   A copy of lines 1 through 4 is placed after line 7. The original lines remain in place, but a copy is added to your text after line 7.

6. Examine Figure 3-16. It shows the effect of the following copy command:

   :1,8 **copy 17**

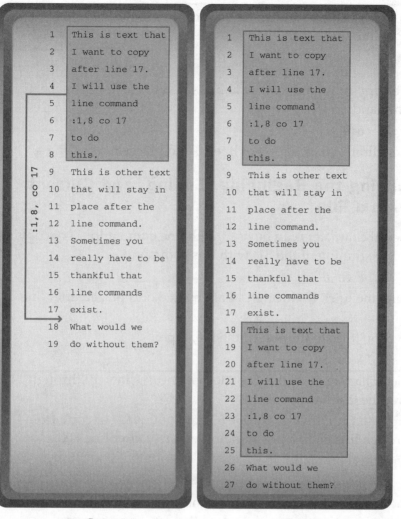

Before   After

FIGURE 3-16   Using line numbers to copy text

Using Line Addresses

Editing commands that begin with a colon (such as *:1,4 copy 9*) operate on a block of text that is identified by its beginning and ending line numbers, which are separated by a comma. Hence, *1,4* specifies lines 1, 2, 3, and 4. Likewise, *57,62* identifies lines 57 through line 62 in the file.

> ● **C A U T I O N :** Always be sure to type the lower number first; the editor does not understand line addresses such as *62,57* or *9,2*.

1. The **copy** command can be abbreviated to **co**. For instance, type this command:

   :10 **co** *4*

   The editor makes a copy of line 10 and places it after line 4.

Specifying the Beginning, Ending, and Current Lines in a File

1. Special characters can be used with line commands. Try copying text to the very beginning of the file with this command:

   :10,14 **co** *0*

   Here, the lines 10 through 14 are copied and placed after line 0 (just before line 1).

2. To copy lines to the end of the file, type:

   :10,14 **co** *$*

   The dollar sign ($) specifies the last line, so lines 10 through 14 are copied after the last line of the file.

   Suppose the cursor is on line 55, and you want to copy from the current line through line 65 to a position immediately after line 80.

3. Type this command:

   :.,65 **co** *80*

   The dot after the colon specifies the current line, that is, the line where the cursor is currently positioned, as the first line address.

Moving Blocks of Text

You have copied text to different locations in the file using line addresses. You can also **move** the text from one location to another.

1. Type this command:

   :1,8 **move** *17*

Examine Figure 3-17 to see the effect. Lines 1 through 8 are moved to the new location, not copied. The same syntax and special characters used for selecting a multiple-line block of text for the copy command are also used for the move command.

2. Before continuing, move another block of text in your file.

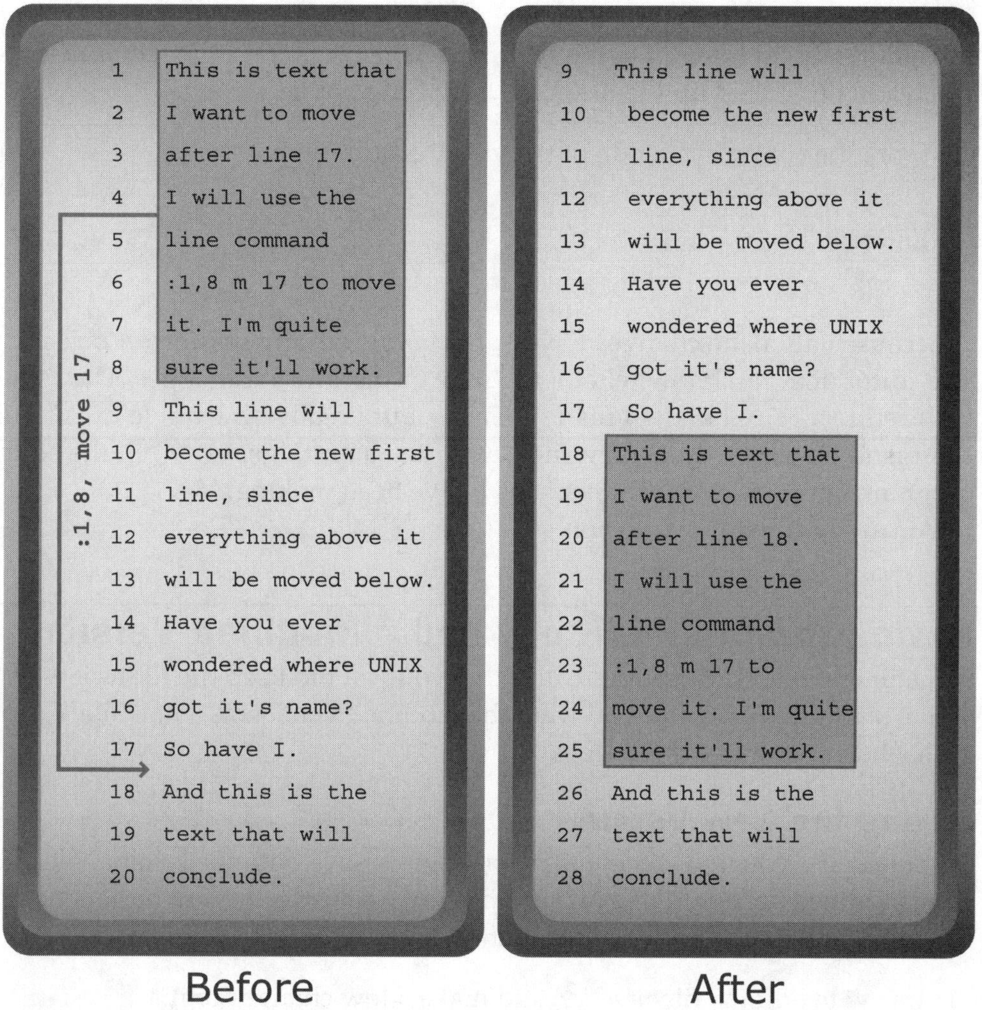

FIGURE 3-17   Using line numbers to move text

3.14 Writing the File and Quitting the Editor

Thus far, you have used **:wq** to write the copy of the file you edited to the disk and quit the editor. We can also write to a different file, abandon changes to the current file, and add content on to the end of an existing file.

Quitting vi Without Saving Changes

By now, you have scrambled your *practice* file. Before continuing, you can quit this editing session, return to the shell, and have the *practice* file remain as it was when you first called up the file at the beginning of this section.

1. From the command mode of the visual editor, type:

   :q
2. Enter:

   :q!

   Because you made changes to your file in this editing session, **vi** objects. The editor does not know whether to save or discard the changes. The **!** says to the editor, "Yes, I know I made changes, but I really do want to quit." This command does not include a write (save), just a quit. It says, "Quit the editor program, but don't write the changes I have been making."

   You are now back in the shell.

Saving the Original Copy and a Modified Version

Sometimes while editing, you realize that you want to keep the file as it was before starting to edit, and you want the modified version as a new file. Keeping both versions requires these steps.

Saving the New Version

In some cases, you may decide that you want to save both the original file and its new, modified version. To save both, you must save the present buffer copy as a new file and then quit the editor without overwriting the original file.

1. Use **vi** to edit the file *practice*, and make a few changes to it:

   vi *practice*

2. To save a copy of the modified version of *practice,* type the following from the **vi** command mode:

   :**w** *newfilename*

   where *newfilename* is any name you want.

A message similar to the following appears on your screen at the bottom of your file:

```
"newfilename" [New file] 18 lines, 150 characters
```

You have instructed the editor to open a new file, *newfilename,* and to write the buffer copy of the file you have been working on to that new file. Figure 3-18 compares writing a file and writing the buffer to a new file.

Protecting the Original Version

The next task is to protect the original version from being written over. The regular (**:wq**) command would write the new version over the old. You would then have two copies of the new version and none of the original. Your objective is to quit the **vi** editor *without* saving the changes to your file.

1. Enter:

   :**q**

   The **:q** is acceptable because you just wrote the file, even though you wrote it to a new filename. The **:q!** works, too.

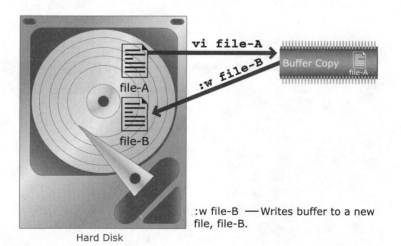

FIGURE 3-18   Saving the new version

2. Use the **ls** command to look at the latest listing of your files.

Your directory now contains a copy of your original file, *practice,* in addition to the modified copy listed under the new filename you chose.

Writing Out Blocks of Text

It is often useful to take portions of the file you are editing and create new files with them. To **write** a block of text from your current file out to a new file, you need two pieces of information:

- The line numbers for the first and last lines of the text you want to write out
- A new filename for the material to be written

1. Start editing *practice* again:

    vi *practice*

2. From **vi** command mode, type this command:

    :1,7 **write** *practice-2*

where *practice-2* is the new filename for the selected text.

The lines specified by the line address (*1,7*) are copied and written into *practice-2.* The text from lines 1 through 7 now exists in two places—in the file you are currently editing (*practice*) and in *practice-2.* See Figure 3-19 for a similiar example.

3. Leave the editor and return to the shell.

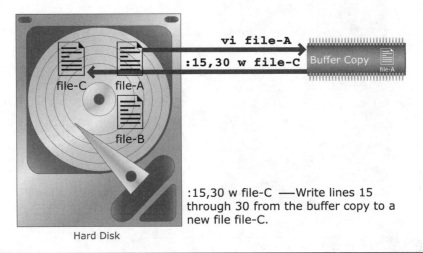

:15,30 w file-C —Write lines 15 through 30 from the buffer copy to a new file file-C.

Hard Disk

FIGURE 3-19 Writing part of an existing file to a new file

4. Examine the new file *practice-2*:

    more *practice-2*

5. Start editing *practice* again with:

    vi *practice*

Writing Over an Existing File

You can use the write command to overwrite, or replace, an existing file.

1. Enter:

    :1,7 **w** *practice-2*

This command is instruction to overwrite *practice-2*, a file that already exists.

See Figure 3-20. The following command will work whether *practice-2* exists or not:

    :1,7 **w!** *practice-2*

Adding to a File

Another type of write command appends text to a file.

1. Enter a command to write lines 5 through 8 to the end of the file *practice-2*:

    :5,8 **w** **>>** *practice-2*

The lines 5 through 8 are added to the end of *practice-2*.

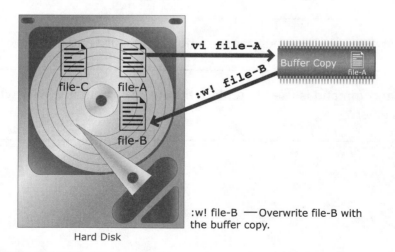

:w! file-B —Overwrite file-B with the buffer copy.

Hard Disk

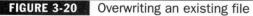

FIGURE 3-20 Overwriting an existing file

◾ Review 4

1. Consider the following scenario. The **vi** editor is started. You want to enter *15 people are in class*, forgetting to enter the **i** command to tell the editor you want to add text (that is, go into append mode). After typing the 15, you realize your mistake and type in an **i**, and then type the intended text again, followed by pressing ENTER and then an ESC. What happens?

   _____

2. What happens when you type *512ix* followed by ESC?

   _____

3. The cursor is at the *a* in the word *Hat.* You are in command mode. What happens when you type in *rob*?

   _____

4. What command joins the next line with the current line?

   _____

5. The cursor is located at the first character of the word *quit*. What happens when you type in *Red* while in command mode?

   _____

6. What command is used to replace one character with many characters you type in until you press ESC?

   _____

7. What command do you type to remove one word and add new text?

   _____

8. What command is used to replace the entire current line with whatever text you enter?

   _____

9. What command deletes text from the cursor to the end of the current line and puts you in append mode?

_____

10. What command deletes text from the cursor to the first occurrence of a specified character _H_ and puts you in append mode to add new text?

_____

11. What command instructs **vi** to find the string _hello_ on the current line and substitute the string _hi_?

_____

12. What command instructs **vi** to check lines 20 through the last, looking for the first occurrence of the pattern _hello_ in each line, and then to substitute the pattern _hi_?

_____

13. What command instructs **vi** to locate every instance of the pattern _bill_ and to substitute the pattern _tom_ through all the lines?

_____

14. What command puts into memory seven lines starting with the cursor line?

_____

15. What command pastes whatever was yanked?

_____

16. What command copies the current line and pastes it below the current line?

_____

17. What command moves the cursor to the 10th line, yanks 6 lines from there, and puts the yanked lines after the 17th line?

_____

18. What command yanks characters on the current line from the cursor to the first instance of the character *H*?

   _____

19. What command copies line 5 and places it after line 10?

   _____

20. What command copies lines 5 through 30 and places them after the last line?

   _____

21. What command copies lines 5 through 30 and places them before the first line?

   _____

22. What command moves lines 5 through 30 after line 100?

   _____

23. What command saves a copy of the current file as a file named *practice1*?

   _____

24. What command saves lines 5 through 30 of the current file to a file named *practice2*?

   _____

25. What command writes out lines 5 through 30 into the existing file *drill*, overwriting the current contents?

   _____

26. What command writes lines 5 through 30 to the end of the existing file *practice*?

   _____

27. Complete the following:

OBJECT	ACTION		
	delete	yank	change
line	dd	_____	_____
_____	_____	yw	_____
To end of line	_____	_____	c$
To the 12th character on the line	_____	_____	_____
_____	_____	y8G	_____

3.15 Interaction with the Shell from Within vi

Once you start editing a file, you are in direct communication with the editor, not the shell. You can, however, instruct **vi** to pass commands to a child shell or to read in the contents of a file.

Reading In Files of Text

When editing a file, a writer or programmer often needs to *read in* the contents of a different file. Pieces of text or programs that are used frequently can be kept in specified files and read into whatever file you are editing when needed. Only a copy is made of the file that is read, leaving the original unchanged.

To read text into the current file, you need to know two things:

- The *name* of the file containing the material you want to copy into your current file
- The *location* (line number) in your current file where you want the new material to appear

For example:

1. From **vi** command mode, type this command:

    :3 **read** *users_on*

    This command instructs the editor to read the file *users_on* and place the text of that file after line 3 in the current file. If you enter the **read** command without specifying a line number, the file will be read in and placed following your current cursor location. The **read** command can be abbreviated as **r**.

2. Try this:

> **:r** *users_on*

Because the read command is a text-changing command, you can undo it. Assume you don't want the inserted text.

3. Simply type:

> **u**

The lines you just read in are deleted from your current file.

Running a Child Shell Command from Within vi

Without leaving **vi**, you can have a shell execute commands.

1. At the command mode, enter:

> **:! date**

The **!** tells the editor to start a child shell and run whatever command follows.

The output of **date** is displayed with the message to press ENTER to continue.

2. Press ENTER. The screen clears and displays the current editing session.

3. Try:

> **:! cal**

This time the **cal** utility is run.

Reading In the Output of a Shell Command Line

In the previous examples, shell commands were run and their output displayed, but it did not affect the file.

You can read the output of a command into the current file.

1. At the command mode enter:

> **:read !cal**

The shell executes **cal**, and its output is added to the file that you are editing, starting with the line that follows your cursor.

2. From command mode, read in the output at a specific address with:

> **:8 r! head -5** */etc/passwd*

The head command reads the first five lines of the */etc/passwd* file, which are read into the current file after line 8.

Recovery from a Misspelled Filename

"Typos"—errors made while typing—are common mistakes when you are entering the name of an existing file. When this occurs, the editor will begin the process of starting a new file using the misspelled name. You can access the correct file without leaving the editor.

1. If you are still editing, put the file away and quit the editor:

   :wq

2. Type the following command, misspelling the name of the file as shown:

   vi *praZtice*

   The editor searches for a file named *praZtice*. Unable to find a file with that name, **vi** starts an editing session for a new file, using the misspelled filename.

   From the command mode you can tell the editor to access the correct file (*practice*) for **edit**ing and to throw away anything you have done in the misspelled file (*praZtice*).

3. Type:

   :edit! *practice*

   and press ENTER.

   This command instructs the editor to abandon the empty file with the misspelled name and start editing the file named in the **:edit!** command.

4. Quit the editor:

   :q!

3.16 Editing Multiple Files

Sometimes you need to edit two or more files at once. But every time you enter **vi** and a filename, you start a new process running the **vi** program. You can avoid this by instructing the editor that you want to edit several files; hence, the **vi** program is started only once.

1. Enter the following shell command line, substituting *file1*, *file2*, and so forth, with names of files from your directory:

   vi *practice users_on today*

   You may see this message:

   ```
   3 files to edit
   ```

2. The first file accessed is *practice*. Make some changes and add text to this file, using **vi** editing tools.

3. When you have finished editing *practice,* enter:

   :w

   which writes all your changes that you made in the buffer copy of *practice*. Notice that this command does *not* include the **q** for quit.

4. The first file has been written; the editor is still active. Now enter:

   :n

   The **:n** instructs the editor to open or access the next file for editing, *users_on*. It follows the series of filenames that you listed when you entered the initial **vi** command.

5. Make changes and write this second file.

6. Continue using the **:w** and **:n** commands as you edit your way through the series of files. When you reach the last file and enter **:n**, you will see the message:

   ```
   No more files to edit
   ```

   or

   ```
   Cannot go beyond last file
   ```

7. You have now edited all the files that you named when you started **vi**. If at this point you want to reedit all the files in the sequence, enter:

   :rew

   This rewinds all the files originally listed and places you at the beginning of the series of files again. You do not, however, have to be at the end of the series of files to enter the **:rew** command. It can be entered at any time during an editing session.

8. When you have finished with this editing session, terminate it by entering:

   :q!

■ Review 5

1. What command instructs **vi** to read in the contents of the file *report* and place the text after line 20 in the current file?

_____

2. What command tells the **vi** editor to start a child shell and run whatever command follows?

_____

3. What command tells the **vi** editor to start a child shell and run the **who** utility?

_____

4. What command do you type to read the output of the **who** utility into the file *practice* while you are in command mode in the file?

_____

5. What command do you type to read the first ten lines of the **who** utility into the beginning of the file *practice* while you are in command mode in the file?

_____

6. You want to edit the file *practice*, but type **vi** *prctice*, misspelling the name of the file. The editor searches for a file named *prctice*. Unable to find the file, **vi** starts an editing session for a new file *prctice*. What command instructs the editor to abandon the new file and start the file *practice*?

_____

7. What command do you type to edit the three files *hello, practice,* and *report* at once, one by one?

_____

8. What command do you type to access the next file for editing while several files are being edited?

_____

9. What command do you type to go back to the first file to reedit all the files in the sequence while editing several files, regardless of which file you are in?

_____

3.17 Customizing the Visual Editor

There are many features of the editor that you can use or not use, as you wish. You can tailor how the editor works for you, using a series of commands that customize the visual editor environment. In this section, you see how to use line numbers, automatic line indenting, special character listings, margin wrap, and other **vi** features.

Employing Line Numbers

Editing blocks of text, moving to a specific line, and identifying your location in a file are all easier tasks if lines in the display are numbered.

1. If you do not have line numbers displayed next to the lines of your *practice* file, request them by entering:

    :set *number*

2. To remove the numbers, enter:

    :set *nonumber*

 N O T E : In **vi**, you may abbreviate the ***number*** command as **nu** and the ***nonumber*** command as **nonu**.

3. Instruct the editor to include the line numbers again using the abbreviations.

4. To determine which editor options are currently on, enter:

    :set

    The display is a list of the options that at this moment are set in the editor.

Setting Automatic Indenting

Sometimes you'll want every line you type to be indented one or several tabs. When you don't want to have to remember to press TAB every time you start a new line, you can set the editor to automatically indent.

1. From command mode, open a new line in your file, and at the left margin, insert a TAB character.

2. Add a word of text.

3. Press ENTER and add another line.

   The new line is at the left margin. No automatic indenting takes place.

4. Leave append mode by pressing ESC.

5. From command mode, enter:

   :set *autoindent*

   or

   :set *ai*

6. Open up a new line, add a TAB, and enter a few characters of text.

7. Press ENTER and add more text.

   Each new line is indented to match the previous one.

Escaping autoindent

Occasionally, automatic indenting becomes a nuisance.

1. Add another line of text that is auto-indented and press ENTER.

   If you cancel *autoindent* for one line, you can move the cursor back to the left.

2. While still in append mode, press:

   CTRL-D

   This moves the cursor one SHIFT-indent to the left. If this doesn't move you back far enough, press CTRL-D again.

3. To shut off *autoindent* altogether, enter command mode by pressing ESC, and then enter:

   :set *noai*

   which sets *noautoindent*.

Requesting Showmode

One difficult aspect of working in **vi** is determining the mode you are in at any given time. On many versions of **vi** you can request that the editor keep you informed of the current mode. Some systems include this feature by default.

1. From command mode of the editor, enter:

   :set *showmode*

   Nothing appears to happen, but the attribute to show the mode has been set.

2. Tell the editor to enter insert mode:

    i

    If your version of **vi** includes *showmode,* the words *INSERT MODE* will appear in the bottom-right corner of the screen.

3. Press ESC.

4. Open a new line below the cursor. The *append* or *insert* mode is labeled.

Ignoring Upper- and Lowercase in Searches

To the editor, *Father* and *father* are different strings of letters, because the uppercase *F* is not the same as lowercase *f.* When you need to, you can instruct the editor to ignore case during searches.

1. From the command mode, enter:

    :set *ignorecase*

    or

    set *ic*

2. Search for all instances of the word *the* by entering:

    /tHe

    Even though the letter *H* is capitalized in the search command, all instances of the word, regardless of capitalization are found when you move through the matches by pressing **n**.

Listing Special Characters

The editor can be instructed to display special characters, such as tabs, in a readable format.

1. From the command mode, enter:

    :set *list*

    In your display, a **$** appears at the end of each line in the text, and tabs are displayed as **^I** throughout the text.

2. Turn listing off by entering:

    :set *nolist*

> **SUMMARY:** To make a set option take effect, you enter **:set option** and press ENTER. To turn off the feature (that is, to return to the state before the option was set), you enter **:set nooption** and press ENTER. To determine what options are currently on, enter **:set** and press ENTER.

Matching Programming Language Special Characters

A common programming error involves improper matching of parentheses and braces. The editor can help.

1. From command mode, enter:

   :set *showmatch*

2. Enter the following text. The first line has four open or left characters. Carefully watch the cursor.

   (xx(xx[xx{yyzz

   end

   }

   ]

   ))

   The editor shows you which opening parenthesis or brace is matched when you enter the closing character.

3. Add another right parenthesis. The workstation beeps, flashes, or in some way notifies you that there isn't a matching open left parenthesis.

   The square bracket [is not matched.

   Being able to match programming characters is useful when you are writing in a variety of programming languages.

Automatically Returning to a New Line

The visual editor processes very long lines, usually 512 characters. The workstation display is only 80 characters wide.

1. To demonstrate how **vi** handles display of long lines, enter the following:

   :set *wrapmargin=0*
   :set *number*

2. Open a new line and start typing real words separated by spaces. Type past the screen's right margin.

   The editor continues displaying the long line on the screen. The remainder of the line does not get a new line number, because it is not a new line, just a continuation.

3. Press ENTER and add another short line.

4. Press ESC and move the cursor up one line.

   The cursor "skips" the extended portion of the long line. The editor forces new lines when a line gets long, if you wish.

5. In command mode of the **vi**sual editor, enter:

   :set *wrapmargin=50*

   or

   :set *wm=50*

   Open a new line and start typing another long line of text. You cannot type lines longer than about 30 characters, at which point the editor automatically returns the cursor to the beginning of a new line, and a new line number is added.

   The *wrapmargin* option allows you to set the position of the screen's right margin, as measured from the right edge of the output, which determines the maximum number of characters the editor can display on a line. Once that limit is reached, each line automatically continues on, or *wraps*, to a new line. The smaller the *wrapmargin* value, the closer to the right side of the screen you can type.

6. A more reasonable *wrapmargin* value uses more of the screen. Enter:

   :set *wrapmargin=10*

When you use the *wrapmargin* option, the editor determines the line length by subtracting the value of *wrapmargin* from the standard line length of 80 characters.

To shut off *wrapmargin*, give it a value of *0*.

Determining the Current Value of an Option

1. From the command mode, enter:

   :set *wm*

At the bottom of your screen, the editor displays:

```
wrapmargin=10
```

Note that the window size may vary depending on your display.

2. When you want to see the current value for an option that has been set, you can enter:

> :set *option*

where *option* is the name of the option whose value you are interested in. The option name and its value are displayed.

Determining the Current Value of All Options

1. To find out the value or state of all options, enter:

> :set *all*

The report indicates what options are on or off and shows the current values for options that accept values.

If you forget the name of one of the **set** options, you can use the **:set** *all* command to obtain a listing.

Customizing vi with the Initialization File

Many programs in UNIX can be customized by recording instructions in a file about how you want the programs to perform. When you call up the visual editor, you can request line numbers on the screen by issuing the **:set** *number* command. You can also put similar instructions in a file that **vi** reads every time it is started up.

The initialization file for the **vi** editor is the file named *.exrc* (for **ex** run control). As soon as you start editing with **vi,** it reads its *.exrc* file. Commands placed in the *.exrc* file determine how **vi** functions.

1. To edit the *.exrc* file, in your home directory type:

> **vi** *.exrc*

If you are using Linux's **vim** editor, the command file is *.vimrc*.

2. Add the following line as text in the file:

> **set** *number*

Do not enter a colon at the beginning of the line; just type the words. If you like having the mode displayed, you can add the same command to your *.exrc* or *.vimrc* file.

> **set** *showmode*
> **set** *wm=15*

Remember that instructions are added as text in the *.exrc* or *.vimrc* files, so do not include the colon.

3. Press ESC to leave append mode.

4. Examine the file. If there are any blank lines, remove them.

5. Write the file and quit the editor with **:wq**. You have created a file named *.exrc (or .vimrc).*

6. Call up another file with **vi**.

> **vi** *practice*

Without your having to ask for them, line numbers appear.

All of the commands within **vi** can be placed in the *.exrc* or *.vimrc* file in your home directory. They will be read in at the beginning of every editing session.

3.18 Having a Single Key Accomplish a Complex Task

The UNIX visual editor allows you to connect one or more commands to a single key, which lets you perform a complex editing task with a single keystroke. In the command mode of **vi**, this is called *mapping.*

1. Begin by editing a file:

> **vi** *practice*

2. A *map* is a set of keystrokes called by a single key. For instance, from command mode, enter:

> **:map** g *1G*

and press ENTER.

3. Now go to the end of the file:

> **G**

4. Enter the mapped key:

> **g**

Because **g** is mapped to *1G*, the cursor moves to the first line in this file as though you executed *1G* itself.

5. Enter:

    :map # Go*This is new text*

    and press ENTER.

6. Nothing appears to happen. Press:

    #

    The editor follows the instruction as mapped:

COMMAND	INTERPRETATION
G	Go to last line in file.
o	Open a line below cursor and enter append mode.
This . . .	Text that is added.

7. To get out of append mode, press:

    ESC

8. To see the current maps, enter:

    :map

Entering Control Characters in Text

In this section, you will be using commands that include *control characters*, such as **^M** for ENTER or **^[** for ESC. It is possible to include them in text files or in maps. Here's how to enter them:

1. While editing a file, open a line:

    o

2. Enter:

    CTRL-V

    On the screen, you see only the ^ symbol displayed.

3. Next, press:

    ENTER

    Displayed on the screen is the control character for the ENTER key:

    ^M

4. Add more text, and while still in append mode, press:

  CTRL-H

5. As expected, the cursor moves back one space. You can also insert the control character for CTRL-H in your text. Try the following sequence:

  CTRL-V

  CTRL-H

A ^H has been added to your screen.

Whenever you wish to insert special characters in your text, precede that character with a CTRL-V.

Mapping Keys in the Command Mode

There are many different uses for mapping in **vi**. Many programming languages include a basic *if-then-else* statement, similar to the following:

```
if X
  then a
  else b
```

When you are writing a program, instead of typing these lines again and again, you can simply map them to a keystroke.

For this example, we will use the @ key as the key to be mapped.

1. From the command mode of **vi**, enter the following **map** command, all on one line. (Recall that in the previous section you learned how to enter control characters by using CTRL-V.)

  :map @ o*if X* CTRL-V ENTER TAB *then a* CTRL-V ENTER TAB *else b* CTRL-V ESC

and then press ENTER.

2. Move the cursor to a line where you would like to add an *if-then-else* statement and press @.

The map Command Syntax

The **map** command takes two arguments: the first argument is the key you would like to map, and the second argument is what you want the mapped key to symbolize.

We started the previous map with an **o**, which is the **vi**sual editor command to **o**pen a new line below and move into the append mode. When the map is invoked, everything from **o** until the ESC character (^[) will be seen as if in append mode.

The words *if X*, *then a*, and *else b* are interpreted as text. The CTRL-V allows you to enter the ENTER and ESC keys into the command sequence. The resulting ^M and ^[produce a carriage return and escape command, respectively.

Using Abbreviations in Append Mode

In command mode, you can use mapping to cut down on the time spent on repetitive editing. You can use **ab**breviations to accomplish the same goal from append mode.

1. From the command mode of **vi**, enter the following all on one line, using CTRL-V to request special characters:

   :**ab** *ift* *if* X CTRL-V ENTER TAB *then a* CTRL-V ENTER TAB *else b*

   and then press ENTER.
2. Move into the append mode with the **o** command.
3. Type a few words, including the abbreviation **ift**. As soon as you type the abbreviation **ift** and one space character, it is expanded to:

   ```
   if X
     then a
     else b
   ```

   The editor displays the current abbreviation.
4. Enter:

   :**ab**

■ Review 6

1. What command do you type to have line numbers displayed next to the lines of the file you are editing?

2. What command do you type to remove line numbers displayed next to the lines of the current editing session?

_____

3. What command do you type to see what options are currently on while you are in command mode?

_____

4. What command instructs the editor to inform you of what mode you are currently in?

_____

5. You want to search for the name _Cassy_ in the file _empinfo_, but there might also be the word _cassy_ in the file. How do you make the editor ignore case during any search?

_____

6. What command instructs the editor to display special characters (for example, a **$** at the end of each line and a tab as ^I throughout the text)?

_____

7. What command makes the cursor flash on the matching open left parenthesis or curly bracket whenever each closing member of the pair is entered?

_____

8. What command instructs the editor to force a new line if you start a new word within the last ten characters on the screen?

_____

9. What command do you type to shut off _**wrapmargin**_ so that a line can be very long?

_____

10. What command do you type to get information showing which options are set and which are not set?

   _____

11. What initialization file is started each time you start an editing session with **vi**?

   _____

12. Assume you frequently open a line for insertion and type the sentence /* *The following is a comment* */. You don't want to repeat the typing of the text every time you want to add it. What command creates a map for the character *c* that opens a line and adds the needed text?

   _____

13. How do you include an ESC key in a map?

   _____

14. What command instructs **vi** to map a # to append the output of the **date** utility after the current line?

   _____

15. In shell programming language, you might type the following heading every time you create a script:

```
#!/usr/bin/ksh
# Thu Sep 13 16:13:43 PDT 2001
# By SUNGGAK KIM
```

   The date and time in the second line is the output of the **date** utility at the point. What mapping makes the task just described possible with a single stroke of ! ?

   _____

16. Where can you put a map so that every time you start editing a file, the editor knows the map?

   _____

17. What mode must you be in to run maps in **vi**?

_____

18. What mode must you be in to run abbreviations in **vi**?

_____

19. What command provides the same result as question 15, but uses an abbreviation **kcode** while in append mode?

_____

3.19 Integrating Features of the Visual Editor

Throughout this chapter, you have used the fundamental visual editor commands to accomplish specific tasks. This final section steps you through a series of modifications in a document to demonstrate how the pieces fit together in an ordinary editing session.

Creating Test Files

Part of this exercise involves reading other files into the one you are editing.

1. If you are still editing a file, write, quit, and return to the shell.

2. Create three test files in your home directory by entering these commands:

who | head -20 > _who-test_
head -20 /etc/passwd > _passwd-test_
ls > _ls-test_

3. Confirm the existence of these files by entering:

ls

Complex Editing with the Visual Editor

The following exercise asks you to make a change and then provides the instruction to accomplish it. Try first to recall the needed command; then check out the written solution. Be sure to complete each step.

1. Use the editor to call up the file *passwd-test*:

   vi *passwd-test*

2. Go to the last line in the file by typing the following:

   G

3. Add two blank lines of text to the end of the file, followed by your name:

   o
   ENTER
   ENTER
   your name

4. Return to command mode:

   ESC

5. Read in the file *ls-test*:

   :r *ls-test*

   Line numbers should be displayed because the editor read the starting *.exrc* or *.vimrc* file.

6. Turn on the line numbers in the display if they are not already there:

   :set *number*

7. Add a line of text after the fourth line in the file and return to command mode:

   4G
   o
   some text
   ESC

8. Find the word *practice,* change it to *practicing,* and return to command mode:

   /practice
   e
   s
   ing
   ESC

9. Read in the file *who-test* at the top of the existing file:

   :0 read *who-test*

10. Copy the whole file, and place the copy at the end of the file:

    :1,$ copy $

11. Go to the first line of the file, and yank a copy of the first six lines. Then put copies after line 6 and at the end of the file:

    1G

    6yy

    6G

    p

    G

    p

12. Go to the first line and delete 5 characters:

    g

    5x

13. Go to the word *root*, replace (substitute) the whole line with the phrase *root is gone*, and then return to command mode:

    /root

    cc

    root is gone

    ESC

14. Go to line 7 and add the word *ADDITION* to the end of the line:

    7G

    A

    ADDITION

    ESC

15. Delete everything from line 10 to the end of the file:

    :10,$ **d**

16. Undo the deletion and bring the text back:

    u

17. Move downward one screen of text:

    CTRL-D

18. Go to the seventh line, and replace (substitute) the first four words with the one word *HELLO*:

    7G

    4cw

    HELLO

    ESC

19. Find a line with a colon, go to the end of that line, and delete all characters except the first 18 characters:

    /:

    $

    d19|

20. Move to the 24th character on a long line, and then yank the remainder of the line, go to the end of the line and put the yanked portion.

    24|

    $

    p

21. Write the current file with the name *garbage*, and then quit the editor without saving the file:

    :w *garbage*

    :q!

■ Conclusion

The visual editor is a complex, command-driven screen editor available on all UNIX systems. When you call up an existing or a new file for editing, you are placed in command mode. From this interpreter, you can issue commands to move around the file, commands to delete text, and commands to enter the append (text addition) mode. There are usually several ways to accomplish every editing objective. You should select a set of commands that meets your needs. More will be added to your repertoire as you work through this book.

At the end of this chapter are command summaries of all commands examined in this chapter.

■ Answers to Review 1

1. **h** or ←
2. **k** or ↑
3. Command mode
4. Command mode
5. /Admin
6. **n**
7. **dd**

8. **x**

9. Anywhere on the line

10. **u**

11. **a**

12. **o**

13. Append mode

14. ESC

15. **:q!**

16. **:wq**

17. Command mode

■ Answers to Review 2

1. **3j** or **3↓**

2. Command mode

3. **7l** or **7→**

4. */wonderful heroes*

5. *?time*

6. **n**

7. **N**

8. **w**

9. **b**

10. **^** or **0**

11. **$**

12. **f***t*

13. *8*| (pipe)

14. **:set** *number* or **:set** *nu*

15. **:set** *nonumber* or **:set** *nonu*

16. *15*G or *:15*

17. **G** or **:$**

18. *1*G or **:1**

19. **:q!**

20. L
21. "(two single quotes)
22. CTRL-D
23. CTRL-B

■ Answers to Review 3

1. *8dd*
2. *5x*
3. **dw**
4. **b2dw**
5. Goes two lines down and deletes three words.
6. **D**
7. **df***H*
8. *:15d*
9. *:2,33d*
10. *:1,$d*
11. **i**
12. **a**
13. **O**
14. Opens a line below the cursor and puts the text *pen* onto the line
15. **A**
16. **I**
17. Inserts the text *mpact* at the beginning of the current line
18. **U**

■ Answers to Review 4

1. *15 people are in class* is repeated in 15 lines.
2. Adds 512 *x*s to the file
3. *Hat* is changed to *Hot*, and the cursor moves to the beginning of the word on *H*.
4. **J**
5. *ed* is typed over the *qu* in *quit*, resulting in *edit*.

6. **s**

7. **cw**

8. **cc** or **S**

9. **C**

10. **cf***H*

11. *:s/hello/hi/*

12. *:20,$ s/hello/hi/*

13. *:1,$ s/bill/tom/***g**

14. **7yy**

15. **p**

16. **yyp**

17. *10G6yy17Gp*

18. **yf***H*

19. *:5* **copy** *10* or *:5* **co** *10*

20. *:5,30* **copy** *$* **or** *:5,30* **co** *$b*

21. *:5,30* **copy** *0* **or** *:5,30* **co** *0*

22. *:5,30* **move** *100* **or** *:5,30* **mo** *100*

23. **:w** *practice1*

24. *:5,30* **w** *practice2*

25. *:5,30* **w!** *drill*

26. *:5,30* **w >>** *practice*

27.

OBJECT	ACTION		
	delete	yank	change
line	dd	yy	cc
word	dw	yw	cw
To end of line	d$	y$	C$
To the 12th character on the line	d12l	y12l	c12l
From cursor to line 8	d8G	y8G	c8G

■ Answers to Review 5

1. :*20* **read** *report* **or** :*20* **r** *report*
2. **:!**
3. **:!** **who**
4. **:read** **!who** or **: r** **!who**
5. :*0* **r** **!who | head** *-10*
6. **:edit!** *practice*
7. **vi** *hello practice report*
8. **:n**
9. **:rew**

■ Answers to Review 6

1. **:set** *number* or **:set** *nu*
2. **:set** *nonumber* or **:set** *nonu*
3. **:set**
4. **:set** *showmode*
5. **:set** *ignorecase* or **:set** *ic*
6. **:set** *list*
7. **:set** *showmatch*
8. **:set** *wrapmargin=10* or **:set** *wm=10*
9. **:set** *wrapmargin=0* or **:set** *wm=0*
10. **:set** *all*
11. *.exrc* or *.vimrc*
12. **:map c o** */*The following is a comment*/*
13. CTRL-V ESC
14. **:map #** **:r !date^M** (^M denotes CTRL-V ENTER.)
15. **:map ! 1GO#!**usr/bin/ksh**^M#** ^[:r!date^M2GJo#
    By SUNGGAK KIM^[
16. **.exrc** or **.vimrc**
17. Command mode
18. Append mode
19. **:ab kcode 1GO#!**usr/bin/ksh**^M#** ^[:r!date^M2GJo#
    By SUNGGAK KIM^[

COMMAND SUMMARY

Starting the Visual Editor from the Shell

vi *filename*   Instructs shell to start **vi** and pass one argument, *filename*, which **vi** interprets as a file to open if it exists in the current directory, or to create if it does not already exist.

vi *file1 file2 file3*   Shell passes **vi** three arguments, which **vi** interprets as files to open. Use **:w** to write a file and **:n** to access the next.

vi +# *filename*   Instructs **vi** to open the file and go to specified line. For example, **vi** +100 *records* is instruction to edit the file *records* beginning on line 100.

vi +/the *filename*   Instructs **vi** to open the file and go to line that contains a target string. For example, **vi** +/Jason *friends* is instruction to edit the file *friends* beginning on the first line containing the string Jason.

view *filename*   Instructs **vi** to open the file for editing, but to deny writing changes unless **w!** is employed.

Cursor Moving Commands

h j k l   Move cursor one space or line left, down, up, or right, respectively.

0(zero)   Moves cursor to the beginning of whatever line it is on.

^(caret)   Like zero, it moves the cursor to the beginning of the current line.

$ Moves cursor to the end of the line.

##G   Moves the cursor to the line specified by the number in front of the **G**. For example, **42G** moves cursor to line 42 in the file.

G   Moves cursor to the last line of the file.

w   Moves cursor forward to the first letter of the next word.

e   Moves cursor forward to the next end of a word.

b   Moves cursor backward to the previous beginning of a word.

- Positions cursor at the beginning of prior line.

+ Positions cursor at the beginning of next line.

12l Positions cursor at column 12 of current line.

L Positions cursor at lowest line displayed on the screen.

M Positions cursor at midpoint on the screen.

H Positions cursor at the highest line on the screen.

' ' Two single quotes moves the cursor to its previous location in the file.

Cursor Positioning Commands (Contextual)

fb Moves cursor forward on the line to next b (or to any other specified character).

Fb Moves cursor backward on the line to previous b (to the specified character).

t# Positions cursor to the right of the first instance of the character # on the line. For example, **t**M moves the cursor to the right of the first M on the line.

T# Moves the cursor leftward on the current line, positioning it just before the first instance of the character # on the line.

/word Moves cursor forward through text to next instance of *word*.

?word Moves cursor backward through text to prior instance of *word*.

n Moves to the next instance of the pattern identified in a previously issued */word* or *?word*.

Display Adjusting Commands

CTRL-D Scrolls the cursor down a block of text in a file.

CTRL-U Scrolls the cursor up a block of text in a file.

CTRL-F   Displays the next screenful of text in a file.

CTRL-B   Displays the previous screenful of text in a file.

z.   Redraws screen.

Setting Display Options

:set number   Instructs the editor to include line numbers as part of the screen display, not as part of the file itself. The abbreviated form of **:set nu** also works.

:set nonumber   Removes line numbers on your screen. You can also use **:set nonu**.

:set showmode   Instructs editor to display append mode information in the lower-right corner of the screen.

:set list   Instructs the editor to place dollar signs at the end of each line, identify tabs as CTRL-I.

:set showmatch   Instructs the editor to briefly move to matching (or [when you enter a closing) or] in a line.

:set window=value   Defines the number of lines drawn on your screen.

:set autoindent   Automatically indents each return. You can also use **:set ai**.

:set tabstop=value   Sets the number of spaces used to display a tab. You can also use **ts**=*value*.

:set wrapmargin=value   Sets the right margin of the display putting in returns when you get within value characters of the margin.

:set ignorecase   Instructs editor to search for strings ignoring the case of the letters in the target.

:set   Shows you all the options you have set.

:set all   Shows you all the set options available.

Text Deleting Commands

dd   Deletes cursor line of text.

#dd   Deletes # number of lines of text.

dw   Deletes one word from text.

#dw   Deletes # number of words from text.

x Deletes the one character under the cursor.

#x   Deletes # number of characters from text.

D   Deletes the rest of the line (from the cursor position on).

:#,#d   For example, :12,37d deletes all lines from 12 through 37, inclusive.

Undo Commands

u   Undo. Reverses last text-change action even if you have moved to a remote portion of the file. In Linux, additional Undo commands reverse previous changes. In BSD's vi, a second Undo undoes the Undo, and brings the change back.

:redo   In Linux, cancels the Undo and redoes the text change. In standard UNIX, a second **u** undoes the first, resulting in a "redo."

U   Undo Reverses all text changes made to current line providing you have not moved the cursor from the line after the changes.

Adding Text to a File

a   (Lowercase) Inserts text starting with the space to the right of the cursor.

A   (Uppercase) Starts adding text at the end of the line.

i (Lowercase) Starts adding text to the left of the cursor.

I (Uppercase) Inserts text at the beginning of the line.

o   (Lowercase) Opens (or inserts) a line below the cursor.

O (Upper case) Opens a line above the cursor.

:#r *filename* For example, **:8r** *report.old* reads the file named *report.old* and places it in the current file after text line 8.

ESC Regardless of which command is used to enter Append/Insert Mode, to leave append mode and return to vi command mode, you need to press the ESC key.

CTRL-V Allows input of control characters. CTRL-V followed ENTER inserts CRTL-M into the file.

Changing Text in a File

cw Changes only the one word under the cursor. (Deletes the word, and then places you in append mode to add text where the word was located.)

s (Lowercase) Substitutes for a single character.

S (Upper case) Substitutes for an entire line.

cc Substitutes for an entire line (same as **S**).

r Replaces the one character under the cursor with the next character typed. Automatic return to command mode.

R Puts editor in Typeover. Replaces characters under cursor with whatever is typed.

C (Uppercase) Changes the rest of the line (from the cursor position forward).

ct# Changes text on the current line up to the target character. For example, **ct***Y* deletes all text on the current line up to the first Y and puts you in append mode to add text in place of the removed text.

cf# Changes text on the current line including the target character. For example, **cf***Y* deletes all text on the current line up to and including the first Y and puts you in append mode to add text in place of the removed text.

cT#   Changes text on the current backward to the target character. For example, **cT**Y deletes all text on the current line from the cursor, backward to the first Y and puts you in append mode to add text in place of the removed text.

cF#   Changes text on the current line including the target character. For example, **cF**Y deletes all text on the current line up to and including the first Y and puts you in append mode to add text in place of the removed text.

Yanking and Putting Lines and Words

yy   Copies or yanks current line into memory buffer. *20***yy** copies current line and next 19 (total 20) into memory. The target lines remain in the file, copies are made in memory for placement in the file with **p**.

dd   Deletes the current line, and places it in the same memory buffer used by **yy**. The target lines are removed from the file, but the **p** command can be used to place them elsewhere in the file.

yw   Copies or yanks current word into memory buffer. *6***yw** copies current word and next five (total six) into memory.

dw   Deletes the current word, and places it in the same memory buffer used by **yw**. Use **p** to place words elsewhere in the file.

yt#   Yank to a character. For example, **yt**B copies or yanks text into memory, starting at the cursor and continuing to just before the first instance of the character B.

yf#   Yank to and include a character. For example, **yf**: copies or yanks text into memory, starting at the cursor and continuing to and including the first instance of the character.

yT#   Yank backward. For example, **yT**N copies or yanks text into memory, starting at the cursor and continuing leftward, to just before the first instance of the character N.

yF#   Yank backward including the target. For example, **yF**J copies or yanks text into memory, starting at the cursor and continuing leftward to and including the first instance of the character F.

p   Puts whatever lines are in memory into the file starting below the cursor line. Puts whatever words are in memory into the file to the right of the cursor.

P   (Uppercase) Puts the yanked or deleted line(s) just above the cursor line. Puts the yanked or deleted word(s) to the left of the cursor.

Text Moving Commands

J   Joins the next line with the current line.

:#,#*move* #   Moves specified lines to target location. *:12,35* **move** *58* moves lines 12 through 35 to after line 58. Can be abbreviated as **mo**.

:1,26 co 82   Copies lines 1 through 26 and places them after line 82. (You select the line numbers.)

Global Editing with the Visual Editor

:s /target/replacement/   Locates the first occurrence of target character string on the current line, removes it, and replaces it with the character string replacement. Only the first instance of the target on the line is modified.

:g /target/s//replacement/   Locates the first occurrence of target character string on all lines, removes each, and replaces them with the character string replacement. The first instance of the target on all lines is modified.

:#,# s/target/replacement/   Makes substitutions on selected lines. For example, **:7,37** s/*march*/*walk*/ examines lines 7 through 37, replacing the first occurrence of the target string *march* in each line with the character string *walk*. The first instance of the target on all selected lines is modified.

:#,# s/target/replacement/g   Makes global substitutions on selected lines. *:1,$* s/*fun*/*joyful*/g locates all occurrence of the target *fun* character string on lines 1 through the end of the file, removes each, and replaces them with the character string *joyful*. All instance of the target on all selected lines are modified.

:s /target/replacement/   Locates the next occurrence of target character string, removes it, and replaces it with the character string replacement. Only the first instance of the target is modified.

:g /target/s/replacement/   Locates the first occurrence of target character string on all lines, removes each, and replaces them with the character string replacement. The first instance of the target on all lines is modified.

:#,# /target/s/replacement/   Makes substitutions on selected lines. *:7,37 /march/s/walk/* locates the first occurrence of the target string *march* in lines 7 through 37, removes each, and replaces them with the character string *walk*. The first instance of the target on all selected lines is modified.

:#,# /target/s/replacement/g   Makes global substitutions on selected lines. *:1,$ /fun /s/joyful/g* locates all occurrence of the target *fun* character string on lines 1 through the end of the file, removes each, and replaces them with the character string *joyful*. All instances of the target on all selected lines are modified.

Editing Tools: Maps, Abbreviations, and Marks

m#   Marks the current line with letter. For example **m***a* marks the current line as *a*. Even if you move the line, it is labeled as *a* and can be addressed.

'#   Addresses the marked line. For example **'***a* takes the cursor to the marked line. The command **'***a*,*$ d* deletes all lines from the marked line a to the end of the file.

:map # command string   Instructs the editor that when you enter # from the command mode, it should be interpreted as a command string. For example, **:map # o**#!*/bin/ksh* instructs the editor that a new command mode instruction exists. When you enter #, it should be interpreted as o, open a new line, then add the text **#!/bin/ksh** to the file. To include returns and other control characters, precede each with a CTRL-V command.

:ab abbreviation char-string   Sets append mode abbreviation. For example, by entering **:abmw** *Milky Way Galaxy* from the command mode, the abbreviation is established. While in append mode, if you enter the string *mw* followed by an ESC, the *mw* is replaced with *Milky Way Galaxy*.

Issuing Commands to the Shell, Without Leaving vi

:!ls   Instructs editor to start a shell that runs the **ls** program. After running the specified program you must press ENTER to return to the editor.

:!ksh   Starts a shell, allowing you to run more than one command. Exiting the shell returns you to the editor.

:0r!spell %   Runs spell on the current file (%) reading the output into the current file starting at line one (after line zero).

:31r!command %   Runs UNIX command (such as cal or date) reading the output into the current file starting at line 31.

CTRL-Z   The csh and ksh command to suspend processing of the current editing session, allowing you to issue commands to your parent shell.

fg   The csh and ksh command to make the suspended editing process active again.

Reading, Writing, and Quitting the Editor

:wq   Writes changes made to a file during that editing session into the disk, quits work on the file, and returns to the shell.

:q   Quits work on a file if no changes or additions have been made.

:q!   Quits work on a file and returns to the shell mode, but does not write changes made during the editing session.

:w filename   Writes the buffer (edited) version of the file to a new file.

:#,# w newtext   For example, **:1,6 w** *newtext* creates a new file named *newtext* and copies text lines 1 to 6 from the present file into *newtext*.

:1,6 w >> oldfile   Appends copy of lines 1 to 6 to end of an existing file named *oldfile*.

:1,6 w! oldfile   Overwrites (replaces) *oldfile* with contents of lines 1 to 6.

4

Using Basic UNIX Utilities

SKILLS CHECK

Before beginning this chapter, you should be able to

- Log onto a UNIX system and issue basic commands
- Use an editor to create and modify files
- Move, copy, and delete files
- Place shell commands in a file and make the file executable
- Identify role of tokens on a command line

OBJECTIVES

After completing this chapter, you will be able to

- Count the words, lines, and characters in a file
- Sort the contents of a file
- Identify and/or remove duplicate lines in a file
- Compare two files by identifying lines common to both
- Translate or remove characters in a file
- Search through files for a string of characters
- Select a portion of each line in a file
- Concatenate files and splice lines together
- Paginate long files
- Join together lines from two or more files that have a common value in the first field
- Make editing changes in the contents of a file, using the stream editor
- Select and modify the contents of a database file
- Do math calculations

Some of the most prominent features on the UNIX system landscape are its powerful utility programs. Powerful utilities locate system information, sort lines, select specific fields, join data files, modify information, and manage files for users. Although each fundamental utility is designed to accomplish a simple task, they can be easily combined to produce results that no single utility could produce by itself. This toolbox of utilities, along with the UNIX features that facilitate using several utilities at once, provide us with a set of powerful solutions to computing problems.

This chapter examines many utilities individually and in basic combinations. File data is manipulated and compared. The basic forms of robust utilities that constitute the core user tools are explored.

In this chapter, you will explore many different utilities. If from previous experience you are comfortably familiar with a specific utility, quickly read the text that describes it, and enter the commands for review. Most experienced users find new aspects of even familiar utilities. Always create any requested files, because they are often used in later exercises. If a utility is unknown or only somewhat familiar to you, carefully read each section and complete the activities. Regardless of your experience, be sure to read each summary, answer the review questions, and examine the command summary at the end of the chapter.

4.1 Extending Utilities Examined in the Tour

Counting elements of files, concatenating files, and viewing files were introduced in the tour. In this first section, you create needed files.

Creating Needed Files

The files you are about to create are used for several exercises in this chapter.

1. Use an editor to create a file named *test-file1* with the following contents:

```
abc  10
def  20
ghi  30
jkl  40
```

2. Create *test-file2* with the following contents:

```
AAA  1A  A
BBB  2B  B
CCC  2C  C
```

Counting Elements of Files

Users often want to know how many lines or words are in a file, how many files are in a directory, or how many users are logged on.

1. Enter the following:

> **wc** *test-file1*
> **wc** *test-file1 practice*

The **wc** utility reports the number of lines, words, and characters in the contents of files. If multiple filenames are given to **wc** as arguments, **wc** reports the number of each element in each file and the total number of lines, words, and characters in all files together.

2. Count the elements of all files in your current directory:

> **wc** *

The shell replaces the * on the command line with the names of all files in the current directory. The shell then interprets all filenames as arguments to **wc**. The **wc** utility then opens each file, counts all elements, and outputs the totals for all files.

The options for **wc** permit selective counts as well.

3. Enter:

> **wc -l** *test-file1*
> **wc -w** *test-file1*
> **wc -wc** *test-file1*
> **wc -l -w** *test-file1*
> **wc -wl** *test-file1*

Counting Elements in Output of Previous Utilities

Using **wc** with other utilities provides useful information.

1. Enter the following commands:

   who | wc

   who | wc -l

   ls | wc

Data is generated by one utility, and its output is redirected to **wc**, which counts elements.

Merging Files with cat

One way to display files, especially if they are short, is with the **cat** utility.

1. Enter the following request to read a file, and display it on the screen:

   cat *test-file1*

   One argument, a filename, is given to **cat**. The **cat** utility opens the file, reads it, and writes each line to its output. In this command, there is no instruction to redirect the output away from the default (the workstation screen), so the output is displayed at the terminal.

2. Provide **cat** with two arguments:

   cat *test-file1 test-file2*

   The **cat** utility interprets all of its arguments as files to open and read. Each line of the first file is read and written to output. When **cat** reads the end-of-file (EOF) character in *test-file1*, it puts that file away and then starts reading *test-file2*, which it also writes to output. No marker is placed between the files. We see the two files as concatenated on the screen.

3. To combine copies of two files into a new third file called *test-file3*, enter the following:

   cat *test-file1* *test-file2* **>** *test-file3*

4. Examine the contents of *test-file3*:

   cat *test-file3*

   This new file consists of the contents of the first file followed by the second.

In this command, we instruct the shell to create a new file *test-file3* and to redirect the output of **cat** to that new file. The **cat** utility is given two arguments, which it interprets as two files. Then **cat** reads each one and writes to output (which the shell connected to *test-file3*). Both files are read and written sequentially. The two input files are con**cat**enated into the output file.

Numbering Lines of Output

Often programmers or data managers want line numbers included in the printout or screen display of a file, but do not wish to actually modify the file by adding the numbers.

1. Enter the following request for **cat** to read a file:

   cat -n *test-file1*
   cat -n *practice*
   cat *practice*

Each line of output is numbered in the display; the original file is not affected. If your version of **cat** does not include the **-n** option, you will be able to number output lines using **pr** when you examine it later.

Examining Files with more

The **more** utility displays long files on the terminal one page at a time. Most recent versions of the **more** utility will search for strings, move forward and backward through a file, and easily shift to the visual editor.

1. Access a large file by entering one of the following:

   more */etc/termcap*

   or

   more */etc/terminfo*

One of these files should exist on your system. The contents of these files are not the primary issue at the moment, their size is. They are large enough to explore with **more**.

(These files contain instructions as to how nearly all manufacturers' terminals work, so programs that interact with terminals communicate reasonably.)

Moving Forward and Backward

1. Press each of the following:

   SPACEBAR

   ENTER

   The SPACEBAR instructs **more** to display the next page of output; the ENTER key adds the next single line to the display.

2. Search for a string by entering:

   /*vt100*

   Like **vi**, the **more** utility interprets the slash as instruction to search through the document for the next instance of the target string that follows the slash.

   The page with the target is displayed.

3. Enter the following:

   b

   b

Each **b** is instruction to move **b**ack one screen of text. With **more**, use the SPACEBAR to move forward through the file, and **b** to go backward.

Obtaining Help

1. Exit **more** with:

   q

2. Use **more** to examine the *practice* file:

   more *practice*

Shifting to the Visual Editor

Once you start displaying a file with **more**, you can easily start editing the file with **vi**.

1. Enter:

   v

   The visual editor is executed, and you begin editing the file at whatever location was current in **more**.

2. Make a change in the file.

3. Exit the editor:

   :wq

   You do not leave **vi** and return to the shell; rather, you return to **more**, examining the file as it was before you made changes with **vi**.

4. Exit **more** with:

   q

5. Look at the file again, to verify the changes you made with the editor are present:

   more *practice*

6. There is more to **more**. Examine the help screen by entering:

   h

   The **more** help screen describes many options we can use with **more**:

<space>	Display next screenful of text.
z	Display next screenful of text.
<return>	Display next line of text.
q or **Q**	Exit from **more**.
b or CTRL-B	Skip backwards one screenful of text.
'	Go to place where previous search started.
=	Display current line number.
/<regular expression>	Search for regular expression.
!<cmd> or **:!<cmd>**	Execute <**cmd**> in a subshell.
v.	Start up **/usr/bin/vi** at current line.
CTRL-L	Redraw screen.

The commands used thus far are included on the help screen. As you proceed, the other options to **more** will become more meaningful.

The **more** utility is a powerful file-examination tool.

7. Exit **more** with:

   q

4.2 Selecting Portions of a File with cut

Data is often arranged in columns in a file. Columns of information, rather than lines, can also be extracted from a file using the **cut** utility.

Creating Example Database Files

1. With the editor, create a new file called *names.tmp*. Because the following exercises require a field delimiter that is the tab character, enter the following text with the fields separated by tabs rather than by spaces:

2. Create a second file called *numbers.tmp* as follows, again with fields separated by tab characters:

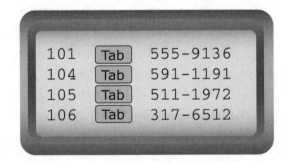

Selecting a Field from a File

The simplest use of the **cut** utility is to extract one field from a file.

1. From the shell, enter the following command line:

   cut **-f2** *names.tmp*

   The **cut** utility outputs the second field of the file *names.tmp*:

   ```
   Nate
   John
   Cassy
   Mary
   Isaac
   ```

2. To select the first field from the *numbers.tmp* file, enter:

   cut **-f1** *numbers.tmp*

   The elements of this command are as follows:

COMMAND	INTERPRETATION
cut	Instruction to the shell to execute the **cut** utility.
-f	An argument passed to **cut** that **cut** sees as the option specifying the extraction of field(s).
1	A number that follows the **-f** option indicates which field(s) to extract. The **1** requests the first field.
numbers.tmp	An argument to **cut** that tells **cut** which file(s) to use as input.

Using Options with cut

The **cut** utility provides several useful options for manipulating data.

Changing the Field Separator

1. Instruct **cut** to use a colon as the field delimiter by entering the following:

   cut -d: -f4 */etc/passwd* | **more**

   The fourth field from the */etc/passwd* file is displayed. Fields are separated by colons in the */etc/passwd* file. The **-d:** instructs **cut** to interpret the colon as the field delimiter as it reads the input.

   Often, data fields are separated by the space character in files. We can instruct **cut** to use any character as the field delimiter.

2. Exit **more** with:

   q

3. Enter the following with a space between the single quotes:

> **cut -d' ' -f1** *test-file2*

The first field from *test-file2* is output.

4. Now enter:

> **cut -d' ' -f2** *practice*

The output is the second word from each line in the file because the spaces determine the fields. The shell interprets spaces on the command line as separators between utilities, arguments, and so on. Because this space is in single quotes, the shell does not interpret it. Rather, the shell passes the space as part of the **-d** argument so **cut** can use it as the field **d**elimiter.

Selecting Multiple Fields

Exact fields and ranges of fields can be output by **cut**.

1. To select two specific fields, enter the following:

> **cut -d: -f1,4** */etc/passwd* | **more**

Fields 1 and 4 are extracted and output.

2. Enter the following to select a range of five fields:

> **cut -d: -f1-5** */etc/passwd* | **more**

Fields 1, 2, 3, 4, and 5 are selected and output.

Selecting Character Ranges

The **cut** utility can be used to select portions of lines based on text character position instead of fields.

1. Enter:

> **cut -c2-50** */etc/passwd* | **more**
> **cut -c1-3** *numbers.tmp*
> **cut -c1** *test-file1*

Starting at the left edge of the line, specific characters, as determined by position, are selected as output.

> **SUMMARY:** The **cut** utility is used to read a file and extract fields, ranges of fields, characters, and ranges of characters. To extract by

fields, each field must be separated by a field delimiter, and, if other than a tab character, the field separator character must be specified. Selection may be made on the basis of a list of fields or characters, or a range of those elements. Options include the following:

-f*list*   Displays fields denoted by list. A *list* consisting of **1**, **4** tells **cut** to display the first and fourth fields of a record, whereas **1-4** requests all four fields.

-d*char*   Specifies a field-delimiting character other than the tab character. Use only when requesting fields with option **-f**.

-c*list*   Displays characters in the positions, denoted by *list*, in a record (for example, the character in position **3**, or characters in positions **5-10**).

4.3 Formatting Output in Columns

Data is often output in one column, leaving most of the screen blank. We can format data into multiple columns as well.

Formatting Output into Multiple Columns

The **column** utility, available on many systems, formats its input into multiple columns.

1. Execute the following command line.

     ls */usr/bin* > *commands*

   Check the contents of *commands* file.
2. Enter:

     more *commands*

   The **more** utility shows the contents of the file in just a single column.
3. Instruct **column** to format it:

     column *commands* | **more**

   The **column** utility displays the contents of its input in multiple columns.

Filling Columns Before Filling Rows

1. Execute the following command line.

    column -x *commands* | **more**

Note the difference between the outputs with and without the **-x** option. The **-x** option instructs **column** to fill the first column before filling the next. Normally, **column** fills the first row, then the second and so forth.

4.4 Putting Lines Together with paste

The **cut** utility cuts out selected data from a file. The **paste** utility, of course, puts data together. This utility is useful when combining lines from various files.

1. Instruct **paste** to operate on the lines of two different files by entering:

    paste *test-file1 test-file2*

The output is as follows:

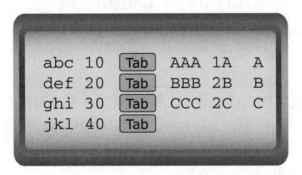

```
abc  10  [Tab]  AAA  1A   A
def  20  [Tab]  BBB  2B   B
ghi  30  [Tab]  CCC  2C   C
jkl  40  [Tab]
```

The **paste** utility reads the first line from the first file into memory, adds a tab character, and then reads in the first line from the second file and outputs the line. The result is that **paste** combines corresponding lines from the two files and outputs the combined line. The second line of the first file is combined with the second line of the second file, and so on, until **paste** reaches the end of both files.

2. Redirect the output from **paste** to a new file using the original text files:

    paste *test-file1 test-file2* **>** *test-fileout*

3. Edit the output:

    vi *test-fileout*

4. From the command mode of **vi**, instruct the editor to display special characters:

> **:set** *list*

Between the pasted lines, the display includes a **^I**, which is the symbol for the tab character. The **paste** utility reads in a line from the first file, adds a tab, then adds a line from the second file. The default output separator is the tab character, but you will soon specify others.

5. Quit the editor and return to the shell.

Recall that **cat** places one file *after* the other. The **paste** command, on the other hand, places them side by side with a separator character included.

6. To see the difference, enter the following commands and examine their output:

> **cat** *test-file1*
> **cat** *test-file2*
> **cat** *test-file1 test-file2*
> **paste** *test-file1 test-file2*

Combining Several Files

The **paste** utility can paste multiple files.

1. Enter:

> **paste** *test-file1 test-file2 numbers.tmp*
> **paste** *test-file1 test-file2 test-file1*

The first line from each file is read and output with a tab added to separate the original lines.

Changing the Output Field Separator

With **paste** you can specify the character used for the delimiter in the output.

1. Have **paste** include a **+** as the output separator by entering:

> **paste -d+** *test-file1 test-file2 test-file1*

The output consists of the lines from the two files pasted together with a **+** character between them.

Essentially, any character can be used as the output delimiter. However, if the character has special meaning to the shell, such as the characters *** $ ~**

& ~ ; " ' or a space, the character must be surrounded by single quotation marks or preceded by a backslash.

2. Enter:

    paste -d'$' *test-file1* *test-file2* *names.tmp*

A dollar sign is placed between the pasted lines in the output.

In addition, **paste** employs other separator characters.

3. Try the following:

    paste -d'*t*' *test-file1* *test-file2*
    paste -d'*n*' *test-file1* *test-file2*
    paste -d'\\\\' *test-file1* *test-file2* *names.tmp*
    paste -d'*0*' *test-file1* *test-file2* *names.tmp*
    paste -d\\' *test-file1* *test-file2* *names.tmp*

t is understood by **paste** to be the tab character; *n* is the newline; \\\\ is the backslash; and *0* is interpreted to be empty (no separator character).

Pasting the Lines of One File Together

The **paste** utility combines lines from two or more files when it is given multiple filename arguments. You can also instruct **paste** to combine multiple lines of one file into a single line of output.

1. Enter the following:

    paste -s *test-file1*

The output from **paste** consists of all the lines from *test-file1* spliced together as one line using the tab character as a separator.

2. Instruct **paste** to use a space as the separator in the output by entering:

    paste -s -d' ' *test-file1*

In this command line, the space must be in quotation marks to tell the shell not to interpret the space and instead pass it to **paste** as an argument.

S U M M A R Y : The **paste** utility connects lines from files in numerical order. The **paste** utility can also be used with options:

-d*char* Change output separator to *char*.

-s   Paste lines together from a single file.

4.5 Searching Files with grep

In our work, we often need to locate lines that contain words or a specific series of characters (called a *string* or *pattern*) in a file. We can search for lines containing strings in one or more files using the **grep** utility. Common uses for **grep** include quickly locating a line with someone's name in a file or identifying which of many files contains a specific string of characters.

Creating a File

1. Use the editor to create a file named *test-g* containing the lines in Figure 4-1.

```
about mother
7ab
About the cat t
-2
a b
^a line
t$ 1234
ttt he
at brother
←──────────── Leave a blank line here.
at
aBc t5t
15-23
They are at -v
Lyle Strand
←──────────── Leave another blank line.
LyleStrand
←──────────── Leave another blank line.
tat
a -2 b
```

FIGURE 4-1   Contents of *test-g* file

Searching Files and Printing Lines

1. Enter the following basic **grep** command line:

   grep *ab test-g*

   All lines containing the pattern or string *ab* in the file *test-g* are located by **grep** and output to the screen. The line containing the word *about* is displayed, as is the line containing the string *7ab*. Because **grep** in its basic form is case sensitive, "About" and "aBc" are not displayed.

2. Enter:

   grep *he test-g*

   The first argument to **grep** is the target; remaining arguments are files to search. All lines containing the string *he* are output.

   The line containing the word *the* is also selected, because **grep** searches for strings. When we see the string *he*, we think of the word *he*. When **grep** sees this target string, it reads it as "the letter *h* followed by the letter *e*." Because **grep** sees two characters as the target, they may be alone or part of any words such as *the*, *they*, and *mother*.

   The **grep** utility also locates lines in a file that do *not* contain a particular string.

3. Enter:

   grep -v *ab test-g*

   In this case, **grep** selects all the lines from *test-g* that do *not* contain the *ab* string.

   The **-v** option tells **grep** to reverse the sense of the search, to reject all target-matching lines, and to output all other lines.

Searching the Output of a Utility

If no files are listed as arguments, **grep** reads from input.

1. Enter:

   sort | *test-g* | **grep** *at*
   who | **grep** *$USER*
   paste *test-file1 test-file2* | **grep** *2*

The lines of the two files are pasted together and output to **grep** which locates lines containing the target 2 character.

2. Enter:

    grep *the*

Only one argument is given to **grep** which interprets it as the search target. With no files to open, **grep** reads from input, which is connected to the keyboard.

3. Enter:

    the
    input
    mother

As you enter a line, it is displayed on the screen. If **grep** finds the target, it writes it to output, which in this case is your screen, producing a second line.

4. To leave **grep**, on a new line enter:

    CTRL-D

Searching Through Multiple Files

The power of **grep** to search multiple files for a target pattern is especially useful when we are certain that we created a file with some known contents, but we cannot recall which of several files contains the target lines.

1. Enter:

    grep *c test-file1 test-file2 names.tmp*

All lines containing a *c* are output.

2. Choose a string that you believe you entered in one or more of your files. Then enter the following command line, substituting your chosen word for *string*, and your chosen filenames for *file1* and *file2*:

    grep *string file1 file2*

3. Search all files in the current directory for the word *the* by entering:

    grep *the* * | **more**

The shell replaces the * in this command line with the names of all the files listed in the current directory. The first argument passed to **grep** is the string *the*, which **grep** interprets as the target. The remaining arguments **grep** interprets as the names of files to open and search.

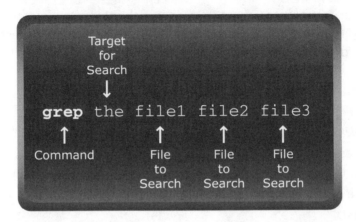

Hence, **grep** looks for the string *the* in all the files in the current directory.

The basic **grep** command line is **grep** *pattern filename(s)* where *pattern* is the target string of characters and *filename(s)* is the name of one or more files to open and search.

Searching for Multiple-Word Targets

Often the goal is to locate a person's name or another target string that contains spaces. The file *test-g* contains the string *Lyle Strand* as text in the file.

1. To locate the line in the file, enter:

    grep 'Lyle Strand' *test-g*

    The quotation marks instruct the shell to not interpret any special characters in the string *Lyle Strand*. The space between *Lyle* and *Strand* would be interpreted as delimiting two separate arguments if the shell were to interpret it. Instead, the shell passes the string *Lyle*(space)*Strand* as one argument to **grep**.

2. Try the command without the quotation marks:

    grep *Lyle Strand test-g* | **more**

Without the quotation marks, the shell passes *Lyle* and *Strand* as separate arguments to **grep**.

ARGUMENT	GREP'S INTERPRETATION
Lyle	The target search string.
Strand	A file to search.
test-g	A file to search.

The **grep** utility then interprets *Lyle*, the first argument, as the search string. To **grep**, all arguments after the search string are interpreted as files to search. **grep** attempts to search *Strand* and *test-g*. Unable to locate the *Strand* file, **grep** displays an error message and then outputs all lines that contain *Lyle* in the file *test-g*.

To pass a multiple-word target to **grep**, enclose the target in single quotation marks so the shell passes it as one argument.

3. As another example, enter:

   grep *'are at' test-g*

Because any shell special character in a target string is open to interpretation by the shell, many users simply quote the target at all times.

Ignoring Case in a Search

As seen earlier, the **grep** utility is case sensitive when you specify the target string in a search.

1. Try:

   grep *lyle test-g*

   No matching lines are returned.

   You can instruct **grep** to ignore case and match the target string, regardless of the case of the letters.

2. Enter the following command line:

   grep -i *lylE test-g*
   grep -i *He test-g*

The lines in *test-g* that contain *Lyle* and *he* are selected because the **-i** option is interpreted by **grep** as instruction to ignore case.

Outputting Only Filenames in a Search

In the **grep** commands executed thus far in this chapter, the output from **grep** is the actual lines in the files that contain the target string, or that don't contain the string if **-v** is used. You can instruct **grep** to just list the filenames where there is a match without displaying the lines.

1. Enter the following optional form of **grep**, with the **-l** (minus el) option:

    grep -l '04' *names.tmp numbers.tmp test**

The **-l** option for **grep** is interpreted by **grep** to mean "list only the filenames that contain the search string, not the matched lines, themselves."

Identifying the Line Number for Each Match

1. To request that **grep** inform you of the location(s) in the file for each match of the target string, enter:

    grep -n '*ab*' *test-g*

With the **-n** option, the output of **grep** consists of the line number and the line content for each match.

Employing Regular Expressions

Some characters have special meaning to **grep**.

1. Enter the following, using single quotes to instruct the shell to not interpret the search string argument.

    grep '*t.t*' *test-g*

All lines that have a *t* followed by any single character, followed by a *t*, are selected. The **.** (period) is the "any single character wildcard" to **grep**.

Identifying the Beginning of a Line

1. Enter:

    grep '^*a*' *test-g*

Every line that starts with the character *a* is selected. The line in *test-g* consisting of ^*a* is not selected, because the *a* is not the first character on the line. The ^ is the "beginning of line" special metacharacter.

2. Tell **grep** to not interpret the metacharacter ^ by entering:

    grep '\^*a*' *test-g*

The line containing the target ^**a** is selected. The \ character is inside single quotes. It is not interpreted by the shell, but passed to **grep** as part of the \^a argument. To **grep**, the \ is interpreted as instruction to not interpret the ^ that follows. The ^ is therefore just a ^ character, not the metacharacter for the beginning of the line.

Selecting Lines with Patterns at the End of the Line

The end of a line can also be specified with a metacharacter.

1. Enter:

    grep '*t*$' *test-g*

All lines that have a *t* followed by the end of the line (designated by the **$**) are selected.

Metacharacters such as these are used in target strings for **grep**. A target employing metacharacters is a *regular expression* and is used by many utilities: **awk**, **sed**, and **grep**. The **grep** utility gets its name from "**g**lobal **r**egular **e**xpressions **p**rint"

Locating Lines of Specific Length

Several metacharacters can be used together to create a regular expression that identifies specific line length.

1. Enter:

    grep -n '^...$' *test-g*

Lines consisting of exactly three characters (any three) between the beginning of the line and the end of the line are selected and output with line numbers.

2. Enter:

    grep -n '^$' *test-g*

All blank lines, with their line numbers, are output.

The **-n** option instructs **grep** to output line numbers. The regular expression ^$ says, "Find lines that have a beginning of line, followed immediately by the end of the line."

A book consisting of a front cover followed immediately by the back cover is a quick read. Regular expressions that incorporate metacharacters ^.$ allow us to specify exactly the lines we want selected. **grep** and regular expressions are covered in Chapter 15, "Selecting Lines with **grep** and Regular Expressions."

> **SUMMARY:** The **grep** utility is used to search through one or more files for lines containing a target string of characters. For a single file, it outputs the selected lines. For multiple files, it outputs the filenames and located lines. Options are as follows:
>
> **grep** without an option   Find *pattern* and output each line that contains it.
>
> **-i**   Make matches ignoring upper- and lowercase.
>
> **-l**   Output only a list of the names of the files that contain *pattern*.
>
> **-v**   Output all lines where *pattern* is *not* found.
>
> **-n**   Output the line **n**umber and the line content for each match.

4.6 Calculating with bc

A powerful calculation utility is available for performing basic arithmetic operations on most UNIX and Linux systems.

Performing Basic Math

At the command line of the shell, call up the calculator:

1. Enter:

   bc

   The screen clears, you are warned not to do your taxes with **bc**, and the cursor is on a new line. There is no prompt. The utility is waiting for input.

2. Enter:

   6 + 9

   And press ENTER.

   The resulting sum of *15* is displayed.

You instructed the shell to execute the **bc** utility. No redirection is specified, so input is connected to the keyboard and output to the screen.

3. Enter the following:

> *1234 + 5678*
> *12 * 12*
> *144 / 3*
> *122 - 4*

The standard add, subtract, multiply, and divide operations are available.

4. Try:

> *2 ^ 6*

The utility calculates 2 raised to the power of 6: 2 * 2 * 2 * 2 * 2 * 2. Thus, 2 raised to the 6th power is *64*.

Using Floating-Point Operations

When we divide integers with **bc**, the result is integer division.

1. Enter:

> *25 / 7*

The answer is *3* because there are *3* whole sevens in *25*, that is, *3 * 7* is *21* remainder 4. The largest multiple of 7 in 25 is 3. By default, remainders and decimals are not reported.

2. Enter:

> **scale**=2
> *25 / 7*

Now the output is of two-decimal-place accuracy.

3. Modify the scale and try again:

> **scale**=4
> *7 / 3*

The command **scale** instructs **bc** how many numbers to the right of the decimal it should provide in the output.

4. Enter:

> *50 / 6*
> **scale**=3
> *50 / 6*
> **scale**=6
> *26 / 17*

The number of places to the right of the decimal is determined by the numeric value assigned to **scale**.

Determining Order of Operations

1. Enter the following to **bc**:

    8 + 2 * 5

    The result is *18* because in **bc** the multiplication operation (*2 * 5*) precedes the addition operation (*8 + 10*).

2. Enter:

    (8 + 2) * 5

    This time the result is *50* because the ( ) force the addition (*8 + 2*) to be completed before the multiplication. To specify the order of operation, use parentheses.

3. Enter:

    (2 + 3) * 4 * (6 - 3)

    The addition (*2 + 3*) and the subtraction (*6 - 3*) are first because they are in the innermost parentheses. The result is *5 * 4 * 3*, or *60*.

4. Enter a CTRL-D to get out of **bc**:

    CTRL-D

■ Review 1

1. If you are using **more** to examine a file and decide you want to look back at the previous page, what do you enter?

   _____

2. From **more**, how can you quickly start editing the current file with **vi**?

   _____

3. What command tells **cut** to output the first five characters of every line from the file *practice*?

   _____

4. What command tells **grep** to look for all lines consisting of only the letter Z followed by any four characters in a file *filename*?

   _____

5. What command instructs **grep** to look through all files in the current directory for lines containing the string *Pat Lloyd* and output just the names of the files that contain a match?

_____

6. How do you get the answer to the following with four-figure accuracy? Add 424 to 79, divide that sum by 161, then raise that result to the 15th power.

_____

7. What command tells a utility to search through every file in the current directory for the name *Catherine Thamzin*?

_____

8. What command results in a listing of the number of words and the number of lines in the files *practice* and *users_on*?

_____

9. What command creates a new file *chapter* consisting of the contents of the files *section1, section2, section3,* and *section4* with all lines numbered?

_____

10. A file called *empnames* contains many employee names, with exactly one name on each line. What command outputs the names in the file in multiple columns, with columns filled before rows?

_____

4.7 Ordering the Lines of a File with sort

The **sort** utility sorts the lines of files or its input following specific criteria and then outputs the ordered results.

Creating a Test File

1. Use the editor to create the file *test-sor* with the content shown in Figure 4-2.

```
abc
1234
mary
75
About town
(Leave a blank line here)
+abc
9
 92
38
_Abc
abc
+777
ZZ
#ZZ
(Leave a blank line here)
zz
my files
?453
?mary
 abc
 96
Mary
^Mary
```

FIGURE 4-2   Unsorted contents of the file *test-sor*

2. Enter the following command to have **sort** read the lines in the file, sort them, and output the results on the terminal screen:

    sort *test-sor*

The resulting material is sorted as shown in Figure 4-3.

In its basic form, **sort** arranges the lines of a file in a sorted order by comparing the first, and when needed, subsequent characters of each line.

If the output is different with upper- and lowercase together, the environment sort variable is set to other than POSIX.

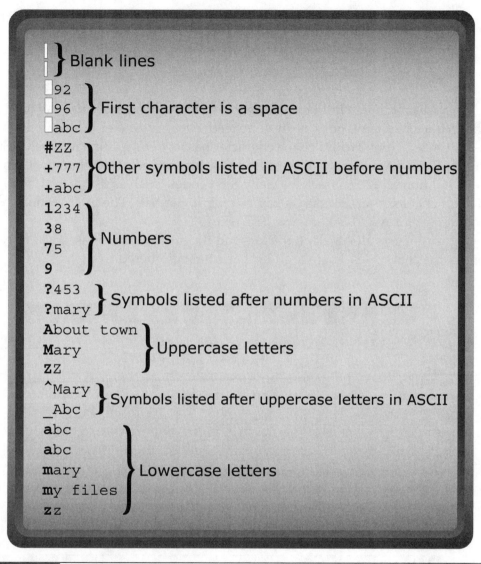

FIGURE 4-3   Sorted version of *test-sor*

3. Enter:

In the bash/ksh:
export LC_ALL="POSIX"
In the csh and tcsh:
setenv LC_ALL "POSIX"

The criterion that **sort** follows to order the lines is the order of the ASCII character set.

4. Examine the ASCII character set by entering this command:

   man *ascii*

Because computers hold only numbers in memory, there is no way to place the character *A* in memory as an *A*. Instead, every character is held in memory as a number, from 0 to 127. Each character has its own specific number. ASCII stands for the American Standard Code for Information Interchange. It is a 7-bit code holding all 128 characters. Many 8-bit codes (such as ISO 8859-1, the Linux default character set) contain ASCII as their lower half. The international counterpart of ASCII is known as ISO 646.

Figure 4-4 lists all ASCII characters and the number that is assigned to each one of the characters. There are 128 characters numbered from 0 to 127.

	0	1	2	3	4	5	6	7	8	9
0	nul	soh	stx	etx	eot	enq	ack	\a	\b	\t
1	\n	\v	lf	\r	so	si	dle	dc1	dc2	dc3
2	dc4	nak	syn	etb	can	em	sub	esc	fs	gs
3	rs	us	sp	!	"	#	$	%	&	'
4	(	)	*	+	,	-	.	/	0	1
5	2	3	4	5	6	7	8	9	:	;
6	<	=	>	?	@	A	B	C	D	E
7	F	G	H	I	J	K	L	M	N	O
8	P	Q	R	S	T	U	V	W	X	Y
9	Z	[	\	]	^	_	`	a	b	c
10	d	e	f	g	h	i	j	k	l	m
11	n	o	p	q	r	s	t	u	v	w
12	x	y	z	{			}	~	del		

FIGURE 4-4 ASCII numbers for characters

To determine the number for a particular character, consult Figure 4-4. You must first locate the character in the body of the table and then read both the number to the left of the row of the character as well as the number at the top of the column. For example, the letter *F* is in row 7 and column 0. Its ASCII value is therefore 70. Likewise, the space (sp) is in row 3 of column 2; therefore, its ASCII value is 32. The + is 43, the *z* is 122, and so on.

The beginning of the ASCII character set is made up of special characters such as *newline*, then some punctuation characters, followed by numbers, more special characters, uppercase letters, six punctuation characters, lowercase letters, and the five programming characters. This is the order **sort** uses to sort the lines of a file, unless you provide sort with specific options to do otherwise.

Sorting in Dictionary Order

The **sort** utility recognizes several sorting options. One option tells **sort** to ignore punctuation and other special characters, using only letters, digits, and spaces in its **sort**.

1. Enter:

   sort -d *test-sor*

   The **d**ictionary sorted output is in Figure 4-5.

The line ^*Mary* is no longer after the uppercase lines with the underscore in the sorted output. It is sorted according to where the *M* fits into the scheme, not the caret. All characters other than *letters*, *numbers*, and *spaces* are ignored in the sort when you use the **-d** option. The sort is based only on letters, numbers, and space characters.

Sorting Regardless of Capitalization

The **sort** program can be told to ignore the case (upper or lower) of the letters in its input when sorting; that is, to **f**old the cases together.

1. For example, enter:

   sort -f *test-sor*

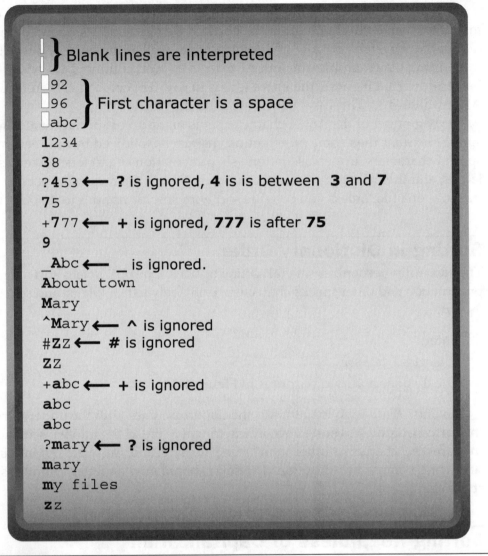

}Blank lines are interpreted

]92
]96 } First character is a space
]abc

1234

38

?453 ⟵ **?** is ignored, **4** is is between **3** and **7**

75

+777 ⟵ **+** is ignored, **777** is after **75**

9

Abc ⟵ **** is ignored.

About town

Mary

^Mary ⟵ **^** is ignored

#ZZ ⟵ **#** is ignored

ZZ

+abc ⟵ **+** is ignored

abc

abc

?mary ⟵ **?** is ignored

mary

my files

zz

FIGURE 4-5   Output of sort with -d option

The output displays the lines in ASCII order, but with upper- and lowercase of the same letter together, as in Figure 4-6.

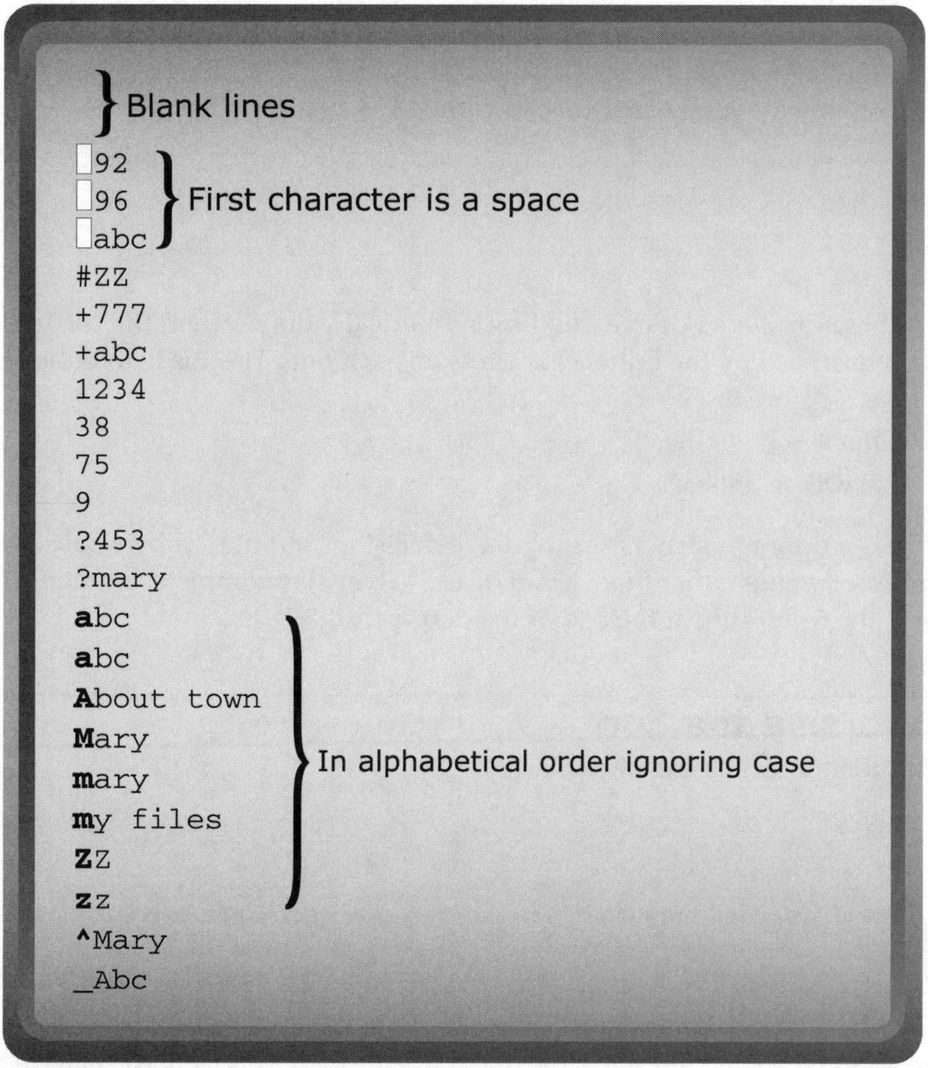

```
    } Blank lines
  □92  ⎫
  □96  ⎬ First character is a space
  □abc ⎭
  #ZZ
  +777
  +abc
  1234
  38
  75
  9
  ?453
  ?mary
  abc   ⎫
  abc   ⎪
  About town ⎪
  Mary  ⎬ In alphabetical order ignoring case
  mary  ⎪
  my files ⎪
  ZZ    ⎪
  zz    ⎭
  ^Mary
  _Abc
```

FIGURE 4-6   Output of sort with -f option

Sorting Based on Numerical Value

When **sort** orders the lines in sorted order, lines consisting of numbers are sorted in ASCII order, not numerical value.

1. Enter:

    sort *test-sor*

    Examine the lines consisting of numbers:

    1234
    38
    75
    9

    These lines are not in ascending numerical value; rather, the sorting is determined by the initial characters on each line. The 1 is before the 3, before the 7, before the 9.

2. Enter:

    sort -n *test-sor*

    The **-n** option instructs **sort** to make decisions about numbers based on numerical value rather than ASCII order. When **sort** completes numerical value sorts, the results are at the end of the output.

Reversing the Sort

The order of sorting can be reversed.

1. Enter:

    sort -r *test-sor*

    The display is in reversed ASCII order, as shown in Figure 4-7.

Sorting by Fields

The **sort** utility generally sorts lines based on the *first character* in each line. If the first characters from two lines match, the second character in each line is examined, then the third, and so on. There is an alternative: you can sort lines based on the contents of specific fields. Many files consist of lines of data that are composed of different fields separated by a character such as a colon, a space, or a tab.

Creating a Data File

To explore sorting lines by specific fields, a data file that contains lines (records), with each line composed of fields identified by a field separator, must be available.

```
zz
my files
mary
abc
abc
_Abc
^Mary
ZZ
Mary
About town
?mary
?453
9
75
38
1234
+abc
+777
#ZZ
 abc
 96  } First character is a space
 92
} Blank lines
```

FIGURE 4-7 Output of sort with -r option

1. Create a file named *respected* containing the following text. Each line for each individual contains five fields separated by spaces. Each field contains different information about that individual. Be sure to include the numbers as the first field.

```
000 Dyllis B. Harvey nurturer
001 Lyle C. Strand mentor
002 James V. Miller dean
003 Marjorie M. Conrad teacher
004 Orin C. Braucher farmer
005 David A. Wass professor
006 Peter M. Kindfield friend
007 Marge M. Boercker writer
```

2. Add one or two other people to the list, using the same five-field format.

Each line in the file provides information about one particular person. Every line, called a *record*, is divided into five information fields that pertain to the person. The following relates the data from the first record to the associated field names:

RECORD NUMBER	FIRST NAME	MIDDLE INITIAL	LAST NAME	DESCRIPTION
000	Dyllis	B.	Harvey	nurturer

A *field* is defined as a series of characters (a word, a number, a string of letters) where each field is separated from the next by some specified or default character. This character is often called the *field delimiter* or *field separator*. The default field delimiter for **sort** is the white space, either the space or tab characters.

Sorting a Data File by Fields

1. Sort the *respected* file according to last name (the fourth field) by entering:

   sort +3 *respected*

The *+3* tells **sort** to count three field separators and then start sorting. Hence, the sort begins at the fourth field.

2. An alternative way to achieve the same result is to use the **-k** option. Enter:

> **sort -k** *4* *respected*

The output is sorted beginning with the fourth field.

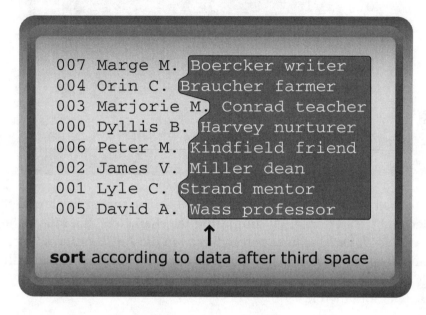

```
007 Marge M. Boercker writer
004 Orin C. Braucher farmer
003 Marjorie M. Conrad teacher
000 Dyllis B. Harvey nurturer
006 Peter M. Kindfield friend
002 James V. Miller dean
001 Lyle C. Strand mentor
005 David A. Wass professor
```

↑

sort according to data after third space

Sorting Starting with One Field

In the previous example, records are sorted based on the values in the fourth field, which contains the last names of the individuals. Because no two records contain the same last name, the sorting is without complication. However, because several individuals in this data have the same middle initial, sorting on the third field raises some issues.

1. Examine how **sort** sorts by field when several records have the same value in the sorted field. Enter:

> **sort +2** *respected*

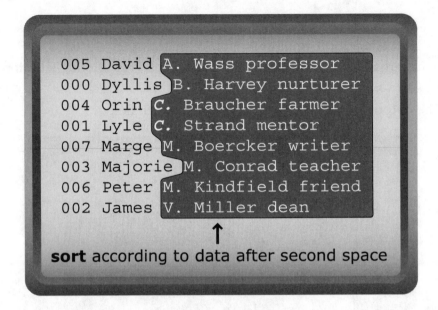

```
005 David A. Wass professor
000 Dyllis B. Harvey nurturer
004 Orin  C. Braucher farmer
001 Lyle  C. Strand mentor
007 Marge M. Boercker writer
003 Majorie M. Conrad teacher
006 Peter M. Kindfield friend
002 James V. Miller dean
```

↑

sort according to data after second space

There are two records with middle initial *C*. The **sort** utility found both *C*'s and decided the sort order by comparing the characters that follow the *C*'s in the next field. *Braucher* comes before *Strand* in the ASCII order, so record 004 is output before record 001. Likewise, the three records for people with middle initials of *M* are arranged based on the contents of the text that follows, last names: *B*, *C*, and then *K*.

Limiting sort

It is possible to instruct **sort** to stop sorting at a given field.

1. Tell **sort** to sort by middle initial by entering:

   sort +2 -3 *respected*

The following display highlights characters that are essential in making the sort decisions:

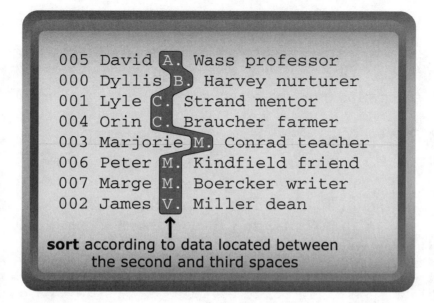

```
005  David  A.  Wass professor
000  Dyllis B.  Harvey nurturer
001  Lyle   C.  Strand mentor
004  Orin   C.  Braucher farmer
003  Marjorie M. Conrad teacher
006  Peter  M.  Kindfield friend
007  Marge  M.  Boercker writer
002  James  V.  Miller dean
```

sort according to data located between
the second and third spaces

This instruction is to count two field separators (**+2**), start sorting, and then stop sorting at the third separator (**-3**), which is really instruction to sort on field 3, the middle initial. The records that have the same value in the sort field (middle initial) are listed in an order that is decided by values in the default first field. *Kindfield* now comes before *Boercker* because it has a lower number in the first field. Thus, the records with *M* in the third field are ordered based on the order of the default first field.

If we tell **sort** to sort lines based on some portion of the record, it breaks ties starting with the beginning of the line unless we tell it to do something else.

Including a Secondary Sort Field

Rather than defaulting to the beginning of the record when there are duplicates in the **sort** field, we can specify another field as a secondary sort, to be examined only in case of a tie in the primary sort field.

1. Request that the third field be the primary sort field, and the second field be the secondary sort field by entering:

    sort +2 -3 +1 -2 *respected*

The output is:

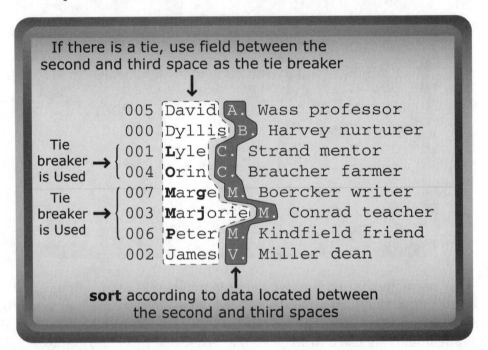

In this version, the records with the same value in the primary field (middle initial) are sorted based on the values in the secondary field, first names. For the two records with *C* in the primary field, *Lyle* is output before *Orin* because *L* precedes *O*.

Three records have a middle initial of *M*, so the first names (field 2) are consulted: *Marge* precedes *Marjorie*, which precedes *Peter*.

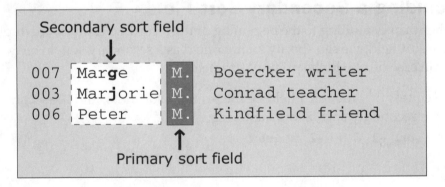

Examining the Code

Review the following command line:

sort *+2 -3 +1 -2* *respected*

This instruction says:

+2	Count two field separators and start sorting each record.
-3	Stop sorting each record at the third field separator. Hence, the third field is sorted.
+1 -2	If the data in the third field results in two or more records with identical data, break the tie by examining the second field of those records (*+1 −2*).

Reversing a Secondary Field

On most systems, each sort field can be handled differently.

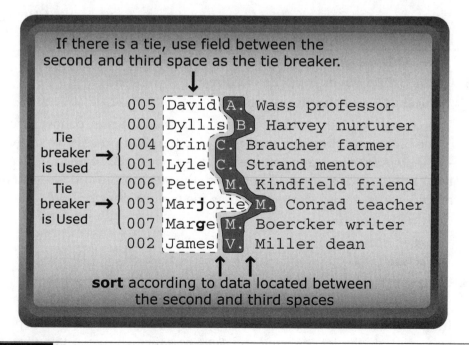

FIGURE 4-8 Reversing secondary order

1. Reverse the sense of the secondary sort field, while leaving the primary field as is, by entering:

    sort +2 -3 +1r -2 *respected*

The output is Figure 4-8. Because the secondary sort is reversed, **Peter** is displayed as the first record with the middle initial of *M*.

With the **sort** utility, we can specify complex sorts based on lines or fields, and we can instruct **sort** to use another field as a secondary sort criteria.

Using sort with a Different Field Delimiter

The file */etc/passwd* contains system information about users.

1. Examine the file by entering the following:

    head */etc/passwd*

    Each line is a series of fields separated by colons:

    ```
    cassy:RstAk9?sMZ4pQb:1991:423:child:/home/cassy:/bin/ksh
    ```

    On some systems, the *passwd* file is quite large; on others it is fairly small.

2. Enter:

    wc */etc/passwd*

3. Create a short file in your current directory by entering:

    head -15 */etc/passwd* > *short-pass*

    This command instructs the shell to start a child process, connect the output of the process to a new file *short-pass*, give the child process two arguments: *-15* and */etc/passwd*, and tell the process to execute the **head** utility. The **head** utility reads at most 15 lines from the *passwd* file and writes them to output, connected to *short-pass*, a new file in your directory.

4. Confirm by entering:

    wc *short-pass*
    cat *short-pass*

5. Have **sort** order the lines in the *short-pass* of the file by entering:

    sort *short-pass*

    In the *respected* file that you used a few steps back, the fields are separated by a space. In the */etc/passwd* and *short-pass* files, the separator character is the colon.

The third field in each record in the password file is the user's unique identification number.

6. To see how **sort** handles the request to sort by specific field when the file does not use white space as a field separator, enter:

    sort +2 *short-pass*

The results are not sorted by the third field, because **sort** is defining fields based on spaces not colons.

7. To request sorting by the third field with fields separated by the colon character, enter:

    sort -t: +2 *short-pass*

The records are now sorted based on the third field, user ID.

The **-t** option instructs sort to use a different character for the field separator. The specified character, the colon, follows the **-t** option without a space between them. The sorting in the previous command is in ASCII, not numerical value. In an ASCII sort, the number 110 comes before 20 because sorting starts with the leftmost character on the line. Character 1 precedes 2 in the ASCII character set.

8. To sort in numerical order, include the **-n** option:

    sort -t: -n +2 *short-pass*

The records are sorted based on the numerical values in field 3.

Redirecting the Output of sort to a File

In the examples entered thus far, the output of **sort** is connected to your workstation screen. As is usually the case, you can redirect the output of a utility to a file.

1. Enter:

    sort *test-sor* **>** *sorted-test-sor*

The **sort** utility sorts the lines from the file named *test-sor*, and the output of **sort** is placed in a file named *sorted-test-sor*. This new file can be edited, manipulated, or examined by other utilities.

2. Examine the *sorted-test-sor* using **more** or **cat**.

Sorting a File and Overwriting

You may be tempted to sort a file and have its output placed back in the file.

1. Enter the following:

   cp *short-pass sp2*
   cat *sp2*
   sort *sp2* > *sp2*

   One of two things occurs. Either you are told the file exists (if *noclobber* is set), or there was no objection, the shell did as it was told, and the file *sp2* is now empty.

2. Enter:

   cat *sp2*

   When we tell the shell to redirect output to an existing file, the shell empties the specified file (unless *noclobber* is set) before executing the utility. By the time **sort** opens the file to sort it, there is nothing there.

   To solve this problem, there is an option we can give to **sort**.

3. Enter:

   cp *short-pass sp3*
   sort *sp3* **-o** *sortedsp3*

   There is no shell redirection in this command line. The shell does not connect the output of **sort** to *sortedsp3*. Instead, three arguments are passed to **sort**.

ARGUMENT	INTERPRETATION
sp3	File to read and sort.
-o	Put output in the file listed as next argument.
sortedsp3	File for output.

Because **sort** reads input first and writes last, we can tell it to read and write the same file without a problem.

4. Enter:

   sort *sp3* **-o** *sp3*
   cat *sp3*

The file is now sorted because **sort** read the file, sorted the lines, and after sorting overwrote the unsorted file with its sorted output.

Although **sort** is a powerful and flexible utility, it sorts only lines. Once it reads in the lines and sorts them, it outputs the whole lines, not just selected portions. Later in this chapter, you will use **cut** and **awk**, utilities that can be used to overcome this limitation. Likewise, **sort**, without the aid of other utilities, cannot easily sort records consisting of multiple lines.

S U M M A R Y : The sort utility takes all lines it receives as input and rearranges them into a variety of orders, based on the following options:

sort (without option)   Sort following the ASCII order.

-r   Reverse the sorted order.

-d   Output based only on letters, numbers, and space characters.

-f   Sorted with uppercase and lowercase of the same letter sorted together (folded); if a tie, uppercase is first.

+n Sort by specific field, where n is the number of field separators **sort** is to count before beginning the sort.

-n Stop sorting at the nth field separator, where n is a number.

-k n Sort by nth field.

-n   Sort by numerical value rather than ASCII order.

-tx Use the character x as the field delimiter, which can be any character.

-o arg Put output in arg filename.

Examining the man Pages

Now that you have explored the **sort** utility and several of its options, examine the manual pages for other **sort** options on your system.

1. Enter:

   man *sort*

2. When you are ready, quit **man** by entering:

> q

3. Explore the **man** pages for some of the other utilities, paying particular attention to their options.

> **man** *wc*
>
> **man** *grep*
>
> **man** *bc*
>
> **man** *man*

4.8 Identifying and Removing Duplicate Lines

Often, when we sort a file containing information such as an index or word list, the resulting output includes lines containing duplicate data. The **uniq** program reads the input and compares each line with the line that precedes it. If the two lines are identical, action is taken.

1. Create a test file called *test-u* consisting of the following:

```
aa
bbb
ccc
aaa
aaa
aaa
bbb
bbb
eee
fff
aaa
```

2. To examine how **uniq** works, enter the following command line:

> **uniq** *test-u*

3. Examine the output:

```
aa
bbb
ccc
aaa
bbb
eee
fff
aaa
```

The **uniq** utility reads a line, then reads a second. If the second line is just like the first, that line is discarded. All duplicate lines that are *not* adjacent to each other remain. Duplicates that are on adjacent lines are reduced to just one copy. If not adjacent, duplicate lines will remain.

Removing All Duplicate Lines

Because the **uniq** utility compares only *adjacent* lines, duplicate lines must be next to each other in the input to be **uniq**ed. One way to be certain all duplicates are adjacent is to first **sort** the file.

1. Examine *test-u*, create a sorted version, and examine it:

> **cat** *test-u*
> **sort** *test-u* > *sor-test-u*
> **cat** *sor-test-u*

2. Now **uniq** the sorted file:

> **uniq** *sor-test-u*

The **uniq** utility reads each line from the file, removes duplicate adjacent lines, and displays the results.

The sorted file has all duplicate lines grouped together. The **uniq** utility removes all but one of each set of duplicates.

3. Sorting and using **uniq** can be accomplished in one step. Enter the following:

> **sort** *test-u* | **uniq**

In this case, after the contents of *test-u* are sorted, the output of **sort** is connected directly to the input of **uniq**, which removes all but one copy of lines that have duplicates.

Identifying the Lines That Have No Duplicates

In *test-u*, there are some unique lines and some lines with duplicates. The duplicates are not all adjacent.

1. Sort the file:

> **sort** *test-u* **-o** *test-u*
> **cat** *test-u*

The file is sorted and overwritten with the sorted version.

2. Use **uniq**:

> **uniq** *test-u*

One copy of all lines is output.

The lines that are unique in the file can be selected as well.

3. Enter the command:

> **uniq -u** *test-u*

With the **-u** option, **uniq** examines the contents of the file and outputs only the lines that have no adjacent duplicate. All copies of lines that have duplicates are discarded. The truly unique lines are the only ones selected.

Identifying the Duplicated Lines

Lines that do have duplicates can be selected and output by **uniq**.

1. Enter the command:

> **uniq -d** *test-u*

With the **-d** option, **uniq** ignores all lines that are unique and outputs one copy of each line that has duplicates.

The **uniq** command with the **-d** option outputs a single copy of each duplicate line, no matter how often it is repeated in the sorted file.

2. Instruct **uniq** to count the number of times each line is in the input:

   uniq -c *test-u*

Each line is output with the count of that line on its left, indicating how many times that line is in the sorted file.

SUMMARY: Unless an option is specified, the **uniq** utility compares adjacent lines in its input, discarding a line if it is a duplicate of the preceding line. If the input is sorted, the resulting output consists of one copy of all unique lines and one copy of all duplicate lines. Options are as follows:

-u Output only the unique lines, discard all of the duplicates.

-d Output only a single copy of the lines that are duplicated; discard the duplicates and all unique lines.

-c Output a single copy of each line with a number to its left indicating the number of times that line is in the input.

4.9 Comparing the Contents of Two Files with comm

Each line in any two files can be fit into one of three categories:

- Lines uniquely in the first file
- Lines uniquely in the second file
- Lines that are in both files

The **comm** utility compares two files, line by line, and identifies in which of the three categories each line belongs. Is it a line found only in the first file, only in the second file, or a line that is in both files?

Creating an Example File

To examine how the **comm** utility compares data, two files of specific content need to be created. In the United States, some states are located on the coast of an ocean; others are not. Some states are in the western part of the United States, and some are not. Some states are *both* in the West *and* on the coast.

1. Use the **visual** editor to create a file called *west* with the following contents:

   ```
   California
   Washington
   Oregon
   Nevada
   Utah
   ```

2. While still editing the file *west*, make sure you are in command mode and enter:

   :set *list*

   This is instruction to **vi** to display special characters including the end-of-line characters.

   A dollar sign appears at the end of each line.

3. If any spaces exist at the end of lines, or if any state name is not spelled correctly or is in the wrong case, correct it.

4. Write the file and quit the editor.

5. Create a second file named *coast*, with the following contents:

   ```
   Florida
   Washington
   Maine
   Oregon
   California
   Georgia
   ```

6. Check to be sure the data is correct with:

   :set *list*

7. Write and quit the editor.

8. For **comm** to work properly, the files need to be sorted. Enter these commands:

   sort *west* > *sor-west*
   sort *coast* > *sor-coast*

Grouping Unique and Common Lines

Consider the following illustration which represents the lines in the two sorted files. Notice that some lines (states) are unique to each file, and some lines are in both files.

There are three groups of lines:

- Lines found in *sor-west* but not in *sor-coast* (western states not on the coast)
- Lines found in *sor-coast* but not in *sor-west* (coastal states not in the west)
- Lines found in both files (western states and on the coast)

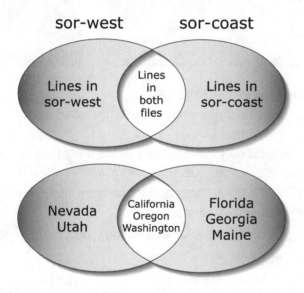

Identifying Unique and Common Lines

1. To identify the common and unique lines in the two sorted files, enter:

   comm *sor-west sor-coast > west-coast*

   This command instructs **comm** to perform the comparison of two files listed as arguments. The output from **comm** is redirected to a new file, *west-coast*.

2. Call up the file *west-coast* with the **visual** editor:

   vi *west-coast*

The output of **comm** is three columns of data:

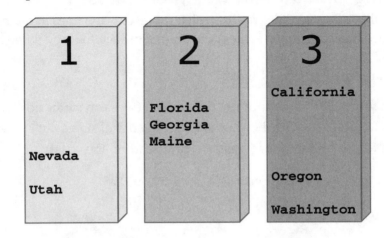

The three columns are as follows:

- The first column contains those lines that are uniquely in the *first* file: *Nevada* and *Utah*.
- The second column contains those lines that are uniquely in the *second* file: *Florida, Georgia,* and *Maine.*
- The third column contains those lines that are in *both* files: *California, Oregon,* and *Washington.*

While editing this output file, again ask the editor to display special characters.

3. From command mode, enter:

> **:set** *list*

The display shows the content with special characters identified. A few of the output lines are included in the next illustration.

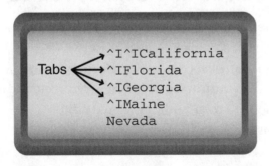

The special character **^I** is the editor's way of displaying the tab character. When **comm** reads *California* as the first line in the first file and then also finds it in the second file, **comm** outputs two tabs and then the line *California*. The two tabs put the line in the third column of output. The line *Florida* is found in the second file only, so **comm** precedes it with only one tab to put it in the second column of output. *Nevada* is only in the first file, so **comm** outputs no tabs before the line. All lines uniquely in the first file, group 1, are against the left margin. All lines in the second file only, group 2, are in the middle because one tab was output in front of each line. All lines in common, group 3, are on the right because two tabs are output in front of each line that is found in both files.

4. Quit the editor and return to the shell.
5. To see how **comm** works, have **comm** compare the original unsorted files, *west* and *coast*:

    comm *west coast*

The output is not correct. Several states that are in common are listed in the output as uniquely in both files. This is a practical impossibility. How did this occur? The **comm** utility compares the files line by line. When **comm** reads the line *California* in the first (unsorted) file and later finds *Florida* as the first line in the second file, **comm** concludes that there can be no *California* in the second file. The logic is this: **comm** assumes that since *Florida* is on the first line of the second file, there can be no other line that starts with a letter before *F* in that file. The input files to **comm** must be sorted first because the **comm** utility was written based on this assumption.

Selecting Unique or Common Lines

The three columns of output are related to the three kinds of lines:

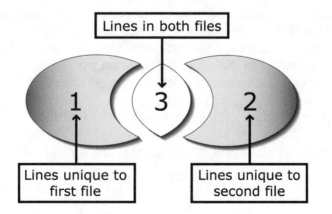

Column 1, group 1, includes the unique lines from the first file; Column 2, group 2, includes lines uniquely in the second file; Column 3, group 3, includes the lines common to both files.

We can select lines common to both files or just those that are unique to one or the other file.

1. Enter:

   comm *-3* *sor-west* *sor-coast*

   This command instructs **comm** to discard group 3, the lines in common in both files. The output is group 1, the lines unique to the first file, and group 2, the lines uniquely in the second file (groups 1 and 2). Those lines found in both files (group 3) are suppressed.

   To list only those lines common to both files—that is, to select group 3—we must leave out groups 1 and 2.

2. Enter this command:

   comm *-12* *sor-west* *sor-coast*

   With the *-12* flag, **comm** suppresses printing of groups 1 and 2, the lines unique to each file. Only those states in the West that are also on a coast are listed—the lines in both files.

3. Likewise, a listing of western states that are not on the coast can be attained by entering:

   comm *-23* *sor-west* *sor-coast*

This flag is an instruction to suppress groups 2, lines unique to the second file, and 3, lines common to both. It outputs only group 1, lines uniquely in the first file.

SUMMARY: The **comm** utility compares the contents of two files, line by line. It reports a table indicating the lines unique to each file, and the lines common to both. Because **comm** works only with one line at a time, input must be sorted. Options are as follows:

-1   Suppress output of lines uniquely in the first file.

-2   Suppress output of lines uniquely in the second file.

-3   Suppress output of lines that are common to both files.

-12   Options can be combined. This combination is instruction to suppress lines unique to each file so that only lines common to both are output.

4.10 Examining Differences Between Files

The **diff** utility indicates how two files are **diff**erent. It reports the lines that are not the same, the location of these lines in their respective files, and what lines you need to add, change, or delete to convert one file to the other.

1. Create a file called *alpha1* containing the following lines:

```
Mary
Robert
Pat
Nancy
```

2. Create a second file, *alpha2*, containing these lines:

```
Mary
Robert P
Pat L
Nancy
Ivan
```

3. Find the differences between *alpha1* and *alpha2* by entering:

   diff *alpha1 alpha2*

The following output is displayed:

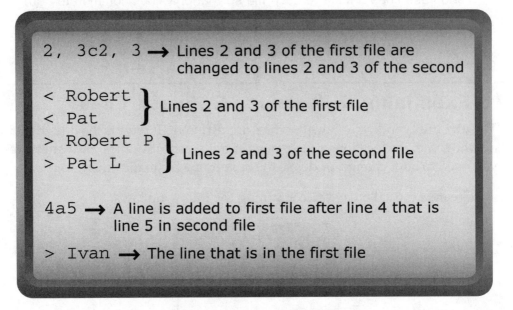

This output contains two kinds of lines. Lines such as *<Robert* indicate that the line *Robert* is in the first file, but not in the second. Likewise, *>Robert P* is in the second file, not the first. A line that include numbers and letters (*2, 3c2, 3*) indicates the location of the differing lines in their respective files and what needs to be done to convert the first file into the second.

4. In contrast to **diff**, the **comm** utility just lists the lines unique to each file and in common to both. Try this command and observe the results:

   comm *alpha1 alpha2*

For more information concerning **diff**, consult the output of **man diff**.

S U M M A R Y : The **diff** utility compares two files and indicates what must be done to the first file to make it match the second. Lines unique to each file are marked. Lines in common are ignored.

4.11 Translating Characters to Other Characters with tr

The **tr** utility reads input and either deletes target characters or translates each target character into a specified replacement character. The output is a translated version of the input.

Translating Specified Characters

The **tr** utility takes two arguments.

1. Enter:

    who | tr *t Z*

   The output of the **who** utility is connected to the input of **tr**. The **tr** utility searches through every character in the input looking for the specified target character (*t*) and then replaces every instance of *t* with Z.

   The output of **tr** remains connected to the screen. Two arguments are given to **tr**. The **tr** utility interprets its first argument as a target character to locate. The second argument is the character used to replace the target. Hence, every *t* that **tr** finds in input is replaced with a Z. See Figure 4-9.

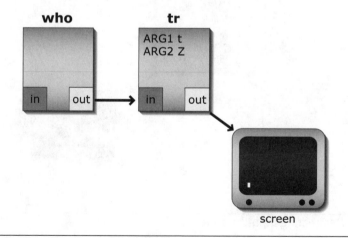

FIGURE 4-9   Redirecting the output of **who**

2. To have a translation made of the contents of the *test-sor* file, enter the following command:

   tr *a Z < test-sor*

   This command line includes the < redirection symbol, which tells the shell to open the file *test-sor* and connect it to the input of **tr**. The utility **tr** is not programmed to open files. In this command line, **tr** is given two arguments, the letter *a* (target) and the letter *Z* (replacement). Each instance of the letter *a* is located by **tr** and replaced with *Z*. The output from **tr** is displayed on the screen. The original file is not altered. See Figure 4-10.

   The **tr** utility makes translations of several characters at the same time.

3. Try this command:

   tr *'Ma7' '| &s' < test-sor*

   The two arguments are in single quotation marks to instruct the shell to pass each argument to **tr** without interpreting any special characters. The < instructs the shell to connect the file *test-sor* to **tr**'s input. The **tr** utility reads from input and makes translations. The translated version of the file is output, in this case, to the screen. The arguments are interpreted by **tr** as target and

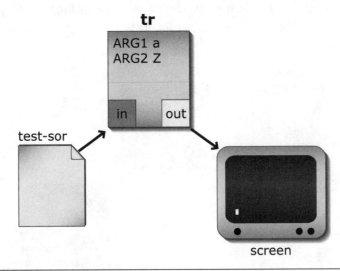

FIGURE 4-10 Redirecting input to a file

replacement characters. All instances of the letter *M* are replaced with a pipe (|). Every *a* is replaced with an *&*, and each *7* character becomes a small *s*.

M	becomes	|
a	becomes	&
7	becomes	*s*

Translating a Range of Characters

With the **tr** utility you can also translate a range of characters such as 0–5 or A–M.

1. For example, enter the command:

   tr '*a-z*' '*A-Z*' < *test-sor*

   Or on older systems:

   tr '[a-z]' '[A-Z]' < *test sor*

   The output, sent to the terminal screen by default, is in uppercase:

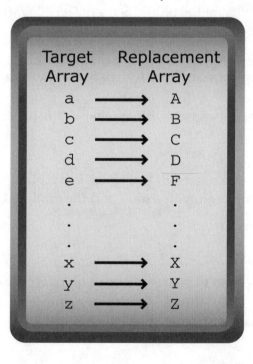

This command instructs the **tr** utility to read from *test-sor* and translate all lowercase alphabetical characters *a* through *z* into uppercase *A* through *Z*.

Deleting Specified Characters

In addition to making translations, **tr** also deletes identified characters.

1. To delete specific characters from *test-sor*, enter:

   tr -d '*cbmZo*' < *test-sor*

Two arguments are given to the process running **tr**: **-d** and *cbmZo*. The file *test-sor* is connected to the input of **tr**. Every instance of each character in the file that matches a character in the second argument is removed.

Employing the tr Utility

The **tr** utility is a useful tool for managing data.

1. Enter the following:

   ls | tr '*a-z*' '*A-Z*'

   The output of **tr** displayed on your screen is an all-uppercase listing of the output of **ls**, which makes old DOS users feel all warm and fuzzy.

2. Enter:

   head *-30 /etc/passwd* | **tr** ':' ' '

   The **tr** utility replaces each **:** with a space and outputs the modified version of the file.

   We can replace every space with another character using **tr**.

3. Enter:

   tr ' ' '+' < *practice*

   Two arguments are passed to **tr**, a space and a plus. Your *practice* file is read, every space is replaced with a plus, and the modified version is output to the screen.

4. Edit practice:

   vi *practice*

   Use your arrow keys to place the cursor on the space between the first and second words.

5. Replace the space with a new line by entering:

   r

   ENTER

   The first word remains on the old line. The rest of the text goes to the next line.

6. Replace the next space with an ENTER.

You could continue replacing spaces with new lines until the file was one word to a line. But there is an easier way.

7. Leave **vi** without saving:

    :q!

8. Enter:

    tr ' ' '\n' < *practice*

The shell interprets the \n as the newline character, ASCII 012. In this case, we are telling **tr** to replace each space in the file with a new line, so every word is output on a line by itself.

SUMMARY: The **tr** utility translates specific characters into other specific characters and translates ranges of characters into other ranges. It also deletes listed characters. If two arguments are given, the characters in the first argument are translated into the characters listed in the second argument, with one-to-one mapping. One option of **tr** is discussed:

-d *argument* Instructs **tr** to delete all instances of each specified character in the argument that follows.

■ Review 2

1. What command tells **sort** to sort the file *junk1* and put the sorted version in *junk1*, replacing the unsorted version?

---

2. A file named *employees* consists of information about employees. Each line is a record for one employee consisting of several fields separated by the % character: lastname, firstname, department, and employeeID, in that order. What command tells **sort** to output the data such that everyone in each department is listed together, alphabetically by last name? Because some employees have the same last name, use the first name as a tiebreaker.

---

3. Using the **man** pages, determine what options accomplish the following:
   a. Tells **sort** to check to see if a file is already sorted, and if so, do not sort it.
   b. Tells **bc** to invoke the math library so you can determine sine, cosine, and so on.
   c. Tells **grep** to output only the number of matches in a file, not the actual matched lines.

   _____

4. What command instructs **tr** to delete all *!.?"&$;*.()*, characters from the file *practice*?

   _____

5. What command instructs **tr** to output a sorted version of the results of **who** in all uppercase?

   _____

6. A file named *awards* consists of lines with only employee ID numbers and last names for employees. Every time an employee gets a commendation letter from a client, another entry is made in the file. What command outputs the employee names and ID numbers and the number of commendations?

   _____

7. You have two report files (*report1* and *report2*) and are not sure which one is the latest version. There are few differences and it is hard to tell what is going on. What command might help?

   _____

8. What command results in a sorting of the file *people*, ignoring case and ignoring punctuation at the beginning of the line?

   _____

9. What command sorts the file *letc/passwd* using the fourth field, group id, as the primary sort and the third field, user id, as the secondary sort?

   _____

10. Consider two files. The first file, *students*, is a sorted list of names of all students enrolled in the school. The second file, *paid*, is a sorted list of names

of students who have paid their tuition. What command lists those students from the first file who have *not* paid their tuition?

_____

11. What command displays the output of **who** in all capital letters?

_____

12. What command would produce a listing of what changes would have to be made in *names* to make it exactly like file *newnames*?

_____

4.12 Listing Names of Files and Directories

The **ls** utility outputs file and directory names listed in the parent directory. You have used it several times to determine the contents of a directory.

1. Enter the following:

> **ls**
> **ls -a**
> **ls -l**   (an el)
> **ls -F**

With no option, **ls** outputs the names of files and directories listed in the current directory, unless their names begin with a period (dot files).

To see all files including the dot files, the **-a** option is used. The **-l** option is instruction to locate all information about each file and include it in the output. The option **-F** is instruction to put a slash in the display after the name of any directory.

The **ls** utility outputs the names either in one column or with names in several columns.

2. Enter:

> **ls -C**
> **ls -1**   (the numeral one)
> **ls -Ca**

The **-C** option is instruction to output names in as many columns as the length of the names permits (longer filenames, fewer columns). The **-1** option is instruction to output filenames one name to a line, all names in the first column.

When you run **ls** and have its output sent to your screen, the multicolumn output is probably the default. Consider what happens when the output from **ls** is redirected to another utility.

3. Enter:

> **ls | more**
> **ls -1 | more**   (the numeral one)
> **ls –C | more**

The default output when **ls** is connected to **more** is to output one filename per column. If we insist on multicolumn output, **ls** obliges.

Redirect the output of **ls** to **wc**.

4. Enter:

> **ls | wc**

The number of lines and number of words are equal. The **ls** output must be one word to a line when it is connected to **wc**.

5. Confirm by entering:

> **ls -C | wc**
> **ls -1 | wc**

The **ls** utility is a powerful, useful tool.

6. Examine the options in the **man** pages:

> **man ls**

4.13 Combining Selected Lines with join

Corresponding lines or records from two files can also be joined together based on the value of a common field. This function of joining records from two or more files based on the "join value" is the core operation in relational database work.

Joining Records Based on Value of the Join Field

1. Examine the contents of the files created in section 4.2, *names.tmp* and *numbers.tmp*, once again. Enter:

> **more** *names.tmp numbers.tmp*

The first column of each file contains the room numbers for each record (101, 102, and so on). The file *names.tmp* relates the room numbers to names of the occupants. The file *numbers.tmp* relates the room number to telephone numbers. Looking at the displayed data, you can determine the phone number for Mary L. She is in room 106, and room 106 has a phone number of 317-6512. By joining those two pieces of information, Mary's phone must be 317-6512.

If your objective were to create a new file that has names and room numbers matched with their respective phone numbers, you would need to **join** all the appropriate records from the two files. Clearly, the field that is used to connect the corresponding lines or records of the two files in this example is the room number, called the *join field.*

2. To output a **join** of the two files, enter:

   join *names.tmp numbers.tmp*

The output is useful information, showing both name and phone number for each room number that has a record in both files:

```
101 Nate H. 555-9136
104 Cassy T.591-1191
106 Mary L. 317-6512
```

The default field for joining records is the first field. When **join** reads the first line from the first file, it finds a 101 in the first field. Reading the first line from the second file, **join** also finds a 101. The join field from both records has the same value, so **join** outputs all fields from both records as a single line. The joining of lines with 104 in the first field is displayed in Figure 4-11.

Examining the Need for Sorted Input

Because **join** compares lines from each file starting at the beginning of each file, one line at a time, the files must be in sorted order in the join field.

1. Modify the *numbers.tmp* file to have the record for room 104 placed as line 1 in the file:

```
104 TAB 591-1191
101 TAB 555-9136
105 TAB 511-1972
106 TAB 317-6512
```

2. Have **join** read the two files and join the appropriate lines:

   join *names.tmp numbers.tmp*

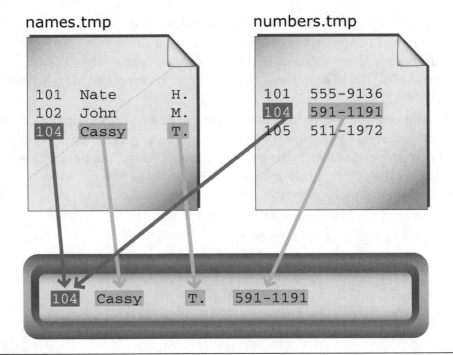

FIGURE 4-11 Record joined by common first field value

The output is quite different. Lines that you know share the same value in the join field are not joined. The **join** utility does not read a line from the first file and compare its join field value to all the lines in the other file. Instead, **join** only compares a line from one file to the first or next line in another file. In this case, the files are not sorted in ASCII order. The **join** utility finds a 104 in the join field of the first line in the second file and concludes that there can be no record with a 101 in the second file because 104 is first. If there were a 101, it would have been before 104. Files must be sorted for **join** to work properly.

Outputting Selected Fields

In the previous example, **join** outputs all fields from both files. We can request output of specific fields.

1. Enter:

   join -o *1.2 2.2 1.1 names.tmp numbers.tmp*

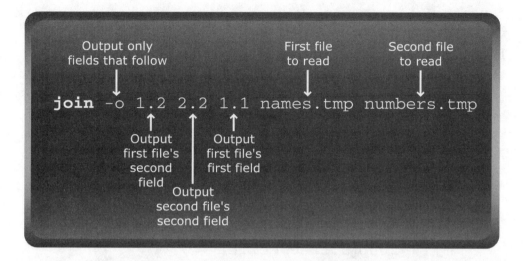

SUMMARY: The **join** utility puts together—joins—lines from separate files if and only if the lines are related to one another through the presence of an identical value in a specified field. Both files must be sorted (in ASCII order) on the specified join fields.

4.14 Editing from the Command Line with sed

When you begin editing a file using the visual editor, the file is read into an editing or buffer space in memory. The whole file is read into memory, and you proceed to make changes anywhere in the file you want to work. Available memory determines the maximum size limit of the file when you are editing using **vi**.

Another way to edit a file would be to read in just one line, make changes, write the line, and read in another. With such an approach, very large files can be edited, because only one line at a time is in working memory. An editor that reads in individual lines works on streams of data and is known as the **stream editor, sed**.

Creating a Sample File

To examine stream editing, we need a file of specific content.

1. Use the visual editor to create a file called *caffeine* with the following contents:

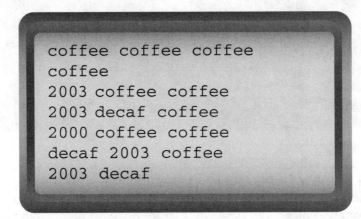

```
coffee coffee coffee
coffee
2003 coffee coffee
2003 decaf coffee
2000 coffee coffee
decaf 2003 coffee
2003 decaf
```

Changing Target Words

Suppose your caffeine addiction has changed flavors, and you want to replace the word *coffee* with the word *chocolate* at every instance where *coffee* occurs in a copy of the file *caffeine*. Without calling up **vi**, you can create a version with the substitutions.

1. Enter the following command:

   sed '**s**/*coffee*/*chocolate*/' *caffeine*

The most common error is leaving out the last / before the last quote. All three slashes are required.

The output comes to the screen; the file itself is not altered. The results show that only the first instance of *coffee* is changed to *chocolate* on each line. The **sed** utility read and modified every line that had *coffee*, but not all instances on each line. This **sed** command contains the following instructions:

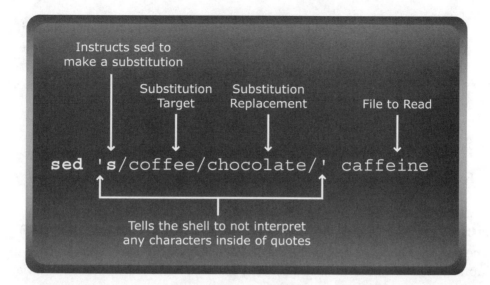

COMMAND	INTERPRETATION
s	Instructs **sed** to make a **s**ubstitution.
/coffee/	The string *coffee* is the target to be searched for on each line. It is the target string to be replaced.
/chocolate/	The replacement string. In cases where there is more than one instance of the target word on a line, only the first is affected.

In summary, the file *caffeine* is not altered. Only the version that is read, modified, and output by **sed** is changed. Not every instance of *coffee* is replaced in the output.

Changing All Instances of the Target

The previous **sed** command modifies only the first instance of the target word on each line it reads as input. You can instruct **sed** to change all instances of a target occurring on each line.

1. Enter the following **sed** command including the **g**lobal request:

    sed 's/coffee/chocolate**/g'** *caffeine*

Each line of the file *caffeine* is read, and each instance of the target string is replaced. The resulting lines are displayed on the screen. The **g** after the replacement string instructs **sed** to **g**lobally affect each line; making substitutions for all instances of the target encountered on the line, not just the first.

2. Enter:

    sed 's/*root***/ROOT/g'** *short-pass* **|** **more**

Each instance of the target string *root* is changed to *ROOT*.

Selecting Lines and Then Making Replacements

The previous **sed** commands instructed **sed** to modify text on any lines of the input. You can request that **sed** act only on lines that meet specified criteria.

1. Enter the following:

    sed '/*2003***/s/***coffee***/***chocolate***/g'** *caffeine*

The */2003/* in front of the substitution specification is the line target. It instructs **sed** to select lines only if they have the string *2003* somewhere on the line. If a line matches and is selected, then look for the substitution target *coffee*. If *coffee* is located on that line, **sed** substitutes *chocolate* for *coffee*. Lines are selected for processing only if the line target string matches; a substitution takes place on the line only if the substitution target is matched. The line with *2000* did not match *2003*, so the string *coffee* is not replaced. Although the last line does match with its *2003*, there is no *coffee* to replace. This command is illustrated in Figure 4-12.

Making a Substitution for the Line Search Target

In the previous example, a target was specified for locating lines, and then a different target for a text substitution was provided. The line target can be used as the substitution target, as well.

1. Enter the following, which does not specify a substitution target:

    sed '/*2003***/s//***2010***/g'** *caffeine*

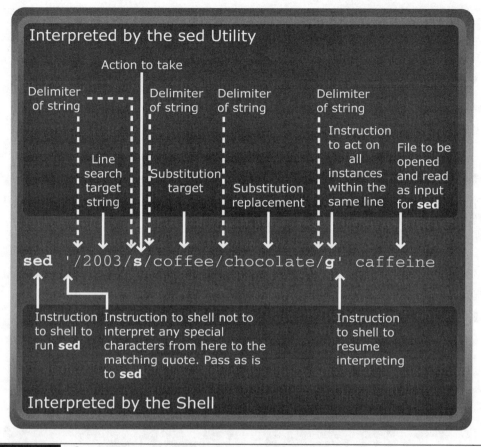

FIGURE 4-12 Components of a **sed** substitution command

Lines are selected if they have the line target string present: *2003*. The *2003* is replaced with the string *2010*. In this command, no substitution target is specified; the two slashes after the **s** have no target between them. When no substitution target is specified, the line selection target is used for substitution. Lines are selected if they contain the line search target string, and then that string is replaced.

2. Enter:

   sed '*/decaf/s//DECAF/*' *caffeine*

Lines that have the string *decaf* are selected, then the *decaf* is replaced with *DECAF*.

Deleting Lines

The **sed** editor will do much more than make substitutions.

1. Enter:

    sed **'/***dec***/d'** *caffeine*

In this case, every line that has *dec* anywhere on the line is deleted.

Using Regular Expressions with sed

The regular expressions examined with **grep** have the same meanings to **sed**.

1. Enter:

    sed **'/^2/s/***coffee***/***chocolate***/g'** *caffeine*

All lines that start with a 2 are selected for operation. If the selected line has *coffee*, it is replaced with *chocolate*, **g**lobally.

2. Enter:

    sed **'/^c/d'** *caffeine*

All lines beginning with *c* are targeted and deleted.

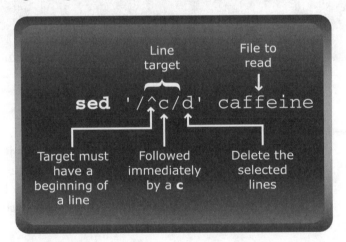

3. Enter:

    sed **'/^$/d'** *test-sor*
    cat *test-sor*

The target specification is "Beginning of the line followed by the end of the line." To be selected, no text can be between the beginning and end of the line. Thus, all the blank lines are selected and deleted.

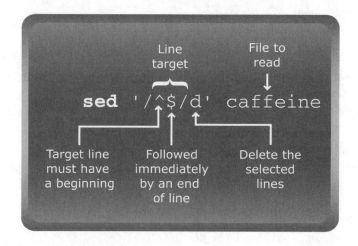

SUMMARY: The **sed** utility takes an input line, makes whatever editing changes are requested, and then outputs that line. It is a **s**tream **ed**itor that uses editing commands and regular expressions. Chapter 16, "Editing the Data Stream with sed," explores more of **sed**'s features.

4.15 Manipulating Data with awk

The output of **who** consists of one line for each user who is logged onto the system. Each line, called a *record*, consists of several fields of information about the user. Likewise, data is often stored in files with individual lines (records) containing multiple fields. The **awk** utility is designed to locate particular records and fields in a database, modify them, perform computations, and then output selected portions of the data. The **awk** utility is particularly useful for information retrieval, data manipulation, and report writing.

The name of the **awk** utility is derived from the names of the programmers who wrote it and many other parts of UNIX: **A**ho, **W**einberger, and **K**ernighan.

1. For this section of the chapter, create a file called *food* and enter the following text:

```
milk   dairy  2.00
hamburger  meat  2.75
cheese  dairy  1.50
```

The *food* file consists of three records. Each record contains three fields: name of product, kind of product, and the price. Each data field is separated from the next by a space, which is the default field delimiter for **awk**.

Selecting Lines and Printing Fields

The **awk** utility does its work by selecting records based on the presence of a specified pattern and then performing a prescribed action on the selected record.

1. Enter the command:

   awk '/dairy/ {print $3}' *food*

   This command line instructs **awk** to select each record in the *food* file that contains the character string *dairy*, and then to perform the action of printing the third field (price) from each of the selected records. In this example, the pattern used to select the lines is not in the field (3) that is output. You can use one field for selection and then output entirely different fields.

   The components of the command line are as follows:

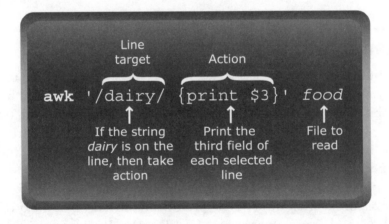

COMMAND	INTERPRETATION
awk	Instruction to the shell to execute the **awk** utility.
' '	Instruction to the shell to not interpret special characters inside the quoted string, but rather to pass the enclosed characters as an argument to the **awk** utility.
/*dairy*/	Instruction to **awk** to select lines that have the string *dairy* anywhere on the line. Lines that contain this pattern are selected for whatever action is specified in the **{ }** section.
{print $3}	Instruction to **awk** to take action on selected lines, namely to output, or **print**, the third field, **$3**. The action, identified by curly braces, is performed on all the lines that have *dairy* in them. The **print** statement is one of **awk**'s many possible actions.
food	This argument tells **awk** which file to read for input.

Multiple fields can be output.

2. Enter:

   awk '/*dairy*/ **{print $3, $1}**' *food*

The third field (a space) and then the first field are output for lines that contain the target string *dairy*.

Changing the Field Delimiter

In the file *food*, the fields in each record are delimited by spaces. Often data files use other characters as field separators. Login information is kept in the */etc/passwd* file, where fields are delimited with colons.

Selecting Specific Data

1. Have the system display your password record by entering the following:

   grep *$USER /etc/passwd*

   If you are on a stand-alone system, the password file is on your system; otherwise, it is on a network server. If you do not get an output line consisting of several fields separated by colons, you are probably on a network server. You will need to issue commands like the following.

2. Request a display from the network server by entering:

   ypcat *passwd* | **grep** *$USER*

The line in *passwd* containing your login ID is selected and output.

We can instruct **awk** to use the colon as the field separator.

3. Enter the following:

   awk -F: '{print $1, $3, $4}' */etc/passwd* | **more**

4. After you have examined a screenful of data, quit **more** by entering:

   q

   The output consists of just the first, third, and fourth fields of all records in the password file.

   The fields are separated by colons in the input; **awk** is instructed to use the colon as the field delimiter because the command line included the argument **-F** followed by a colon. However, **awk** displays its *output* using its default output field separator, a single space.

   The **awk** utility will also match a specific field.

5. Enter:

   awk -F: '$1 == "*root*" {print $1, $3}' */etc/passwd*

   This command is detailed in Figure 4-13.

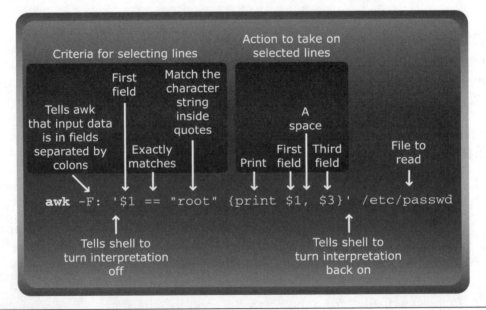

FIGURE 4-13 Using the awk utility

S U M M A R Y : The **awk** utility locates records that are stored in rows and columns (records and fields) in files (databases). It modifies records, performs computations, and outputs selected fields. One option is examined:

-F_char_   Changes field delimiter to _char_.

The **awk** utility is explored further in Chapter 17.

4.16 Sending Output to a File and to Another Utility

When you construct a command line, the output of a utility can be sent to only one of three places, the default terminal, a file, or another utility. Using redirection, output from a utility is redirected to one place. It cannot be sent to both another utility *and* a file. There are times when we want to have the output of a utility sent to a file for later examination, and at the same time have the output redirected to another utility or the screen. Because output cannot be sent to two places by the shell, another utility was created to accomplish this goal.

1. Count the files of your home directory by entering:

    ls | wc -l

    When you run the **ls** command above, the output of **ls** is passed to **wc**, which counts the number of words. The output of **wc** is displayed on the screen.

2. Enter the following:

    ls | tee *current-files* | **wc -w**

    The output of **wc**, the number of files in the current directory, is displayed on the screen.

3. Examine the contents of your new file, *current-files* by entering:

    more *current-files*

    The file *current-files* contains the output of the **ls** utility.

    The **tee** utility reads from input (the output of **ls**) and then writes each line to output, which is connected to **wc**. In addition, **tee** writes a copy of each line to memory. After reaching the end of input, **tee** writes the buffer copy of all lines to a new file. Then, **tee** interprets its argument (*current-files*) as the name to give the new file that contains a copy of all lines processed. In this case, a copy of all the lines **tee** read from input is also written to the file *current-files*.

4. We can use the screen as the output of **tee**:

    cal *2003* | **tee** *yr2003*

The **cal** utility is given *2003* as an argument. The **tee** utility is given *yr2003* as an argument. To **cal**, *2003* is a year. So, **cal** outputs the calendar for the year *2003*.

To **tee**, the *yr2003* argument is instruction to write the buffer copies of all lines read to a new file called *yr2003*. The **tee** utility reads from input (output of **cal**) and writes to its output, which is connected to the screen and also writes each line to memory (buffer). See Figure 4-14.

> **SUMMARY:** Like a plumber's tee that sends water in two directions, the **tee** utility sends what it reads from its input in two directions: to a file named as an argument and to standard output. Standard output is connected by default to the workstation screen or it can be redirected to another utility, or even to another file. The **tee** utility does not modify the data in any way.

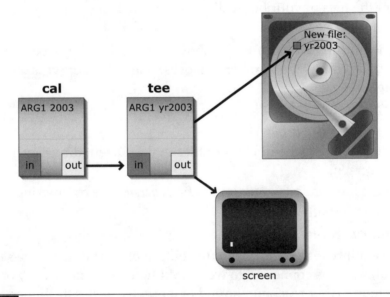

FIGURE 4-14 Examining redirection with **tee**

4.17 Determining What Kind of File

On UNIX systems there are many different kinds of files: text files, executable binary files, database files, e-mail messages, postscript files, tar files, directories, font files, and so on.

Determining a File Type

We can check what sort of file the */etc/passwd* is.

1. Enter.

   file */etc/passwd*

   The output reports that */etc/passwd* is an ASCII text file.

   ```
   /etc/passwd: ASCII text
   ```

2. Now request information about some other files:

   file */usr/bin/passwd*
   file */bin/ls*

   The programs **ls** and **passwd** are binary. They are executables we run when we enter **ls** or **passwd** at a command line.

```
/bin/ls: ELF 32-bit LSB executable, .....
```

Passing Multiple Arguments to file

The **file** utility will report on many files.

1. Enter:

   file *new_script* */tmp* ~

4.18 touching Files

Whenever a file is created, the system keeps track of the creation time. Whenever it is modified, that time is recorded as well. We can create empty files to use the timestamps for record keeping.

1. Enter the following command:

   touch *newfile1A newfile2B*

2. Get a long listing of these files:

    ls -l *new**

Note the modification time at the 6th through 8th fields. They are the date and time at the moment of the file creation.

Updating Modification Time of a File

Check a long listing of your files.

1. Enter:

    ls -l *users_on*

The output is something like

```
-rw-r--r--   1 sk      users      260 Aug 15 16:20 users_on
```

You can change the modification time without actually changing the file.

2. Enter:

    touch *users_on*

3. Get a long listing of *users_on* again.

    ls -l

The output lists a new modification time, namely when you **touch**ed it. Note that only modification time is updated.

4.19 Employing Multiple Utilities to Achieve Broader Goals

Each UNIX/Linux utility accomplishes only one, usually simple task. The **sort** utility sorts lines. Period. If we want to sort the words in a file, we must first modify a copy of the file so that only one word is on each line. Then when **sort** sorts the lines, it is sorting the words. The **ls** utility displays the names of files listed in a directory, not a count of the files. To count the files in a directory, we must run **ls** and then redirect the output to **wc**. To achieve more complex goals, we must employ one utility to do its thing, accomplishing part of the task, then pass the output to other utilities that work on the output of the first utility and complete the goal.

Counting Directories

There is no utility that outputs the number of subdirectories listed in a directory. The **ls** utility can identify directories, but does not provide a count.

1. Enter:

   ls -F | more

   The **-F** option instructs **ls** to put a slash after each directory name in its output. When **ls** sends its output to another utility such as **more** or **grep**, **ls** puts one filename on each line of output.

   We can pass the output of **ls** to **grep** and tell **grep** to look for lines containing a specific target.

2. Enter:

   ls -F | grep /

   The output of **ls** is redirected to **grep**, which looks for lines that include a slash somewhere on the line. Matched lines (the directories) are output.

3. Count the number of directories:

   ls -F | grep / | wc -l

   The number of subdirectories listed in the current directory is output.

4. Create an alias:

   In the ksh or bash shells:

   alias *numdir*=**'ls -F | grep / | wc -l'**

   In the **csh** or **tcsh** shells:

   alias *numdir* **'ls -F | grep / | wc -l'**

5. Try the alias:

   numdir

Determining the Unique Users on a System

Every user on a system logs on using their login name at a port at a given time. If a person logs on more than once, there are multiple entries for that user in the output of **who**.

1. Examine the output of **who** to see if anyone is logged on at least twice:

   who | sort

If there are no users with multiple login sessions, you might (it's not essential) log on again yourself in one of the following ways.

- If you are using the graphical interface, each terminal window you have open is a separate login. Open another window.
- If you are on Linux, use CTRL-ALT-F3 (or F4) to access another virtual console, and log in again. Stay logged on but return to the original console (probably virtual console CTRL-ALT-F1).

The output of **who** is a series of fields. If a user is listed more than once, then some of the data in the fields will be different. Each login is at a different time, from a different port.

2. Enter:

who | awk '{print $1}'

The output of **who** is redirected to **awk**, which prints only the first field.

3. Sort the output of **awk** with:

who | awk '{print $1}' | sort

The output of **awk** (the first field from **who**, i.e., login names) is redirected to **sort**, which sorts the lines.

4. Count the number of times each line is in the output of **sort**:

who | awk '{print $1}' | sort | uniq -c

The output of **sort** is redirected to **uniq**. The **-c** option to **uniq** is instruction to count the number of times each line is present in the input. The output from **uniq** is one copy of each line and the number of times that line was in the input, which is the number of times each user is logged on.

Listing All Words Used in a File

A text file consists of several words to the line, the same word in different lines, sometimes capitalized, sometimes lowercase. In the tour, you created a file named *practice* that contains many words.

1. Display the file *practice* in all lowercase letters:

tr 'A-Z' 'a-z' < *practice*

The shell connects the file *practice* to the input of **tr** and gives **tr** two arguments, *A-Z* and *a-z*, which **tr** interprets as instruction to locate all uppercase letters and replace each with its lowercase equivalent.

2. Replace spaces with newline characters:

   tr *'A-Z' 'a-z'* < *practice* | **tr** ' ' *'\n'*

   In this command line, the output of a process running **tr** is redirected to a second process also running the code for **tr**. The second **tr** is given the arguments a *space* and a *\n*, which **tr** interprets as instruction to locate each space in the file and replace it with a newline character. Words on a line are separated by spaces. When a space is removed and a newline character is inserted as a replacement, the next word is moved to the new line. Each word is now on a line by itself.

3. Sort the output:

   tr *'A-Z' 'a-z'* < *practice* | **tr** ' ' *'\n'* | **sort**

   The output from **sort** is a list of all words in the file *practice* in alphabetical order. Punctuation is still included, blank lines are output, and duplicates are listed. In the next chapter, a script is created to accomplish this task more thoroughly.

■ Review 3

1. How would you output only the first two fields of */etc/passwd* using **awk**?

   _____

2. Two files have fields of data separated by spaces for a company:
   File: *employee*
   Fields: empID lname fname yearhired
   File: *job*
   Fields: empID dept jobtitle date salary

   Considering that *employee* and *job* need to be sorted first, what commands result in a new file called *working* that consists of each employee's last name, first name, department, and job title?

   _____

3. What **sed** command outputs all lines of a file named *ohio*, quitting at the line containing *"Otterbein College"*?

   _____

4. What command line instructs **sed** to replace all instances of the string *"UCB"* with the string *"University of California"* on all lines where *"UCB"* is at the beginning of the line in the file *alma_matter*?

   _____

5. What command instructs **awk** to output the home directory, user login name, and user ID for the first 20 users in the *passwd* file?

_____

6. What single command line accomplishes the following? The output of **who** is passed to **sort**, while at the same time, writing a copy of **who**'s output to a new file named *who.out* and the output from **sort** is passed on to **wc** and written to *sort.out*, which is a new file. Finally, the **wc** utility outputs the number of lines, words, and characters in the sorted **who** to the screen.

_____

7. Imagine you found a file named *README* in a directory and tried to read the file using a text editor. But the editor couldn't properly display the contents. Instead, what you got was a bunch of weird characters. To properly view the contents of the file, you need to find out what sort of file it is. What command will tell you what type of file *README* is?

_____

■ Conclusion

In this module, you used a variety of UNIX utilities and employed basic versions of several utilities that are examined in detail in later chapters. The utilities took input, made transformations (such as selecting, modifying, or combining data), and then output results.

Each of these utilities completes its basic task well. To have a utility work in specific ways, you must employ options for the utility, called by arguments like *-flag*. More complex tasks are accomplished by passing the output of one utility to another, refining the output data. Often it is efficient to put complex commands that involve multiple utilities in script files, to have them executed by entering the script's name rather than the complex command, which, conveniently, is the subject of the next chapter.

■ Answers to Review 1

1. **b**
2. **v**
3. **cut -c1-5** *practice*
4. **grep '^Z....$'** *filename*
5. **grep -l 'Pat Lloyd'** *
6. Start **bc** then enter **scale=4;** ((424 + 79) / 161) ^ 15

7. **grep** '*Catherine Thamzin*' *

8. **wc -wl** *practice users_on*

9. **cat -n** *section[1-4]* > *chapter*

10. **column –x** *empnames*

■ Answers to Review 2

1. **sort** *junk1* **-o** *junk1*

2. **sort -t**'%' *+2 -3 +0 -1 +1 -2 employees*

3. The answers are as follows:

   a. **sort -c**

   b. **bc -l**

   c. **grep -c**

4. **tr -d** '*!.?"&$;*.(),*' < *practice*

5. **who** | **sort** | **tr** '*a-z*' '*A-Z*'

6. **sort** *awards* | **uniq -c**

7. **diff** *report1 report2*

8. **sort -fd** *people*

9. **sort -t:** *+3 -4 +2 -3* /*etc*/*passwd*

10. **comm -23** *students paid*
   or
   comm -13 *paid students*

11. **who** | **tr** '*a-z*' '*A-Z*'

12. **diff** *names newnames*

■ Answers to Review 3

1. **awk -F:** '{print $1, $2}' /*etc*/*passwd*

2. **sort** *job* **-o** *job*
   sort *employee* **-o** *employee*
   join -o *1.2 1.3 2.2 2.3 employee job* > *working*

3. **sed** '/*Otterbein College*/q' *ohio*

4. **sed** '/^*UCB*/s/*UCB*/*University of California*/g' *alma_matter*

5. **head** *-20* /*etc*/*passwd* | **awk -F:** '{print $6, $1, $3}'

6. **who** | **tee** *who.out* | **sort** | **tee** *sort.out* | **wc**

7. **file** *README*

COMMAND SUMMARY

awk *pattern* {*action*} *filename*   Performs the action on all records in *filename* that contain *pattern*.

cat *file1 file2 > file3*   Creates new *file3* with the contents of *file1* and *file2*.

comm *file1 file2*   Compares *file1* to *file2* and shows the lines common and unique in each of two files.

cut *option filename*   Outputs selected fields from *filename*.

diff *file1 file2*   Shows lines that are different in each file and how to modify the first file to match the second.

grep *expression filename*   Outputs all lines in *filename* that contain the *regular expression*.

join *file1 file2*   Files first must be sorted. **join** combines lines from *file1* and *file2* that contain the same value in common fields.

paste *file1 file2*   Combines line 1 from *file1* with line 1 from *file2*, and so on.

pr *filename*   Paginates named file (*filename*).

sed *command filename*   Executes specified **sed** editing command(s) on *filename*.

sort *filename*   Sorts the contents of the file *filename*.

tee *filename*   Reads from input and then writes both to output and to a file *filename*.

tr *string1 string2 < filename*   Reads input and translates each character *string1* characters into *string2* characters.

uniq *filename*   Removes duplicate adjacent lines from *filename*.

wc *filename*   Counts words, lines, and characters in *filename*.

Using Multiple Utilities in Scripts

Before beginning this chapter, you should be able to

- Edit files with **vi** and create basic shell scripts
- Create, copy, remove, rename, display, and print files
- Select strings with **grep** and fields or characters with **cut**
- Translate characters with **tr** and sort lines of input
- Output the beginning of a file with **head**
- Output the last portion of a file with **tail**
- Identify unique and duplicate lines in a file with **uniq**
- Obtain system data with **date**, **cal**, **hostname**, and **id**
- Edit data using **sed** and manipulate data with **awk**
- Connect records that have equal values in the join field
- Paste together records and concatenate files
- Employ **tee** in a pipeline to read data from its input, write to a file, and write to output
- Identify which lines in two files are unique to each file and which are in common

After completing this chapter, you will be able to

- Combine basic utilities to accomplish complex tasks
- Create shell scripts that use utilities to output formatted, relational data from more than one file
- Create a script that filters and modifies data
- Construct scripts incrementally
- Identify errors in scripts and repair them

Powerful UNIX/Linux utilities are employed by users everyday around the world to accomplish complex tasks. At the shell prompt, we enter commands that use one or several utilities in combination to read data, to identify particular portions to output, and to alter, sort, or delete information. This chapter investigates how to create several powerful shell scripts that employ multiple utilities to accomplish complex data manipulation and retrieval tasks. Putting utilities together in scripts to accomplish specific goals is a fundamental, useful, and exceedingly important set of abilities.

5.1 Employing Utilities to Obtain Information

Often when we need to collect basic information, we enter a series of commands. By placing the commands together in a script, we can repeat the series, avoiding errors and saving time.

Outputting Data About the User

We often issue specific commands to get information about our login session.

1. Use the visual editor to create a file named *mydata*:

   vi *mydata*

2. Add the following content:

   echo '*id output:*'
   id
   echo
   echo '*who entry:*'
   who | **grep** *$USER*
   echo
   echo '*present directory:*'
   pwd
   echo

```
echo 'current system:'
hostname
echo
echo 'current processes:'
ps
echo 'search path:'
echo $PATH
```

3. Write the file and return to the shell by pressing ESC and entering:

   :wq

4. At the shell, make *mydata* executable and run it:

   chmod +x *mydata*

   mydata

> **N O T E :** When you enter **mydata**, the commands in the script should run. However, if you get an error message like "*mydata* not found," the shell is not looking in the current directory for *mydata*. You can inform the shell that *mydata* is in the current directory and that you want it executed by entering:
> **./mydata**
> The script's output is displayed on the screen.

5. Tell the shell to redirect the output of *mydata* to a file:

   mydata **>** *me_A*

   or

   ./mydata **>** *me_A*

6. Examine the file:

   more *me_A*

   The contents of the file consist of data generated by the programs in *mydata*, namely information about your present login session. Every time you run the script, the shell executes each command in the script, one after the other. The output from the script goes to your screen unless you redirect it to a file or utility.

5.2 Listing Directories and Files Separately

The **ls** utility outputs the names of the files and directories that are listed in the current directory. Nearly every file you have created thus far has been listed in the directory you are "in" when you log on, your *home directory.*

The output of **ls** does not list directory names together and then filenames together. Rather, the output is filenames and directory names mixed together, sorted by name, date, or size. We can write a script to produce a listing of all directory names together in alphabetical order followed by all filenames, also in order.

Identifying Directories

1. Make sure you are in your home directory, and then create three new directories:

   cd

   mkdir *Resumes Papers Recommendations*

   The **mkdir** command makes directories. It can make multiple directories at one time, because **mkdir** interprets all arguments as names to assign to new directories.

2. Confirm that the new directories exist in your current directory:

   ls -F | more

   The directories listed in your current directory are displayed with a slash at the end of the name. Because the output of **ls** is passed to the **more** utility, the output of **ls** is one filename to a line.

   The **ls** utility is passed one argument, **-F**, which **ls** interprets as an instruction to identify the nature of the objects in the directory, and in particular, to identify directories by attaching a / to the directory names in the output.

Selecting Only Directories or Files

1. Select only those lines that contain directory names from the output of **ls**:

   ls -F | grep /

The output of **ls** is passed to **grep** one filename to each line. The **grep** utility is given one argument, the **/**, which **grep** interprets as the target search string. Only those lines containing a slash match the target and are output by **grep**, namely the directory names. Filenames do not have a trailing **/**, so they are not selected.

Many systems include the utility **column**, which formats output into columns.

2. Request that the output be put into columns by entering:

   ls -F | grep / | column

Interpretation by the Shell

Redirect output of ls to input of grep

Redirect output from grep to input of column

Pass -F as an argument to ls

Pass / as an argument to grep

Execute ls utility

Execute grep utility

Execute column utility

```
ls    -F  |  grep  /  |  column
```

Tells ls to include / on directory names in output. ls outputs one filename to a line.

Tells grep to search for lines that include the target / character

Reads input and formats data into columns

Interpretation by ls, grep, and column

The **grep** utility outputs lines that have directory names. The output of **grep** is redirected to the utility **column**, which formats the data into as many columns as is practical to display. The **column** utility is not available on all systems. If it is not on your system, just use the previous command.

The shell starts three child processes to execute this command line. The output (o) of the first process running **ls** is redirected to the input (i) of the second process running **grep**. The output of the second process is redirected to the input of the third process running **column**. The output of the third process remains connected to the screen.

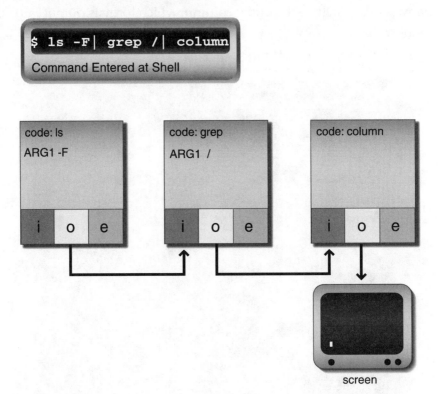

We can reverse the way **grep** works.

3. Tell **grep** to reject directories and select only files by entering:

   ls -F | grep -v / | column

   In this command line, **grep** is given two arguments. The **-v** option to **grep** is instruction to identify lines that meet the search criteria of having a slash on the line, *then to reject those matching lines, and to output all the lines that do not match.* Because filenames lack the slash, they are the output of **grep**.

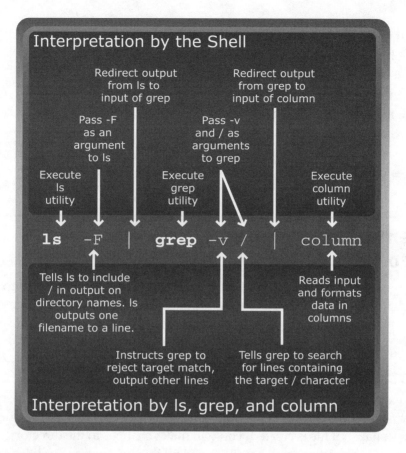

Creating a Script

1. Use the editor to create a script named *lsdf* (**l**ist **d**irectories and **f**iles), and then enter the following contents:

    echo
    echo
    echo 'Directories are:'
    ls -F | grep / | column
    echo
    echo 'Files are:'
    ls -F | grep -v / | column
    echo

2. Make the file executable and run it:

> **chmod +x** *lsdf*
>
> *lsdf*

The names of directories are listed first, then the files. They are not mixed in one alphabetical listing the way **ls** operates.

This script uses **echo** to output empty lines and the *"Directories are:"* or *"Files are:"* information. The real work is done by **ls**, **grep**, and **column** in the two lines that output either just directories or just files.

5.3 Identifying Changes Made to Files in a Directory

When we work on projects or need to keep data secure, it is helpful to determine what changes have occurred to the files and subdirectories listed in a directory. Have any new files been added? Any permissions changed? Any files renamed?

Creating a Target Directory's Files

In this exercise, you will first create a series of files in the *Resumes* directory, and then make a file that contains a "snapshot" of information about the files in the directory. After the snapshot file is created, you will make changes to the directory's contents, and then make another snapshot file. You will then use various utilities to identify the differences between the information in the two snapshot files.

In an earlier step, you created a directory named *Resumes*.

1. Make *Resumes* your current directory and confirm your location:

> **cd** *Resumes*
>
> **pwd**

2. While in *Resumes*, create several files by entering:

> **date** > *today*
>
> **cal** > *month*
>
> **who** > *logged.on*
>
> **id** > *mylogin*
>
> **head -5** */etc/passwd* > *short-passA*
>
> **cp** *month month.bak*

3. Confirm you created all six files with:

   ls -l

4. You are currently in the *Resumes* directory. Return to your home directory and confirm your location:

   cd
   pwd

Collecting Data About Files in a Directory

The next step is to create a file or snapshot in your home directory that contains data about all files listed in the *Resumes* subdirectory. You are in your home directory.

1. Enter:

   ls -l *Resumes*

   A long listing of information about the files listed in the *Resumes* directory is displayed. When **ls** is given a directory name as an argument, it reports on the files listed in that directory.

2. Redirect the output of **ls** to a snapshot file:

   ls -l *Resumes* **>** *file.info1*

3. Examine the contents of *file.info1* with:

   more *file.info1*

   The contents of *file.info1* contain information about each file listed in the directory *Resumes*, including permissions, date modified, owner, and so on. It is a snapshot of the current status of all files in the *Resumes* directory.

Modifying the Directory's Contents

The next task is to make changes to files listed in the *Resumes* directory.

1. Change back to the *Resumes* directory:

   cd *Resumes*
   pwd
   ls

2. Modify aspects of the files by entering:

> **chmod -w** *today*
> **mv** *month month2*
> **date** > *new.date*
> **who** >> *month.bak*
> **ls -l**

The directory now has one added file, one file with a new name, one file with altered permissions, and one file with added content.

3. Return to your home directory and confirm your location:

> **cd**
> **pwd**

Comparing Current File Information with the Original

The contents of the *Resumes* directory have been modified.

1. Create a second file containing information about the files listed in *Resumes*:

> **ls -l** *Resumes* > *file.info2*

The files *file.info1* and *file.info2* are the two files in your home directory that are snapshots of *Resumes*. They contain information about each of the files listed in the *Resumes* directory before and after you made changes.

2. Have **diff** identify the differences in the two snapshot files:

> **diff** *file.info1 file.info2*

The output from **diff** is a series of lines that describe what is different between the two files. The two snapshot files contain information about the contents of the directory *Resumes* at two different times. The differences in the contents of the two files reflect the changes that were made to the files in the directory.

The snapshot files are created in your home directory rather than in *Resumes*, so the contents of the snapshots will not be seen in the output of **diff**.

5.4 Creating a Complex Word Analysis Script

By employing several utilities in a script, we can accomplish tasks much more complex than any single utility can accomplish.

This pipeline feature of UNIX is very useful and is central to effectively manipulating data with UNIX utilities. As Peter said while running the Pickled Pepper utility, "primitive programs prove positively powerful when properly piped." As we examine in a later chapter, shell scripts can be very complex structures involving decisions and intricate data handling.

Regardless of how extensive a program is after it is completed, the program starts out as a simple, basic script that accomplishes a limited task. After the initial version of the script works, additional code is added to increase its power. As more functionality is added, the script is debugged, and then more functionality is added. By first making a small program work, then adding more incrementally, the programmer can more easily control the development of the script and more quickly detect errors.

Determining the Number of Unique Words in a File

It is sometimes instructive when examining our writing to know what different words we are using in a file. This exercise guides you through the creation of a complex script that reads a file and outputs a list of unique words that are in the file, the number of times each word is used, and the total number of unique words employed.

The **uniq** utility removes duplicate adjacent lines from its input. It outputs both the unique lines and single copies of any lines that were duplicates and adjacent. If the same words are in a different order on two adjacent lines, **uniq** will not delete one of the lines, because the two lines are not identical. The **uniq** utility only deletes a line if it is adjacent to another identical line.

If each line contains only one word, the lines must be sorted for **uniq** to remove duplicate adjacent lines (words). The goal of this script is to prepare data from a file so that **uniq** can work properly: punctuation and blank lines must be removed; differences in case for the same word must be reconciled; and the words must be one word to a line in a sorted order.

Removing Punctuation

In text files, punctuation characters often are attached to some of the words. Because *friend* is not the same as *friend?* with a question mark, all punctuation must be removed.

1. Create a file of some length by entering:

   cat *practice support.names practice > manywords*

2. Edit the file *manywords* and add a paragraph of any text:

   vi *manywords*

3. Write and quit the *manywords* file:

   :wq

4. Use the editor to create a new file named *wordsUsed*:

   vi *wordsUsed*

5. Enter the following line in *wordsUsed*:

   tr -d '?."!:,();' < *manywords*

6. Write the file and quit the editor:

   :wq

7. Make the script executable and run the script:

   chmod +x *wordsUsed*

   wordsUsed **| more**

   The output from **wordsUsed** is the contents of *manywords* with punctuation characters removed. See Figure 5-1.

Examining the Code

The components of the **tr** command line are as follows:

COMPONENT	DESCRIPTION
tr	Instructs the shell to execute the **tr** utility.
-d ' '	Pass **tr** two arguments: **-d** and the characters inside the single quotes. The **-d** is interpreted by **tr** as instruction to delete all characters listed as the second argument. The single quotes tell the shell to pass the punctuation characters uninterpreted to **tr** as the second argument.
?.":,();	The contents of the second argument. Hence, **tr** searches for literal *?.":,( );* characters in the input and deletes those characters.
< *manywords*	Instruction to the shell to open the file *manywords* and connect it to the input of **tr**. The **tr** utility only reads from its input. It does not interpret an argument as a filename. We must have the shell connect the file to **tr**'s input.

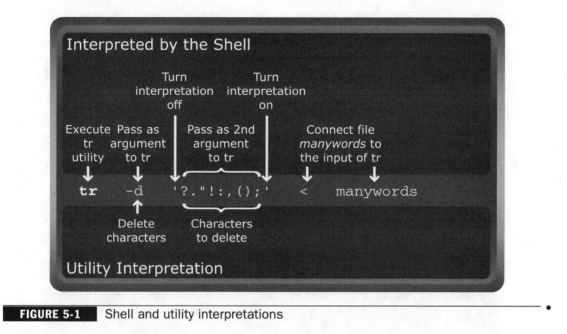

FIGURE 5-1 Shell and utility interpretations

Making All Characters Lowercase

Once the punctuation characters are removed from the data, there is still the matter of capital letters. Some words are capitalized and others are not. To properly remove duplicates, each duplicate word must match case, as well as characters. A simple solution is to just make the whole file lower- or uppercase.

1. Use **vi** to edit the file *wordsUsed*, and add a backslash to the end of the first line:

    tr -d '?."!:,();' < *manywords* \

2. Add a second line to the script:

    | **tr** '*A-Z*' '*a-z*'

3. Run the script and examine its output:

    wordsUsed | **more**

    The output is a copy of the data from the file *wordsUsed* with all characters in lowercase. See Figure 5-2.

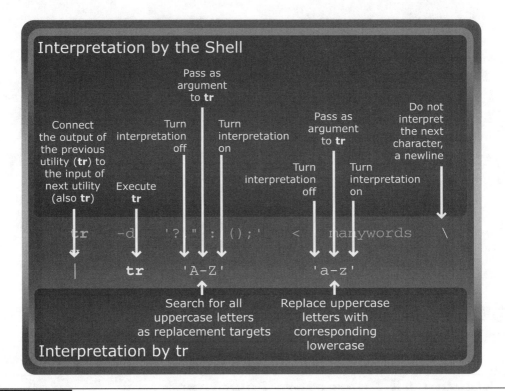

FIGURE 5-2 Shell and tr interpretations

Examining the Code

The components of the added text are as follows:

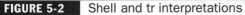

COMPONENT	INTERPRETATION
\	Instruction to the shell to not interpret the special meaning of the next character, which is a newline. Without an end-of-line character that the shell can interpret to mean the "end of command," the shell keeps reading from the next line in the file as though both lines were actually one. Hence, multiple lines in the script are seen by the shell as one line of input.
|	Instruction to connect the output of the previous process, which is running **tr**, to the input of the following process, also running **tr**.

COMPONENT	INTERPRETATION
tr	Execute the second **tr** utility.
' '	Instruction to the shell to not interpret the enclosed characters as having significance to the shell. The text between the quotes is passed, as is, to **tr** as an argument.
A-Z	The first quoted argument passed to **tr**. The **tr** utility interprets *A-Z* to be instruction to search for all uppercase letters as targets for replacement.
a-z	The second quoted argument passed to **tr**, which is interpreted by **tr** as the replacement characters. All uppercase letters are replaced with their matching lowercase letters.

Putting Each Word on a Line

The output of the script has many words on each line. We want to remove duplicate words, not duplicate lines. But **uniq** works only on lines. To remove duplicate words with **uniq**, we must modify the data so that each word is on a line by itself. To accomplish this task, we need to use the code for a newline character in the *ASCII character set*.

1. Examine the ASCII characters and their associated codes by entering:

   man *ascii*

   The character with *012* beside it is the *newline* character. Lines in a file are separated by this character so that terminals and printers are able to display individual lines. The alternate name for newline is the **\n**, which is often used.

2. Modify the script *wordsUsed* to include the following lines:

   tr -d '?.":,( );' < *manywords* \
   | **tr** '*A-Z*' '*a-z*' \
   | **tr** ' ' '\n'

The spaces and quotes must be carefully entered.

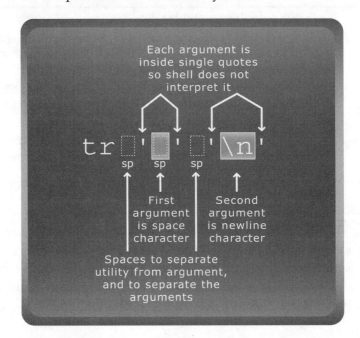

3. After completing the changes, run the script *wordsUsed*:

   wordsUsed | **more**

Examining the Code

The additions to the script are as follows:

COMMAND	INTERPRETATION
\	Instructs the shell to not interpret the newline character at the end of the second line in the script.
|	Connect the output of the previous process running **tr** to the input of the next process, also running **tr**.
tr	Run the **tr** utility, which locates target characters and replaces them with other replacement characters.
' '	Pass to **tr** a first argument consisting of one space. The **tr** utility interprets this first argument to be the character to locate and replace by the character listed in the second argument.

COMMAND	INTERPRETATION
\n	Pass to **tr** a second argument, **\n**. The **tr** utility interprets this second argument as the replacement character. The \n is the **ascii** character newline. The target character, each space, is replaced with the newline character everywhere in the file. The resulting output of **tr** consists of every word from the input file on a new line.

Each word is output on a line by itself. If there were places in the file with two spaces next to each other, both are changed to newlines. So there are probably blank lines in the output as well.

Replacing Tabs with Newlines

The previous version of *wordsUsed* changes all spaces to newlines, resulting in most of the text being output one word to a line. However, if you have any TAB characters in the file, they remain.

We can replace the TAB characters with newline characters, too.

1. Modify the last line to search for both spaces and TAB characters:

   | **tr** ' \t' '\n\n'

2. Run the script again and examine the results:

   wordsUsed | **more**

   The script's last line instructs **tr** to locate spaces and replace them with newlines, and to locate TAB characters (\t) and replace them with newlines, also.

Removing Blank Lines

The output includes whatever blank lines were in the input file and any that were added when double spaces became two new lines. We can remove the blank lines.

1. With **vi**, include the **sed** utility in *wordsUsed* by modifying the script to read as follows:

   tr -d '?."!:,();' < *manywords* \
   | **tr** '*A-Z*' '*a-z*' \
   | **tr** ' \t' '\n\n' \
   | **sed** '/^$/d'

2. Run the script again:

wordsUsed | **more**

Blank lines are removed from the output data.

Examining the Code

One line consisting of the following is added to *wordsUsed*:

COMMAND	INTERPRETATION
\	The \ is placed at the end of each of the previous three lines. Each backslash instructs the shell to not interpret the newline that follows. As a result, the shell interprets all four lines of the file as *one* command line.
|	Connect the output of **tr** to **sed**.
sed	Execute the **sed** utility.
' '	Instruction to the shell to pass the enclosed string to **sed** as an argument without interpreting any special characters.
/^$/d	The argument passed to **sed**, which **sed** interprets to mean "locate lines that consist of a beginning ^ and ending $ with no text in between (blank lines), and then delete (**d**) those lines."

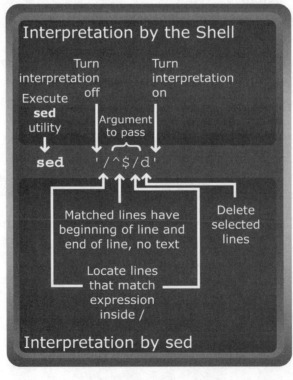

Sorting the Lines

At this point, the output consists of all the words in the file, in their original order, in lowercase, without punctuation, and without blank lines. The word *the* is in several places in the file.

For **uniq** to remove duplicate lines, they must be adjacent. It's time to sort.

1. Modify the script as follows:

    tr -d *'?."!:,();'* **<** *manywords* \
    | **tr** *'A-Z'* *'a-z'* \
    | **tr** *' \t'* *'\n\n'* \
    | **sed** *'/^$/d'* \
    | **sort**

2. Rerun the script to confirm the effect of the sorting:

    wordsUsed | **more**

    All lines containing the same word are output on adjacent lines.

Examining the Code

The added commands are as follows:

COMMAND	DESCRIPTION
\	Instructs the shell to not interpret the newline that follows.
|	Connect the output of **sed** to the input of the next utility, **sort**.
sort	Run the **sort** utility, which sorts all lines it receives from **sed**. Because every word is on a line by itself, the output is a sorted list of words from the file, one word to a line. If the file contains ten instances of the word *the*, they are listed on sequential lines.

Removing Duplicates

At last, the data is ready for **uniq** to toss out the duplicates.

1. Modify the script:

    tr -d *'?."!:,();'* **<** *manywords* \
    | **tr** *'A-Z'* *'a-z'* \
    | **tr** *' \t'* *'\n\n'* \
    | **sed** *'/^$/d'* \
    | **sort** | **uniq -c**

2. Write and quit the editor, and then run the script:

    wordsUsed | **more**

All duplicate lines are removed in the output.

Examining the Code

The addition to the script is:

COMMAND	INTERPRETATION
|	Connect the output of **sort** to the input of **uniq**.
uniq -c	Run the **uniq** utility, passing it the **–c** option. **uniq** outputs all unique lines, only one copy of duplicate adjacent lines, and the number of duplicates for each line it encountered. Multiple lines containing the same word are reduced to just one line containing that word with the number of times that line was present in the input. The output consists of a list of all the words that are in the file with the number of instances of the word.

Listing Most-Used Words First

The output from **uniq** consists of a listing of all words in the *manywords* file and the number of times each was in the file, such as:

```
12   a
2    about
4    at
2    bill
1    box
6    can
2    charlie
```

It is probably more useful to output the words based on their frequency. Modify *wordsUsed* to include a final **sort**:

    tr -d '?."!:,( );' < *manywords* \
| **tr** '*A-Z*' '*a-z*' \
| **tr** ' \t' '\n\n' \
| **sed** '/^$/d' \
| **sort** | **uniq -c** \
| **sort -rn**

1. Run *wordsUsed*:

   ***wordsUsed* | more**

   The script now outputs the words with the highest number of occurrences at the top of the list. This time, the output of **uniq** is piped to another **sort**, which sorts the lines based on the number that is at the beginning of each line. To follow numerical sort rather than ASCII, we include the **-n** argument. **sort** normally outputs the lowest numbers first. To see the most commonly used words on the top of the list, we reverse the sort order with the **-r** option.

Writing to Both a File and the Next Utility

The resulting unique lines (words) are displayed on the screen. The last addition to the *wordsUsed* script has the output of **uniq** sent to a file and also to **wc** to count the total number of lines (unique words) employed.

1. Complete the script *wordsUsed* so it looks like this:

   tr -d '?.”!:,();' **<** *manywords* \
   | **tr** '*A-Z*' '*a-z*' \
   | **tr** ' \t' '\n\n' \
   | **sed** '/^$/d' \
   | **sort** | **uniq -c** \
   | **sort -rn** \
   | **tee** *words.out* | **wc -l**

2. Run the script:

   ***wordsUsed* | more**

   The total number of lines in the output of **sort**, which is the number of different words in the file, is displayed on the screen.

3. Examine the contents of the new file, *words.out*, which is in your current directory:

   more *words.out*

   The file *words.out* contains a list of all unique words and the number of times each is in the file *manywords*.

Examining the Code

The addition to the script is:

COMMAND	INTERPRETATION
\	Do not interpret newline.
I	Connect the output of **uniq** to the input of the next utility, **tee**.
tee	Run the **tee** utility, which reads from its input and then writes to output and saves a copy in memory, to be written to a file when it has read all input.
words.out	The name of the file **tee** creates. A copy of all the input that **tee** receives is written to this file.
I	Connect the output of the previous utility, **tee**, to the input of the next utility, **wc**.
wc	Run the **wc** utility.
-l	Instruction to **wc** to count and display only the number of lines, ignoring the number of words and characters. Because each word in the input is on a line by itself, the output from **wc** is the number of different words employed in the file.

Reviewing the Completed Script

There is no utility in UNIX that lists the unique words used in a file. By piping several utilities together, we can list the unique words, how many times each is used, and the total number of words.

In summary, the program accomplishes the following:

COMMAND	INTERPRETATION
tr -d '?."!:,();' **<** *manywords* \	Removes punctuation.
I **tr** '*A-Z*' '*a-z*' \	Makes all characters lowercase.
I **tr** ' \t' '\n\n' \	Replaces spaces with newlines and TABS with newlines.
I **sed** '/^$/d' \	Removes blank lines.
I **sort** I **uniq -c** \	Sorts the data, removes duplicate lines.
I **sort -rn**	Sorts by number of times each word is in the file.
I **tee** *words.out* I **wc -l**	**tee** reads from input and writes to output and to the *words.out* file. Output from the **tee** utility goes to **wc**, which counts the number of lines (which are words, in this case).

The diagram in Figure 5-3 identifies how the data is passed and transformed by the script's utilities. The arguments passed to each utility are labeled ARGS.

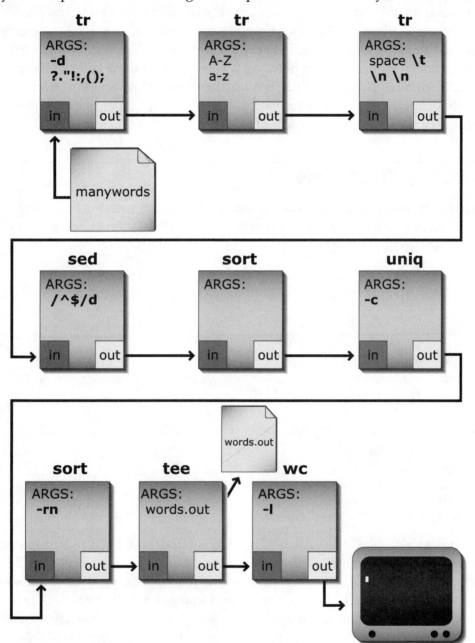

FIGURE 5-3 The flow of utilities and arguments

5.5 Obtaining Relational Data

For many installations, computers are relational database engines. Many large-scale database application programs are used in Linux/UNIX, including Mysql, Postgress, and Oracle. Project data is stored in files with records related to each other by values in a join field. As was introduced in Chapter 4, "Using Basic UNIX Utilities," the **join** utility is available for creating smaller, less complex database applications. The following exercise develops an application to maintain records of gifts to a nonprofit school.

Creating Data Files

1. Use the editor to create a file named *support.contrib* with the following contents. Be sure to include the *000   0AMNT   0YEAR* first line.

   vi *support.contrib*

   ```
   000    0AMNT    0YEAR
   001    1500.    2001
   001    1600.    2003
   001    2000.    2002
   002    1750.    2001
   002    3800.    2002
   003    2300.    2003
   003    2500.    2001
   004    1000.    2003
   004    5000.    2002
   ```

2. Create a second file *support.names* with contents of:

   ```
   000    0LASTNM    0FIRSTNM
   001    Boercker   Marge
   002    Mayfield   Mel
   003    Sears      Robert
   004    Hach       Phila
   ```

   Look at both files. The structure of each is important. Each record in one file corresponds to a record in the other file via the ID field (the first field). Because Marge Boercker is 001 in the *support.names* file and 001 gave 1500 dollars in 2001 in the *support.contrib* file, we conclude that Marge gave the 1500 dollars.

   When developing an application, short data files like these that have obvious joins relating a limited amount of data are used to make verification of the structures easier. If a program has a bug, it is easier to spot.

Creating a Basic join Script

The data in the *support.names* file describes the contributors. The data in *support.contrib* describes the amount and year of each contribution. The data in both files is related by the ID number, which is the first field of each file. To use **join** to join together the records from the two files based on their common field, the records must be sorted by ID. The following script accomplishes a join of the data.

1. Make copies of the data files in case you make an error later:

    cp *support.contrib support.contrib.BAK*
    cp *support.names support.names.BAK*

2. Use the editor to create a file named *support.script* with the following contents:

    sort -n *support.contrib* **-o** *support.contrib*
    sort -n *support.names* **-o** *support.names*
    join *support.names support.contrib*

3. Make the script executable and run it:

    chmod +x *support.script*
    support.script

    The output shows that ID 001 is Marge Boercker and that she gave 1500 dollars in 2001. The first and last name come from one file. The years and contribution amounts come from the other file. The records are related by the ID values. The output consists of the lines from each file joined together based on the value in the ID field. See Figure 5-4.

Examining the Code

The shell passes four arguments to **sort**:

    sort -n *support.contrib* **-o** *support.contrib*

ARGUMENT	SORT'S INTERPRETATION
support.contrib	Read files *support.contrib* and sort the lines.
-o	After sorting, put the output in the file with the name that is the next argument.
support.contrib	Name of file to receive sorted output.

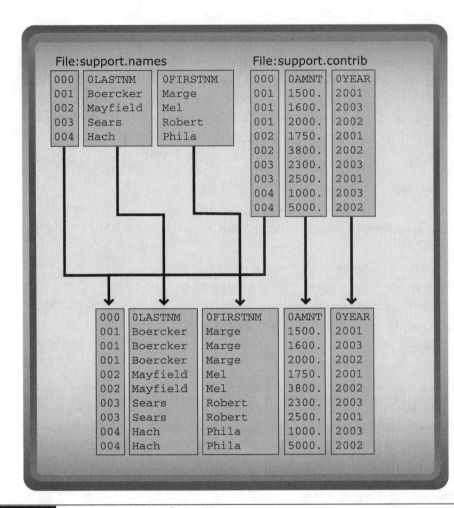

FIGURE 5-4 Looking at a join of the data

The first two lines of the script tell **sort** to sort each file and overwrite each with the sorted versions. In the future, the user can add data to either source file and it will be automatically sorted every time the script is executed. The last line runs **join**, giving **join** the two sorted files as arguments. **join** reads each file. Records from both files containing the same value in the join field are output together as one line, as demonstrated in Figure 5-4.

The first line of output is the title of each column. Because the 0 is the first character of the first line in both files, it is always sorted as the first line of output, because the 0 is before the rest of the digits in the ASCII table.

Modifying the Output of the join

All columns of data are output including the *ID*, which we don't need to display.

1. Modify *support.script* to select output fields:

   sort -n *support.contrib* **-o** *support.contrib*
   sort -n *support.names* **-o** *support.names*
   join -o *1.3 1.2 2.2 2.3 support.names support.contrib*

2. Run the modified script:

   support.script

   The output this time is only the *first name, last name, year,* and *amount* for each record. The *ID* is left out. These data are output because the arguments to **join** specify just fields 3 and 2 from the first file (*1.3 1.2*) and fields 2 and 3 from the second file (*2.2 2.3*), as shown in Figure 5-5.

Examining the Code

The crucial line is

   join -o *1.3 1.2 2.2 2.3 support.names support.contrib*

OPTION	INTERPRETATION BY JOIN
-o	Output only selected fields.
1.3	Output the first file's third field.
1.2	Output the first file's second field.
2.2	Output the second file's second field.
2.3	Output the second file's third field.

Sorting the Output by Contributor

The output is joined and has been reduced to the essential data. The records are sorted by ID, even though ID is not in the output. The resulting records are not

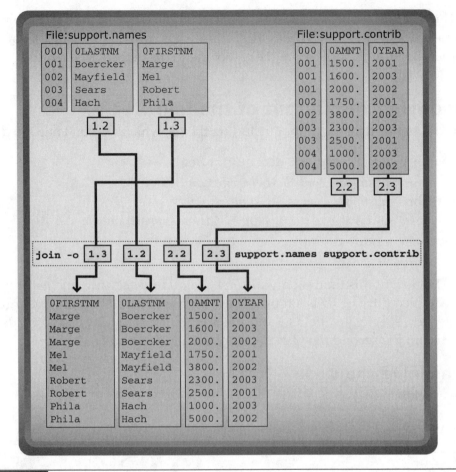

FIGURE 5-5 Selecting output fields

sorted by person or year. To sort the records by last name and year, we must direct **sort** to use primary and secondary sort fields.

1. Modify the *support.script* to be:

   sort *support.contrib* **-o** *support.contrib*
   sort *support.names* **-o** *support.names*
   join **-o** *1.3 1.2 2.2 2.3 support.names support.contrib* \
   | **sort** *+1 -2 +3 -4*

2. Run the script:

   support.script

A brief examination of the data reveals that each person made multiple contributions over several years. The output is now sorted primarily by contributor's last name (field 2 in the input to sort). The secondary sort field used to order the records for each contributor is the year a contribution was made (field 4). The records for years that a contributor made a contribution are output together.

```
0FIRSTNM  0LASTNM  0AMNT  0YEAR
Marge   Boercker  1500.  2001
Marge   Boercker  2000.  2002
Marge   Boercker  1600.  2003
Phila   Hach 5000.  2002
Phila   Hach 1000.  2003
Mel  Mayfield  1750.  2001
Mel  Mayfield  3800.  2002
Robert  Sears  2500.  2001
Robert  Sears  2300.  2003
```

```
$ join -o 1.3 1.2 2.2 2.3 support.names support.contrib \
| sort +1 -2 +3 -4
```

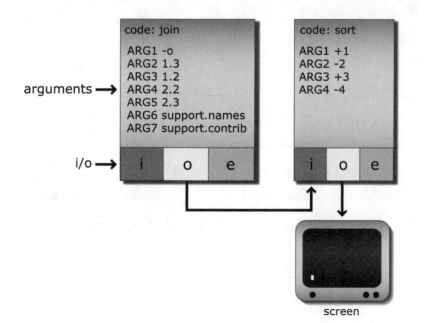

screen

Examining the Code

The role of each argument to **join** and **sort** is identified in the following illustration.

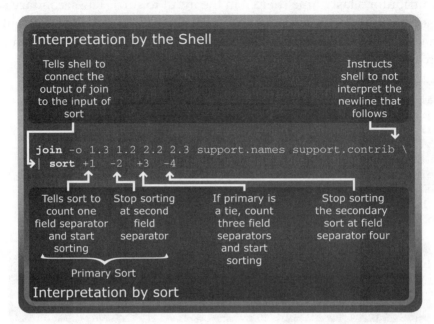

■ Review

1. Examine the following script, *n-on*:

   **who | sort **
   **| awk '{print $1}' **
   | uniq | wc -l

   What will be in the output of *n-on*?

   _____

2. Where will output of the *n-on* script be sent?

   _____

3. How does the shell interpret each of the following in *n-on*?

   a. who

   _____

  b. \

  _____

  c. '{print $1}'

  _____

  d. |

  _____

  e. wc

  _____

  f. –l

  _____

4. What does **join -0 2.3 1.1 2.2** *file1 file2* mean?

  _____

5. When the shell reads the *n-on* script, how many command lines does it find?

  _____

Conclusion

The scripts created in this chapter use utilities to locate and manipulate data. By creating a script that connects the output of one utility to the input of another, we can accomplish complex tasks. By building a script incrementally, we can see what each utility accomplishes and locate errors more quickly.

Answers to Review

1. The number of users logged on
2. To the screen
3. The answers are as follows:
   a. Utility to execute
   b. Do not interpret the character that follows the backslash (\ ), the newline.

     c. Do not interpret **{print $1}**, but instead pass it as an argument to the
        awk utility.

     d. Redirect the output of the utility on the left to the input of the utility on
        the right.

     e. Execute the **wc** utility.

     f. Pass **–l** as an argument to **wc**.

4. Join *file1* and *file2* based on values in the first field. Output second file's
third field, first file's first field, and second file's second field.

5. There is only one command line, which spans several input lines because
the newline characters are not interpreted.

Creating and Changing UNIX Directories

6

O B J E C T I V E S

After completing this chapter, you will be able to

- Create a directory
- Change to a directory
- Use the complete pathname for a file
- Identify the role of inodes, data blocks, and directories when managing files
- Specify the path to a file relative to a user's home directory
- Use parent and current directories in path specifications
- List a file in more than one directory
- Move directories and their contents
- Remove directories

In this chapter, you create and use new directories, called *subdirectories*, listed in your home directory, and then create and access files within these subdirectories.

The UNIX/Linux *file system* or *directory structure* allows us to create files and directories accessed through a hierarchy of directories. For example, a letter to a client named Forbes on July 2, 2002, can be a file named *Forbes7.2. 2002* listed in a directory named *Clients.* The *Clients* directory can be listed in another directory, *Correspondence,* which is located in your home directory. Such an arrangement is essential for locating information quickly on the system. If you are an experienced DOS/Windows user, the directory structure examined in this chapter will be familiar, because the DOS file system is similar to the UNIX file system. The workstation screen is a small porthole through which we look into our collection of files. When a carefully designed hierarchical file system is in place, we can access the needed information with minimal effort.

6.1 Employing Directories to Create Order

Managing files in directories requires a set of important, fundamental skills because nearly everything on the system is a file, and all files are accessed through directories. In the tour of a UNIX/Linux system in Chapter 2, you created directories and then changed directories into the directories you made. This chapter examines those skills in much more detail, including an investigation into how the file system really works.

A collection of information stored electronically on the hard drive of a system is a *file.* The data stored in files can be accessed, modified, copied, and removed. In the same sense, a library's shelves contain books of information stored on paper. Those books can be accessed, copied, removed, and even modified. In a library, the cards in the card catalog or records in the online catalog provide users with information about the books and their location in the stacks. Similarly, in UNIX/Linux there is an "index card" or *inode* that contains all the information available about each file, including the location of the actual file on the disk.

Files are not actually "in" directories. Files are in *data blocks* on the hard drive. The only things in a directory are the names and the inode numbers (index card) for each of its files.

Re-examining the Home Directory

Nearly everything you have created thus far has been listed in the one directory you access when you log on, your *home directory*.

1. Log on now to your account. As you have experienced before, you are automatically in your home directory.

2. Enter:

   pwd

   The path from *root* to your home directory is displayed.

   You are given the same place to work each time you log in, because the path to this directory is the sixth field in the record for your account in the */etc/passwd* file.

3. Enter:

   grep $USER /etc/passwd

   or

   ypcat passwd **| grep $USER**

   The sixth field is the path to your home directory.

4. List your current files:

   ls

   The files you create are listed in your home directory.

5. Create a new file by entering:

   who > *f-name*

   The new file *f-name* contains the login names and other information concerning users currently logged onto the system. You do not specify where the new file is to be located. As a default, the file is created and listed in your current directory, which at the moment is your home directory.

6. Ask for a listing of the filenames in your current directory. Enter:

   ls

   The names of the files you have created appear on the screen. If you have only a few files, this listing is brief. However, if you have many files, this listing fills up the screen and is difficult to read. By using a well thought out directory structure, you can store related files together in different directories and then have shorter listings in each directory.

All filenames you include in a command refer to files listed in your current directory, unless you specify otherwise. The following illustration shows the relationship between your home directory and some of the files probably listed in your home directory.

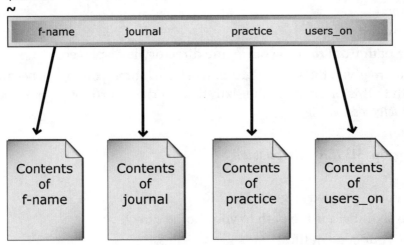

home directory
$HOME
~

f-name   journal   practice   users_on

Contents of f-name   Contents of journal   Contents of practice   Contents of users_on

7. If your home directory does not have files named *practice, journal, users_on*, and *f-name*, create them now using an editor, because they are needed in exercises in this chapter. Append a few lines of any content to each file.

Examining How Files Are Listed in Directories

People often think of UNIX directories as holding files much like physical file cabinets contain files. Although this "folder" metaphor is commonly used, it is inaccurate and misleading. A directory does not actually contain files. Rather, a directory only contains the names of files and the number of the "index card" or inode that contains all the information we need about the file. The **ls** command reads the names of the files listed in the current directory and then outputs those names. The total contents of a directory can also be shown.

1. To see the actual contents of your current directory, enter:

   ls -i

```
21188 f-name
51234 journal
44333 names.tmp
```

```
66554 number.tmp
87666 ordered_1
42233 phon
33773 practice
55666 prtest
77665 test_file
91919 users_on
```

Your output includes very different numbers. But the directory contents are structured the same: filenames and inode numbers.

For each of its files, the directory contains only the name of that file and a number that leads to the inode for that file. The inode contains information about that file and the addresses of the data blocks on the hard drive where the file is actually located.

Inodes are small pieces of memory on the hard disk. Each inode simply stores information about the file (such as its owner, permissions, date created…) as well as the addresses of the blocks on the disk where the data that is the file is actually located. A directory contains only a filename and an index number for each of its files and directories. Nothing else.

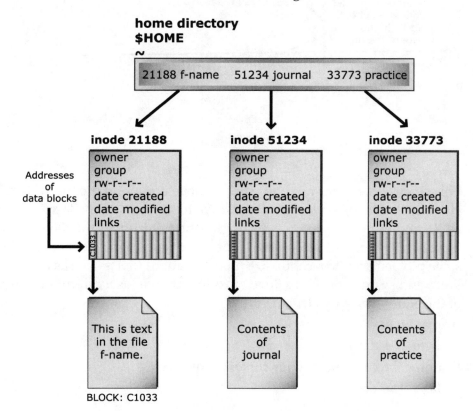

Each user's home directory is just a file containing the name and inode number of each file the user created for this directory. The inode contains the remainder of the information about the file and the addresses needed to locate the data.

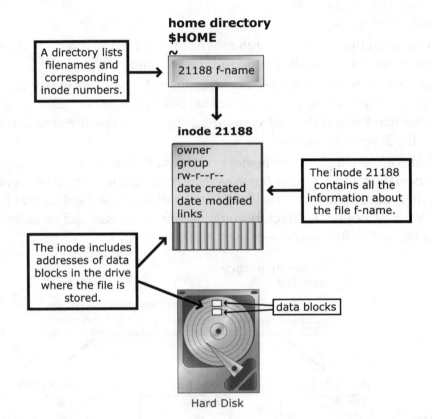

home directory
$HOME
~

21188 f-name

A directory lists filenames and corresponding inode numbers.

inode 21188

owner
group
rw-r--r--
date created
date modified
links

The inode 21188 contains all the information about the file f-name.

The inode includes addresses of data blocks in the drive where the file is stored.

data blocks

Hard Disk

This chapter examines not only how to move around in the file system, but also how the inodes make it all work. We have found in the last 20 years of UNIX and Linux education that people who think about the file system by including the role of directories, inodes, and data blocks are better able to solve problems and conceptualize more advanced topics such as permissions, links, and so on. Hence, we developed this chapter as a careful investigation of the entire directory structure.

2. Add another file:

   who > *users_test*

3. Examine the contents of your current directory:

   ls -i | more

The new filename, *users_test,* and its index (inode) number are added to the current directory.

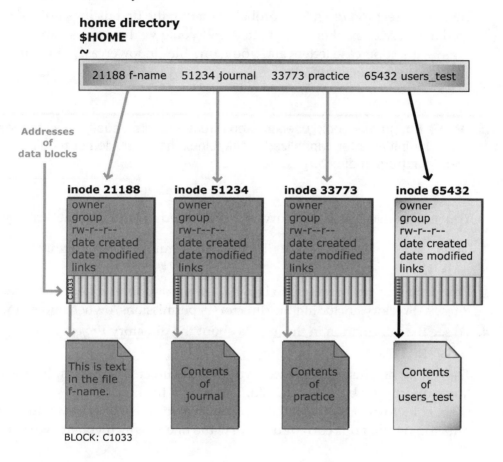

Creating Directories

Usually when we create or make directories, they are listed in the current directory.

1. Create a new *Projects* directory by entering:

   mkdir *Projects*

   The command **mkdir** accomplishes but one task, it **ma**kes a **dir**ectory. The new directory is listed in whatever directory we are "in" when we create the new one. Each new directory we create, often called a *subdirectory,* can list additional files and other directories.

2. Obtain a listing of the contents of the current directory by entering:

> **ls | more**

The new directory, *Projects*, is probably among the first listings unless you used a lowercase *p* when you created it. If you give directories names that begin with uppercase letters and you name files in lowercase, directories are listed first when **ls** is run.

N O T E : In this book, user-created directories are usually given names with the initial letter capitalized. UNIX/Linux, however, do not require capital letters in directory names.

You just created a new directory, which is listed in your current directory.

3. Obtain a complete listing that includes inode numbers by entering:

> **ls -i**

Projects has an inode unique to it, where all information is kept about the *Projects* directory, including the directory's permissions, owner, and so forth.

4. To see the information in the inodes about the **d**irectory *Projects*, enter:

> **ls -ld** *Projects*

The following illustration depicts your home directory. The graphic for your home directory is bordered in bold. The one for the new *Projects* subdirectory is not bold, to indicate that although you created a new directory, your home directory is still your current directory, the one in which you are working.

home directory
$HOME
~

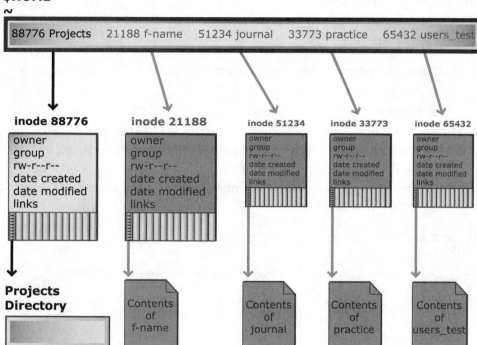

5. Enter:

   pwd

   You remain in your home directory.

Changing Directories

We inform the shell when we want to change to a different directory, that is, make it the current directory.

1. Change your current directory to the newly created *Projects* directory by entering:

   cd *Projects*

   The **cd** or change **d**irectory command instructs the shell to locate the directory listed as an argument (*Projects*) and to make it the current directory. The following illustration indicates that your current directory is no longer your home directory. The subdirectory *Projects* is now your current directory and is shown outlined in bold.

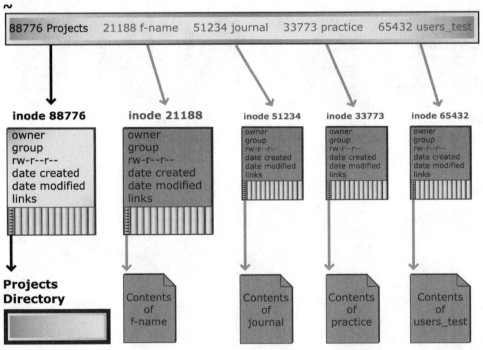

Examining the Path to Your Current Directory

Regardless of your location in the file system, you can always identify your current directory.

1. You are in *Projects.* Confirm your location by entering:

pwd

The output is the absolute *path* from the top of the file system (***root*** or ***/***) to your current directory. The topmost directory, called ***root***, is symbolized by the first forward slash (*/*) in the pathname. All other directories from ***root*** to the current directory are separated by slashes. The *path* is a list of directory names separated by the */* (slash) character. In this example, the last directory listed is *Projects.* The one before it is the parent directory of *Projects,* which in this case is your home directory. Your home directory is listed in its parent directory, and so on to ***root***.

The **pwd** command prints the pathname of your current or working directory.

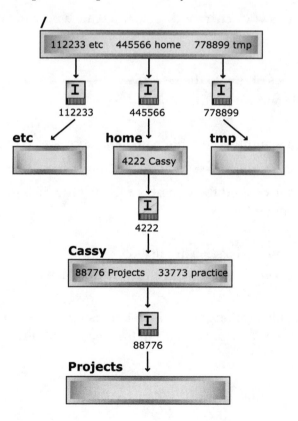

Listing the Contents of the Current Directory

On several occasions, you have obtained displays of the names of files listed in whatever directory was your current directory at the time.

1. List the contents of the directory that is now your current directory (*Projects*), with the usual command:

    ls

    Nothing is listed. You have no ordinary files in the new *Projects* directory. The files that appeared when you last entered **ls** still exist, but they are not in this directory. The **ls** command displays only the names of the files listed in your *current* directory. You changed your current directory to be *Projects*, leaving your home directory by typing the **cd** *Projects* command.

Creating Files Within a Subdirectory

1. With *Projects* as your current directory, create a new file named *testing*. Enter:

    vi *testing*

2. Add a few lines of text to the new file.

3. Write the file and return to the shell.

    :wq

4. With **vi**, create another new file named *practice*, and add the following:

    ```
    This is a file practice in the Projects directory.
    ```

5. After you have created the two new files, list the filenames in the *Projects* directory by entering:

    ls

    The files *practice* and *testing* are listed.

6. As usual, the contents of the directory include filenames and inode numbers:

    ls -i

   The following illustration shows the relationship between your home directory and its files. The files you just created in the *Projects* subdirectory are included.

home directory
$HOME
~

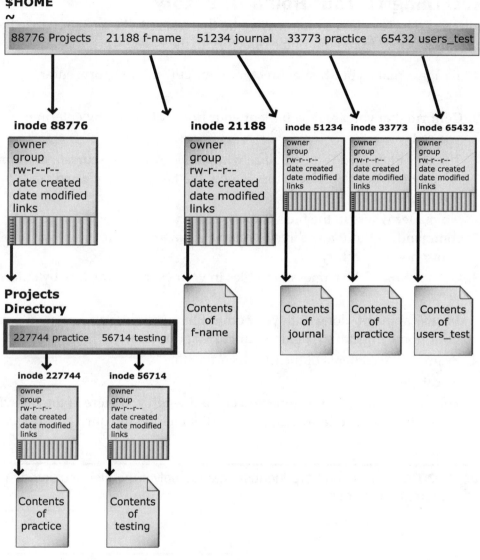

Returning to Your Home Directory

You used the command **cd** *subdirectory* (in this case, **cd** *Projects*) to change the current directory from your home directory to the *Projects* directory.

1. To again make your home directory your current directory, enter:

   cd

2. Confirm that you are now back at your home directory by entering:

   pwd

   The output of **pwd** is the same as when *Projects* was the current directory, except that your home directory is now the last directory listed, and *Projects* is not listed at all.

   No matter where in the file system we are currently working, the **cd** command, without any directory name as an argument, returns us safely to our home directory.

3. Get a listing of the names of the files in your current directory by entering:

   ls

   Projects appears, along with your other files, including a file named *practice*. Your home directory is again your current directory.

4. Examine the contents of the file *practice* with:

   cat *practice*

   This file *practice* is not the one you created when you were in the *Projects* directory, but the one created in an earlier chapter in your home directory.

> **N O T E :** Files can have identical names only if the files are listed in different directories.

Distinguishing Between Files and Directories

In this book, directory names have an uppercase first letter to distinguish them from ordinary filenames. The **ls** utility provides another way to identify directories.

1. From the shell, type the command:

   ls -F | more
   ls -C -F | more

2. Examine the output of **ls** with the **-F** option. Directory names are displayed with a slash appended to the end, such as *Projects/*. The slash character is not a filename extension, but just a character added to the display by **ls** in the output to indicate the nature of the object.

   Filenames displayed with an asterisk (*) at the end are *executable* files, such as the scripts you created earlier.

The **ls** command interprets the **-F** option as instruction to display all files and directory names, identifying directories with a slash, executables with an asterisk, and so on.

Listing the Contents of a Subdirectory

We often run **ls** to determine the contents of the current directory. We **cd** to a new directory and then run **ls** to list its contents. You can list the contents of *Projects* without **cd**ing into it.

1. Enter:

   ls *Projects*

   The *Projects* directory is read, and the filenames listed in it are displayed on the screen. To list the contents of a subdirectory without leaving the parent directory, enter the **ls** command with the name of the subdirectory as an argument.

When **ls** is given a *directory_name* as an argument, it displays the contents of the directory called *directory_name*, provided *directory_name* is listed in the current directory.

Obtaining Information about a Directory or Its Contents

You are in your home directory and have a subdirectory *Projects.*

1. Obtain a long listing of the content of *Projects*:

   ls -l *Projects*

   The files, permissions, owners, and so on, of the files listed in *Projects* are displayed.

2. Obtain information about the **directory** *Projects*, not its contents, by entering:

   ls -ld *Projects*

This time the permissions, and so on, about the directory *Projects* itself are displayed, not information about the files listed in *Projects*.

Without the **-d** option, the **ls** command returns a listing of information about the contents of the target directory. When passed the **-d** option, **ls** provides information about the directory itself.

Recursively Listing Directory Content

The **ls** utility lists files in the current directory. We can list both the current directory files and the contents of subdirectories.

1. Enter:

    ls -R -C | more

    All files listed in the current directory are output. The directories listed in the current directory are also displayed as are the files listed in each subdirectory. The **-R** option to **ls** is instruction to **R**ecursively descend through the directory tree.

6.2 Managing Files in Directories

To impose order on the chaos of an untamed home directory, we create subdirectories and list files in them.

Moving a File into a Subdirectory

What really happens when we move a file from one directory to another?

1. List all files that start with an *f* and their inodes in the current directory:

    ls -i *f**

    The output includes a listing of the *f-name* file. The name and inode are listed.

    Record the inode for *f-name* _____

2. Move the file to the *Projects* directory with:

    mv *f-name Projects/*

3. List the files in your home directory:

   ls

   The file *f-name* is no longer listed.

4. List the contents of the *Projects* directory:

   ls -i *Projects*

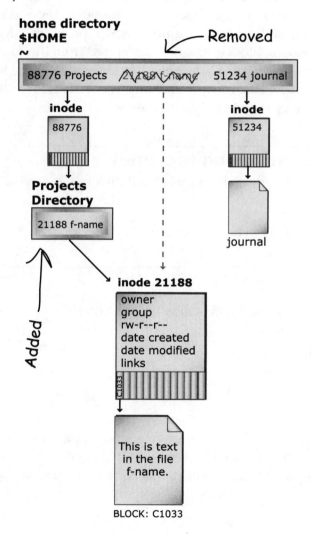

Your files *practice, testing,* and *f-name* are listed. The listing for the file *f-name*, including its inode number, was moved to the *Projects* directory. The inode for *f-name* as it is listed in *Projects* is the same inode that was listed for *f-name* in the home directory before it was moved.

When you issue the command **mv** *file directory*, the system cannot move the electronic file into the subdirectory, because directories do not contain files. Instead, the name and the inode number (which provides information about the file including the data block addresses) are erased from the current directory and are written in the subdirectory. The new directory now lists the file's name and the same inode number. This process of changing the directory where a file is listed to another directory is obviously called **moving the file.**

Copy Files into Subdirectories

Copying a file and putting the copy in a subdirectory is somewhat like moving a file.

1. Create a new file in your current (home) directory:

    cd
    cal > *month*
    ls -i

2. Copy *month* into the *Projects* directory by entering:

    cp *month Projects/*
    ls -i *Projects*
    cd *Projects*
    cat *month*
    cd

The copied file does *not* have the same inode number as the original. When we copy a file, a second electronic version is created. The copy has its own inode, permissions, and data blocks that contain the new file's actual content. Each file now has a life of its own.

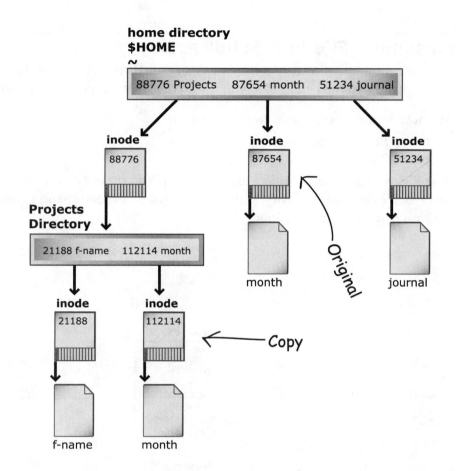

The syntax of the commands you just used to **move** or **copy** files from the current directory to a subdirectory is as follows:

mv *filename subdirectoryname* (listing is moved, same inode)
cp *filename subdirectoryname* (second file is created with new inode)

> **S U M M A R Y :** If a **cp** or an **mv** command is given one or more file name arguments followed by a last argument that is a directory, the files are moved or copied into the directory, with the files retaining their original names. In fact, it is the listing for a file that is moved. If a copy is created, a new listing is written in the target directory. If a file is moved, it retains its inode number. If a file is copied, the copy is given its own, new, unique inode.

Accessing a File in a Subdirectory

You are in your home directory. Listed in this home directory is a subdirectory
Projects. You moved the listing of *month* from your home directory to *Projects.*

1. Without leaving home, you can access *month*:

> **more** *Projects/month*
>
> **pwd**

The file *month,* listed in *Projects,* is displayed. You do not change directories,
but reach into a subdirectory and access the file. This command is really
a significant set of instructions:

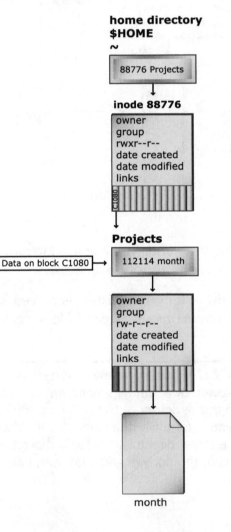

month

- Look in the current directory for a subdirectory named *Projects* and identify its inode number.
- Locate the inode that has the correct number.
- Check on permissions.
- If permitted to access the directory, get the directory's address from the inode.
- Open the directory *Projects.*
- Look in *Projects* for a file named *month.*
- Identify the inode associated with *month.*
- Examine permissions from *month*'s inode, and if permitted to read the file, get from the inode the data block addresses of the data blocks that hold the file.
- Read the file from the data blocks.

You have been following this format for some time when you entered commands like **more** */etc/passwd.*

Avoiding Mistakes When Moving Files into Directories

When you are moving a file into a subdirectory, what happens if you misspell the directory name?

1. In your current (home) directory, create a new file *trouble.*

    date > *trouble*
    more *trouble*
    ls -i *t**

    Record the inode for *trouble* _____

2. In the next command, you attempt to move *trouble* into the *Projects* directory, but misspell *Projects* as *ProjectZ.*

    mv *trouble ProjectZ*

3. Get a listing of the files in the *Projects* directory:

    ls *Projects*

    The file *trouble* is not there.

4. List the files in the current directory:

    ls -F

    The file *trouble* is missing; it was moved, but to where? A new listing named *ProjectZ* is in the current directory. It is not a directory.

5. Examine the file *ProjectZ*:

> **more** *ProjectZ*
> **ls -i** *ProjectZ*

When you issued the command **mv** *trouble ProjectZ*, there was no directory *ProjectZ*, so the file *trouble* was renamed to *ProjectZ*, which retains its inode, the same one that *trouble* had before.

If the **mv** utility is given two arguments, it changes the name of an existing file (argument one) to a new name (argument two), unless the second argument is a directory. If the second argument is a directory, the name and inode number listing for the file (argument one) is moved into that directory. In this example, there is no directory named *ProjectZ*. The **mv** utility simply changes the name of *trouble* to a new filename, *ProjectZ*.

6. Change the name of the file back to *trouble*:

> **mv** *ProjectZ trouble*

7. To avoid this problem, enter the **mv** command with a slash after the directory name:

> **mv** *trouble ProjectZ/*

This slash informs **mv** that you want the listing for file *trouble* to be moved into a *directory* named *ProjectZ*. This time, the shell cannot find a directory named *ProjectZ*, so on most systems it displays an error message. With the */* at the end of the last argument, **mv** interprets the argument as a directory name. When it cannot find a directory of that name, it cries foul. Without the */* at the end of *ProjectZ*, there is no insistence that *ProjectZ* be a directory. The argument does not match a directory name and so is seen as simply the new name for the file in a rename request.

Changing Filenames When Moving Files

In the commands you've used so far in this chapter, the files kept their original names in the new directory listings. You can also change the name of a file as you move it.

1. Create a file and move its listing into a subdirectory, with a new filename, by entering the following:

> **touch** *junkness*
> **ls -i** *j**

Record the inode number of the file *junkness* _____

> **mv** *junkness Projects/treasure*
> **ls -i** *Projects*

The file that was *junkness* in the current directory is now listed in the *Projects* directory under a new name, *treasure*. It retains the same inode. It is the same file. One directory's junk is another directory's treasure.

The syntax for the command to move a file listing from the current directory to a new directory and also change its filename is **mv** *filename subdirectory/newfilename.*

The **mv** command really does mean **move**, but it moves the *listing* for a file or directory to another directory. It does not move the file's contents. The file or directory remains on the drive in the data blocks where it always was. It does not move; just its listing moves.

Removing Files from Subdirectories

You have just used the **mv** command to move the listing of a file from the current directory into a subdirectory without changing directories. You can remove (delete) files from a subdirectory in essentially the same way.

1. Try this series of commands to remove the files *treasure* and *month* from the *Projects* directory:

   > **ls** *Projects*
   > **rm** *Projects/treasure Projects/month*
   > **ls** *Projects*

   The files *treasure* and *month* are removed.

   > **cd** *Projects*
   > **ls**

   In fact, the inodes are consulted to identify the data blocks used by both files; then, the entries for both files are removed from the *Projects* directory. The blocks are then released so that others can use them.

Creating Subdirectories Within Subdirectories

Earlier in this chapter, you created the *Projects* directory as a subdirectory of your home directory. You can also create a subdirectory to be listed in the *Projects* directory.

1. Check to see that the *Projects* directory is still your current directory by entering:

   pwd

2. Create a new subdirectory to be listed in *Projects*:

   mkdir *Code*
   ls -i

   The new directory is created and listed with its own inode in the current directory.

3. Leave the *Projects* directory, and change to your new *Code* directory:

   cd *Code*

4. Make sure the *Code* directory is your current directory with:

   pwd

   This time the output of **pwd** consists of the path to your home directory, followed by */Projects/Code*. The new subdirectory, *Code*, is listed in the *Projects* directory. The *Projects* directory is listed in your home directory, and your home directory is listed in some other directory, and so on, to the topmost directory, */* (***root***).

5. Use an editor to create a file named *report3* in your current directory (*Code*) that contains the following:

   This is report 3 created in the Code directory.

6. Write the file and quit the editor:

   :wq

7. List the files in the current directory by typing:

   ls
   pwd

   You now have the file named *report3* listed in the *Code* directory, which is listed in the *Projects* directory, which is listed in your home directory. At this point, your directory structure should look like the following illustration.

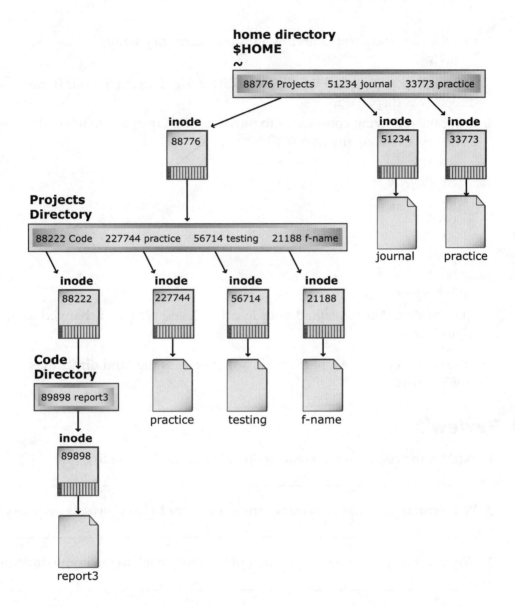

Moving Through the File System

You are in the *Code* directory.

1. Change your current directory back to your home directory with:

   pwd
   cd
   pwd

2. List the files and directories in your home directory with:

   ls -F

   A complete listing of all the files and directories located in your home directory is displayed.

3. Enter the following commands to move through the path to the *Code* directory and view the *report3* file:

   pwd
   cd *Projects*
   ls
   pwd
   cd *Code*
   pwd
   ls
   cat *report3*

   At each step, you confirmed your location, listed files, and changed to a subdirectory.

   In the next section, we will examine how to access files and directories more efficiently.

■ Review 1

1. What is the command to create a directory named *Proposals*?

   _____

2. What command changes your current directory to the *Proposals* directory?

   _____

3. What command changes your current directory back to the home directory?

   _____

4. What shell command can you enter to identify your current directory?

_____

5. What **ls** command option tells **ls** to distinguish files from directories in its output?

_____

6. Your home directory is your current directory, and you enter the command **cd** *Projects*. You then create a file named *confused*. What directory will list the *confused* file?

_____

7. How is it possible to have two files with the same filename in your account?

_____

8. Assume your home directory is your current directory. What command will move a file named *florence* to a directory named *Proposals*, which is a subdirectory of the home directory?

_____

9. Assume you want to move the file *ideas* from the current directory to a subdirectory named *Work*, and you enter the following command:

   mv *ideas work*

   When you examine the *Work* directory, the file is not listed there. Where is it?

_____

10. In the current directory, what command would list the files of a subdirectory named *Cows* and distinguish between files and directories?

_____

6.3 Using Pathnames to Manage Files in Directories

In the previous section, you moved through the directory system by entering a series of **cd** commands, such as **cd** *Projects* and **cd** *Code*. Each **cd** command changed one directory. There is an explicit way to reach distant directories using one **cd** command with a complex argument.

Accessing a Subdirectory

1. Make your home directory your current directory:

   cd

2. Change your current directory from your home to the *Code* directory in a single step, by typing the following command. (A common error is to enter spaces between the directory names and the / character. The full path is one argument, no spaces.)

   cd *Projects/Code*

3. Check the path to your current directory by entering:

   pwd

   Your current directory is now *Code*.

   The command **cd** *Projects/Code* is instruction to change your current directory to a subdirectory (*Projects*) and then move on to its subdirectory (*Code*).

   The *Projects/Code* argument is a list of directories that describes where a directory or file is listed. *Projects/Code* is a pathname. In this case, *Projects* is listed in the current directory, and *Code* is listed in *Projects*. This path instruction tells the shell to look in the current directory for a listing of *Projects,* then to look in *Projects* for a listing for *Code,* and finally to make *Code* the current directory.

   The shell keeps track of your current directory. A filename or directory name in a command line refers to a file or directory listed in the current directory. *Pathnames* are the mechanism used to tell the shell what path to follow to access a file or directory that is *not* listed in the current directory.

Using Pathnames with Utilities

Pathnames can also be used as arguments to utilities. After the previous exercise, your *Code* directory is now your current directory.

1. Enter:

   ls

   A few steps back, you created a file in the *Code* directory called *report3*.

2. Change directories to your home directory by typing:

   cd
   pwd

3. Type the command:

   vi *report3*

   This command results in one of two events. Either the editor begins the process of creating a new file called *report3* in your home directory, or, if at some earlier time you created a file named *report3* in the home directory, the editor will access that file. In either case, however, you do not access the *report3* file that is listed in the *Code* directory.

4. Leave the unwanted file and return to the shell by entering:

   :q!

   To get to the desired *report3* file that is listed in the *Code* directory, you could change directories to your *Code* directory and then edit the file. Or, you could use the more efficient pathname.

5. Use **vi** to edit the *report3* file listed in your *Code* directory without changing your current directory from your home directory. Enter:

   vi *Projects/Code/report3*

   The argument passed to **vi** is the pathname to the file *report3*. The file is *report3*, listed in *Code*, which is listed in *Projects*, which is listed in the current directory.

6. Make some changes or additions to *report3*, leave the file, and return to the shell.

7. Examine the following illustration as you read the following examination of how the argument *Projects/Code/report3* is interpreted:

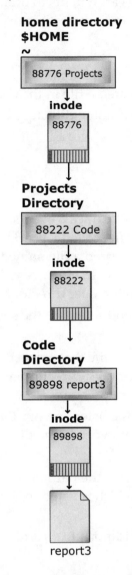

- Look in the current directory for a *Projects* listing.
- Identify the inode number associated with *Projects*.
- Locate the appropriate inode on the hard drive.

- Open *Projects'* inode, check permissions, and if permitted, obtain the address of the data block that holds the contents of the *Projects* directory.
- Open the data block holding the contents of *Projects.*
- Locate an entry in *Projects* for the directory *Code.*
- Identify the inode number associated with the *Code* directory listed in *Projects.*
- Locate the *Code* directory's inode on the hard drive.
- Open the inode and determine where on the drive the block is located that holds the data for the *Code* directory.
- Open the *Code* directory data block.
- Look through *Code* for an entry for *report3.*
- Identify the inode number for the inode for *report3.*
- Locate *report3's* inode on the drive.
- Open *report3's* inode, check permissions, and identify the address of the block on the drive where the file's contents are located.
- At long last, open the correct data block, and read the file into a buffer for **vi** to edit.

8. Confirm your present location:

    pwd

    Your current directory is still your home directory. Even though you worked on the file listed in a different directory, you did not change your current directory from your home directory to that directory. When you wrote the file with the **:wq** command, it was written to its original directory, not to your current directory. However, what happens when you write to a new file from **vi**?

9. Again edit *report3*:

    vi *Projects/Code/report3*

10. Make another change in the file.

11. From the command mode of **vi**, write and quit with:

    :w *report3-new*

    :q

12. List the files whose name begins with the letter *r* in your current directory and in *Code*:

    ls *r**

    ls *Project/Code/r**

From **vi**, a new file is written to the *current* directory, unless you specify a path to some other directory.

13. Once again, edit *report3*:

    vi *Projects/Code/report3*

14. This time specify where to write a copy using a pathname. Enter:

    :w *Projects/r3*

15. Exit **vi**:

    :q

16. List the files in *Projects*:

    ls *Projects*

    The file *r3* that you created from within the editor is listed there.

> **N O T E :** A pathname of a file combines both a directory path to the directory where the file is listed and the file's name, all separated by slashes. By using the file's pathname, we can work with any UNIX utility on a file not listed in the current directory.

Copying Files into Other Directories Using Paths

Pathnames are particularly useful with the **cp** and **mv** commands. You can copy or move files from one directory to another. In this exercise, you copy the file *journal* to the *Code* directory and give it a new name.

1. Make sure your home directory is your current directory:

    cd

2. Type the following command (leaving no spaces between the names and the / characters):

    cp *journal* *Projects/Code/journal2*

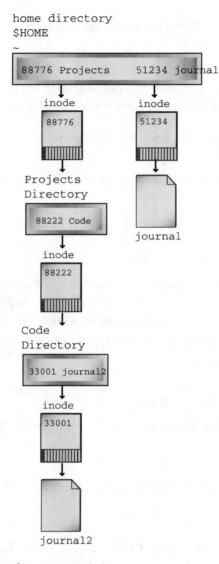

With this command, you are giving **cp** two arguments that tell the **cp** utility to use the appropriate inodes to:

- Locate the file *journal* that is listed in the current directory.

- Open the *Projects* directory to obtain information on the location of the *Code* directory.
- Open the *Code* directory.
- Make a copy of *journal* (from the current directory), and list the copy in the *Code* directory, giving the new copy the name *journal2*.

3. List the journal file and associated inodes with:

    ls -i *journal*

4. Change from your home directory to the *Code* directory by entering:

    cd *Projects/Code*

5. Confirm that *journal* was properly copied and listed in its new directory as *journal2*:

    ls -i

    Because *journal2* was created as a copy of another file, a duplicate electronic copy of the file is made. The new directory listing includes a new inode number that contains information needed to locate this new copy. Both the original and the copy can be edited independently.

6. Examine the file with:

    cat *journal2*

    It has the same file contents.

7. Finally, return home and create another directory named *Docum*:

    cd
    mkdir *Docum*

8. Change to the *Docum* directory and create a new file:

    cd *Docum*
    touch *readme*

    The file system now looks like that depicted in the following illustration.

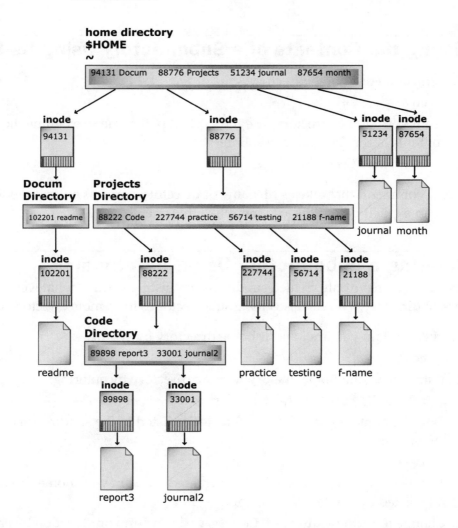

SUMMARY: The general form of the **cp** command as used earlier is as follows:

cp *filename   Directory1/Directory2/newfilename*

where *filename* is a file in the current directory; *Directory1* is listed in the current directory; *Directory2* is listed in *Directory1;* and *newfilename* is the new name given to the copy of *filename* when it is listed in its new home, *Directory2.* You don't need to include the *newfilename* in the command. Omitting the *newfilename* results in the copy of the file having the same name as the original file. Duplicate names are acceptable because the second file is in a different directory.

Listing the Contents of a Subdirectory Using Its Path

1. Return to your home directory:

   cd

2. From your home directory, use the explicit pathname to examine the contents of the *Code* directory. Enter:

   ls *Projects/Code*

Any command that takes a filename or directory name as an argument can be given an explicit pathname argument like this one.

Creating a Subdirectory Using a Pathname

Thus far, you have only created subdirectories, listing them in whatever was the current directory. You can also create subdirectories for remote directories.

1. Make certain you are in your home directory by typing:

   cd

2. Without leaving home, make one more directory by entering:

   mkdir *Projects/Corresp*

3. Find the names of the files and directories listed in the subdirectory, *Projects*, by entering:

   ls -F *Projects*

   The new directory *Corresp* that you created while in your home directory is now listed in the *Projects* directory.

4. Change to the new directory *Corresp*, and confirm your location by entering:

   cd *Projects/Corresp*
   pwd

5. Create a file named *replies* in the *Corresp* directory, and add a few lines of text to it:

   vi *replies*

6. Save the file and return to the shell.

7. Leave the *Corresp* directory and return to your home directory with:

   cd

Your directory hierarchy now matches the structure shown in the following illustration.

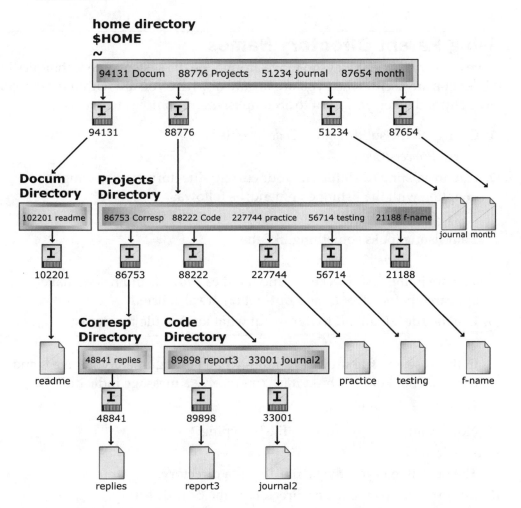

8. Make sure you are in your home directory by typing:

pwd

You can change directories to directories located below the current directory, and you can change from a subdirectory back to your home directory. You have not yet, however, changed from one subdirectory to another subdirectory located on a different branch of a directory tree (from *Code* to *Docum,* for instance). The special characters introduced in the next section allow for changes of this kind.

Using Parent Directory Names

There are very efficient ways to move around the file system. The techniques in this section are useful when you are unsure of where you are within the directory hierarchy and when you want to accomplish more complicated goals.

1. Change to the subdirectory *Code* by entering:

    cd *Projects/Code*

2. Obtain a listing of all files in your current directory by including the **-a** option with the listing command, as follows:

    ls -a

    Your listing looks something like this:

    .   ..   *journal2   report3*

    You are in the *Code* directory, and the files *journal2* and *report3* have appeared before. Dot (.) and dot-dot (..) are also listed.

3. Use the **file** command to figure out what kind of file the dot is:

    file .

    In this case, the **file** utility examines whatever argument you give it and reports what kind of object it is. You receive a message indicating:

    ```
    .: is a directory
    ```

4. Now examine the dot-dot (..) file by typing:

    file ..

    The output tells you the .. file, too, is a directory.

5. Confirm that your current directory is the *Code* directory:

    pwd

6. Display the inodes with all the files and directories listed in the current directory:

    ls -ai

7. Change to the dot (.) directory by typing the command:

    cd .

8. Determine the path to the dot directory by typing:

    pwd

    The output of **pwd** says that your current directory is again *Code*. But *Code* was also your current directory before you typed the **cd .** command.

9. Obtain a listing of the contents of the dot directory:

    ls .

    The files listed in the current directory are displayed.

    The single dot is the "name" for your current directory used in the listing. The dot is how your current directory accesses itself. Every directory refers to itself as the . directory. It's the personal pronoun of Cyberville.

10. Determine the path to your current directory by typing:

    pwd

11. Change your current directory to the dot-dot directory by typing:

    cd ..

12. Confirm your present location with:

    pwd

    You are now in the *Projects* directory. *Projects* is the parent directory of the *Code* directory where you were located before. The command **cd ..** changed your current directory from *Code* to the *Projects* directory, *Code*'s parent.

    In a directory, the .. (dot-dot) is the listing for its parent directory. The parent directory is the directory located one level above your current directory and is the directory that lists the current directory's name and inode.

13. Examine the inodes for the files and directories listed in the *Projects* directory:

    ls -aiF

    The output lists the inodes for *Projects* (the . directory), the subdirectory *Code*, and various files.

14. Compare the results with the inodes listed in the *Code* directory:

    ls -ai *Code*

The *Code* directory is accessed through its inode.

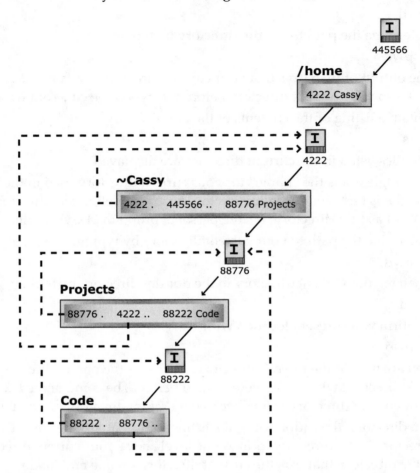

In *Code,* the **.** inode has the same inode number that the parent directory, *Projects,* lists next to its subdirectory, *Code.* To *Project,* the *Code* directory is the same inode that **.** is in *Code.*

My daughter refers to herself as "Me" (.), and I refer to her as "Cassy." We both address the same person.

15. Now move up two directories with:

> **pwd**
> **cd ../..**
> **pwd**

At any directory level, when you type **cd ..** you change directories to the (parent) directory; hence, typing ../.. moves to the grandparent.

16. Change directories to your home:

> **cd**

17. Confirm your location:

> **pwd**

18. Move to your home's parent and confirm:

> **cd ..**
>
> **pwd**

You are probably in a directory named *home* or a subdirectory of it. The home directory is no one's home, but lists many users' homes. (Should it have been called *city* or *homes*?)

19. Go to the parent of home:

> **cd ..**
>
> **pwd**

When we create a directory, it is listed in the current directory unless we specify otherwise. Return to your home and create a new directory.

20. Enter:

> **cd**
>
> **mkdir** *Skye*

It is listed in the current directory.

21. Enter:

> **ls -iF**

What are the contents of the new directory as soon as it is created?

22. Enter:

> **ls -ai** *Skye*

When a directory is created, it gets two listings: itself (the **.** directory) and its parent (the **..** directory). When we create directories, they are part of the file system because the parent knows the newly created subdirectory's inode, and the subdirectory knows its parent's inode.

Changing to Root's Parent Directory

An interesting issue is presented when we are at the top of the file system and ask to **cd** to its parent.

1. Change directories to *root*:

> **cd /**

2. Confirm your location:

   pwd

3. Change to *root*'s parent:

   cd ..

4. Examine where you are located:

   pwd

   You are at *root*. The reason why you stay at *root* when you **cd** to *root*'s parent is in the inode listing.

5. Enter:

   ls -ai

   The inode for *root* is 2; the inode for *root*'s parent is also 2. When you **cd** to *root*'s parent, you access the same inode as the directory you are in: *root*. The parent of *root* is *root*.

> **S U M M A R Y :** It is possible to change directories in both directions within the file system. The command **cd** *subdirectory* changes from a directory to the subdirectory. The directory name must be specified, because several directories may be listed in one parent directory. The **cd ..** command changes from a subdirectory to its one and only parent directory. The dot-dot can be used because each directory has only one parent directory. The dot specifies the current directory. The **/** placed at the beginning of a path is instruction to start the path at *root*.

Copying Multiple Files to Subdirectories

Thus far, you have used the **cp** and **mv** utilities in several ways. You changed the names of files and copied files within the same directory. You have also used these utilities to move or copy a single file into a subdirectory, as with the **mv** *practice Projects/* command. This section examines how to use **mv** and **cp** to move and copy multiple files into other directories.

Both **move** and **copy** commands have been used thus far with two arguments, such as **cp** *file1 newfile1* or **mv** *file1 DIR1 / file1A.*

1. Make sure you are in your home directory, and try entering a **cp** command with these three filenames as arguments:

   cd
   cp *practice journal f-name*

The **cp** utility displays a usage error message telling you only two arguments are acceptable, unless the last one is a directory.

Commands with more than two filename arguments, such as **cp** *file1 file2 file3,* are ambiguous. Should the new *file3* contain both of the other files? Or is *file1* copied and given two names? Because no clear meaning is attached, an error message is displayed.

2. Commands such as the following, however, *do* make sense. Enter:

> **cp** *practice journal Docum/*
> **ls** *Docum*

Although three arguments are given to **cp**, the last argument is a directory, not a file. The meaning is clear: copy both files (listed as the first two arguments) into the destination subdirectory (listed as the last argument).

Both the **cp** and **mv** utilities accept more than two arguments, providing the last argument is the destination directory.

3. Create a new directory called *Archives* by entering:

> **mkdir** *Archives*

4. Copy several of your files into the *Archive* directory by entering:

> **cp** *users_on practice journal l* Archives/*
> **ls** *Archives*

All the files listed as arguments, including all files that have names beginning with an *l* in your current directory, are copied.

Moving Multiple Files

Likewise, you can use **mv** to move multiple files into a directory. Both **mv** and **cp** can affect many files as long as the last argument is a directory.

1. While you are in your home directory, create several new files by entering:

> **touch** *cassy dimitri owen danny monika*
> **ls** -i

2. Move all five files to your *Docum* directory by entering:

> **mv** *cassy dimitri owen danny monika Docum/*
> **ls** i

Because *Docum* is a directory that exists, and it is the last argument in the command line, all argument filenames and inode listings are moved into that directory. They are no longer listed in the current directory.

3. Confirm that the listings have been moved. Enter:

    ls i *Docum/*

Moving Files into a Parent Directory

1. Change directories to the *Code* directory, a subdirectory of *Projects*, which is in turn a subdirectory of your home directory, by entering:

    cd
    cd *Projects/Code*

2. Confirm your current directory:

    pwd

3. Examine the listing for *report3*:

    ls -ai *report3*

Record the inode number for *report3* _____

4. Move the listing for a file from the *Code* directory into its parent, the *Projects* directory. Enter:

    mv *report3* **..**

The last argument is a directory, namely the parent directory, so it is acceptable.

The **mv** utility moves the listing for the file *report3* from the current directory into the **..** directory. Because the *Projects* directory is the parent of *Code*, you have just moved the name and inode number for the file *report3* from *Code* into *Projects*.

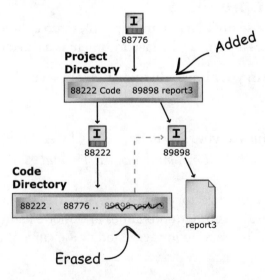

5. Return to the *Projects* directory:

> **cd ..**
>
> **pwd**

6. Confirm that the listing for *report3* was moved into *Projects*:

> **ls -i**

The listing for *report3* is now in *Projects*. It is the same file; it has the same inode. A file is not affected when we move it. All we do is change the listing for the file from one directory to another.

7. Move *report3* back to *Code*:

> **mv** *report3 Code*

8. Create three files, and then move them to your parent directory:

> **touch** *megan daniel betty*
>
> **ls -i**
>
> **mv** *megan daniel betty* **..**
>
> **ls -i**

The directory **..** is a directory listed in the current directory. Because the last argument in the command line is a directory, namely the **..** parent directory, all three files are moved into the specified directory.

9. Change to your parent directory, and confirm that the listings have been moved with:

> **cd ..**
>
> **ls**
>
> **ls -i**

The file listings of names and inodes are moved from the current directory to its parent.

Examining the Full Path to Directories

1. From your home directory, identify the path to your current directory:

> **cd**
>
> **pwd**

The full path starts at **root**; the / directory then lists all directories to your current directory. It is something like:

> */home/cassy*

The files in your current directory are easily listed or accessed.

2. Enter:

    ls

    cat *practice*

   The same file can be accessed using its full path and name.

3. In the following command, replace */home/cassy* with the path to your home directory from the previous **pwd** command:

    cat */home/cassy/practice*

   This instruction says to start at *root* (*/*), find home, in home find *cassy*, and in *cassy* find *practice*. The fact that you happen to be in one of those directories is irrelevant.

4. Go to */tmp* and create a directory using your login name:

    cd */tmp*

    mkdir *$USER*

5. Change to your new directory:

    cd *$USER*

6. Make a subdirectory in your current directory, make that subdirectory your current directory, and then confirm your location:

    mkdir *Mydir*

    cd *Mydir*

    pwd

   If all is well, you are in */tmp/yourlogin/Mydir*.

7. While in the *Mydir* directory, create a file:

    date > *myfile*

    ls

    pwd

8. Now return home:

    cd

9. Access the file you just created using its explicit full path:

    more */tmp/$USER/Mydir/myfile* (Use either *$USER* or your actual login name.)

   The full or absolute path starting at *root* identifies any file explicitly.

Because no two objects can have the same name in a directory, all files are uniquely identified by the absolute path. If two objects have the same name, they must be in different directories so that the absolute paths are different.

Explicitly Calling Your Home Directory

In shells other than **sh**, we can identify the home directory in the following way.

1. Change directories to *tmp*:

   cd **/tmp**
   pwd

   Your present working directory is **/tmp**.

2. Without changing directories, obtain a listing of the files in your home directory by typing the following command:

   ls ~

   The filenames listed in your home directory are displayed.

3. Examine your current directory path:

   pwd

   Your current directory is still in **/tmp**. The ~ is interpreted by the shell as the path to the user's home directory. Hence, you are given a listing of the files in your home directory, while remaining elsewhere.

4. Access a file that is in your home directory without changing directories. Enter:

   more ~/practice

   This is instruction to examine your home directory, look there for a file *practice*, and display it.

5. Go directly to the *Code* directory by entering:

   cd ~/Projects/Code
   pwd

   The argument *~/Projects/Code* is instruction to examine your home directory for a directory named *Projects*, follow the inode to the *Projects* directory, look in *Projects* for the directory called *Code*, and make *Code* your current directory. This works because the C shell and all shells developed after it define the tilde (~) as the path to the user's home directory.

6. Enter:

   echo ~

   The shell interprets the ~ and replaces it with its value: the path to your home directory.

7. Try:

echo *~/Projects*

The shell replaces the ~ with the absolute path to your home directory, then adds */Projects* to that path. The result is the absolute path to the *Projects* directory.

8. Enter the following:

echo *~/..*
echo *~/Projects/Code*
echo *~/ABCDE*

Including Other Users' Logins in Directory Paths

In the previous exercise, you used the tilde (~) to indicate your home directory. It can also be used to specify *any user's* home directory. On UNIX/Linux systems, the system administrator can log on as the user *root*, after entering the appropriate password. Once login is complete, a shell is started and the current directory is set to *root*'s home directory, as specified in the */etc/passwd* file.

1. Examine the *root* entry in the password file by entering:

grep *root /etc/passwd*

You'll see a display much like the following:

```
root:wAbLL/MiFOxBI:0:1:Operator:/root:/bin/ksh
```

The fields of this line are separated by colons. The sixth field is the home directory of *root*, usually */root* on Linux or */* on UNIX.

2. Request a listing of the path to the home directory for *root* by entering the following command. Do not put a slash or a space between the ~ and the user ID *root*.

echo *~root*

The path to the home directory of the user *root* is displayed.

3. Obtain a listing of the contents of the home directory of another user on the system by entering the following command, where *otherlogin* is the login ID of a friend:

echo *~otherlogin*
ls *~otherlogin*

The contents of the home directory of the user whose name you specified are displayed if you have appropriate permission. If you do not have permission to access another user's account, you can use the same approach on your own account.

4. Substitute your login name for *mylogin* in the following command line:

   ls *~mylogin*

 SUMMARY: The tilde used alone is interpreted by modern shells as the path to your home directory. The tilde attached to the login name of any actual user is interpreted to be the path to that user's home directory. Paths to files listed in a user's home directory may be specified starting with the tilde.

For the tilde to work, the shell must determine where the home directory for your colleague, *otherlogin,* is located.

5. Request a display of the */etc/passwd* record for *otherlogin*. Enter:

   grep *otherlogin* */etc/passwd*

   or

   ypcat passwd | **grep** *otherlogin*

   When you use the tilde, the shell consults the */etc/passwd* file data to locate the path to the user's home directory. The next to last field in */etc/passwd* is the home directory for *otherlogin.*

6. The key is the fact that the shell interprets the tilde as a special character with a specific meaning. Enter:

   echo ~
   echo *~nobody*

   The home directory information from the *passwd* file is displayed.

   The preceding tilde is interpreted by the shell as the home directory of the user; the tilde attached to a user login name is interpreted as the path to that user's home directory.

   People often attempt to use the tilde to change directories to a directory that is an ordinary directory, not a user's home directory.

7. For example, attempt to go to the */tmp* directory with the following command:

   cd *~tmp*

The error message indicates there is no user on the system named *tmp.* Although there *is* a *tmp* directory, there is no user *tmp*; hence, there is no *home* directory for a user *tmp.*

■ Review 2

At this point, we have specified directories using a variety of instructions. In the following table, a **cd** command including its argument is on the left. Fill in the result of entering the specified **cd** command on the right.

Command	Result
cd ..	Change to parent directory.
cd ../bill	
cd ~	
cd ~/bill	
cd ~bill	
cd ~bill/bill	
cd /bill	
cd bill	

6.4 Accessing Files in Remote Directories Using All Methods

Because the **cd** command allows you to move around a UNIX file system, at any moment, your current directory could be any directory you have permission to access anywhere on the system. Likewise, you can reach from wherever you are to any other directory to access a file. When you want to access a file that is not located in your current directory, you must specify a path to the file: either an absolute path from *root* or a relative path from your current directory, or the path from a user's home directory.

Summarizing Methods for Accessing Directories

In the previous sections, you examined several ways to specify a file's location. The following bulleted list shows summary commands for examination. Make sure you are in your home directory.

1. Enter:

    cd

We can identify a file in many ways:

- **Current Directory:** Locate a file in the current directory by using its name. For example:

wc *practice*

This is enough information to uniquely identify a file if the file is listed in the current directory.

- **Path from Current Directory:** Specify the path to a file starting with a directory that is listed in the current directory:

wc *Projects/Code/report3*

This is an instruction to look in the current directory for a listing for *Projects*; open the directory *Projects,* and then locate the requested subdirectory, open it, and so on. A path to a file beginning at the current directory is termed a *relative path*; it will be different depending on your current location.

Among the directories listed in your current directory is the parent **..** directory. Paths starting with the parent are actually starting in the current directory because the parent is listed here as the **..** directory; for instance, **cat** *../file* looks in the current directory for the inode of **..** and then opens it and accesses the *file*.

Sometimes we need to identify a file in the current directory by using *./scrA,* which instructs the shell to look in the current directory for a file named *scrA*.

- **Start at Root:** Specify a path to a new file starting at *root,* regardless of your current directory:

touch */tmp/$USER/newname*
ls -l */tmp/$USER/newname*

This is an instruction to examine the *root* directory for the requested subdirectory, *tmp,* and open it, and so on. A path starting at *root* is the *absolute path* to the file.

- **Start at Home:** Specify a path beginning at your home or any other user's home directory. The path to a file starting at home is the same regardless of your current directory. For instance:

wc *~/practice*

It makes no difference what directory is your current directory if you start the path at a user's home:

wc *~otherlogin/practice*

where *otherlogin* is some other user. This argument is instruction to look up the home directory for the user *otherlogin* in the *letc/passwd* file and then to use the path to that home directory in the command, plus whatever additional path is specified.

Perform the following exercises to explore more examples of the various ways to provide a path to a file.

Specifying the Path Starting in the Current Directory

1. To access a file or directory that is listed in the current directory, you simply specify its name. Enter:

   wc -l *practice*
   ls *Projects*

   When you want to access a file or directory listed in a directory that is listed in your current directory, you specify the directory, then a slash, then the target file or directory.

2. Make sure you are in your home directory, and then create a new file in the *Projects* directory called *actions*:

   cd
   vi *Projects/actions*

3. Add text that is a brief description of how to access files at a distance.

4. Write the file and quit the editor:

   :wq

5. Obtain a listing of the files in the current directory with:

   ls

   The file *actions* is not listed in the current directory.

6. List the contents of the *Projects* directory:

   ls *Projects*

   The new file is listed in *Projects*.

 S U M M A R Y : A *subdirectory* is a directory listed in the current directory. In all instances where you want to access a subdirectory, you just specify its name. It is listed in the current directory, so the shell locates it.

A common mistake is to use a slash in front of the requested directory—for instance, **cd** */Projects*. This is instruction to start at *root* and look there for the directory *Projects*. The requested directory is not found in *root*, and an error message is presented. The other common error is to use a backslash rather than a slash, for some unknown reason.

7. Change to the *Projects* directory:

    cd *Projects*

8. Obtain a word count of the *users_on* file, which is listed in your parent directory. Enter:

    wc *../users_on*

    Because the .. directory is listed in the current *Projects* directory, it can be used as the starting point for the path to a file in one of its subdirectories.

9. Enter:

    pwd

    The output indicates that you remain in the *Projects* directory.

10. Access the *readme* file, located in *Docum*, which is in your parent directory:

    wc *../Docum/readme*

    This command is instruction to look in the current directory for a dot-dot directory (your parent), then to look in .. for the directory *Docum*, and then to look in *Docum* for a file named *readme*.

11. Enter **cd** to return to your home directory.

12. The same procedure is available for specifying subdirectories of directories listed in the current directory, such as:

    ls *Projects/Code*
    wc *Projects/Code/journal2*

Specifying the Absolute Path to a Directory

Within any directory, all files and/or directories must have unique names. Except for */ (root)*, all files and directories must be listed in another (parent) directory. The result of these two conditions is that every file on the system must have a unique pathname from */ (root)*.

1. Identify the absolute path to your present directory:

    pwd

The output of **pwd** is something like this:

```
/home/cassy
```

2. Change to the *Code* directory:

> **cd** *Projects/Code*

3. Obtain the absolute path:

> **pwd**

4. Ask for a display of the file *journal2* located in the current directory by entering:

> **cat** *path-to-this-directory/journal2*

Using the *cassy* example from earlier, you would enter:

> **cat** */home/cassy/Projects/Code/journal2*

Every file has a unique, absolute pathname. It always starts at **root** (/) and includes the appropriate subdirectories.

> **S U M M A R Y :** Every absolute pathname starts from **/** (**root**). The absolute path to every file in a directory consists of the path to the directory followed by a slash and the file's name. For example, the file *passwd* located in the **etc** directory has an absolute pathname of **/etc/passwd**.

Specifying Paths Using Home Directories

The path specification can start at any user's home directory and proceed from there.

1. Change to the **/tmp** directory by entering:

> **cd** */tmp*
>
> **pwd**

2. Without changing directories, get a listing of the files in your *Code* directory by entering:

> **ls** *~/Projects/Code*

This command line is instruction to:

- Access the user's home directory
- Locate a listing for *Projects*
- Use the inode to access *Projects*

- Locate a listing for *Code* in *Projects*
- Read from *Code* to determine the names of all files listed there

The starting point is the path to the home directory for the user who issued the command.

Returning to the Previous Directory

Many shells allow us to change directories and then return to our previous location, no matter where that is. The **bash** and **ksh** shells maintain the previous directory path as the value of a variable. The **tcsh** maintains a list of previous directories in a list that can be accessed.

Going Back to Last Current Directory Using bash and ksh

These shells keep the path to the current directory and the previous directory in variables:

1. If you are not using a Bash or Korn shell, start one for this exercise.
2. Confirm your present location:

    pwd
    echo $PWD

3. Change directories and confirm location:

    cd /tmp / $USER
    echo $PWD
    pwd

4. Enter the following:

    echo $OLDPWD
    cd $OLDPWD
    echo $PWD
    pwd

    The value of the variable *PWD* is the path to the current directory and the variable *OLDPWD* is the path to the previous current directory. The *OLDPWD* variable can be used as an argument to **cd** to return to the previous directory.

5. An alternative way of specifying the previous directory on many **bash** and **ksh** shells is a - argument:

    cd /tmp
    pwd

    cd -

    pwd

6. If you started a child **bash** or **ksh**, exit it to your login shell.

Returning to Previous Directories Using the tcsh

The **tcsh** shell does not use a variable, rather a *stack* of previously visited directories. As users we must instruct the shell to add a directory to the stack.

1. If you are not communicating with a **tcsh**, start one now.

2. Make sure you are at your home directory:

    cd

3. Enter:

    pushd */tmp*

    pwd

    pushd */etc*

    pwd

You have changed directories to */etc* and have added previous directories to the list.

4. Enter:

    popd

    pwd

    popd

    pwd

With each **popd** you go to the directory on the top of the stack.

Accessing Directories Using All Methods

The activities in this section utilize the various methods of path specification you have explored in this chapter. It is suggested that you examine each instruction and try to accomplish the goal before reading the solution that follows.

1. Make sure you are in your home directory, and then obtain a display of the names of the files listed in the *tmp* directory, which is listed in *root*:

    cd

    ls */tmp*

2. List the files in the directory in *tmp* that has your login name:

    ls */tmp/$USER*

3. Confirm that you are still in your home directory:

    pwd

4. Copy your file *practice* to the */tmp/$USER/* directory, and give the file a new name, *practice2*:

    cp *practice* */tmp/$USER/practice2*

5. Without changing directories, obtain a listing of the files in */tmp/$USER*:

    ls */tmp/$USER*

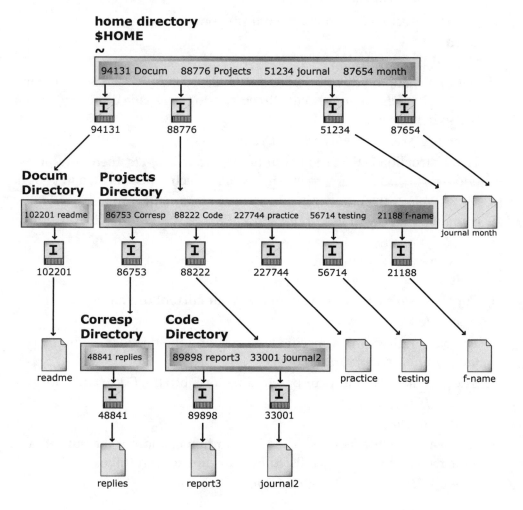

6. Change directories to */tmp/$USER*, confirm your location, and obtain a listing of files:

   cd */tmp/$USER*

   pwd

   ls

7. Copy the file, *practice2* (which you just created here) back to the *Code* directory, which is in *Projects* in your home directory, and obtain a listing of the files in *Code*:

   cp *practice2* *~/Projects/Code*

   ls *~/Projects/Code*

8. Change directories to **root** and confirm your location:

   cd /

   pwd

9. Without changing directories, copy the file *report3*—which is located in *Code*, in *Projects*, in your home directory—to the *Docum* directory, which is also in your home:

   cp *~/Projects/Code/report3* *~/Docum*

   This instruction is to start at your home, locate *Projects*, then *Code*, and then find *report3*. Lastly, copy *report3* to *Docum*, which is also located in your home.

10. Make *Projects* the current directory, and create a file named *greeting* containing the word *hello*, but list it in *Projects'* parent directory. Confirm.

    cd *~/Projects*

    echo *hello* **>** *../greeting*

    ls *..*

11. Copy the file back from the parent to your current directory:

    cp *../greeting* *.*

    The parent directory is specified with *..* , and the destination directory is the current directory, dot.

12. Copy all files listed in your parent directory into the *Docum* directory:

    cp *../** *~/Docum/*

    ls *~/Docum/*

13. Run **wc** on the file *users_on* listed in your home, and put the output in a file named *num_users_on* listed in your directory in */tmp*:

    wc *~/users_on* **>** */tmp/$USER/num_users_on*

14. Create a file named *friend-listing* in your *Projects* directory, containing the filenames listed in the home directory of a friend:

ls *~login-of-friend* **>** *~/Projects/friend-listing*

15. Make *Projects* your current directory and confirm that the file was created:

cd *~/Projects*
pwd
ls
more *friend-listing*

■ Review 3

1. Assume your current directory is not known. What command changes your current directory to a directory named *Education*, which is listed in a directory named *Proposals*, which is listed in your home directory?

_____

2. From your home directory, what command do you enter to edit a file *mikekirby* that is listed in the *Proposals* directory?

_____

3. From any directory, how can you create a directory *Rejected*, listed in the *Proposals* directory in your home directory?

_____

4. How would you copy a file *selquist* from your home directory into *Education*, a subdirectory of the *Proposals* directory?

_____

5. What command changes directories to the parent directory?

_____

6. What command changes to the *Marilyn* directory listed in your home directory?

_____

7. Assume that directories *Programs* and *Letters* have the same parent directory and that you are currently in the *Programs* directory. How do you change your current directory from *Programs* to *Letters*?

   _____

8. How would you move the file *report7* in the current directory to the parent directory?

   _____

9. How can you copy all files from the current directory to the parent?

   _____

10. Given that you are located in your home directory, what are three different ways you can create a directory named *Junkyard* in a subdirectory called *Location* that is in your home directory?

    _____

11. You are in your home directory, using the **vi** editor to edit a file called *client-list* that is under *Proposals/Contracts/*. You end the session; which directory are you in now?

    _____

12. What command do you issue to use the **vi** editor to edit the file *cats* in the home directory of the user named *Chris*?

    _____

13. What command will copy a file called *rhino* to a subdirectory *Africa* and rename the file *elephant*?

    _____

14. What command would move the file *vans* from the subdirectory *Transportation* in the home directory of the user named *kim* to the */tmp* directory, renaming the file *cars*?

    _____

15. The following diagram illustrates a hypothetical file system. The two home directories are for Melissa and Isaac.

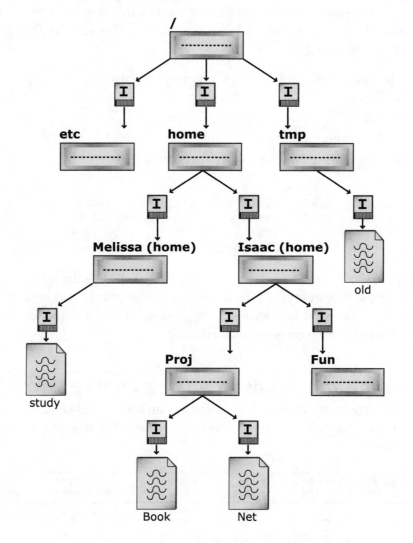

a. Assume you are in the directory *Melissa* and want to go to the directory *Isaac* on the right. What command would you enter?

_____

b. You are in *Melissa's* home and want to copy *old* to *Proj*.

_____

6.5 Examining the Long Listing for Files

Thus far, when you needed to see the current permissions and other information about your files, you entered the **ls -l** command. In this section, the different parts of the long listing are examined.

1. Obtain a long listing of the files in your home directory by typing the following:

   cd

   ls -l | more

The **ls -l**ong listing has the following components:

```
total 13
drwxrwxrwx 4 cassy staff  4096  Nov 13 17:04 Projects
-rw-rw-rw- 1 cassy staff  1452 Sep 7   11:58 journal
-rw------- 1 cassy staff  1064 Sep 2   21:14 practice
-rw-rw-rw- 1 cassy staff  6100 Oct 12 11:32 users_on
```

The first piece of information seen here (*total 13*) indicates the total number of data blocks used by everything in the current directory. In this case, 13 blocks are used. Each line that follows is the long listing of information for one file or directory listed in the current directory.

Identifying the Fields in a Long Listing Entry

In a long listing entry, or *record,* the information for each file or directory is divided into seven fields. In the example just discussed, the first record's fields are as follows:

PERMISSIONS FIELD	NO. OF LINKS	FILE'S OWNER	FILE'S GROUP	SIZE IN BYTES	DATE OF LAST MODIFICATION	DIRECTORY OR FILENAME
drwxrwxrwx	4	cassy	staff	544	Nov 13 17:04	Projects

Links

The second field in each record is a number that indicates the number of directories where that object (file or directory) is listed. You created the *Projects* directory in your current directory. There are four directories that have entries that refer to the *Projects* directory: *Projects'* parent directory lists *Projects;* the *Projects* directory lists itself as the **.** directory; and the two subdirectories of *Projects* each have a listing for its parent, *Projects,* as the **..** directory.

Files generally have a *1* in this field, indicating that they are listed in their current directory only. If a file is listed in two directories, it is *linked* to both directories and has a *2* in this field, and so on.

Owner

The third field of the long listing is the login name of the owner of the file (in some contexts, the owner is called the user). In this example, *cassy* is the name of the file's owner.

Group

The fourth field is the name of the group to which the owner of the file is assigned. In this example, the group is *staff*. Groups are used to gather together various users who need to share access to the same files. Groups in UNIX are like families in a town—the group is a name for several users who in some way are connected together and can share resources. Every user belongs to at least one group. Access to a file can be granted for all users in a group and denied to users who are not members of the group. In the */etc/passwd* file, each record's fourth field is that user's group number.

1. To see what group you are in, enter:

   groups

2. To see what groups are on your system, enter:

   more */etc/group*

Size

The fifth field of the **ls -l** output is the length of the file in bytes.

Modification Date

The sixth field identifies the date the file was last altered.

Filename

The last field is the name given to the file.

6.6 Managing Files from More Than One Directory

Whenever you create a file, the filename and inode number are listed in a directory, namely, its parent. A listing for a file in a directory is a *link* to the file. In these exercises, you have accessed each file from the parent directory either by specifying the file's name, or by including the parent directory in the pathname to the file. If a directory just links us to our files, can we list or link a file to multiple directories? For example, can we put the name and inode number for a file in several directories, allowing us to access the file from any one of the directories? Of course.

Listing a File in a Second Directory

1. Make sure you are in your home directory:

   cd

2. Use the **visual** editor to create a file named *testing-links*:

   vi *testing-links*

3. Add the following text:

   This file is listed in my home directory.

4. Write and quit the editor:

   :wq

5. Confirm that the name and inode for *testing-links* is listed in the current directory, your home directory, by entering:

   pwd
   ls -i *testing-links*

   Record the inode number of *testing-links* _____

6. Change directories to the *Archives* subdirectory, and get a listing of its files:

   cd *Archive*s
   ls

   At this point, the file *testing-links* is not listed in *Archives*.

7. List the files in your parent directory:

   ls ..

   The output indicates *testing-links* is listed in the parent directory, your home.

8. Instruct the shell to also list the *testing-links* file in the current directory, but use the name *testing2*:

   ln *../testing-links testing2*

   The file is being listed in or **linked** to a second directory. There are two arguments to the **ln** command: the target file and the name the file is to have in its new listing in the current directory. In this example, the file is given a different name in the second directory. It could be the same name, if you wish.

9. Obtain a display of the files now listed in your current directory:

ls -i

The *testing-links* file listed in the home directory is also listed in this directory with a new name, *testing2*. The file *testing2* is listed with the same inode number associated with *testing-links* in the parent directory. It is the same file, just listed in two directories, with different names but connected to the same inode.

10. Access the file *testing2*:

vi *testing2*

11. Add the following line:

And now listed in Archives, too.

12. Write the file and quit the editor with:

:wq

13. Return to your home directory:

cd

14. Examine the *testing-links* file from your home directory:

more *testing-links*

The line you added when you accessed the file from the *Archives* directory is in the file. It is the same file listed or linked to two directories. The following illustration describes the linked file.

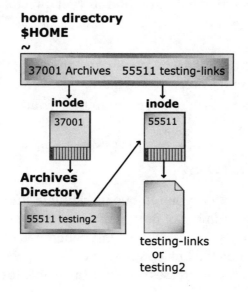

home directory
$HOME
~

| 37001 Archives 55511 testing-links |

inode **inode**
| 37001 | | 55511 |

Archives
Directory

| 55511 testing2 |

testing-links
or
testing2

15. Examine the original and linked files using **ls**:

>   **ls -li** *testing-links*
>   **ls -li** *Archives/testing2*

They are equivalent listings. Both access the same inode, and both report the file is linked to two directories.

16. Use the **file** utility to explore the files:

>   **file** *testing-links*
>   **file** *Archives/testing2*

There is no hint that one was the original, the other a link.

Both listings, *testing-links* and *testing2*, are associated with the same inode number—they are the same file. There is only one file with one inode; however, it is listed or linked to two directories and can be accessed from either.

Removing Linked Files

Every file's "index card," the inode, keeps track of the number of directories that list it. Each instance of a file listed in a directory is one link.

1. Obtain a long listing of the file in the current directory with:

>   **ls -l** *testing-links*

In the listing, the field to the right of the permissions is the number of links or the *link-count*. The file *testing-links* has two links: the current directory and the *Archives* directory.

2. Remove the file *testing-links* from the current directory by entering:

>   **rm** *testing-links*
>   **ls**

Although it was originally created in this directory, the file is now removed and not listed in this directory anymore.

3. Does that mean it is also removed from the *Archives* directory? Enter:

>   **ls -l** *Archives*

The link count is back to 1. The file is now listed only in *Archives*.

>   **more** *Archives/testing2*

When you remove a file, you remove its listing in the specified directory. If after the removal the number of links remaining is one or more, the file is kept on the hard drive in its data block(s). Only when it is no longer listed in any directory (that is, when the link count goes to zero) is the file actually removed (that is, the data blocks' addresses are made available for new use).

Linking a File to a Directory Using the Original Name

You do not have to link files by giving the new link a new name.

1. Link another file with:

      ln *users_test Archives*
      ls -i *users_test*
      ls -i *Archives/users_test*
      ls -l *users_test*

   If **ln** is given a directory as its target (second) argument, the file is listed in the target directory using the same name of the original listing. The link count in the output of **ls -l** reflects that the file is listed in two directories.

Linking Multiple Files

The **ln** utility will link several files at a time.

1. Change to your home directory and issue:

      ln *megan daniel betty Archives*

2. List your current files with link count and inodes:

      ls -il *megan daniel betty*

3. List the files in the *Archive* directory:

      ls -il *Archives*

   All the files listed as arguments to **ln** preceding the target directory (*Archives*) are now listed in the Archives directory as well as the current directory. They have the same inodes in the listings in both directories.

 SUMMARY: A file can be linked to multiple directories using the **ln** command. The first argument is the current filename; the second argument is the new directory where the file is to be listed. A file is removed from any linked directory with the **rm** command. When it is removed from the last directory that lists it, the file is actually removed. Only files can be hard-linked in this way.

Linking Files with Symbolic Links

The links you created in the previous exercises listed the actual inodes for a file in two directories. Links created in this way are called *hard links* because the inode is hard-coded into the various directories that list the file. As will be examined later, hard links do not work for some files, and only the superuser can create hard links for directories.

An alternative method for linking an existing file to another directory does not list the linked file's inode in the second directory.

1. Make sure you are in your *Projects* directory:

    cd ~/Projects
    pwd

2. Create a link to the *journal* file from *Projects* by entering:

    ln -s ~/journal

3. Examine the inodes of the two files:

    ls -i *journal*
    ls -i ~/*journal*

    They do not have the same inode number.

4. Confirm that both links actually access the one file with:

    echo "*In Projects File*" **>>** *journal*
    cat ~/*journal*

    When you add text to the file listed in *Projects*, and then read the same file listed in your home directory, the added text appears because you are writing to and reading from one file.

    A symbolic link or soft link is created when we use the **-s** option to **ln**. A *symbolic link* is a small file in the current directory that contains the information needed to locate the linked file wherever it is actually listed.

5. Examine the long listing of the symbolic link with:

    ls -l *journal*

    The output is like:

    ```
    lrwxrwxrwx  1 cassy    users    6 Oct 24 16:47 journal
    -->/home/cassy/journal
    ```

    The initial character is not a **d** for directory, not a **-** for file, but an **l** for symbolic link. The arrow indicates that the filename *journal* in the current directory is a link to the file *journal* in *cassy*'s home directory listed in *home,* listed in /. This is clearly a different creature. The link is a small file in the current directory containing a pointer to the inode of the real file wherever it is located.

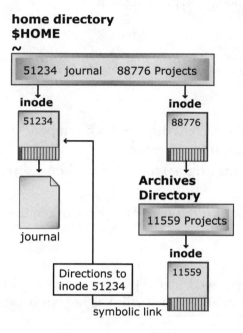

6. Ask for a description of *journal* listed in the current directory:

> **file** *journal*

The output from **file** is:

```
journal: symbolic link to /home/cassy/journal
```

Both of these commands report that *practice* is not a regular file the way hard links are. Rather, *journal* is a symbolic link in the current directory with its own inode.

Removing a Symbolic Link

Removing the link is like removing a file.

1. Enter:

> **rm** *journal*
> **ls**

The entry for *journal* (the symbolic link) is removed from the current directory.

Removing a File that Has a Symbolic Link

In the last exercise, you removed the link to a file. What happens if you remove a file that has a symbolic link pointing to it?

1. Enter:

   date > *~/realfile*
   ln -s *~/realfile rf*
   ls -l *rf*
   cat *rf*

   The entry *rf* in the current directory is a symbolic link to the real file named *realfile* listed in the home directory.

2. Remove *realfile*, the original file, from the home directory:

   rm *~/realfile*

3. Examine the effect on the symbolic (soft) link in the current directory:

   ls -l *rf*
   cat *rf*

   The real file is removed, so the pointer (symbolic link) points to nothing. It is a broken link. The symbolic link is not equivalent to the file it links.

Linking Directories

On some systems, the superuser *root* can use a **-d** option to the **ln** utility and create hard links to directories in other directories. Ordinary users cannot create directory hard links. Ordinary users can, however, create symbolic links to directories.

1. You are presently in the *Projects* directory:

   pwd

   One of the directories listed in your home is the directory *Docum*.

2. Link the *Docum* directory to your current directory with:

   ln -s *~/Docum*

3. List the contents of the current directory:

   ls -F

   The *Docum* directory is listed as a subdirectory of your current directory; however, note that it has an @ following it instead of a /, denoting that it's a symbolic, or *soft*, link.

4. List the contents of *Docum*:

    ls *Docum*

The filenames listed in *Docum* are displayed.

5. Change directories to *Docum* and confirm your location:

    cd *Docum*

    pwd

6. Create a file:

    touch *filefromProjects*

7. Change to your home directory and list its files:

    cd

    ls

The *Docum* directory is listed in your home directory.

8. List the contents of the *Docum* directory:

    ls *Docum*

The file you created when you accessed the *Docum* directory from *Projects* is listed.

9. List the contents of *Projects*:

    ls *Projects*

The archives directory is listed in *Projects,* too.

10. Confirm that the contents of both *Docum* directories listings are the same:

    ls -i *Docum*

    ls -i *Projects/Docum*

You can now access the *Docum* directory from your home or from *Projects.*

Users often link system directories for easy access.

11. Link the *tmp* directory to your home:

    cd

    ln -s */tmp tmp*

12. List the contents of your current directory:

    ls -l | more

The *tmp* directory is now listed in your home.

13. List the contents of your *tmp* and of */tmp*:

    ls *~/tmp*

    ls */tmp*

You now have the */tmp* directory listed as *tmp* in your home.

> **S U M M A R Y :** *Hard links* are used to make equivalent links to a file from two or more directories. If the original file is removed, the listing in the second directory still accesses the file.
> *Symbolic* or *soft links* are used to link directories or files to another directory. A symbolic link is a pointer in a small file in another directory that points to the inode of the original file. The original file and the symbolic link have their own unique inodes. When the original file or directory is removed or moved to a different location, the symbolic link points to nothing and is broken.

Examining the Reason for Symbolic Links

When a hard drive is partitioned in preparation for installing Linux or UNIX, usually several unique sections or partitions are created. Each partition holds part of the UNIX/Linux directory tree.

1. To see what partitions are employed on your system, enter:

   mount

   The hard drive partitions and where they are mounted are listed.

   The information displayed is like:

```
/dev/hda2     on     /
/dev/hda3     on     /home
/dev/hda5     on     /tmp
/dev/hda6     on     /usr/bin
```

One partition is labeled "/" and holds the core of the hierarchical directory tree. On some systems there is only the / file system, rather than multiple partitions.

If there are additional partitions, they are mounted onto the / file system, giving the user a complete directory tree to use. Often, / and */home* and */usr/bin* and */tmp* are on separate partitions and are mounted when the system starts up.

Most of each partition on the hard drive is formatted into small pieces of memory called *data blocks,* often 1024 bytes in size. Data blocks hold the actual data that we call files. In addition to the data blocks in a partition on a drive, space is set aside in each partition for the inodes that manage the files in that partition. Each partition, holding one file system, has a set of *unique* inode numbers for that partition. And that's the problem. If a system has */home* as a specifically separate partition and */tmp* as another, there could be a file in each partition having the same inode. Inodes are unique only within a single partition file system, but can have duplicates in another partition. Because inode 12345 refers to one file in the */tmp* file system partition and refers to a different file in */home,* creating a hard link in */home* to the file that has inode 12345 does not link it to the file in */tmp,* but links it to the file of that number in the */home* file system.

A *symbolic link* is a small file in a directory on one file system partition that points to the correct file system and then the correct inode for the linked file. We can use hard links only for files within the same file system. Symbolic links link directories and files in the same or different file systems.

Lastly, inodes are the key to UNIX/ Linux file system mastery. What is a file? Is it just the data, or is a "file" also its characteristics, its permissions, owner, creation date, group, size, and so forth? If we want to think of the file as embodying all of its characteristics, not just the data in the data blocks, then *the inode is the file.* The inode contains the whole of a file, including its descriptive characteristics and the addresses of the blocks where the file data reside. The network is the computer; the inode is the file.

6.7 Moving and Removing Directories and Their Contents

You have used the **mv** command to move files into directories and to rename files within a directory. As we have seen, a directory is just a file that contains the names of other directories and files, with their associated inode numbers. Many file management operations are performed by modifying the contents of a directory. For instance, to change the name of a file is to change its entry in its parent directory. To create a new directory is to create an entry in one directory that includes the new directory name and its inode number so that the shell can **cd** to or access the new directory.

Because directories are just files, it seems reasonable that we can change the name of a directory and move it in the same way we move and change names of other files. We can, so read on, Macduff.

Changing a Directory's Name

Directories are named initially by the owner when they are created. The name can be changed.

1. Make sure you are in your home directory and that the *Projects* directory is listed:

   cd

   ls -F

2. Identify the inode for the *Projects* directory:

   ls -id *Projects*

   Record *Projects'* inode number _____

3. Change the name of the *Projects* directory by entering:

   mv *Projects Old-projects*

4. Obtain a listing of the contents of your current directory:

   ls -F

   There is no *Projects* directory listed in your home directory anymore. However, *Old-projects* is listed.

5. Examine the contents of *Old-projects*:

   ls -F *Old-projects*

   The contents are not changed; only the name of the directory is different. There is one place the directory is named: the entry in your home directory. That entry was modified to read *Old-projects* instead of *Projects*.

6. Examine the inode number for *Old-projects*:

   ls -id *Old-projects*

   You changed the name for the *Projects* directory in the current directory, but the new name is attached to the same inode number. The entry points to the same directory, just using a new name.

home directory
$HOME
~

88776 Old-projects P~~rojects~~

inode 88776

owner
group
rw-r--r--
date created
date modified
links

Old-projects

7. Change the name of *Old-projects* back to *Projects*:

   mv *Old-projects Projects*
   ls -id *Projects*

   The two directories use the same inode.

Moving a Directory

Every user directory is listed in a parent directory. You can move a directory to a different location in the hierarchical file structure, that is, list it in a different parent directory.

1. Obtain a listing of the files and directories in the current (home) directory:

   cd
   ls -F

   The directories *Projects* and *Archives* are both listed.

2. Note the inodes referenced by *Projects* and *Archives*:

    ls -id *Projects*

    ls -id *Archives*

Enter the inode for *Projects* _____

Enter the inode for *Archives* _____

3. Move the listing for the *Projects* directory from your current directory to the *Archives* directory:

    mv *Projects Archives*

    ls

    ls *Archives*

Projects is no longer listed in the current directory, but is listed in the *Archives* directory. The following illustration depicts the directory structure before and after the move.

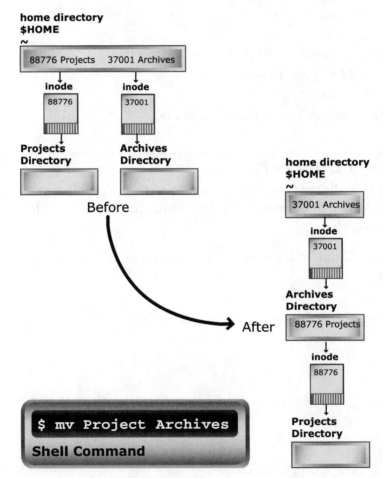

Your current directory, which is the parent directory of its subdirectories, contains the subdirectories' names and inode numbers. You can change the directory where a directory is listed. If you change the listing, you "move" the directory. Inodes remain the same for each directory.

4. Examine the contents of *Projects,* now listed in *Archives*:

    ls *Archives/Projects*

When a directory is moved, its contents are undisturbed. Moving a directory is just moving the listing for the directory from one parent directory to another. It does not affect the "child" contents of the moved directory. The two parent directories are affected. One directory loses the listing for the moved directory, the other directory gains a listing. The directory that is moved has a new parent directory in its listing. Moving a directory does not affect the moved directory's subdirectories.

5. Revisit the inodes:

    ls -ai *Archives*
    ls -ai *Archives/Projects*

The *Projects* directory in *Archives* has the same inode number as . in *Projects.* Yes, *Projects* sees itself as the same inode that the parent (*Archives*) sees as *Projects.* Even though the directory is moved, it keeps its inode number.

In *Projects,* the .. directory has the same inode number as the . listing in *Archives. Projects* sees *Archives* as its parent.

6. Move the *Archives* directory back to your home directory by entering:

    mv *Archives/Projects* ~
    ls -ai *Archives*
    ls -ai *Projects*

The listing for *Projects* is moved from *Archives* to your home directory. Both now see your home directory as their parent.

6.8 Removing Directories and Files

In UNIX/Linux, we remove directories using specific commands, just as we remove files.

> **CAUTION:** Always use remove commands with great care, because often it is difficult if not impossible to recover lost items. Make sure you are in the appropriate directory for each of these activities.

Removing an Empty Directory

Two commands are available for removing a directory. The first command removes an empty directory—a directory with no files listed in it.

1. Make sure you are in your home directory with:

   cd
   pwd

2. List the files and directories in your home directory with:

   ls -F

3. Create a new directory by typing:

   mkdir *Dirempty*
   ls -F
   ls -id *Dirempty*

4. Check to see if there are any files in the *Dirempty* directory by typing:

   ls *Dirempty*

5. Remove the empty directory *Dirempty* by typing the command:

   rmdir *Dirempty*

6. Confirm that the *Dirempty* directory is gone by typing:

   ls -F

7. Attempt to remove the *Archives* directory even though it contains files:

   rmdir *Archives*

The error message indicates that the *Archives* directory is not empty, and **rmdir** does not remove directories that list other files or directories. Leave it as is.

Removing a Directory and Its Files

You have seen how the **rmdir** command removes only empty directories. With an alternate command, you can remove directories that are either empty or that contain listings of files.

We will attempt to remove the directory *Code* from the *Projects* directory.

1. Change to the *Projects* directory:

    cd *~/Projects*

2. Double-check that you are in the proper directory and that *Code* is listed:

    pwd ; ls

3. Attempt to remove the *Code* directory. Type:

    rmdir *Code*

    The directory cannot be removed with **rmdir** because it contains files. You receive an error message:

    ```
    rmdir: Code: Directory not empty
    ```

4. To remove the *Code* directory *and* its files, type:

    rm -r *Code*

    The **-r** option of the command instructs **rm** to recursively remove files. The utility starts by removing files from the directory, then enters a subdirectory and removes its files, then removes the empty subdirectory, and so on, recursively down through the target directory's subdirectories.

5. Confirm that *Code* has been removed by typing:

    ls -F

    Not only is the *Code* directory removed, but so are all the files listed in the directory and any subdirectories you might have created in *Code*.

C A U T I O N : The **rm -r** command has significant impact and should be used very carefully. Double-check that the directory you are removing doesn't contain any subdirectories that you may need. Move anything you want to keep to another directory before you use the **rm -r** command.

---

6. To demonstrate the power of **rm -r**, carefully enter the following commands to create a series of directories:

    mkdir *DIR10*
    touch *DIR10/skye*
    mkdir *DIR10/DIR20*
    mkdir *DIR10/DIR21*
    mkdir *DIR10/DIR20/DIR30*
    date > *DIR10/DIR20/today*
    cp * *DIR10/DIR20/DIR30*

The structure just created is described in the following figure.

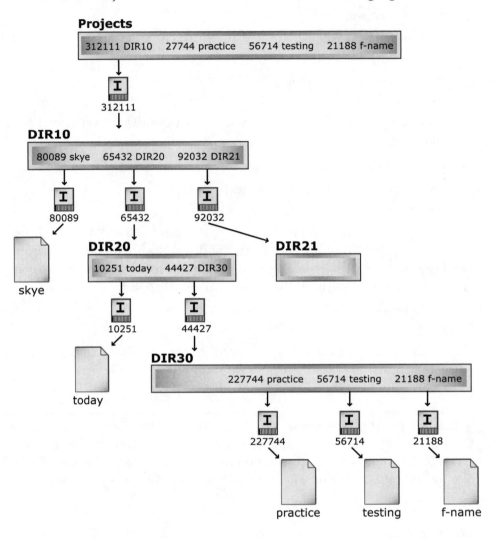

7. Check with the following:

   ls
   ls *DIR10*
   ls *DIR10/DIR20*
   ls *DIR10/DIR20/DIR30*
   pwd

8. Now attempt to remove the directory tree with:

> **rmdir** *DIR10*
> **ls**
> **rm** *DIR10*
> **ls**
> **rm** **-r** *DIR10*
> **ls**

The **rm** **-r** directory command removes all files and directories starting with the target directory and recursively descending through all subdirectories.

■ Review 4

1. What command would you enter to move the file *eakins*, which is in your current directory, so it's listed in your home directory?

   _____

2. What is the difference between the commands **rmdir** and **rm** **-r**?

   _____

3. Assume you are in the *Projects* directory, which has the subdirectories *Old-projects* and *New-projects*. What is the command to move the *Bookproject* directory from *New-projects* to *Old-projects*?

   _____

4. You are in your home directory, where there is a file named *users_on*. What command will list the file in both your home directory and in the subdirectory *Projects*?

   _____

■ Conclusion

In this chapter, you moved around the file system, created directories, copied and moved files into directories, accessed files using the special directory characters (. .. / and ~), and employed absolute pathnames. You listed files in multiple directories and removed directories in the file system. By storing files in subdirectories, we can organize and manage files, keep old copies of files, and remove groups of useless files. Files are accessed by specifying the path to the file. If no pathname is specified, the current directory is searched. The *root* directory, a home directory, the parent directory, and the current directory can all be used as starting points for the path to a file. The absolute pathname for a file is the list of directories, beginning with *root*, that are traversed to access the file.

Directories, because they are a type of file, can be moved, removed, and renamed, largely using the same commands. Treating and maintaining a well-defined and functional file structure is a necessary condition for the effective and efficient use of a system.

■ Answers to Review 1

1. **mkdir** *Proposals*
2. **cd** *Proposals*
3. **cd**
4. **pwd**
5. **ls -F**
6. *Projects*
7. The files exist in different directories.
8. **mv** *florence Proposals/*
9. The file *ideas* was renamed *work* and remains the current directory. UNIX is case sensitive.
10. **ls -F** *Cows*

■ Answers to Review 2

cd ..	Change to parent directory.
cd ../*bill*	Change to parent directory and then change to its subdirectory *bill*.
cd ~	Change to the user's home directory.
cd ~/*bill*	Change to the directory *bill*, which is a subdirectory of the user's home directory.
cd ~*bill*	Change to the home directory of a user named *bill*.
cd ~*bill/bill*	Change to the directory *bill*, which is a subdirectory of the user *bill*'s home directory.
cd /*bill*	Change to the directory named *bill*, a subdirectory of /.
cd *bill*	Change to the directory *bill*, which is a subdirectory of the current directory.

■ Answers to Review 3

1. **cd** *~ / Proposals/Education*
2. **vi** *~ / Proposals/mikekirby*
3. **mkdir** *~ / Proposals/Rejected*
4. **cp** *~/selquist ~/Proposals/Education*
5. **cd** *..*
6. **cd** *~ / Marilyn*
7. **cd** *../Letters*
8. **mv** *report7 ..*
9. **cp** ** ..*
10. **mkdir** *Location/Junkyard*
    mkdir *./Location/Junkyard*
    mkdir *~/Location/Junkyard*
11. You are in your home directory. You do not actually move to another directory unless you use **cd**.
12. **vi** *~Chris/cats* (Note that there is no slash between the ~ and *Chris*.)
13. **cp** *rhino Africa/elephant*
14. **mv** *~kim/Transportation/vans /tmp/cars*
15.
    a. **cd** *../Isaac*
    b. **cp** */temp/old ~Isaac/Proj*

■ Answers to Review 4

1. **mv** *eakins ~*
2. **rmdir** only removes empty directories, but **rm -r** removes a directory and all of the files and subdirectories.
3. **mv** *New-projects/Bookproject Old-projects*
4. **ln** *users_on Projects*

COMMAND SUMMARY

cd *pathname*   Changes to the directory specified by *pathname.*

pwd   Displays the full pathname of your current directory.

mv *filename path/newfilename*   Moves the listing for the file named *filename* into the directory specified by *path* and renames the file *newfilename* if it is specified.

mv *directoryname path/new_directoryname*   Moves the listing for the directory named *directoryname* into the directory specified by *path* and renames the moved directory *new_directoryname* if it is specified.

cp *filename path/newfilename*   Puts a copy of *filename* into the directory specified by *path* and names the copy *newfilename* if it is specified.

ls -a   Displays a list of files and subdirectories in your current directory, including files with names beginning with a period/dot.

ls -F   Displays the names of files in your current directory and places a / after directory names. Executable files are displayed with a *.

ln   Creates a listing of a file in another directory. The **ln** without an argument creates a hard link; the inode is the same in both locations. It is one file listed in two directories. Files in different file systems cannot be hard linked.

ln -s   Creates a soft link, or listing of a file or directory in a second directory. A soft link can list directories and files in a different file system in a second directory.

ls -ld   Outputs a long listing of information about the directory itself, not its contents.

ls -i   Lists filenames and their associated inodes in the current directory.

mkdir *directory*   Creates a new directory called *directory.*

rmdir *directory*   Removes *directory*, but only if it contains no files or subdirectories.

rm -r *directory*   Removes *directory*, as well as everything it contains.

Accessing and Changing Previous Commands

S K I L L S   C H E C K

Before beginning this chapter, you should be able to

- Rename, copy, and remove files
- Use several utilities in one command line by redirecting output
- Change directories throughout the file system
- Access and modify files using the **vi** editor
- List the currently running processes

O B J E C T I V E S

After completing this chapter, you will be able to

- Repeat commands already executed
- Modify previous commands
- Add elements to commands and reexecute them
- Print commands without having them executed
- Edit previously entered commands
- Access arguments from previous command lines

The fundamental way to accomplish tasks using a Linux or UNIX system is to interact with a shell by typing commands from the keyboard. The shell interprets what we enter and executes the needed commands. While interacting with the shell, we often need to cycle through a series of commands, repeat a command, or reenter mistyped commands. Sometimes we need to enter a series of commands that differ only slightly from one another. In each of these cases, having to retype command lines may take significant energy and time, often leading to frustration as we make new errors. To improve our efficiency and dispositions, all modern shells keep track of commands we issue, allowing us to repeat and/or modify previously executed command lines without having to reenter them.

7.1 Surveying Shells and Features

We don't all drive Model T Ford automobiles, although in its day the Model T was a good means of transportation. Modern cars accomplish the same tasks as Model Ts, but offer useful new features. However, not all modern cars have incorporated the same additional features. Likewise with shells. The original shell was created by Steve Bourne in the early 1970s. Although **sh** is much closer to the modern shells than a Model T is to modern autos, the analogy still holds. The Bourne shell, **sh**, includes all the essential basic features that we see in modern shells: prompting the user for input, redirection of output, variable evaluation, command substitution, starting of child processes, and a wealth of programming features such as **for** loops and **if then else** decision making.

However, the **sh** shell includes no code that allows us to modify previous commands, no aliases, no history, and no command-line editing. A few years after the Bourne shell was written, Bill Joy, at the University of California at Berkeley, became tired of retyping commands and wrote the C shell, **csh**. This new shell included aliases, command history, a way to modify previous commands, noclobber, and a set of programming tools that handled a variety of features differently than the **sh** shell. Although the alias and history features improved the environment, the **csh** provided no way to actually edit previously entered command lines. In the mid-1980s, a group of programmers mostly at universities solved the problem by modifying the **csh** to allow users to change previously entered command lines by using editor instructions. They also added other user-friendly features. A different group of programmers at the Free Software Foundation found the **sh** programming environment more useful, but the **csh** command-line history and alias features essential to better living. They rewrote the **sh** to include the **csh** user-friendly features. This new version of the Bourne shell was aimed at breathing new life into **sh**, so they called it the **bourne again shell** (**bash**). Then David Korn wrote the **ksh** to include all the features of alias, history, and command-line editing, but use a different syntax for invocation.

So, how to best examine all this?

We recommend you first determine what shells are available on your system, then work through the first history portion of this chapter using either a **csh**, **tcsh**, or **bash**. Then, using a **ksh**, work through the exercises in that section. Finally, examine the command-line editing section using one of the shells that support that feature—a **ksh**, **bash**, or **tcsh**.

Determining the Available Shells

We can ask your current shell to locate the various shell programs available on your system in the directories listed in your path.

1. Enter:

   which sh

   If the path to the executable displayed is for **sh**, the **sh** Bourne shell is available on your system.

2. Enter:

   which csh
   which tcsh
   which bash
   which ksh

   If you do not have a **ksh** on your system and you are running Linux, you can install it. On most Linux distributions, the Korn shell is called **pdksh** (public domain **ksh**) in the **rpm** packages. The most current instructions for adding **pdksh** are available at the **www.muster.com** web site.

Checking On Needed Files

The exercises in this chapter utilize files created in previous chapters: *practice* and *journal*. If you do not currently have files by those names, create junk files of any content with those names now.

7.2 Using the History Feature with csh, tcsh, bash, and ksh

Modern shells maintain a listing of commands that we previously entered, allowing us to repeat, modify, and in some shells, edit previous commands. This *history* feature permits us to rerun commands once we enter them correctly and to make slight changes to long commands without retyping the whole line. This section first examines how history works with the **csh**, **tcsh**, and **bash** shells, then examines how to repeat commands with the **ksh** shell.

Reexecuting Commands with csh, tcsh, and bash

The Bourne (**sh**) shell does not maintain a history list. The **ksh** history works differently and is examined in the next section.

1. Determine what shell you are using:

   echo $$

   ps

   The PID of your current shell is the output of the **echo** command; the output of **ps** tells you what that shell is.

   If you are working with an **sh** or **ksh** shell, you should start a child shell by typing one of the following commands:

2. To start a C shell, enter:

   csh

3. To start a **tcsh** shell, enter:

   tcsh

4. To start a **bash** shell, enter:

   bash

   These commands tell your current shell to start up a child or subshell. You will use either this new shell or your shell to run the exercises in this chapter. We recommend completion of this section using one of the C shells or **bash**, then looking at the **ksh** in the next section.

   Regardless of which shell you have chosen, when you want to leave the subshell and return to your original login shell, just type the **exit** command.

Instructing the Shell to Keep a History List

From the time the **bash** shell and **tcsh** shells are started, they begin maintaining a history list of commands you enter. Some **csh** shells do not keep track of the commands you enter unless you request it.

   1. If you are using the C shell, enter:

       set *history=40*

   This C shell command instructs the shell to start maintaining a list of up to 40 commands.

Inspecting a List of Past Commands Issued

The history feature keeps a record of the exact command lines that you enter, in the order that you enter them.

   1. Type each of the following shell command lines:

       date
       who | wc -l
       cd
       ls -F
       wc *practice*
       cal *1752*
       cat *practice*

   These command lines are recorded in the history list maintained by your shell.

   2. Examine the list by entering:

       history

   The output of **history** is similar to the following. (Of course, the numbers on the left of your output will be quite different if your shell executed other commands.)

```
1   set history=40
2   date
3   who  |  wc  -l
4   cd
5   ls  -F
6   wc practice
7   cal 1752
8   cat  practice
9   history
```

The last command line on the history list is the last command that you entered. All of the commands that you typed appear on your screen as output from the **history** command. If **history** were already functioning when you began these exercises, you will see previous commands listed in the output as well. Each command on the list has an associated *event number* on the left.

There are several ways to access the history list and reissue a command. You can request the shell to:

- Repeat the most recently entered command
- Reissue a command identified by its event number
- Reexecute a command by specifying part of the command name

Repeating the Most Recent Command

1. Review the *practice* file by typing the following display command:

   cat *practice*

   The **cat** utility reads the *practice* file and displays it. To see it again, we need to repeat the command.

2. When your shell prompt reappears, enter:

   !!

   The file *practice* is displayed on your terminal screen again, because the **cat** command is repeated.

   In the **csh**, **tcsh**, and **bash** shells, we repeat the last command by entering double exclamation points (also known as *bang-bang* or *double bang*).

3. Enter:

   date
   !!
   cal
   !!
   history
   !!

Executing Commands by Event Number

Several of the remaining exercises use the history list of previously entered commands. The numbers that appear on your workstation at the left-hand side of every line, the event numbers, are determined by the specific commands that you recently entered. In each exercise, consult your history list and use the correct event numbers.

1. To examine the history list, type:

   history

2. Select one of the commands to repeat. Place its event number in the following command instead of *event_number*:

   !event_number

   For instance, to repeat the command associated with event number *4* at the command line, enter (without a space):

   !4

   The shell examines the history list and executes the command with the specified number.

3. Call up your history list again by typing:

   history

   The commands !! and !*event_number* are not listed. The shell instead lists the actual command that was repeated.

4. To see if someone new has logged on, repeat the **who | wc -l** command by using its event number from the history list.

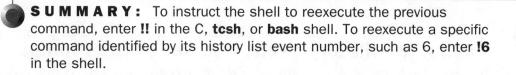

> **SUMMARY:** To instruct the shell to reexecute the previous command, enter **!!** in the C, **tcsh**, or **bash** shell. To reexecute a specific command identified by its history list event number, such as 6, enter **!6** in the shell.

Reexecuting Commands Selected by Part of the Line

Often, you'll need to repeat a command but cannot recall the event number. One way to handle this is by typing **history**, locating the correct event number, and then typing the appropriate ! command. As is usually the case with UNIX, there is an alternative, and more efficient, way.

1. To repeat a previous command, enter:

   !h

   This command tells the shell to repeat the last command entered that begins with the letter *h*, namely the **history** command, producing a list of the commands you recently entered.

Sometimes it may be necessary to type more than one letter of a previous command to correctly specify the command you want repeated.

2. Again, examine the history list:

   history

   You have entered several commands that start with a letter *w* and are included in the list.

3. Enter:

   !wc

   This time the **who** command line is not reexecuted, but the **wc** line is.

4. Enter:

   !c

   The last command that starts with a *c* is executed, probably **cat** *practice*. If you want the command **cal** *1752* reexecuted, the *!c* does not work.

5. Enter:

   !cal

   The last command starting with *cal* is executed.

6. Compare the output in each of the following:

   !w
   !wc
   !wh

Adding the History Event Number to the Prompt

It is useful to know what event number the shell is giving to each command as you enter it. You can change the shell prompt to include this information.

1. From the shell, type one of the following commands:

   In the C or **tcsh** shell, enter:

   set *prompt*='\! % '

   In the **bash** shell, enter:

   PS1='\! $ '

   Notice that there is a space on both sides of the percent and dollar sign in these two commands. The *bang* (exclamation mark) tells the system to read the last event number from the history list, add one to this number, and display it. The prompt then displays each event number as you work; this arrangement for the prompt remains until you change the prompt again or log out.

> **N O T E :** Prompt specifications can be made to take effect each time we log on. To do this, we'll need to modify the *.cshrc* file (for a C shell) or the *.tcshrc* for the **tcsh**, or the *.bashrc* for a **bash** shell. Details about modifying these files are in Chapter 20, "Modifying the User Environment."

Selecting Arguments from Previous Commands

Another way to reduce typing of command lines is to reuse arguments from previous commands. The **csh**, **tcsh**, and **bash** shell include this feature.

Selecting All Arguments

1. Display the contents of *practice* and *journal*:

    cat *practice journal*

2. Run a word count on these same two files by typing:

    wc !*

    The output is the **wc** information on the same two files.

    We can easily verify how the shell interprets the **!*** in the last command.

3. Enter:

    history

    The shell expanded the **!*** characters in the **wc** command to be the arguments from the previous command.

    The **!*** is interpreted by these shells as "Put all arguments of the previous command right here." In this case, **!*** is expanded into *practice journal*, the arguments in the previous (**cat**) command.

4. Enter:

    !w
    head !*
    ls -l !*

Selecting the Last Argument

1. Create a directory *Conservatory* by entering:

    mkdir *Conservatory*
    ls -ld !$

    The long listing for the directory *Conservatory* is output by **ls**.

2. Copy the file *journal* to the directory *Conservatory*:

   cp *journal* **!$**

   The **!$** is interpreted by the shell as instruction to take the last argument in the previous command line and substitute it here. Because *Conservatory* is the last argument in the previous command, the file *journal* is copied to the *Conservatory* directory.

3. To move to the *Conservatory* directory, type the following command:

   cd !$
   pwd

4. View the history list to verify that the shell evaluated the **!$** as the last argument on the previous command line.

   To select the last argument in the previous command, use the **!$** at the appropriate location in the current command.

5. Return to your home directory:

   cd

   The shell allows us to use the previous command's last argument in the middle of a new command:

6. Enter:

   !ls
   ls !$
   cp *practice* **!$**/*newpractice*

   The file *practice* is copied to the *Conservatory* directory and given a name of *newpractice*. The **!$** is replaced with the last argument from the previous command, the directory name.

Modifying Previously Entered C Shell Commands

In addition to repeating commands, C shell's **history** feature can be used to modify previous commands before reissuing them.

Adding to the Previous Command Line

The **history** feature allows us to add additional instructions to a previously executed command line, and then reexecute it.

1. Enter:

   cal *9 1752*
   !! > *sept1752*
   history

After running the **cal** command, the shell ran **cal** again and redirected its output to the new file *sept1752*. The history listing shows the command generated by the shell as it interpreted the **!!** command, namely **cal** *9 1752 > sept1752*. The shell interpreted all characters after the **!!** as characters to be added to the previous command.

2. For a more interesting example, enter:

> **who**
> **!! | sort**
> **!! | grep** *$USER*
> **!! | tr** *'a-z' 'A-Z'*
> **!! >** *who-me*
> **history**

The output of **history** shows how the shell adds whatever is after the **!!** to the previous command and then executes it. Each successive command shows the additional tokens that are added.

3. Enter:

> **cat** *practice journal* | **wc**
> **!! -c**

The **-c** is added to the end of the previous command line and it is executed. Any string or tokens can be added with the history mechanism in these shells.

Adding to Any Previous Command Line

1. To count the number of words in *practice*, enter:

> **wc -w** *practice*

2. To count the words in both *practice* and *journal,* enter:

> *!w journal*

This command is instruction to access the history list, locate the most recently executed command that begins with *w*, append the word *journal* to the command line, and execute the newly constituted line. The command that is executed is:

> **wc -w** *practice journal*

Another way to perform this task is to look at the history list and type a command line that includes the event number of the earlier command line.

3. Enter:

> **history**

4. Find the event number that matches the command **history**, and use it for the next command. The command line you need to type is in this format:

!event_number > *command-hist*

where *event_number* is the event number you located in the history output.

This command instructs the shell to look in the history list for the command line associated with the number you selected and to add to that command line the redirection and filename information that followed the *!event_number* in the command line.

> **S U M M A R Y :** To recall and append to a previous command line in a C or **bash** shell, type the appropriate recall command followed by the string to be appended.

Making Modifications to Command Lines

Creating command lines can be complex and prone to mistakes. A later section of this chapter guides you through using editor commands to edit previously entered commands while using a **ksh**, **bash**, or **tcsh** shell. This section explores how to quickly make minor modifications. If you do not have access to one of the three shells that permit command line editing but have access to a **csh**, the following modification technique is the only way you have to make corrections.

1. Type the following command, spelled exactly as written with a **tq** as the second utility:

who | **tq** *'a-z'* *'A-Z'*

The shell complains that there is no utility **tq**.

2. Type the following line. (The caret character [^] is usually SHIFT-6 on the keyboard.)

*^q^r^*

This command line tells the shell to locate the first occurrence of the letter *q* on the previous command line, substitute the letter *r* for the *q*, and execute the modified command line. The altered command line appears on your screen before being executed:

```
who  | tr  'a-z'  'A-Z'
```

This option also works with more than one letter or word and with spaces.

3. Enter:

   ^who^cal^

   The modified command is displayed and executed:

   ```
   cal | tr 'a-z' 'A-Z'
   ```

Changing the Utility and Options Within a Command

1. A commonly used **sort** option, **-d**, requests the utility to **sort** in **d**ictionary order. Type:

   sort -d *practice*

2. Another option is **-r**, for a **sort** in **r**everse order. To change your **sort** and do it again without having to retype the whole command line, type:

   ^d^r^

3. A third **sort** option is **-f**, for a **sort** in which the lines beginning with upper- and lowercase letters are **f**olded together. Change your command line to utilize this option by typing the following and be sure to include the - characters:

   ^-r^-f^

   The command line **sort -r** *practice* contains three instances of the letter *r*. If we had issued **^r^rf^** the shell would have changed the first one on the line. (An *r* to *f* substitution would have changed the spelling of *sort* to *soft*.) To avoid the problem, the **-r** was specified in the substitution request to indicate that the minus sign and letter *r* are to be replaced with a minus sign and the letter *f*.

Printing the Command Line Without Executing It

Often, it is useful to look at a previously entered command without having it reexecuted. You can have a command line printed to the screen and added to the history list without executing it.

1. Tell the C shell to display a previous command without execution. Type:

   !c:p

   The **!c** portion of this command instructs the shell to locate the last command beginning with a *c*. The **:p** at the end of the line prints the command on the terminal screen and adds it to the history list without executing it.

2. Make a change in this command line using the **history** syntax for the last command by entering:

   ^cal^ls^:p

   This printing allows you to confirm that the command formatted properly.

3. Execute the command line that you just corrected and printed by typing:

!!

The double bang tells the C shell to execute the last command, even if it previously was only printed on the screen and never executed.

> **S U M M A R Y :** The **:p** command can be appended to any command line. It instructs the shell to print the command line to the screen without executing it. The command is also added to the history list even though it isn't executed.

Accessing History with the Korn Shell

The Korn shell, **ksh**, includes a history feature that allows us to repeat the last command, repeat a command by history number, and repeat by providing a part of the command line. We can also add redirection information to a previous command. There is no way to add a string of characters to a previous command or to make modifications like the caret feature in the C/**bash** shells.

Repeating Previous Commands

1. Start a Korn shell by entering:

ksh

A child **ksh** shell starts. If you do not have access to a **ksh**, proceed to the next section, "Using Editing Commands to Modify the History."

2. Enter:

date
r
ls
r
cal
r

The **repeat** command in the **ksh** is the **r**, not the *double bang* of the other shells.

3. Enter:

r *d*
r *ca*

Commands are repeated if a portion of the command is given as an argument to the **r** command.

4. Likewise, examine the history and reexecute a command by its history number:

> **history**
> **r** *event_number*

For example:

> **r** *3*

reexecutes the third command on the history list.

The history commands for repeating previous command lines in all shells are summarized in the following illustration:

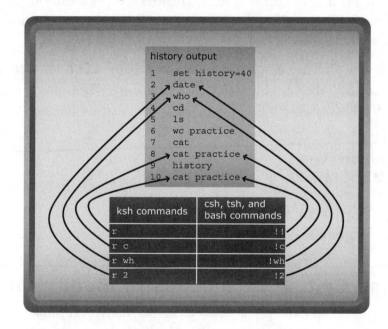

Adding to Any Previous Command Line

Most versions of the Korn shell permit making some additions to a previously issued command, using the **r** command.

1. Enter:

> **cat** *practice*
> **ls**
> **who**

2. Now enter:

   r | wc

   The Korn shell adds the | and **wc** arguments to the previously issued **who** command line. The output is a count of the words, characters, and lines in the output of **who**.

   In the **csh** and friends history mechanism examined earlier, we could add any token or character string to a previous command. Not so with **ksh**.

3. Instruct the Korn shell to locate the last command that began with a **w**, and add a **-c**. The goal is to issue the **who | wc -c** command.

   r w -c

   The Korn shell issues an error statement and does not provide a count of the characters in the output of **who**. The **ksh** accepts additions to previous commands using the **r** command *only* if the first new addition is one of the redirection symbols |, >, >>, or <.

Specifying the Length of the History List in the Korn Shell

In the **ksh** shell, the variable **HISTSIZE** determines the number of commands kept in the history list.

1. Enter:

   history | wc
   HISTSIZE=80
   history
   history | wc

   The history size now has been set to record 80 event numbers.

7.3 Using Editing Commands to Modify the History

The **tcsh, bash,** and **ksh** shells allow us to use many **vi** commands to make modifications to previous commands. Although the way we inform the shells we want to use the editing feature depends on which shell we are using, there is little difference in the behavior of the shells once they are informed.

Requesting the Command Editing Feature

1. Tell your shell you want to use command-line editing.

   In the **ksh** or **bash** shells, enter:

   set -o vi

In the **tcsh** shell, enter:

    bindkey -v

2. Enter the following commands:

    ls -F
    cal
    date
    history

Repeating Commands

At this point, you have at least four commands in the history list. When you entered the **set -o vi** or **bindkey** command, we agreed to a fiction with the shell. The agreement is that we can think of the history list as though it were a file, and we can use **vi**sual editor commands to modify command lines "in" the history "file," and the shells agree to follow those instructions.

We enter another command. It gets added to the end of the commands in the history list. We add another, it gets added. It is as though (fiction) we are editing a history "file," adding new lines with each command we enter. Assuming the fiction, we must be in append mode of the editor. To go to command mode so we can move about the file, we need to press ESC.

1. Press ESC.
Nothing happens.

2. Press:

    k
    k
    k
    k

Each press of **k** moves the "cursor" up one line in the history "file."

3. Once you have selected a command line that you wish to rerun, press ENTER.

The shell is accepting most **vi** commands, but not all. In **vi**, we can move the cursor using the **h**, **j**, **k**, and **l** keys, and we can use the arrows. On most systems, the shells that have the editing feature accept only the **h**, **j**, **k**, and **l** keys and do not interpret the arrows properly. We can stop ourselves from using the arrows by putting a piece of paper or a Post-it over the arrows until the urge passes.

4. Again, press:

    ESC

You have told the shell that you want to be in command mode.

5. Move up and down the list with:

> **k**
>
> **k**
>
> **k**
>
> **j**
>
> **j**

6. Land on some command and reissue it by pressing ENTER.

Making Changes in Previous Command Lines

In addition to returning to a previous command and executing it again, we can use the commands of the **visual** editor to modify a command before we reexecute it.

1. Press:

> ESC

2. Move up through the history list by pressing **k** until you are at the **cal** command line.

Depending on the shell you are using, the cursor is either at the *c* at the beginning of the command (**ksh** and **bash**) or at the *l* at the end of the command (**tcsh**).

3. Tell the shell you want to add text to the end of the file:

> **A**

4. Add a space and the year *1752*.

5. Press ENTER to execute the modified command.

The capital **A** is the **vi** command instructing the shell to add text to the end of the line. You added the text *1752* to the original command line. When you pressed ENTER, you instructed the shell to leave the **vi**-like command mode and run the newly modified shell command.

6. Enter:

> **who | awk '{print $1}'**
>
> **history**

Each new command keeps showing up on the history list.

7. Enter:

    ESC
    k
    k

The **who | awk** line should be in view.

8. Move the cursor around the command line by entering **vi** commands such as:

l (el)	Move right one character
h	Move left one character
w	Move one word right
b	Move one word left

9. Move the cursor to the *1* in the **$1**.
10. Replace the *1* with a *2* by entering:

    r2

11. Execute the modified command by pressing ENTER.
12. Now, issue the following command, complete with errors:

    grape *$USERS /etc/password*

13. Press ESC, then **k**, and use the editing commands to turn **grape** into **grep**, remove the **S** from *USERS*, and fix the *passwd* spelling.
14. Press ENTER and run the command.
15. Using the editing feature, change the target from *$USER* to *root*, and have the output of the command redirected to a new *root-pw* file.

Essentially, all the basic commands from **vi** are available with the shells for command-line editing. The more we edit previous commands rather than simply retyping the command line, the more efficient and capable we become. Rather than make mistakes in long commands, learning the editing skill is worth the effort. Using the editor commands with the shell to fix an error removes the error. Retyping the command fixes the error…and introduces new ones.

Making the Editing Feature Available with Each Shell

You can issue the **bindkey -v** command to each **tcsh** shell you use and a **set -o vi** to every **bash** or **ksh** shell you use, or you could place those commands in the appropriate startup files. Depending on your setup, reasonable places to start are as follows:

1. Make sure you are in your home directory:

   cd

2. List your housekeeping files:

   ls -a

If you log onto a **bash** shell and there is a *.bashrc* listed, put the **set -o vi** as the last line in the *.bashrc* file; otherwise, add it to the *.profile* file.

If you use a **ksh**, you might put the same line in the *.kshrc* if you have one. If not, putting it in the *.profile* will inform a **ksh** at login that you want the editing feature.

The **tcsh** reads the file *.tcshrc* if there is one, and *.cshrc* if there is no *.tcshrc* file.

7.4 Summarizing the Features of the Shells

This chapter examines how the several shells handle history, command modification, and command-line editing. The following illustration summarizes the features available in each shell:

Feature	Shells				
	sh	csh	tcsh	bash	ksh
><:;&	yes	yes	yes	yes	yes
noclobber	no	yes set noclobber	yes set noclobber	yes set -o noclobber	yes set -o noclobber
alias	no	yes alias h history	yes alias h history	yes alias h=history	yes alias h=history
history	no	yes !	yes !	yes !	yes r
Command Modify	no	yes ^^^	yes ^^^	yes ^^^	no
Command Editing	no	no	yes bindkey -v	yes set -o vi	yes set -o vi

◼ Review

1. What command will reexecute the last command you entered?

   _____

   _____

2. What command would you execute to increase your history list to *100*?

   _____

   _____

3. What command would you use to instruct the shell to print the last command you entered but not actually execute it?

   _____

   _____

4. What command could you use if you wanted to reedit the last file you edited with **vi**?

   _____

   _____

5. If you have just run the **spell** command on your file *journal* and want to place all misspelled words in a separate file called *journal.errors*, what command would you use?

   _____

   _____

6. Suppose you have entered the command

   cat *food nip litter*

   What would you type if you wanted to use **pg** instead of **cat** and execute it as your next command?

   _____

   _____

■ Conclusion

The history mechanisms of the C and Korn shells establish how many commands are recorded, allow us to make substitutions in the command line, to recall commands and arguments, and to edit previous commands without retyping them. All this saves time and effort.

This chapter introduced some of the more useful features of the history mechanism and command line editing. For additional information, refer to the *csh* and *ksh* **man** pages or consult Chapter 20, "Modifying the User Environment."

■ Answers to Review

1. In the C shell: **!!**
   In the Korn shell: **r**

2. In the C shell: **set** *history=100*
   In the Korn shell: *HISTSIZE=100*

3. In the C shell: **!!:p**
   In the Korn shell: ESC and then press K once

4. In the C shell: **!***v*
   In the Korn shell: **r** *v*

5. In the C shell: **!!** > *journal.errors*
   In the Korn shell: ESC
   k
   A > *journal.errors*

6. In the C shell: **^cat^pg^**
   In the Korn shell: ESC
   k
   cw
   pg
   ENTER

COMMAND SUMMARY

C Shell

set *history=#*   Sets the length of the history list to be # number of previous commands.

!!   Executes previous command.

!!*string*   Reexecutes the last command that started with *string*.

!!:*p*   Prints last command on the screen, but does not execute it.

!#   Repeats command that was assigned to the # event number.

!# *string*   Reexecutes the command with event number # (from the history list), but with *string* appended to the end of the command.

!*letter*   Repeats last command that began with the specified *letter*.

^*string1***^***string2***^**   Looks for the first occurrence of *string1* in the last command, substitutes *string2* for it, and reexecutes the command.

^*string1***^***string2***^:***p*   Looks for the first occurrence of *string1* in the last command, substitutes *string2* for it, prints the command line, and places the revised command line in the history list *without* executing it.

set *prompt=string*   Sets the shell prompt to *string*. If there is a ! (preceded by a backslash) embedded within *string*, the command number of the command about to be entered will be included in the prompt.

Korn Shell

HISTSIZE=#   Sets the value of the history list variable to be # number of previous commands.

ESC   Puts you into **vi** control (command) mode for retrieving and modifying previously entered commands. Note, in the **ksh** and **bash** shells the **set -o vi** must be set.

r   Repeats previous command.

r l *command*   Adds pipe and *command* to previous command.

r #   Repeats # command.

r *aa*   Repeats last command beginning with *aa*.

8

Specifying Instructions to the Shell

OBJECTIVES

Upon completion of this chapter, you will be able to

- Establish where utilities read input, write output, and write error information
- Use the command line to pass complex arguments
- Employ filename expansion characters
- Use the shell's special characters to communicate your intentions
- Identify the function of complex command lines
- Employ local and environmental variables
- Modify the search path
- Control interpretation of special characters
- Redirect output and error messages
- Employ startup files to tailor how the shell functions
- Instruct the shell to use the output of one command line as part of another

The various shells interpret our commands to accomplish tasks we specify. When the shell produces a prompt on the terminal screen, it is asking us what we want to do next. We type in a response requesting that some program(s) accomplish a task. Providing our request exactly follows the shell's grammar rules, the shell does as we ask and starts whatever program(s) we request. After the programs complete their work, the shell pops back up and asks what's next.

We have to "talk shell language" when we issue commands if we want to be understood. The shell interprets the grammar (*syntax*) of command lines in very specific ways, and of course, it does what we *say*, not what we intend. When we properly make requests, communicating our intentions exactly, the shell does as we intend, and we get work done.

This chapter examines how we can ask for and get exactly what we want. To make sense out of communicating with the shell, we will carefully examine how the shell interprets the commands and special characters we issue.

But our goal is more than syntax mastery. Execution of a program is a complex event in any computing environment. Fortunately, in Linux and UNIX we can explore how the shell interprets our commands, how child processes are started, how the correct code is executed, and how to troubleshoot errors. If we know how the shell functions, we can more effectively make requests.

The fundamental components of a UNIX or Linux computing system are hardware, files, and processes. The hardware, consisting of the central processing unit (CPU), storage devices, working memory, connecting bus, keyboard, terminal, and cables, could be used to run any one of several computing systems. When the hardware is running UNIX/Linux, the core program, called the *kernel*, schedules the CPU's work on the processes in the queue, allocates primary memory, and handles the input/output of terminals, disk drives, and other peripherals. The kernel program virtually defines UNIX and Linux. (This complex, extensive program has consumed an enormous number of programming hours. There is, however, no truth to the rumor that programmers who spend their time removing the rough edges from the kernel are called Kernel Sanders.)

This chapter's exercises begin with a detailed examination of how the shell interprets a command line to determine how many processes to start; how to redirect input, output, and error messages; how to pass arguments; and how to execute the code. The second section explores how the shell expands portions of command lines by interpreting filename wildcards, variables, and other special characters. The last section examines how the shell and child processes interact in the execution of complex command lines.

8.1 Examining Shell Command-Line Execution

When you are logged onto UNIX, you do not communicate directly with the kernel. Rather, you tell the shell what you want, and the shell translates your requests into the proper kernel *calls,* which instruct the kernel to do the work. When you request that the shell run a utility, the shell asks the kernel to start a new process, redirects input and output, passes arguments to the process, and locates the compiled utility program code in a file on the file system on the hard disk. The shell then instructs the process to run the appropriate code.

The login shell, just another utility, is started when you log on and exits when you log out. We often start other shells and exit them as needed. The shell's job is to interpret our instructions. The shell is the interface between us, other utilities, the file system, and the kernel. Each shell process executes code that resides in a file in a system directory. The shell process gets CPU time, follows instructions in the code file, sends output and error messages to your terminal, and generally behaves like any other utility.

One of the shell's primary functions is to read each command line you issue, examine the components of the command line, interpret those pieces according to its rules of grammar (syntax), and then to do what you request.

Interacting with the Shell

Obviously, the basic way we communicate with the shell is to enter a command line from the keyboard that requests execution of utilities. When we examine the events carefully, even a simple command communicates a lot of information from our heads to the shell. A continuous cycle takes place.

1. At the shell prompt, enter:

   echo *HELLO*
   ls

   First, you typed the individual characters *e c h o   H E L L O* and then pressed ENTER. The shell executed a new process, passed it the string of characters *HELLO* as an argument, and told the new process to execute the code for **echo**. The shell did not send a new prompt to your screen until after **echo** completed its work. Then at the new prompt, you entered an *l* followed by an *s* and then another ENTER. The shell went through the steps needed to execute **ls**, and the output from **ls** appeared on the screen.

   • The shell displays a prompt.

- We enter a command and press ENTER.
- The utility runs, or we get an error message.
- The shell displays a new prompt.

Every time we ask for a utility to run, we are instructing the shell to start a child process to execute the code that is the utility.

2. Compare the **PIDs** for the **ps** utilities in the following:

   ps
   ps

The output should include both your shell and the **ps** with their process identification numbers. Each time we run a new **ps**, it is a new process.

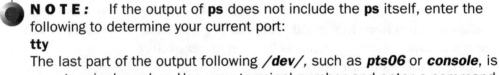

N O T E :   If the output of **ps** does not include the **ps** itself, enter the following to determine your current port:
tty
The last part of the output following **/dev/**, such as **pts06** or **console**, is your *terminal number.* Use your terminal number and enter a command like one of the following:
ps -t console
or
ps -t tty03
or
ps -t pts06
The **ps** should now be included. This is explored carefully in Chapter 11, "Controlling User Processes."

3. We are not always successful. Enter:

   wc -z *users_on*

The same cycle of events takes place, but when **wc** starts, it does not recognize the option **-z** and then exits sending an error message to your screen. A new shell prompt appears.

Examining Communication with the Shell

A lot happens between your entry of a command line and the execution of the utility. The shell must interpret each aspect of the command line.

1. Enter the command:

   ls

   The shell interprets these two characters as a request to execute the **ls** utility. Why not interpret the command as instruction to read the contents of a file named **ls**? Or to move the cursor to a lower section? Or to evaluate a variable named **ls**?

   Entering **ls** results in the execution of a program, a *utility*. Where is the utility code located? How does the shell find it?

   The **ls** utility locates the names of the files in your current directory and then formats a listing as output. The output comes to your screen. Why not write the results to a file? Why doesn't the output appear on someone else's display?

2. Enter the command:

   ls -l

   The output is a long listing of the files in the current directory. Is **ls -l** a different utility than **ls**, or is it the same code acting in some optional manner?

3. Make a mistake, leaving out the space between the utility and its option as you enter the following command line:

   sort-r users_on

   We get an error message indicating that the command *sort-r is not found.* But we know the **sort** command does exist. Why the complaint?

4. Enter:

   sleep 5

   Why does the shell wait until after the **sleep** is finished to present a new prompt? How does it know when **sleep** has concluded its work?

To explore this set of questions and related issues, we will carefully examine a series of familiar commands.

Parsing Basic Command Lines

The shell proceeds through a series of specific steps after we issue commands. When the shell receives a line of input from a user or file, the shell first decides whether the user intends the input line to be a command by itself or a part of a multiline command. The shell determines the number of processes to start, starts the child processes, passes arguments, does redirection of input and output, and finally tells the child processes what utility code to execute.

Identifying Complete Commands

When we type a command line, as soon as we press ENTER, the cursor moves to the next line, and the line that we typed is passed to the shell for interpretation.

1. Enter the following on two input lines:

   who
   | sort

   If we try to put a command on two input lines, the shell interprets the first line as a complete command and executes it, if it can, then attempts to interpret the second line as a command in itself. In this case, the shell complains bitterly about the second line not starting with a utility. The shell is programmed to interpret the ENTER as signaling the end of a complete command that it should start interpreting.

   Carefully examine how the shell responds to the following. To make it clear when to press ENTER, we explicitly specify it in this exercise.

2. Type the following commands:

   ls \ENTER
   -l ENTER
   history ENTER

   A long listing is displayed as though you entered the **ls -l** command on one line. The history output shows that even though the command **ls -l** was entered on two input lines, the shell interpreted them as one command line. The \ is interpreted by the shell as instruction to *not interpret* the special meaning of the single character that immediately follows. You pressed ENTER immediately after the backslash, so the ENTER is not interpreted by the shell. Because the shell does not find an *end-of-line character* indicating that it is a complete command, the shell reads additional input on the next line. When the shell encounters an ENTER that it can interpret, after the **-l**, the shell processes the two input lines as one command line.

3. As a more complex example, type in the following with an ENTER at the end of each line, all preceded by \ except the last:

   who \
   | tr \
   -d \
   12345 \
   | sed *5q*

The shell interprets the five lines of input as one command line because we told it to not interpret the first four ENTER keys. The shell interprets only the fifth.

4. Examine the history:

   history

Although we had many input lines, they are all part of one command line.

Identifying Command-Line Tokens

When we enter commands such as **ls -l**, we usually include several words or *tokens* on the command line. The shell interprets some tokens as utilities, others as arguments, others as files. How does the shell identify a string of characters as being a token in the first place? If a command line consists of one word or token, it is easy. The ENTER identifies the end of the command and therefore certainly identifies the end of the single token. But how does the shell identify individual tokens in a long command line?

Thereisnomusicwithoutthesilencebetweenthenotes.
There is no music without the silence between the notes.
ThereisnoEnglishwithoutthespaces.

We know the shell uses white space to identify the words or tokens of a command line.

1. Enter:

   grep*thepractice*

   The error message that appears is instructive. To the shell, this is a single token line, and the first token is always the program to run. Therefore, the shell complains that the *grepthepractice command is not found*.

2. Enter:

   grep *the practice*

   The spaces tell the shell how to divide the line into tokens.

3. Enter the following, including the several spaces between the tokens:

   ls   -l
   who | grep $USER

Both command lines run as though we included only one space between the tokens. The shell interprets one or more spaces as separating the tokens on the command line. "One space, Two space, Red space, Blue space," it makes no difference. One or many more spaces indicate where one token ends and another starts.

We are not limited to spaces when we want to specify multiple tokens.

4. Enter the following without spaces:

     who | wc>_filewho_

Even though there are no spaces around the | and > redirection characters, the shell still identifies the **who**, **wc**, and _filewho_ as separate tokens on the command lines. The shell interprets >, <, and | as special characters that control input and output for the utilities and files that are adjacent. The shells recognize them as instructions, not part of filenames, so spaces are not needed. We usually include spaces in command lines around each token or redirection to make it easier for humans to read the code.

5. Enter:

     echo _$USER$USER$USER_

The shell recognizes the $ as starting a new variable, even though no spaces delimit them.

Identifying Utilities to Execute

One of the first steps the shell must accomplish when it interprets a command line is to determine how many child processes to start. The shell must identify which tokens on the command line are the utilities to be executed because each one is executed in a child process.

Interpreting the Initial Word on a Command Line

Whatever string of characters we provide first on the line is interpreted by the shell as instruction or a utility to execute.

1. Enter the following at the prompt:

     abcde _fghij_

The shell responds that the utility _abcde_ is not found. The string _abcde_ is the first token on the command line, so from the shell's perspective, it must be a utility. Unable to locate _abcde_ in the system directories that the shell searches for utilities, the shell reports the _cannot find_ error message.

2. Try:

     _users_on_ **sort**

While we clearly intend the file *users_on* to be sorted, the shell draws no such conclusion. The first token must be a program or instruction.

Because C shell family variables are set using a different syntax than shells in the Bourne family (**sh**, **bash**, or **ksh**), the following works only in a Bourne type shell.

3. If you are using a C shell, start *one* of the following **sh** family shells:

   bash

   or

   ksh

   or

   sh

4. In an **sh** family shell, create a variable by entering:

   a=date
   echo $*a*

   This almost looks like we are violating the "first token is a program or instruction" rule.

5. Try the following, which includes spaces around the equal sign:

   b = hello

   The error message indicates that the command *b* is not found. The shell interprets the first token as the instruction. The space following the *b* makes it the first token.

6. Remove the spaces around the equal sign:

   b=hello
   echo $*b*

   Without the spaces, the first token includes the equal sign; thus, the shell interprets the first token as an instruction to create a variable. With spaces, there is no = in the first token. For that reason, variables are created in the **sh** family of shells with no spaces around the equal signs.

7. Evaluate the value of the variable:

   echo $*a*

   When $*a* is entered as an argument to **echo**, the value *date* is displayed on the screen.

8. Enter:

   $*a*

Interpretation of the command consisting of only the variable displays the current date and time. When the shell interprets the $a variable, it replaces the $a with its value on the command line. So in the first example the value, *date*, is passed as an argument to **echo**. In the second command line, the $a is replaced by its value, *date*, which is the first token on the line and is interpreted as the utility to execute.

Unless it is a shell built-in instruction like creating a variable, the first token is seen as a utility to execute.

If you started an **sh** family shell, you may want to exit from it now and return whenever needed. Alternatively, you can stay in it and exit both shells at logout.

Interpreting the Token Following a Pipe Redirection Symbol

The initial token on a line is the first utility. Many times, you have redirected (piped) output from one utility to another.

1. Enter the following commands:

   who | wc
   **who > ** *wc*
   ls -l *wc*
   more *wc*

   In the first command line, **wc** is placed after the pipe. The shell interprets **wc** as a utility to be executed and connects the output from **who** to the input of **wc**. The second command line includes *wc* after the > redirect. In this case, the shell does not interpret *wc* as a utility; rather, it is seen as the name to give a new file. The output of **who** is written to the new file *wc* when the *wc* follows a redirect. When the **wc** is the first token, it is seen as a utility. It is not the name **wc** that tells the shell to execute a utility, it is the location of **wc** on the command line that makes the difference. The first three rules of real estate are right: *location, location, location.*

2. As a further example, enter:

   ls | *abcde*

   The shell attempts to execute the utility *abcde* and pass it the output of **ls**. The shell again complains that the utility does not exist.

A word or token placed immediately after a pipe or at the beginning of a command line is interpreted by the shell as a utility to be executed.

Interpreting Tokens Following Semicolons

You can have the shell independently run one utility after another on a single command line without redirecting output from one to another.

1. Enter the following:

    ls; cd */tmp*; **ls; cd**

    The shell runs the **ls** utility and then, after the **ls** is completed, the change directory is accomplished. After you are in */tmp*, a new **ls** is run. After **ls** produces a list of files in the current directory, */tmp*, a final **cd** brings you home. There is no output redirection. Each segment separated by semicolons is an independent pipeline or command. They are run one after another as though you entered them one after another at the prompt.

2. Enter the following:

    cal *1752* > *yr1752* ; **sleep** *3* ; **ls -l** *yr1752* ; **wc** *yr1752*

    The semicolons separate the commands or pipelines on the one input line. When the first is finished, the second is executed, and so forth.

3. Enter:

    listz ; **date**
    sleep *2* ; **date**
    zzzz ; **sleep** *2* ; **listz** ; **date** ; **sleaze** *2* ; **sleep** *3*

    The shell interprets the semicolon as making no restriction on success or failure of the previous command. As soon as execution of the command to the left of the semicolon is completed, execution of the command to the right is started, whether the first is successful or not.

    The first token after a semicolon must be a utility.

Interpreting Tokens Following Logical AND Conditional Execution

You can run a command based on the successful outcome of the preceding pipeline in the same command line.

1. Have the shell run the following:

    daxx && echo *HI*

    You see an error message that the command *daxx is not found*. The command following the **&&** is the **echo** *HI*, which is not executed.

2. Enter:

> **wc -z** *practice* **&&** **echo** *HI*
> **wc -l** *practice* **&&** **echo** *hello*
> **date** **&&** **xxxxx**

The **&&** is interpreted by the shell as instruction to run the command that follows only if the preceding command line executes successfully. In the first command, the shell complains that:

```
wc: invalid option -- z
```

and so **echo** *Hi* is not run. The second command runs fine because **-l** is a valid option for **wc**, and once that is run successfully the **echo** *hello* is run. In the third command, **date** is successful. There is a **date** command, and once it is run, the shell tries to run the **xxxxx** command and complains:

```
xxxxx: command not found
```

A token following **&&** must be a utility.

Interpreting Tokens Following Logical OR Conditional Execution

We can also require conditional execution based on failure of the previous command.

1. Enter:

> **xxxx | |** **echo** *HI*
> **date | |** **echo** *HI*

An error message is delivered that *xxxx is not found*, but this time the **echo** command *is* executed. The **date** utility runs successfully, but the **echo** is not executed. If the command to the left of the double pipes is successful, the command after the | | does *not* execute. The shell interprets the | | as instruction to execute the command line following the | | only if the preceding command on the line fails. If the left is successful, the command to the right is not executed.

The token following a | | is a utility.

Conditional Execution Summary

Conditional Execution Using **&&**

- If the preceding command is successful, execute the command that follows.
- Likewise, if the preceding command is not successful, do not execute the command that follows.

Conditional Execution Using | |

- If the preceding command is not successful, execute the command that follows.
- Likewise, if the preceding command is successful, do not execute the command that follows.

Conditional Execution Using ;

- When the previous command is completed, whether successfully or not, execute the command that follows.

The impact of these conditional execution special characters is that the first token after a | | or && or a ; begins a new command or pipeline; hence, it must be a utility.

Interpreting Tokens in Command Substitution

We tell the shell that a token or string of characters is a variable by placing a $ in front of the variable name string.

1. Enter:

   echo *I am $USER with a home directory at $HOME*

   Because variables are clearly marked, they can be placed anywhere on the command line. Utilities are placed in command lines at the beginning following a pipe or after one of the conditional execution symbols. Often it is useful to execute a utility in another location on a command line.

2. Enter the following commands and compare the results:

   echo *today is* **date**
   echo *today is* `date`

   The resulting output of the second command line includes the output of the **date** utility, not the word *date*. If your output is *today is date* after issuing both commands, you probably used regular quotes, not backquotes. The backquote character is usually on the same key as the ~ character, often in the upper left of the keyboard.

   The shell first has the **date** utility executed and then replaces `**date**` on the command line with the output of **date**. The **echo** utility received as arguments *today is Fri April 23 14:31 2003*, which it sends to output, connected to the terminal. This is an example of shell *command substitution*. The shell interprets the backquote character as instruction to have whatever is inside the backquotes executed first. The shell then replaces the backquotes and command line that they enclose with the output they generated.

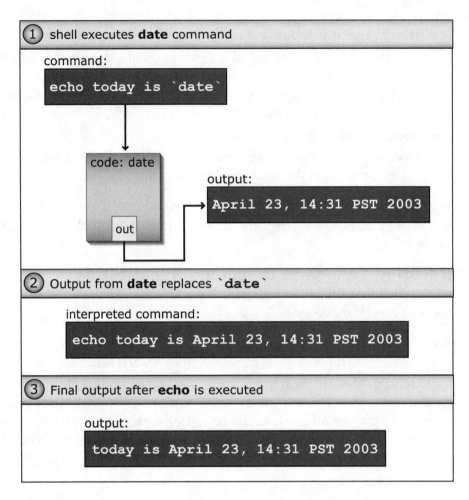

In addition to the backquotes, there is another syntax that instructs the shell to do command substitution.

3. Enter:

   echo *today is* **$(date)**

   The shell first executes the command line inside the $( ) and then removes the $( ) and its enclosed command from the command line, replacing them with the output.

4. List the files in the current directory:

   ls

5. Create a file named *some-files*, and include in it a line of text listing the names of four files in the current directory. For example, your *some-files* file might have this line:

first-file names lost-days west

6. After creating *some-files*, enter:

  ls -l `` `cat ``*some-files*`` ` ``

  ls -l $(cat *some-files***)**

The shell first executes the **cat** *some-files* command and then removes the command **cat** *some-files* from the command line. In its place, the shell puts the output that the command generated. This command substitution creates an executable command line of:

```
ls   -l   first-file   names   lost-days   west
```

The four filenames and **-l** are passed as arguments to **ls**, which creates a long listing of information about the four files:

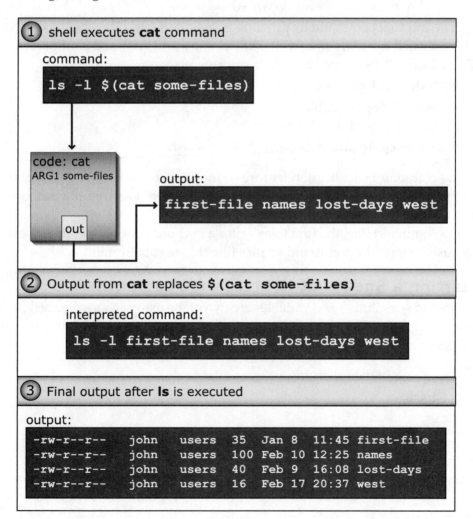

7. Have the shell use command substitution by entering:

> **wc `cat** *some-files*`
> **wc $(cat** *some-files***)**

The lines, words, and characters are counted in all four files whose names are in the file *some-files*. The shell interprets the backquotes as instruction to execute the enclosed command and replace the backquoted string in the command line with its output.

8. Try the following commands:

> **echo** *My current directory is* **`pwd`**
> **echo** *My current directory is* **$(pwd)**
> **echo** *there are* **`who | wc -l`** *users on*
> **echo** *there are* **$(who | wc -l)** *users on*

The internal command or pipeline is executed first. The shell takes the generated output, removes the backquotes and enclosed command, replacing the command with its output.

9. Include a utility that does not exist in a command substitution:

> **echo** *today is* **`aabbzz`**
> **echo** *today is* **$(aabbzz)**

The shell complains that *aabbzz does not exist*.

The command substitution feature of modern shells allows us to include the output of a command anywhere in a command line. We are not limited to just first token, after pipe, and so forth.

In a command line, the first token after a backquote or after **$(** must be a utility because it starts the command or pipeline that is substituted.

Starting a Shell that Is More Communicative

Command substitution and variables are two of the many actions the shell performs when interpreting the command lines we enter. We can start a shell that tells us what it is doing as it goes along.

1. Enter one of the following:

> **bash -x**

or

> **tcsh -x**

or

> **ksh -x**

2. Ask the shell to interpret variables by entering:

> **echo** *I am* **$USER** *at* **$HOME**

The output resembles the following:

```
+ echo I am john at /home/john
I am john at /home/john
```

The shell received your command line. It interpreted the variables, replacing them with their values. The shell then output the line beginning with the **+**, which is the shell telling us what interpretation it accomplished. The last line is the output from running the interpreted command line.

3. Examine how the shell does command substitution:

> **echo** Today is `` `date` ``
> **echo** Today is **$(date)**

First, the shell runs **date**, and then takes the output and places it in the command line, removing the `` `date` `` or **$(date)**. The **echo** command line is then executed with the output of **date** as part of its arguments.

4. With the **-x** shell in operation, try:

> **echo** *My current directory is* `` `pwd` ``
> **echo** *My current directory is* **$(pwd)**
> **echo** *there are* `` `who | wc -l` `` *users on*
> **echo** *there are* **$(who | wc -l)** *users on*

Each step of the shell's execution of the command lines is displayed with **+** lines, the final output is displayed without.

5. Whenever you want to exit the talkative shell, just enter:

> **exit**

Identifying Utilities on the Command Line

Examine the following schematic of a command line. Each blank line represents a token. What is each one (utility, file, argument)?

> _____ | _____ && _____;_____`\_\_\_\_\_ | \_\_\_\_\_` || _____

If a token is first on the command line, what is it? After a pipe? Following a semicolon? After a double ampersand? A double pipe?

In this example, every token must be a utility.

> utility | utility && utility ; utility `utility | utility` || utility

In summary, utilities are:

- The first command or token in a command line
- The token that follows a pipe (the utility to receive input)
- The token that follows **&&** (the utility to run if the previous utility is successful)
- The token that follows a semicolon (the utility to run after the command to the left of the semicolon is complete)
- The token that follows a ` (the utility to run for output to replace a backquoted command line)
- The token following **$(** another form of the command substitution syntax
- The token that follows **| |** (the utility to run if the previous utility is *not* successful)

Starting Processes to Run Utilities

Thus far, in this exploration we have examined how the shell receives a command line (pipeline); identifies the tokens using spaces, redirection, and other special characters; and identifies which tokens are utilities. The shell then starts child processes that will ultimately run all utilities. If the command pipeline contains three utilities, the shell must start three child processes.

1. Examine your current processes by entering:

    ps | sort | uniq

The output includes the shell(s), probably the **ps**, and a process running each of the other utilities, **sort** and **uniq**. The shell starts a child process for each utility on the pipeline the shell is interpreting.

The shell you are using is an active process, running in the foreground. The kernel has assigned it a **Process ID**entification number (**PID**) so it gets CPU attention when its turn comes up. The shell maintains variables and their values in memory; the code to run was located and is being executed. The input to the shell process is connected to your keyboard. Error messages and output from the shell come to your screen. The resources allocated to a running process are called a *process space* or a *process image*. The following depicts your shell process:

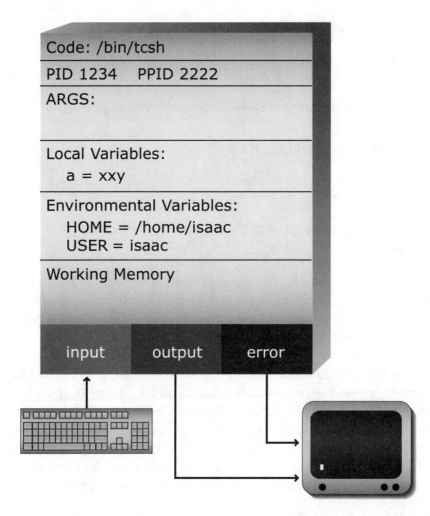

When you issue a command to run a utility, such as **ls**, the shell interprets the command line and then starts a child process that will ultimately execute the utility **ls**, which is no simple task.

The first thing the shell does is request that the kernel make an *almost* exact copy of its own process space. The copy of the process space includes the environmental variables, such as your user ID, your search path, and your home directory. Environmental variables are passed to child processes from the parent. Each time the shell starts a child process, it issues a kernel *call* that starts a child process, known as a *fork*.

Initial Input, Output, and Error Connections

The new (child) process space is a *copy* of the shell. Hence, the input, output, and error are connected to your screen and keyboard, as they are for your shell process.

1. Enter a command line that calls for no redirection:

   wc

2. Enter a few lines of text, such as:

   1 2 3 4
   second line
   third

3. Tell **wc** you are through with the end-of-file character:

   CTRL-D

The shell determined that one child process was needed. When it was started, it inherited from the shell the keyboard for input and the screen for output and error. After the process started executing the **wc** code, it read whatever you entered as input, counted, and wrote its results to output, which was still connected to your screen because we made no request to redirect it.

Because the child process inherits the shell's input, output, and error destinations, when the process later runs, you receive its output, not your neighbor and not a file, unless you choose to redirect the output. No matter how many processes you start after you log in, they are your login shell's child processes. They have you listed as the USER, your terminal for output, because your shell has that information. When child processes are created, they inherit information and input/output error connections from the parent.

Initial Code in Child Processes

At this point, the child shell is a copy of your shell and even has access to the same shell code as your current shell. The child process is not told the new code to execute until all redirection and argument passing "plumbing" is completed.

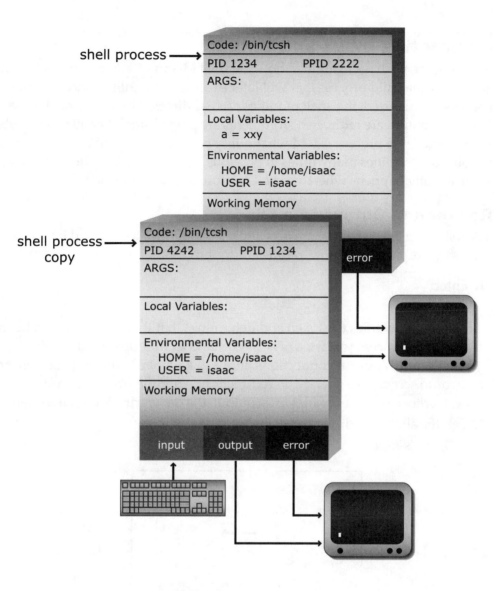

Redirecting Input and Output

At this point, we have examined how the shell identifies tokens, counts utilities, and starts one child process that will later execute each utility. Once the child processes are started, the shell modifies each as directed by the command line. Input and output are redirected, arguments are passed, and after all that plumbing is completed, the process is told what utility code to execute. We have redirected the output of utilities many times in previous exercises. This section examines what actually happens when the shell interprets redirection.

Redirecting Output to a File

The following exercises discuss how the shell identifies tokens and how child processes are called when we redirect output to files.

1. Enter:

   ls

   The shell identifies the token and determines that there is one utility; hence, one child process is started. The shell starts a child process that inherits the shell's input/output connections: input to keyboard, output to screen, and error to screen. We specify no redirection. After the process runs the **ls** code and writes the names of files to its output, the data is displayed on the terminal.

2. Tell the shell to redirect the output:

   ls > *ls-files*

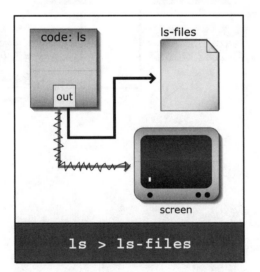

The shell's job is to interpret the command line. In this case, there is redirection instruction: the redirect symbol and a token that follows it, namely, **>** *ls-files*. The shell interprets the **>** as instruction to redirect the output for the new process away from the workstation screen and to attach it to the file named after the **>**, in this case *ls-files*. With the plumbing done, the process is told to run the **ls** utility. When the process has completed its tasks, it writes the listing to its output, which the shell previously connected to the file.

Redirecting Output to an Existing File

When you redirect the output of a utility to a *filename*, the shell creates the new file. What happens when the file you specify already exists depends on the shell you are using and how the *noclobber* variable is set.

1. Make sure *noclobber* is off, so the shell will clobber (overwrite) existing files when redirecting output.

   In the C family shell, enter:

   > **unset** *noclobber*

   In the **ksh** or **bash** shell, enter:

   > **set +o** *noclobber*

   When you redirect the output of a utility to an existing file, the Bourne shell (**sh**) interprets your command as instruction to overwrite the existing file, and there is no telling it otherwise. The **ksh**, **bash**, **csh**, and **tcsh** overwrite the existing file if the shell option *noclobber* is turned off.

2. Enter the following:

   > **head -10 /etc/passwd >** *testing*
   > **more** *testing*
   > **cal >** *testing*
   > **more** *testing*

   In each case, the shell starts a child process, redirects the output as specified, then later tells the process to execute a utility's code. If the file exists when the shell is redirecting output, the shell deletes the contents of the file and attaches it to the output of the utility.

   When you enter commands such as **sort** *file*, the **sort** utility reads the contents of *file* and outputs a sorted version. The original file itself is not sorted.

Often, we need to sort a file and want the file itself sorted, not just a copy on the screen. There is a temptation to redirect the output back to the file and to enter a command, as shown next.

3. Make a copy of *practice,* and then sort it using redirection, as follows:

   cp *practice pract-2*
   more *pract-2*
   sort *pract-2* > *pract-2*

4. Now examine the contents of *pract-2*:

   more *pract-2*

The shell first completes the interpretation of a command line, does all output redirection, and *then* executes the utility. In the **sort** command you just entered, the > *pract-2* is instruction to redirect the output of **sort** to an existing file. The shell empties the existing file before it attaches the output of **sort** to the file. The process running **sort** is then started and given the argument *pract-2*, which **sort** interprets as a file to read. When **sort** opens the file, it finds it is empty, making sorting quite easy. Be careful. Many an important file has been lost by accidentally overwriting it with output.

Protecting Existing Files

When we set the *noclobber* variable on, we are instructing the shells to not overwrite files by redirecting the output from a utility.

1. Set the *noclobber* variable *on* by entering one of the following commands:
   In the C family of shells:

   set *noclobber*

   In a **ksh** or **bash** shell:

   set -o *noclobber*

   At this point, the shell is told to not overwrite using redirection. What choice does it have when we later instruct the shell to redirect to a file?

2. Enter:

   who > *testing*

   The shell complains that the file exists and processes no further.

Escaping noclobber in the Shell

There may be times when you actually do want the shell to overwrite a file while you have the *noclobber* variable set *on*. You can specifically instruct the shell to overwrite a file even though you set *noclobber*.

1. Instruct the shell to overwrite using the output of a utility.

   C shell family:

   > **date** >! *testing*

   ksh or **bash** shell:

   > **date** >| *testing*

2. Confirm that the file was overwritten:

   > **more** *testing*

   By placing the exclamation point (!) after the output redirect symbol (>) in the command, you instructed a C shell to overwrite the file, if it exists. In the **bash** and **ksh** shells, the >| is instruction to overwrite even if **noclobber** is set.

Adding to an Existing File

With *noclobber* set, you cannot redirect the output of a utility to an existing file, but you can still *append* the output to the end of an existing file.

1. Enter:

   > **cal** >> *testing*
   > **more** *testing*

   The output of **cal** is at the end of the *testing* file.

Avoiding Accidental Removal of Files with Other Utilities

The *noclobber* feature is an instruction to the shell, not to other utilities.

1. Make sure there is no alias for **cp**, and copy a file onto *testing*:

   > **unalias cp**
   > **cp** *practice testing*

2. Examine the contents now:

   > **more** *testing*

   Even when *noclobber* is turned on, you can still accidentally destroy files using utilities such as **cp** or **mv** if you copy or move an existing file and use the name of another existing file as the second argument. The shell is not redirecting output; *noclobber* has no effect.

3. Enter:

   cp **-i** *practice testing*

4. You are prompted to confirm your choice to rename (and thus, overwrite) *testing*. Do not overwrite the *testing* file. Enter:

   n

To protect yourself from accidental removal of files with the **cp** and **mv** utilities, employ the **-i**, inquire, option to the utilities.

Employing Default Input

If a utility needs input to sort or count, we usually supply a filename argument or redirect something to the input of the process. What really takes place when we do not specify input?

1. Enter:

   wc > *junk-wc*

   The shell starts one process, connects the output to a new file named *junk-wc*, and then tells the process to execute the **wc** code. No file is listed as an argument, so **wc** does not open a file for data. Lacking a file to read, **wc** reads from input. The command line makes no request to redirect the output from a previous utility or file to input, so when **wc** reads from input, it finds your keyboard. Whatever you type is the input.

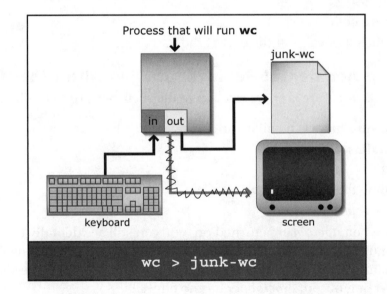

2. Enter:

> **grep** *the*

Only one argument is passed to **grep**. Because **grep** always interprets its first argument as the target search string, **grep** knows what to look for. No files are provided as additional arguments, so **grep** reads from input, which is still connected to the keyboard because it has not been redirected elsewhere.

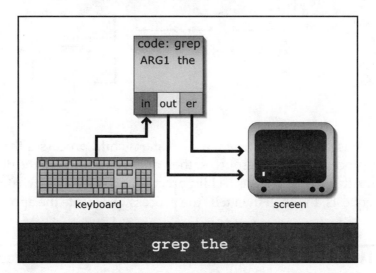

Redirecting Output to Another Utility

You have also, in previous exercises, told the shell to redirect output of a utility to the input of another utility.

1. Enter:

> **who** | **grep** *yourlogin* | **wc -l** > *n-on*

This command line tells the shell to start three child processes and to connect the output from the first child process to the input of the second. Then the shell is to connect the output from the second to the input of the third, and the output of the third to the file *n-on*.

After arguments are passed to the processes, the shell ultimately tells each process what utility code to execute. The **who** utility creates a list of logged-on users and writes to its output. The first process's output is connected to the input of the second process, running **grep**. This **grep** process selects all lines it reads from input that includes your login and writes them to output, which is connected to the input of the third process, running **wc**. After **wc** counts the number of lines it reads from its input (the output of **grep**), **wc** writes its results to its output, which is redirected to a file *n-on*.

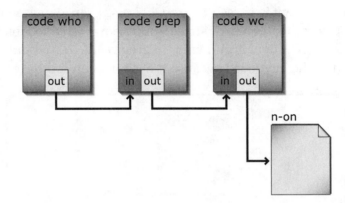

All of that is possible because the shell starts child processes that are copies of its own process space or resources, then does redirection of the default output and input. After the shell starts a child process and completes whatever plumbing the user requests, the shell then tells the process to execute the appropriate code.

> **S U M M A R Y :** Redirecting input and output from the default (workstation) destination to files and other utilities is one of the functions of the shell. The shell's output, input, and error are connected to your workstation. Creating a new process begins with making a copy of your shell's process space. The input, output, and error are therefore initially connected to your workstation and remain there unless you instruct the shell to redirect one or more of them to another utility or to a file.

Redirecting Error Messages

When the shell or a utility is unable to perform a command, an error message is issued. Unless you redirect it, error output is displayed on your workstation screen.

1. Enter:

   ls *xxxxA practice*
   wc *xxxxA practice*

The shell starts the child process, passes arguments, and then instructs the process to execute the correct code. When a file named *xxxxA* cannot be located, the child process sends an error message out the *standard error* door, which is connected to the terminal.

These error messages can be redirected from your screen into a file. The various shells work differently in this regard, as shown next.

Redirecting Error in Bash, Korn, and Bourne Shells

You can redirect standard error of child processes into a new file in **sh** family shells.

1. Make sure you are in a shell that is in the **sh** family.

2. Redirect standard errors into a file named *myerrors* by entering the following command:

   ls *practice xxxxA* **2>** *myerrors*

   With the **2>** errors added to the command line, no error message is displayed, even though you do not have an *xxxxA* file and the process running **ls** generates an error.

3. Examine the contents of the file named *myerrors*:

   more *myerrors*

   The error message was redirected to the file.

4. Redirect output and error messages to different locations:

   ls -l *practice xxxxA* **>** *lsoutput* **2>** *lserror*
   more *lsoutput*
   more *lserror*

   To the **bash, ksh,** and **sh** shells, **1>** or **>** is instruction to redirect output to a file, whereas **2>** is interpreted as the redirection instruction for the error messages of the process.

Redirecting Both Error and Output Together

You can redirect standard error and output into the same file in **sh** family shells.

1. To redirect *both* standard error and standard output to the same file, enter the following command:

   ls -l *practice xxxxA* **>** *outerr* **2>&1**

2. Examine the result by entering:

>   **more** *outerr*

The file contains both the long listing of the *practice* file and the error message that *xxxxA is not found*. The **2>&1** is instruction to connect the error (**2**) to the same place the output (**1**) is connected.

Redirecting Error in the C Shell Family

The C shells do not support redirecting the error independent of standard output. We can redirect both error and output away from the terminal.

1. In a **csh** or **tcsh**, enter:

>   **ls -l** *practice xxxxA*
>   **ls -l** *practice xxxxA* **>&** *outerr2*

In the C shell, the **&** after the redirection symbol tells the shell to route the standard error, along with the standard output, to the named file.

2. Or, route the errors and output to the next utility:

>   **ls -l** *practice xxxxA* **| wc**
>   **ls -l** *practice xxxxA* **|& wc**

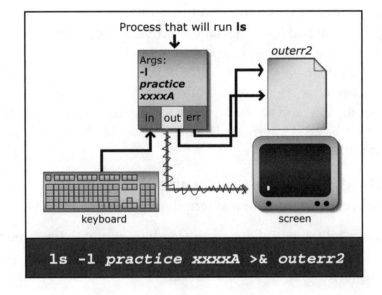

Passing Arguments to a Processes

Another task performed by the shell in interpreting your commands is to pass arguments to the utility being run. In an earlier exercise, you entered **ls-l** and received a message that the command was not found.

1. Examine the following command line:

    ls -l *practice*

When you enter this command, including the space between the **ls** and the **-l**, the output is a long listing of the file *practice*. As you have experienced, the shell uses the space as one of the ways to identify the pieces of a command line. The **ls** is the first token on the command line, so from the shell's view, it must be a utility. The **-l** is the second token. The string of characters *practice* is the third. These second and third tokens are the two arguments—strings of characters that have no special meaning to the shell. They are not the first token, and they do not follow a redirection symbol. Thus, they cannot be utilities. They do not follow >, so the shell does not see them as files to use in redirection. The shell is programmed to pass all leftover strings to the preceding utility as arguments for the utility to interpret. To **ls**, the **-l** argument has special meaning; it is instruction to produce a long listing.

The **ls** utility interprets any arguments not preceded by a minus sign, such as *practice*, as the names of files. The result of this command, then, is production and output of a long listing of information about the file *practice*.

Any tokens left over on a command line when the shell has completed its interpretation are passed as arguments to the associated utility. Each utility interprets its arguments in its own way.

Using Options as Arguments

Command options, as well, are interpreted as arguments by the shell. We often specify more than one option to a utility on a single command line, each preceded by a minus sign, each as separate arguments.

1. Enter the following multiple-argument command line:

    ls -a -l

The shell passes two arguments to the utility. These arguments are options that tell the **ls** utility to output a long listing of **all** the files in the current directory.

2. We can also specify two or more option flags on the command line as one argument:

ls -al

sort -rd *practice*

Only one argument, **-al** or **-rd**, is passed to each utility; however, the utility interprets the one argument as instruction to follow the code of two options.

Comparing the Shell's View of Options with the Utility's View

Options have meaning to the utility; from the shell's view, however, the options are just arguments to be passed to the utility.

1. Examine the following utilities and their arguments. Enter them if you wish:

ls -l

wc -l

pr -l *15 practice*

In all three instances, the shell passes the same argument, but it is interpreted very differently by the three utilities. To **ls**, the **-l** means produce a long listing. To **wc**, the **-l** is instruction to just output the count of lines in the input. To **pr**, the **-l** is instruction to make the page length equal to whatever argument follows.

Expanding Tokens on the Command Line

When the shell is interpreting the command line, there are several special characters that instruct it to expand the line. For instance, the wildcard * character tells the shell to include (at that location in the command line) all filenames. Variables are interpreted. The shell completes expansions and modifies the lines as appropriate.

1. If you are not communicating with a shell in the **-x** mode, start one now:

ksh -x

or

bash -x

or one of the others.

2. Enter the following:

ls -l *u**

who | grep *$USER*

The shell first expands the filename expansion *u** to all filenames that match, then places those names on the command line. Each is then interpreted as an argument to pass to **ls**.

The shell interprets *$USER* variable and replaces the variable name with its value. Your login name then becomes an argument that is passed to **grep**. To **grep** the string of characters it read as argument *1* is interpreted as the search string. All lines matching your login are output.

3. And enter:

> **who | awk '{print $1}'**

The shell does not interpret the **$1** in this command line, but passes it as part of the argument to **awk**. The first single quote instructs the shell to turn off interpretation of all special characters, so the string **{print $1}** is not interpreted; rather it is passed as a literal argument to **awk**.

Following this overview of command-line interpretation, the next section looks in detail at expansions.

Specifying the Code to Execute

After you enter a command that requests a utility be run, and the shell interprets the redirection and completes argument passing, the shell must locate the code for the program. The C shell variable *path* and the **sh** shell family variable *PATH* contain a list of directories that are searched by the respective shells to locate the code for a utility.

1. List the value of your search *path* variable by entering:
   In the C shell:

   > **echo $path**

   In the **sh** family:

   > **echo $PATH**

   The list of directories displayed shows the places the shell checks for the utilities you include in any command line. Notice that one of the directories in your path is */bin*.

2. List the contents of */bin*:

   > **ls -F /bin**

   The directory is full of the executables we know and love.

3. Obtain a long listing of the code file for the **ls** utility. Enter:

   ls -l */bin/ls*

   The output is similar to the following:

   ```
   -rwxr-xr-x 1 root   65536 Jun 23 2003 /bin/ls
   ```

   This file contains the executable program **ls**. It is the compiled version of the program, which includes a lot of machine-readable control characters that will disrupt a workstation dramatically if you try to display the file using ordinary file-reading utilities.

4. Examine the character strings in the file by entering:

   strings */bin/ls*

   A list of disjointed words and phrases is displayed. The **strings** utility ignores all machine code and outputs only the *strings* of ASCII characters that it finds. The displayed output from **strings** consists of the error messages and other character strings included in the binary file of **ls**.

Locating the Code

To run a utility, you can provide the shell with the path to the utility code file, rather than have the shell check the path to find the code.

1. Enter:

   /bin/ls -l

   When you provide the absolute path to a utility, the shell does not have to use the search path to locate the utility.

2. Locate several programs:

   which *ls*
   which *xterm*
   which *date*

Starting Code Execution

Once all the argument passing and redirection plumbing are completed, the shell has finished most of its work. The shell now tells each process what code it is to execute. While execution takes place, the shell waits for the process to complete before presenting a new prompt, unless we executed the command line in the background.

Instructing a Process to Execute Different Code

You have access to other shells on your system, probably **bash**, **tcsh**, and **ksh**. If you are not certain which shells are available, you need to identify at least two for the following exercises.

1. Enter:

   > **which** *ksh*
   > **which** *csh*
   > **which** *tcsh*
   > **which** *sh*
   > **which** *bash*

   If the shell responds with the path to the executable file, you can run that shell.

2. Have the current shell output its **PID**:

   > **echo $$**
   > **ps**

3. Identify what kind of shell you are running:

   Circle original shell: *bash tcsh csh sh ksh*

4. Start a child C shell, examine a list of processes, and get the **PID** for the new shell:

   > **csh**
   > **ps**
   > **echo $$**

   The list of processes includes the new child shell and the original shell and its parent.

5. Note the **PID** number for your new **csh** shell.   PID:_____

6. Enter:

   > **exec sh**
   > **ps**
   > **echo $$**

7. Note the **PID** for the **sh** shell.   PID:_____

   A process was running the code for the **csh** shell. You entered **exec sh**, and the same process is now running the code for **sh**.

8. Tell the process to stop reading the code for **sh** and to start executing the code for another shell:

   Enter whichever of the following uses another shell available on your system:

   > **exec bash**

   or

   > **exec ksh**

   or

   > **exec tcsh**

9. List your processes again:

   > **ps**
   > **echo $$**

   The same process has changed the code it is executing again. We are not starting child processes. The same process is active through all the previous steps. It has the same **PID**. However, the code that it is executing changes with each time we issue the command **exec**.

10. Instruct the process to return to executing the code you started with and the shell you circled in step 3 of this section.

    > **exec** *(original shell)*

Having the Process Execute the Correct Code

When the shell starts a child process, it is a copy of most aspects of the shell. Environmental variables, input, output, and error connections and code are all the same as the shell has. One of the last tasks is to tell the child process the correct code to execute.

Enter the command line:

> **grep** *the practice* **|** **sort -r** > *practice-the*

- The shell finds an ENTER at the end of the command line and concludes it is a complete command line to be executed.
- The shell finds a token at the beginning of the line and one after a pipe, concluding that two child processes need to be started.

- The two child processes are started, each with input connected to the keyboard, output to the screen, and errors to the screen.

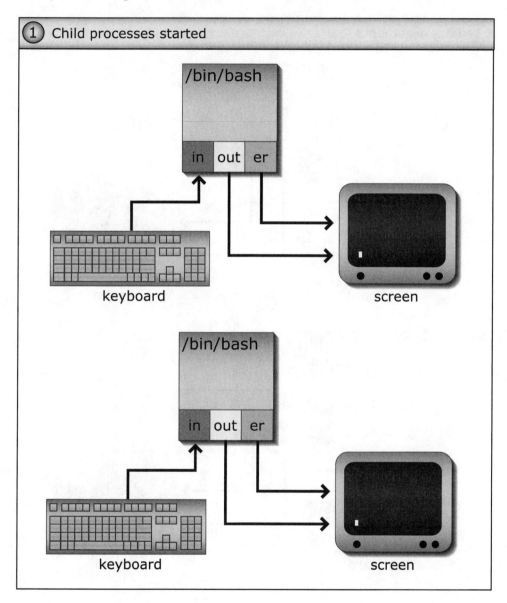

① Child processes started

- The shell passes arguments to the appropriate processes. The first process gets two arguments, *the* and *practice*. The second process gets one argument, **-r**.

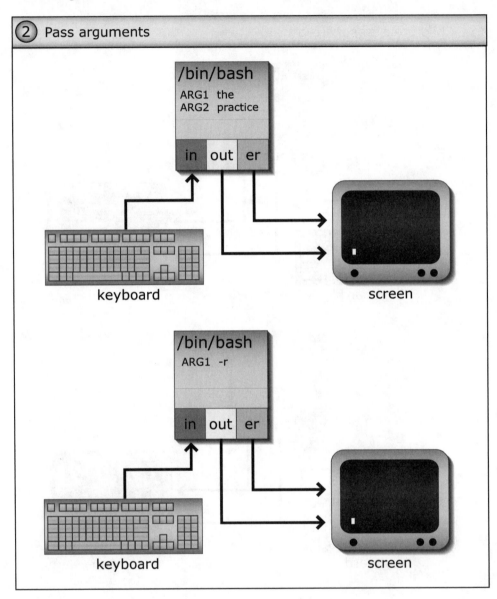

- The shell handles redirection. The | tells the shell to connect the output from the first process to the input of the second. The > tells the shell to connect the output of the second process to the file *practice-the*.

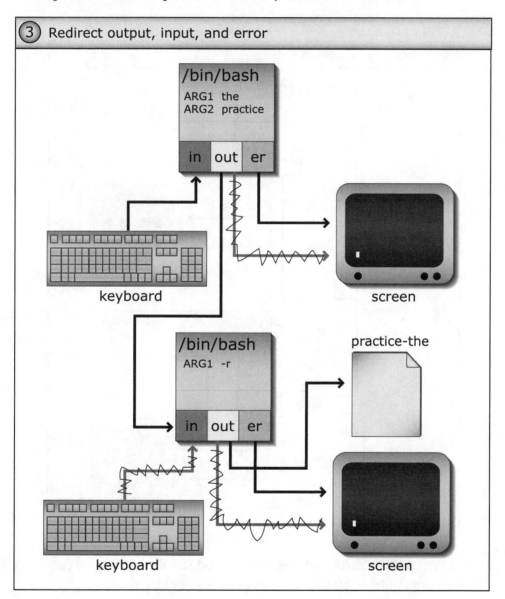

With the plumbing completed, the shell must tell each process the correct code to execute:

- To the first process, the shell issues the command: **exec grep**
- To the second process, the shell issues: **exec sort**

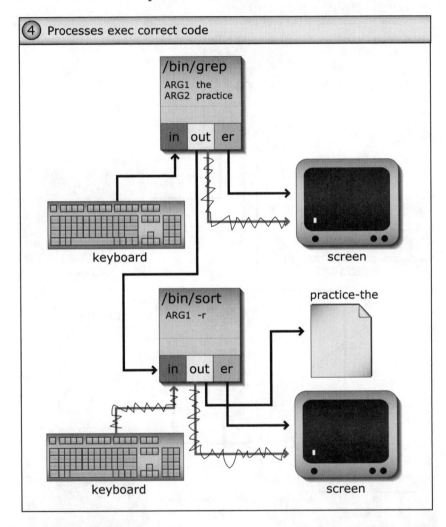

The two child processes start executing the code for the two needed processes. The shell waits until notified that both processes have exited.

- The first process, running **grep**, interprets its first argument as the search string, the second as a file to open and search. It locates all lines containing the string *the* and writes them to output, which the shell connects to the second process' input.

- The second process, running **sort**, interprets the **-r** as instruction to list its sorted lines in reverse order. It completes the sort and writes to output, which is connected to the file named *practice-the.*

As each process completes its work, it exits, notifying the shell. The shell displays a new prompt and we go on.

Examining the Exit Code

When a process is exiting, it tells its parent how things went.

1. Enter:

>**date**
>**echo $?**
>**wc -zz** *users_on*
>**echo $?**

The **date** utility ran successfully; it reported an *0* as its exit code. The variable **?** is interpreted by the shell as the exit code of the last process. There is no option to **wc** named **-z**, so **wc** exits and tells the shell that things did not go well. Exit codes other than zero are error codes.

- Try:

>**grep** *xxxx* */etc/passwd*
>**echo $?**

There is no output from **grep**. No error message, either. But **grep** reported an error exit code to the shell (*1*).

- In contrast, try:

>**grep** *aa* */etc/xxxx*
>**echo $?**

There is no file named *xxxx* in the */etc* directory. However, the exit error code is different, (*2*), conveying a different message. From **grep**, an exit code of *1* indicates that the file was located, but no matches were found. An exit code of *2* conveys the message that the file could not be located.

Every time a process completes its execution and exits, it informs its parent that it was successful with an exit code of *0* or unsuccessful with an exit code of other than zero. No additional information is passed to the parent process, just the exit code. Much like a kid coming home from a date. When asked by the parents "How did it go?" the reply is only "Fine." or "Terrible." Don't look for more.

Identifying the Function of Command-Line Tokens

The shell is programmed to ascribe the role of each command-line token or word *based on its location* in the command line.

Consider the following schematic of a command line. Each blank line represents a token. What role must each token have?

_____ _____ | _____ ; _____ _____ ` _____ _____ `

The various tokens have specific roles:

- The first token on a command line must be a utility to execute.
- The token that follows a pipe, semicolon, or backquote must be another utility.
- Any tokens left must be arguments to the foregoing utility.

Thus, the roles for each token in this example must be

utility *argument* | **utility** ; **utility** *argument* `**utility** *argument*`

This schematic represents a command line such as:

ls -l | wc -l; grep *alec* `**cat** *somefiles*`

Yes, the **cat** must be a utility and *somefiles* an argument. The backquoted command line **cat** *somefiles* is executed first, and its output replaces the backquoted command on the command line. The command line then looks like:

```
| ls -l | wc -l; grep alec first-file names lost-days west
```

Each token in the output of the command substitution is an argument passed to **grep**.

Here's another example. Each token plays a specific role in the following command line:

_____ _____ | _____ $_____ > _____ ; _____ > _____

The tokens following the > must be files, and a variable is evaluated. Once evaluated, the variable's value is passed to the previous utility as an argument.

Using the Model to Interpret Command Lines

We issue commands to the shells. We want work to be done. By considering how the shell interprets commands, we can formulate our request more effectively.

Completing Plumbing Before Execution

The key is the fact that the shell does the redirection and passing of arguments (plumbing) before telling the child process to execute the code.

1. Make sure *noclobber* is off:

   In **bash** or **ksh**:

   > **set +o** *noclobber*

   In **tsch** or **csh**:

   > **unset** *noclobber*

2. Enter:

   > **ls** *j**

   The files in the current directory with names starting with a *j* are listed.

3. Enter the following complete with error:

   > **wc -z** *users_on* **>** *junk-wc1*
   > **ls** *j**

   Even though the utility complains that the option does not exist, the new file *junk-wc1* is created. The shell starts a child process, passes arguments, and handles redirection. It creates the file and connects it to the output from the child process. *Then* it tells the process to execute the code for **wc**, which complains about the -z option and exits. The file was created by the shell before execution of the code.

4. Enter:

   > **daxxx >** *junk-wc2*
   > **ls** *j**

   Plumbing is completed first. The file is created and connected to the child process' output. Then, when trying to execute the code, the shell could not find the utility **daxxx** and the child process was ended.

5. Turn *noclobber* back on:

In **bash** or **ksh**:

   set -o *noclobber*

In **tsch** or **csh**:

   set *noclobber*

6. Enter:

   daxxxx > *junk-wc2*

   The shell complains that the file *junk-wc2* already exists. It does not complain that the utility cannot be found. The shell started a child process and then ran into trouble trying to complete the plumbing. Since the file already exists, the shell complains and exits without even trying to locate the **daxxxx** utility.

7. Try:

   daxxxx >> *junk-wc2*

   The redirection plumbing is successful, so the shell now encounters a problem executing a program that does not exist.

8. And finally, try:

   daxxxx > *junk-wc3*

   The command is not found.

   Enter:

   date > *junk-wc3*

Now the shell complains that the file exists. It was created in the previous step when the shell could not find the utility.

Instructing a Utility to Read Input

We tell the shell to connect input and output, but does the child read from input just because it is there?

1. Output only five lines of a file:

   head -5 *coast*

2. Sort all lines in a file:

   sort *coast*

   The child process is given an argument. To **sort**, the argument is a file to read and sort.

3. Read a file twice and sort the lines:

   sort *west coast*

   Two arguments, two files.

4. Provide no files to sort, and the child process reads from input:

   head *-5 coast* | **sort**

   The output from the process running **head** is connected to the input of the process running **sort**. Because **sort** has no filenames to open, it reads from input, the output of *head*.

5. Connect output to **sort**'s input and also pass it an argument:

   head *-5 west* | **sort** *coast*

   The output is the sorted version of *coast* with each line present only one time. The output of **head** is not read and sorted and included in the output. Because **sort** has an argument, it opens that file and sorts it. The fact that the shell connected the output of **head** to **sort** is not noticed because **sort** does not read from input when it has an argument filename.

   Of course, we can tell **sort** to read from input as well as the file argument.

6. Enter:

   head *-5 west* | **sort** *- coast*

When utilities such as **sort** receive a minus sign as an independent argument, they interpret it to mean *read from input*. In this example, **sort** reads from input and read the file.

Providing Ambiguous Redirect

This example is best examined in a **tcsh** or **csh**.

1. If you are not interacting with a **tcsh** or **csh**, start one.

2. Consider the following command before pressing ENTER:

   who *> who-junk1* | **sort** *-r*

   We are telling the shell to start two child processes and to connect the output from the first process to a new file, *who-junk1*. We are also asking to connect the output of the first process to the input of the second. How can the output be redirected to two places?

3. Press ENTER and see how the shell responds.

   The **csh** family agrees it is ambiguous and quits.

4. Try the command again in a **ksh** or **bash** shell.

These shells ignore the second redirection request and simply connect the output of **who** to the file. It doesn't really do as we want; it doesn't complain either.

Changing How the Shell Executes a Command

In the analysis of command-line interpretation covered thus far, we have considered only commands executed in the foreground. We can also have the shell run processes in the background and temporarily interrupt execution.

Running a Command Line in the Background

When you enter a command line, the shell interprets it, executes needed utilities, and waits until the utilities complete their work. You can ask the shell to interpret, execute, and *not* wait, but instead to present a new prompt to you for continued interaction.

1. Enter the following command and observe the results:

sleep 5

When **sleep** has counted to 5, it exits. Your shell's wait is over, so it presents a new prompt.

2. Put **sleep** in the background by entering:

sleep **200** &

When you enter this **sleep** command line with the **&**, the shell immediately presents a new prompt. You can enter a new request. A command consisting of utilities, arguments, and redirection terminated by an ENTER is called a *job*. With the **&**, the whole *job* is placed in the *background*. The CPU still works on the job. The shell does not wait for the **sleep** to finish, but instead displays a prompt immediately.

3. List your current processes:

ps

The child process running the **sleep** is among the processes. It will continue until it counts to *200* and exits, a little more than three minutes.

Suspending a Job

Modern shells allow us to *suspend* a job in midstream and return to it later.

1. Start editing a file:

    vi *practice*

2. Add a line of text to the *practice* file.

3. Return to the command mode of **vi**:

    ESC

    and then press:

    CTRL-Z

    The shell presents a prompt, and the **vi** display is no longer active.

4. Enter:

    ps

    The **vi** job is still in the list of processes. It is suspended, not killed.

    The output shows that **vi** is still a process on your process list; however, it is not active. It gets no CPU attention, but it is not destroyed, either.

> **N O T E :** If the CTRL-Z does not suspend the job in your shell, enter **stty -a** and in the output locate **susp=** (*value*). Whatever is listed as the *value* should be used in this exercise instead of CTRL-Z.

5. Bring the job back into the *foreground* by entering:

    fg

6. Put the file away and quit the editor:

    :wq

We can suspend the processing of a foreground job and return momentarily to the shell using CTRL-Z. To bring the job back into the foreground, we enter **fg**. It is much like photography. I load my camera and start taking pictures. Then I hang the camera around my neck and concentrate on other tasks. I don't remove the film or put the camera away. It is in the background. Later I bring it into the foreground and take more pictures.

Identifying Multiple Processes in One Pipeline

Being able to suspend a job allows us to examine aspects of how the shell works. Processes are started as part of the shell's interpretation of a command line.

1. Enter the following:

   sort | **grep** *aaa* | **tee** *bb* | **wc**

   Four processes are started. Because this command line does not specify an input source for **sort**, it reads whatever you enter at the keyboard as input data.

2. Enter the following text:

   baaa
   abab
   aaaahhh

   The job is in the foreground. We are giving input to **sort**, not to the shell.

3. Suspend the **sort grep tee wc** job by entering:

   CTRL-Z

   The shell prompt is displayed.

4. Request a list of processes currently running, with:

   ps -l

   All four of the processes that you requested in the last command—**sort**, **grep**, **tee**, and **wc**—are still running. They were not told to exit. The job was suspended, the processes get no CPU attention, but they are not gone. The output of **ps** shows that each utility included on the command line is executing in its own child process and that all have the same parent, your shell. They have the same number in the **PPID** field that your shell has in the **PID** field.

5. Bring the job back to the foreground by entering:

   fg

6. With the job in the foreground, enter another line:

   This is all.

7. Inform **sort** that you are finished:

   CTRL-D

   The output from the job consists of the lines entered before and after the job was suspended.

When we ask for a utility to be executed, the shell starts a child process to run the code. If we don't say otherwise, it is executed in the foreground. The shell waits until the child exits before interacting with us. We can also put the job in the background, where it continues execution, even though at the same time we continue interacting with the shell in the foreground to do other tasks. If a job is in the foreground, we can suspend it with CTRL-Z and interact with the shell. If a job is suspended, no work is done on the processes that constitute the job, but it is not destroyed either. It just sits until we ask for it to return to the foreground with **fg**.

The topic of process control and suspension is examined in detail in Chapter 11.

8.2 Shell Command-Line Expansion

The previous section examined how the shell walks through interpreting command lines that we issue. Simple commands work as described. If we issue more complex lines, the shell must expand tokens to their meaning. In the previous sections, you explored how the shell interprets command lines, matches filenames, and executes processes to run the requested utilities. Several aspects of command lines are given to the shell in a sort of shorthand notation. We say we want the number of lines, words, and characters in all files in the current directory by entering **wc** * at the prompt. The shell must expand the wildcard * to match all filenames. Variables, command substitutions, filenames, and special character expansions are part of the shell's features.

Using Shell Characters to Expand Filenames

You can create filenames that contain common base names with number or letter extensions. Then, by entering shell commands that contain special characters, you can match and select the filenames in groups. As the shell examines each command line you enter, it looks for the special characters. Some characters are interpreted as *wildcard* characters and used for matching unspecified characters of a filename. Other characters are used to select a range of characters for matching with filenames. This feature is often referred to as filename *expansion* or filename *matching,* because you can select many filenames while entering only one name with special characters embedded.

Matching Filenames Using Wildcard Characters

We often name files using a scheme that creates a relationship among the files. Using wildcard characters, we can list groups of filenames that have similar characteristics.

1. For instance, create empty files with the following commands that employ **touch**:

   touch *chap chapter2 chapter5 summaries*
   touch *chapter chapter3 chapter5A chapter57 chapter62*
   touch *chapter1 chapter4 index chapterA chapterR chapter2-5*

   The **touch** command changes the date associated with an existing file named as an argument. If the file does not exist, **touch** creates it as an empty file. It is a quick way to create files.

   This is another place where interacting with a shell using the **-x** option is very useful.

2. Enter:

   ksh -x

   or

   bash -x

   or whatever shell you want, with a **-x** option.

3. Obtain a long listing for a selection of these files:

   ls -l *chap**

   This command contains the asterisk * wildcard character, which matches any character. The first **+** line shows that the shell matches the string *chap** with names of files in the current directory. It replaces *chap** on the command line with all the filenames that begin with the characters *chap* followed by zero or more additional characters of any kind. Thus, the files named *chap*, *chap62*, and so on, are selected. The matched filename strings are passed to **ls** as arguments. The **ls** utility then produces its long listing about those files listed as arguments.

   The shell interprets the * and replaces it with the long list of filenames. Those names are passed to **ls**, which does its job. It is as though you entered the command line including all the filename arguments at the keyboard.

   The question mark **?** is a more limited filename-matching character.

4. Enter the following command:

    ls *chapter***?**

This time, neither *chapter* nor *chapter5A* is selected, because the **?** character matches any one character. There must be one and only one character, but it can be anything.

The ***** and **?** are two of the special metacharacters interpreted by the shell.

As the shell interprets the command line, it does not open files. It just matches the filenames with the string of regular and metacharacters you enter, and then passes this list of matching filenames as arguments to whatever utility precedes the arguments on the command line.

5. To explore how the shell interprets the command line, enter:

    wc *chap**

The shell interprets the filename expansion * and replaces the *chap** with all filenames that match. The names are passed to **wc** as arguments, so **wc** outputs a count of the elements in each file (0).

6. Try:

    wc *****

All files are counted.

Selecting Filenames Within a Range

You can have the shell match filenames that include letters or numbers that fall within a specified range.

1. Enter:

    ls *chapter*[2-5]

In this case, the files *chapter2*, *chapter3*, *chapter4*, and *chapter5* are selected, but neither *chapter1* nor *chapter5A* is included in the output. The number *1* is not included in the specified range, and the filename *chapter5A* has a character after the number, which is not specified in the requested range. The file *chapter2-5* does not match, because the [2-5] on the command line is interpreted by the shell as instruction to match one character in the range of 2 through 5, not the three-character string *2-5*. The square brackets tell the shell to match any filename that has the letters *chapter* followed by one and only one number in the range 2-5.

2. To include *chapter5A* in the match, change the command to:

    ls *chapter*[2-5]*

Adding the * tells the shell to expand the filename *chapter* to include one character from the list of numbers 2, 3, 4, 5, and then zero or more of any other characters.

You can select filenames that contain more than one specified range of characters.

3. Try this command:

   ls *chapter[0-9][0-9]*

The selected filenames now include *chapter57* and *chapter62*, because they are the only filenames that start with *chapter* followed by one digit and then followed by another digit.

The characters listed in the brackets need not be a range. A list of acceptable values works, too.

4. Enter:

   echo *chapter[R3A1]*

The output is *chapter1*, *chapter3*, *chapterA*, and *chapterR*.

Using the Curly Brace Expansion Characters to Specify Filenames

The curly brace characters, { and }, are also used by the **bash** shell and modern **ksh** shells for matching and creating multiple filenames from one pattern.

1. Enter the following:

   echo *chapter{1,3,5A}*

2. Use the curly braces to attempt to select all files in a range:

   echo chapter{1-7}

The curly braces match existing filenames if each match is specified in the braces, but will not expand ranges.

The curly braces can be used to expand a range for creating files or directories.

3. Create five new files by entering:

   touch *ABC{1,2,3,4,16}*

   ls *AB**

The shell creates new files with the name *ABC* as the base name, and then adds each of the strings in the curly braces. Hence, new files are created with names *ABC1*, *ABC2*, *ABC3*, *ABC4*, and *ABC16*.

You may wish to make multiple directories that all begin with the same name.

4. Enter:

    mkdir *Newprojects-{one,two,three}*

5. Now examine the results:

    ls

The shell created three new directories with the same base: *Newprojects-one*, *Newprojects-two*, and *Newprojects-three*.

In the command you just entered, the curly braces around the strings *one*, *two*, and *three* tell the shell to use each portion to create a new file or directory name.

Creating and Using Local Variables

Throughout the previous chapters, we have been employing variables to hold information. We created variables, changed their values, and evaluated them.

This section takes a careful look at variables of two different kinds. If a shell keeps a variable private and does not give the information to child processes, it is a *local* variable. If the shell does pass a variable and its value to its child processes, the variable is an *environmental* variable.

Examining How Both Families of Shells Work

For the following exercises, we suggest you complete the tasks first in a shell in the C family and then in a shell in the **sh** family by choosing one of the following approaches:

- Employ two windows on the graphical interface, one with a **csh** or **tcsh** shell running, and one with either a **bash** or **ksh** shell.
- Or, use virtual terminals accessible through the F keys to have one terminal running a **csh** or **tcsh** shell, and one terminal running either a **bash** or ksh shell.
- Or, operate in one shell, start a child of the other type when needed, and exit it back to the current shell after exploring what happens in the other.

Evaluating Existing Variables

When your shell was started, it was given the names and values of many variables. You have been using them in commands such as these:

    echo *$HOME*
    echo *$USER* (or **echo** *$LOGNAME*)
    who I **grep** *$USER*

1. Ask for a listing of many of the current variables and their values by entering:

   set | more

   and

   env | more

The variables displayed are available to you because they are in your shell's memory.

Creating and Changing Variables

The two families of shells each use their own syntax for creating a variable.

1. Depending on your current shell, enter one of the following commands:

   In a **csh** or **tcsh**:

   set *AA=200*

   In a **ksh, bash,** or **sh**:

   AA=200

   These commands instruct the corresponding shell to place in memory the variable named *AA* with a current value of *200*.

2. Ask the shell to evaluate the variable in a command line by entering:

   echo *$AA*

   The value of the variable *AA* is output to the screen.

   The shell interprets the **$** character as instruction to locate in the shell's memory a variable that has the name of the character string that follows the **$**, namely *AA*. Once the variable and value are located, the shell replaces the *$variable-name* (*AA*) with the variable's value on the command line. After the variable evaluation is completed, the command line reads: **echo** *200*. When executing **echo**, the shell passes one argument, 200, the value of the evaluated variable. The **echo** utility reads its arguments and writes them to standard output, in this case, connected to your screen.

   A variable's value is not etched in stone.

3. Enter one of the following commands:

   In a **tcsh** or **csh**:

   set *AA=wonderful*

In a **bash, ksh,** or **sh:**

AA=wonderful

4. Evaluate the *AA* variable again by entering:

echo *$AA*

The new value assigned to the variable is reported.

5. List your current variables:

set | more

The new variable *AA* is listed as one of the variables in your shell's memory.

Setting the Value of a Variable to Include Spaces

For programming purposes and user convenience, we often need to set the value of a variable to include characters that are special to the shell, such as spaces. In previous chapters, you created a series of files whose names are used in the next exercise.

1. List your files:

ls

If the files used in the next command are not in your current directory, use names of files that are.

2. Enter one of the following:

In **ksh** or **bash** or **sh:**

files='practice west coast respected'

In **tcsh** or **csh:**

set *files='practice west coast respected'*

3. With the variable set, ask the shell to evaluate it and list the current variables:

echo *$files*

set | more

The variable *files* consists of several tokens or words separated by spaces.

A variable of this sort is useful.

4. Enter:

    wc $files

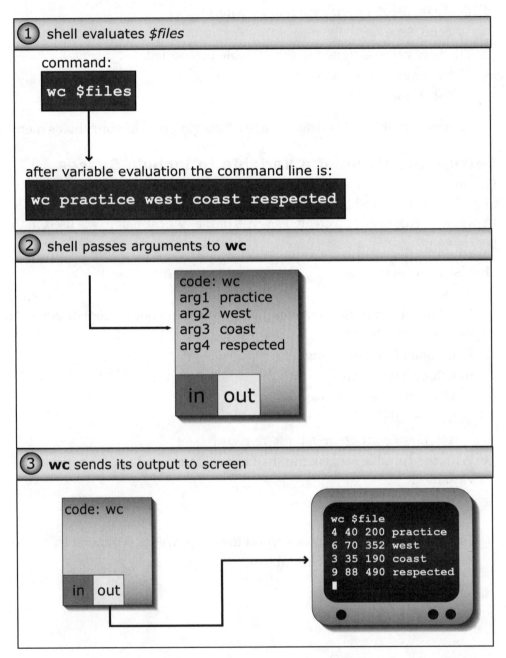

5. Try two other commands:

    ls -l *$files*
    head -3 *$files*

In each case, the shell replaces the variable with its value. Hence, the commands as executed are:

    ls -l *practice west coast respected*
    head -3 *practice west coast respected*

The job of the shell is to replace a variable with its value on the command line.

6. Try:

    $files

The shell replaces the dollar sign and variable name with the value:

    practice west coast respected

The token *practice* is the first one on the line, so the shell interprets it as the utility to execute. The result: *Command not found.*

Passing Environmental Variables to Child Processes

Variables created as we just created *AA* are in the shell's memory and are available as long as that shell exists. They are *local variables*; they are not passed to child processes. The shells allow you to pass user-created variables to child processes, but the mechanisms employed by the shells are different.

Creating a C Shell Family Environmental Variable

In the **csh** and **tcsh** shells, local and environmental variables are separate entities having lives of their own.

1. Make sure you are in one of the C shells.
2. Create or modify the local variable *AA*:

    set *AA=hello*

3. Instruct the C shell to create a new environmental variable, *BB*, by entering:

    setenv *BB 6060M*

The C shell syntax for setting environmental variables is:

    setenv *variable-name variable-value*

Two arguments are given to **setenv**; no equal sign is used.

4. Ask the C shell to list all of its environmental variables by entering:

    printenv | more

or

    env | more

The variable *BB=6060M* is included in the list.

5. Start a child C shell and evaluate the variables. Enter:

    csh
    echo *$AA*
    echo *$BB*
    printenv | more

or

    env | more

The output includes the value for *BB* but not for *AA*. As the child shell is started, it is given the environmental variable *BB* and its value, but is not given the local variable *AA*. When the child process (and it could be *any* child process) is created, the environmental variables and their values are given to the child process. The local variables are *not* passed to a child process.

6. Start a "grandchild" process:

    sh
    echo *$BB*

A child shell does not have to be the same type to inherit environmental variables. The environmental variable created with **setenv** in the C shell is passed to its child's child, a Bourne shell, **sh**.

7. Exit the current shell and the child C shell, returning to the shell (**tcsh** or **csh**) where you created *AA* and *BB*:

    exit
    exit

Listing Variables in the csh and tcsh Shells

When you enter the command **set**, the C shells list local variables. When you enter **env** on some systems and **printenv** on others, environmental variables are listed.

1. In your current C family shell, list the local variables:

    set | more

The local variable *AA* with a value of *hello* is included in the output of **set**. The environmental variable is not listed.

2. List the environmental variables:

> **env | more**

or

> **printenv | more**

The environmental variable *BB* with a value of *6060M* is output. The local variable is not.

Resolving Variable Conflicts in the csh and tcsh

When you created the environmental variable *AA*, you gave it the value of *hello*.

1. Ask the shell to evaluate the *AA* and *BB* variables with:

> **echo $*AA***
> **echo $*BB***

The local variable *AA* has a value of *hello*, and the environmental variable *BB* has a value of *6060M*.

2. Create a local variable with the same name, *BB*:

> **set** *BB=localvalue*

3. Evaluate the variables again:

> **echo $*AA***
> **echo $*BB***

In this C shell, you have two variables called *BB*—one local variable to which you assigned a value of *localvalue* and one environmental variable that you gave a value of *6060M*.

4. Tell the C shell to display its local variables:

> **set | more**

Only the local variables are listed.

5. Ask for the C shell's environmental variables by entering:

> **printenv | more**

or

> **env | more**

The variable *BB* is on both lists but with different values. The local variable *BB* was created using **set** *BB= localvalue* and is in the list displayed when you enter **set**. The environmental variable *BB* was created with **setenv** and is displayed when you enter **env** or **printenv**.

When you request evaluation of any variable, the C shells check the list of local variables first. If the variable is located there, the local value (in this case, *localvalue*) is used. If the variable is not found in the local list, then the C shell examines the environmental variable list where the value (*6060M*) is located. The result is that in the C shell, a local variable takes precedence over an environmental variable of the same name.

6. Create a child and ask for the value of *BB*:

    csh
    echo $*BB*

The environmental value is displayed. When a child process is created, the parent's environmental variables are given to the child. Local variables are not passed to a child, so in this exercise, the environmental value is the only one available.

7. Exit the child and return to its parent:

    exit

Removing Variables in the C Shell

At this point, you have a local variable and an environmental variable named *BB*.

1. Remove the local *BB* variable:

    echo $*BB*
    unset *BB*

2. List the current local variables:

    set

    BB is not there.

3. Request that the shell evaluate the variable *BB* and then list the current environmental variables:

    echo $*BB*
    printenv

    or

    env

The display says that *BB* is still a variable and has a value of *6060M*, which is the value you gave *BB* when you created the environmental variable. Even though you removed the local C shell variable several steps back, the environmental variable *BB* still exists. Its value is used when the variable cannot be located in the local list. *BB* is listed with the environmental variables.

4. Instruct the shell to remove the *BB* environmental variable by entering:

    unsetenv *BB*

5. Confirm the environmental variable is gone with:

    echo *$BB*
    printenv

or

    env

To remove a local variable in the C shell, enter **unset** *local-variable.* To remove an environmental variable in the C shell, enter **unsetenv** *environment-variable.*

Passing a Variable from an sh, ksh, or bash Shell to a Child

In the **sh** family of shells, there is only one mechanism for creating a variable. Once a local variable is created, though, we can make it available to child processes.

1. Access a **ksh** or **bash** or **sh** shell.
2. Create two new variables by entering:

    Var2=hello
    LL=Fun
    export *LL*

3. Create a child shell of any kind. Enter the appropriate command for a shell:

    csh or **ksh** or **sh** or **bash**

4. Evaluate the variables:

    echo *$Var2*
    echo *$LL*

The exported variable *LL* is available to the child process; the local is not. Using **export** *variable_name* makes the variable an environmental variable.

Modifying an Environmental Variable

We created the *LL* variable in the shell that is this shell's parent. The next steps will modify the value and then examine what happens when a new child shell is started.

1. Modify the *LL* variable's value:

   LL=evenmorefun
   echo *$LL*

   The new value is in the shell's memory.

2. Start a "child of the child" process and evaluate the *LL* variable:

   sh
   echo *$LL*

   The variable is passed with its new value. Once you tell a **sh** family shell to export a variable, the variable is given to all child processes and all their child processes, and so on. All descendent child processes receive the variable and whatever is its current value.

3. Exit from the two child shells, and return to the shell where you created *LL*:

   exit
   exit

4. Evaluate the variable we have been traveling with:

   echo *$LL*

The value of the variable is *Fun*, as it was when you created it in this shell. Child processes do not pass variable values to their parents. Although we changed the value of *LL* in a child shell, it did not report the change to the parent. The parent retains its original value.

Creating and Exporting in One Command

We can create and export a variable at the same time.

1. In a shell in the **sh** family, enter:

   export *newvar=enoughalready*

2. List the environmental variables:

   env | **more**

The creation and exporting are accomplished in one command line.

Listing Variables in the ksh, bash, and sh Shells

With the **ksh**, **bash**, and **sh** shells, the **set** command gives you a listing of *all* variables.

1. **set** | **more**

   Variables that are exported and those that are local are both included in the output of **set**.

2. To list only the exported variables in an **sh** shell, try each of the following:

   env | **more**

   or

   export | **more**

   The **set** command instructs the **sh** family of shells to list all variables, both local and environmental. The **env** command lists only environmental variables.

Removing ksh, bash, and sh Variables

The **sh** family of shells removes variables using the same **unset** command:

1. To remove the environmental *LL* variable in the Korn shell, enter:

   unset *LL*

2. Enter:

   set
   env

   LL is gone.

   Once *LL* is removed, it cannot be exported. It is not available in local or any child shells.

Removing Variables by Exiting the Shell

1. Create a child shell of any kind, for example, a C shell.

2. Set the value of a new variable:

   csh
   set *college*='*A great experience*'
   echo *$college*

   The value of the variable *college* is in the child shell's memory.

3. Exit the child shell and return to its parent, and then evaluate the variable *college* in the parent shell with:

   exit
   echo *$college*

When a child shell exits, it takes its memory of all variables with it. Parents are not informed of variables set in child processes.

Summary of Shell Features

Shell	ksh, bash, sh	tcsh, csh
Create local variable	a=xxx	set a=xxx or set a = xxx
Create environmental variable	b=yyy export b or export b=yyy	setenv b yyy
Remove local (C shell family)	--------	unset a
Remove environmental (C shell family)	--------	unsetenv b
Remove variable regardless of whether local or environmental (sh family)	unset a unset b	--------
List ALL variables (sh family)	set	--------
List environmental variables	env	env
List local variables (C shell family)	--------	set
Make local into environmental	export	--------

Determining the Command-Line Role of a Variable

So far in these examples, the variables were placed on the command line as arguments to the **echo** utility. Using arguments with **echo** is a good way to have the shell evaluate variables and display the result. The location of a variable among the other tokens on the command line determines the ultimate role of that variable's value in the execution of the command.

1. Set the value of a new variable to the name of a utility. Enter one of the following commands:

In a C family shell:

    set *L=ls*

In an **sh** family shell:

    L=ls

2. Instruct the shell to evaluate the variable using it as an argument by entering:

    echo $L

3. Have the shell evaluate the variable when it is the first token on the command line. Enter:

    $L

The names of the files in the current directory are displayed. When you enter *$L* and press ENTER, the shell is passed the command line **$L** for interpretation. It interprets the **$** as a request to evaluate the variable *L*. The shell consults its memory and determines that *L* has a value of the character string **ls**, which is then placed on the command line, replacing the *$L* token. The *$L* was the first token on the command line. When the **ls** replaces the variable on the command line, it becomes the first token. Because the first token must be a utility, the **ls** is interpreted as the **ls** utility string. The shell executes **ls**, which lists the filenames in the current directory.

4. Change directories and repeat the command from step 3. Enter these commands:

    cd */tmp*
    $L

The names of the files in the **/tmp** directory are displayed. The variable is again evaluated to be *ls* and the **ls** utility is run, because of the location of **ls** on the command line. The shell keeps the variable names and values in its memory, not in a file. Therefore, regardless of your current directory, shell variables are available.

5. Change back to your original directory.

The **$L** variable results in the **ls** utility being executed, because the shell does all the plumbing before execution. If the shell were to look for utilities before evaluating variables, the shell would complain about not finding the utility **$L**.

6. At the shell prompt, set two variables, each consisting of a string of characters that includes a space.

In a C family shell, enter:

> **set** *CC='-l -i'*
> *set DD='practice coast'*

In an **sh** family shell, enter:

> *CC='-l -i'*
> *DD='practice coast'*

7. Confirm the values by entering:

> **echo $CC**
> **echo $DD**

Now each variable has a value that consists of two strings of characters separated by a space.

8. Employ the variables in the following command lines:

> **ls $CC**

The variable *CC* has a value of *-l -i* when the shell evaluates it. Thus, after the variable's value is substituted, **ls -l -i** is the result. The shell executes **ls** and passes it the two arguments. The output is a long listing (**-l**) with inode numbers (**-i**) included for each file.

9. Extend the use of variables with the following commands:

> **echo $CC**
> **echo $DD**
> **ls $CC $DD**

A long listing, with inodes for the files *practice* and *coast*, is output. The shell evaluates all variables, creating the command line **ls -l -i** *practice coast.*

10. Variable interpretation can be carried to the limit with:

> *$L $CC $DD > $L*

As a result of this command line, the shell interprets the *$L* variable (created several steps back) as **ls**, the *$CC* as **-l -i,** and *$DD* as *practice coast*. After expansion, the resulting command line is:

```
ls -l -i practice coast > ls
```

The shell replaces the variables on the command line, then interprets the resulting values as whatever is appropriate for that location on the line.

Interpreting Role of Expanded Tokens on the Command Lines

In previous exercises, we expanded the value of a variable to provide an argument to a utility. If the variable has a value that includes several tokens, the outcome is more complex.

1. Enter:

   wc *$DD*

   The shell replaces the variable *DD* with its value *practice coast*. Now the shell passes *two* arguments to **wc**, which interprets each as a file to open and examine. The original variable becomes two arguments.

   Filename expansion also produces multiple tokens.

2. Create a directory to play in:

   mkdir *ShellTest*
   cd *ShellTest*
   ls

   You are now in a directory that contains no ordinary files.

3. Create three small files with:

   cal *>* *a*
   head *-10* */etc/passwd* *>* *b*
   cp *~/coast* *c*

4. Enter:

   grep *a b c*

   Given three arguments, **grep** interprets the first as the target search string. It sees the second and third arguments as files to examine. It does not locate lines in *a* that contain the character *a*. To **grep**, the first argument is the target and the remainder are filenames.

5. Ask to search for *a* in all files:

   grep *a* *

   The shell replaces the * with the filenames, *a b c,* so the command line is:

   ```
   grep   a   a   b   c
   ```

The first argument is *a*, so that is the target. The second, third, and fourth arguments (*a b c*) are seen as files. All three are examined.

6. Carefully examine the output from the following:

    grep *

The shell replaces the * with filenames *a b* and *c* and then passes all three as arguments to **grep**, which interprets the first argument (*a*) as the target and the remainder (*b* and *c*) as files to open.

8.3 Customizing How the Shell Functions

The shell includes a wide variety of customizable features that you can use or not, as you see fit. This section examines how, as a user of the shell, you can modify the path of directories the shell searches when you issue a command, specify the contents of the shell's prompt, and include instructions in the startup files to tailor how the shell behaves.

Using and Modifying the Search Path

When we issue a command, the shell must locate the code to execute. The directories in the *path* and *PATH* variables are searched for the chosen executable when we issue a command.

1. Enter:

    **echo $*PATH*

Changing the path Variable in the C Shell

The *path* variable can be changed to add new directories.

1. In your home directory, create a directory named */bin* if you do not already have one there:

    cd
    mkdir *bin*

2. Modify your path with the following command:

    set *path=($path ~/bin)*

    Whenever the shell sets the value for a variable in a line like this, it starts by evaluating the right-hand side. Once the new value is determined, the shell assigns it to the variable listed on the left. The variable *$path* is evaluated first. The string *~/bin* is added to the list of directories in the path, and then the new path is assigned to the variable *path*. The result is that the value of *path* becomes the current path plus *bin* located in your home directory.

3. Confirm the new value for *path*:

      echo $path

4. Create a script named *2day* in the *bin* directory of your home directory. It should contains one line:

      date

5. Make the script executable and run it to confirm that it works.

6. Change directories and attempt to run the script by entering these commands:

      cd /tmp
      2day

   Even though the script is in your C shell path, the C shell does not find *2day*.

7. Enter:

      rehash

8. Now run the script:

      2day

   The C family of shells cheats. Instead of looking in all the directories in the path every time you enter a request for a utility, the shells keep a listing of the utilities in your path and which directory they are in. When a C shell is started, it searches the complete path and creates a cheat sheet (*hash table*) of utilities and their directories. The shell creates its list when it is started, when we change the directories listed in the *path* variable, or when we instructed the shell to do so with **rehash**. Once the table is created, the shell can locate a utility much faster, because it only needs to consult the table, rather than a dozen directories.

   Once you modify the contents of a path directory, you must either log out and log back in, or enter the **rehash** command, to get the shell to re-create its table of utilities to reflect your changes.

Examining Elements of the Search Path in the C Shell

1. Make sure you are in a **csh** or **tcsh** shell.

2. To examine your current path, enter:

      echo $path

   The output is a series of directories, such as:

```
(/usr/local/bin /usr/X11R6/bin /bin /usr/bin  .)
```

The directories to be searched are separated by spaces. The . is the current directory, wherever you are in the file system.

The *path* variable is a local variable. Normally, you assign its value in one of the *startup* files so that its value is available to each shell you create.

In addition to *path*, the C shell also maintains (but does not use for locating commands) the environmental variable *PATH*. This variable contains the same information as *path*, but in a format that is acceptable to other shells, such as the **ksh**, **bash**, and **sh**. Because *PATH* is an environmental variable, it is passed when you request a child shell in the **sh** family. In the C shells, the two variables are intertwined, in that whenever you change the value of one, the other is automatically updated to reflect the change.

Whenever we add a new directory of commands or load a new application on a system, the path administrator either puts the new commands in a directory currently in the user path, or changes the path for the users to include the directory where the new commands are located. We will modify the path to include a local directory.

Adding the Current Directory to the Path
If the current directory is not listed among the directories in the path, you can add it.

1. Enter:

   set *path=($path .)*

First, the current value of the variable *path* is evaluated, the space and dot are then added, and this new value is assigned to the variable *path*.

Modifying the Path in the ksh, bash, and sh Shells
Unlike the C shell, the **sh** family of shells maintains only one path variable, *PATH*.

If you are not in a **ksh** or **sh** or **bash**, enter one of them to do the following.

1. In an **sh** family shell, enter:

   echo $PATH

   The format of the shell *PATH* variable is the same as the C shell's *PATH* variable. The directories in the path are separated by colons.
2. Add a new directory to the existing Korn shell path list by entering:

   PATH=$PATH:~/sh-bin

   In this case, you are adding *~/sh-bin* to the end of the string of directories in your path.

3. Create a new script in your *~/sh-bin* directory and make it executable.

4. Change directories to */tmp* and run the script.

Because the Korn shell actually checks the directories listed in the *PATH* variable rather than referring to a hash table, when we modify the path, the shell can immediately locate the script.

Including the Current Directory in the sh Shells' Paths

A colon (:) at the beginning or end of a path string is interpreted by the **sh** family of shells as instruction to search your current directory. You can also place an empty field using two colons (::) or explicitly request the current directory, anywhere in the path, using a dot. If your current directory is to be included in your *PATH* variable, for security reasons it is best to have it listed last, as in:

```
PATH=/bin:/usr/bin:/usr/local::
```

If your current *PATH* does not include the current directory, you can add it.

1. Enter:

   PATH=$PATH:.

The old *PATH* is evaluated. The colon dot is added, and then the resulting construction is assigned to the variable *PATH*.

Creating Personalized Shell Prompts

The shell displays its prompt, we respond, the shell rewards us by doing as we ask, the shell displays a prompt, we respond. Pavlov would be proud. The original prompts were single-character messages: $ in the **sh** and the % with the **csh**. Modern shells allow us to customize them extensively. For example, you may want to have the full pathname of your current directory displayed as a prompt. Unfortunately, if you were to set the prompt to include your current directory, when you then change directories, the prompt would indicate you were still in the previous directory. The next sections describe how you can tailor your prompt in the various shells.

Modifying the Prompt in the tcsh Shell

The **tcsh** provides for quite elaborate tailoring of the prompt.

1. Enter:

      set *prompt*='! %c %% '

   The prompt now includes the current command history number, the name of the current directory, and a percent followed by a space.

2. Change directories to */tmp*:

   The prompt reflects both the new history number and new current directory.

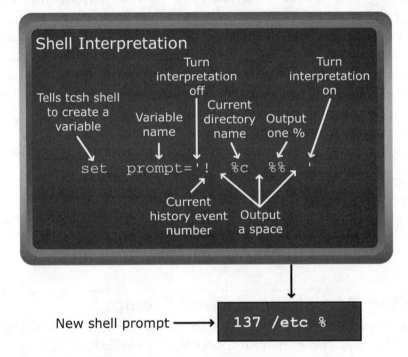

New shell prompt ⟶   137 /etc %

The shell variable *prompt* is evaluated each time the prompt is displayed, and all internal % variables are evaluated at that time. When you change directories, the prompt is reevaluated and the new directory is included in the display.

   The **man** and **info** pages for the **tcsh** describe the collection of variables you can use in constructing a prompt.

Modifying the Prompt in the ksh and bash Shells

1. Enter the following:

      echo $PWD

   The value of the variable *PWD* is the current directory.

2. In a **ksh**, enter the following:

    PS1='! $PWD $ '
    cd /tmp
    cd

The value in the variable *PS1* is used by the **ksh** as its prompt. Whenever it is time to display the prompt on the screen, the shell first evaluates any variables in the contents of the prompt variable and then displays the results. The *PWD* has a value equal to the path to the current directory. Every time you change directories, *PWD* is reset. Because the variable *PWD* is evaluated at every prompt display, the prompt includes the current directory. Essentially, any variable can be included in a **ksh** prompt.

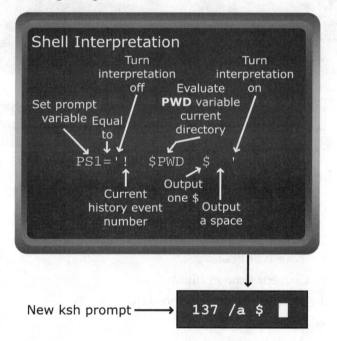

New ksh prompt ⟶   137 /a $

Modifying the Prompt in a bash Shell

The **bash**, like the **tcsh**, provides a wealth of tailoring possibilities.

1. Enter:

    PS1='\! \W $ '

The prompt includes the current history event number (**\!**), current directory (**\W**), the dollar sign, and then a space.

2. To see some of the power of the **bash** features, enter:

    PS1='\h \t \d \W \n \! *bash$* **'**

The prompt includes the current host, time, date, and current directory on the first line, followed by the history event number and *bash $* on the second line.

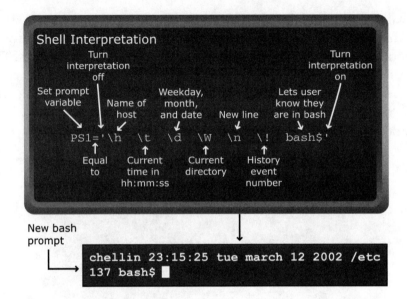

3. Change directories and return home:

    cd */etc*

    cd

The prompt variables just used are:

- **\h**   Name of host
- **\t**   Current time in hh:mm:ss
- **\d**   Weekday, month, and date
- **\W**   Current directory
- **\n**   New line
- **\!**   History event number

The **man** and **info** pages on **bash** describe the full collection of prompt variables in the section titled *PROMPTING*.

Modifying the Secondary Prompt in the sh Shells

When we enter a command that is incomplete, the shell presents a secondary prompt to ask for the remainder.

1. For example, in a **ksh** or **bash**, enter:

   **ls > **

   And immediately press:

   ENTER

   The shell displays a secondary prompt, usually a > to indicate that the shell is waiting for the remainder of the command line.

2. Complete the command:

   -F

   and press ENTER.

3. List the current shell variables:

   set

   Among the local variables are:

   PS1

   PS2

   The value of the *PS1* variable is the string the shell presents as its primary prompt every time it is ready for your next command.

   The *PS2* variable is the string the shell displays whenever it needs the remainder of a command line. It is currently > by default.

4. Enter:

   PS2='-2-$ '

   With the secondary prompt modified, try it.

5. Enter:

   **ls **

   -F

   This version of the secondary prompt is clearly a prompt, not a redirect. Later you can modify the startup files to have every shell employ the tailored prompts.

Modifying the Prompt in a csh Shell

The **csh** provides a much more limited set of prompt tailoring options.

1. Enter:

   set prompt='! *csh% '*

   The prompt includes the history event number, the string *csh %*, and a space.

8.4 Employing Advanced User Features

Built into the shell are several features that make issuing commands more efficient. Previously, we have used history, command-line editing, aliases, and user-created variables to issue command-line instructions more effectively. The shells also provide built-in shell variables, filename completion, and a method for creating a path of directories for file location. Collectively they provide powerful assistance when using the shells.

Employing Shells of Both Families

For the following exercises, we suggest you complete the tasks first using a shell in the C family and then again with a shell in the **sh** family. Choose one of the following approaches:

- If you are using a graphical interface, start two windows. In one window, execute a **csh** or **tcsh**, and in the other window, start a **bash** or **ksh** shell. As you complete the exercises in both windows, you can compare how they behave.
- If you are using Linux without graphics, you can use virtual terminals accessible through the F keys. Start a **tcsh** in one virtual terminal, and start a **bash** or **ksh** shell in the other terminal.
- If you are not in Linux and using a terminal, you are limited to one shell at a time. We suggest you operate in one shell and complete the exercises; then start a child of the other type and examine the exercises again.

Employing Shell Options to Customize Interaction

In earlier exercises, you instructed the shell to modify its behavior using shell built-in variables such as *noclobber*. The shell interacts differently depending on whether a variable is present in the C shells, or is turned on in the **bash** and **ksh** shells. When *noclobber* is set on and you redirect the output of a utility to an existing file, the shell does *not* overwrite it and the shell quits processing. When *noclobber* is off, the shell does redirect output to an existing file, but overwrites the contents.

In the C family of shells (**csh, tcsh**), operational variables are set by entering a command such as:

> set *noclobber*

and turned off with a command such as:

> unset *noclobber*

The variables are listed among all local variables in the C shell family when we enter:

> set

In the **ksh** and **bash** shells, we communicate about shell operational variables by entering commands that turn options on such as:

> set -o *noclobber*

We turn options off with commands like:

> set +o *noclobber*

We list the various operational variables with:

> set -o

Many variables can be set that modify the way each shell operates.

Requesting the Shells to Complete Filenames

Because typing command lines with absolute accuracy is difficult to do, a useful feature allows us to give only part of a file or directory name and then ask the shell to complete it. Operation of this feature differs among the shells. The **tcsh**, many versions of the **csh**, and the **ksh** all provide this feature, with some twists.

1. For these exercises, create three files by entering:
   > **touch** *zadigAAA zadigBBB*
   > **ls** > *zzzzCCC*
   > **ls** -l *z**

   The three files are listed.

The next several sections examine the use of file completion in each of the shells.

Instructing the tcsh Shell to Complete Filenames

This section examines file completion using the **tcsh** shell. If you do not have access to one, skip down to the following sections that guide you through these exercises using the other shells.

1. Make sure you are communicating with a **tcsh** shell.
2. Inform the **tcsh** shell that you want the *filename-completion* feature turned on by entering:

   set *filec*

   When the variable *filec* exists in the environment of the **tcsh**, the shell will search for matching filenames.

3. Type the following *but do not press* ENTER:

   ls -l *zz*

4. Instead of ENTER, press TAB.

   The command line on the screen changes to:

   `ls -l` *zzzzCCC*

   The command in its modified form just sits there. The shell is not executing it yet.

5. Press ENTER to have the command line executed.

   When you enter part of a filename and press TAB, the shell examines the filenames in the current directory, completes the name, and displays it. You can add more to the line, or simply press ENTER and execute it.

6. Enter:

   tr *'a-z' 'A-Z' zz*

   and press TAB.

   The shell completes the *zz* filename to *zzzzCCC*.

7. After the filename is completed, add **| more** to the line so it reads:

   `tr  'a-z'  'A-Z'  zzzzCCC  |  more`

8. Press ENTER to execute the command.

Completing Filenames That Have the Same Beginning

When we provide enough of a filename to uniquely identify it, the shell simply completes the name. What happens if more than one name meets the partial name criteria?

1. Enter:

    ls -l *za*

and press TAB.

The shell attempts to complete the filename by examining the names of files in the current directory. However, the shell cannot distinguish between two existing filenames that start with *za*, namely, *zadigAAA zadigBBB*. At this point, some shells display as much of the name as matches both files. Some shells simply beep or flash; others list the files that match, and then display the incomplete command line and wait for more information.

You need to give the shell more characters—enough to uniquely identify the filename.

2. Enter:

    A

and press TAB.

The command line changes to employ a complete filename:

```
ls  -l   zadigAAA
```

3. Press ENTER to run the command.

4. Attempt to expand a filename that does not exist:

    ls *Zx5*

and press TAB.

If no filename in the current directory matches the characters you enter, the shell beeps or flashes.

Employing Other Directories in Completion

We can also have the shell complete directory names and filenames in directories other than your current directory.

1. Enter:

    ls -l */t*

and press TAB. The display is now

```
ls  -l  /tmp/
```

2. List the contents of */tmp* by pressing ENTER.

A long listing of the files in the */tmp* directory is produced.

We can ask for filename completion anywhere on the command line. The filename completion feature looks for matching file or directory names in directories specified on the command line. You can continue this process of entering characters and using TAB to produce a full pathname of a file or directory.

3. Enter:

   wc /e

   and press TAB.

   The display is changed to read:

   ```
   wc  /etc
   ```

4. Add:

   /pa

   Press TAB again.

   The file is not uniquely identified.

5. Add another letter:

   s

   and press TAB.

6. When you have provided enough of the *passwd* filename to uniquely identify it, press ENTER.

Completing Executable Filenames

The first token on a command line is a utility. We can ask the shell to provide a list of matching utility names using filename expansion.

1. Enter:

   wh

   and press TAB.

> **N O T E :** If more than one command starting with *wh* exists, you must press TAB twice to see all the options.

The shell responds with all commands in your *path* that start with **wh:**

```
whatis where whereis which while who whoami
```

and then displays the command as you have constructed it thus far.

2. Complete it with an *o* or just clear the command by pressing BACKSPACE.

3. Try:

   gr

   followed by pressing TAB twice.

   The collection of commands that start with **gr** is displayed.

4. Enter:

   who | g

   followed by pressing TAB twice.

   A long list of utilities that start with **g** is presented.

5. Add one character:

   r

   followed by pressing TAB twice.

   The collection of commands that begin with **gr** is much smaller.

6. Complete it by adding:

   e

   followed by pressing TAB twice.

   Then add:

   $USER

We can use filename completion with files, directories, files in directories, and with executables.

Filename Completion in the Korn Shell

The filename completion feature of the **ksh** shell functions in the same manner as in the C shells once you turn it on.

1. Start a **ksh** either in another window, or as a child shell.

2. Set the filename-completion variable in the Korn shell by entering:

   set -o *vi*
   set -o *vi-tabcomplete*

3. Go back and run through the same exercise in filename completion with the Korn shell as you did with the C shell.

Filename Completion in the bash Shell

The **bash** shell probably includes filename completion by default.

1. Try it:

   ls */t*

   And press TAB.

2. If file completion does not work, try:

   set -o *vi*
   set +o *posix*

3. Work through the exercises listed for the **tcsh** employing a **bash** shell.

   File completion is a useful way to improve effectiveness in a command-line environment.

Filename Completion in the csh Shell

Many C shells include filename completion but use the ESC key to trigger completion of filenames.

1. Go back through the exercises listed as **tcsh**, but use ESC instead of the TAB that is specified in each exercise.

Setting a Search Path for Locating Directories

When we want to run a utility, we just enter its name. The shell searches through the directories listed in the *PATH* or *path* variable and locates the utility we requested. When we want to change directories, however, we must explicitly state the path to the directory as an argument to the **cd** command. We enter command lines like **cd** */etc* or **cd** ~ or **cd** */home/cassy/Projects*. A feature available in modern shells allows us to designate directories in remote parts of the file system that the shell should access by name, as though they were in the current directory.

1. Create the following directories and files:

   mkdir */tmp/$USER*
   date > */tmp/$USER/dateintmp*

2. Make sure you are in your home directory:

> **cd**
> **ls**

There is no directory with a name equal to your *login* name. (If there is, change its name before entering the next step.)

3. Depending on your current shell, enter one of the following:

In **tcsh**:

> **set** *cdpath=/tmp*

In **bash, ksh**:

> *CDPATH=/tmp*

The directory path variable now has just one directory that will be searched.

4. Attempt to change directories to a directory with the name of your *login* by entering:

> **cd $USER**
> **pwd**

You are in the directory */tmp/$USER*, though you did not explicitly indicate */tmp*. The shell examines the current directory and then the list of directories in the directory path variable *cdpath* or (*CDPATH*) for the target directory. It found the directory in */tmp*.

When you enter a **cd** command, the shell searches first in the current directory. If no directory is located that matches the name, the shell then searches directories in the path listed in the C shell **cdpath** or the Korn/Bash shell **CDPATH** variable. The procedure is analogous to searching the directories in the *path* or *PATH* variable for requested utilities.

You can include multiple directories in your directory search path.

In a **bash** or **ksh**, a colon separates the two tokens.

5. Enter the following, including a colon between the */tmp* and */* in the value:

> *cdpath='/tmp:/'*
> **echo $cdpath**

6. Go to a directory in root by entering:

> **cd** *bin*
> **pwd**
> **cd** *etc*
> **pwd**
> **cd**

The format of both *cdpath* and *CDPATH* is the same, respectively, as that of *path* and *PATH* variables. Colons separate the tokens in *CDPATH* and spaces in *cdpath*. The directories are searched in the order that they are listed. Many versions of the C shell family accept only one directory name in the *cdpath* variable.

Evaluating Shell Variables

In addition to the variables examined earlier in all shells, the **bash** and **ksh** shells have built-in variables that are useful in interacting with the shell.

Built-in Variables in the bash and ksh Shells

We use the **ps** command to identify the current processes and their parents. These shells also maintain the parent's *PID* in a variable.

1. In a Korn or Bash shell, enter:

   echo $$
   echo $PPID
   ps -l

2. The shells keep track of the length of time they have been "alive":

   echo $SECONDS
   date
   echo $SECONDS

   The shell maintains a variable named *SECONDS* with a value of the number of seconds since the shell was started.

3. Execute a child shell and check on its age.

4. In the **bash** shell, another variable allows you to execute any command just before it displays the prompt:

   PROMPT_COMMAND=cal

   Every time you enter a command, the shell will run **cal** just before displaying the new prompt.

5. Enter a few commands.

6. To turn the prompt command feature off, enter:

   PROMPT_COMMAND=

Customizing Shell Startup Files

Do you want file completion? A particular prompt? A series of aliases? The designers of UNIX/Linux refuse to make decisions like that for you. Instead, tools are provided that allow you to customize the shell as you see fit. Whenever a shell is started, it reads startup files to see how you want it to behave.

1. List all the files in your home directory:

    ls -a

Included in the output is the set of files with names that begin with a period, the *dot files*. Each dot file is a run control file for a specific utility or shell. We can add instructions to these files to modify the *PATH*, set variables, add aliases, and so on. The various shells read different files. This topic is examined in more detail in Chapter 20, "Modifying the User Environment."

Customizing the csh Shell

When you start a **csh**, it reads a system file in the */etc* directory and the *.cshrc* file in your home directory. If you make additions to the end of the *.cshrc* file, you can customize how the **csh** behaves.

1. Use the editor and make additions to the *.cshrc* file, such as:

    set *prompt*='! % '
    alias cp 'cp -i'
    set *history=200*
    set noclobber
    set ignoreeof

    Whenever you start a new **csh** shell, it reads the *.cshrc* file.

2. Start a child **csh** and examine its variables.

Customizing the tcsh Shell

If a *.tcshrc* file exists, the **tcsh** reads it. Otherwise, it reads the *.cshrc* file. You could include lines such as the following at the end of a *.tcshrc* file or add them to the *.cshrc* file if there is no *.tcshrc* file.

1. Use the editor to access the *.tcshrc* file and make additions to the end of the file that include all lines just listed for the *.cshrc* and the following:

   bindkey -v
   set *prompt*='! %c %% '
   set *filec*

2. The other variables, aliases, and history settings suggested for the *.cshrc* file can be included here as well.

When you next start a **tcsh** shell, these customizations should be in effect.

Customizing the bash Shell

The **bash** reads the file *.bashrc* whenever it starts.

1. With the editor, create or make additions to the *.bashrc* file:

   set -o *vi*
   set -o *ignoreeof*
   set -o *noclobber*
   PS1='\! \t \W \! *bash$* '
   PS2='-2-$ '

When you next start a **bash** shell, these settings should be in place.

Customizing the ksh Shell

Usually, systems are set up so that the **ksh** reads the *.kshrc* whenever it is started.

1. Use the editor to modify or create the *.kshrc* file and to add lines such as the ones listed earlier for the *.bashrc* file.

2. In a Linux **ksh**, add:

   set -o *vi-tabcomplete*

   Older korn shells do not have this feature.

3. Start a new **ksh** shell and examine the settings:

   set -o

The settings you listed in the *.kshrc* should be in effect. If the **ksh** did not read the *.kshrc* file, an environmental variable is not set. Do the following:

1. Add the following line to the end of the file *.login* in your home directory:

   setenv *ENV* ~/.kshrc

2. Add the next line to the *.profile* file:

   export *ENV=~/.kshrc*

3. Log out and when you return, the Korn shell should behave properly.

   The **ksh** is programmed to read at startup whatever file is the value of the *ENV* variable. The lines you just added make certain that all shells carry the environmental variable *ENV* as equal to *~/.kshrc*, so whenever you start a **ksh**, it inherits the needed variable and value.

There are several other files read by each shell, some system files, and other local files examined in Chapter 20, "Modifying the User Environment."

■ Review

1. What is a token? How does the shell decide where one token ends and another begins?

   _____

2. What is the result of running the following?

   **wc `cat** list`

   _____

3. What are each of the following tokens?

   _____ | _____ _____ < _____ | | _____ `_____` _____

4. What is the result of running the following?

   cat *file1 file2* > *file1*

   _____

5. How can you overwrite a file if *noclobber* is set in the C shell? In the Korn shell?

   _____

6. How do you create a local variable named *tuesday* with the value *8-5* in the C shell? In the Korn shell?

   _____

7. How do you create an environmental variable called *OCT* with the value *NOT_PAID* in the C shell? In the Korn shell?

   _____

8. You have a global variable *LEVEL* in the Korn shell with value *one*, and you start a child Korn shell. In the child shell, you enter the command

LEVEL=two. You now start another child (grandchild) shell. What is the value of *LEVEL* now?

9. How do you enable filename completion in the Korn shell?

10. You want to find all records containing the string *friend* in some files. You know that their names begin with *monica*, followed by some character followed by one number (*0, 1, 2,* or *3*), followed by one other number (*3, 4, 5, 6, 7,* or *8*), followed by more characters. What is the shortest command to find the records?

11. What does the following accomplish:
   CDPATH=/MLA/Projects

12. How do we tell the **bash** and **ksh** shells to set the primary prompt and the secondary prompt?

■ Conclusion

The UNIX shells are powerful command interpreters that read your command lines and take requested actions, including redirecting output, evaluating variables, performing command substitution, passing arguments, and executing utilities. Special characters are interpreted or not interpreted depending on whether and how they are quoted. Words or tokens in command lines have meaning to the shell based on their location in the line, on the content of the tokens, and on their relationship to other tokens. We can modify the primary and secondary prompts, create a list of directories that the shell searches for files as though they were in the current directory, instruct the shell to complete partial filenames, and modify startup files that control how the shells behave.

■ Answers to Review

1. A token is a string of characters (word) separated from other strings by white spaces, redirection symbols, or other special characters.

2. The shell initially executes `cat list` and replaces the string with the results. Whatever text is generated by the **cat** command becomes arguments to the **wc** utility.

3. **utility** | **utility** *argument* < *file* | | **utility** `utility` *argument*

4. If *noclobber* is set, the shell issues an error message warning you that the file you want to create already exists. If *noclobber* is not set, the shell empties *file1* to receive data, and **cat** combines empty *file1* with data from *file2* and puts it in *file1*.

5. In the C shell, use >!

   In the Korn shell, use > |

6. C: **set** *tuesday=8-5*

   Korn: *tuesday=8-5*

7. C: **setenv** *OCT NOT_PAID*

   Korn: *OCT=NOT_PAID*

   export *OCT*

8. two

9. **set -o** *vi-tabcomplete*

10. **grep** friend monica?[0-3][3-8]*

11. In **bash** and **ksh**, include the directory */MLA/Projects* in the directory search path.

12. Primary is *PS1* and secondary is *PS2*. *PS1*='*prompt string*'

COMMAND SUMMARY

Input, Output, and Error Redirection Characters

| Redirects output from prior utility to next utility.

< Opens file on the right of symbol and connects it to the input of the utility on the left.

> Redirects output of utility on the left into the file named on the right.

>> Output from utility on the left is appended to the file on the right.

>! Redirects output of utility on the left into file on the right; overrides *noclobber* feature (C shell).

>| Redirects output of utility on the left into file on the right; overrides *noclobber* feature (Korn shell).

>& Redirects the combination of standard output and standard error to the file on the right (C shell).

2> Redirects standard error to the file on the right (Korn shell).

2>&1 Redirects the combination of standard output and standard error to the file on the right (Korn shell).

Command-Line Control Characters

; Command separator. Executes each pipeline separated by ; as a separate command, although they are on the same command line.

& Causes the command to be run in the background.

&& Executes pipeline on the right when pipeline on the left executes successfully.

|| Executes pipeline on the right when pipeline on the left does not execute successfully.

` command ` or **$(** *command* **)** Denotes beginning and end of command to be run and replaced by its result prior to the execution of other elements on the command line.

Interpretation Controlling Characters

" "   Turns off (and on) shell interpretation of most special characters.

\   Turns off interpretation of next single character.

/ /   Turns off and on interpretation of essentially all special characters.

Filename-Matching Characters

*   Expands to match any number of any character (except . as first character in a filename) to be matched.

?   Expands to match any one character.

[ ]   Defines list of characters from which one is to be selected for matching.

{ }   Defines string for matching or for generating new file or directory names.

${ }   Evaluates variable named in curly braces and merges with adjacent string.

Shell Variable Commands

In the C Shell

set *variable=value*   Initializes or changes the value of local variable to *value*.

setenv *variable*   Initializes or changes the value of environmental variable to *value*.

set   Displays all local variables and their values.

printenv *variable*   Displays environmental variable and its value.

printenv   Displays all environmental variables and their values.

env   Displays all environmental variables and their values.

unset *variable*   Removes local variable.

unsetenv *variable*   Removes environmental variable.

In the Bourne and Korn Shells

variable=value   Initializes or changes value of *variable*.

export *variable*   Makes *variable* environmental.

set   Displays all local variables and their values.

printenv   Displays all environmental variables and their values.

env   Displays all environmental variables and their values.

unset *variable*   Removes *variable* (local and therefore environmental).

Initializing Shell Operational Variables

set *filec*   Turns on filename completion (C shell).

set -o *vi-tabcomplete*   Instructs shell to complete filenames when user enters TAB.

set *noclobber*   Prevents overwriting files with redirection (C shell).

set -o *noclobber*   Prevents overwriting files with redirection (Korn and Bash shells).

set -o   Instructs shell to list current values of shell operational variables.

set cdpath=(/path)   Sets path for user's **cd** command search (C shell).

CDPATH=/path   Sets path for user's **cd** command search (Korn shell).

Job-Control Commands

CTRL-Z   Suspends currently running foreground job.

fg   Brings last suspended or backgrounded job to the foreground.

bg   Places suspended job in the background (will resume running there).

ps   Lists current processes.

Setting File and Directory Permissions

S K I L L S C H E C K

Before beginning this chapter, you should be able to

- Access and leave the system
- Create and display files
- Name, copy, and remove files
- Execute basic shell commands
- Redirect input and output
- Access and modify files using an editor
- Use the UNIX directory file system
- Create basic shell scripts

O B J E C T I V E S

After completing this chapter, you will be able to

- Determine the permissions various kinds of users are granted for files
- Change permissions for a file
- Examine how permissions limit access to a specific file
- Change permissions for access to a directory
- Examine how permissions limit access to a specific directory
- Change how the system assigns default permissions for new files and directories
- Modify permissions for whole directory trees
- Assign permissions appropriately to achieve security goals

Contemporary UNIX/Linux systems manage files that can vary greatly in their importance—from state secrets to casual notes. To maintain appropriate security, files on each system are given different levels of protection. For instance, if a file contains plans for a new product, then only a few users should have access to read the file. Its availability must be restricted. In contrast, a memo intended for everyone must be accessible by all employees.

UNIX/Linux systems routinely store information in files. They run programs that are in files. How system programs behave is usually prescribed in a control file. Whether or not a user has access to a file is determined by a *set of permissions* for the file. Even workstation terminal displays and other hardware are managed and have permissions as though they were files. By changing a file's permissions, the owner of a file determines which users can read, modify, delete, and/or execute the file. Fundamental UNIX security for users and for the system is the result of carefully prescribing which users have access to each file and directory. Access is determined by the permissions assigned and the subsequent effect of each permission setting. This chapter investigates how to modify file permissions and explores how these permission settings permit and deny access.

9.1 Describing File Permissions

A person working on a UNIX/Linux system issues commands, enters data, writes programs, changes directories, and obtains information. All these activities are accomplished by accessing files that are utilized in three ways:

1. When we examine the contents of a file with utilities such as **more**, **cat**, and **vi**, we *read* the file's contents. The file is not changed, only read. When we use **ls** to list the contents of a directory, we are reading the directory.
2. When we have completed editing a file using **vi** and we type **:w**, we *write* the file, making changes. When we enter **who >>** *file*, we add the output of **who** to the file. We write to it. When we add a file to a directory or change a filename, we write the name in the directory.
3. When we enter the name of a shell script, we start or *execute* a new child process that reads the command file (shell script) and then runs whatever commands are in it.

If a user owns a file, that user may either allow or deny any of the three permissions: read, write, or execute. The owner can modify the permissions on a file for the three classes of users: the owner or *user*, other members of the owner's *group*, and all *other* users (people not in your group).

The first portions of this chapter examine using letters (mnemonics) to modify the permissions for the three classes of users, followed by an in-depth look at using numbers to specify the permissions. The next sections investigate the effects of file and directory permissions on user activities, followed by an examination of how files and directories are assigned their initial permissions. The last section guides you through modifying permissions for all files in a whole directory tree.

Examining the Permissions Field

A great deal of information is packed into the permissions field.

1. Reexamine the permissions for all the regular files in your home directory by entering:

   ls -l

   In the permissions field, there are ten slots for each file. For example:

   ```
   -rwxr-x--x
   ```

   Every slot is occupied either by a minus sign or by a letter. If the first slot is a **-**, then the object is a file. If it is a **d**, then the object is a directory. In the last nine slots, a minus sign indicates that the particular permission is denied. If a letter appears in the slot, it indicates that a permission is allowed. The letters you see will usually be *r*, *w*, or *x*, and for some files you might also see *b*, *c*, *l*, *p*, *s*, *S*, *t*, or *T*.

2. For example, enter:

   ls -ld */tmp*

   The result is usually:

   ```
   -rwxrwxrwt   /tmp
   ```

   The *t* in the */tmp* directory permissions is a special permission called the *sticky bit*, which we will examine later.

Directory

The first slot indicates whether the listing is for a directory, a plain file, or a special UNIX file. The first character in the permissions field for the file *users_on* is a minus sign, indicating that *users_on* is a regular file. The file *Projects* is a directory, as indicated by the **d** in the first character location.

In addition to the **d**, this location may also hold a **b**, **c**, **p**, or **l** for some system files. These characters indicate the special nature of the file, which is of interest to the system administrator.

1. For example, enter:

   ls -l */dev* | **more**

   Note that there is a *c* or *b* at the beginning of many permissions fields, which indicates whether the device processes data one **c**haracter or **b**lock at a time.

File Permissions

The remainder of the permissions field is divided into three sets of three slots each. Depending on how your account is set up, the permissions for *practice* could look like this:

```
-rw-r--r--
```

Following the first dash, there are three sets of three permissions. The first set, *rw-*, determines what you as owner (user) of the file can do with the file:

- The first of these three slots contains either an **r**, indicating the owner has read permission and can view the contents of the file, or a minus sign to indicate that read permission is denied.
- The second slot contains either a **w**, indicating the owner has write permission and can alter the contents of the file, or a minus sign to prevent the owner from altering the file.
- In similar fashion, the third slot indicates whether a child shell can be started to execute the commands in the file. An **x** means the owner has execute permission; a minus sign indicates the owner does not.

In summary, the presence of an **r**, **w**, or **x** in the first set of permission slots, or permission bits, indicates that the associated permission is allowed; a minus sign indicates that this permission is denied for the owner of the file.

File Permissions for Group and Other

When you create a file of any kind, you are the owner of that file. As owner, you have the power to set permissions for three kinds of users: yourself (*user* or owner), for the rest of the users who are in the same *group* as you, and for any *other* users who have access to the system (that is, users not in your group).

1. Again, display the permissions for the files in your current directory by entering the following command:

   ls -l

   In the long listing output that appears, the name of the owner and group are the third and fourth fields. (If the group name is not displayed, try **ls -lg**.)

   The same read, write, and execute permissions apply to users who are in the owner's group and to other users. The middle three positions determine the read, write, and execute permissions for users who are members of the same group as the owner. This is done so that people working on the same project can have access to the same files and resources and can also place different restrictions on the rest of the system's users. The last three slots indicate the permissions assigned to everyone who has an account on the system, but who is not the owner nor in the owner's group.

   For example, consider the following permissions field:

   ```
   -rwxr-xr--
   ```

   The object is a regular file; the user (owner) has read, write, and execute permission for the file.

User	Group	Other
rwx	r-x	r--
The owner of the file	Users in the same group as the owner (rest of group)	Users *not* in the same group as the owner (else)

   Other members of the same group as the owner have read and execute permission, but not write permission. They can execute a child process to run the commands in the file. Although they can see the contents the file, they cannot alter them. All other users have permission to read, but not to write or execute. Every file has an associated permission field for user, group, and all others on the system.

   Consider the following permissions, and then fill in the missing information. The answers are at the end of the chapter.

Permission Field	TYPE	USER	GROUP	OTHER
drwxr-x---	directory	rwx	r-x	---
-rw-rw-r--				
-r-xr-----				

In summary, the three permission fields have the following meaning:

- *Type*   The first bit describes the file as directory, ordinary, and so on.
- *User*   Bits 2, 3, and 4 determine what the owner can do with the file.
- *Group*   Bits 5, 6, and 7 determine what users who are in the owner's group can do with the file.
- *Other*   Bits 8, 9, and 10 determine what users who are not the owner nor in the owner's group (other) can do with the file.

Employing Read and Write Permissions

1. Examine the permissions of an old file such as *practice* by entering:

   ls -l *practice*

   The permissions displayed for this file are probably:

   ```
   -rw-rw-rw-
   ```

   or

   ```
   -rw-r--r--
   ```

   The first **rw-** indicates that the current permissions attached to the *practice* file allow you, as owner, read and write permission, but not execute permission.

2. Start editing the file with the visual editor:

   vi *practice*

   You are able to read the file. Its contents are displayed on the screen.

3. Make a change in the file by opening a new line and adding text, such as:

   These are two new lines
   I am adding to the file practice in this permissions chapter.

4. Write the file and quit the editor with the **:wq** command.
   You are able to make the changes to the file because you have **w**rite permission.

   To access the contents of a file, you must have **read** permission for that file. To make changes or modify a file, you need **write** permission for the file.

Changing Permissions for a File to Read Only

As you saw earlier when touring the system, you can restrict access to a file. For example, you (as owner) might want to be permitted to read a letter but not to change it in any way. To prohibit changes, you remove the *write* permissions for that file.

1. Change the permissions, removing the write permission on the file *practice* by typing:

   chmod -w *practice*

2. Obtain a listing of the new permissions, with:

   ls -l *practice*

   The **chmod -w** *filename* command is instruction to change the **mode**, or permissions, for the file by removing the **write** permission (minus **write**).

chmod	Instruction to **ch**ange the **mod**e or permission
-w	Remove **w**rite (minus **w**rite)
practice	From the file *practice*

Because you did not specify whether you wanted to modify the user, group, or other, it is removed from all three. The **chmod -w** command is described in the following illustration.

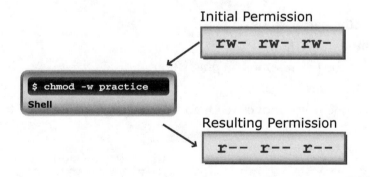

3. Use **vi** to call up the *practice* file again.
   You can access a file with **vi** because you have read permission.
4. Delete a line.

5. Attempt to write the file with the usual **:wq** command. The resulting error message is something like:

```
File is read only
```

or

```
Permission denied
```

You cannot write the buffer copy of the file that you have modified back to the original file, because you do not have write permission. You still have read, so you are able to read the file; but without write, you cannot alter the file's contents.

To return to the shell, you could quit the editor without writing, or write the changed buffer copy to a new file. On many systems, **:w!** works. Because you are the owner of the file, you are allowed to change the permissions on the file to include write. You could change the permissions as owner, so the system allows you to insist on writing with the **:w!** command.

6. Quit without attempting to write by typing the editor command:

   :q!

Changing Permissions for a File to Write Only

With one command, you can change the permissions for the *practice* file to add write permission and deny read.

1. Modify the permissions on *practice* by entering:

   chmod -r+w *practice*

2. Examine the permissions on *practice*:

   ls -l *practice*

The argument **-r** removes read, and the **+w** adds **write** to all three classes of users.

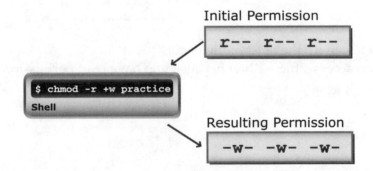

Initial Permission
```
r-- r-- r--
```

```
$ chmod -r +w practice
Shell
```

Resulting Permission
```
-w- -w- -w-
```

3. Attempt to read the file:

> **cat** *practice*

The shell responds with an error message:

```
practice:  Permission denied
```

This error message indicates you do not have read permission on the file; hence, you cannot read its contents.

However, you still have write permission for the file. It is possible to write to a file, even if you cannot read it.

4. You can instruct the shell to connect the output of a utility to the end of an existing file. Type:

> **date >>** *practice*

This command specifies the output of **date** to be appended to the *practice* file. Because you have write permission for the file, you can add text.

5. Attempt to determine whether the addition was made to the file. Enter:

> **more** *practice*

You are not allowed to examine the file, because you do not have read permission for the file. You can add to it; you just can't see what you did.

Adding Read Permission to a File

In the previous exercise, you limited the permission to only write for the file *practice*.

1. Reset the permissions for *practice* to allow reading. Enter:

> **chmod +r** *practice*

2. Use **more** to confirm that you are able to read the file.

The date is the last line. It was added when you only had write permission for the file.

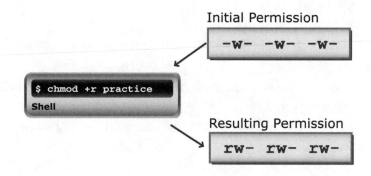

Initial Permission

```
-w-  -w-  -w-
```

```
$ chmod +r practice
Shell
```

Resulting Permission

```
rw-  rw-  rw-
```

9.2 Using Execute Permissions with a File

As you saw in earlier chapters, shell commands can be placed in a file and run all at once. This technique of creating command files, or *shell scripts,* can make work more efficient and reduce errors.

Creating a File of Shell Commands

Shell scripts are created just like any other file, usually with an editor.

1. Ensure that you are in your home directory:

   cd

2. Create a new file named *inform* by entering:

   vi *inform*

3. Place the following lines in the *inform* file:

```
date
pwd
echo You have the following processes
ps
echo current process is $$
```

4. Write the file and return to the shell:

   :wq

Telling the Shell to Read a Script

When we enter a command at the shell prompt, the shell interprets the line we enter, executes it, gives us another prompt, and then we enter another command. At this point, several commands are in the *inform* file. We can instruct the shell to read the file and execute each of the commands it contains.

1. Enter at the (C shell):

   source *inform*

   or (Korn and Bourne shells use the dot as the source command):

   . *inform*

   The result is that the current shell runs each of the commands in the file as though you just typed them.

2. At the shell prompt, request that the shell inform you of its process ID (PID):

   echo $$

The PID of your current shell is the same PID that was reported when you ran the *inform* script. Your current shell executes the commands in the *inform* script when you source it.

Running a Script by Entering Its Name

To run a shell script like any other UNIX command, we type its name and press ENTER.

1. From the shell, type:

   inform

 NOTE: If you get an error message that says:
command not found
it means your path does not include searching for *inform* in the current directory. Enter the following command to tell the shell the script is in the current directory:
./inform

Either way, when you enter *inform* or *./inform*, you receive an error message such as:

```
inform:   execute permission denied.
```

Although the file contains valid shell commands, the shell does not execute them, because you do not have execute permission on the file.

2. Examine the permissions of *inform* by entering:

   ls -l *inform*

   You have read and write only; clearly, that is not enough. Once you have written a file full of commands, you cannot execute it by calling its name unless you have execute permission on the file. But what does *execute* really mean?

Changing Permissions to Make a File Executable

The error message you received in the preceding exercise lets you know that the shell attempted to execute a child shell to run the commands in the file *inform*, but found that you did not have execute permission, and an error message appeared. This is only a plain, ordinary, nonexecutable file. You need to change the permissions for *inform* to execute it by calling its name.

1. To make *inform* executable, type:

   chmod +x *inform*

   The **+x** option instructs **chmod** to grant execute permission for the file.

2. Examine the permissions now:

   ls -l *inform*

   There is an **x** in the third field, indicating it is executable by you. Likewise, **x** is granted to group and other.

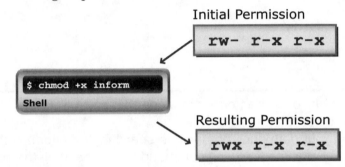

Initial Permission

`rw- r-x r-x`

`$ chmod +x inform`
Shell

Resulting Permission

`rwx r-x r-x`

3. Execute the **inform** shell script by typing:

   inform

   You are treated to the display of the current date and time, the path to your current directory, your current processes, and the PID of the shell that is executing the script. All the shell commands that you wrote in the **inform** file are run. The PID of the shell that ran the script this time is not your current shell. It has a different PID.

4. Look at the output of **ps** when the script runs. An additional shell (probably an *sh* or *bash*) is included, and its PID matches the one that ran the script.

> **SUMMARY:** When you execute a script by entering its name, a child shell is started. The child shell reads the script and runs the listed commands. In contrast, you can have your current shell read the script and execute whatever commands are in it by sourcing the file. When you source a script, the current shell must read the file. Read is sufficient permission for sourcing. No child shell is started, so no **x** is needed. To start a child shell to run a script, the user must have execute permission. The child shell must read the file instructions; hence, read must also be on. To have a script run by a child process, the owner must change its permissions (or file mode) to include both execute and read permissions—execute to start a child, and read so the child can read the instructions.

Determining Who Can Modify Permissions

Throughout these chapters you have changed the permissions of *practice* and other files. For system security reasons, there are limits to what files you can affect.

1. Determine who you are by entering one of the following commands:

    whoami

    or

    who am i

    or

    id

    The output includes your login name.

 **N O T E :** If you are ***root***, exit and log back on as an ordinary user; then continue with step 2. Doing the following as ***root*** could damage your system.

2. Determine the current permissions of the file *date* in the */bin* directory by entering:

    ls -l */bin/date*

    The output shows that although everyone can execute the **date** utility, you are not the owner of the */bin/date* file; **root** is the owner.

3. Attempt to modify the permissions on the system file by entering:

    chmod +w */bin/date*

    An error message indicates that you are not the owner of the file. Only the owner can change file permissions.

4. Enter:

    ls -l */bin/date*

    The permissions are not changed.

9.3 Changing File Permissions Using Mnemonics

There are two ways to change the mode or permissions for files using the **chmod** command. One method is to use **chmod** with letter arguments for the permissions, such as **-w**, **+x**, and **-r**, to add or remove permissions. You have already used this method several times. The other, numerical, method will be examined in the next section.

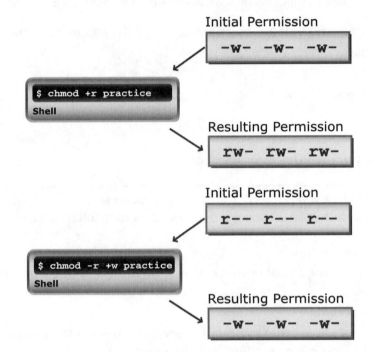

Initial Permission

-w- -w- -w-

$ chmod +r practice
Shell

Resulting Permission

rw- rw- rw-

Initial Permission

r-- r-- r--

$ chmod -r +w practice
Shell

Resulting Permission

-w- -w- -w-

This mnemonic assignment method allows us to set permissions for each type of user in several ways.

Assigning Specific Permissions

1. Create a test file with:

   date > *permtest*

2. Check the current permissions with:

   ls -l *permtest*

Assigning to All Users

1. Assign full permissions for the file to all three classes of users:

   chmod a=rwx *permtest*

2. Check the new permissions with:

   ls -l *permtest*

The command is instruction to assign permissions for **all** three permission sets and to set them to equal to **rwx**.

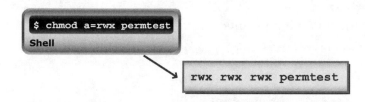

```
$ chmod a=rwx permtest
Shell
```

```
rwx rwx rwx permtest
```

3. Modify all permissions again with:

    chmod a=r *permtest*
    ls -l *permtest*

Using **a,** all three types of user permissions are set to just read.

Assigning to One Type of User

This approach also permits assignment of permissions to each class: **u**ser or **g**roup or **o**ther.

1. Try the following:

    chmod ug=rw,o=r *permtest*
    ls -l *permtest*

The classes **u**ser and **g**roup are assigned **r**ead and **w**rite, while **o**ther users are assigned **r**ead only.

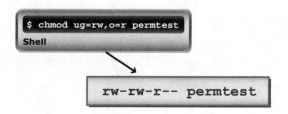

```
$ chmod ug=rw,o=r permtest
Shell
```

```
rw-rw-r-- permtest
```

2. Specify each assignment with:

    chmod u=rwx,g=rx,o=r *permtest*
    ls -l *permtest*
    chmod u=rwx,go= *permtest*
    ls -l *permtest*

When permissions for a type of user are set to nothing, such as **go=**, no permissions are granted; in that case, both **group** and **other** are --- permissions.

3. Assign the following permissions:

   chmod a=rwx *permtest*
   ls -l

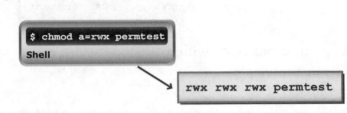

```
$ chmod a=rwx permtest
Shell
```

```
rwx rwx rwx permtest
```

4. Now assign only group and other:

   chmod g=r, o= *permtest*
   ls -l

   Group is given read permission, and other has all permissions removed. User, since it is not given any new assignment, retains whatever permissions it had before the **chmod** command.

5. Explore a little further with:

   chmod ug=rwx,o=r *permtest*
   ls -l *permtest*

6. Now try:

   chmod g=u *permtest*
   ls -l *permtest*

   The **group** permission is assigned the permissions currently given to the **user**. Permissions for one type of user can be assigned to another.

7. Enter:

   chmod u=r,o= *permtest*
   ls -l *permtest*

   No new assignment is given to group, which retains its current permissions.

Adding and Deleting Permissions

In the previous exercises, you assigned specific new permissions to the *permtest* file that took effect regardless of the current permissions. You can also add or subtract a permission without affecting the remainder of the current permissions.

1. Enter these commands:

   chmod a=rwx *permtest*
   ls -l *permtest*
   chmod -x *permtest*
   ls -l *permtest*

   The **x** permission is removed from all three permission sets.

2. Modify just one class of permissions:

   ls**chmod g-w** *permtest*
   ls -l *permtest*

   The **write** permission is removed from **group**.

3. Enter:

   chmod u-w,o-r *permtest*
   ls -l *permtest*

   In this example, **u-w,o-r** is instruction to **chmod** to remove **w** from **user** and to remove **r** from **other**. A comma separates instructions, and no spaces can be included.

4. Enter:

   chmod u+wx *permtest*
   ls -l *permtest*

   The argument **u+wx** is instruction to add **w** and **x** to **user**.

5. Enter:

   chmod u-x,o+r *permtest*
   ls -l *permtest*

   The **u-x,o+r** tells **chmod** to remove **x** from **user** and add **r** to **other** users.

Permissions can be assigned to **u**ser, **g**roup, and **o**ther, or specific permissions can be added and subtracted from whatever the current permissions happen to be.

S U M M A R Y : In summary, the types of users are:

u	User
g	Group
o	Other
a	All

The permissions that can be set are the usual suspects:

r	Read
w	Write
x	Execute
–	None

The actions that can be used are:

=	Assigns permissions
–	Removes permissions
+	Adds permissions

Use commas to separate assignment units.

9.4 Changing File Permissions Numerically

To specify permissions for all three types of users, the other essential method employs numbers that convey the permission information. Once the basics are mastered, this is the more easily used alternative and is essential for more advanced topics.

1. Examine the permissions of the *inform* file by typing:

   ls -l *inform*

2. Type the following:

   chmod *700 inform*

3. Examine the permissions now granted by displaying a long listing for the file:

   ls -l *inform*

   The output is:

   ```
   -rwx------cassy staff July 14 9:37 inform
   ```

This set of permissions indicates the user has full read, write, and execute permission for the file. The group and other users have no access.

Using Numerical Permissions for Read, Write, and Execute

1. Enter the following:

   chmod *400 inform*
   ls -l *inform*

2. Only an **r** is present in the owner's permissions field. The *400* grants read only to the owner.

3. Change the permission again and examine the results by entering the following commands:

   chmod *200 inform*
   ls -l *inform*

   Only write permission is granted to the owner.

4. Now assign only execute permission by entering:

   chmod *100 inform*
   ls -l *inform*

5. Deny all permissions by entering:

   chmod *000 inform*
   ls -l *inform*

The basic number permissions you just used are as follows:

Number	Permission
4	read
2	write
1	execute
0	deny all

Using the numerical approach (as in **chmod 700**) to modify the permissions for a file allows you to numerically specify the exact permissions you want to be granted, regardless of the current permissions. The number *700* grants **rwx** to owner and nothing to group and other.

Assigning Combinations of Permissions

Users seldom grant only one of the three permissions to a file. Often a combination, such as read and write, is specified.

1. Change the permissions for *inform* to include both **read** and **write** for the owner by entering:

   chmod *600 inform*

2. Examine the resulting permissions:

   ls -l *inform*

   The owner has **read** and **write**.

   Combination permissions are specified using the sum of the values for the specific permissions.

Permission		Number
read	=	4
write	=	2
read and write	=	6, which is (4 + 2)

3. Try the following:

   chmod *754 inform*

   The result is:

   ```
   rwxr-xr--
   ```

   7 sets the permissions for owner to be **rwx**.
   5 sets the permissions for group to be **r-x**.
   4 sets the permissions for other to be **r--**.

This result confirms what you saw previously. Look at the user and group fields. The **7** produced **rwx**, while the **5** produced **r-x**. The numerical difference between **7** and **5** is **2**. The difference in the permissions between **7** and **5** that result is **write**, which we know is **2**.

Look at the permissions for other. Clearly, **4** is read. The difference between group (**5, r-x**) and other (**4, r--**) is *1*, which must be the missing permission, execute.

The numbers *0*, *1*, *2*, and *4* are assigned permission values as follows:

Number	Permission
0	Assigns no permissions
1	Allows execute permission
2	Allows write permission
4	Allows read permission

Identifying All Possible Combinations of Permissions

In the following list, the numbers *1*, *2*, and *4* are used in combinations that add up to produce *3*, *5*, *6*, and *7*. Each of the combinations of *1*, *2*, and *4* adds together to produce a number that no other combination yields. All possible numbers from *0* to *7* are uniquely specified.

This set of unique numbers is used with **chmod** to establish the permissions for files.

The primitives (*0*, *1*, *2*, and *4*) can be added together to grant any combination of permissions. The basic permissions for a file are as follows:

Number	Permission
0	Grants no permissions
1	Grants execute permission only
2	Grants write permission only
3	Grants write and execute permission (2+1)
4	Grants read permission only
5	Grants read and execute permission (4+1)
6	Grants read and write permission (4+2)
7	Grants read and write and execute permission (4+2+1)

Thus, combinations of the three numbers *1*, *2*, and *4* can be used to express the eight possible combinations of execute, write, and read permissions.

Each number *0* through *7* translates into a unique set of permissions.

1. Try each of the following:

   chmod *700 inform*
   ls -l *inform*
   chmod *600 inform*
   ls -l *inform*
   chmod *500 inform*
   ls -l *inform*
   chmod *300 inform*
   ls -l *inform*
   chmod *400 inform*
   ls -l *inform*
   chmod *700 inform*
   s -l *inform*

4r	2w	1x	chmod value	Resulting Permissions
-	-	-	0	---
-	-	1	1	--x
-	2	-	2	-w-
-	2	1	3	-wx
4	-	-	4	r--
4	-	1	5	r-x
4	2	-	6	rw-
4	2	1	7	rwx

Turning Switches On and Off

Permission bits are either on or off. It is a standard computer operation. The very basis of computer science is the on/off switch. If there is just one switch, only two values are possible: *on* and *off*. We can view *on* as *1* and *off* as *0*.

If we have two switches, more values are possible.

If we consider the first switch to represent the value *1* when it is on and the second switch to represent the value *2* when it is on, then the following is possible:

Switch 2	Switch 1	Value
Off	Off	0
Off	On	1
On	Off	2

And if both are on, 2+1=3.

Switch 2	Switch 1	Value
On	On	3

Likewise, if there are three switches, the values from 0 to 7 are possible:

Switch Value = 4	Switch Value = 2	Switch Value = 1	Result Value
Off	Off	Off	0
Off	Off	On	1
Off	On	Off	2
Off	On	On	3
On	Off	Off	4
On	Off	On	5
On	On	Off	6
On	On	On	7

Because we assign *4* to mean read, *2* to mean write, and *1* to be execute, then the table looks like this:

4 read	2 write	1 execute	chmod value	Resulting Permissions
Off	Off	Off	0	---
Off	Off	On	1	--x
Off	On	Off	2	-w-
Off	On	On	3	-wx
On	Off	Off	4	r--
On	Off	On	5	r-x
On	On	Off	6	rw-
On	On	On	7	rwx

9.5 Changing Permissions for Group and Other

The numeric values used to set file permissions can be used to specify permissions for any of the three sets (user, group, and other) in the permissions field.

1. Enter the following command to add full permissions for your group only:

    chmod *070 inform*

2. Check the permissions for *inform*. Type:

    ls -l *inform*

    The group permissions include read, write, and execute permission for the group (*7*). Users and others are denied all access (*0*).

3. Type the following command, which grants full permissions to everyone:

    chmod *777 inform*

4. Check how you have changed the permissions for *inform* with:

    ls -l *inform*

    The permissions now show **read**, **write**, and execute for user, group, and all other users.

5. First enter the **chmod** command to change the *inform* file's permissions. After each change, examine the results using the **ls -l** *inform* command.

    chmod *640 inform*
    chmod *750 inform*
    chmod *744 inform*
    chmod *732 inform*

With three numbers of values *0* through *7*, such as *750*, you can specify which of three permissions, **r**, **w**, and **x**, are granted to three classes: user, group, and other.

Determining Which Permissions Apply

Permissions are usually most restrictive for other, less so for group, and least restrictive for the owner of a file. If they are not—if group actually has more permissions granted than owner—it raises some interesting questions.

1. Change the permissions for *inform* to be **rwx** for other, **r-x** for group, and grant no permissions to yourself, the owner.

    chmod *057 inform*
    ls -l *inform*

    The permissions displayed are:

    ```
    ---r-xrwx
    ```

You, as owner, appear to have no granted permissions. But you are in your group. Are you granted your group's permissions?

2. Attempt to execute and read the script:

> *inform*
>
> **cat** *inform*

You have no access to the file.

The process of determining permissions for a file or directory begins with establishing whether you are the owner. If the answer is yes, you are granted the owner's permissions as determined in the first three permission bits. The question of what group you belong to—of what the group permissions are— is never raised; you pass the owner test and are given the owner permissions. Period. The same thing happens with respect to members of your group. They fail the owner test, but then pass the group test. They get the group permissions. If other users attempt to access this file, they fail to be the owner, fail to be in the group, and are then assigned the "else," or other, permissions.

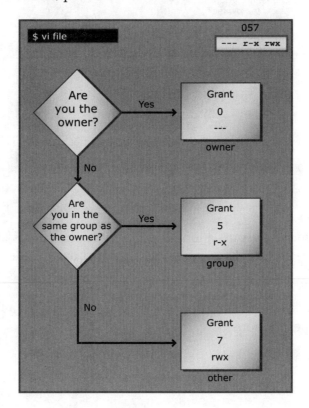

3. Change the permissions back so you can execute the script:

   chmod 754 *inform*

4. Run it again:

   inform

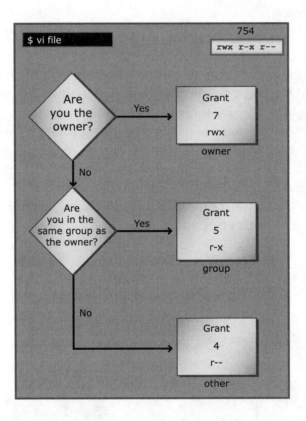

■ Review 1

1. What command outputs a long listing of your filenames in the current directory, including the permissions attached to each file?

   _____

2. What permissions are granted to each class of users for a file with the following permissions?

   r-x------

   _____

3. The file *practice* has no permissions at all. What permission should be assigned to this file so you (the owner) could add text to the end of the file?

_____

4. Consider a file with the following permissions:

rwxr-xr-- *scriptfile*

Who can run each of the following? (Enter **y** for yes or **n** for no.)

	USER	GROUP	OTHER
source *scriptfile*			
scriptfile			
echo date >> *scriptfile*			

5. Consider the following conditions:

- You, the owner, can access the file with **vi** and write changes.
- The file contains a series of shell commands such as **ls** and **who**. When you enter the file's name at the command line, the commands listed in the file are run.
- Members of your group cannot make changes to the file, but when they issue the file's name to the shell, the commands in the file do run. Other users can use **cat** or **more** on the file, but when they issue the filename to the shell, the commands in the file do not run.

What permissions must this file have?

_____

6. What permission would you *deny* to **g**roup and **o**ther so they cannot execute or source a script?

_____

7. How can you execute commands in the file *hi* without giving the file **x** permission?

_____

8. How do you identify which objects are directories in the output of **ls** with a long listing?

_____

9. You are in the same group as Sam, Tom, Bill, and so on. The permission field on a file you own named *answer* is **----r-----**. Who can read the file?

_____

10. There are several commands in the script *inform*. What minimum permissions for the script are needed to run the commands by entering its name?

   _____

11. What commands remove **r** permissions and add **x** permissions to the file *inform*?

   _____

12. Assume users *unx0l, unx02, unx03* are in a group and *ora0l* and *ora02* are in another group. Suppose *unx02* has a script file named *inform* containing commands with a permission of **765**. Answer the following questions:
   a. Who can read the file *inform*?

   _____

   b. Who can execute the commands in the file *inform* by sourcing the file?

   _____

   c. Who can execute by entering *inform*?

   _____

   d. Who can change the contents of the file *inform*?

   _____

13. What would the resulting permissions be if the following command were executed?
      chmod u=rx,g=x,o= *inform*

   _____

14. The file *simple* has a permission field of -rwxr--r--. What command removes **w** from the user and adds **x** to group and other?

   _____

15. In the following table, insert the appropriate **chmod** value or resulting permission.

chmod Value	Resulting Permission
700	rwx --- ---
	r-- --- ---
200	
	rw- --- ---
	--x --- ---
000	
500	

16. In the following table, insert the appropriate resulting permissions based on the **chmod** value.

Command	Resulting Permission
chmod 777 *inform*	rwx rwx rwx
chmod 751 *inform*	
chmod 640 *inform*	
chmod 660 *inform*	
chmod 000 *inform*	
chmod 444 *inform*	
chmod 754 *inform*	
chmod 420 *inform*	

9.6 Exploring the Effect of Granting Different Permissions

In this exercise, you change the permissions on the *inform* file to all possible combinations and examine what you can do to the file as a function of the resulting change in permissions.

1. Change the permissions of *inform* to **rwx** for you, the owner:

> **chmod** *700 inform*

2. Now attempt to read the script:

> **more** *inform*

3. Try to add a new word to the bottom of the script file:

> **echo** *date* >> *inform*

4. Execute the script:

> *inform*

5. Have your current shell read and execute the commands in the script. Bourne and Korn shell users, use the dot command; C shell users, use **source**:

> **.** *inform*

or

> **source** *inform*

The **date** command is the last one run, the result of appending the word *date* to the end of the file in the previous step.

6. List the permissions of *inform*:

   ls -l *inform*

   All of these commands were successful with permissions of **rwx**. Put a **y** in each of the boxes associated with each command under the *700* permissions in the following table.

7. Change the permissions on *inform* to *600* with:

   chmod 600 *inform*

8. Issue the commands in the following table to determine whether you can display, modify, and list the file. In each case, enter **y** if successful or an **n** if not.

9. Proceed by changing the permissions on *inform* to *500*, run the commands and enter **y** or **n** in each block of the table. Then proceed to *400*, *300*, and so on.

	700 rwx	600 rw-	500 r-x	400 r--	300 -wx	200 -w-	100 --x	000 ---
chmod 700 *inform*								
more *inform*								
echo *date* >> *inform*								
inform								
.inform (**source** *inform*)								
ls -l *inform*								

What permissions are essential for executing a script by entering its name? What permission is needed to source a file? What permission is needed to add text to a file? What permission is needed to have **ls** list the file?

Examining the Results

From the previous exercise, we can conclude:

- To access the contents of the file, we need **read** permission.
- To add content to a file, we need **write** permission.
- Both **read** and **execute** are required to run a script by entering its name. We need execute to start a child shell and then if the child is to read the script to see what is to be done, we need read.
- When we ask the current shell to read a file and execute its contents—either using the C shell **source** command or Bourne/Korn's dot command—we need only read permission. No child shell is started; the current shell is used.

There is no need for execute permission. The current shell just reads the file as though we just typed the commands.

- Regardless of the permissions on the file, we can use **ls** to list the filename and its current permissions.

This illustration examines the relationship between the current directory, the *inform* file listed in the current directory, its inode (also listed in the current directory), and the data blocks that hold the data of file *inform*. The **ls** utility does not access the file to produce a listing of the filename and its permissions. That information is not in the file; rather, the filename is listed in the current directory along with the file's inode number. The permissions and so on for the file are in the file's inode. The inode is read not the file. Changing the file permissions on a file determines what we can do to the file. The permissions are recorded in the inode.

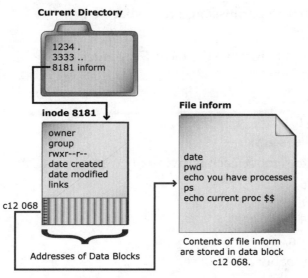

Current Directory

```
1234 .
3333 ..
8181 inform
```

inode 8181

```
owner
group
rwxr--r--
date created
date modified
links
```

c12 068

Addresses of Data Blocks

File inform

```
date
pwd
echo you have processes
ps
echo current proc $$
```

Contents of file inform are stored in data block c12 068.

1. Enter:

    ls -i *inform*

Removing Files

What file permission is needed to remove a file?

1. Create a junk directory by entering:

    mkdir *Junkperms*

2. Make *Junkperms* your current directory:

   cd *Junkperms*

3. Create a series of files by entering:

   touch *old7 old6 old5 old4 old3 old2 old1 old0*

4. Modify the permissions as follows:

   chmod *700 old7*
   chmod *600 old6*
   chmod *500 old5*
   chmod *400 old4*
   chmod *300 old3*
   chmod *200 old2*
   chmod *100 old1*
   chmod *000 old0*

5. Confirm that all permissions are as specified:

   ls -l *old**

6. Now attempt to remove the file *old7* by entering:

   rm *old7*

7. List the files:

   ls -l *old**

   The *old7* file is gone.

8. Continue to remove each individually:

   rm *old6*
   ls -l *old**
   rm *old5*
   and so on.

   You are probably asked:

   ```
   rm: remove write-protected file 'old5'?
   ```

   Answer by typing an **n**.

   Whether a user can remove a file is determined by whether the user has **write** permission on the file as well. If you grant other users write for a file, they can remove the file as well. Without write, you usually cannot remove a file. A special case occurs when a user who requests that a file be removed is also the owner of the file and has not granted themselves write for the file. The owner could grant write then remove the file; **rm** saves the step by saying, in essence, "You do not have write permission and cannot remove the file without changing permissions to include write; however, because you are the owner and could change the permissions, I'll remove it if you say so."

9. List your current files:

   ls -l

   All files that initially had a **write** permission were removed.

10. Go back to your parent directory with:

    cd ..

9.7 Modifying Directory Permissions

When you type **ls -l**, the output reveals that directories have the same kind of permissions field as regular files, except there is a *d* in the leftmost position. The owner of the directory has the power to change the permissions, which in turn affect access to the directory in much the same way as the permissions affect file access. The owner determines which users have read, write, and execute access to the directory. Assigning permissions to directories is done with the same letters and numbers that are used for assigning permissions to files.

Directories are special files containing two things for each file or directory listed in them: the name of each file (or directory) and for each, an associated inode number that leads us to the inode for the file. Permissions for directories determine what you can and cannot do to the directory itself. For instance, what permission would you expect is needed on a directory that would allow you to change the name of a file listed in that directory? What permission is needed on a directory to run **ls** to output the names of the files that are listed in the directory? In this section, we examine how to modify directory permissions and what powers are granted and denied with each permission.

Using Permissions to Control Directory Access

The owner of a directory has the power and responsibility for setting the directory access permissions. Directory permissions, like file permissions, include read, write, and execute.

1. Create a new subdirectory, *Mybin*, in your home directory by typing:

   cd
   mkdir *Mybin*

2. Examine the specific permissions attached to *Mybin*.

   ls -ld *Mybin*

   The **d** option instructs **ls** to provide a listing of information about the directory itself, not its contents.

   Earlier, you examined the total contents of a directory and found two things for each file, a filename and an inode number.

3. Display the contents of your current directory now with:

   ls -i

   The display is a list of the current directory's filenames and associated inodes. This is the total content of the directory—filenames and their associated inodes.

   The directory contains filenames and related inode numbers. The inode contains all the information about a file including permissions, owner, the date it was created, links, and addresses of data blocks on the hard drive where the file's content resides. There is nothing in the file's data blocks except the contents of the file—not even its name. We access the file by first getting its inode number from the directory, then examining the inode for permissions and data block addresses, and finally going to the correct blocks on the drive to access the file itself.

4. Copy the *inform* file into the new *Mybin* subdirectory by entering:

   cp *inform Mybin*

5. Change to the *Mybin* directory and create eight test files by entering the following commands:

   cd *Mybin*
   touch *old0 old1 old2 old3 old4 old5 old6 old7*

6. Run the *inform* file to make sure it is executable:

   inform

   If it is not executed, change its permissions to **700** so it is.

7. Return to the parent directory:

   cd ..

Listing the Files in a Directory

At the moment, your current working directory is the parent of *Mybin*.

1. Obtain a listing of the files in *Mybin* by entering:

   ls *Mybin*

   The output on your screen is not the files listed in your current directory, but the files listed in *Mybin*. You can read the filenames that are listed in *Mybin*.

   The current directory lists itself (inode 1234 .), its parent, and also the child directory, *Mybin*, with an inode of 8555. To access contents of *Mybin*, the inode accessed first is 8555, which contains the information about the directory *Mybin*, including the permissions and data block addresses. The data blocks for *Mybin* contain the filenames and inode numbers for the files listed in *Mybin*. To find the permissions for a file such as *inform*, we need to open and read the inode associated with the file *inform* that is listed in the *Mybin* directory.

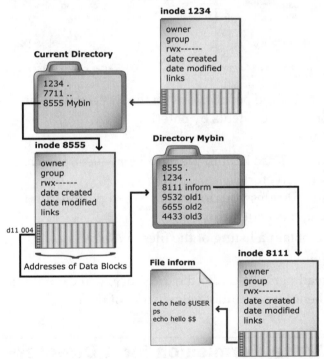

In summary, permissions for the directory *Mybin* are in the inode whose number is listed next to *Mybin* in the current directory. Permissions for files that are listed in the *Mybin* directory are in inodes listed next to the filenames in *Mybin*.

2. Change the permissions of the *Mybin* directory to be only write and execute with:

   chmod *300 Mybin*

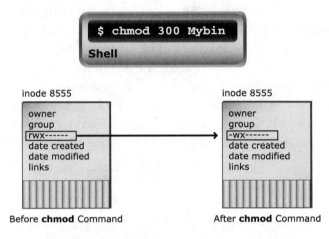

inode 8555

owner
group
rwx------
date created
date modified
links

Before **chmod** Command

inode 8555

owner
group
-wx------
date created
date modified
links

After **chmod** Command

3. Instruct **ls** to list the permissions on the directory *Mybin*, rather than the permissions of its contents by entering:

   ls -ld *Mybin*

   The permissions are kept in the inode for *Mybin*, which is accessed from your current directory.

   The output indicates you do not have read permission for the directory, only write and execute (**d-wx------**).

4. Attempt to obtain a listing of the files in *Mybin*.

   ls *Mybin*

   Without read permission for the directory, you cannot read the directory's contents; hence, you cannot get a listing of its files.

Denying Write Permission for a Directory

With a file, write permission must be granted before a user can modify the contents of the file. The same is true for directories.

1. Modify the permissions on *Mybin* to exclude write, and examine the results:

   chmod *500 Mybin*
   ls -ld *Mybin*

   The directory has only read and execute for the owner; write is denied.

2. Obtain a listing of the files in *Mybin*.

   ls *Mybin*

   You can list the directory's contents because the filenames are kept in the directory, and you still have read permission on the directory. You are reading the directory itself to obtain the list of names of its files.

3. Attempt to change the name of the file *old5* by entering:

   mv *Mybin/old5 Mybin/old5.bak*

Without **write** permission, you cannot modify the contents of the directory. You cannot change the name of a listed file, remove a file, or add a new file. To make any of those changes requires at least modifying the content of the directory (that is, writing).

Examining the Need for Execute Permissions

The directory permissions **read** and **write** are similar to the same permissions on regular files. The execute permission, however, has a very different impact on a directory than it has on a file.

1. Change the mode of *Mybin* to read and write only:

   chmod *600 Mybin*
   ls -ld *Mybin*

   Only read and write are permitted. Execute is denied.

2. Attempt to change directories to *Mybin*.

   cd *Mybin*

   The shell returns an error message similar to the following:

   ```
   Mybin: Permission denied
   ```

   Execute permission for a directory determines whether you can make the directory your current directory.

3. Confirm you are still in the parent of *Mybin*:

   pwd
   ls -ld *Mybin*

4. Attempt to read the script *inform*, which is in *Mybin*:

   cat *Mybin/inform*

   ```
   Mybin: Permission denied
   ```

Without execute permission, you cannot **cd** into a directory, nor can you use the directory in a path to reach a file or directory that is listed in it. You cannot read *inform,* because you cannot get through the directory *Mybin* to get to the file. Although you still have read permission on the *inform* file itself, you cannot get through the parent directory to access the file without execute permission on the directory. You cannot get to the file.

SUMMARY: To **cd** to a directory, or to use the directory in a pathname, you must have execute permission for that directory.

Examining the Effect of Directory Permission

In this section, you will examine the effect of assigning various permissions to the directory *Mybin,* keeping track of the results in the following table.

Starting in your home directory, you will assign the first permission to *Mybin* listed at the top of the table and then will try each of the commands listed in the left column. In the appropriate columns of the table, write down whether the command was executed without error producing the requested information.

	700 rwx	600 rw-	500 r-x	400 r--	300 -wx	200 -w-	100 --x	000 ---
chmod 700 Mybin								
ls -ld Mybin								
ls Mybin								
ls -l Mybin								
cat Mybin/inform								
echo date >> Mybin/inform								
Mybin/**inform**								
who > Mybin/new7								
rm Mybin/old7								
cd Mybin								
if **cd** Mybin works, then... — **pwd**								
ls								
inform								
more inform								
cd ..								

1. Change the mode to the needed permission by entering:

   chmod *700 Mybin*

   Enter a **y** in the table reporting that you can change the permission.

2. Confirm the permissions for the directory *Mybin* by entering:

    ls -ld *Mybin*

Enter a **y** in the table.

3. Obtain a listing of *Mybin*'s files by entering:

    ls *Mybin*

Enter a **y** in the table.

4. List the contents of the directory *Mybin*, including its permissions, owner, and so on, by entering:

    ls -l *Mybin*

5. From the parent directory, read the *inform* file, which is in *Mybin*:

    cat *Mybin/inform*

6. Add the word *date* to the existing file *inform* (note double redirect):

    echo date >> *inform*

7. Request that the *inform* script be run:

    *Mybin/***inform**

8. Create a new file in *Mybin* called *new7* by entering the following:

    who > *Mybin/new7*

9. Remove an old file by entering:

    rm *Mybin/old7*

10. Change directories to *Mybin*:

    cd *Mybin*

    pwd

If the **cd** to *Mybin* was successful and you are in *Mybin*, do the following steps. Otherwise, go to "Continuing the Exploration..." after step 14.

11. List the files:

    ls

12. Run the script:

    inform

13. Read inform:

    more *inform*

14. Return to the parent directory:

    cd ..

Continuing the Exploration of Directories with 600 to 000 Permissions

1. Change the permissions of *Mybin* to **600**.

   chmod **600** *Mybin*

2. Repeat the previous exploration steps, using *new6* in step 8 and *old6* in step 9 when appropriate. Write the results in the figure under *600*.

3. Continue with each successive permission (and use the appropriate files, that is, *newfile5* and *oldfile5* with parameter *500*) until the table is completed.

Examining the Results

These data tells us a great deal about the impact of permissions on directory access. Consider the diagrams as you review the results.

ls -ld *Mybin*

This command is a request to list permissions for the directory itself. These permissions are kept in the inode for the directory *Mybin*. The name *Mybin* and its inode number are listed in the current directory. Whether we can be in the current directory to access inodes or go through the current directory is determined by the permissions on the current directory. Regardless of the permissions on *Mybin*, we can ask what those permissions are because the permissions for the directory *Mybin* are in an inode listed in the current directory, not in *Mybin*, and we are not changing the permissions on the current directory.

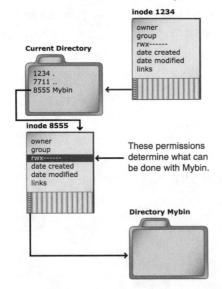

inode 1234

owner
group
rwx------
date created
date modified
links

Current Directory

1234 .
7711 ..
8555 Mybin

inode 8555

owner
group
rwx------
date created
date modified
links

These permissions determine what can be done with Mybin.

Directory Mybin

ls -l *Mybin*

To provide a long listing of the content of a directory, we must read the filenames from the directory *Mybin* and then get the permission and other information about each file from the inodes, which are also listed in *Mybin*. To get through *Mybin* to the various file inodes, we must have execute permission for the directory. Therefore, to do an **ls -l**, both **r** to read the filenames and **x** to access the inodes are needed.

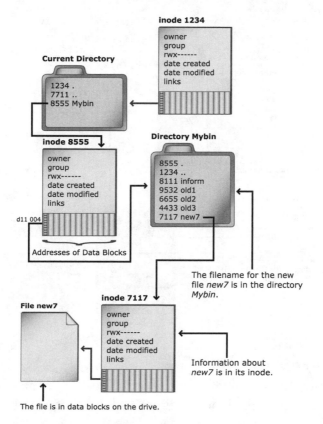

cat *Mybin/inform*
echo *date* >> *Mybin/inform*

As long as we have execute on *Mybin*, we can go through *Mybin* to reach *inform*. Though we only have **x** on the *Mybin* directory, we can still read, write, and execute the file *inform* because we have **r**, **w**, and **x** on *inform*. The **x** on *Mybin* permits us to get to *inform*. What we can do with *inform* is determined by the permissions on that file, not on its directory.

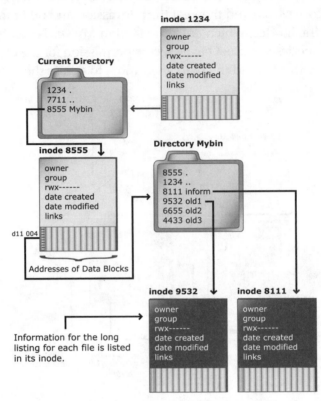

inode 1234
owner
group
rwx------
date created
date modified
links

Current Directory
1234 .
7711 ..
8555 Mybin

inode 8555
owner
group
rwx------
date created
date modified
links

d11 004

Addresses of Data Blocks

Directory Mybin
8555 .
1234 ..
8111 inform
9532 old1
6655 old2
4433 old3

Information for the long listing for each file is listed in its inode.

inode 9532
owner
group
rwx------
date created
date modified
links

inode 8111
owner
group
rwx------
date created
date modified
links

rm *Mybin/old7*
date > *Mybin/new7*

To add or remove a file from the directory, we need **w** to modify the directory's contents and **x** to reach the inode to either add the needed data for a new file or get data block addresses to release them if the file is removed.

> **S U M M A R Y :** These exercises reveal the following:
> —To list the contents of a directory with **ls**, we need read permission.
> —To create files in or remove them from a directory (thus, write to the directory file and reach inodes to describe the file), we need both write and execute permissions.
> —To make a directory the working directory with **cd**, or to pass through it as part of a search path, we need execute permission on the directory.
> —To get a long **ls** listing, both read and execute are needed. Although read permission is enough to run **ls**, it is not enough to run **ls -l**. The

information needed for the long listing is not held in the directory itself. Only the filenames and inode numbers are in the directory. The permissions, owner, and so forth, are listed in the inode. The only way to access the inode is through the directory, which requires execute permission.

Limiting Execute in a Path

Execute permission has important consequences for directories.

1. Make the permissions **rwx** for the owner of the *Mybin* directory, and then add a new directory named *Testing*:

   chmod *700 Mybin*
   ls -ld *Mybin*
   mkdir *Mybin/Testing*

2. Change directories to *Testing*, add a file there, check your location, and return to the current directory:

   cd *Mybin/Testing*
   date > *today*
   pwd
   cd *../..*
   pwd
   ls *Mybin/Testing*

   You are able to change directories through *Mybin* to *Testing*.

3. Change the permissions of *Mybin* to deny execute:

   chmod *600 Mybin*
   ls -ld *Mybin*

   Attempt to change to the *Testing* directory:

   cd *Mybin/Testing*

Because you do not have execute on the *Mybin* directory, you cannot use it in a path to reach its subdirectory *Testing*. *Testing* and its files are unreachable if there is no execute on its parent. Though the permissions on *Testing* are wide open, you cannot get to it without **x** on its parent.

Granting Execute Permission Only

You have seen that, without execute permission, you cannot change into or through a directory. Is execute enough?

1. Change the permissions for the directory *Mybin* to be only **x**:

   chmod *100 Mybin*
   ls -ld *Mybin*

2. Attempt to change directories to *Mybin*, get a listing of its files, and then change directories to *Testing* and get a listing there:

   cd *Mybin*
   pwd
   ls
   cd *Testing*
   pwd
   ls
   cd *../..*

With only execute permission on a directory, you can **cd** into it, but you cannot get a listing of its files. You can also change directories from it to a subdirectory. Once in the subdirectory, the permissions on that subdirectory are in effect.

When I was 13, I was in the kitchen when my mother asked if she could get some of her things out of a family closet that was in my room. I replied that it was the holiday season, and I was making presents in my bedroom. I didn't want anyone looking around in there. Mom said she wanted into the closet, not my room. I said, "But Mom, you have to go *through* my room to get to the closet." She replied, "I'll go through your room *blindfolded*." Once she was in the family closet, she could turn on the light, take the blindfold off, and get what she needed. I granted her execute but not read or write permission to my room. Once she passed through my room into the closet, where she had full **rwx** permission, she could do as she wished.

Establishing Directory Permissions for Group and Other

The permissions on directories are specified for user, group, and other, in the same fields of the long listing that are associated with file permissions.

1. Restore full permissions to owner for *Mybin* by typing:

   chmod *700 Mybin*
   ls -ld *Mybin*
   ls -l *Mybin*

With the present permissions, no ordinary user except the owner of the directory can obtain a listing of the files in *Mybin* using **ls**. (Of course, the super user [*root*] can access a directory regardless of its permissions.) Members of the group and others cannot **cd** to *Mybin* or use that directory in a path to access any files in it or below it—regardless of the permissions granted for the individual files.

2. Allow all users in your group to have execute permission to your directory *Mybin*. Enter:

> **chmod** *710 Mybin*
> **ls -ld** *Mybin*

This command changes permissions to allow the owner total access to the directory. Members of the group cannot run **ls** or create files in the directory. However, they can **cd** into it. Other users who are not in your group are denied all access.

3. If you have *root* power and know how to add a user, add another user, then log in as that user and try to access the directory.

4. If you logged in as a different user, log out and log back in as yourself.

5. Allow your group and others to change directories into *Mybin* and to obtain listings of files. Enter the following:

> **chmod** *755 Mybin*
> **ls -l** *Mybin*
> **ls -ld** *Mybin*

SUMMARY: The **chmod** program modifies the permissions for files and directories. In a numerical argument such as *754*, the first number (*7*) assigns permissions for the owner/user, the second number (*5*) assigns group permissions, and the last number (*4*) assigns permissions to other users.

9.8 Changing Permissions for Files in All Subdirectories

Thus far, you have changed the permissions for individual files. The **chmod** utility can be used to change the permissions for *all* files in a directory and even for all of its subdirectories.

1. Issue the following commands to change to your home directory and then to create a subdirectory that contains several files, another subdirectory, and additional files:

   cd
   mkdir *DIR-A*
   ls -ld *DIR-A*
   cd *DIR-A*
   touch *A AA AAA monica*
   ls -l *
   mkdir *DIR-B*
   ls -ld *DIR-B*
   cd *DIR-B*
   touch *B BB BBB olenka*
   ls -l *
   cd
   ls -l -R *DIR-A*

The resulting files and directories are illustrated in the following figure. The new directory, *DIR-B*, contains a series of files with limited permissions. *DIR-B* is listed in the *DIR-A* directory, which is listed in your home directory.

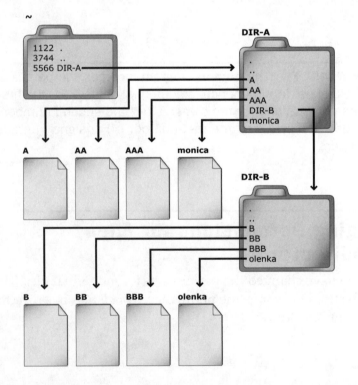

2. Change the permissions for *all* the files in *both* directories by issuing one command:

    chmod -R 777 *DIR-A*

3. Check the permissions of the directories and files:

    ls -ld *DIR-A*

    ls -l *DIR-A*

    ls -ld *DIR-A / DIR-B*

    ls -l *DIR-A / DIR-B*

The **-R** option to the **chmod** utility is instruction to start at the named directory and **R**ecursively descend down through the directory tree to change the permissions for all the files and directories it encounters.

■ Review 2

1. What are the minimum permissions that allow the user to read and have the current shell execute commands in a file?

    _____

2. What minimum numerical permission do you need to execute commands in a file by sourcing the filename?

    _____

3. What permissions on a file do you need to get a long listing of the file?

    _____

4. The file *inform* has a numerical permission of *754*. Consider the following questions:

    a. Who has what permissions?

    user:

    _____

    group:

    _____

    other:

    _____

    b. Who can change the permission of the file?

    _____

    c. Who can change the contents of the file?

  _____

5. What is the minimum permission required to pass through a subdirectory?

  _____

6. What information is kept in a directory?

  _____

7. What minimum permission(s) for a subdirectory do you need to list the contents of the subdirectory?

  _____

8. You are in a directory. What minimum permission for the current directory do you need to be there and list the contents of the directory?

  _____

9. What minimum permission for a subdirectory do you need to create files in the subdirectory?

  _____

10. What minimum permissions for the file or directory are needed to do the following successfully?

    a. cat *Mybin/inform*

      Mybin:

  _____

      inform:

  _____

    b. date > *Mybin/newfile*

      Mybin:

  _____

    c. echo *date* >> *Mybin/today* (*today* already exists.)

      Mybin:

  _____

      today:

  _____

    d. touch *Mybin/hello* (**touch** creates a new file, *hello.*)
       Mybin:

       _____

    e. rm *Mybin/hello*
       Mybin:

       _____

       hello:

       _____

    f. ls -1 *Mybin/hello*
       Mybin:

       _____

       hello:

       _____

    g. ls -l *Mybin*
       Mybin:

       _____

    h. ls -ld *Mybin*
       Mybin:

       _____

11. Fill in the missing data in the following table.

chmod Argument	Resulting Permissions
777	
	r-xr-xr--
640	
400	
	rwxr-xr--

9.9 Identifying Other Permissions

When cruising around the file system, you will sometimes see permissions **s** and **t** for files, rather than **r**, **w**, or **x**. The **s** and **t** permissions can only be set by the superuser, not by ordinary users. This section introduces these remaining two permissions. For a detailed account of these superuser permissions, consult the **man** section on **chmod** in Section 2 of the *Reference Manual,* or look in a good system administration text.

Running Programs as Root

The executable *passwd* file is a program that users run to change their passwords. The binary is located at */usr/bin/passwd* or */bin/passwd*. Encrypted passwords are kept in the password file */etc/passwd* or in */etc/shadow*, depending on your system. Ordinary users do not have write permission to these password files.

1. Enter the following commands:

    ls -l */etc/shadow* (You may not have this file on your system. It is used in more secure installations.)

    ls -l */etc/passwd*

    The superuser, *root*, is the owner and has write permission. Ordinary users do not have write.

    Even though you lack write permission to the password files, you have probably run the *passwd* program to change your passwords, thus changing the contents of one of these files.

2. Examine the permissions in the password-changing program file:

    ls -l */usr/bin/passwd*

    On a network system, examine the permissions for */usr/bin/yppasswd*. The output includes one or more unusual permissions:

```
-r-s--x--x   3   root  94208   Jun 29 1995  /usr/bin/passwd
```

This output indicates that the file's owner is *root*. The owner has read permission, and also has an **s** instead of an **x** in the execute field. Group and other each have execute permission, but not read. The **s** in the owner field indicates that when anyone who has permission to execute this program executes it, the program runs as though *root* is running it—that is, with the identity of *root*, not the identity of the person who actually requested that the program run. An ordinary user runs *passwd*, the **s** tells the system that while running the *passwd* program, the user has *root*'s identity. Because the *passwd* changing program runs as *root*, and because *root* does not have write permission for the *password* data file, any user running *passwd* has the power to change the user's password in the protected file. This is called *set user ID*.

Setting Group ID

Often programs on systems need to be available to any member of a specified group. The programs are owned by a member of the group, but other group members have execute authority. If the administrator wants other users not in the specified group to run the specific program, the set group ID is turned on for that program. If the execute permission slot for group for an executable program contains an **s**, then others with execute permission for the program run the program as though they were a member of the group, though they obviously are not.

Requiring Ownership to Remove a File

Directories can have special permissions.

Assume the permissions in a directory were **rwxrwxrwx**. If a person not in your group creates a file in the directory, you could remove the file because you have write and execute in the directory. The same goes for the */tmp* directory:

    ls -ld */tmp*

In this case, the last permission bit is a *t*, which changes the rules. With the *t* set for a directory, it prohibits a user who has write permission on the directory from removing or changing the name of files belonging to another user. This is called the *sticky bit set*. When the sticky bit is set on a directory, only the owner of a file can delete or change the name of the file in that directory.

9.10 Setting Permissions When Files and Directories Are Created

In UNIX, we create files in three ways: we copy an existing file into a new one; we use a utility such as an editor or **tee** to create a file; or we specify that the output of a utility be sent to a new file, using redirection in a shell command. When we run **ls -l** after creating a new file, the new file has permissions already set, without ever specifying them. We are not consulted first; the initial permissions are automatically assigned to the new files and directories.

Examining the Default Permissions

Thus far in this chapter, you have examined how to change the existing permissions to new permissions on files and directories. This section investigates how the initial settings are established.

Earlier in the chapter, you created the command file *inform*. The operating system initially set the permissions for you, the owner, as read and write. At that point, you were not able to execute the file. At creation, permission settings were included for other users who were members of your group and for all others. These default permission settings are determined by the **umask** value.

As you will see, the **umask** is so named because its value determines which permissions are *masked* from being set.

1. To ensure that you can access the files used in the following exercises, check to make sure you are in your home directory:

   cd

2. Obtain the current setting of **umask** by entering:

   umask

   A number such as *22* or *022* is displayed.

This **umask** setting determines the value of permissions for new files as they are created. Changing the **umask** has no effect on an existing file. The **umask** setting is initially determined by default on the system, but can be modified from the shell command line, or through entries in a user's startup files. For some hollow reason, especially in late October, people often enter **unmask**, but the command is **umask**. (True, it happens.)

Specifying Directory Permissions

To explore how directory permissions are affected by **umask**, the following exercises guide you through changing **umask** values and creating new directories.

1. Create a new, empty directory for these next exercises and make it your current directory:

   mkdir *DIRS*
   cd *DIRS*
   pwd
   ls

2. You are about to change the value of the **umask**. First, write down the present value so that you can change it back later.

   Original **umask** value: _____

3. Reset the **umask** to *000* by entering:

   umask 000

4. To confirm that you have changed the **umask**, type:

   umask

   The **umask** is now set at *000*, which may be displayed as *0*. (It doesn't make much difference whether a checking account balance is $0 or $0000. dollars.)

5. With the **umask** at *000*, create a new directory and determine its permissions:

   mkdir *DIR000*
   ls -ld *DIR**

   The output is:

   ```
   drwxrwxrwx  DIR000
   ```

   The permissions of the directory are wide open—readable, writable, and executable by everyone.

   When the **umask** is set to *000*, nothing is masked out, and all permissions are granted for new directories.

   The **umask** is *000*, so no gates are closed. Because no permissions are masked, all nine permissions are granted to the new directory.

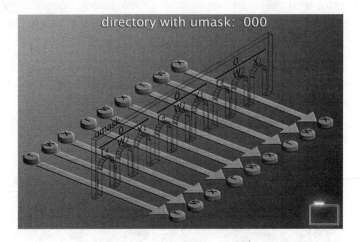

directory with umask: 000

Creating a Directory with Write Masked

A directory created while **umask** is *000* has full permissions granted to user, group, and other.

1. Change **umask** to be *022* and request confirmation:

   umask *022*
   umask

2. With the **umask** at *022*, create a new directory and examine its permissions:

   mkdir *DIR022*
   ls -ld *DIR**

   This new directory, created while the **umask** is **022**, has permissions of:

```
drwxr-xr-x
```

The owner has **rwx**, the group **r-x**, and others **r-x**. What permissions are missing or *mask*ed? Nothing is masked from the owner, *0*. Group is missing **write** permission (2), and other is missing **write** (2). The missing or masked permissions are *022*.

   The directory *DIR000* retains its full permissions. It was created while the **umask** was *000* and is not affected by the change of **umask**. The **umask** affects the permission when files and directories are created, not after. Once they are created, we change permissions with **chmod**.

   The following figures summarize how permissions are determined for a new directory when the **umask** is *022*. The two doors, **w** for group and **w** for other, are closed.

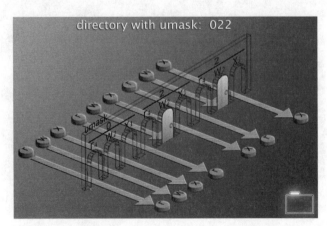

directory with umask: 022

Permissions masked when the **umask** is set to *022* are as follows:

- *0*   Nothing is masked from the *owner's* permissions.
- *2*   The permission **write** is masked from *group*.
- *2*   *Other* is also missing **write**.

umask	Owner	Group	Other	
000	rwx 421	rwx 421	rwx 421	Directory permissions granted if nothing was masked.
022	0 ---	2 -w-	2 -w-	Permissions masked by **umask** at current setting.

Masking Different Permissions for Group and Other

In the last exercise, when a new directory was created, the write permission was masked for group and other, because there were 2s in the second and third fields of **umask**.

1. Change the **umask** by entering:

   umask *037*

2. Create another directory:

   mkdir *DIR037*

3. Check the directory's permissions:

   ls -ld *DIR**

   This time the directory's permissions are:

   ```
   drwxr-----DIR 037
   ```

   The *owner* has full **rwx**, the *group* has just **read**, and *others* are granted no permissions. The directory's permissions are *740*: read, write, and execute for the owner, and read for the group. With the **umask** set at *037*, no permissions are masked for the owner, write and execute (*2+1=3*) are denied to group, and all (*4+2+1=7*) permissions are denied to other users.

The following figure summarizes how permissions for a new directory are determined when the **umask** is *037*. Although all permissions are possible for a directory, the mask doors of 0, 2+1, 4+2+1 are closed.

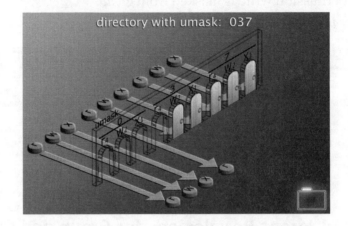

directory with umask: 037

4. Change the **umask** to the following values. With **umask** as a value, create a directory, and then examine the permissions for that directory.

umask value	Resulting Directory Permission
023	d _ _ _ _ _ _ _ _ _
066	d _ _ _ _ _ _ _ _ _
027	d _ _ _ _ _ _ _ _ _

Because nothing is masked for user (owner), and directories are created with full permissions if nothing's masked, the user gets **rwx**. Group has a mask of 2, hence the **w** is masked, so group gets read and execute. Other has a mask of 3, which masks 2 (**w**) and 1 (**x**), so the only permission granted is read, 4.

In this figure, all permissions are "launched," but the unmask doors 0, 2, 2+1 are closed with resulting permissions of rwxr-xr--.

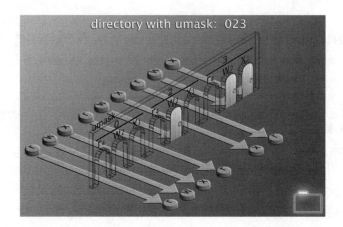

directory with umask: 023

S U M M A R Y : If the **umask** is set to *000*, no permissions are masked, and any directories created have full **rwx** for all users. A nonzero in any field of **umask** specifies the permissions that are denied to the owner, members of the group, and others depending on which field is not zero. The **umask** values and resulting permissions are as follows for each of the three fields.

Directory unmask Value Results

Umask Value	Result
0	Denies no permissions hence, grants all three permissions, **rwx**.
1	Restricts execute permission only, granting **r** and **w**.
2	Restricts write permission only, granting **r** and **x**.
3	Restricts write and execute permission only, granting **r**.
4	Restricts read permission only, granting **w** and **x**.
5	Restricts read and execute permission (4 + 1), granting **w**.
6	Restricts read and write permission (4 + 2), granting **x**.
7	Restricts read, write, and execute (1 +2 + 4), granting no permissions.

Identifying File Permissions with Nothing Masked

A particular **umask** setting results in different permissions for files than it does for directories.

1. To examine the resulting *file* permissions when nothing is masked, change the **umask** value to *0* by typing:

   umask *000*

2. Create a file named *file000*:

   date > *file000*

3. Check the mode of *file000*:

   ls -l

   At this point, the file is readable and writable by everyone.

   When the **umask** is set to *000*, nothing masked, the default permissions for a new file are *666* (readable and writable by owner, group, and others). Even though the **umask** is set to *000*, nothing masked, when files are created, they do not have execute permission. No one, not even the owner, is granted execute permission for a file until it is specifically added using the **chmod** command.

Denying Write for New Files

The **umask** is used to mask permissions for new files in the same way it masks directory permissions.

1. Set the **umask** to *022* by entering:

   umask *022*

2. Create another file called *file022* and check its permissions:

   touch *file022*
   ls -l

   The permissions are **r**ead and **w**rite for owner, and **r**ead alone for group and others (*644*).

   When the **umask** is set to *000* and you create a file, the file's initial permissions are as open as possible without granting execute (*666*). When you reset the

umask to *022* and create a new file, the new file has permissions of *644*. The write (*2*) is masked or denied for group and other.

The following figure summarizes how initial permissions are granted to files when the **umask** is *022*. Only read and write are possible, to be limited by closing **unmask** doors.

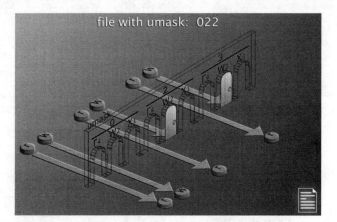

File Permissions When Execute Is Masked

At file creation, execute is never granted to a file. If **umask** also *masks* execute, what is the result when files are created?

1. Set the **umask** to *023* by typing:

   umask *023*

2. Create another file named *file023* and check its permissions:

   touch *file023*
   ls -l

   The new file created while **umask** is *023* has permissions of:

```
-rw-r--r--
```

This result is exactly the same as when the **umask** was set to *022*. The only difference between the two is that *023* calls for masking the execute permission for other users. Because files are not granted execute at creation—at all—it makes no difference whether the **umask** masks or doesn't mask execute for files.

The following table and figure summarize how permissions are granted to a new *file* when the **umask** is masking execute. At file creation, execute is not granted; hence, there is none to be masked. Masking execute for files is irrelevant.

umask	Owner	Group	Other	
000	rw 42-	rw 42-	rw 42-	File permission granted when nothing is masked.
023	0 ---	2 -w-	21 -wx	Permissions masked by **umask** at current setting
	42 rw-	4 r--	4 r--	Resulting file permissions

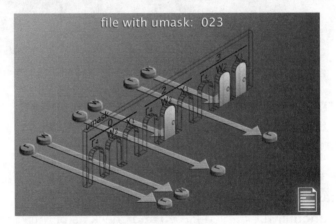

file with umask: 023

Predicting Permissions for Files

In this exercise, you change the **umask**, calculate the permissions for a file, and then check the permissions.

1. Set the **umask** to *037*:

   umask *037*

2. Create another file named *file037*:

   touch *file037*

3. In the following table, write down the permissions you expect *file037* to be granted at creation.

umask	Owner	Group	Other	
000	rw- 42-	rw- 42-	rw- 42-	File permissions granted when nothing is masked
037				Permissions masked by **umask** at current setting
				Resulting directory permissions

4. Check the new file's permissions against what you wrote in the table. Type:

ls -l *file037*

ls -l

The file's permissions are **read** and **write** for owner, and **read** for group (*640*). The **umask** works as expected: the file is not **writable** or **executable** by the group; nor is it **readable**, **writable**, or **executable** by others.

 S U M M A R Y : If the **umask** is *000*, new files are created with read and write for user, group, and other. The execute permission is not granted at file creation. When the **umask** is not *0*, permissions are masked for new files. Although *2* masks write and *4* masks read, the *1* for execute has no effect, because execute is not granted when files are created. There is nothing to mask.

Predicting Permission for Files and Directories

Because file and directory permissions are affected differently for the same **umask**, it is useful to compare the results.

In this next exercise, you will predict and compare permissions for files and directories using the **umask** values specified in the next table.

1. Predict the permissions for a file and a directory when **umask** is *022*.

2. Modify **umask** and create a directory to verify your prediction.

3. Predict each **umask**'s effect; verify by changing the **umask** and creating directories and files.

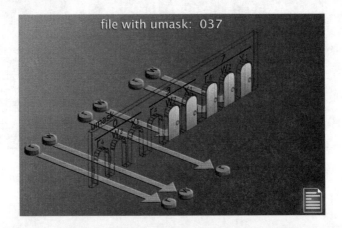

file with umask: 037

Resulting Directory Permissions	umask	Resulting File Permissions
drwxrwxrwx	000	rw-rw-rw-
	022	
	023	
	033	
	037	
	077	
	777	

9.11 Inheriting Permissions When Files Are Copied

Clearly, the **umask** affects permission when new files are created, but does it affect all new files? Whether the **cp** command retains permissions when files are copied depends on the version of UNIX you are using.

1. Set your **umask** to 777, return to your home directory, and create two files:

   umask 777
   cd
   touch *newfile777*

who > *who-file777*
ls -l **777**

Notice that, at this point, new files are created with no permissions granted at all.

2. Earlier in this chapter, you created a new file, *inform*, in your home directory that contained several shell commands. You made it executable and then executed it. Examine the permissions for the *inform* file:

ls -l *inform*

3. Make a new file by copying the *inform* file:

cp *inform inform1*
ls -l *inform1*

Because you have read permission for inform, you can copy it into *inform1*.

4. Attempt to execute the new file. Type:

inform1

If this new file is executable, proceed to step 5; otherwise, do the following:

rm *inform1*
cp -p *inform inform1*

The **-p** option on some systems tells **cp** to copy permissions as well as contents.

5. Check the permissions of both files. Type:

ls -l *inform inform1*

The file *inform1* is assigned the permissions that *inform* had when *inform1* was copied.

When you copy a file, the new copy of the file has the same permissions as the original. The **umask** has no effect on files that are created by copying other files. If you do want to have **umask** take effect when making a duplicate file, you can use a utility other than **cp**.

6. For instance, copy the file *inform* to a new file named *inform2* using the **cat** utility. Enter:

cat *inform* > *inform2*

7. Attempt to execute the new file:

inform2

You cannot execute the file.

8. Check the permissions:

ls -l *inform2*

The new file has the permissions determined by the **umask**. In this instance, you instructed the shell to redirect the output of **cat** to a new file. The shell follows **umask** instructions when creating files.

9. Before continuing with the upcoming Review section, go back to the earlier section "Identifying File Permissions with Nothing Masked" and find the original **umask** value that you recorded. Reset the **umask** back to that value. Or, just log off and log back on.

■ Review 3

1. What command sets the **umask** permission fields so that no one other than the owner can write to the file, but everyone can read the file?

   _____

2. What command sets the **umask** permission fields so that the owner can read, write, and **cd** to a directory and everyone else can only **cd** into them?

   _____

3. If **umask** is *022* and the permissions on a file named *scriptA* are **rwxr-x- - - -**, what are the permissions for the resulting files when you enter the following commands?

   a. **touch** *abc*

   _____

   b. **mkdir** *def*

   _____

   c. **who** > *ghi*

   _____

   d. **cp** *scriptA scriptB*

   _____

   e. **wc** *scriptA* > *wcA*

   _____

4. If **umask** is set to *000*, who has what permissions for newly created files and directories?

	USER	GROUP	OTHER
files			
directories			

5. The **umask** is set to *067*. Now you create a directory *Club* and a file *members* under the directory by typing:

   mkdir *Club*
   who > *Club/members*

   What are the resulting permissions for *Club* and *members*?
   Club:

   _____

   members:

   _____

6. Consider the following scenario:

   date > *today_date*
   cat *today_date*
   umask *777*
   cat *today_date*

   Will the second **cat** command be successful? Why or why not?

■ Conclusion

The UNIX/Linux operating system includes a collection of files. Some are essential for system operation; others contain valuable information. Still others are powerful programs that should be employed only by certain users. Many files are simply useful to one or more users.

Each file and directory has an associated set of permissions that determines what users can do to the file or directory. The owner of a file or directory has the power to modify permissions.

Files and directories are granted initial permissions at creation determined by the **umask** setting at the time the file or directory is created. Changing the **umask** has no effect on current files or directories, but determines the permissions for new files/directories. When files are copied, permissions are copied as well.

For a file, read permission is needed to access the file's contents with a utility, write is needed to make changes in the file, and execute is needed to start a child shell to run the commands in the file. If the file is a script, execute is necessary, but not sufficient. The child shell must read the file to see what to do, so read is also required. The contents of a directory must be read to run **ls**; hence, read permission is needed. To add a file, remove a file, or change a file's name, the user must have write and execute permission in the directory to modify the directory contents and to access the inode to modify information about the file. To **cd** into a directory or include the directory in a path, the user must have execute permission.

Two methods are available for changing the permissions: letters (**chmod +x**) and numbers (**chmod 700**).

■ Answers to Table in "File Permissions for Group and Other"

PERMISSION FIELD	TYPE	USER	GROUP	OTHER
drwxr-x—	directory	rwx	r-x	—
-rw-rw-r–	file	rw-	rw-	r–
-r-xr——	file	r-x	r–	—

■ Answers to Review 1

1. ls -l
2. Read and execute permission for the user, but not write permission. None to group or other.
3. w
4.

	USER	GROUP	OTHER
source *scriptfile*	Y	Y	Y
scriptfile	Y	Y	N
echo *date* >> *scriptfile*	Y	N	N

5. rwxr-xr--
6. read
7. **source** *hi* (bash and c shells) or **.** *hi* (Korn and Bourne shells)
8. The permission field starts with **d**.
9. Everybody in your group except you

10. r and x

11. **chmod -r+x** *inform*

12.

    a. *unx01, unx02, unx03, ora01, ora02*

    b. *unx01, unx02, unx03, ora01, ora02*

    c. *unx02, ora01, ora02*

    d. *unx01, unx02, unx03*

13. -r-x--x---

14. chmod u-w, g+x, o+x *simple*

15.

700	rwx – – – – – –
400	r – – – – – – –
200	–w– – – – – –
600	rw– – – – – –
100	– –x – – – – –
000	– – – – – – – –
500	r–x – – – – –

16.

COMMAND	RESULTING PERMISSION
chmod 777 *inform*	rwxrwxrwx
chmod 751 *inform*	rwxr–x– –x
chmod 640 *inform*	rw–r– – – – –
chmod 660 *inform*	rw–rw– – – –
chmod 000 *inform*	– – – – – – – –
chmod 444 *inform*	r– –r– –r– –
chmod 754 *inform*	rwxr–xr– –
chmod 420 *inform*	r– – –w– – – –

■ Answers to Review 2

1. read
2. *444*

3. none

4.

    a. User: r w x
       Group: r x
       Other: r

    b. User

    c. User

5. x

6. Names of files and their inode numbers

7. r

8. rx

9. wx

10.

    a. **cat** *Mybin / inform*
       Mybin: x
       inform: r

    b. **date** > *Mybin/newfile*
       Mybin: wx

    c. **echo date** >> *Mybin/today* (*today* already exists.)
       Mybin: x
       today: w

    d. **touch** *Mybin/hello* (**touch** creates a new file, *hello*.)
       Mybin: wx

    e. **rm** *Mybin/hello*
       Mybin: wx
       hello: Nothing

    f. **ls -1** *Mybin/hello*
       Mybin: x
       hello: Nothing

    g. **ls -1** *Mybin*
       Mybin: rx

    h. **ls -ld** *Mybin*
       Mybin: Nothing

11.

777	rwxrwxrwx
554	r–xr–xr– –
640	rw–r– – – – –
400	r– – – – – – –
754	rwxr–xr– –

■ Answers to Review 3

1. umask *022*

2. umask *066*

3.
    a. rw-r--r--

    b. rwxr-xr-x

    c. rw-r--r--

    d. rwxr-x---

    e. rw-r--r--

4.

	USER	GROUP	OTHER
Files	rw-	rw-	rw-
Directories	rwx	rwx	rwx

5. *Club*: **710** or -rwx--x---
   members: **600** or -rw------

6. Yes. The **umask** will only affect newly created files and directories. Changing the **umask** will not change previously created files and directories.

COMMAND SUMMARY

source *filename*   Will run a script in the C shell.

**. *filename*   Will run a script in the ksh or bash shells.

whoami   Displays the information about who you are and your current login name.

id   Shows your UID and GID (information about you and the group to which you belong).

chmod mode *filename*   Changes the permissions on *filename* to those represented by *mode.*

chmod -w *filename*   Removes the write permissions for all classes of users.

chmod + *filename*   Adds the execute permissions to all classes of users.

chmod a=rwx *filename*   Changes all permissions for all classes to read, write, and execute.

chmod u=rwx,g=rx,o=r *filename*   Changes permissions to read, write, and execute for user; read and execute for group; and read for others.

chmod u=rwx,go= *filename*   Changes permissions to read, write, and execute for user; and removes all permissions for group and others.

umask *mode*   Changes the default permissions for newly created files and directories. Initial permission value is equal to **777** masked by *mode* for directories, and a permission value equal to **666** masked by *mode* for plain files.

Mode Summary

r   Allows read permission for designated user.

w   Allows write permission for designated user.

x   Allows execute permission for designated user.

4   Allows read permission for designated user.

2   Allows write permission for designated user.

1   Allows execute permission for designated user.

Obtaining Help from Online Resources

10

S K I L L S   C H E C K

Before beginning this chapter, you should be able to

- Access and leave the system
- Execute basic shell commands
- Redirect output from a utility to another utility or file

O B J E C T I V E S

After completing this chapter, you will be able to

- Display the online manual pages that describe specific commands and files
- Search for online manual pages by keyword or regular expression
- Navigate around the **info** database to obtain information about utilities
- Identify and access useful Internet sites

U NIX and Linux systems include an extensive collection of powerful utility programs, system features, application languages, and support libraries. These diverse and complex facilities are too numerous and feature-rich to remember in detail. While working, we often need to employ the exact syntax of a particular option or command format for a utility. The needed information is available from the *UNIX Programmer's Manual*, often called the *UNIX Reference Manual*, which is available online. Additionally, Linux systems and some UNIX systems provide help accessed by a utility called **info**, which obtains information concerning many commands and features from an online database. The Internet also provides a wealth of resource information concerning UNIX and Linux. This chapter examines how to access information in the manual through the **man** command, locate appropriate help from the **info** database, and access resources on the Net.

10.1 Accessing the Programmer's Manual

The Reference Manual is an indispensable part of a functioning system. It contains readily available, detailed documentation on the uses and functions of all standard utility programs, many application programs and libraries, as well as information on UNIX system files and system programming libraries. The Reference Manual also contains supplementary information on related special files and commands for each entry. In addition, examples and error conditions are often provided.

Displaying and Searching Through a Manual Entry

From the shell, you can request that individual manual entries be written on the workstation screen.

1. Examine the online manual entry for the **cat** utility by entering:

    man *cat*

    Every manual entry follows the same basic organization. The top line of the output includes the name of the utility, followed by a number in parentheses that refers to the section of the manual where the entry is located. Words at the left margin in all uppercase letters, such as "NAME" and "SYNOPSIS," introduce the various sections of the entry. The NAME section has a brief description of the utility.

2. Advance through the manual pages for the **cat** utility:

   SPACEBAR

3. Quit the **man** utility:

   q

4. Examine the manual entry for **sort**:

   man *sort*

   We can move around the manual entry using **more**'s navigation commands.

5. Enter:

   SPACEBAR
   SPACEBAR
   ENTER
   b
   b
   q

Because the **more** utility is employed to display the **man** pages, all of the usual text display commands from **more** work. Pressing the SPACEBAR advances one screen of text at a time, pressing ENTER advances one line of text at a time, and pressing **b** scrolls back one screen of text.

Searching Through a Manual Entry

Often, manual entries are very long, and it is difficult to access the portion that contains what you want. We can search for specific words.

1. Call up the manual entry for *sort* again.

   man *sort*

2. With the first part displayed, search for the word *field* by entering:

   /field

   Press ENTER and the display advances to the first page that includes the word *field*.

3. Press **n** to advance to the next instance of the word *field*.

   We can search with the */target* command and we quit with **q**.

   Entries in the manual tend to follow the structure of a newspaper story: usually the most critical information comes first. By reading just the first few sections, you can examine the most important features of the utility.

4. To exit the **man** utility, enter **q**.

5. Examine the manual entries for a few of the commands you have used, such as **date**, **wc**, **more**, **who**, **vi**, **grep**, and **awk**. Take special note of the options available for each utility.

Searching for Manual Entries Using Keywords

On most systems, we can have the **man** utility search the online manual database for all entries containing a specific keyword. In the NAME section of each utility's manual entry is the utility's name and a brief description of what the utility accomplishes. We can have **man** search the manual pages' descriptions for keywords. Usually, the description lines are kept in a separate database for easy access.

1. Do a keyword search for the word *edit* to see which entries relate to text editors.

>   **man -k** *edit* **| more**

   or

>   **apropos** *edit* **| more**

   Among the many entries listed, you will find your old friends **vi**, **vim**, **sed** and **ed.** Search the manual table of contents for the word *copy* by typing:

>   **man -k** *copy* **| more**

   Each of the lines in the output contain the string *copy,* either in the title or in the brief description that follows. The keyword may be any combination of letters. Some of the entries in the **man -k** output do not contain *copy* as a separate word; instead, *copy* is part of anther word. When doing a keyword search, **man -k** searches for all instances of the string you provide as the target.

2. Do similar searches using the keywords *move, print, help,* and *file.*

10.2 Outputting Manual Pages to a File or Printer

The output of **man** is normally sent to the screen. You can also instruct the shell to redirect the output of **man** to a file or to the printer.

1. Redirect the manual entry for **man** by entering this command:

>   **man man >** *man.manpage*

2. Examine *man.manpage* with the editor by entering:

> **vi** *man.manpage*

Included in the output on many systems are a number of control characters needed to display the file properly on the screen. They make the output difficult to read in a file or when printed. Depending on various local settings of the printing and spooling of print jobs, your print out of the **man** output may include control characters.

One way to dispose of these characters is to redirect **man** output to an intermediary utility that cleans up the control characters.

3. Quit the editor.

4. From the shell, try each of the following commands. One should work on your system.

> **man** *who* | **colcrt** > *who.manpage*
> **man** *who* | **col -bx** > *who.manpage*

5. Examine the output by entering:

> **vi** *who.manpage*

6. To print the output of **man**, enter one of the following commands:

> **man** *who* | **colcrt** | **lpr**
> **man** *who* | **col -bx** | **lpr**

The **colcrt** and **col** utilities remove the terminal control characters.

10.3 Locating Information with info

The **info** utility provides access to a wealth of information about commands and system features. The **info** database and its user interface provide detailed descriptions of many system files, programs, and options in a navigable online environment. The **man** utility requires that you know exactly what command you are looking for or a precise word that might describe the actions of a command or file. However, in some situations the word that comes to mind is not the word that is used to describe the topic in the manual pages. The **info** utility offers a way to browse through a hierarchical tree of descriptive informational pages, which often provide us with answers to questions we did not realize we were asking.

Accessing the info Program

A large database of help files that contains a wealth of information about all aspects of the system is included in Linux systems.

1. Try the following command:

   info *sort*

   A page of information about the **sort** utility is displayed. Make a quick read. It contains much of the same information as the **man** pages.

2. To leave **info**, enter:

   q

3. Examine another entry:

   info *ls*

4. Page down by entering:

   SPACEBAR

   SPACEBAR

   ↓ [DOWN ARROW]

5. To page up, one of the following should work:

   DELETE

   or

   BACKSPACE

6. Leave **info** by entering:

   q

Examining info From the Top

We can access information about various utilities and system features through the **info** database. If we do not give **info** a topic argument, it starts by displaying a top level file.

1. Enter:

   info

   The **info** command always invokes a file from the **info** database. In this case, the file *dir* is displayed, which describes the top of the **info** database tree. Your screen probably looks something like the following:

```
File: dir        Node: Top       This is the top of the INFO tree

   This (the Directory node) gives a menu of major topics.
   Typing "q" exits, "?" lists all Info commands, "d" returns here,
   "h" gives a primer for first-timers,

* Menu:

Texinfo documentation system
* Info: (info).                      Documentation browsing system.
* Standalone info program: (info-stnd).    Standalone Info-reading program.
* Texinfo: (texinfo).           The GNU documentation format.
* install-info: (texinfo)Invoking install-info. Update info/dir entries.
* makeinfo: (texinfo)Invoking makeinfo.       Translate Texinfo source.
* texi2dvi: (texinfo)Format with texi2dvi.    Print Texinfo documents.
* texindex: (texinfo)Format with tex/texindex. Sort Texinfo index files.
```

Each file or node contains information about a specific topic. This node contains the menu to access the top-level nodes of major files in the **info** database. The major filenames are preceded by one asterisk in the beginning of the line and followed by the filename, in parenthesis, where the topic information is kept. The screen identifies your current location in the **info** database tree. In this case, you are reading file *dir* and you are located in the "Top" node. This screen also provides some information about the program, and then presents the beginning of the long menu of topics.

2. Move around the pages by pressing:

   ↓ DOWN ARROW
   ↓ DOWN ARROW
   ↑ UP ARROW
   SPACEBAR
   SPACEBAR
   DELETE   (or BACKSPACE)

Returning to the Top of the Node

1. No matter where in the file you are located, you can return to the top of this node with:

   b

   The information and menu at the beginning of the node is presented again.

2. Go deep into the node by pressing a series of SPACEBARs.

3. Return to the top:

   b

Obtaining Help About Info

The **info** program includes its own **help**, which is an **info** node.

1. Enter:

    CTRL-H

    or

    ?

2. Move around this help section with the ARROW keys, as well as the SPACEBAR and DELETE.

    As you can see, there are many commands available to the **info** utility.

3. To leave this help screen press:

    l   (el key)

    You are back at the file *dir* because it is the last node you examined.

4. Exit **info** by pressing:

    q

Selecting Information by Making Menu Choices

In the last exercise, you scanned the contents for the top-level node of the **info** database tree. The system information data is kept in files accessed through the menus listed in the top node of the database tree.

1. Start **info** again:

    info

2. Press the DOWN ARROW to move through the text of the top node until the cursor is at one of the options (with an asterisk on its left) that you find interesting.

3. With the cursor on top of the chosen line press:

    ENTER

    Now you are located in the top of whatever file you chose.

4. Exit the **info** program.

    q

    A second way to access menus is available.

5. Enter:

    info *bc*

    The top of the node for the **bc** calculator program is displayed. It consists only of menu options.

6. To select the *Examples* option, enter:

   m *exa*

   and press the ENTER key.

   The **m** tells the program you want a menu. Provide enough of the menu's name that uniquely identifies it. After you press ENTER, Scotty beams you there.

7. Exit **info**.

Examining the Database Files

1. Request information about the **wc** utility:

   info *wc*

2. Page down several times:

   SPACEBAR
   SPACEBAR
   SPACEBAR
   SPACEBAR
   SPACEBAR
   SPACEBAR

   At this point, you probably left the information concerning **wc** and are into information concerning another utility. The **info** database is a complex set of files that are related in various ways.

3. Change to the directory that holds the **info** files by entering the following:

   cd */usr/share/info*
   ls

   The *share/info* directory contains files that are accessed by **info**. Most are *zip* files, compressed so they take up less space. The file named *dir* is listed, and it is not compressed.

4. Examine *dir* with:

   more *dir*

   This is the file that is the top-level node of the information tree. It has all the menus for selecting other files.

5. Exit the **more**:

   q

6. List the directory contents again and then examine one of the files:

    ls

    zcat *which**

    q

The **zcat** utility uncompresses and displays compressed files. The output is the contents of the file that contains information about **which**. The **info** command facilitates our accessing the information in this directory.

Summary of Navigation Through info

The nodes are set up like a tree. You can descend to certain subtopics, you can move to the following or **ne**xt node or **previous** node in the same level, or you can ascend to a node above the level you are in. If you are in the *Top* node of a file and try to go up the tree from there, you exit that file and end up at the *Top* node of file *dir*, the highest node of the **info** database tree.

1. Enter:

    info

The top node of the **info** tree is displayed once again.

2. Enter:

    h

A mini-tutorial on how to use **info** is provided. Read this section and follow the steps provided there. Although the steps may appear simple at first, they quickly become more complex.

Summary of Frequently Used Node Navigation Commands

n	Takes you to the next node in the current level.
p	Takes you to the previous node at the same level.
u	Takes you up one level of the current node.
d	Takes you back to the *Top* node of file *dir*.
l	Takes you back to the last node you were at.
b	Takes you to the beginning of current node.
DOWN ARROW	Moves one line down at a time.
UP ARROW	Moves one line up at a time.
SPACEBAR	Moves forward a page.
DELETE OR BACKSPACE	Moves backward a page.
q	Quits info.

10.4 Accessing Internet Resources

The Internet is a fluid assembly of more information than we can assimilate in several lifetimes. The key to success lies in being able to access what you want by narrowing your search. Unfortunately, search engines bring up a lot of chaff with the wheat. To save you trouble and get you started, we maintain a list of sites that we find useful. With time, new sites are developed, others go to bit heaven. Therefore, some sites on the following list may not be available or useful as you access them. To obtain our latest recommended site list, see the instructions that follow the list.

Examining Helpful Internet Sites

The following sites provide a sample of the wealth of available information.

- For recent news in the Linux world:

    http://www.linux.org/
    http://linux.com/

- For interactive web tutorials and information on designing and developing courseware in the UNIX/Linux worlds:

    http://www.muster.com

- For Linux code documentation:

    http://www.linuxdoc.org/

- For recent software updates and information on how to configure the GNOME GUI:

    http://gnome.org/

Locating Current List of Internet Sites

We maintain our *Helpful Internet Sites* page with annotated names and addresses of the sites our students find useful.

1. Using your browser, go to:

    www.muster.com

2. At the home page, locate *Services* and click on:

    Links to Sites

    The current list of our *Helpful Internet Sites* is displayed and active. Copy the list to your system and then browse away.

■ Review

1. What command displays the manual entry for **man**?

   _____

2. What command would you type to search the **man** table of contents for all references to the word *file*?

   _____

3. What command will display the info page for **ls**?

   _____

4. When you're in the **info** pages, what keystroke will take you to the top node regardless of where you are?

   _____

5. What happens when you press **u** while in the info pages?

   _____

6. You are at the bottom of a node. What happens when you press **b**?

   _____

■ Conclusion

Three major sources of information and help for users were explored in this chapter: the **man** pages, the **info** help system, and sites on the Internet. Each source of information provides a wealth of resources for users who have questions, need to locate a utility to accomplish a task or solve a problem, or just learn more about the system and its resources.

■ Answers to Review

1. **man** *man*
2. **man -k** *file* | **more**
3. **info** *ls*
4. **d**
5. It takes you to the node listed under *Up* on your current node.
6. It takes you back to the top of the text in the current node.

COMMAND SUMMARY

man -k word(s)   Displays all lines in the table of contents containing any word listed in *word(s)*.

info *command_name*   Displays the information from the info database describing the mode for *command_name*.

n   Displays the next node.

p   Displays the previous node.

u   Displays the node that is listed as the Up node.

l   Displays the node for menu_item

b   Scrolls back to the top of the current node.

q   Quit info.

Summary of Info Navigation Commands

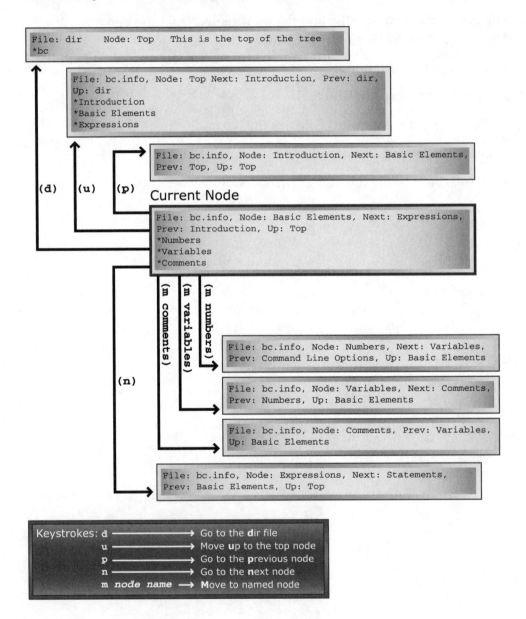

```
File: dir      Node: Top   This is the top of the tree
*bc
```

```
File: bc.info, Node: Top Next: Introduction, Prev: dir,
Up: dir
*Introduction
*Basic Elements
*Expressions
```

```
File: bc.info, Node: Introduction, Next: Basic Elements,
Prev: Top, Up: Top
```

(d) (u) (p)

Current Node

```
File: bc.info, Node: Basic Elements, Next: Expressions,
Prev: Introduction, Up: Top
*Numbers
*Variables
*Comments
```

(m comments) (m variables) (m numbers)

```
File: bc.info, Node: Numbers, Next: Variables,
Prev: Command Line Options, Up: Basic Elements
```

(n)

```
File: bc.info, Node: Variables, Next: Comments,
Prev: Numbers, Up: Basic Elements
```

```
File: bc.info, Node: Comments, Prev: Variables,
Up: Basic Elements
```

```
File: bc.info, Node: Expressions, Next: Statements,
Prev: Basic Elements, Up: Top
```

Keystrokes: d ——————→ Go to the **d**ir file
            u ——————→ Move **u**p to the top node
            p ——————→ Go to the **p**revious node
            n ——————→ Go to the **n**ext node
            m *node name* —→ **M**ove to named node

Controlling User Processes

OBJECTIVES

After completing this chapter, you will be able to

- Display information about processes
- Describe the life cycle of a process
- Terminate problem processes
- Suspend and activate processes
- List, background, foreground, suspend, and kill jobs

At any moment, one to several users are logged onto a running Linux or UNIX system doing a variety of tasks. A user may be editing a file in one window and searching the Web in another. At the same time, other users are performing system administration tasks, updating a database, and creating web pages. The system itself is also running tasks, handling central processor scheduling, reading and writing to the disk, sending mail, printing jobs, and completing other system functions. Each of these running programs is a separate process that includes reading instructions, accessing computer memory, reading from input, evaluating arguments, performing calculations, and writing to output.

Because UNIX and Linux provide numerous users the opportunity to run many different programs at the same time, management of those tasks is essential. When UNIX was designed, multitasking was a main objective. The goal was to allow several tasks to be accomplished at the same time. The problem was keeping all the activity straight. Processes were the solution.

In this chapter, you will investigate how the hardware and software execute utilities via processes, how to monitor and control separate processes, and how to manage several processes connected by pipes as one job.

11.1 Processing Processes

A *process* is the code, data, CPU activity, memory accesses, and other events associated with an instance of a program's execution. When we request **date**, a process is started that follows the instructions in the file */bin/date*, the code for the utility **date**. Some processes take only a short time to complete; others run continuously. All processes, however, go through a life cycle that begins when they are started and that ends when they exit.

You log onto your system. A shell process begins. You enter commands to the shell. The shell interprets the commands you type, executes the utilities requested, waits, then after the utilities are finished, asks you what you want to do next. Many processes that maintain the system's functionality (printing, accepting logins, serving web pages) are started when the system is booted. When we enter a command line at the shell prompt and press ENTER, the shell starts a new child process, completes redirection of input and output, passes arguments, and finally instructs the process to execute the appropriate program's code that was specified in the command line. We start child processes all the time: **vi**, **cat**, and **who**, for instance, are utilities run in child processes. When we start a child shell by entering **tcsh** or **bash**, a child process is started that runs the shell code. The shell is just another program or utility.

When a utility such as **vi** is being executed by several users (or several times by the same user), each execution of the program is a separate process.

Obtaining Detailed Information on System Processes

In previous chapters, you used **ps** to display information concerning processes that are owned by you. We can use **ps** to examine all processes running on your system, regardless of who owns them.

1. Enter the following commands:

    ps -aux | more
    ps -ef | more

    One or both of the previous command lines probably resulted in a long list of all the processes currently running on the system. The output lists the ID of each process, what code it is running, who the owner is, and other data. Several of the processes belong to *root*, because *root* is the owner of many system processes.

    We can request that **ps** list only the processes owned by a particular user.

2. Enter:

    ps -u *root* **| more**

    The wealth of processes started when your system booted up, and owned by *root*, are described.

3. List all processes owned by you:

    ps -u *$USER*

    This list identifies all the processes you own running in any terminals.

Identifying Processes Connected to a Terminal

If you are using a graphical environment, processes that you own manage the various graphical components. If you are on a terminal or interacting through a terminal window, all current processes started through this terminal can be identified. Most user processes need to read input from and write output to a terminal display. Thus, most user processes must be informed of the *tty* or port to which they are attached. This data is stored with each process and is displayed as part of the output of the **ps** command.

1. Start a process, having it execute in the background with:

   sleep 1000 &

2. At the shell prompt, determine what terminal port you are using:

   tty

   The output is something like */dev/console* or */dev/tty09* or */dev/pts/04*.

3. Use the portion of the *tty* output after the */dev/* for your *port* in the following:

   ps -t *port*   (where *port* is like *console* or *tty/09* or *pts/04*)

   The output probably shows the running processes, your shell, the **sleep**, and the **ps**. If you are running the graphical interface or have logged in more than once, there may be more processes. The output is probably like the following:

P I D	T T Y	T I M E	C M D
8464	pts/04	00.00	**bash**
9312	pts/04	00.00	**sleep**
9627	pts/04	00.00	**ps**

4. Using the output displayed on your terminal from the **ps** command, fill out the following chart for your shell, the **sleep**, and **ps**:

P I D	T I M E	C M D
		sleep
		ps

In this exercise, you recorded three pieces of information for each process:

- The PID or *process identification number*
- The CPU time the process has consumed
- The command code being executed by the process

PID   The numbers in the PID column serve as **Process IDentification** numbers. As each process is created, it is assigned a unique PID beginning with 0 at system startup. If 1,207 were the PID of your **ps** process, it might or might not be the $1,208^{th}$ process started on your system since the last time the system was rebooted. PID numbers do not simply increase forever. Each system has a maximum process identification number. When this number is reached, the numbering starts over again from the first *available* number greater than 1. As a result, a process with a lower PID may have been started after one with a higher PID.

TIME   This is the CPU time used by the process so far. Because systems are quite fast, this is often zero.

CMD   The items listed in this column are the names of the utilities associated with each of the processes you have running.

On most systems, when you run **ps**, one of the processes listed is **ps**. When the **ps** utility is running, it lists all the processes that are running at that time. Thus, it lists itself.

1. Run the **ps** utility again using your port data to list processes attached to your terminal, and fill out the following chart based on this new output:

    ps -t *port*   (where *port* is like **console** or **tty09** or **pts/04**)

PID	CMD

Compare the PIDs for the shell process in this and the previous table. It is the same PID, and, therefore, the same shell process as before. You did not exit the shell; it is continuing to wait on your every need.

Compare the PIDs for the **ps** process in the two tables. They are different because when the **ps** completed its work the first time, it output its results and quit. The second instance of executing the **ps** utility is a new one; hence, a new PID.

When a user enters a utility name at the shell prompt, a process is created to carry out the instructions contained within the utility. The process completes its task, writes its output, and dies. If the user then enters the same command name again (as you just did with the **ps** command), a new process is created with a new PID.

Starting a New Shell Process

Most processes live short, happy lives executing utilities. They perform their functions and then die.

1. Log out and then log back on.
2. After logging back on, identify your current port:

   tty
3. After you have logged on again, get a list of the processes you are running:

   ps -t *port*   (where *port* is like *console* or *tty09* or *pts/04*)

   The PID of your current shell is different from the PID of your previous login shell, which you noted in the tables on the previous pages.

   This is a new shell process. It has a new PID. When you logged out, you exited the old one. The shell process that you are now using was created when you logged on.
4. Start a child shell, determine its port, and examine the currently running processes:

   csh
   tty
   ps -t *port*   (where *port* is like *console* or *tty09* or *pts/04*)
5. Ask your current shell for its PID:

   echo $$

   Every shell maintains a variable that contains its PID. We access it with **echo $$**.

   The parent shell is still alive, so is the child. You are communicating with the child shell.
6. Exit the child:

   exit

   When you enter the command **exit** or CTRL-D, the shell process finally does what all processes do when they reach the end of a file or receive an **exit** command—it dies.

Obtaining Detailed Data About User Processes

The **ps** utility provides a great deal of information about the status of processes and their relationships.

1. To generate a long listing of your current processes, enter:

> **ps -l**   (minus el)

Following are descriptions of some of the fields in this display. The **man** pages provide information about **ps** on your system and are an essential resource.

Flags (F)

This mysteriously named field contains a number indicating what **F**lags or options are set for the process. For this purpose, the only meaningful number is the one that indicates that the process is in memory. Which of your processes is in memory? Certainly **ps** is—it must be in memory when it is running, and it must be running while it is performing its function. And probably the shell that is running, **csh** or **ksh**, is in memory. Most processes are in memory at any given moment.

State (STAT)

The State field contains an uppercase letter indicating the state of the process. The most common states are sleeping (S), and running or runnable (R). Other states are idle (I) and traced (T).

Size (SZ)

The **SiZe** field contains a number that indicates the size of the process in memory. If you can read hexadecimal (base 16), you can use this field to determine the relative sizes of processes. Depending on which system you are using, the process size may be given in kilobytes, blocks, or pages. Details such as process size unit of measurement are best determined by checking the manual pages of your system.

Command(CMD)

This label refers to the actual command being run by the process.

Identifying the Genealogy of Processes

A process is much more than a series of instructions for the CPU to follow. Important data is associated with each process, including the workstation (*tty*) to which it is attached, a list of open files to which it can write, and other pertinent information. When you create a process, it inherits most of this information from its *parent process.*

1. Enter the following commands to explore how processes keep track of their parents:

    ps -l
    csh
    ps -l

2. Using the new subset of fields displayed by the **ps -l** command, fill in the following chart:

P I D	P P I D	T T Y	C M D
			_____(Parent shell)
			csh
			ps

Essentially, each process is created, or spawned, by a previously existing process—its parent process. Each process knows its own PID and the PID of its parent. Specifically, in the table you just created, the PPID (**Parent PID**) associated with the **csh** process is identical to the PID associated with **csh**'s parent, whatever shell process (**csh**, **sh**, or **ksh**) you were in when you started the **csh**. The shell process executed the **csh** and is the parent of the **csh** process. When we ask a child for the name of his or her parent, we get the same answer as when we ask the parent for his or her own name.

Processes inherit data from their parent process. When you log onto the system, your first process, usually the shell process, is started up by the login program. From then on, every utility or executable filename that you type in is executed by a process that is a child (or *n*th grandchild) of your shell process. Because each new process that is created is a child process, it inherits data (such as *tty*, user ID, current directory) from the parent process. Variables that are exported are passed to the child shell.

Ending Foreground Processes

Generally, once a process is under way, it runs until it is finished, unless you issue a keyboard interrupt, log out, or you instruct the process to die.

Identifying the Interrupt Setting

One of the important settings for your terminal is the *interrupt,* which tells processes to exit. Usually, the interrupt is set to CTRL-C, but it may be set to another key sequence.

1. Perform a sanity check. See what the setting is for your system:

   stty -a

   The output is a long list of settings for your terminal and keyboard interaction with the system. One of the settings is probably:

   ```
   intr  =  ^C
   ```

   which indicates the *interrupt* is set to CTRL-C. If you have some other value, use it in the following exercises for CTRL-C.

Interrupting a Process from the Keyboard

If we start a process, we can end it with a signal.

1. Start a process by entering:

   sleep *100*

   The program is running in the foreground; you are not presented with a new prompt. At this point, you could wait nearly two minutes (100 seconds), or you can tell the shell to issue the interrupt signal to the process.

2. Enter:

   CTRL-C

   The sleep dies and the shell asks what's next.

3. Ask for the exit status from the sleep:

   echo $*?* (or **echo $status)

   The variable *?* is interpreted by the shell as the exit code of the last process. The status reported is probably *130* or *1*, indicating that the process did not end successfully, but was terminated.

4. Start a utility with the keyboard as input:

   wc

5. Enter a few lines and then on a new line, indicate you are through entering data with the end-of-file character:

   CTRL-D

The output of **wc** is displayed, reporting the number of lines, words, and characters that you entered as input.

6. Run **wc** again. After entering text, exit **wc** using the *interrupt* instead of the EOF:

wc
A few lines of text
CTRL-C

The process exits, the shell prompt is displayed, but no output is generated by **wc**. When we issue a CTRL-D, we are saying, "end of file, there is no more input, do your counting and report." In contrast, the CTRL-C interrupt signal tells the process to stop all operations, die, and be gone. No output is generated; the process just croaks.

Telling a Process to Quit

Another keyboard signal that users can employ to stop a foreground process is *quit*.

1. Start a foreground process:

sleep *300*

No prompt is displayed; the sleep process is running in the foreground.

2. Instruct the process to *quit* with:

CTRL-\   (CTRL and backslash)

The sleep process quits; a new shell prompt is displayed. The *quit* signal destroys the process and sometimes makes a copy of the CPU memory associated with the process at the time of its hasty exit, called a *core* file.

3. List your files and remove the *core* file if it is there:

ls

The *interrupt* and its stronger brother *quit* are available to users to force a process running in the foreground to exit.

Ending Processes Not in the Foreground

When a process is running in the foreground, we can issue *interrupt* and *quit* signals from the keyboard. If a process is running in the background, what is the impact of the *interrupt* and *quit* signals?

Interrupting and Quitting

Start another process.

1. Enter:

   sleep *500* **&**

   The **&** appended to the command line tells the shell that the command should not be run as the current job, but rather should be executed in the background while the shell attends to other tasks we request.

2. With the sleep running in the background, enter:

   ps

3. Attempt to issue the *interrupt* and *quit* signals:

   CTRL-C
   CTRL-\
   ps

   The *interrupt* and *quit* signals from the keyboard have no impact on the process. We are not able to send keyboard signals to a process if it is not the foreground process.

4. Examine the output from the last **ps** and identify the *PID* of the sleep process.

5. Kill the sleep process using its *PID* in the following:

   kill *-2* *PID*

   The shell responds with

   ```
   [1]   Interrupt    sleep 500
   ```

   indicating that the process ended as a result of an interrupt.

   The **kill** command sends one of several *signals,* which are like bad news telegrams to processes. For instance, many utilities can be killed from the keyboard by entering the keyboard interrupt character, CTRL-C. The very same effect can be achieved by sending *signal 2* (**kill** *-2* *PID*) to the process. In fact, the keyboard interrupt character CTRL-C just sends *signal 2* to the foreground process that is attached to your terminal. When you press CTRL-C with no process in the foreground, the shell process itself gets the *interrupt*. Wisely, the shells are programmed to *catch* the interrupt signal and to do nothing special with them. Upon receipt of a signal, a process may be programmed to forestall its demise by *catching* the signal, or it may follow the signal's instruction and exit. Not all utilities can catch signals.

The *-2* option to **kill** instructs it to issue the *interrupt* signal to whatever process is associated with the argument *PID*. We can also enter instructions to **kill** to send the same *quit* signal to a process as we send from the keyboard with CTRL-\.

6. Start another process, identify the *PID*, and kill it with the *quit* signal as an argument to **kill**:

    sleep 600 &

    ps

    kill -3 *PID*   (the *PID* of the sleep process)

    The shell confirms the process was ended with a *quit.*

The CTRL-\ from the keyboard sends the same *quit* signal to the current foreground process that **kill -3** sends to any process identified by its *PID.*

Sending the Terminate Signal

There are many different signals that can be sent to processes using the **kill** command. Some are useful to users.

1. Enter:

    sleep 200 &

    The *PID* of the **sleep** is listed on the screen.

2. Use **sleep**'s *PID* in the following:

    kill *PID*

    When we use the **kill** *PID* command without an argument, we are issuing the default **kill** signal. The default signal is *signal 15*, the *Software Terminate* signal. It is a friendly message to the program that is running to put its toys away and exit. The response you got from the shell indicates that the process was terminated by the signal.

3. Start another process, identify its *PID*, and terminate it with the *Software Terminate* argument (*-15*) and the *PID* of the process:

    sleep 500 &

    kill -15 *PID*

Using the *-15* argument or no argument results in sending the same *Software Terminate* signal.

Hanging Up on a Process

Sometimes killing a process with the default *Software Terminate* signal has no effect, because the process catches that signal, or because of the peculiarities in the way signals get delivered by the system. In these situations, the process continues to run and to appear in the output of **ps**. Often, by sending a different, stronger signal, you can have the process exit.

1. Once more, type the command:

   sleep *200 &*

2. Identify the PID of the sleep process and kill the process with:

   kill *-1 PID*

   ps

The output indicates that the process was terminated with *signal 1*, the *Hangup* signal, which breaks the communication links of a process. Like people, most applications quit when they have been hung up on.

Aborting a Process

Likewise, we can end a process using the *abort* signal.

1. Enter:

   sleep *200 &*

   ps

   kill *-6 PID*

   The process is aborted.

2. Start a child shell. Determine its **PID** by entering:

   echo $$

3. Attempt to kill the shell by entering:

   kill *PID*

   echo $$

4. If the shell catches the terminal signal, try the following until the child shell is terminated. Once the shell exits, start a new one and try the other signals.

   kill *-2 PID*

   echo $$

   kill *-3 PID*

   echo $$

   kill *-6 PID*

echo $$
kill *-1 PID*
echo $$
kill *-9 PID*
echo $$

If you are using a graphical interface, start some processes in one window. Then, from another window, identify the *PID*s, and use the **kill** command with arguments to end the processes you started in the first window.

Listing All Signals

Although only a few signals are needed by users, the system employs a large variety.

The signals we mainly use are:

Signal **1**	Hangup; closes process communication links
Signal **2**	Interrupt; tells process to exit
Signal **3**	Quit; forces the process to quit
Signal **6**	Aborts the process
Signal **9**	Kills the process; cannot be caught
Signal **15**	Software Terminate (default signal for **kill**); tells application running in process to exit

When you need to kill a process, start with **kill** and no argument, which is the same as (*-15*), and then increase the power with *-2*, then *-3* and *-6*. If nothing else works, enter **kill** with a *-9* argument. *Signal 9* is special; it cannot be caught by the process. So unless another process is involved, the process ends. However, you should always try one or more of the other signals first, because processes need to go through some cleanup procedure before they exit. Sending them *signal 9* prevents them from performing the cleanup operations.

We can list all the available **kill** signals for the current system.

1. Enter:

    kill -l   (minus el for list signals)

11.2 Managing Jobs

A command line that instructs the shell to start several processes with output from the first connected to the second, and so forth, is often called a *job*. All modern shells allow us to start, suspend, make active, and kill all processes associated with a job.

Part of effective process management is the ability to switch from one task to another. Suppose you need to print a file, but you're in the middle of writing a long letter with the editor. When you're running one program, you cannot start a new program without terminating the first program, unless you are in a graphical environment or are using virtual terminals. You could kill the editing session, or you could finish the letter before printing the file, or you could open a new window or virtual terminal. In most environments, you can move from one program to another without killing the current program.

Suspending a Job

Begin by starting to edit a new file.

1. Enter:

   vi *joy*

2. Type a line such as the following:

   Bill Joy has made enormous contributions to our field.

3. Return to command mode of the editor:

   ESC

4. While in command mode, press:

   CTRL-Z

   The shell responds with the message

   [1] Stopped

   or

   [1] Suspended

   This output includes *[1]*, which is the number associated with this *job* you just *suspended* with the CTRL-Z command. The shell then displays a new prompt showing it is ready for new instructions.

5. List your current processes:

   ps -l

   The **vi** process is still there, although you are not actually editing the file at the moment. The process that is running **vi** is now *suspended* (the technical term is Traced [T] and it appears as the status code in the output).

   You are sitting at your desk reading a book. The phone rings. You insert a bookmark in the book, put it down, and answer the phone. You don't put the book back on the library shelf or give it back to its owner and lose your place. With a bookmark in the book, you can return to the exact place you left off when you are ready to continue. By keeping the book around and using a bookmark, you are really suspending the job of reading the book. Picking the book up and starting again is bringing the reading process into the foreground, making it active.

   Likewise, we can request that a suspended UNIX/Linux job be made active again.

6. Enter:

   fg

   The **vi** process editing the file *joy* becomes active, exactly where you left off before you suspended the process.

7. Add some more text.

8. Return to command mode and then suspend the **vi** process again:

   ESC
   CTRL-Z
   ps

Identifying Jobs that Are Running or Suspended

You just started **vi** in the foreground and then suspended it. Start the following jobs in the background.

1. Enter:

   sleep *1500 &*

   A message similar to the following is displayed:

   ```
   [2]  11407
   ```

   and the shell prompt reappears.

2. Enter:

    sleep *60 &*

    [3] 11422

The bracketed numbers [2] and [3] are the *job numbers* for each background job. Following the job number is the PID for the process.

3. Now list the current processes:

    ps -u *$USER*

The **ps** utility displays information about each individual process.

Another utility lists the jobs that are running or suspended.

4. Enter:

    jobs

The **vi** job is listed as job *[1]* and is "Stopped" or "Suspended." The **sleep** jobs *[2]* and *[3]* are running, even though they are in the background. In less than a minute, the **sleep** *60*, job *[3]*, will be finished and exit. A suspended (or stopped) job is not running, but it is not killed, either. The system keeps track of where the program stopped its execution (bookmark) and can restart it at the same point later. No computer time is consumed by the process while it is suspended.

Examining the Listing of Multiple Jobs

The **jobs** command lists all jobs that are either suspended or in the background in the current shell.

1. At the shell prompt, enter:

    grep *the* I **tr** *'a-z'* *'A-Z'* I **uniq** I **sort**

Because only one argument is passed to **grep**, it is interpreted as the target search string. No filename argument is provided, so **grep** reads from input connected to the keyboard. Whatever you enter is searched by **grep**, passed to **tr**, then passed to **uniq**, and finally passed to **sort**, which displays its output on the screen.

2. Enter the following text, being sure to include all the *the* strings.

    what is this?
    the cat
    FATHER
    THE cat

> *the dog*
> *father*
> *The dogs*

3. Instruct the shell to suspend the whole job with:

   CTRL-Z

   The shell responds with the suspended information either on one line or across several:

   ```
   [3]  Stopped    grep the | tr 'a-z' 'A-Z' | uniq | sort
   ```

   At this point you have, either running or suspended, the **vi**, one **sleep** (unless you are very speedy, the **sleep 60** has surely exited), and the processes in the recently suspended **grep** jobs.

4. Confirm by listing the jobs:

   jobs

   A list of jobs appears, similar to the following:

   ```
   [1]  -     Stopped    vi joy
   [2]        Running    sleep 1500
   [3]  +     Stopped    grep the | tr 'a-z' 'A' 'Z'| uniq | sort
   ```

   The output shows that the whole **grep** command line is job *[3]*. The **jobs** command is a shell built-in command. It lists all jobs that are running in the background or that have been suspended. The **jobs** output is divided into four columns: the job number, the order (the + marks the lead job and the – marks the second job), the status (running in the background or stopped), and the command being executed.

Comparing Jobs and Processes

1. Examine your current **jobs** and processes using the long listing to get the *PID*s and *PPID*s:

   jobs
   ps -l

   The single job [3] that started with **grep** is seen as one job and this job consists of many processes. Every job can include one to many processes. If the job is more than one process, pipes connect them. Note that all the processes associated with job *[3]*, the **grep** job, have the same Parent *PID*—your current shell.

Changing the Status of Jobs

When we start a job, it is either in the background or the foreground. We can suspend a foreground job. We can also make a suspended job the foreground job or change it to the background.

Bringing a Suspended Job into the Foreground

While your job is suspended, you can give any instructions to the shell that you wish. You can edit files, run other utilities, or even edit other files.

1. Check the date and time by typing:

   date

2. Restart your **grep** job again by typing:

   fg

   The system responds with

   ```
   grep the | tr 'a-z' 'A-Z'| uniq | sort
   ```

   You are back at the same place, entering data to be read by **grep**.

3. Enter another line to **grep**, such as:

   When will the output be displayed?

4. On a new line, end the input with the end-of-file marker:

   CTRL-D

   The output is a unique, uppercase, sorted list of the lines you entered containing the string *the*. The whole collection of processes is suspended and brought into the foreground.

5. Bring the suspended **vi** job to the foreground:

   fg

6. Quit this job by typing:

   :q!

7. Review the jobs that are still pending:

   jobs

   The **sleep** *1500* job is most likely running in the background.

Moving a Background Job into the Foreground

1. Start another job in the background:

   sleep *30* **&**

2. Confirm that **sleep** *30* is running in the background:

   jobs

3. Bring the job into the foreground with:

   fg

   The **sleep** *30* becomes the foreground job. No shell prompt is displayed. The **sleep** job does not start over, but continues as the foreground job until it completes counting to *30*. You can terminate this job using CTRL-C, or simply wait until sleep expires.

4. List your current jobs:

   jobs

   You probably have another **sleep** still listed in the background.

5. Bring that job into the foreground and terminate it with:

   fg
   CTRL-C

6. Continue cleaning up until **jobs** produces no output.

Putting a Suspended Job into the Background

We often start a job in the foreground and then realize we should have put it in the background. One solution is to kill it and start over. Another is to suspend it, and then put it in the background.

1. Use **vi** to create a script named *scr-long* with the following contents:

   echo *hi $USER* 1
   sleep *10*
   echo *hi $USER* 2
   sleep 15
   echo *hi $USER* 3
   sleep 15
   echo *hi $USER* 4
   sleep *10*
   echo *hi $USER* 5

2. Make *scr-long* executable:

   chmod *700* *scr-long*

3. Start the script in the foreground by entering its name:

> *scr-long*

You have no prompt. It is running in the foreground.

4. Suspend the process with:

> CTRL-Z

5. List the jobs:

> **jobs**

The *scr-long* script is suspended. It proceeds no further.

6. Instruct the shell to move the process from suspended to background with:

> **bg**

The shell responds with:

```
[1]   scr-long &
```

After the bracketed number, the response to your **bg** command is the name of the command that you just moved into the background. The ampersand (**&**) denotes that the command line is being run in the background. The script outputs the arguments you listed to **echo**, sleeps and runs **echo** again, and so forth.

7. As the script is running, enter:

> **ps**
> **jobs**

The script is now running in the background. You started it in the foreground, suspended it, and then pushed it into the background.

8. Try the following:

> **sleep** *200*
> CTRL-Z
> **jobs**
> **ps**

The **sleep** is suspended.

9. Attempt to put it in the background:

> **bg**
> **ps**

With some shells, it dies. If the **sleep** is built into the shell, it cannot be put in the background from a suspended state.

10. Try:

   /bin/sleep 200
   CTRL-Z
   jobs
   ps
   bg
   ps
   jobs

When we use the utility **sleep**, we can suspend and change to the background.

Recalling the Most Recent Jobs Specifically

So far, you have manipulated only the lead job. Surely we can access the other jobs without killing the lead jobs in succession.

1. Make sure you have several jobs pending by typing:

   sleep *200* **&**
   sort | **grep** *'a-z'*
   CTRL-Z
   sleep *150*
   CTRL-Z
   vi *practice*
   CTRL-Z
   jobs

The **vi** *practice* job is the most recently suspended job, and it is marked with a plus sign. The **sleep** *150* job is the next most recently suspended and is marked with a minus sign.

Previously, you brought the lead job into the foreground by typing **fg**. This time bring the lead job specifically into the foreground by typing:

   fg %+

The %+ argument to **fg** in the command line specifies the lead job. Because the **vi** practice is the lead job, it is brought to the foreground and is now the current job.

2. Add a few lines of text.

3. Escape to command mode and suspend the **vi** process again by entering:

   CTRL-Z

4. Check the job status:

   jobs

   The lead job **vi** *practice* is again marked with the plus, and the second lead job is marked with the minus.

5. Foreground the second lead job by entering:

   fg %-

   The %- is the symbol for the job following the lead job. In the example, the suspended **sleep** *150* job follows the lead job. This command tells the shell to bring it into the foreground.

6. Re-suspend the current job by pressing:

   CTRL-Z

7. Enter:

   jobs

Note that **sleep**, which was the second lead job, is now the lead job (marked with a +). This is because it was the last job suspended.

Recalling Jobs from the Jobs List

We can specify any job on the job list and bring it into the foreground.

1. Have the shell display a list of the current jobs. Type:

   jobs

   The output is a listing of all of your stopped or background jobs.

2. Place the job listed as having job number *2* in the foreground by entering:

   fg %2

   The %2 specifies the job with the job number 2, which is brought to the foreground.

3. Re-suspend the job with CTRL-Z.

4. Similarly, bring the fourth job to the foreground. Type:

   fg %4

   Job number *4* is brought to the foreground.

5. Suspend it again with:

   CTRL-Z

   Another way to bring jobs to the foreground is by using the job name instead of its number.

6. Enter:

    fg %sort

7. Re-suspend it by typing:

    CTRL-Z

You can even use the first letter of the job name.

8. Enter:

    fg %v

The suspended **vi** job is now brought to the foreground. If you have more than one job that begins with the same letter, add one or more characters in order to differentiate the job you desire to bring to the foreground.

9. Re-suspend this job by typing:

    CTRL-Z

 S U M M A R Y : A suspended job is not running at all. A background job is running, but it's not running in the foreground so you can interact with a shell. In general, to recall a particular job into the foreground, you type the **fg** command in this format:
fg *%job_name*
or
fg *%job_number*
where *job_number* is the number of the job for the chosen command line listed in the output from the **jobs** command. The job number is not the PID for the process.

Moving a Specific Suspended Job to the Background

We can also move a job into the background. The procedure is similar to the way we move a suspended job into the foreground.

1. Start *scr-long* and then suspend it:

    scr-long
    CTRL-Z

2. Put a long **sleep** in the background:

    sleep 500 &

3. List the current jobs:

    jobs

The process running *scr-long* is suspended, not running in the background. You can change its status.

4. Identify the job number for the *scr-long* that is suspended, and use it for the # in the following command:

>   **bg %#**

5. Use the **jobs** command to verify that the *scr-long* job is now running in the background:

>   **jobs**

You can also use the name of a suspended job to push it into the background by typing:

>   **bg** *%job_name*

 SUMMARY: In general, to move a foreground job into the background, you must first suspend it, and then type the **bg** command in the following format:

bg *%job_name*

or

bg *%job_number*

where *job_number* is the number of the chosen job listed in the jobs command output.

Killing a Particular Job

Earlier, we killed the current foreground job using CTRL-C (the interrupt signal) and killed specific processes using the *PID* as an argument to the **kill** command. In this section, we examine how to terminate or kill stopped jobs and jobs running in the background.

1. Find out what jobs you have pending by typing:

>   **jobs**

2. Kill the most recent job in the job list by entering:

>   **kill %+**

3. Examine the list of jobs again:

>   **jobs**

The job probably exited; if not, increase the power of the signal.

Another way to kill a job is by using the job number.

4. To kill job number 2, type:

kill %2

A message is displayed that indicates that the job has been killed.

To avoid killing the wrong jobs, first check the currently running jobs, using the **jobs** command before using **kill**. Try this now. Type:

jobs

5. Kill one of the other jobs, using its job number as the # in the following:

kill -1 %#

You can also use the name of a suspended job to kill it by typing:

kill %*job_name*

 S U M M A R Y : The **kill** command takes the same arguments as the **fg** and **bg** commands. To kill the most recent job, use **kill %+**. To kill the second most recent job, use **kill %-**. In general, to kill a particular job, you use the command **kill %*job_number*** or **kill %*job_name*.** You may kill the wrong job if you are not particularly careful. If you run **jobs** to determine the rank or job number of the job you want to kill, and the **+** job is running in the background, that job could finish before you enter the **kill** command. If this happens, you may kill the wrong job.

11.3 Exiting When Jobs Have Been Stopped

Job control is a very useful method for managing processes. Because background jobs and stopped jobs remain invisible to you until the jobs either write to the terminal or are finished, you might forget that processes other than the current one are running. UNIX job control provides a method of warning you of stopped or running background jobs when you attempt a **logout** or **exit** of the process.

1. Type the **jobs** command to make sure there are jobs running in the background or stopped.

2. If you do not have any stopped jobs, add:

vi *testfile* **&**

3. Issue the command to exit your shell:

exit

The shell responds with an error message:

```
There are suspended jobs.
```

or

```
There are stopped jobs.
```

In addition to the issue of stopped jobs remaining in the queue, you have not exited the shell. The assumption is that you have forgotten about your stopped jobs, so you are informed that there are stopped jobs, and the current shell remains active.

> **CAUTION:** This gives you a chance to decide whether to kill any of the unresolved jobs. Text editors and database programs are good examples of programs you do not want to kill. However, if you were able to log off without resolving these programs, they would continue. When you logged on again, you would not be able to access the process from your new shell. You would then have to kill the process and lose any work done.

4. Check your jobs now by typing:

jobs

5. If you don't care whether the jobs continue running, you can ignore them and exit anyway by typing **exit** again:

exit

When you make this second request, the shell exits even though there are stopped jobs.

■ Review 1

1. Describe the life cycle of the process that would execute the command **who**, located in */bin*.

_____

_____

_____

2. Consider the following scenario: You log onto your system on *tty23*. The system starts a **csh** for you that has a PID of *1056*. Then you start a shell script (the script is executed by a **sh** with a PID of *1080*) that in turn executes **who** (a PID of *2020*).

   a. What is the PPID of the **who** process?

   _____

   b. What is the PPID of the process executing the script?

   _____

   c. With information provided, can you determine with what *tty* the **who** process is associated?

   _____

3. Let's say you start a process that appears to be taking too much time. You decide to terminate the process, but find that typing CTRL-C doesn't do anything. How do you determine the **PID** of the wayward process? Hint: **ps -t** *nn* lists processes attached to *tty nn*.

   _____

   _____

   _____

4. Once you determine the PID of the process in question 1, how do you kill it?

   _____

   _____

   _____

5. What would happen if you entered the following sequence of commands to your shell:

   who > */dev/null* **&**
   sleep *100* **&**
   mail margaret < */etc/motd* **&**

_____

_____

_____

6. What command would you use to start up a **ps** in the background?

_____

For the next three questions, refer to the following listing:

```
[2]          Stopped    sort /etc/passwd
[3]    -     Stopped    vi .cshrc
[4]    +     Stopped    more .login
[5]          Running    find / -name foo
```

7. What command would you use to bring the **vi** editor to the foreground?

_____

8. What is the command you would use to kill the **more**?

_____

9. What is the command you would use to get this listing?

_____

■ Conclusion

UNIX and Linux are really just files, processes, and hardware. When we do work, it is by executing processes. The various commands used for process management provide us with exceedingly valuable tools for accomplishing work and troubleshooting. Users launch processes, kill processes, move them from foreground to background, suspend them, and start them again to accomplish complex computing goals.

■ Answers to Review

1. The file */bin/who* exists on the disk. You type in the **who** command. The system loads the utility from the disk into main memory. The CPU executes the instructions in main memory, resulting in a list of users currently logged

on to be printed on your terminal. When the last name is printed (the instructions are finished), the process dies, and the space in main memory taken up by the process is freed for use by other processes.

2. The answers are as follows:

   a. 1080

   b. 1056

   c. Yes: *tty 23*

3. Log onto another screen or workstation. From the second terminal, run *tty* to identify the port for the second session. Then run **who** to find your original session, being careful to avoid the entry containing the port you just started. Next, run **ps -t** *nn*, where *nn* is the port of your original session. Look for the name of the process causing the problem in the COMMAND column.

4. You can **kill** the wayward process with **kill** *PID*, where *PID* is the Process IDentification number you found from **ps**. If this doesn't work, try **kill -1** *PID*. Failing even that, use **kill -9** *PID*. Finally, log out of your second session.

5. The **who** command would execute, but its output would disappear; *margaret* would receive a copy of the message of the day (motd) in the mail, and your prompt would be returned in roughly 100 seconds, after all of the above commands are complete.

6. **ps &**

7. **fg %3** or **fg %-**

8. **kill %4** or **kill %+**

9. **jobs**

COMMAND SUMMARY

ps   Lists processes that you own.

ps -l   Generates a long listing of your processes.

ps -f   Outputs a full listing of processes that you own.

ps -u *login*   Lists processes that are owned by the user whose login ID is *login*.

ps -t *nn*   Lists processes that are associated with the workstation *tty*.

ps -ef   Prints information about all processes.

ps -aux   Prints information about all processes.

kill *PID*   Terminates a process by sending a Software Terminate signal.

kill -*1* *PID*   Hangs up communication links to a process.

kill -*2* *PID*   Ends a process by sending a Process Interrupt signal.

kill -*3* *PID*   Brings a process to a conclusion by issuing a Process Quit signal.

kill -*6* *PID*   Instructs a process to end by issuing the Abort Process signal.

kill -*15* *PID*   Software Terminate signal (default).

kill -*9* *PID*   Kills a process. Usually the last form of **kill** to try. Cannot be ignored, but may not allow the utility to clean up.

CTRL-C   Kills the current foreground process by sending the Interrupt signal.

CTRL-   Kills the current foreground process by sending the Quit signal.

CTRL-Z   Suspends the current job.

fg %*job_num*   Brings the job with number *job_num* into the foreground. Without an argument, **fg** brings the most recently *stopped* job into the foreground.

bg %*job_num*   Puts the job with number *job_num* into the background. Without an argument, **bg** moves the most recently *stopped* job to the background.

jobs   Prints a listing of all of the *stopped* and *background* jobs under control of the current shell.

kill %*job_num*   Kills the job with job number *job_num*. Without an argument, **kill** kills the most recent *stopped* job.

Managing, Printing, and Archiving Large Files

12

S K I L L S   C H E C K

Before beginning this chapter, you should be able to

- Create, copy, move, and remove files
- Issue complex commands to the shell
- Access and modify files using the editor
- Use job control to run processes in the background
- Kill processes using their PIDs

O B J E C T I V E S

After completing this chapter, you will be able to

- Examine files, running little risk of harming them
- Paginate and add headers to files
- Locate files by name or other characteristics in the file system
- Create and manage archives of directories and their files
- Copy files to floppy disks and retrieve them
- Send files to specific printers and remove them from queues
- Split a large file into several small pieces and reassemble the file

As we use Linux and UNIX systems to accomplish work, we often create large files that we need to manage in several ways. We need to effectively view files, format and paginate files, split files into smaller pieces, copy individual files or whole directory trees to backup media or archives, and locate and recover lost files. This chapter examines how to accomplish those tasks.

12.1 Viewing Long Files Safely with vi

Files vary greatly in size and importance. Users often need to effectively examine files without running the risk of damaging them.

Creating a Long File

To complete the exercises in this section, you need to have a text file that is at least 200 short lines long.

Create a new file containing a list of the names of the files in your home directory.

1. Enter:

   > **mkdir** *Long*
   > **cd** *Long*
   > **ls** ~ > *longfile*

   To make the file longer, the next command takes the first 25 characters from each of the lines in your *practice* file and adds them to the end of *longfile*.

2. Enter the following, which uses double-redirects to add to the file:

   > **cut -c 1-25** *~/practice* >> *longfile*
   > **more** *longfile*

   The first 25 characters from each line in your *practice* file in your home directory are read and added to the end of *longfile*.

3. Add the names of the files listed in */bin* by entering the following:

   > **ls** */bin* >> *longfile*

4. Examine the file, determine the number of lines, and keep adding the filenames listed in */bin* until *longfile* is at least 200 lines long:

> **more** *longfile*
> **wc -l** *longfile*
> **ls** */bin* >> *longfile*
> **wc -l** *longfile*
> **ls** */bin* >> *longfile*

5. Instruct **cat** to add numbers to the left of all lines in a copy of the file:

> **cat -n** *longfile* > *nlongfile*
> **more** *nlongfile*

The file is reasonably long and has a number at the beginning of each line in the file.

Effectively and Safely Viewing Files

The **more** utility provides several useful commands for viewing files, including the slash (/) for searching, SPACEBAR to go forward, and **b** to go back a screen. Users often become so familiar with **vi** and its extensive *move around* features, that they simply use **vi** instead of **more** to examine files. Unfortunately, users often automatically use the write-quit :**wq** when ending an editing session and unintentionally make and save changes, modifying files that they just wanted to view.

Another way to use the visual editor to examine files is to start **vi** in *safe* or read-only mode.

1. Enter:

> **view** *nlongfile*

The visual editor starts and the beginning of the file is displayed. Even though you have write permission on *nlongfile*, the editor announces that you are in read-only mode.

At this point, you can move about the file using the full range of **vi** movement commands, such as:

COMMAND	INTERPRETATION
H, **M**, and **L**	Move to the highest, middle, and lowest line in the display.
CTRL-D, CTRL-B, CTRL-U, CTRL-F	Move the display by whole or half screens.
w, **e**, **b**	Move in word increments.

COMMAND	INTERPRETATION
:set number	Add line numbers to the display.
39G	Go to the 39th line.
fX	Move to the first **X** on the line.

2. Attempt to delete a line.
   Most versions of the editor warn you that you are changing a read-only file. You have the same choices that **vi** offers whenever you edit a file lacking write permission:

:q!	Quit the editor without saving changes.
:w!	Write the file, saving the changes, and quit the editor.
:w *newfilename*	Save the file in a new file.

3. Leave **view** and return to the shell by whatever method you choose.

4. If you just want to examine a file and wish to avoid accidentally changing it, use **view**. That puts you in the editor, editing the file as though the file were read-only. Later, you can force the editor to write changes to the file, but it takes a clear signal, employing the **!**, which usually protects us from ourselves.

12.2 Splitting Long Files

Sometimes a file is too long to fit onto a floppy or to be processed by a utility. We could use **sed** to break the file into pieces and invent a naming scheme for the parts that could be used to quickly reassemble the pieces. Or we could use **split**. Let's use **split**.

1. Enter:

   wc *nlongfile*

   The total number of lines, words, and characters in the file is calculated and output to the screen.

2. Split the file into small files with:

   split -20 *nlongfile lf+*

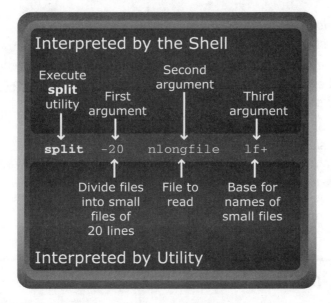

3. Examine the contents of the current directory with:

   ls

   ls *lf**

4. Examine the pieces:

   more *lf+aa*

   wc ** lf **

   Each file, except for the last one, has 20 lines in it. The first 20 lines of the *longfile* are in file *lf+aa*, the next 20 in *lf+ab*, and so forth.

   We now have the file split into pieces of specified size; the pieces have extensions starting with *aa* and going through the alphabet as far as needed.

5. Reassemble the file:

   cat *lf+** | **more**

   The file is displayed in the original order, because the filenames *aa*, *ab*,… are in ASCII order, the same order the shell uses for the filenames when it replaces the * in the command line.

6. Remove the pieces and then have the file split into much smaller pieces:

   rm *lf+**

   split -5 *nlongfile slong*

> **ls** *slong**
> **wc** *slong**

The *nlongfile* file is divided into small files of five lines each, each file with a name beginning with s*long* and ending with *aa* through *az*, then *ba* through *bz*, and so on.

7. Enter:

> **cat** *slong** | **more**

The file's pieces are read and assembled into the right order.

Very long files can be split, placed in media with limited file size capacity, then reassembled in a target environment.

12.3 Paginating Long Files

If you have been printing files, you have been using either the **lp** or the **lpr** utilities to spool files for printing. Both **lp** and **lpr** queue jobs and pass files to the printer. If the file is larger than a page, the file is divided into pages only by the separate sheets of paper. There are no margins separating the text from the top or bottom of whatever the printer defines as a page, and usually the pages are not numbered. Even the task of *paginating* a file involves formatting the text.

When we want to make decisions about how text is formatted, we must invoke one of several formatting utilities to act on the data from a file. Manipulating layout with one utility and printing with another is typical of UNIX utilities. Each utility has a focus, doing its job well and carrying no extra baggage. In this section, we examine the **pr** utility that outputs a file in pages to the screen or printer.

Printing and Paginating a File

The **pr** utility's basic function is to read a file and output paginated text.

1. Enter:

> **pr** *nlongfile*

The output whizzes by on your screen. Like the **cat** utility, the **pr** utility just sends its output without pausing.

2. To see the output one screenful at a time, redirect the output of **pr** to **more**:

> **pr** *nlongfile* | **more**

The output of **pr** is in 56 text lines to a page. Each page has a header at the top and blank lines at the bottom. The header contains the date and time the file was last modified, the filename, and the page number.

3. Redirect the output of **pr** to the printer managing program:

> **pr** *nlongfile* | **lpr**

The file *longfile* is now printed on your default printer. Because most printers use 66-line pages, each page contains 66 lines; this includes the page header, 2 blank lines at the top of the page, 5 blank lines at the bottom of the page, and 56 lines of text.

Modifying the Length of Pages

You can change the default page length used by the **pr** utility to any reasonable length (a minimum of 11 lines, to a maximum of 2,147,483,647).

1. Enter the following with a **-l** (minus el) option:

> **pr -l** *20 nlongfile* | **more**

The option **-l** followed by the number *15* is instruction to **pr** to output pages consisting of *20* lines, including header and footer, which take up 5 lines each.

Printing and Paginating Multiple Files

We can also give **pr** several files as options.

1. Return to your home directory and paginate several files:

> **cd**
>
> **pr** *practice users_on scrA* | **more**

Each file is paginated by **pr** and then sent to **more** to be output separately.

You can also use **cat** to combine files, then use **pr** to paginate the resulting data.

2. Type:

> **cat** *practice users_on* | **pr** | **more**

The two files are concatenated, paginated, and displayed one screen at a time.

By replacing **more** with **lpr** or **lp**, the combined data is paginated and printed.

Modifying Page Layout

The basic use of the **pr** utility is changed with options that instruct **pr** to modify the page header, output just a portion of a file, use multiple columns, add numbers, and otherwise alter the layout.

Customizing Page Headers

By default, **pr** puts a header on each page. You can change the content of the header.

1. Change the header for the original file without numbers, *longfile*, by entering:

    pr -h *'My test file' Long/longfile* | **more**
    pr -h *"$USER longfile" Long/longfile* | **more**

    Instead of just the name of the file, *longfile*, the header title for each page is now whatever you place after **-h** on the command line.

    The title argument following the **-h** option can include spaces or other shell special characters, provided the argument is quoted.

Creating Numbered Listings

In an earlier section of this chapter, you used **cat -n** to produce output that had numbers included to the left of each line. In many earlier versions of UNIX, the **-n** option is not available with **cat**.

Another way to obtain line-numbered output is with **pr**.

1. Enter the following:

    pr -n *Long/longfile* | **more**

    Every line, including any blank lines, is numbered in the output.

    Depending on the version of UNIX you are using, either **pr -n** or **cat -n** outputs numbers. In recent versions and in Linux, both utilities work.

Skipping Pages from the Beginning

When examining very long listings, you might want to pass over the first several pages and paginate the remainder.

1. Enter the following command, and do not include a space between the + and the page number. It is one argument.

    pr +3 *Long/longfile* | **more**

The resulting output starts on the third page, as specified by the *+3* in the command line. Pages 1 and 2 are skipped.

Printing Multiple Files Side by Side

With **pr** we can compare two or more files by printing them side by side on the same page.

1. Enter:

   pr -m *coast west* | **more**
   pr -m *coast test-sor* | **more**

   The two files are displayed side by side in two columns.

In the output, long lines are not split up. Any line that does not completely fit within a column is truncated.

Printing One File with Multiple Columns

We can instruct **pr** to output one file in two or more columns.

1. Output the file *longfile* in three columns on the screen:

   pr -3 *Long/longfile* | **more**

   In the three columns just displayed, any lines longer than the column width are truncated, as occurs with multiple files.

   We can provide quite complex instructions to **pr**.

2. Enter:

   pr +2 -h *"File Comparison"* **-m** *coast west*

The components of this command are identified in the following illustration:

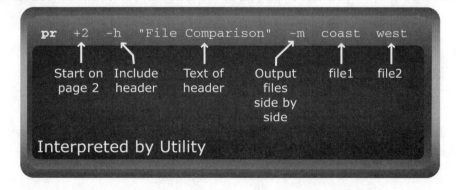

S U M M A R Y : The **pr** utility is used to read one or more files and format (paginate) output with headings into one or more columns. Options are as follows:

pr without option	Provides a header that displays the filename, page number, as well as date and time of last modification of the file.
-h *title*	Allows you to replace the filename in the **h**eader with a *title* of your choosing.
-m *file1 file2*	Outputs files side by side. Lines may be truncated.
-# (*#* is any number)	Outputs the file in # columns. Lines may be truncated.
-n	Add **n**umbers to each line.
-l *#*	(minus el number) Sets page length to # lines.

12.4 Printing Your Heart Out

One of the first devices attached to an early UNIX system was a printer. No matter how electronic our age becomes, printers continue to sell. This section examines the various options available to tailor printing of files and output from previous utilities in a pipeline.

Printing a File

You have been sending files to the printer using either the **lp** or **lpr** commands in previous exercises. The **-d***printer* and **-P***printer* portions of the following commands request a specific printer. Type one of the following commands (substituting the name of your printer for *printer*).

lp -d*printer practice*

or

lpr -P*printer practice*

In the following exercises, we will specify only **lp** or **lpr**. If you need to designate a printer, add the **-d** or **-P** options.

Printing the Output of a Pipeline

As with most other UNIX utilities, you can connect the output of another utility to the input of the print utility, using a pipe. Here are two examples.

You can print the contents of the current directory without first creating a file. Have the shell connect the output of **ls** directly to the input of **lp** or **lpr**.

1. Type one of the following commands depending on whether **lp** or **lpr** is running:

   ls | lp
   ls | lpr

   The output of the **ls** utility is sent directly to the **lp** or **lpr** utility, which sends the data to the printer exactly as if that output had been stored in a file. This piping feature allows you to make a hard copy of online information.

   If your system has the online UNIX manual, you can obtain a hard copy of the manual pages describing any utility.

2. Type one of the following commands:

   man wc | col -bx | lp -d*printer*
   man wc | colcrt | lpr -P*printer*

   The **col -bx** and **colcrt** utilities remove control characters that are of value to terminals but make reading a printed version difficult.

Sending Your Job to a Different Printer

If you have more than one printer available, you can explicitly select a specific printer when you issue the print command. If you do not have an alternative printer, skip ahead to the next section.

1. Type one of the following commands where *printer2* is the name of the second printer on your system:

   lp -d*printer2 practice*

   or

   lpr -P*printer2 practice*

   These commands allow you to choose your printer. When one printer is down or occupied, you can send your print requests to another. Installations often use different queues for different printing styles, such as landscape, portrait, letterhead, and so on.

Printing Multiple Copies

Suppose you need a copy of your *numbers.tmp* file for several of your colleagues. You can send the file to the printer once for each copy you need, but a more efficient way is to issue a single command line asking for multiple copies.

1. For example, request five copies of a file by typing one of the following command lines:

   lp -n5 *west*

   The option **-n5** tells **lp** to print five copies of the file.

   Or type:

   lpr —#5 *west*

   The option **—#5** instructs **lpr** to print five copies of the file.

Adding a Title Line to the Banner Page

Each of the jobs you just printed probably was preceded by a *banner page*, also called a *burst page*, containing information about the printer and about the user issuing the print request. If you want, you can add a title line to this banner page.

1. Add your title and print the *numbers.tmp* file again. Type one of the following commands:

   lp -t"*numbers file***"** *numbers.tmp*

   or

   lpr -P*printer* **-J"***numbers file***"** *numbers.tmp*

   The formats of the two print commands are as follows:

   lp -d*printer* **-t***title filename*

   or

   lpr -P*printer* **-J***title filename*

Notice there is no space between the **-t** or the **-J** and the *title*.

Checking the Status of Print Jobs

On some systems, print jobs are sent faster than the printer can produce the output. Each new job is added to the list of jobs to be done (the *queue*). UNIX lets you check your specific print job, or all jobs from all users in the printer queues.

The *spooler* is the program that administers print requests. The spooler receives print requests from multiple users and sends jobs one at a time to the printer. It is the spooler that makes it possible for the system to process simultaneous print job requests from several users.

When you type a print command followed by a printer designation and filename, the spooler processes your request, assigns a request number to the job submitted, and queues the job for printing at the specified destination. If the printer you specify is free, the print request is passed to the printer, and the file starts printing. Otherwise, the job must wait for the printer to be available.

You can search the printer queue for the status of any job you send (printed, printing, or waiting).

1. Send the file *practice* to the printer, using the print command appropriate for your system. Your file *practice* is now queued for printing, waiting for its turn to be printed.

2. Examine the queue by typing one of the following commands:

   lpstat

   or

   lpq -P*printer username*

   where *username* is the login name of your current account, and *printer* is the selected printer.

If few people are using the printer, your print job is printed immediately upon request. There would be no trace of it in the output of **lpstat** or **lpq**.

Canceling a Print Request

Just as you can send a request to a printer, you can also cancel that request.

1. From the command line, type one of the following commands:

   lpstat -t

   or

   lpq -P*printer*

2. Enter the following command to remove jobs from the queue:

    cancel

or

    lprm

All your printing jobs are removed from the queue.

The programs that manage print queues are the *print spoolers*, **lp** and **lpr**. We use the **lp** and **lpr** commands to add print jobs to queues, to display status information about queues, and to remove print jobs from queues.

12.5 Locating Files with find

As you create more complex directory structures, it becomes easier to lose files. Fortunately, UNIX provides a utility that searches through directory trees to locate files.

Locating Files by Name

The file *practice* is located in several of your directories. All files can be located using **find**.

1. Make sure you are in your home directory:

    cd

2. Ask **find** to locate each file with the name *practice* and inform you of their pathnames by entering:

    find ~ -name *practice* **-print**

The **find** utility may take some time to complete its work. As **find** is examining directories, it reports to your workstation both its output and any error information that is appropriate. You may see the pathnames of files named *practice*, as well as information about which directories you cannot examine because of their assigned permissions.

Following are explanations of each part of the command line in the preceding example.

COMMAND	INTERPRETATION
find	Instructs the shell to execute the **find** utility, which searches a target directory and all of its subdirectories.
~	This argument specifies the starting point directory—in this case, your home directory. The result is a search of all directories listed in your home directory, which includes your home directory and all its subdirectories.
-name *practice*	Instructs **find** to locate all files with the specified name *practice*. In addition to locating files by name, **find** can also locate based on the criteria of age, owner, permissions, size, etc.
-print	Specifies that the full pathname of each occurrence of the file(s) matching the selection criterion should be output. In addition to printing, **find** can be instructed to remove located files, change file permissions, or employ essentially any shell file-manipulation command.

Locating Files by Owner

The **find** utility is used to locate files based on a variety of criteria.

Determine whether you have a directory in */tmp* named the same as your user login name.

1. Enter:

   ls -ld */tmp/$USER*

   If a long listing for your directory in */tmp* is displayed, make sure the permissions allow you to **rwx** the directory.

   If you do not have a directory in */tmp* of your login name, create one.

2. Enter:

   mkdir */tmp/$USER*

3. Copy three more of your files to the directory you created in */tmp*:

   cp *practice names.tmp users_on* */tmp/$USER*

4. Create a subdirectory of your directory in */tmp*:

   mkdir */tmp/$USER/Hall*

5. Add two files to the new directory:

touch */tmp/$USER/Hall/candlestick*
touch */tmp/$USER/Hall/colmustard*

You now own several files located in */tmp*'s subdirectories.

6. Instruct **find** to locate files owned by you by entering:

find */tmp* **-user** *$USER* **-print**

The paths to all files in */tmp* that you own are displayed.

The result of this command is a display of all files belonging to the selected owner that are located in the directory tree that has */tmp* at the top.

COMMAND	INTERPRETATION
find	Instructs the shell to run the **find** utility.
/tmp	This first argument to **find** instructs **find** to start its search in the /tmp directory and search all directories below that.
-user	An option to **find**, instructing it to search for files by owner, not by name or any other criteria.
$USER	This argument directly follows the **user** argument and is interpreted by **find** to be the user whose files should be located. The shell replaces *$USER* with your login name. All files belonging to this user in the directory tree starting at */tmp* are located.
-print	Once files are located, this action takes place; in this case, the path to the selected files is output.

Putting find's Output in a File

In the previous exercise, the **find** utility completed a search of the directory tree below */tmp* and displayed the output on the screen.

1. Instruct the shell to redirect the output of **find** to a new file:

find */tmp* **-user** *$USER* **-print** > *my-tmp-files*

2. After **find** completes its search, examine the output file:

more *my-tmp-files*

The *my-tmp-files* contains a listing of the pathnames for the files you own in */tmp* or any of its subdirectories. The error messages, if any, went to your screen and not to the file.

Using Error Redirection with find

When we search for a file with **find**, the screen usually fills with many error messages, prohibiting us from further work. We can redirect all error output from jobs running in the background.

1. Enter:

   In a C shell:

   find .. -name *temp* **-print >&** *mytemp* **&**

   In an **sh** family shell:

   find .. -name *temp* **-print 2>** */dev/null* **1>** *mytemp* **&**

The **find** utility looks for all files named *temp* in all directories starting with your parent directory. If a *temp* file is found, its full pathname is placed in the *mytemp* file.

In a C shell, when error messages occur—for instance, when a directory cannot be accessed—these error messages are also placed in the file with the output. The **&** at the end instructs the shell to execute the process in the background.

In the Korn shell, errors are sent to the "bit bucket in the sky," */dev/null*. All systems have a */dev/null*, which accepts any input we give it, but never writes it anywhere. When we want output neither saved nor on the screen, we redirect it to */dev/null*.

Locating and Removing Files by Owner

The **find** utility can be used to perform actions other than printing.

1. Enter:

   find */tmp* **-user** *$USER* **-exec rm {} \; -print**
   ls */tmp/$USER*

The execution of this command results in the deletion of all files belonging to the selected owner that are located in the directory tree with */tmp* at the top.

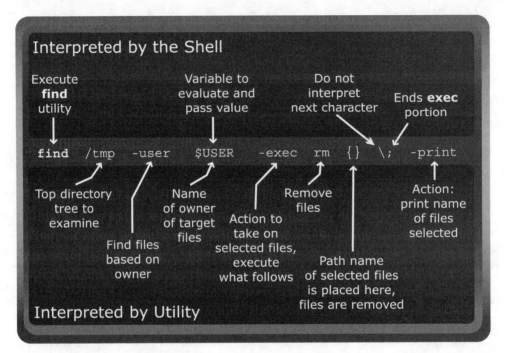

The preceding command line is interpreted as follows:

COMMAND	INTERPRETATION
find	Instructs the shell to run the **find** utility.
/tmp	The first argument to **find**, instructing it to start its search in the */tmp* directory and search all directories below that.
-user	An option to **find**, instructing it to search for files by owner, not by name or any other criteria.
$USER	Shell interprets *$USER*, replaces it with its value—your login name—and passes the login name as an argument to **find**. This argument directly follows the **user** argument and is interpreted by **find** to be the user name whose files should be located. All files belonging to this user in the directory tree starting at */tmp* are located.
-exec	Instruction to execute the command that follows on all files located.
rm	Command to run the **rm** utility.

COMMAND	INTERPRETATION
{}	Placeholder for the located filename(s). Each filename that **find** locates meeting the selection criteria is substituted into the command following **exec** at the position of these curly braces. Hence, all located files become arguments to **rm**, and they are removed.
\;	Tells **find** where the **exec** command ends. A semicolon (;) is always required to identify the end of the **-exec** portion of the **find** command. The backslash before the semicolon is required to tell the shell to not interpret it. If there were no backslash, the shell would interpret the **;** as a command separator and run everything up to the **;** as one command.
-print	Instruction to **find** to output the path to all files that meet the search criteria.

The **find** utility, with the **-exec** option, is used to execute any command utilizing the filename(s) that are selected.

The **find** utility is a powerful search tool. It allows us to search through specified directory trees, based on a variety of criteria, and then perform actions on the located file. The **find** utility is used to create backup copies of all files owned by a user, to locate large, old, unused files, and so on.

12.6 Archiving Long Files

As we use a Linux or UNIX system for more important work, the need to put copies onto transportable media grows. We often want to drop a file onto a floppy to take it to a meeting, back up important work for safety, create an archive for historical purposes, or to transfer data to a new environment.

Copying Files to and from Floppy Disks

Most Linux systems provide or have access to a set of programs called **mtools**, which facilitate copying files to the floppy drive without going through the process of mounting the drive, a topic examined in a system administration text.

1. Locate a floppy formatted in DOS.
2. Put the floppy in the floppy drive.
3. Make sure you are in your home directory:

   cd

4. Request a list of files that are on the floppy by entering:

> **mdir**

If a brief list of the disk's contents is displayed, you have **mtools** available. Continue. If you see an error message that mtools is not found, skip this section and locate someone to help install **mtools** if you are on Linux. See the **www.muster.com** site.

Copying a File to and from a Floppy

1. Enter:

> **mcopy** *practice* **a:**

This command instructs the shell to run **mcopy** and give it two arguments: a filename from the current directory and the *a:*, which is an agreed-on name for the floppy.

2. List the contents of the floppy:

> **mdir**

A copy of the file *practice* is listed as residing on the disk.

3. Change directories to another directory, such as:

> **cd** *~/Long*
> **ls**

4. Copy the *practice* file from the floppy to the current directory with:

> **mcopy a:***/practice* .
> **ls**

The file *practice* is copied from the *a:* drive to the current directory.

Copying All Files

We can select all files from a directory and copy them to the floppy.

1. Enter:

> **cd**
> **mcopy** * **a:**
> **mdir**

As many files as could fit on the floppy are copied from the current directory.

Removing Files from a Floppy

1. List the files on the floppy:

> **mdir**

2. Select several files to remove and use their names in the following:

   mdel *file1 file2*

3. To remove all files from the floppy, enter:

   mdel *
   mdir

4. To remove directories from a floppy, enter:

   mdeltree *directoryname*

Formatting a Floppy Disk

Additionally, we can format a floppy in DOS format using the command **mformat**, which formats the *a* drive.

A copy placed on a floppy with **mcopy** is just a copy of the file. Attributes such as permissions are not included in the copy. When you copy a file from a floppy, the permissions for the newly copied file adhere to whatever the default umask setting is.

Creating Archives

One of the workhorse archiving utilities is **tar**, originally a tape archiving program. It has been so reliable that it is used extensively to make archive files on most systems. The advantage of a **tar** archive over a floppy disk copy is that a **tar** archive retains file attributes such as permissions.

1. Make sure you are in your home directory:

   cd

2. Create a **tar** archive of the files in your home directory by entering:

   tar -cvf *archfile.tar* .

   This command instructs **tar** to:

   <u>c</u>reate an archive in

   <u>v</u>erbose mode, displaying filenames being archived, then use a <u>f</u>ile to hold the archive.

   archfile.tar is the filename. The extension *.tar* is not required, but it's a good idea to use so that you can easily differentiate your tar files.

   . is the source directory, in this case your current directory, from which all files will be archived.

3. List the contents of the **tar** archive with:

    tar –tf *archfile.tar*

4. Create a new directory and make it your current directory:

    mkdir *Backups*
    cd *Backups*

5. Move the archive to the current directory:

    mv *../archfile.tar* .

6. Extract the directory tree from the archive:

    tar –xvf *archfile.tar* .

    This command is instruction to:

    e<u>x</u>tract the structure from the archive in <u>v</u>erbose mode, from a <u>f</u>ile.

7. List the files:

    ls -l

    All the files listed in your home directory, including permissions, directories, ownership, and so forth, are maintained by the **tar** archive.

8. Return to your home directory:

    cd

12.7 Surveying Backup and Archiving Utilities

Backing up information on a UNIX/Linux system is essential for security of data. Users need to back up and archive files, directories, or whole sections of file systems for preservation or to transfer to another system.

Many utilities are designed to facilitate making a backup or media copy of the file system. The various utilities work in different ways. Different utilities do each of the following:

- Transfer files intact to or from media, or
- Create an archive, which is a single file that contains other files plus information about them, such as their filenames, owners, timestamps, and access permissions, or
- Create a compressed file using an established compression algorithm The compressed file can be transferred to media or another file system or to a different computer on the network, or
- Create an archive file consisting of versions of the target files and file information. In addition, the files are automatically compressed.

The following list of utilities describes the various Linux and UNIX utilities available for backup, archiving and compressing data. Each is described briefly so you can decide which might be appropriate for your needs. Several of the most useful were examined in earlier exercises. Systems vary in terms of the utilities that are available and how they are implemented. For specifics on the use of these utilities, we suggest you consult your system's manual pages.

Transferring Files to and from Media

These utilities just transfer data from one media to another. There is no archiving, no compressing.

- **dd**   Copies files to media, making user-specified conversions such as block size that are appropriate for the media. This utility is especially useful for raw tape reading.
- **mcopy**   Copies files to and from floppy disk in DOS format, with no compression and no archive construction.

Archiving or Restoring Files Without Compression

Each utility in this group either creates an archive or restores files from an archive, retaining the system information about the files.

- **ar**   Creates, modifies, and extracts files from an archive file on the file system. This is often used to manage programming libraries.
- **ranlib**   Generates an index for an archive.
- **dump**   Makes appropriate backup copy archives of files from a file system to tape, disk, or other backup media. Files are in standard character format, in an archive, but not compressed.
- **restore**   Allows files to be brought back onto the system with appropriate ownership, permissions, and so forth, from a dump tape.
- **archive**   Locates articles from Usenet archives and copies them to a local directory tree (UNIX only).
- **tar**   Reads all specified files and directory trees and creates a single file archive that is the same size as the original files. Although there is an archive created, no compression takes place. The **tar** file can be written to media, copied to another file system, or compressed with a compression utility.

Files can be extracted from the archive, using **tar** with the **-x** option, or with **cpio**.

- **cpio** Copies files into and from **cpio** or **tar** file archives.
- **shar** Creates an archive for a directory and all its contents in flat ASCII character format, which can be mailed and unpacked with */bin/sh*. Directories, permissions, ownerships, and so on, survive archiving, mailing, and unpacking.
- **rpm2cpio** Converts some Linux Packages (RPM) archives to **cpio** archives.

Compressing and Uncompressing Files and Archives

Utilities that compress data (files or archives) use complex algorithms to reduce the size of the object.

- **compress** Uses an algorithm representing commonly used character strings with a generated number list to reduce the effective size of a file. No archiving or writing to media takes place.
  Compressed files are given a "dot-Z" extension and can be restored with uncompress, **gunzip**, or **gzip -d**. The compress utility is largely being replaced by **gzip**.
- **uncompress** Uncompresses files that were created with **compress**. This utility is being replaced by **gunzip**.
- **macunpack** Extracts Macintosh files from an archive.
- **gzip** Compresses files and adds .gz extension. This utility is often used to compress a **tar** archive for transfer between systems. Files can be uncompressed using **gzip -d**, **gunzip**, or **zcat**.
- **gunzip** Uncompresses files that were compressed with **gzip**.
- **compact** An older compression scheme uses a .C extension, produces less compression, and does not work with other compression utilities (UNIX only).
- **uncompact** Uncompresses files built by compress (UNIX only).

Compressing and Archiving Files

The previous utilities created archives or compressed files. The following utilities are used to create archives of compressed files, then to uncompress selected files from the archive as needed:

- **zip**   Creates an archive of a directory tree and its files in compressed format. It works like a combination of the UNIX commands **tar** and **gzip**. It is available on UNIX, VMS, MS-DOS, OS/2, Windows NT, Minix, Atari, and Macintosh.
- **unzip**   Uncompresses a file, directory, or archive that was compressed with **zip**. It can be used as a filter for extracting from a ZIP archive in a pipe line.
- **zipinfo**   Lists detailed information about a ZIP archive.
- **zmore**   Displays a zipped file one page at a time by unzipping data as needed.
- **zcat**   Behaves like the UNIX **cat** utility. It accesses specified files from a zip archive, reads them, uncompresses the data, and writes it to output. The archive is not affected, just read.
- **zcmp**   Compares two files from a zip archive by uncompressing the data and passing it to **cmp**. The archive remains compressed.

■ Review

1. Assume you have **rwx** permissions on a file named *secret* and enter the command

   view *secret*

   You delete a line from the file and enter **:wq** to quit the editor. What happens?

   _____

2. What command prints the file *nlongfile* starting with page 2, putting three columns to a page?

   _____

3. What command instructs **find** to locate all files named *core* anywhere in your home directory and its subdirectories and then removes the files?

   _____

4. What command sorts the output of **ps -aux** and divides it into a series of small files, named *ps-aa*, and so forth, each file containing ten or fewer lines?

   _____

5. What is the difference between copying all the files from a directory to a floppy using **mcopy** and creating a **tar** image of all the files in a directory and putting it on a floppy?

■ Conclusion

Linux/ UNIX provide essential tools that facilitate our viewing, paginating, printing, locating, copying to floppy, and making archives. Each tool examined in this chapter has even greater usefulness that is described in the **man** pages of each tool.

■ Answers to Review

1. You are told the file is read-only because you started **vi** using the **view** command.
2. **pr +2 -3** *nlongfile* **| lpr**
3. **find ~ –name** *core* **-exec rm** {} **\;**
4. **ps -aux | sort | split** *-10 ps-*
5. The files will be available either way, however information such as permissions, ownership, and so forth, is retained only in a **tar** archive.

COMMAND SUMMARY

Printing Commands

lp -dprinter filename   Requests that the file *filename* be printed on the destination printer *printer*.

lp -dprinter -nnumber filename   Specifies number of copies to be printed, where *number* is the number of copies desired.

lp -dprinter -ttitle filename   Specifies that *title* be printed on the banner page.

lpstat   Produces a report on the status of all your print requests.

cancel -P printername jobnumber   Cancels the specified print request (whether printing or not), where *printername* is the printer and *jobnumber* is the ID of the requested job.

cancel   Removes all jobs of user being printed on *printer*.

lprm   Removes all jobs of user being printed on printer.

lpr -Pprinter filename   Requests that the file *filename* be printed on the destination printer *printer*.

lpr -Pprinter -#number filename   Specifies the number of copies to be printed, where *number* is the number of copies desired.

lpr -Pprinter -Jtitle filename   Specifies the banner to be printed on the banner page.

lprm -Pprinter jobnumber   Cancels print request if it is not printing.

Command Summary for pr

-l #   Instructs **pr** to output data in pages of # lines.

-h headertext   Instructs **pr** to put *headertext* on the top of each page of output.

-n   Instructs **pr** to put line numbers on each line of output.

+#   Instruction to start printing on page # in the file.

-#   Instruction to output file in # columns to a page.

Command Summary for split

-# *targetfile outname*   Instructs **split** to read *targetfile* and divide the contents into files of # lines named *outnameaa, outnameab,* etc.

Command Summary for find

-print   Outputs the path to all matched files.

-exec   Runs whatever command follows *-exec* on the command line for each matched file.

-user *username*   Locates files owned by user *user name*.

Command Summary for mtools

mdir   Lists contents of floppy in drive *a*.

mcopy   Copies file(s) to or from drive (*a:*) to or from directory.

mformat   Formats drive in DOS format.

Command Summary for tar

c   Creates archive.

v   Instructs **tar** to be verbose and display the name of each object as it is read or written.

f   Instructs **tar** to read from or write to a file.

x   Extracts data from an archive.

t   Reports on table of contents of archive (contents).

II

Programming in the Shell with Power Utilities

Special Characters and Programming Structures

13

Before beginning this chapter, you should be able to

- Rename, copy, and remove files
- Use several utilities in one command line by redirecting output
- Change directories throughout the file system
- Access and modify files using the **vi** editor
- Give proper instructions to the shell to execute complex command lines
- Use command substitution, filename expansion, and variable evaluation
- Diagnose command lines considering shell generation of child processes
- Identify currently running processes and parents

O B J E C T I V E S

After completing this chapter, you will be able to

- Have the shell interpret or not interpret special characters as needed
- Employ command-line arguments with shell scripts
- Use program control statements at the command line and in scripts
- Perform basic arithmetic operations in the shell
- Employ special characters to turn off interpretation of other special characters

The various shells that we use to interact with UNIX and Linux are powerful, feature-rich utilities that interpret our requests to execute programs, execute instructions in shell scripts, and interpret complex programming statements. We instruct the shells to interpret and not interpret special characters, to employ built-in features, and to execute scripts that include decision-making program control statements. This chapter examines the built-in features, special character interpretation, and basic programming structures of the **sh** family of shells: **sh**, **bash**, and **ksh**.

This chapter begins with an exploration of how the **sh** shells employ quoting to turn off and on the interpretation of special characters. The next sections examine how basic arithmetic operations are performed and how arguments are passed to scripts. This chapter concludes with a section investigating programming features available to use both at the command line and in scripts.

13.1 Shell Interpretation of Special Characters

When the shell interprets a command line, many characters have special meaning, including * & $! > | < [ ] ; ~ and spaces. We use a $ to designate a variable to be evaluated in commands such as **echo** *$PATH*. The shell interprets the $ as instruction to locate the variable *PATH* and replace the string *$PATH* with the variable's value on the command line. The shell then passes the value as an argument to **echo**. In other commands, the shell replaces the * with the names of all files in the current directory. When the shell interprets a command line, it must make sense out of whatever special characters we include as instructions.

We have also issued commands that told the shell to not interpret specified special characters—by placing them in single quotes or following backslashes.

To Be Interpreted or Not to Be Interpreted...

That is the question. Whether 'tis nobler in the mind to evaluate a variable and replace it with its value, or to leave it be, and thus be passed as a dreaded, unworthy character string.

The shell interprets three special characters as instruction to turn off interpretation of other special characters.

1. Start a communicative shell by entering one of the following:

   ksh -x

   or

   bash -x

   The shell now performs all interpretations and displays the results before having the child process execute the utility.

2. Enter:

   echo *

   To the shell, the * is the filename-matching character. It is a special character that is interpreted by the shell as instruction to locate all filenames in the current directory consisting of zero or more of any character—all filenames. The shell then replaces the asterisk on the command line with all the names that match. The filenames are then arguments passed to **echo**. As usual, **echo** simply reads its arguments and writes them to output.

3. Now tell the shell to not interpret:

   echo *
   echo "*"
   echo '*'

   If the * follows a backslash or is inside single quotes or double quotes, the shell does not interpret the *'s special meaning. The * is just an asterisk that is passed as an argument to the child process that will run **echo**. When **echo** runs, it writes its arguments (the asterisk character) to output, which is still connected to the screen.

   The output from these commands demonstrates a particularly important aspect of the way the shell functions, namely, the output is just the asterisk. The backslash and quotation marks are *not* included in the output. The special characters \\, ", and ' are instructions to the shell. They convey the message to *turn interpretation off* specific strings that follow. They are not part of the strings to be left uninterpreted; they are the instruction to not interpret.

4. Carefully examine the results of the following:

   echo $HOME $HOME $HOME
   echo \\$HOME $HOME $HOME

   The shell interprets special characters, unless we tell it not to. The backslash instructs the shell to turn off interpretation of any special meaning attached to one and only one character, the one that immediately follows. It is the kryptonite for one character. In the second line, only the first *$USER* is not interpreted; only the first $ follows a backslash.

5. As you enter the following examples, identify where interpretation is turned *off* and where it is turned back *on*:

> **echo** '*$HOME $HOME*' *$HOME*
> **echo** *my files are:* *
> **echo** '*my files are:* *'
> **echo** *my files are:* *

At this point, the double and single quotes behave the same: the first one turns *off* interpretation, and the next matching quote turns it back *on*. There are differences in the behavior of single and double quotes, as we shall soon explore.

Turning Interpretation Off and On

These three characters—backslash, a pair of single quotes, or a pair of double quotes—have special meaning to the shell; namely, to turn interpretation off when reading a specified character or string of characters.

To communicate our intentions to the shell successfully, we have to think like the shell.

1. Enter the following, carefully placing single quotes where specified:

> **touch** *zza1 zza2*
> **echo** ' *zza** ' *zza** ' *zza** '

Is the middle *zza** buried inside two quotes or not quoted at all?

The middle string is interpreted.

When the shell reads a command line and encounters a single quote, it turns off interpretation of essentially all special characters until it encounters the next matching quote.

To make sense out of "shell quoting," imagine the shell maintains a series of on/off switches associated with the special characters. For each character, interpretation is either on or off.

CHARACTER	INTERPRETATION
'	The shell starts at the left end of the command line and finds a single quote. The shell turns off interpretation of essentially all special characters. (Interpretation of the * character is off.)
zza*	Because interpretation is off, all characters are passed to **echo** uninterpreted.
'	Shell finds the matching single quote and turns interpretation back on.
zza*	Interpretation is on, so the filename matching takes place, and a series of filenames are matched and given as arguments to **echo**.
'	Interpretation is turned off.
zza*	This string is passed uninterpreted.
'	Interpretation is turned back on.

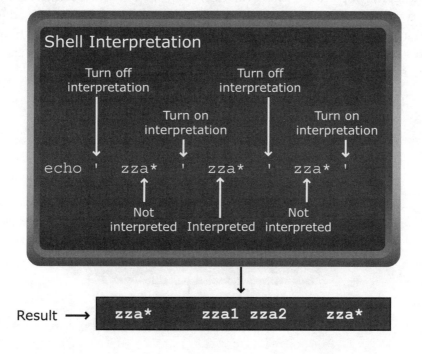

2. As another example of the "on-off" nature of shell interpretation, enter:

> echo *$USER* ' *$USER* ' *$USER* ' *$USER* '

The first and third instances of **$USER** in this command line are interpreted, and the variable values are passed to **echo**. The second and fourth instances are not interpreted, and the string *$USER* is passed uninterpreted to **echo**. The shell always begins command-line processing at the left with interpretation switched on. Interpretation moves from left to right. When the first single quote is encountered, interpretation is switched off.

At first glance, the third **$USER** appears to be deep inside quotation marks. In reality, it is not quoted at all. The first **$USER** is interpreted, and its value is passed to **echo** as an argument. When the shell encounters the first single quote, it turns interpretation *off*. Hence, the second **$USER** is not interpreted, but is passed to **echo** as the literal argument *$USER*. At the second single quote, the shell turns interpretation back *on*. The third **$USER** is interpreted as a variable. This **$USER** is replaced with its value, which is passed to **echo** as an argument. The last instance of **$USER** is enclosed in quotes like the first and passed literally to **echo**. The last single quote turns interpretation back on, so the ENTER is interpreted.

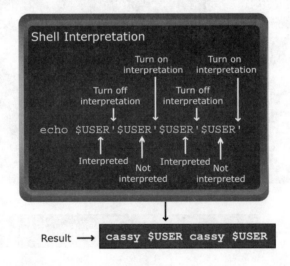

Result → cassy $USER cassy $USER

3. Enter:

> echo '* *$USER*   *$HOME*' *$USER* *$HOME* '*$USER*'

Interpretation is turned *off* at the first single quote, *on* at the second, *off* at the third, and *on* at the fourth. If interpretation is *off* when a character is encountered, the character is passed as a literal character argument to **echo**.

Examining the Effect of Quoting on Special Characters

In the following table, characters that are special to the shell are listed in the far-left column. Across the top, the column heads are the three characters that turn off interpretation. The table contains some information about how the asterisk is interpreted. In the remainder of this section, we examine whether a special character is interpreted or not interpreted with respect to the single quotes, double quotes, and backslash. As you explore each of the following exercises, fill in the table.

Shell	inside "	inside '	Following \
*	Not interpreted	Not interpreted	Not interpreted
[ ]			
{ }			
<			
&			
|			
>			
;			
$			
spaces			
newline			
'			
"			
\ (sh)			
\ (csh)			
`			
!(csh)			
!(bash)			

Interpretation of Filename-Matching Characters

1. Create two files in your current directory:

   touch *perry1 perry2*

2. Evaluate the filename-matching characters:

   echo *perry* perry[0-9] perry{1,2} perry?*

   The shell interprets all filename expansion characters if they are not quoted.

3. Tell the shell to turn off interpretation with single quotes:

   echo *'perry* perry[0-9] perry{1,2} perry?'*

   The shell does not interpret any filename expansion character if it is inside single quotes.

4. Turn off interpretation with double quotes:

   echo *"perry* perry[0-9] perry{1,2} perry?"*

   Likewise, the shell does not interpret any filename expansion character if it is double quoted.

5. Turn off interpretation of the filename expansion special characters using backslashes:

   echo *perry* perry\\[0-9\\] perry\\{1,2\\} perry\\?*

   The shell turns off interpretation of every filename expansion character when they follow backslashes. If a filename-matching special character is inside single or double quotes, or follows a backslash, it is not interpreted, but is passed as an ordinary character.

6. Fill in the blanks in the previous table indicating that the [, {, and ? are not interpreted following \ or inside single or double quotes.

Interpretation of Redirection and Conditional Execution

We know the shell interprets all < & | > ; characters if they are not quoted.

1. Tell the shell to turn off interpretation with single quotes, double quotes, and backslashes:

   echo ' < & | > ; '
   echo " < & | > ; "
   echo \< \& \| \> \;

The shell does not interpret any redirection or conditional execution character if it is in quotes or following a backslash.

2. Fill in the blanks in the summary table indicating that the <, &, |, and ; are not interpreted following \ or inside single or double quotes.

Interpretation of Variables

Variables can be interpreted or not interpreted depending on how they are quoted.

1. Place a variable in the clutches of the "don't interpret" characters with:

   echo *$HOME $HOME*
   echo *\$HOME $HOME*
   echo *'$HOME $HOME'*
   echo *"$HOME $HOME"*

   The backslash and single quotes both instruct the shell to not interpret variables. However, if a variable is inside double quotes, the shell interprets it anyway.

2. Try:

   echo *"I am *** $USER who are you?"*
   echo *'I am *** $USER who are you?'*

   Inside single quotes, all special characters are not interpreted. Inside double quotes, the variable **$** is interpreted.

3. Fill in the table indicating that variables are interpreted inside double quotes, but not interpreted inside single quotes or following a backslash.

   Because the shells interpret variables inside double quotes, we can pass many characters to a utility uninterpreted, yet evaluate variables.

4. Enter:

   who | **sed** *"s/$USER/*guru*/"*

The shell replaces the variable with its value, then passes the modified argument to **sed**. After **sed** locates the target string of your login name, **sed** replaces the target with the string *guru* and outputs the line.

Interpretation of Spaces

In previous exercises, we issued commands that included spaces inside single quotes. The following exercises focus on whether the shell interprets spaces when they are quoted.

1. Enter:

   ls -l
   ls\ -l
   ls' '-l
   ls" "-l

   When the shell is instructed to not interpret a space, it is then just a literal space. Where, the shell asks, is the utility **ls**_space_**-l**?

2. Try:

   echo *A* *B*
   echo '*A* *B*'
   echo "*A* *B*"
   echo *A*\ \ \ \ \ *B*
   sort *users_on*\ *practice*
   sort *users_on*' '*practice*

   The shells do not interpret spaces when they follow the backslash or are inside single or double quotes.

3. Fill in the table indicating that spaces are not interpreted.

Interpretation of the Newline

We press ENTER at the end of every command line we issue. The shell interprets it as the end-of-command marker. The next few exercises demonstrate some differences among the shells.

At this point, you are probably communicating with a member of the **sh** shell family.

1. Start a C shell by entering:

   tcsh

   or

   csh

2. Enter:

   echo '*$USER*

   and without a closing quote, press ENTER.

In a C shell, you receive an error message that it found unmatched quotes. The shell interprets the first single quote as instruction to turn interpretation off. The shell is not told to turn interpretation back on with a matching single quote before you pressed ENTER, so it complains.

Now examine the same events in a **bash** or **ksh** or **sh** shell.

3. Either start a child shell with **bash, ksh,** or **sh,**

or

if your parent shell is appropriate, exit the current shell and return to the parent.

4. In a **bash** or **ksh** or **sh** shell, enter:

> **echo ' $USER**

and without including the closing quote, press ENTER.

The shell responds with its secondary prompt. When a member of the **sh** family of shells receives an incomplete command, it displays the secondary prompt to ask for the remainder. In this case, the shell turns off interpretation when it encounters the first single quote. When you press ENTER, the ENTER is not interpreted, because interpretation is off. The shell is still waiting for an ENTER to interpret as the end of the command.

5. Type an asterisk and a closing single quote:

> *** '**

Press ENTER.

The * is not interpreted; it is inside quotes and is passed as-is to **echo** as an argument.

Interpretation of Single and Double Quotes

We have examined how the shell interprets many characters when placed inside single quotes and double quotes. Can we turn off interpretation of the quotes themselves?

1. Enter:

> **echo "'"**
> **echo '"'**

The shell passed the enclosed quote in each case. The shell does not interpret single quotes if they are inside double quotes; nor does it interpret double quotes inside single quotes.

2. Now try:

    echo \\'
    echo \\"

The output is the uninterpreted quotation characters. The shell interprets the backslash as instruction to not interpret the single character that follows, so the quotes are not interpreted, but passed as arguments to **echo**.

If the shell were to interpret the quotes following backslashes, the output would be quite different. Interpreting the quotes would result in turning interpretation off; the ENTER would not be interpreted. The C shells would complain, and the **sh** shells would present a secondary prompt. Instead, the quotes are passed as arguments to **echo**. The shell interprets the quotation marks as ordinary characters without any special characteristics if they follow a backslash.

3. Enter:

    echo *I'm in $HOME*

We get a secondary prompt in an **sh** family shell and a complaint in a C shell. The apostrophe in *I'm* is just an apostrophe to us, but to the shells it is a single quote. Interpretation is turned off. The variable is not interpreted. Because interpretation is never turned back on, the ENTER is not interpreted. If you are in a C shell, you received an error message. The **sh** shells present a secondary prompt.

4. If you have a secondary prompt, enter a closing single quote and press ENTER.

5. Instruct the shell to not interpret the single quote apostrophe by entering:

    echo "I'm in $HOME"

The single quote is not interpreted, but the variable $HOME is—because the shell interprets $ special characters inside double quotes.

Interpretation of the Backslash by sh Shells

This is another place where the two families of shells behave differently.

1. Access an **sh** family shell.

2. Enter:

    **echo **

The shell does not interpret a backslash following a backslash.

3. Examine the following command *without pressing* ENTER:

   echo '\'

One of two things will happen when you ask for this line to be executed:

   - If the shell does not interpret the backslash inside single quotes, then the backslash character should be passed as the argument to **echo** and displayed on the screen.
   - If the shell were to interpret the \ inside the single quotes, what would happen? The backslash is instruction to not interpret the character that follows, in this case, the closing quote. Without a closing quote, interpretation remains off and the **sh** family of shells would not find an ENTER to interpret as the end of command line, presenting the secondary prompt.

4. Have the shell examine the command by pressing:

   ENTER

The backslash is passed as an uninterpreted character. The **sh** family of shells does not interpret backslashes inside single quotes.

5. Examine the same question with double quotes by entering:

   echo "\"

The shell presents the secondary prompt. The first double quote instructs the shell to turn off interpretation of most characters. The second double quote should have turned interpretation back on so the ENTER would be interpreted. But the ENTER was not interpreted. The second double quote must have been turned off by the backslash.

If a backslash follows another backslash or is inside single quotes, it is not interpreted by an **sh** family shell. If a backslash is inside double quotes, the **sh** shell does interpret it.

Well, mostly.

6. Try the following:

   echo "*abc\def*"

If a backslash is in front of a character that has no special meaning to the shell, the backslash is not seen as instruction to turn off interpretation of a special character, so in that case, the backslash is passed uninterpreted.

7. A full demonstration of this feature is:

echo "$USER \\$USER *"

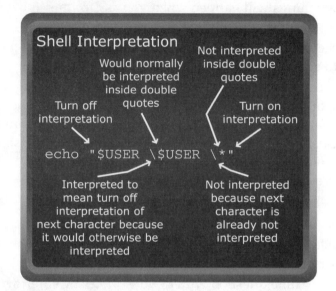

In the **sh** family of shells, if a backslash is inside double quotes and precedes a character that has special meaning to the shell, the backslash is interpreted and turns off the interpretation of the character that follows. If a backslash is inside double quotes and precedes a character that would otherwise not be interpreted, the backslash itself is not interpreted, but passed as a backslash itself .

8. Enter the results in the summary table.

Interpretation of Backslash in the C Shells

1. Access a member of the C shell family.
2. Enter the following:

   echo '\\'
   echo "\\"
   **echo **

The C shells do not interpret backslashes inside single or double quotes or following backslashes.

Interpretation of Command Substitution

1. Enter the following commands and observe the results:

> **echo** *today is date*
> **echo** *today is* `` `date` ``
> **echo** *'today is* `` `date` ``*'*
> **echo** *"today is* `` `date` ``*"*
> **echo** *today is \\`date\\`*

The shells interpret the backquote character as a request to perform command substitution. It says, "Replace the backquotes and their included command with the results of running the included command." If the backquotes are preceded by a backslash or inside a pair of single quotes, the backquotes are not interpreted, but passed as part of the argument. Inside a pair of double quotes, however, the backquotes are interpreted.

2. Fill in the appropriate fields in the table.

Interpreting the History Special Character

In the C shell family and **bash**, the ! history substitution character has power.

1. Try each of the following in **csh** and then in **bash**:

> **cal 2 2004**
> **!!**
> **echo !!**
> **!c**
> **echo '!!'**
> **!c**
> **echo "!!"**
> **!c**
> **echo \\!!**

Shells in the C family interpret the history mechanism ! even when inside single or double quotes. Only the backslash is interpreted as instruction to turn the ! off. In **bash**, the ! is interpreted inside double quotes.

Passing File Expansion Characters
That Lack a Match in an sh Shell

There is an additional difference between the shells.

1. Enter the following command in a C family shell:

> **echo** *zABC[1-4]*

The C shell informs you there is no match with the files in the current directory.

2. Access a member of the **sh** family of shells and enter:

echo *zABC[1-4]*

When an **sh** family shell is given filename expansion instructions and finds no matching files, it *passes the instruction uninterpreted* as an argument to the utility. Shells in the C shell family complain that there is no match, whereas shells in the **sh** family pass the uninterpreted string as the argument.

Summarizing Interpretation Control Characters

The table you created in the previous exercises contains your results when experimenting with quoting. The following illustration provides a summary:

Shell	inside "	inside '	Following \
*	Not interpreted	Not interpreted	Not interpreted
[ ]	Not interpreted	Not interpreted	Not interpreted
{ }	Not interpreted	Not interpreted	Not interpreted
<	Not interpreted	Not interpreted	Not interpreted
&	Not interpreted	Not interpreted	Not interpreted
|	Not interpreted	Not interpreted	Not interpreted
>	Not interpreted	Not interpreted	Not interpreted
;	Not interpreted	Not interpreted	Not interpreted
$	Interpreted	Not interpreted	Not interpreted
spaces	Not interpreted	Not interpreted	Not interpreted
newline	Not interpreted	Not interpreted	Not interpreted
'	Not interpreted	-	Not interpreted
"	-	Not interpreted	Not interpreted
\ (sh)	Interpreted if next character would be interpreted	Not interpreted	Not interpreted
\ (csh)	Not interpreted	Not interpreted	Not interpreted
`	Interpreted	Not interpreted	Not interpreted
!(csh)	Interpreted	Interpreted	Not interpreted
!(bash)	Interpreted	Not Interpreted	Not interpreted

It looks like a lot of data to remember. However, it can be summarized as follows:

- The backslash turns off interpretation for all special characters. Period. All shells, all characters.
- The single quotes turn off interpretation of all special characters for all shells, except the **!** in C shells.
- The double quotes turn off interpretation of all special characters except: **$** (variables) and backquote (command substitution) in all shells and:
    - \ (backslash) in front of an interpretable character in the **sh** family of shells and **bash**.
    - **!** (history substitution) in the C shells.

Another way of summarizing is to describe the powers for each family:

sh shells	All three ways of turning off interpretation turn off all special character interpretation, except that inside double quotes the following are interpreted: **$** and the "back brothers."—the backquote (`) is always interpreted, and the backslash (\) is interpreted if it precedes a character that would otherwise be interpreted. In **bash**, history **!** is interpreted inside double quotes.
C shells	All three ways of turning off interpretation turn off all special character interpretation, except that the **$** and backquote are interpreted inside double quotes, and the history **!** is interpreted inside single or double quotes.

Passing Special Characters to Utilities

When we want to give instructions to a utility, we must communicate through a shell.

To **grep**, the **$** is interpreted as *end of line*. To **awk**, the same character signifies the field. To the shell, it indicates that a variable follows. We have to specify which process is to interpret any special character we employ.

1. Enter:

    grep '*a$*' *west*
    who | **awk** '{ print *$1* , *$3* }'

    These commands work because the shell passes important information, uninterpreted, as arguments to the child processes executing **who** and **awk**. Without the single quotes, the shell would interpret the **$** characters. With the single quotes, we can use **$** to communicate with the utilities.

Mixing Single and Double Quotes to Pass Information

Many utilities expect quotes to be included in their arguments. How do we comply?
By including both single and double quotes on a command line, we can examine
their interactions.

1. Enter the following command:

    echo ' *"$USER"* '

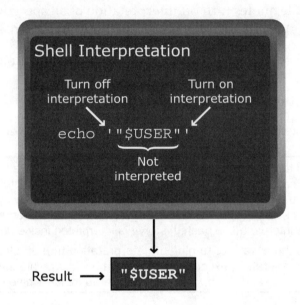

The shell interprets the first single quote as instruction to turn off
interpretation of the double quotes and **$** variable characters. Thus, the
argument *"$USER"* is passed as an uninterpreted string of characters to
echo as an argument.

2. Reverse the order by entering:

    echo " *'$USER'* "

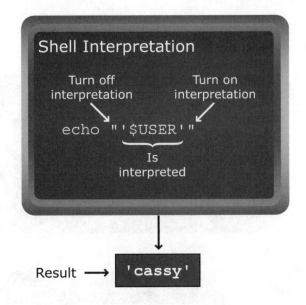

In this case, the output is the user login name surrounded by single quotes. The shell interprets the first double quote as instruction to turn off interpretation of the single quotes, but to interpret the $. Hence, the variable evaluation takes place. The argument sent to **echo** is the value of the evaluated variable surrounded by the uninterpreted single quotes.

The key here is that although *$USER* is surrounded by single quotes on the command line, those single quotes are inside double quotes, and therefore have no special meaning.

3. Examine a more complex version:

   echo '*$USER*"*?' *$USER* ' "*$USER*" '

Examine this command line from the left. The first single quote turns interpretation *off*, so the string *$USER*"*? is passed uninterpreted. The next single quote turns interpretation back *on*, and *$USER* is evaluated to be your login ID. The third single quote turns interpretation back *off*, so the string

"*$USER*" is passed literally. The last single quote turns interpretation back *on*, so the ENTER is evaluated.

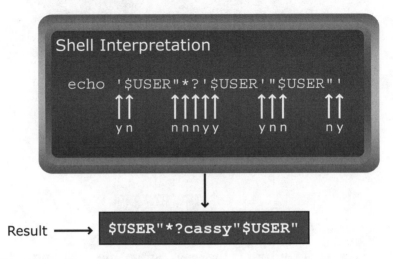

Result ⟶ $USER"*?cassy"$USER"

Deciphering Complex Command Lines

When a command line includes several of the special characters and several of the characters that affect interpretation, it gets rather messy.

1. In a **ksh** or **bash**, enter:

   echo '* $USER \' " Today's date is \" `date` \" $USER *"

   If we first determine where the shell turns interpretation *off* and *on*, then the output becomes more obvious.

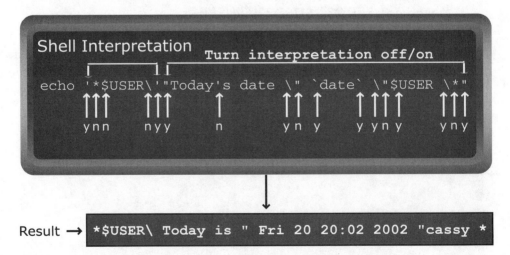

Result → *$USER\ Today is " Fri 20 20:02 2002 "cassy *

Not Interpreting Special Characters in Variable Values

Because the shells interpret variables but not most other special characters inside double quotes, we have some powerful opportunities.

1. In a shell of the **sh** family, enter:

   *aa=z**

   set

   echo $*aa*

   The shell first expands the *z** to the list of filenames that start with the letter z and then assigns those names as the value of the variable *aa*. The variable list output and the variable evaluation confirm the assignment.

2. Instruct the shell to not interpret the special character at variable assignment. Enter:

   aa='z'*

   set

   Clearly, the value of the variable is now *z**, not the actual filenames.

3. Enter:

   echo $*aa*

   The output from **echo** is the names of the files that start with z. First, the shell interpreted the variable and replaced it with its *z** value. It then also expanded the asterisk to match filenames. The shell cannot do everything at once; it must evaluate special characters in some order. The shell completes variable expansion, the *aa* is replaced by *z**, then the shell does filename expansion, replacing the *z** with the names of matching files. The filenames are passed to **echo** as arguments.

4. Enter:

   echo "$*aa*"

   The shell interprets the variable and replaces it with the *z** on the command line, inside the double quotes. The shell does not interpret an * inside double quotes, so this time the asterisk is passed uninterpreted as an argument to **echo**. Inside double quotes the shell interprets the variable but not special characters in the value of the variable.

5. As another example, enter:

   bbb='AA   BB'

   set

   The new variable *bbb* has a value of *AA   BB*.

6. Enter:

   echo $*bbb*

The shell replaces the variable *bbb* with its value *AA   BB*. Therefore, the modified command line is:

   `echo    AA         BB`

The shell then interprets the spaces between the *AA* and the *BB* as separating two arguments. The shell passes *AA* as the first argument to **echo** and *BB* as the second. The child process starts executing the **echo** code and outputs its first argument, *AA*, followed by a single space and the second argument, *BB*.

The shell interprets the $ as instruction to interpret the variable. Because the variable's value includes spaces, the shell interprets the spaces as token delimiters, resulting in two arguments being passed to **echo**.

7. Instruct the shell to interpret $ but not to interpret other special characters:

   echo "$*bbb*"

   The shell interprets the variable, but does not interpret special characters (the spaces) in its value inside double quotes. The shell therefore passes one argument including the spaces.

13.2 Examining Shell Programming Features

The shell special variables and characters that turn interpretation *off* and *on* coupled with built-in programming features lay the groundwork for complex shell programs.

Passing Arguments to a Script

In addition to the built-in variables examined earlier, the shell is programmed to interpret special variable names.

1. Use the editor to create a script called *argtester*, and add the following eight lines:

```
echo hello $USER
echo 'The contents of variable $1 is '        $1
echo 'The contents of variable $2 is '        $2
echo 'The contents of variable $3 is '        $3
echo 'The contents of variable $0 is '        $0
echo 'The contents of variable $* is '        $*
```

       echo *'The contents of variable $# is '*   **$#**
       echo *'The contents of variable $$ is '*   **$$**

2. Make the file executable and run it:

       chmod **755** *argtester*
       argtester *Butch Kaye Jason Amber Brandon Corrinne*

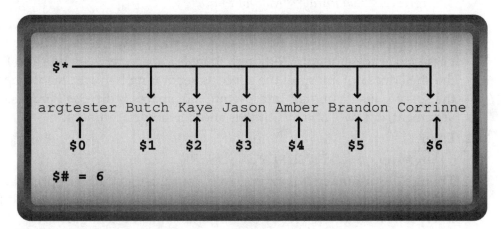

3. Run the script again by entering:

       argtester *Peter Ann Noah Karuna*
       argtester *red blue heliotrope yellow*

The child shell interprets the arguments it receives as:

Variable	Value of Variable
$1	Argument 1
$2	Argument 2
$3	Argument 3
$4	Argument 4, and so forth...
$0	Argument 0, the script that is running
$*	All arguments
$#	Number of arguments
$$	PID of current process (running the script)

Examining Complex Arguments

The *argtester* script allows us to examine how the shell interprets command-line arguments.

1. Enter the following:

   argtester "Bob Purdy" "Margot Smith"

   The results of the **echo $1** and **echo $2** lines in the script are displayed. The shell interprets the command line as containing only two arguments to be passed to **echo**—not four. Although there is a space between Bob and Purdy, the shell does not interpret the space as separating two arguments, because the space is inside quotes. Interpretation of spaces is off. *Bob Purdy* is one argument, not two. *Margot Smith* is another single argument.

2. Enter:

   argtester ' $USER'$USER'z* $USER'*

   Though the argument is constructed by putting together interpreted and uninterpreted portions, there are no spaces that the shell is permitted to interpret. Hence, there is only one argument passed to *argtester*.

3. Try:

   argtester 'Kenny   Tray'

   The results are instructive. Clearly, *argtester* received only one argument, but by the time it is displayed on the screen, it no longer has multiple spaces between the first and last names.

   Edit the script *argtester* and modify the first line to include double quotes around the last *$1* so it reads:

   echo *'The contents of variable $1 is '*   *"$1"*

4. Save the file and quit the editor.

5. Enter:

   argtester 'Kenny   Tray'

   This time the argument is displayed complete with spaces as argument 1. The *$1* is in double quotes in the script so the variable is interpreted but not resulting spaces. However, the evaluation of $* shows that the shell did interpret the spaces; there are no double quotes around the $* in the script.

6. Modify the script to double quote all the argument variables, $2, $3, and so forth, at the ends of each line.

7. Enter:

   argtester 'Kenny   Tray'

The output consistently shows one argument with appropriate spacing.

8. Enter:

argtester '$1 == "'$USER'" {print $4}'

Only one argument is passed to *argtester*. There are no spaces the shell is permitted to interpret. The value of the variable *$USER* is interpreted. It is outside the single quoted sections. After interpretation, the value of USERS is "quoted".

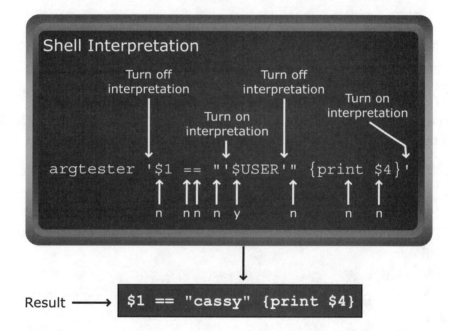

Result ⟶ `$1 == "cassy" {print $4}`

Interpreting Some Characters in an Argument

The **bc** utility performs basic calculations reading instructions from input, usually attached to the keyboard. To employ **bc** in a script or as a part of a command line, we still need to communicate through the input.

1. Enter:

echo "8 * 9" | bc

The shell starts two processes, passing an argument including the uninterpreted * to **echo**. The **echo** utility reads its argument and writes it to output, the input of **bc**, which performs the calculation and outputs the results. The shell does not interpret the * because it is inside double quotes. We need the * to be passed to **bc** as instruction to multiply.

2. Enter:

   a=7

   echo "(2+$a) ^ $a" | **bc**

The shell interprets the variable **$** inside double quotes, but does not interpret the other special characters, so the correct command is constructed and given as an argument to **echo**, which passes it on to **bc**'s input, namely:

| (2+7) ^ 7

To **bc**, this is instruction to raise *9* to the power of *7*, or *9*9*9*9*9*9*9*.

Creating a Variable with User Input

At the command line, we create variables explicitly by telling the shell the name of the variable and the value to assign.

1. Enter:

   a=1122

   echo $a

   The **sh** family of shells also creates variables with input read from the user.

2. Enter:

   read *xxx*

   No prompt is displayed; however, the shell is waiting for input.

3. Enter:

   160AA

   and press ENTER.

4. Evaluate the new variable:

   echo $*xxx*

   A new variable named *xxx* is created with a value of *160AA*. In this instance, the shell interprets the **read** command as instruction to create a new variable, using the argument to **read** as the new variable's name, and then to assign the variable the value of whatever the user types in, until the next ENTER.

   The same procedure can be used to modify the value of an existing variable.

5. Enter:

   read *xxx*

   and type:

   This is the new value for xxx

6. Evaluate the variable:

    echo $*xxx*

The shell interprets the argument to the **read** command as the name of a variable and interprets whatever the user types until the next ENTER as the value to assign to the variable. If the variable exists, its value is modified. If the variable does not exist, the shell creates it. A variable consisting of many words is acceptable.

Performing Arithmetic with let

The utility **bc** performs complex calculations, but the **sh** family of shells performs basic arithmetic internally using a built-in command, **let**.

1. For these exercises, be sure to communicate with a member of the **sh** family: **bash**, **ksh**, or **sh**.

2. Enter:

    aa=12
    echo $*aa*
    let *aa=20*
    echo $*aa*

The **let** built-in command is used to assign values to variables and to perform arithmetic calculations.

3. Enter:

    let *aa=$aa+12*
    echo $*aa*

In the **let** command, the shell first evaluates the value of the variable *aa*, then adds *12* to the value. The resulting *32* is assigned to the variable *aa*. The steps are evaluation, calculation, then assignment.

4. The **let** command can be executed as double parentheses. Enter:

    ((*aa=$aa-6***))**
    echo $*aa*

5. To complete a **let** operation and display the results in one statement, enter:

    echo $((6+3))
    echo $((*aa*3***))**

The shell performs the operation inside the **(( ))** and then passes the results to **echo** as an argument.

Making Decisions in the Shell

The shells are more that just interpreters of our wishes. They are full programming languages.

Most of the shell programming accomplished today is written in the **sh**, **bash**, **ksh** family of shells. This section examines several fundamental functions in **sh** family shell programming; however, mastery of **sh** family programming makes mastery of C shell programming easy because the differences are just in syntax.

Obtaining a Report on How Things Went

We write command lines, press ENTER, and give them to the shell. The shell interprets what we enter, starts child processes, then completes redirection of input-output and passing the arguments. With plumbing completed, the shell instructs the child processes to execute the correct program code. After the program completes execution, it sends an exit status message to its parent and exits.

1. Enter:

   date
   echo $?

   The shell runs **date**, which sends an exit code at exit. We ask the shell to tell us the exit code from the last process that it ran; we are told *0*, indicating that all was successful when **date** ran.

2. Enter:

   wc -z *practice*
   echo $?

   The **wc** utility does not recognize option **z**, so it complains through an error message that is written out the error door, connected to your screen. As **wc** exits, it sends the exit code to the shell. All did not go well. The message is not a zero.

3. Examine how **grep** sends error codes to the parent depending on its success:

   grep $USER *users_on*
   echo $?

   When **grep** locates the requested file and finds at least one line that matches the target, it reports a zero exit code to its parent process. If you no longer have the *users_on* file created in the second chapter, create it again with:

   who > *users_on*

4. Request that **grep** search for a target that is not on any lines in the file:

   > **grep** *XX558 users_on*
   > **echo $?**

   When **grep** can locate the requested file but cannot match any lines with the target string, it reports an exit code of *1*.

5. Request that **grep** search through a nonexistent file:

   > **grep** *$USER xxxx*
   > **echo $?**

   If **grep** cannot find the file listed as an argument, **grep** sends an error code of 2 when it exits. Why? Because that is what the programmer decided. As programmers, we define the meaning of error exit codes. If the program is successful, we are to exit with *0*. Unsuccessful? Not zero.

6. Use the editor and create a short script named *short-scr* consisting of:

   > **echo** *hi $USER*
   > **exit** *7*
   > **who**
   > **sleep** *5*
   > **cal**

7. Make it executable, run it, and check the exit code:

   > **chmod** *755 short-scr*
   > *short-scr*
   > **echo $?**

   The output is the greeting from **echo**. The **exit** runs and passes the *7* exit code to the parent shell. When we ask the parent shell for its last child exit code, the answer reported is *7*. Because the shell exits at the **exit** line, the code following the **exit** is not run. There is neither execution of **who**, nor **sleep**, nor **cal**.

IF You Are Good at Grandmother's, THEN We'll Stop at the Park, ELSE a Nap

Our parents taught us the **if**...**then**...**else** program structure (and its more intense, abbreviated form, **if**...**else**), along with **while** *it is raining, wear the boots,* and **for** *each guest, prepare a place setting, including napkin.* We just have to learn the syntax for each new language. The **if**...**then**...**else** structure that our parents so carefully taught us takes the following syntax in an **sh** shell.

1. At the shell prompt of an **sh** family shell, enter the following command lines:

   if date
   then
   echo *it worked*
   echo *Congratulations $USER*
   else
   echo *it failed*
   fi

   As soon as you enter the concluding **fi**, the **date** program runs, followed by the outputs from **echo**: both *it worked* and *Congratulations login-name.* The **date** program runs successfully, providing the shell with a *0* (success) exit code. Because the exit from the program following the **if** is a zero, the code following the **then** is executed.

2. At the command line prompt, enter a program that fails after an **if**:

   if dazate
   then
   echo *it worked*
   else
   echo *it failed*
   fi

   The program following the **if** is unsuccessful; therefore, the code following the **then** is executed.

   The full command structure can be executed on one command line.

3. At the shell prompt, enter:

   if date; then echo *it worked* **; else echo** *it failed* **; fi**

Every process sends an exit code to its parent as it exits. We use the exit code to make decisions. The process running **date** was successful, returning an exit code of *0*, so the statements following the **then** were executed. If the exit were not zero, the **else** statements would have been executed.

Making Decisions and Exiting with a Code

Every program produces an exit code when it ends.

1. Carefully enter the following, with a space between each token:

   [6 -eq 7]
   echo $?

   The statement *six is equal to seven* is evaluated. If it is true, an exit code of *0* is returned. If false, a *1*. The exit code is *1*, so the statement 6 -eq 7 is false.

2. Enter:

   [6 -ne 7]
   echo $?

   Because the statement *six is not equal to seven* is true, the exit code is *0*.

3. Enter:

   [6 -lt 7]
   echo $?

   The statement *six is less than seven* is true, so the exit code is *0*.

4. Enter:

   [3 -gt 4]
   echo $?

   False, *3* is not greater than *4*.

5. Enter:

   [6 -ge 7]
   echo $?

   False, *6* is not greater than or equal to 7.

But Where Is the Utility?

The last several examples examined the exit code status after running lines that have statements inside brackets such as:

   [7 -eq 7]

We enter statements like these to the shell and get exit codes. If we are asked what are the elements in a command line that looks like the following:

___   ___   ___   ___   ___

we immediately respond:

   util arg arg arg arg

The problem is, we don't expect a program to have a name like [, so we are caught off guard.

1. In a **tcsh** or **ksh**, enter:

   which [

   The usual response is:

   ```
   /usr/bin/[
   ```

2. Obtain a listing of the [in */usr/bin* by entering:

   ls -l */usr/bin/*[

   The output indicates that the bracket points to a file named **test**. Brackets are another name for the **test** command.

3. Enter the following without a space between the left bracket and the six:

   [6 **-ge** 7]

   The error message indicates that the command [6 is not found. There was no problem finding the [command, but [6 is another matter.

4. Leave out the last space:

   [6 **-ge** 7]

   The closing right bracket must be an argument unto itself. Because we are dealing with a utility, each argument must be identified explicitly with spaces.

Testing Strings and Files

The test utility is a powerful tool for making program decisions.

1. Enter:

   [*hello*]
   echo $?

   Any string of text inside the brackets is evaluated as true. For that reason, we can evaluate whether a variable has a value.

2. Enter:

   [*$USER*]
   echo $?

   The shell evaluates the variable and replaces it with its value. Because a single string of characters is inside the brackets, the **echo $?** evaluates as **0** true.

3. Enter:

   echo *$ABCD*

The variable does not exist; no value is passed to **echo**.

4. Enter:

> [*$ABCD*]
> **echo** *$?*

The variable does not exist. No value is placed inside the brackets. *1*, false, is returned.

5. Enter:

> [**-f** */etc/passwd*]
> **echo** *$?*

It is true that there is a file named */etc/passwd*, so the exit code is *0*.

6. Enter:

> [**-f** *xxyy55*]
> **echo** *$?*

You probably have no file of that name. Exit code *1*.

Making Decisions Based on Exit Codes

1. At the command line in an **sh** family shell, enter the following lines:

> **if** [**-f** */etc/passwd*]
> **then**
> **echo** *File Exists*
> **else**
> **echo** *File does not exist*
> **fi**

The test brackets return a *0* exit code. The file exists. Statements between **then** and **else** are executed.

2. At the command line, enter:

> **if** [*345* **-gt** *297*]
> **then**
> **echo** *345 is greater than 297*
> **else**
> **echo** *345 is not greater than 297*
> **fi**

The test returns a *0* because the statement "*345 is greater than 297*" is true. Statements following **then** are executed.

3. Enter:

> **if [-f** */etc/xxxx* **]**
> **then**
> **echo** *file exists*
> **else**
> **echo** *file does not exist*
> **fi**

The file does not exist.

For All of These Objects, Do Those Things

1. Enter:

> **ls**

If you do not have the files named in the following commands in the current directory, either return to your home directory where they should reside, or use four filenames that are listed in the current directory.

Usually, we ask the shell to run a utility on a file, then on another file. Sometimes we have several files and several utilities we want executed.

2. At the command line of an **sh** family shell, enter the following lines:

> **for** *xx* **in** *users_on west coast*
> **do**
> **head -3** *$xx*
> **ls -l** *$xx*
> **wc** *$xx*
> **done**

The output indicates that the **head, ls,** and **wc** utilities are executed first with the file *users_on*, then with *west*, and finally *coast*. The shell runs all the utilities operating on the first file, then all the utilities on the second file, and continues until it runs out of files.

As usual, we learned this as children. The load of laundry is dumped on the bed. Pick up one piece of clothing, fold it, decide where it goes, and put it away. Pick up another piece of clothing, go through the same fold, decide, put away loop. Continue until you run out of clothing on the bed.

The example **for** loop you just ran first creates a new variable, named *xx*, then assigns *xx* the value of the first string following the **in**, namely, *users_on*. With the value of *xx* in place, the shell runs through all the commands in the **do**...**done** section of the code. Then the shell assigns to *xx* the next value listed after the **in** and again goes through the **do**...**done** commands with the new value. The **for** loop continues until all arguments after the **in** are processed.

```
          ①       ③       ⑤
for xx in users_on west coast
do
     head -3 $xx ⎫
     ls -1 $xx   ⎬ ② ④ ⑥
     wc $xx      ⎭
done
 ⑦
```

① Assign **xx** value of **users_on**
② Run do to done code
③ Assign **xx** value of **west**
④ Run do to done code
⑤ Assign **xx** value of **coast**
⑥ Run do to done code
⑦ Exit

While This Is True, Keep on Doing That

While it is raining, keep your raincoat on. As soon as it stops raining, we know to take it off.

1. Use the editor to create a script named *counting*, and add the following lines:

   aa=0
   clear
   while [$*aa* -le *10*]
   do
   echo $*aa*
   sleep *1*

```
((aa=$aa+1))
done
echo "Th Th Th That's All Folks"
echo
sleep 1
```

2. Make it executable and run it.

Here's what happens:

- The variable *aa* is initially set to a value of zero.

- The shell evaluates whether *aa* is less than or equal to *10*.

- It is true that *aa* is less than or equal to 10, so the **do**...**done** code is executed:

  - The value of *aa* is displayed.
  - The **sleep** counts to *1* and exits.
  - **let** adds one to the value of *aa* (we're using the *(( ))* form of **let**).

- The **while** evaluation takes place again, the loop runs again.

- Once the value of *aa* reaches *11*, the **while** loop is not executed.

- The code following the loop is executed.

Take This Branch

The **for** loop is instruction to take all actions listed for each object selected. The **case** structure executes one and only one of several options, based on the value provided. For example:

Do you want to eat:

a) Chinese
b) Pizza
c) Mexican
d) Italian
e) None of the above

1. At the shell, enter:

   case *A* **in**
   A) **date ;;**
   B) **cal ;;**
   C) **ls ;;**
   D) **who | wc -l ;;**
   esac

2. Reexecute the previous exercise, changing the first line to:

   case *D* **in**

The **case** structure looks for a value before the **in**, which it matches with one of the possible branches. The *A* in the **case** line instructs **case** to execute the line *A*) **date**, so the utility is executed.

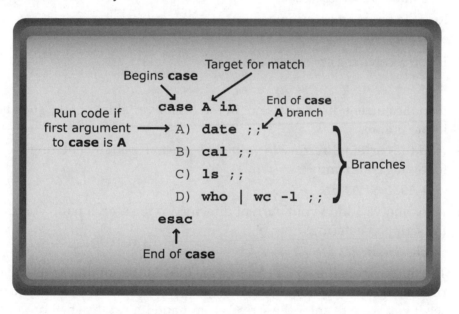

13.3 Creating Shell Scripts

When writing shell scripts, it is most efficient to start with a simple portion of the script, make it work, and then add additional features. If the script fails after a new feature is incorporated, we know the error is related to the code we just added. These scripts are designed to be executed in a member of the **sh** family of shells.

Developing a Basic Script that Employs an Argument

This script is developed in stages beginning with a single line, growing to a script that decides what to do based on the presence or absence of an argument.

1. Create a new file named *checkuser* containing the following line:

   who | grep $USER | wc -l

2. Make *checkuser* executable by entering:

   chmod 755 *checkuser*

3. Run the script by entering:

   checkuser

4. If you receive the error message:

   ```
   checkuser: not found
   ```

   then the current directory is not in the *PATH* variable that the shell uses to locate utilities.

5. Add the current directory to your shell's search path by entering the following command:

   PATH=$PATH:.

6. After you've added your current directory to the search path, you can run the script by entering:

   checkuser

   The output from the script *checkuser* is the number of times that the user running the script is logged on. This output is identical to what you would see if you were to enter the script's command line at the shell prompt.

Examining the Code

When you run the *checkuser* script, the various components of the command line are interpreted as follows:

COMMAND	INTERPRETATION
who	Instruction to the shell to execute the **who** utility.
|	Instruction to the shell to connect the output of **who** to the input of the next utility, **grep**.
grep	Instruction to the shell to execute the **grep** utility.
$USER	Instruction to the shell to evaluate the variable USER and place its value on the command line, replacing the string $USER. The shell then passes the value of the variable (your login ID) to **grep** as an argument. To **grep**, the first argument is interpreted as the target string to look for in the input. Only lines that contain your login ID are output by **grep**.
|	Instruction to the shell to connect the output of **grep** to the input of the next utility, **wc**.
wc	Instruction to the shell to execute the **wc** utility.
-l	Instruction to the shell to pass the argument -l to **wc**. The **wc** utility interprets -l as instruction to output only the count of *lines* it receives as input, not characters or words.

Echoing Fixed Strings in a Shell Script

The **echo** utility reads all its arguments and writes them to standard output, usually connected to the workstation display. Programmers often use **echo** commands in shell scripts to send information to the user.

1. Edit the executable file *checkuser* to match the following:

   echo *The number of times you are currently logged on is:*
   who | **grep** *$USER* | *wc -l*

2. Run the script again:

   checkuser

   Including the **echo** command line makes the script's output a bit more friendly, but as you will see, the real power of using **echo** in a script lies in displaying more essential information.

Modifying and Running the Script to Obtain Information

1. Modify all lines in the *checkuser* script as follows so that it includes reading input from the user:

   echo *Please enter the login name of the user you want to check*
   read *name*

> **echo** *The number of times $name is currently logged on is:*
> **who | grep** *$name* **| wc** *-l*

2. Run the modified script:

   checkuser

3. When prompted, enter the login ID of a user who is currently logged on (it could be yourself) and then press ENTER.

Originally, *checkuser* produced a count of current logins for the user who ran the script. Now, it will do the same for any login name entered by the user when asked by the script.

Examining the Code

The *checkuser* script now contains the minimum components needed for an interactive shell script.

COMMAND	INTERPRETATION
read *name*	Instruction to create a new variable called *name* and assign it the value of whatever is read from the keyboard
echo *The...$name...is:*	Information line written to the screen, including the value of the variable *name*

Modifying the Script to Process Command-Line Arguments

Command-line arguments can be used to pass information as needed in scripts.

1. Reduce the script *checkuser* to the following lines:

   > **echo** *The number of times $1 is currently logged on is:*
   > **who | grep** *$1* **| wc** *-l*

   The **read** statement and the **echo** command line requesting input are removed, and a new element—the variable statement *$1*—is added as an argument to **grep** and to **echo**.

2. Run the modified script by entering the following command, replacing the argument *loginname* with your login name or the login of a user currently logged on:

   checkuser loginname

   Output should resemble the following:

   ```
   The number of times loginname is currently logged on is: 1
   ```

In this version of the script, the shell is asked to evaluate the variable *$1*, a *positional parameter,* which has the value of the first argument on the command line, the *loginname* you entered. In the script, *$1* always has the value of the first command-line argument, regardless of where in the script it is used.

3. Run *checkuser* again using the login name of a user currently logged on.

Making Decisions in Shell Scripts

Logic control structures such as "if this is true, then do this" add power and flexibility to a script. The script in this next example examines whether it is given a first argument. If so, it uses the value of the first argument in its work. If not, it prompts the user for necessary input and then runs.

1. Modify *checkuser* to match the following:

> **if ["*$1*"]**
> **then**
> *name=$1*
> **else**
> **echo** *Please enter a login name to check*
> **read** *name*
> **fi**
> **echo** *The number of times $name is logged on is:*
> **who** | **grep** *$name* | **wc** *-l*

2. Run the modified script by entering the following command line, replacing *loginname* with the login name of a user currently logged on:

> *checkuser loginname*

The output from *checkuser* is information about the number of times the user you specified as an argument to the command is logged on.

3. Now run the script without an argument:

> *checkuser*

4. When prompted by the script, enter a login name.

In this version of *checkuser*, the output is information concerning the login ID you enter when prompted.

Making Decisions Using if-then-else

The essence of this script is how the value of the variable *name* gets assigned. The variable is given whatever is entered as an argument at the command line, or if there is no argument, the variable is assigned whatever value is entered after the script prompts the user. The decision pivots on whether an argument is included by the user on the command line.

The following table analyzes the elements of the decision-making structure in the final version of *checkuser*. The **echo** line has been truncated to fit the table.

COMMAND	INTERPRETATION
if ["$1"]	If there is a value for the $1 variable...
then	Then do the following...
name=**$1**	Set a new variable, *name*, assigning it the value of the variable **$1**, the first argument from the command line...
else	Otherwise do the following.
echo *Please*...	Display the message "Please..."
read *name*	Set value of the variable *name* to be the user's input from the keyboard.
fi	End of the **if** structure.

The overall **if-then-else** structure translates as follows: "**if** the first argument exists, **then** set the value of *name* to it; **else** prompt for it and set the value of *name* to whatever is entered." All **if** structures are terminated with **fi**. If an argument is passed on the command line, then **$1** exists and control passes to the **then** portion of the structure. The shell creates a new variable, *name,* and assigns it the value of the variable *$1* (which is the login name included as the first argument on the command line). If the argument is *not* included on the command line, the variable *$1* does not exist, and control moves to the **else** statement. The action specified in the **else** is the **echo** prompt and the **read** command, which gets the needed information for the variable *name* from the user.

Either by supplying a command-line argument or by answering the script's inquiry, the variable *name* is created and assigned a value. The shell then replaces *$name* with its value in the argument to **echo** and as an argument to **grep** in the remaining lines of code.

Developing a Script That Asks and Does As We Say

A basic menu script presents alternatives, asks what we choose, and does as we request.

1. Create a script named *get-pass* and enter the following text:

   ```
   clear
   echo "1) grep $USER /etc/passwd"
   echo "2) ypcat passwd | grep $USER"
   echo "3) who | sort | awk '{print $1}' | uniq -c"
   echo "What command do you want to run?"
   echo Select 1 2 or 3
   read choice
   echo you selected number $choice
   ```

2. Make the script executable and run it:

   ```
   chmod 755 get-pass
   get-pass
   ```

   The script presents a menu, asks which choice we want, and then confirms what we chose. At this point, no action is taken.

3. Add the following lines to the end of the script:

   ```
   case $choice in
   1)
   grep $USER /etc/passwd
   ;;
   2)
   ypcat passwd | grep $USER
   ;;
   3)
   who | sort | awk '{print $1}' | uniq -c
   ;;
   esac
   ```

4. Run the script again:

   ```
   get-pass
   ```

The menu is presented, the script waits for your answer, and then, depending on the choice you make, runs the called-for command line. It only runs one time. A full menu with a loop to keep running is examined in Chapter 20, "Modifying the User Environment."

```
clear ◄── Clears screen
echo 1) grep $USER /etc/passwd                    Outputs menu
                                                  and requests to
echo 2) ypcat passwd | grep $USER                 screen

echo 3) who | sort | awk  '{print $1}' | uniq -c

echo "What command do you want to run?"

echo Select 1 2 or 3.

read choice ◄── Creates variable choice containing what the user enters

echo you selected number $choice ◄── Displays user's choice

case $choice in ◄── Choice is replaced with whatever the user enters

1) ◄── If user enters 1, code between ) and ;; is executed

grep $USER /etc/passwd

;;

2) ◄── If user enters 2, code between ) and ;; is executed

ypcat passwd | grep $USER

;;

3) ◄── If user enters 3, code between ) and ;; is executed

who | sort | awk  '{print $1}' | uniq -c

;;

esac ◄── End of case
```

■ Review

1. What will be the output for user Cassy if the following commands are entered in a **bash**, **sh**, or **ksh**?

```
echo '***  '$USER'  ***'
echo "**\"$USER\"  `date`  \$USER  '$USER'  *"
```

_____

_____

2. What does each of the following mean to the shells?

   a. $6

   _____

   b. $$

   _____

   c. $*

   _____

   d. $#

   _____

   e. esac

   _____

   f. while

   _____

3. What option is employed when starting a shell to have it display the command line after interpretation but before execution?

   _____

4. What does the third ' in the following accomplish?

   echo \' '$USER' \'

   _____

5. What is the output of **echo**?

   a=6
   (($a * $a))
   ((a=$a + 4))
   echo $a

   _____

6. Write a program called *prod* that takes two integer arguments and outputs the result of the first integer multiplied by the second.

   _____

   _____

7. If a user enters the following in an **sh** shell, what does **echo** display?

   [*6* -ge *6*]
   echo $?

   _____

■ Conclusion

The **sh** shells are powerful programming environments that provide users with important features that allow us to make complex specifications. We can have the shell interpret special characters, or pass them uninterpreted to child processes running utilities. The **sh** family of shells interprets no special characters if inside single quotes or following a backslash. Inside double quotes, the $ variable and backquote ` are interpreted, as is the backslash. We can pass arguments to child processes to make differences in operation or to have data for evaluation. The shells also make **if**, **for**, **while**, and **case** decisions that can be used to alter how data is treated or how programs are executed.

■ Answers to Review

1. *** cassy ***

   **"cassy" Saturday Apr 23 14:31:01 PST 1991 $USER 'cassy' *

2. The answers are as follows:

   a. Sixth argument

   b. Current process's PID

   c. All arguments

   d. Number of arguments

   e. End-of-case

   f. Evaluate exit code after running command that follows. If *0*, run all statements inside **do** to **done**. Evaluate again.

3. **-x**

4. It turns interpretation back on. (The first and fourth ' are not interpreted.)

5. 40

6. #This is *prod*

   echo $(($1 * $2))

7. 0

   Because it's true that 6 is greater than or equal to 6.

COMMAND SUMMARY

Turning Interpretation Off and On

' ' First **'** turns interpretation off for all special characters in all shells except **!** in **csh** family. Second turns interpretation back on.

**** In all shells, turns interpretation off for any special character that immediately follows.

" " First turns interpretation off for nearly all special characters; second turns interpretation back on. Exceptions: In **csh** family, the command substitution (`` ` ``), history (**!**), and variable (**$**) are interpreted inside double quotes. In the **sh** family, command substitution, variables, and the backslash preceding an otherwise special character are interpreted inside double quotes. In **bash**, history (**!**) is interpreted.

Passing Arguments to Child Processes

$1 First argument on command line. Arguments one through nine are accessible in this form. For arguments after the ninth, add curly braces; for example, ${10} is used for the tenth argument.

$* All arguments on command line.

$# Number of arguments on command line.

$0 The 0th argument is the name of the command or script being executed.

Making Calculations

let Performs arithmetic calculations in the form of **let** *a=a+8*.

(( )) Completes arithmetic calculations inside double parentheses.

Programming Statements

read *xxx* Creates or updates variable listed as argument, with whatever user enters until ENTER.

$? Variable contains value of exit code of whatever program was last executed.

[ ] Alternate form of test command. Reports *0* to parent process if statement inside brackets is true, reports *1* if statements are false.

[-f *xxx* **]** Tests whether *xxx* is a file. If it is a file, bracket returns a *0* exit code.

[x **-eq** y]   Reports true if *x* is equal to *y*.

[x **-ne** y]   Reports true if *x* is not equal to *y*.

[x **-gt** y]   Reports true if *x* is greater than *y*.

[x **-lt** y]   Reports true if *x* is less than *y*.

[x **-le** y]   Reports true if *x* is less than or equal to *y*.

[x **-ge** y]   Reports true if *x* is greater than or equal to *y*.

[string]   Reports true if a single string is present.

Program Control

if...then...else

if *command*	Runs command and obtains exit status.
then *command*	If exit status is **0**, commands after **then** are executed.
else *command*	If exit status is not **0**, commands after **else** are executed.
fi	End of **if**.

while

while *command*	Runs command and obtains exit status.
do	If exit status is **0**, code following **do** is executed.
(commands)	
done	End of **do** loop.

case

case xx *in*	Starts **case**, reading value after **case** and before **in**
a*)* *command* *;;*	If **xx** matches **a**, command is executed
b*)* *command* *;;*	If **xx** matches **b**, command is executed
esac	End of **case**

Employing Aliases and Functions

14

Before beginning this chapter, you should be able to

- Utilize the UNIX directory hierarchy system
- Access and modify files using the **vi** editor
- Employ basic utilities
- Issue complex commands to the shell

O B J E C T I V E S

After completing this chapter, you will be able to

- Create and use nicknames or aliases for commands
- Build aliases that contain multiple commands
- Make permanent aliases
- Use the original command after it has been aliased
- Remove previously created aliases
- Pass arguments to C shell aliases
- Employ Korn shell functions
- Pass arguments to functions

When we issue commands to the shell, we often use a set of command lines repeatedly. If these command lines are lengthy, they can be tedious to retype. In modern shells, you can save time and avoid errors by assigning abbreviations or aliases that are interpreted as nicknames for lengthy commands.

In our daily lives, we create aliases. When nine-year-old Rachel Reed calls home and asks for Dad, "Dad" is an agreed-upon alias for Harry Reed at that phone number and address. Once an alias is defined as the nickname for a command or a series of commands, we can use this alias instead of, or as well as, the command or command line.

14.1 Using Temporary Aliases

The simplest use of the **alias** command is to assign a nickname to a utility that already exists. Often the alias is an abbreviation for the sake of convenience. The utility can then be called by its shorter alternative name as well as by its original name.

Giving a Command an Alternative Name

In modern shells, you can obtain a list of commands that you have entered.

1. Log on to your system.
2. Determine what shell is currently running:

   ps
   echo $$

   The PID reported is the PID of your current process, your shell.

   We suggest you work through this chapter using both a **ksh** or **bash** and then a **tcsh** shell. Either open a second terminal window and have a tcsh running in one and a **ksh/bash** in the other, or complete a section of the chapter using one shell, and then go through it again using the other.

3. In either shell, enter the following:

   ls
   who | wc -l
   date
   history

4. The **history** command can be abbreviated by using an alias. Depending on the shell you are using, enter one of the following shell command lines.

   In a shell that is in the C family (**tcsh** or **csh**), enter:

   > **alias** *h* **history**

   With the C shells, two arguments are passed to **alias**. These arguments are the new nickname and the command name.

   In the **ksh** and **bash** shells, enter:

   > **alias** *h***=history**

   With the **ksh** or **bash** shell **alias** command, **alias** is given one and only one argument. The equal sign in the argument must be between the alias name and the command on the right. There cannot be spaces on either side of the equal sign, because they would be interpreted as delimiters of multiple arguments. The format is the same as assigning variable values, except it is an argument to **alias**. You have assigned a new name, or alias, *h*, to be equivalent to the **history** command.

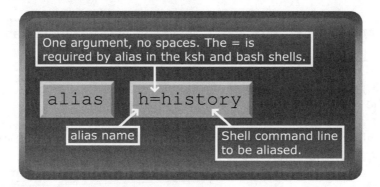

5. To compare the two commands, enter:

   > **history**

6. Verify that *h* is interpreted the same way by typing:

   > *h*

   The two commands, **history** and *h*, can now be used interchangeably.

   Suppose you previously worked on a different system where there was a command called **list** that gave you the same information the **ls** utility provides.

7. Enter the commands:

list

The output indicates the **list** command cannot be found on your system. (If your system does have the utility **list**, use **LIST** in these exercises instead.)

8. You can create an alias for **ls** called *list* by typing the following:

In the C shell family:

alias *list* **ls**

In the Korn/bash shells:

alias *list*=**ls**

9. From either shell, type:

list

The output is the same as if you had typed the **ls** command, because *list* is an alias for **ls**, which is the utility executed by the shell. With this alias, you can continue to use both the command **ls** and the alias name *list*.

 SUMMARY: The basic command lines for creating an alias for a command are as follows:
In the C shell family:
alias *nickname* **command**
In the Korn/bash shells:
alias *nickname*=**command**
In both shells, the nickname becomes a new way to execute the command. The difference is the equal sign.

Creating an Alias for a Command Including an Option

When an aliased command uses options, we can pass those same options to the alias you created for that command.

1. Enter:

list -l
list -F

The standard options apply. We can also include an option in the alias itself.

2. Depending on which shell you are using, enter one of the following command lines.

In the C shell family:

    alias *ls* **'ls -l'**

In the Korn shell:

    alias *ls=***'ls -l'**

3. Try out the new alias by typing:

    ls

The output is a long listing of the files in your current directory. When you type the command **ls**, the long listing of the current directory appears on the screen, just as if you had typed the **ls -l** command, because the shell replaces **ls** with the command **ls -l** on the command line.

To employ an alias that includes spaces, you must enclose the whole string in single quotes so that the shell does not interpret the spaces when the alias is created.

Listing Defined Aliases

You can instruct either shell to display all current aliases and their meanings.

1. To examine the aliases you established, enter:

    alias | *more*

The command **alias** with no arguments is a request to display the current aliases and their definitions. The list you see should look something like the following. Notice that the aliases you defined are on the list. There may be others.

In the C shell:

```
h    history
list    ls
ls    'ls -l'
```

In the Korn shell:

```
h='history'
list='ls'
ls='ls -l'
```

You can also request the definition of a single alias.

2. Find the definition of the *list* alias by typing:

    alias *list*

The definition of the *list* alias is displayed on the screen. By checking to see if an alias exists before you create one with that name, you can avoid conflicts overwriting a useful alias.

Examining How Aliases Work

Each time you enter a command that contains an alias, the shell replaces the alias with its definition before execution.

1. A few steps back, you aliased *list* to just **ls**. Try it now:

   list

   The output is not that of **ls** but of **ls -l**.

   When the shell interprets your command line, it looks for the command you enter in the current alias list. In this example, the shell finds that *list* is aliased to **ls**. It then checks the alias list again. It finds that **ls** is an alias for **ls -l** and then runs the command.

   Where the shell keeps information is important. Aliases are not kept in files but in memory. *Shell scripts* are files containing a series of commands. A *variable* is a named value stored in the memory of a shell. An *alias* nickname for a command line is also held in the memory of the shell.

Adding Command-Line Tokens to an Alias

An alias can include arguments in the definition. Can we also add options for the original command as arguments to an alias?

1. Use the **ls** alias to display a long listing of the contents of the **/** directory by typing:

   ls /

   The shell replaces the **ls** with **ls -l**, interprets the command line as **ls -l /**, and then executes it.

   The output is a long listing of the contents of the **/** directory.

2. For another example, use the **list** alias to display all of the dot files in your home directory by entering:

   list -a

After the shell replaces an alias with its definition, the shell processes the modified command line normally, passing the arguments to the utility.

The shell makes the alias substitution and then interprets the command line as:

ls -l -a

A process is started, given **-l** and **-a** arguments. The child process executes **ls**, which then displays a long listing of your home directory, including the dot files (such as *.login*, *.cshrc*, *.kshrc*, and *.profile*).

Using the Original Command, Not Its Alias

In your shell, **ls** is presently an alias for the **ls** command with the -l option. Perhaps you want to run the **ls** command with no option, but don't want to remove the alias.

One way to sidestep the effects of an alias is to use the complete pathname of the original command.

1. Enter the full path to **ls**:

   /bin/ls

   The program **ls** that is listed in */bin* is executed, not the alias **ls -l**.

   We can also accomplish the same thing by specifically instructing the shell *not* to interpret the alias.

2. Enter the command:

   \ls

   The output is from **ls**. The shell does not run the alias **ls -l**. The backslash is interpreted by the shell as instruction to use what follows as a command name, not an alias.

Removing a Temporary Alias

We can remove aliases from the memory of the shell.

1. Remove the alias *list* by typing:

   unalias *list*

2. Verify that the *list* alias is gone by typing:

   alias

   The alias *list* no longer appears among the aliases your shell has in memory.

Overwriting an Alias

We can redefine an alias:

1. Enter the following:

   In the C shell family:

   > **alias** zz **'sleep 2'**

   In the **ksh** or **bash** shells:

   > **alias** zz=**'sleep 2'**

2. Try the alias:

   > zz

3. Create a new zz alias with:

   > **alias** zz **date**

   or

   > **alias** zz=**date**

4. Enter the alias again:

   > zz

   The **date** utility runs.

When you use an alias name that is already in use, the new one overwrites the old in the shell's memory.

Abandoning Temporary Aliases

You have an alias, *ls*, that is defined as **ls -l**, which outputs a long listing of files.

1. Confirm it still works by typing:

   > *ls*

2. Log off the system and log back in.

3. Once you are logged in again, enter:

   > ls

   You get the usual output of **ls**, not the **alias**.

4. Obtain a listing of defined aliases by typing:

   > **alias**

   None of the aliases that you defined before logging out still exists.

When you define an alias from the command line, that alias remains in the memory of the shell until you do one of the following:

- Exit the shell (logout or exit).
- Delete the alias from memory.
- Overwrite the alias with a new one.

When you log out, the shell you are using dies, and with it, all temporary information; hence, the aliases disappear.

14.2 Making Aliases Permanent

All aliases are temporary because they exist in the working memory of the shell. When you log out, kill the shell, or explicitly delete the alias, the alias is gone. You can also place the commands that create aliases in a file and then instruct your shell to read that file.

Saving Aliases

We can save aliases you create in a file.

1. Create a file called *.aliases.csh* in your home directory:

   cd
   vi *.aliases.csh*

2. Enter the following lines:

   alias *h* **history**
   alias *ll* **'ls -F'**
   alias *t* **date**
   alias *a* **alias**

3. Save the file.

4. Create a second file called *.aliases.ksh*:

   cd
   vi *.aliases.ksh*

5. Enter the following:

   alias *h*=**history**
   alias *ls*=**'ls -F'**
   alias *ll*=**'ls -l'**
   alias *t*=**date**
   alias *a*=**alias**

6. Save the new *.aliases.ksh* file and return to the shell.

After saving your alias definitions in a file, you can have the shell read the file every time you log on or whenever you instruct the shell to read it.

7. Start a child bash shell:

bash

8. List your aliases in the new shell:

alias

The output of **alias** shows only those aliases that are predefined in your system files. Depending on your system administrator, you may not have any predefined aliases, or you may have many—but the aliases you just created are not listed. The aliases you defined in one of the *.aliases* files have not been read by your current shell.

9. Instruct the bash shell to read your *.aliases.ksh* file. Type the following commands:

. *~/.aliases.ksh*

The source (dot) command instructs the ksh shell to read each line in the file as though it were entered from the keyboard. In this case, each line of the *.aliases.ksh* file is an **alias** command, so by reading the file, you tell the shell to store each of the aliases in the shell's memory.

10. Confirm that the aliases in the *.aliases.ksh* file now exist in the current shell's memory by typing:

alias

The output contains each of the aliases you defined in the *.aliases.ksh* file.

11. Start a csh or tcsh shell, and have the shell read the *aliases.csh* file by entering:

tcsh
source *~/.aliases.csh*

12. Confirm the aliases are now available:

alias

The **source** command in the C shells and the dot command in the bourne, bash, and korn shells instructs the shells to read a file, in this case the aliases file. By reading the file, the instructions for creating aliases are read.

Every time you start a shell, you could instruct the shell to read the file and make your aliases operational.

Making Aliases Permanent

Instead of explicitly telling the shell to read the aliases file by typing the appropriate source command, you can place them in a startup file to be read whenever a shell is started.

You can modify each of your startup files so that the appropriate *.aliases* file is automatically read each time the shell is started. The startup files are

SHELL	CONTROL FILE
csh	*.cshrc*
tcsh	*.tcshrc* or if there is none, *.cshrc*
bash	*.bashrc*
ksh	*.kshrc*

1. Using **vi**, edit the appropriate startup file in your home directory. Depending on what shell you are using, add one of the following lines:

   In the *.cshrc* or *.tcshrc*, go to the end of the file and add:

   source *~/.aliases.csh*

   In Korn shell's *.kshrc* or Bash's *.bashrc*, go to the end of the file and add:

   . *~/.aliases.ksh*

2. Save the file and return to the shell.

3. Exit each child until you log out.

4. Log back in and enter:

   alias

Each of your saved aliases and their definitions should be included in the list. If you wish, you can add more permanent aliases to your files.

> **NOTE:** If your shell does not read the startup file and its aliases, some setup changes need to be made. Those will be discussed in Chapter 20, "Modifying the User Environment," or see a system administrator for help.

14.3 Working with Complex Aliases

We have defined basic aliases for single commands. We can also create and use aliases that contain a series of commands.

Creating an Alias for a Sequence of Commands

An alias is an effective shortcut for a complex series of commands.

1. Define an alias called *status*:

    In the C shell family:

    > **alias** *status* **'history; pwd; ls -l; date'**

    In the Korn or bash shells:

    > **alias** *status*=**'history; pwd; ls -l; date'**

    The command in step 1 defines *status* to run four utilities that:

    - Execute the shell command history
    - Displays the working directory
    - Outputs a long listing of the directory
    - Displays the date and time

    The semicolon is used to separate commands on the single line. Any number of commands may be used in the definition of an alias. The single quotes tell the shell not to interpret any character as having special meaning; hence, the commands listed inside are all part of the alias definition. They get interpreted when you run or call the alias.

2. Use the new *status* alias:

    > *status*

    All the components of the alias are run.

3. Create the following aliases and then run them:

    In the C shell family:

    > **alias** *ll* **ls -l**
    > **alias** *ls* **ls -F**
    > **alias** *yr* **'cal** *2003***'**
    > **alias** *myps* **'ps -ef | grep $USER'**
    > **alias** *proj* **'cd** ~/Projects**'**
    > **alias** *code* **'cd** ~/Projects/Code**'**
    > **alias** *friend* **'who | grep** *friend-login***'** (Replace with the login name of a friend)

    In the ksh or bash shells:

    > **alias** *ll*= *ls* **-l**
    > **alias** *ls*= *ls* **-F**

> **alias** *yr*='**cal** *2003*'
> **alias** *myps*='**ps -ef** | **grep** *$USER*'
> **alias** *proj*='**cd** *~/Projects*'
> **alias** *code*='**cd** *~/Projects/Code*'
> **alias** *bill*='**who** | **grep** *friend-login*' (Replace with the login name of a friend)

14.4 Avoiding an Alias Loop

A common error when using the C shell is defining an alias that is already defined as an alias and which calls the new alias. Confused? So is the shell.

Before you can practice avoiding an alias loop, you must create one.

Defining an Alias Loop

One form of the alias loop is a direct loop.

1. In a C shell, enter:

   alias *ll* **ls**
   alias *ls* **ll**

2. Try the aliases:

   ls
   ll

   The alias is defined as another alias that is defined as the first alias. It is clearly a loop.

3. Remove both aliases:

   unalias *ls*
   unalias *ll*

   Create an alias *ls* so that it first prints the name of the current directory and then lists its contents.

4. In the C shell, type:

   alias *ls* '**pwd; ls**'

5. Test the *ls* alias.

   ls

   You probably (depending on your system) get an error message, such as:

   ```
   Alias loop.
   ```

When you enter *ls*, the shell first determines that *ls* is the nickname for **pwd; ls**.

After the shell replaces an alias with its definition, the shell again examines the command line for aliases to be replaced. The command **pwd** has no alias, but *ls* is the alias **pwd; ls**. After another cycle, the command would become **pwd; pwd; pwd; ls**. The shell could continue looping, replacing one self-referencing command with another. Instead, it complains and quits.

In an earlier step, you created an alias for *ls* when you entered:

    alias *ls* **'ls -F**

The definition for *ls* is **ls -F**.

This is also a self-referencing alias loop, and you might think that it should not have worked. However, to allow for just such aliases, the shell does not reexamine the alias list for commands in a definition if the command is placed first in the definition.

Investigating Alias Looping in the Korn Shell

You do not encounter alias looping in the **ksh/bash** shells because they handle aliases differently.

1. In the Korn shell, type:

    alias *ls*=**'pwd; ls'**

2. Now enter:

    ls

The *ls* alias does not cause an "alias loop" error message to be displayed, as it did in the C shell. Rather, the alias functions as expected, displaying your full current directory name and a listing of all the files there. Although the Korn shell, like the C shell, reexamines the command line after the *ls* alias expansion, the shell does not look in the alias list for *any* instance of the **ls** command within the expansion itself. Because the alias list is not re-referenced, there is no alias loop. The shell finds the system **pwd** and **ls** utilities and then runs them.

■ Review 1

1. What is the simplest use for the **alias** command?

2. When the command **alias** is used without any arguments, what happens?

   _____

3. How would you alias **ls** to get a list of all files, including dot files, listed in a directory when you type **ls**?

   _____

4. What command removes the existing alias *list*?

   _____

5. Why don't aliases take effect immediately after you enter them in your *.aliases* file?

   _____

6. How do you turn an alias off?

   _____

14.5 Passing Arguments to an Alias in the C Shell

The most significant difference in alias operations among the shells is how they handle (or don't handle) arguments that we want to incorporate into an aliased command.

   If a user enters arguments on a command line after an alias, the shell simply adds the arguments to the aliased command.

1. For example, in a C shell, enter:

   alias *yr* **cal**

2. Use the alias with an argument for a year, such as:

   yr 2005

   The shell replaces *yr* with its alias and adds the argument from the command line, ultimately running the **cal** utility with an argument 2005.

   If we want the argument placed somewhere other than the end of the alias, the solution is very different. To put an argument in the middle of the alias defined command line, we use special characters to indicate where the argument should be placed.

Passing One Argument to a C Shell

In the csh or tcsh (you must be in one of these shells), we can create aliases that specify the location for data passed as arguments.

1. Create the following alias:

    alias *userpass* **'grep \!^** */etc/passwd'*

2. Run the alias with an argument:

    userpass root

    The record in */etc/passwd* that contains the string *root* is selected and output. The user tells the shell to use an alias named *userpass* and to give it the command-line argument *root*. The argument to the alias is placed at the **\!^** in the alias definition and then the alias command line is executed.

> **N O T E :** We can pass arguments in this way with the **csh** and **tcsh** shells. The bash and ksh do not pass arguments to aliases; they use a different structure called a *function* to accomplish the same goal. Using functions in the ksh and bash shells is examined in the next section of this chapter.

Suppose you want to create an alias called *where* that would locate a file, providing it is located in a subdirectory of your home directory. You want to display the absolute path to the file as the result of typing the alias *where* with a *filename* argument. The usual way to accomplish this is to use the **find** command in the following way:

    find ~ **-name** *filename* **-print**

This instructs **find** to start looking in your home directory (~) and all its subdirectories for files with the name *filename* and to print the absolute pathname of each file it finds that matches the criteria.

3. Define the *where* alias for locating files by typing:

    alias *where* **'find** ~ **-name \!^ -print'**

    The **\!^** tells the shell to expect an argument (only one) when it is used as a shell command.

4. Test the *where* alias by typing:

    where practice

In this command, *practice* is the name of the target file. The ***where*** alias effectively expands into the following complete command:

> **find ~ -name** *practice* **-print**

5. Try the following aliases using an argument from the command line:

> **alias** *on* **'who | grep \!^ | wc -l'**
> **alias** *cap* **'cat \!^ | tr "a-z" "A-Z"'**
> **alias** *pasw* **'grep \!^ /etc/passwd'**

or

> **alias** *pasw* **'ypcat** *passwd* **| grep \!^'**

Passing Multiple Arguments with the C Shells

In many situations, you will want to pass multiple arguments to a **csh** or **tcsh** shell. For example, suppose that instead of removing files with the **rm** command, you want the **rm** to be an alias that moves files to a special directory called *TRASH*. By doing this, you can still have the files on hand, but they will be clearly designated as *TRASH*. You could then throw out the trash occasionally.

> **N O T E :** All uppercase letters are used for this directory name to clearly indicate that *TRASH* is not a file, nor is it an ordinary directory.

1. Create the *TRASH* directory in your home directory by entering:

> **mkdir ~/TRASH**

2. Define a ***trash*** alias that accepts multiple arguments by typing:

> **alias** *trash* **'mv \!* ~/TRASH'**

Here the **\!*** construct indicates that one or more arguments are to be passed to **mv**.

3. Create two files:

> **date** > *temp1*
> **echo** *junk* > *temp2*

You now have two files, *temp1* and *temp2*, listed in the current directory.

4. Use the new ***trash*** alias to "remove" the two files to the *TRASH* directory:

> ***trash*** *temp1 temp2*

The shell accepts two arguments, *temp1* and *temp2*, and places them in the alias as arguments to **mv** in the middle of the ***trash*** alias definition. Both files are moved into the ~/*TRASH* directory.

5. Confirm that the two files are no longer listed in your current directory with:

ls

6. Confirm that the files are listed in the *TRASH* directory with:

ls ~/TRASH

At this point, you could alias **rm** to the definition of the *trash* alias, and then because **rm** would move unwanted files to the *TRASH* directory, you would be able to "undo" the removing of files.

The *trash* alias is not a simple nickname alias; it accepts arguments and places them in the middle of the alias definition.

14.6 Employing Functions in the bash and ksh Shells

Using the ksh and bash shells, we can create only simple aliases. For example, we can alias the string *ll* to **ls -l**. We can use the alias in a command line that adds arguments to the end of the alias definition such as *ll file1 file2*. But in the **bash** and **ksh** shells, we cannot pass arguments and have them inserted in the middle of the alias definition command line the way we did in the *trash* example using the **tcsh** or **csh** shell.

The ksh and bash shells use a different feature, called functions, to accomplish the same goal.

Defining and Using Functions at the Command Line

1. If you are not communicating with a **ksh** or **bash**, start one of them now.

The **korn** and **bash** shells allow us to define a block of code in memory and execute it by calling its name.

2. Enter:

numfiles()
{
ls | wc
}

At this point, you have instructed the shell to define a function. The name *numfiles* now refers to the code inside the curly braces. It is not a file; it is not a script. The function is just defined in memory.

3. Request the function be run by entering:

numfiles

The number of files in the current directory is calculated and output because *numfiles* is defined as **ls | wc** in the previous step.

Passing Arguments to a Function

We can pass arguments to functions.

1. Enter:

   pasw()
   {
   grep *$1 /etc/passwd*
   }

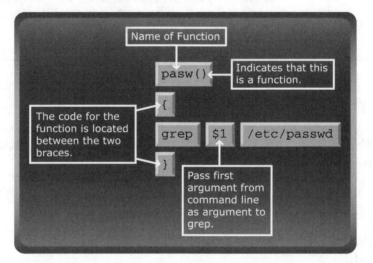

2. Enter:

   pasw root

   The line from the */etc/passwd* file that contains the string *root* is output.

3. Enter:

   add()
   {
   echo *"$1 + $2"* | **bc**
   }

4. With the *add* defined, run it passing two numbers as arguments:

   add 48 73
   add 580 360

Functions are in the memory of the shell. Arguments to functions are the usual *$1*, *$2*, *$**, and so forth.

The following table examines the code:

add()	This line tells the shell that **add** is the name for a new function. The shell interprets the **()** as indicating the object is a function.
{	This indicates the beginning of the body of code that is run whenever the function is called.
**echo "$1 + $2"	bc**	This is the body of the function; namely, it runs the **echo** utility, passing it two arguments: the value of the first argument from the command line (*48*) and the second argument (*73*). The output from **echo** is passed to **bc** which performs the calculation.
}	This indicates the end of the function definition.

Employing a File of Function Definitions

In the **ksh** and **bash** shells, we can define the code for functions in a file and then have the shell read the file, much like we defined aliases in a file and had the shell read them.

1. Using the visual editor, create a file called *myfunctions*:

   vi *.myfunctions*

2. Add the following lines to the file:

   mult()
   {
   echo "$1 * $2" | bc
   }
   lsf()
   {
   ls -F $1 | grep *
   }

3. Write the file and quit the editor.

4. Without changing the permissions on the file *myfunctions,* have your shell read the file by entering:

   . *~/. myfunctions*

Your shell read the file and now has the functions in memory.

5. To get a listing of the functions in a Korn shell's memory, enter:

   functions

   or in a Bash shell

   typeset -F

   The function definition you entered at the command line and those you wrote in the file *myfunctions,* which the shell just read, are in the shell's memory. They are listed as output to the **functions** or **typeset** commands.

6. Use the function by entering:

   mult 12 6

   lsf $HOME

   The product of 12 and 6 is output as are the script files in your home directory.

   When you ask for the function to be executed, your shell runs the code that is in its memory as the function definition. The argument on the command line is passed to the function and incorporated as **$1**.

7. Edit the *myfunctions* file again and add the following function:

   trash()
   {
   mv $* ~/*TRASH*
   }

8. If the directory ~/*TRASH* does not exist, create it.

9. Instruct your shell to read (source) the *myfunctions* file:

   . ~/*. myfunctions*

   The *trash* function is now in memory.

10. Confirm with:

    functions

11. Create two junk files, remove them with *trash*, and confirm they are in the *TRASH* barrel:

    date > *junkfileA*
    echo *junk* > *junkfileB*
    ls *junkf**
    trash junkfile[AB]
    ls *junkf**
    ls ~/*TRASH*

Whatever arguments are passed to the function are treated by the function as arguments to **mv**. The files are moved to the *TRASH* directory.

The shell interprets **$*** as all arguments from the command line. The function *trash* moves unwanted files to the *TRASH* directory. Occasionally, check *TRASH* and really remove the oldie moldy files.

12. Add another function to the *.myfunctions* file:

    pwr()
    {
    echo "*$1* ^ *$2*" | **bc**
    }

13. Have your shell read the functions:

    . ~/.myfunctions

14. Try the math functions with:

    pwr *3 4*
    pwr *2 16*

    In this function, the shell interprets **$1** as the first argument, **$2** as the second, and passes them to **echo**. The argument to **echo** is read and written to output, connected to **bc**'s input. The value of the first number raised to the power of the second is calculated and output.

Specifying Complex Functions on the Command Line

We introduced functions by entering basic examples from the command line. The following example utilizes multiple arguments in a function.

1. At the shell prompt, enter:

    cap()
    {
    cat **$*** | **tr** '*a-z*' '*A-Z*'
    }

2. List functions:

    functions

3. Try it with:

    cap users_on practice .myfunctions

All files listed as arguments are passed to **cat**, which reads them and passes their contents as input to **tr**, which changes all lowercase letters to uppercase.

Functions in the **bash** and **ksh** shells are powerful tools that can be defined in a file or on the command line. They reside in the memory of the shell-like aliases and are destroyed when the shell exits.

To maintain the functions, either have your shell read the functions file by including the following line in the *.kshrc* and *.bashrc* files, or enter the line after logging in:

> **.** *~/.myfunctions*

■ Review 2

1. Suppose the output of the **who** command on your system is almost always more than a screenful, and you want to pipe the output of **who** through the **more** command. What command would you type to make the alias?

   _____

2. How can we define a function called *locat* that takes two arguments, the first is the path to the starting directory for a **find** command, the second is the name of a file you want to locate.

   _____

3. Write a C shell alias called *collect* that takes many filenames as arguments and concatenates all of those files into a new file named *collectedfiles* in the current directory.

   _____

■ Conclusion

The **alias** command is useful in nicknaming commands or assigning special names to a series of commands. This renaming ability allows for the creation of abbreviations or names that are more easily remembered. Arguments may be passed into aliases through the use of the special \!^ and \!* notations in the C shell only. Functions in the Korn and Bash shells permit the passing of arguments and accomplish the same goals as aliases.

■ Answers to Review 1

1. Assigning new names to commands that already exist.
2. A list of all **alias** names and their definitions is displayed.
3. **alias** *ls* **'ls -a'**

   or

   alias *ls*=**'ls -a'**
4. **unalias** *list*
5. The shell hasn't read the file.
6. Use the **unalias** command or a backslash in front of the alias.

■ Answers to Review 2

1. In the C shell:

   alias *who* **'who | more'**

   In the Korn shell:

   alias *who*=**'who | more'**
2. *locat*()

   {

   find **$1 -name $2 -print**

   }
3. **alias** *collect* **'cat \!* >>** *collectedfiles***'**

COMMAND SUMMARY

Commands for Communicating on a Network

alias *name* **command**   (C shell) The *name* is aliased to the *command*.

alias *name*=**command**   (Bourne and Korn shells) The *name* is aliased to the *command*.

alias *name*   Displays the alias for *name* if there is one.

alias   Displays all aliases.

alias *name* **'cmd; cmd'**   (C shell) The *name* is aliased to a sequence of *cmd*s (commands).

alias *name*=**'cmd; cmd'**   (Bourne and Korn shells) The *name* is aliased to a sequence of *cmd*s (commands).

alias *name* **'command** \!^'   (C shell) The *name* is aliased to a one-argument *command*.

alias *name* **'command** \!*'   (C shell) The *name* is aliased to a multiple-argument *command*.

unalias *name*   Removes an alias.

name()   Defines the *name* for a function.

{ }   Encloses function definition.

$1   First argument from command line, its value replaces **$1** in the function.

Selecting Lines with grep and Regular Expressions

15

T he ability to search for words or character patterns in programs or with the UNIX editors is an essential set of skills. However, when we use an editor to search for a word, we have to open the file and read it into the editor's memory space or buffer. The buffer size limits the size of files that we can edit. Fortunately, there are powerful utilities that can be used to search for a target in a file or in an entire directory of files *without* reading the whole file into memory. These search capabilities are offered by the utility **grep**, short for **g**lobal **r**egular **e**xpression **p**rint family of programs, which are derived from the UNIX editor, **ed**.

This chapter examines the major features of **grep**, including the use of special characters to extend the search capabilities. Two additional related utilities are also explored: a faster search utility called **fgrep** and a utility that uses an extended set of search characters, called **egrep**. These three members of the **grep** family of utilities solve different problems, helping us select and extract appropriate records and data from input or files.

In Chapter 3, we used **grep** to search a file for lines that contained a target string of characters. Some searches employed special characters that identified the beginning- and end-of-line. The **grep** utility accepts instructions to select lines based on a wide range of logical criteria. The expressions used by **grep** for such complex searches are also employed by other utilities, including **awk** and **sed**. This chapter examines the search criteria used by **grep** and then compares **grep**'s functionality with that of its cousins, **fgrep** and **egrep**.

15.1 Creating an Example File

The exercises in this chapter use **grep** to search for specific targets in a file. To keep things orderly as you work through the chapter, we suggest that you first create a directory to hold data and programs associated with the advanced utilities.

1. If it does not already exist, create a new directory named *Power-utilities*.
   mkdir *Power-utilities*

   This directory, used to store **grep** data and command files created in this chapter, will later be used in conjunction with **sed**, **awk**, and shell programming.

2. Make *Power-utilities* your current directory:
   cd *Power-utilities*

> **NOTE:** For the exercises in this chapter to work properly, the lines in several test files must be entered exactly as they are presented here, including all blank lines. (That is, insert a blank line where it says, "INSERT BLANK LINE HERE".

3. Create an example file called *testexpr1A* that contains the following fairly ridiculous lines (or download them from **www.muster.com**):

```
7534
a5a
abcthea
^ac$
cccccc
t9R
        INSERT BLANK LINE HERE
theaters cbca
the dog
25%*4/;_\$
abbabba
        INSERT BLANK LINE HERE
a
bc
33334448888
        INSERT BLANK LINE HERE
6bc0M
7a
^7 4
abc
ab
^^^^^^^^^^^^^^
^66
```

4. Create a second test file called *testexpr2B* with the following contents:

```
The cat
The cats
THE horse
about town
a^^
^a
t9R
m7bc9
        INSERT BLANK LINE HERE
^the
She is at 3749
```

```
said that
the carrot is not edible
theaters
        INSERT BLANK LINE HERE
b a7
b7
        INSERT BLANK LINE HERE
1234
a
M4MMMMTT
throughout history...
the zephyr flew
```

5. And finally, create a third test file called *testexpr3C* with the following contents:

```
mother
brother
father
sister
a5BT
abbb
7BATS
        INSERT BLANK LINE HERE
Before we left
7bbbb
abbbb
This is the end $
[0-9]Boy
a
aa
333BBB444ccc
coast starlight
        INSERT BLANK LINE HERE
aaa
7-r +4 \5
ab
abb
```

6. Check each file to be certain it is precisely correct.

15.2 Modifying How and Where grep Searches for Lines

Two tasks we often need to accomplish are:

- Identifying the lines in a file that contain a word or string of characters
- Determining which of several files contains a particular word or string of characters

Finding Patterns Rather Than Words

In earlier chapters, you used **grep** to search a file and select lines that contained a target string of characters. For instance, we can instruct **grep** to search through the *testexpr* files you just created and look for lines containing the target anywhere on the line.

1. Enter:

    grep *a testexpr1A*

2. Compare the results with the file's contents. Enter:

    cat *testexpr1A*

   The output from **grep** that is displayed on the screen shows all of the lines in the file *testexpr1A* that contain the target string or pattern *a* somewhere in the line. The lines containing a match to the target are selected and output by **grep**. The lines that are output contain the target string somewhere on the line.

Searching Through Several Files in a Directory

The **grep** utility searches through all files whose names are listed as arguments.

1. Enter the following:

    grep *a testexpr1A testexpr2B*

   The search target is the character string *a* because *a* is the first argument passed to **grep** when the shell interprets the command line. The **grep** utility is programmed to interpret the first argument (not option) it receives as the search string, or *target string,* and all other arguments as the names of files to be opened and searched.

2. Enter:

    grep *a testexpr** | **more**

   The shell replaces the *testexpr** with all filenames in the current directory that begin with *testexpr*. The shell then passes the string *a* as the first argument to **grep**, followed by the filenames that are the remaining arguments. **grep** examines the lines in all files listed as arguments, searching for the target string *a*.

The **grep** utility searches all lines that it reads and outputs every line that contains a match to the target string, as well as the name of the file that contains the line.

Displaying Line Numbers for Matched Lines

Whenever **grep** outputs lines it selects from a file, the whole line is displayed. If more than one file is searched, **grep** lists the name of the file where each match is found.

We can tell **grep** to provide line numbers for selected lines.

1. Enter:

       grep -n *a testexpr1A*

    Each line containing an *a* is output next to the line number from the file.

2. Examine all three files:

       grep -n *a testexpr**

    The **-n** option instructs all members of the **grep** family to output line numbers.

3. Enter:

       grep -n *he testexpr2B*

    This number option is particularly useful when working with large files or when selecting blank lines.

Examining All Files in a Directory Tree for Matches

We can instruct the **grep** utility to examine the files in a directory and all of its subdirectories.

1. Enter:

       grep –r *the* ~ **| more**

 N O T E : If you are using a graphical environment with lots of files in your home directory, this could be an extensive search. Bail out at any time with **q**.

The lines containing the string *the* in all files in the home directory and all subdirectories are output. The **–r** argument is interpreted by **grep** as the option to recursively examine the files in the target directory and the files in all subdirectories of the target directory, selecting lines with the target string.

Listing Just Names of Files in a Directory That Contain Matches

The **grep** utility is programmed to work in several optional ways. For instance, instead of displaying the contents of all matched lines, you can have **grep** list just the names of the files that contain a match.

1. Enter:

     grep -l *the testexpr**
     grep -l *dog testexpr**

2. Enter the following request to list all files that contain a match in your home directory:

     grep -l *the* **~/* | more**

   The names of all files in your home directory that contain the target string *the* are listed as output. The **-l** option to **grep** tells it not to display matched lines, but just to list the names of all files that contain at least one match.

3. Try:

     grep -r -l *the* **~ | more**

   grep recursively searches the directory tree starting at the user's home and lists the names of the files that contain the target.

Counting the Number of Matches

In addition to the **-l** option's information on the names of files that have matches to the target, it is sometimes important to determine the number of matches in each file.

1. Enter:

     grep -c *the testexpr**
     grep -c *a testexpr**

With the **-c** option, the output of **grep** consists of two fields: the name of *all* files it examined, and a count of the number of matches in each file, even if there are no matches.

Matching Whole Lines

Another option to **grep** allows us to insist that the whole line match before it is selected.

1. Enter:

> **grep -n -x** '*The cat*' *testexpr**

The **-x** option instructs **grep** to select lines that match exactly. If there is anything more on the line (for example, the *s* in the line *The cats*), it is not chosen.

Reversing the Sense of a Search

We can instruct **grep** to locate all lines that match certain search criteria. We can also tell **grep** to select all lines that do *not* match the criteria.

1. Enter:

> **grep** *bc testexpr1A*
> **grep –v** *bc testexpr1A*

The first command results in **grep**'s locating all lines that contain at least one instance of the target string *bc* somewhere on the line. The **–v** option instructs **grep** to output all lines that do *not* contain a match of the target. That is, to reject all lines that do have a match, and output all lines that do not have a match. The **–v** reverses the sense of the search.

Locating Targets That Include Minus

If we want to look for a string *-r* in a file, **grep** would see it as an option, not the target. An option to **grep** instructs it not to interpret the minus sign as option indicator.

1. Enter:

> **grep -n -e** *-r testexpr**

Any line that has a *-r* string somewhere on the line is selected and output. The **-e** option to **grep** instructs it to interpret what follows, *-r*, as just a character string, not as an option to recursively search files.

2. Look for lines with a *-9* string:

   grep -n -e *-9 testexpr**

15.3 Searching for Lines Using Basic Metacharacters

In string searches like the previous examples, **grep** interprets each character in the target string as a character to be matched exactly as it examines each line of input. Several utilities, including **grep**, interpret certain characters as having special meaning rather than as literal characters to be matched. These special characters, called *metacharacters*, symbolize a rule that is applied in the search for a specified string. Because a target string can utilize metacharacters, it is called a *regular expression*.

Selecting Lines Having a Pattern at the Beginning of the Line

You can specify a target string as well as where on the line the string is located.

1. Enter the following:

   grep '^*a*' *testexpr1A*

2. Compare the results of the **grep** command in step 1 with the contents of the first test file by entering:

   cat *testexpr1A*

All lines beginning with the character *a* are output. Lines that contain an *a* elsewhere are not selected.

In particular, the line containing the literal characters ^*a* is not selected. The fact that an exact match with the string ^*a* in the line did not result in the selection of that line indicates that the ^ (caret) does not match a caret; it has special meaning. It is a metacharacter.

The target string ^*a* is enclosed in single quotes to instruct the shell to pass the enclosed characters to **grep** as they are, rather than to interpret any of them as a special shell character.

Used in a search, the caret is interpreted by **grep** to mean the beginning of a line. The expression ^*a* means "look for the beginning of a line, then if the first character after the beginning of line is an *a*, select the line."

A *regular expression* is a string of characters. Regular expressions used in searches usually include characters that are searched for literally. A regular expression may also include special characters such as the caret (**^**) that are not searched for literally, but instead are interpreted as specific instructions regarding the search.

3. Reverse the sense of the search with:

> **grep -v '^a'** *testexpr1A*

All the lines that start with an *a* are rejected; all other lines are selected.

4. Try the following:

> **grep '^7'** *testexpr1A*
> **grep -v '^7'** *testexpr1A*

We can select lines that have a character at the beginning of the line, or with **-v** select all lines that do not have the target character at the beginning of the line.

The caret can be used in front of any string to locate lines with that string placed at the beginning of the line.

5. Examine all files by entering:

> **grep '^ab'** *testexpr**

All lines that start with the exact string *ab* are selected.

Even the caret character can be selected if it is at the beginning of the line.

6. Enter:

> **grep -n '^^'** *testexpr1A*
> **grep -n -v '^^'** *testexpr1A*

Locating Lines Having a Pattern at the End of the Line

A different metacharacter is used to specify *end-of-line*.

1. To locate lines in the file that end with a particular string, enter:

> **grep -n 'c$'** *testexpr1A*

2. Reverse the sense of the search:

> **grep -n -v 'c$'** *testexpr1A*

When used in a search pattern, the dollar sign ($) is not just a character to be matched. Although the string *c$* is in the file, it is not selected. The **$** in the search pattern is interpreted by **grep** to mean "end of line."

The **$** is instruction to the shell to evaluate a variable. When not interpreted by the shell and passed to **grep**, the **$** also has the special meaning to **grep** of "end of line." To instruct the shell to pass the **$** character to **grep** without interpreting it as a shell instruction, the string is placed inside single quotes. Several special characters have special meaning to each of the shells, and different shells may have different special characters. Thus, many users simply put the target string inside single quotation marks every time to ensure the shell does not interpret any part of the target string. As a result, the shell always passes the enclosed string to the utility without interpreting any shell special characters.

3. Enter:

   grep '*^the*' *testexpr1A*

   This is instruction to search for the string *the* only at the beginning of a line.

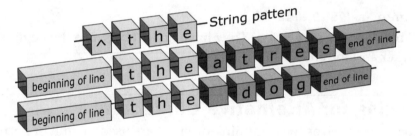

4. Enter:

   grep '*that$*' *testexpr**

   This is instruction to **grep** to look for the string *that* located only at the end of a line.

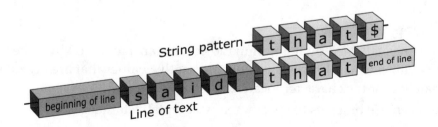

Locating Lines of Specific Content

The **-x** option allows us to specify the exact contents of a line for matching. Because the end and beginning of a line can be specified with metacharacters, even greater power for selecting lines is available.

1. Enter the following:

    grep -n '^*a*' *textexpr1A*

    All lines with an *a* character at the beginning of the line are selected and output with line numbers.

2. Employ both beginning- and end-of-line markers:

    grep -n '^*a*$' *textexpr1A*

    All lines consisting of just one *a* character are output.

    The regular expression says to look for lines that have a beginning-of-line, one *a* character, then the end-of-line.

3. Require that lines have a beginning right next to the end, with no characters in between:

    grep -n '^$' *textexpr1A*

    All blank lines are selected. They have no text between the beginning-of-line marker and the end-of-line marker.

Searching for Alternative Characters

Metacharacters such as the beginning-of-line ^ are used to limit or narrow the scope of pattern searches. The caret says to "begin the definition of the target only at the beginning of the line." Metacharacters can also be used to expand searches rather than narrow them.

When searching for a string, we may want to list more than one possible value that could match *one* character location in the target string.

1. Enter:

    grep '*a*[*b7*]' *testexpr**

    The lines returned by this command contain an *a* followed by either a *b* or a *7* character. The brackets contain alternative values that are acceptable as matches for the character location.

    You can use brackets to specify many acceptable targets.

2. Enter:

    grep '[*bg6B4*]' *testexpr1A*

This time the search pattern matches lines containing any one of the characters listed in the brackets.

3. Enter:

    grep [*ac7*]*b*[*bc*] *testexpr**

Lines are output only if the line contains an *a*, *c*, or a *7*, followed by a single *b*, followed by either a character *b* or *c* on the line. The following illustration examines some representative lines from the output.

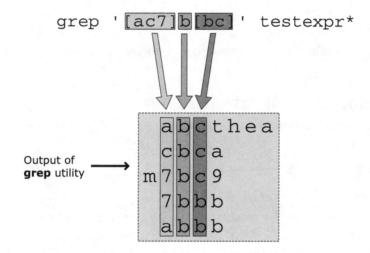

Any character listed between the [and the] is acceptable for a match of one character at the specified location.

Ignoring the Case of a Letter When Searching

A common application of metacharacters that expands the search using a regular expression is to find targets regardless of letter case.

1. Instruct **grep** to search for the string *he* preceded by either a capital or lowercase *t*. Enter:

    grep '[*Tt*]*he*' *testexpr2B*

In this case, **grep** selects all lines containing either the string *The* or the string *the* in the file *testexpr2B*. It does not select the line with *THE*.

grep matches any one of the characters enclosed in the brackets ([ ]). The brackets contain an expanded list of characters that are acceptable for that single position in the target string.

We can also tell **grep** to ignore case throughout the search.

2. Enter:

> **grep -i** *tHe testexpr2B*

All lines with the string *the* regardless of capitalization are selected. The **–i** option instructs **grep** to ignore case when making a search.

3. As another example, enter:

> **grep -i** *b testexpr**

Lines with a letter *B* or *b* are selected and output.

Matching Any Character

One of the most important metacharacters—the dot—expands to match any single character.

1. Enter the command:

> **grep -n** '.' *testexpr2B*

As you can see by the resulting output, the command did not locate only the lines with dots. The dot metacharacter is interpreted by **grep** to mean "match any single character." This metacharacter, when used by itself, causes **grep** to find a match in every line containing any character. The only lines not selected are blank lines.

2. Now try the reverse:

> **grep -v -n** '.' *testexpr2B*

The blank lines are returned. Lines that have a character in them are rejected. All other lines are selected.

Searching for Any Single Character

The dot is designed to work in combination with other characters. We can use **grep** to find the lines that contain any character at the beginning of the line.

1. Enter the following command:

    grep '^.b' *testexpr**

    Lines that start with any character followed by a character *b* are selected. The dot requires that one character, any character, be located in its specified position for a match.

2. Try:

    grep '^...$' *testexpr**

    Lines consisting of three and only three characters are matched.

Instructing grep to Treat a Metacharacter as Ordinary

Sometimes we need to instruct **grep** to match a literal character that **grep** would normally interpret as a metacharacter. To accomplish that goal, we need to do two things:

- If the shell attaches special meaning to the character, we must get the shell to pass it uninterpreted.
- We must instruct **grep** to treat the character as an ordinary character, not a metacharacter.

Suppose you needed to locate all lines that contained a literal caret.

1. Enter the following:

    grep '^' *testexpr1A*

    Because the caret is placed inside single quotation marks, the shell does not interpret it, but instead passes it as a literal caret to **grep**. However, **grep** interprets the caret as a metacharacter that means "search for beginning of line." Since all lines have a beginning of line, all lines are returned. This includes the blank lines because a blank line is a line starting with a beginning of line character followed immediately by an end of line character.

    To locate all caret characters, rather than the beginnings of all lines, we must instruct **grep** to interpret the caret literally—as an ordinary character, not as a metacharacter.

2. Enter:

    grep '\^' *testexpr1A*

    This time, because the backslash and caret are inside the single quotes, they are passed to **grep** uninterpreted by the shell as the first argument. Hence, the first argument that **grep** receives is \^, which to **grep** is the target search pattern. Like the shell, **grep** reads the backslash as instruction to interpret the very next single character as an ordinary character, not a metacharacter. In this example, the next character is the caret, so lines containing a literal ^ are selected and output.

3. To locate lines that contain a **$** sign, enter:

   grep '\$' *testexpr1A*

   Here the string \ $ is inside single quotes, so the shell passes it uninterpreted to the **grep** utility. The backslash is instruction to **grep** to not interpret the special meaning of the next character (the $) and to interpret it literally.

   All lines containing a literal $ are selected. Preceding any character with the backslash forces **grep** to accept that character literally, ignoring any metacharacter traits the character might have.

Instructing grep to Not Interpret Metacharacters

One member of **grep**'s family is **fast grep** (**fgrep**), which is faster because it interprets all characters literally, performing no metacharacter expansion.

1. Try:

   fgrep '^' *testexpr**
   fgrep '$' *testexpr**

   No backslash is included, because **fgrep** ascribes no special meaning to any character.

2. Enter:

   fgrep '\$' *testexpr**

   Only one line is selected, because only one contains the target string literal *backslash* followed by a literal *dollar sign*.

   In Linux, the **fgrep** functionality is also available as an option to **grep**.

3. Enter:

   grep -F '$' *testexpr**

   The **-F** option to **grep** is instruction to operate Fast by not interpreting any metacharacters.

Locating an Explicit Word

Along with its turn-off-interpretation function, the backslash is also associated with certain characters to give them special meaning. In searching for a specific word, for instance, you can use the symbols for *beginning-of-word* and *end-of-word* to limit the selection to literal words only, not strings contained in words.

1. To search for the specific word *the*, enter the command:

   grep '\<*the*\>' *testexpr1A*

   When a string is enclosed by \< and \>, **grep** recognizes the string not as instruction to search for a \ followed by a < character, but as instruction to match only exact, literal occurrences of the enclosed string. The string must be self-contained (not part of a larger word), but it may be located next to punctuation or at the beginning or end of a line. All lines containing the string are output to your screen.

   Many versions of **grep** also provide an alternative method for selecting words.

2. Enter:

   grep -w *the testexpr1A*

   The **-w** option instructs **grep** to select lines that contain the target as a word itself, not as part of another word. With the **-w** option, word boundaries are determined by spaces, punctuation, and beginning or ending of lines.

3. Enter:

   grep '\<*the*' *testexpr**

   This time, any line that contains the string *the* at the beginning of a word is selected.

■ Review 1

1. What command would list the files in the current directory and all subdirectories with the number of lines in each file that include the string *security*?

   _____

2. What command outputs the lines with their line numbers in the file *project* that have a space as the first character?

   _____

3. What command instructs **grep** to locate lines with a $ at the beginning of the line?

_____

4. What command instructs **grep** to output all lines in the file *practice* that contain the word *McKinney*, regardless of how it is capitalized?

_____

5. What command instructs **grep** to output all lines, with line numbers, in the file *testexpr* that consist of exactly two characters?

_____

15.4 Locating Characters in a Set

Selection of lines based on whether they contain a string solves only some of the search problems we must handle. We can also define a set of characters such as "all digits" or "all characters except digits," and search for lines that have at least one character matching the defined sets.

Locating a Range of Characters

1. To locate lines that contain at least one number followed by the character *B*, enter the following command:

   grep '[0123456789]B' *testexpr3C*

   The lines containing one number followed by the letter *B* are selected. The lines containing only digits are not selected, because there is no *B* following a number.

   This regular expression specifies that lines should be selected if somewhere on the line two characters match the criteria: The left character must be a member of the set of characters in the brackets, *0* through *9*, and the character on the right must be a *B*.

   The rather laborious format of listing every number from *0* through *9* in the brackets can be replaced by using a bracketed *range of numbers*.

2. Enter:

   grep '[0-9]B' *testexpr3C*

The dash between the *0* and the *9* is a metacharacter that tells **grep** to create a set of characters in the range zero through nine. If any one member of the *0-9* set is present to the left of a *B* character, the line is a match. If **grep** did not interpret the dash as a metacharacter, it would match any line that has one of the three characters: *0*, *–*, or *9* to the left of a *B*.

3. Try the same argument with **fgrep**:

    fgrep '*[0-9]B*' *testexpr**

    or

    grep -F '*[0-9]B*' *testexpr**

    fgrep interprets the target as literal characters to be matched, so **fgrep** matches any line that contains the exact string.

    The presence of the dash in a range is essential.

4. Enter the following:

    grep '*[09]*' *testexpr**
    grep '*[0-9]*' *testexpr**

    The results of a search using *[09]* as the target (no dash) produces only lines that have either a *0* or a *9* somewhere on the line. The expression *[0-9]* matches any single number from *0* to *9* inclusive, resulting in the selection of all lines containing at least one number somewhere on the line.

Exploring Specific Target Sets

The **grep** utility can be very exact in its selection of lines based on a set of targets.

1. Enter each of the following:

    grep '*[ab]*' *testexpr3C*

    All lines containing at least one *a* or *b* somewhere on the line are selected.

2. Enter:

    grep '*^[ab]*' *testexpr3C*

    All lines starting with either an *a* or *b* are selected.

3. Enter:

    grep -v '*^[ab]*' *testexpr3C*

    All lines starting with either an *a* or *b* are rejected; all others are selected.

4. Enter:

    grep '*^[abcdefg]*' *testexpr3C*

    All lines beginning with any of the characters in the set *a* through *g* are selected.

5. Enter:

   grep **'^[a-z]'** *testexpr3C*

   All lines beginning with any character from the set *a* through *z* are chosen.

6. Enter:

   grep -v **'^[a-z]'** *testexpr3C*

   All lines beginning with any character from the set of characters *a* through *z* are rejected, and all other lines are chosen.

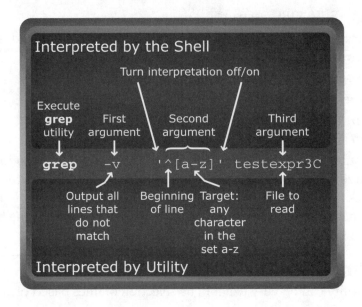

7. Enter:

   grep **'^[0-9]'** *testexpr3C*

   All lines beginning with a character in the set *0* through *9* are selected and output.

8. Enter:

   grep -v **'^[0-9]'** *testexpr*

All lines beginning with a character in the set *0* through *9* are rejected; all other lines are selected and output.

Searching for Lines Using a Range and an Explicit List

The use of brackets to enclose search parameters provides considerable flexibility. For example, both a range *and* an explicit list can be passed to **grep** in a single set of brackets as defining a set of acceptable match characters.

1. Enter:

   grep '[25A-Z]' *testexpr1A*
   grep '[25A-Z]' *testexpr**

   This regular expression is instruction to **grep** to select lines that include at least one of the characters in the target set—namely, a *2* or a *5* or any uppercase alphabetic character. The **grep** utility outputs all lines that contain at least one of the set of target characters.

2. As an alternative example, enter:

   grep '^[a0-5m-z]' *testexpr3C*

   Lines that begin with an *a*, or a digit from *0* through *5*, or a lowercase letter from *m* through *z* are selected. If any one of the characters in that complex set is at the beginning of a line, it satisfies the match condition and the line is selected.

3. Enter:

   grep **–v** '^[A-Z0-9a-z]' *testexpr3C*

   All lines that begin with an uppercase letter, or a digit, or a lowercase letter are rejected, all others are selected.

Searching for Specific Targets

Using the brackets carefully, very specific targets can be matched, letting you select particular lines from a very large file.

We can specify the contents of part of a line.

1. Enter:

   grep '[*a-z*][*0-9*][*A-Z*]$' *testexpr1A*

   With this target argument, **grep** looks for lines on which the last three characters meet the criteria specified, namely a lowercase letter followed by one number, followed by one uppercase letter and the end of the line. Each set of brackets is an instruction telling **grep** what set of characters are appropriate matches for one character in the target line.

Searching for Characters Not in a Set

The previous examples defined target sets of specific characters that if matched resulted in the line's selection and output. We also can define the set of target characters as all characters other than some other defined set. Read on.

1. Enter the following:

   grep '[*a-z*]' *testexpr1A*

   We have seen this before. The set of target characters consists of the set of all lowercase letters. If any one of the characters in the lowercase target set is on a line, the line is chosen.

2. Enter:

   grep -v '[*a-z*]' *testexpr1A*

   This reverse search says that if any one of the target lowercase letters is on a line, we reject the line and select all other lines. If even one lowercase letter is present, the line does not qualify.

Examining Parts of a Set

The set of all characters consists of the lowercase letters *a* to *z*, the uppercase letters *A* through *Z*, digits *0* to *9*, punctuation characters, and other characters like >, ^, (, +, #, and so forth.

Consider the following illustration.

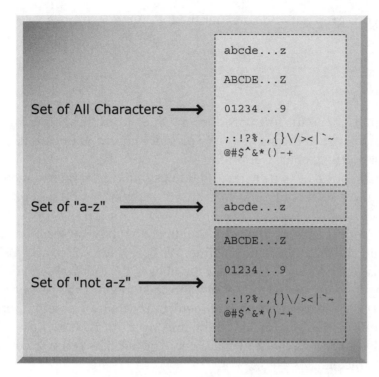

We can divide the set of all characters into two sets, the set (*a-z*) and the set of all other characters. The set (*a-z*) contains only the lowercase letters *a* through *z*. The set of (*all others*) contains the digits, uppercase letters, punctuation, and other characters. Every character is either in the set (*a-z*) or in the set (*all others*). A more precise way of describing the set of (*all others*) is to call it the set of (*not a-z*) characters. The set of all characters consists of the two subsets of (*a-z*) characters and (*not a-z*) characters. A character *m* is in the set (*a-z*) and the % is in the set of (*not a-z*):

Set	(a-z)	(not a-z)
Sample Members:	moghtcbswqxmlya	7R+M?/';2#VG&~}|*FP

Put on your **grep** hat and consider the following four lines:

```
abcde
 a8bcd
  ab cde
   234567#
```

A request is made for us to produce the lines from these four that have at least one character in the set (*a-z*). We produce copies of lines 1, 2, and 3. Each has at least one (*a-z*) character on the line.

A second request asks us to select all lines that do *not* have a member of the set (*a-z*). We select only line 4 because it is the only line that has no (*a-z*) characters.

A third request asks us to produce all lines that have at least one member of the set (*not a-z*) somewhere on the line. We select lines 2, 3, and 4. There is no (*not a-z*) character on line 1. The *8* is a member of the (*not a-z*) set; line 2 is selected. Yes, there are members of the set (*a-z*) on this line, but that is not the search question. The presence or absence of members of that set is not important. There is at least one (*not a-z*) character on the line, the criteria. It is chosen. The third line contains a space, a (*not a-z*) character. Chosen. The last line consists of only (*not a-z*) characters. Selected.

We specify the (*not a-z*) set in regular expressions as **[^a-z]** with the caret inside the brackets.

1. Enter:

   grep '[^a-z]' *testexpr1A*

   Lines that have at least one character from the set (*not a-z*) are chosen. Many of the selected lines contain lowercase letters. This is *not* another way of saying if there is a lowercase letter, reject the line. Instead, a positive selection is being made. Lines that have at least one character from the specific set of (*not a-z*) characters are chosen.

   In summary, the set of all characters consists of uppercase, lowercase, punctuation, digits, computer characters, and so on. The set can be divided into two subsets. In this case, the set of "all characters" can be thought of as containing the two sets:

   - Lowercase characters *a* through *z* called set (*a-z*)
   - All other characters: often called set (*not a-z*)

   The sets (*a-z*) and (*not a-z*) together form the set of (*all characters*).

The last **grep** command looked for the [^*a-z*] regular expression. When the caret is the first character inside brackets, it is a regular expression that says "select all lines that have at least one character from the set (*not a-z*) somewhere on the line." This does not say "reject lines that contain a character in the set (*a-z*)." Rather, it says, "If there is at least one character from the (*not a-z*) set on the line, select the line." If a digit or an uppercase letter or some piece of punctuation or a space is somewhere on the line, it is a member of the (*not a-z*) set and the line is chosen. It is of no consequence whether there are lowercase letters on the line. This regular expression does not say reject lines that contain them. It *does* say locate lines that have at least one character that is not *abcdefg...xyz*.

2. Enter:

> **grep** '[^*ab*]' *testexpr1A*

This time, all lines are chosen that have at least one character on the line that is in the set (*not ab*), that is neither an *a* nor a *b* character. If there is a *c* or a *7* or anything on the line in the set of (*not ab*), the line is selected and output. There may also be *a*'s and *b*'s on the line, but that is not the search criterion.

3. Reverse the sense of the selection for the last two command lines:

> **grep -v -n** '[^*a-z*]' *testexpr1A*
> **grep -v -n** '[^*ab*]' *testexpr1A*

With the **-v** option, **grep** rejects lines that match the criterion and selects all others. In the first command line, **grep** is instructed to see if there is a (*not a-z*) on the line (a digit or space or uppercase). If there is at least one (*not a-z*) character on the line, then **grep** *rejects* the line and selects all others, sending the lines and their line numbers to output. In the earlier search for lines that had at least one (*not a-z*) character, the blank lines did not match. This time the sense of the search is reversed, blank lines are selected.

In the second command line, if there is a character from the set (*not ab*) anywhere on the line, reject the line. Select all others. Blank lines are selected.

4. Select all lines that have a character from the set of digits, (*0-9*) and not digits, (*not 0-9*):

> **grep** '[*0-9*]' *testexpr1A*
> **grep** '[^*0-9*]' *testexpr1A*

5. Confirm by displaying the rejected lines:

> **grep -v** '[^*0-9*]' *testexpr1A*

The regular expression [*0-9*] is interpreted by **grep** as instruction to locate lines containing at least one character in the set (*0123456789*).

The regular expression [^*0-9*] is seen as instruction to look for lines containing at least one character in the set (*not 0-9*). A line may or may not have a digit; this makes no difference. What matters is whether there is a lowercase letter or punctuation or other (*not 0-9*) character on the line.

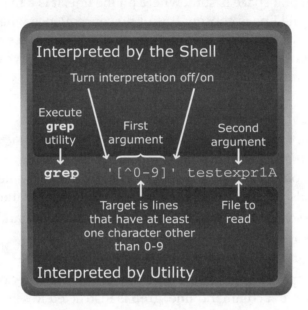

6. Employ the *not in this set* expression in conjunction with the beginning-of-line:

   grep '^[^*a-z*]' *testexpr1A*

   All lines that have a (*not a-z*) character as the first character on the line are chosen. Blank lines contain no characters and are not selected. The caret has two distinct meanings in this regular expression. The first caret (outside the brackets) is interpreted to mean *beginning of line,* and the second caret (inside the brackets) is instruction to look for a *not-* set of characters.

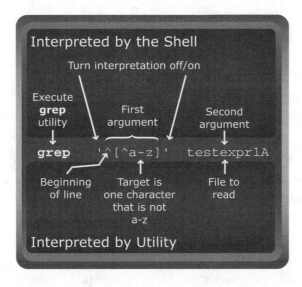

7. Output the lines rejected by the previous command:

   grep -v '^[^a-z]' *testexpr1A*

   Lines beginning with a (*not a-z*) character are rejected; all others are selected. Blank lines are output. Without the **-v** option, blank lines were not chosen. With the **-v** option, the previously rejected lines are output, so the blank lines are displayed.

Using Brackets to Search for Literal Metacharacters

Brackets are used to define a "list of acceptable characters." Matching a single character from the bracketed list results in selection. Metacharacters, as well as ordinary characters, can be included in a bracketed list.

1. Enter:

   grep '[\2$^]' *testexpr*

   Lines containing the characters \, 2, $, or ^ are returned. All the characters enclosed by brackets in this example are treated as ordinary characters in the search by **grep**. When the caret (**^**) is the first character in brackets, it is the set negation metacharacter. In any other position inside brackets, it is just a caret.

2. To search for a *]* or *^*, enter this command:

> **grep '[ ]^]'** *testexpr**

When the right bracket, *]*, is the first character enclosed by brackets, it is treated as an ordinary character for searching. When the *^* is not the first character in brackets, it is seen as an ordinary character.

You can take **grep** searches to the extreme and impress all your friends by locating all lines that do *not* begin with a caret.

3. Time for *carotene*, enter:

> **grep '^[^^]'** *testexpr1A*

All lines that start with a character other than a caret are returned. Each caret in the preceding command performs a unique function. The first signifies the beginning of a line. The second—the one immediately following the left bracket—is the set negation caret. The final caret is the search target. All lines that start with a caret are selected.

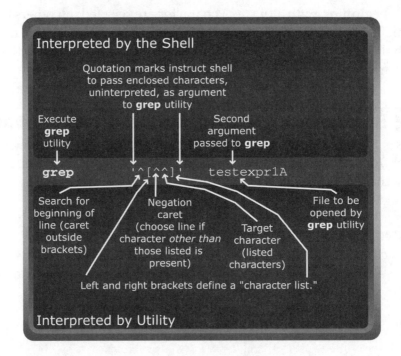

4. Compare the following:

    grep '\^' *testexpr1A*

All lines that contain a literal caret are selected.

    grep -v '\^' *testexpr1A*

All lines that contain a literal caret are rejected; all other lines are selected.

    grep '[^^]' *testexpr1A*

All lines that contain at least one character that is not a caret are selected. One character from the (*not* ^) set is enough.

    grep -v '[^^]' *testexpr1A*

All lines that contain at least one *not-caret* character are rejected; all other lines are selected.

    grep '^[^^]' *testexpr1A*

All lines that begin with a character from the set of (*not* ^) are selected.

    grep -v '^[^^]' *testexpr1A*

All lines that begin with a character from the set of (*not* ^) are rejected, and all other lines are selected.

Searching for Character Repetitions

In the previous exercises, you searched for target characters based on matches to characters, ranges, literal metacharacters, and characters symbolizing the beginning or end of a line. Additional, more complex search possibilities are available, including locating explicit words and multiple instances of specific or undefined characters.

Searching for multiple instances of target characters is an important **grep** feature.

1. Enter the following commands:

    grep '*ab*' *testexpr3C*
    grep '*ab**' *testexpr3C*

In the output from the first command, all lines that have *ab* on the line are selected.

If there is text before or after the *ab*, it's not an issue. In the output from the second command that employs a *, all lines that contain an *a* are selected, not just lines that contain *ab*.

The asterisk is interpreted by **grep** to mean any number, including none, of the previous character. The *, a powerful expanding metacharacter, can match zero, one, two, or fifty occurrences of whatever character precedes it. This interpretation is quite different from how the shell interprets the asterisk (called a "splat") in filename expressions.

2. Enter:

   grep '^*ab*$*' *testexpr3C*

   The output is all lines consisting only of an *a* character followed by zero or more of the character *b* and then the end-of-line character. The line *abc* does not match.

3. As a variation, enter:

   grep '^*abb*$*' *testexpr3C*

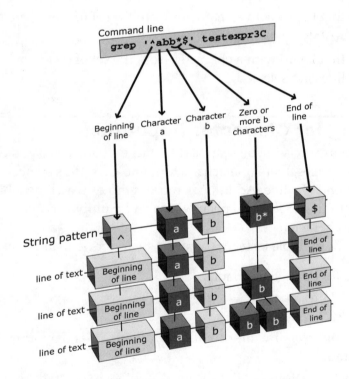

This time there must be a beginning-of-line followed by *ab*, and then zero or more *b*'s and the end of line. There must be one *b*, and there may be many.

When using the *, keep in mind its rather open-ended expandability (zero or more of the preceding character). For example, enter the following command:

> **grep** '*ab*' *testexpr3C*
> **grep** '*abb**' *testexpr3C*

The output is the same. Any line containing the string *ab* is matched. The added instruction of *b** has no impact, because it makes no difference if there are zero or more added *b* characters.

4. To match lines with at least two *b* characters, enter this command:

> **grep** '*abbb**' *testexpr3C*

We must tell **grep** to match *abb* and then zero or more others.

5. The effects are clearest when ends of line are used:

> **grep** '*abbb*$*' *testexpr3C*
> **grep** '*abb*$*' *testexpr3C*
> **grep** '*ab*$*' *testexpr3C*

This last command line results in all lines that have one *a* followed by zero or more *b* characters. What happens if we tell **grep** to select lines with zero or more of the character *a* anywhere on the line?

6. Enter:

> **grep** '*^a**' *testexpr3C* | **wc -l**
> **wc** -l *testexpr3C*

The line count is the same. All lines are selected, because all lines have zero or more *a*'s.

7. Confirm that no lines are rejected:

> **grep** -v '*^a**' *testexpr3C* | **wc -l**

Matching Any Number of Any Characters

The . and the * metacharacters can be combined to match any sequence of characters.

1. Enter:

> **grep** '*e.* r*' *testexpr**

This command tells **grep** to locate all lines that contain an *e* followed by zero or more characters, followed in turn by an *r* anywhere on the line. Spaces are also characters, so lines are matched when the *e* is in one word and the *r* is in another.

To explore how the dot metacharacter works, examine the following:

2. Enter:

    grep '.' *testexpr1A*

All lines that have any content have a character that matches.

3. Reverse the sense of the match:

    grep -v '.' *testexpr1A*

Only blank lines are output, because they have no characters to match the wildcard.

4. Employ multiple dots defined by beginning and end of line:

    grep '^...$' *testexpr**

All lines that consist of three and only three characters are selected.

5. Select lines with zero or more of any characters:

    grep '^.*$' *testexpr3C*
    grep '^.*$' *testexpr3C* | **wc**
    wc *testexpr3C*

All lines including the blank lines qualify as having zero or more of any character.

6. Look for lines that have at least one character:

    grep '^..*$' *testexpr3C*

The beginning-of-line is followed by a character, followed by zero or more characters. Lines with at least one character are chosen.

7. Locate blank lines:

    grep -v '^.*$' *testexpr3C*

Lines with at least one character are rejected; only lines that do not have a character (blank lines) are selected.

Employing Complex Regular Expressions

Examine each of the following, predict what it will do, enter it, examine the output, and then read our comments:

1. Enter:

    grep '^.[0-9].$' *testexpr1A*

This regular expression instructs **grep** to locate lines that are three characters long, consisting of any character followed by a *0* through *9* (digit), followed by a third character, which can be any character.

2. Enter:

   grep '^[^0-9][0-9][A-Z]*$' *testexpr2B*

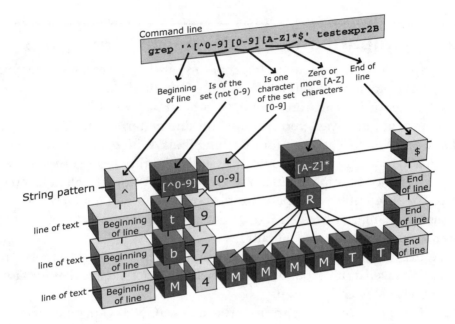

The first character on the line is not a digit, followed by a digit, then zero or more uppercase letters, then the end-of-line.

3. Enter:

   grep '^a.*a$' *testexpr**

   Lines are selected if the first character is an *a*, followed by zero or more of any characters, followed by another *a* at the end of the line.

4. Enter:

   grep '^[^a].*a$' *testexpr**

   The beginning of the line is not an *a*, followed by any number of any characters, and an *a* at the end of the line.

   Locating words that begin and end with a *t* requires a more precise target.

5. Enter:

   grep '\<t[a-z]*t\>' *testexpr**

Locate words that start with a *t* and end with a *t* and have any number of letters between them. Recall that the [*a-z*] matches any single letter, and the * matches any number of occurrences of the preceding character. When used together, they match any number of any letter. The \< and \> are instructions to match whole words, not parts of words.

15.5 A Comparison of grep, egrep, and fgrep

The **grep** utility has limitations. It accepts arguments, is reasonably fast, and interprets metacharacters. But it looks only for a single target and does not read a file for instructions or search patterns. A bit of history...

In the beginning was **grep**, a command-line pattern-matching utility that uses a basic set of metacharacters for matching lines. With **grep** we are limited to one search at a time. There is no logical OR and no ability to read files for targets.

A faster, more compact version of **grep w**as developed, called **fgrep** or **f**ast **grep**. The **fgrep** utility accepts multiple targets and will read a file for targets. It is somewhat faster because it does not interpret or expand metacharacters. **fgrep** interprets its targets literally.

A third version—**extended grep** or **egrep**—accepts multiple targets, processes the basic as well as an expanded list of metacharacters, reads files for targets, but is somewhat slower than **grep**.

The GNU programming group wrote a new (GNU) version of **grep**, which integrates the three **grep** utilities into one **grep** that behaves like **egrep** in its normal mode and like **fgrep** when given a **-F** option. It is GNU's **grep** that is provided on Linux distributions. In the remaining exercises, we will explore the **grep** family features.

Selecting Lines That Match Two Criteria

We can use any version of **grep** to select a line when one criteria is matched as well as another (logical AND). **grep** accomplishes logical AND searches in two ways. We can pipe the output from one **grep** process directly to another, or in some cases we can explicitly include both criteria in one regular expression employing metacharacters.

1. Enter the following:

 grep '^*a*' *testexpr**
 grep '^*a*' *testexpr** | **grep** '*b*$'

The first **grep** process locates all lines that begin with the character *a*. The lines selected can have anything after the initial *a* character. The output from the first **grep** is passed directly to the second **grep**, which selects only the lines that have a *b* at the end of the line. Because lines that are ultimately output were selected by both **grep** processes, the lines had to pass both tests— a logical AND.

We can accomplish the same goal with careful use of metacharacters.

2. Employ one process:

> **grep** '^*a.*b$* ' *testexpr**

All lines that begin with a letter *a*, then have zero or more of any characters and end the line with a *b* character, are selected.

3. Compare the following:

> **grep** *a testexpr1A* | **grep** *b*
> **grep** '[*ab*].*[*ab*]' *testexpr1A*

The results are *not* the same. In the first example, all selected lines have both an *a* and a *b* somewhere on the line. The second regular expression is satisfied in several ways: a line with two *a*'s, or an *a* and a *b*, or two *b* characters. The regular expression says that there must be an *a* or a *b*, followed by zero or more of any characters, followed by either an *a* or a *b*.

Selecting Lines If One of Several Targets Matches

In contrast to the logical AND, where both criteria must be met, we can also select lines if either one of two criteria is satisfied. This logical AND operation is available only with **egrep** in standard UNIX and with the **-E** option to GNU **grep** in Linux.

1. Enter (standard UNIX or Linux):

> **egrep** '*a*|5' *testexpr1A*

or (Linux):

> **grep** -E '*a*|5' *testexpr1A*

All lines containing at least one *a* or one 5 somewhere on the line are selected. As long as one criterion is matched, the line is chosen.

The pipe in this command is interpreted by e**x**tended **grep** as instruction to select lines if they match either criterion, in this case, the presence of either an *a* or a 5.

The pipe | is interpreted by **egrep** as the logical OR operator.

2. Enter:

>   **egrep** '^*a* | *a*$' *testexpr1A*

All lines with either an *a* at the beginning of the line or an *a* at the end of the line are selected.

3. Enter:

>   **egrep** '^[^*a-z*] | *bb*$' *testexpr3C*

All lines that either begin with a character other than *abcd...z* OR have two *b*'s at the end of the line are selected.

Searching for Targets Listed in a Command File

Unlike **grep**, both the **fgrep** and **egrep** utilities can read a file containing several search targets and then can search other files for those targets.

Creating a Target File

With **grep** you must list the search target as the first argument on the command line. But with both **fgrep** and **egrep**, targets can be read from a file.

1. Create a file named *targs* containing the following lines:

```
ab
37
coast
zeph
^C. *C$
```

> **C A U T I O N :** Be sure to remove any blank lines accidentally entered.
> If an **egrep** target file contains a blank line, an error results.

Employing a Target File

1. With the *targs* file created, you can enter the following command:

>   **fgrep -f** *targs testexpr**

All lines that match any one of the strings in the *targs* file are selected.

The **-f** option informs **fgrep** that the next argument is a file to be read that contains target strings to match. In this example, the file is *targs*, which is opened and the list of targets read. All targets in the *targs* file are then processed individually, as though you had entered a series of individual

grep commands. The normal line-matching process then takes place, with resulting matches going to standard output.

2. Now attempt the same command with **egrep**:

   egrep -f *targs testexpr**

   The **egrep** utility returns the same lines as did **fgrep**. Both **egrep** and **fgrep** accept command files for instructions.

3. Try to have **grep** read the command file:

   grep -f *targs testexpr**

   Most standard versions of **grep** display the error message that tells you that **grep** does not recognize the **-f** option. It does not read from a target file. If you are using GNU's **grep**, probably on a Linux system, the results are the same as **egrep**.

Using Extended Expressions with egrep

In addition to the standard metacharacters interpreted by **grep**, the **egrep** utility is programmed to interpret additional or extended metacharacters.

1. So you can experiment with **egrep**'s extended metacharacters, create a new file called *test-extend* that contains the following text:

```
x
Y
4
04
x4
xY
xxY
xYY
xY
Yx
Yx444
xY4
xYY
xYY4
xYa4
0xYxY4a
0xYYYY4
0xYxYxYxYxY4
ac
abc
abbc
```

Specifying One or More of a Previous Character

The **grep** utility interprets the metacharacter * as an instruction to "match zero or more of the previous character." With **egrep**, you can use the "*one* or more" operator to make a match only if there is at least one of the previous character.

1. Enter:

   egrep '*xY*+' *test-extend*

   or

   grep -E '*xY*+' *test-extend*

   Lines that contain *xY*, *xYY*, or *xYYYY* are displayed. The + metacharacter tells **egrep** to match if the line contains an *x* followed by one or more *Y* characters.

2. Substitute a * for the + in the preceding command:

   egrep '*xY**' *test-extend*

   The output includes the lines containing an *x* followed by zero or more *Y* characters. Thus, lines with just an *x* are output also.

Identifying a Character as Optional

The * is interpreted as any number including zero of the previous object; the + means at least one of the previous object.

1. Enter:

   egrep '*ab*?*c*' *testextend*

   Lines are selected that have an *a* followed by zero or one *b* characters and then a *c*. The ? is the metacharacter that is used to indicate that an object is optional—zero or one, not two or more, of the object to the left.

Grouping Characters for Searches

With **egrep**, parentheses are used to define a substring that can then be manipulated by other metacharacters.

1. Try the following grouping of characters:

   egrep '*0*(*xY*)+*4*' *test-extend*

   This regular expression instructs **egrep** to search for the pattern *0*, followed by at least one, possibly more, occurrences of the string *xY*, followed by a *4*.

The search pattern is expanded by defining the substring xY with parentheses, and then operating on the substring with the "one or more" operator, +. Thus, the resulting display includes lines that contain a 0 followed by at least one or more instances of the string xY followed by a 4.

Matching an Exact Number of Repetitions of a Target

In the previous exercises, we matched zero or more characters, at least one character, and zero or one characters. We can also specify exactly the number to match.

Creating One Last File

1. Use the editor to create a new file *testexpr4D* with the following contents:

```
a
aa
aaa
aaaa
aaaaa
aaaaaa
123456
ABCDEF
Xa
axa
```

Reviewing Metacharacters for Matching

1. Enter:

> **grep** '*a****' *testexpr4D*

All lines are output.

The * is interpreted as matching zero or more of the character *a*. Because all lines have zero or more *a*'s, all are output.

2. Enter:

> **grep** '*aa****' *testexpr4D*

All lines with at least one *a* and zero or more additional *a*'s located anywhere on the line are selected.

3. Enter:

> **grep** '^*aa****$*' *testexpr4D*

All lines consisting only of one *a* plus zero or more additional *a*'s are selected.

4. Switching to **egrep**, enter:

> **egrep** '^a+$' *testexpr4D*

All lines consisting of at least one *a*, possibly more, are chosen.

5. Enter:

> **egrep** '^aa?$' *testexpr4D*

All lines that consist of an *a* and maybe a second *a* are chosen. The regular expression says, "locate the beginning-of-line, an *a*, then zero or one additional *a*'s, then the end-of-line."

Specifying Number of Characters to Match

1. Enter:

> **egrep** 'a{1}' *testexpr4D*

All lines that contain one *a* somewhere on the line are selected.

2. Enter:

> **egrep** 'a{2}' *testexpr4D*

All lines containing two *a*'s anywhere on the line are chosen. (If a line has three *a*'s, it is also true that it has two *a*'s.)

3. Enter:

> **egrep** '^a{2}$' *testexpr4D*

Lines consisting only of two *a*'s are selected.

4. Enter:

> **egrep** '^a{2,6}$' *testexpr4D*

If a line consists of 2, 3, 4, 5, or 6 *a*'s, the line is selected.

5. Enter:

> **egrep** '^a{3,}$' *testexpr4D*

All lines consisting of three or more *a*'s are matched.

Of course, the expansion characters may be used with any object.

6. Search through all the *testexpr* files:

> **egrep** '^[a-z]{3,6}$' *testexpr**

All lines from any of the files consisting of three to six lowercase characters are chosen.

A Summary of the grep Family of Utilities

The following table summarizes the various capabilities of the **grep** family.

CAPABILITY	GREP	EGREP	FGREP	GNU GREP
Finds command-line patterns	Yes	Yes	Yes	Yes
Finds targets listed in files	No	Yes (-f)	Yes (-f)	Yes (-f)
Finds multiple patterns	No	Yes	Yes	Yes (-E)
Interprets regular expressions	Yes	Yes	No	Yes
Interprets extended regular expressions	No	Yes	No	Yes
Interprets all characters literally	No	No	Yes	Yes (-F)

Kissing grep Goodbye

Examine the following **grep** command lines, determine what they accomplish, and then try them out.

1. Enter:

    grep '^*root:***'** /etc/passwd

    All lines in the password file that have the string *root:* located at the beginning of the line are located.

2. Enter:

    who | head -*10* **| awk '{print $1}'** > *on-names*
    egrep -w -f *on-names* /etc/passwd

    or

    ypcat passwd | egrep -w -f *on-names*

    The login names from up to ten users are pulled from the output of **who** and placed in the file *on-names*. The second command line has **egrep** use the file of user names as targets for a search of the password file. The password records for the ten users logged on are displayed.

3. Enter:

> **find** ~ **-name** *users_on* **-exec grep** *$USER* {} \;

The **find** utility examines the names of all files in directories starting in your home directory. Every time **find** locates a file with the name *users_on*, it passes the path to the file as an argument to **grep**, which searches all lines in the file and outputs those lines that have a match to the value of the **$USER** variable, the user's login name.

4. Enter:

> **who** | **egrep** '*nancy* | *bob* | *pat* | *mary* | *lefty*'

This command line has **egrep** select alternative matches in the output of **who**.

■ Review 2

1. What command searches for lines in file *outline* that contain any of the following but no other chapters?

> *chapter1 chapter2 chapter3 chapter4*

_____

2. What command instructs **grep** to locate lines in *file* that have the string *2002* anywhere on the line, followed by any number of any characters, followed by *2004* at the end of the line?

_____

3. What command instructs **grep** to select all lines from *file* that have two or more adjacent spaces anywhere on the line?

_____

4. What command instructs **fgrep** to search through */etc/passwd* for all usernames located in *targ-file*?

_____

5. What command instructs **egrep** to locate all lines that have at least one (*a* to *z*) character on the line in file *prog6*?

_____

6. What is the command line if you want to search the file named *sizes* for lines containing the words *large*, *Large*, *medium*, *Medium*, *small*, or *Small*?

7. What will the following accomplish?

   egrep '^[^*a-zA-Z*]|[A^$0-9]$' *testexpr**

8. What command instructs **grep** to output all lines in the file *practice* that do not have any digits on them?

9. How would you locate instances of the word *is* in all files in your home directory?

10. What command has **grep** search for any of the following characters:
    ^ [\ ? M t
    anywhere on the line?

■ Conclusion

Using **grep** to search through input for lines that contain a specified string of characters is an essential UNIX activity. The **grep** utility facilitates selecting lines based on criteria that you specify and outputs the matched lines, line numbers, line counts, or only filenames where matches occur. Regular expressions are search strings composed of ordinary characters and metacharacters, which **grep** interprets as instructions to locate specific words, select targets by location on the line, match a range of characters, accept any number of added characters, and so forth. A faster version of the utility, **fgrep**, does not interpret metacharacters, but does read a file for a list of targets to search for. The extended version, **egrep**, reads a file of targets like **fgrep**, interprets metacharacters like **grep**, and also interprets additional metacharacters allowing for more explicit searches.

■ Answers to Review 1

1. **grep** **-rc** *security*
2. **grep** **-n** '^ ' *project*
3. **grep** '^\$' *file*
4. **grep** **-i** *mckinney practice*
5. **grep** **-n** '^..$' *testexpr*

■ Answers to Review 2

1. **grep** *'chapter[1-4]' outline*
2. **grep** *'2002.*2004$' file*
3. **grep** *'   *' file* (There are three spaces before the *.)
4. **fgrep** **-f** *targ-file* **/etc/passwd**
5. **egrep** *'[a-z]+' prog6*
6. **egrep** *"[Ll]arge | [Mm]edium | [Ss]mall" sizes*
7. This regular expression has an OR metacharacter in the middle. It says to select lines if the beginning of the line is not an upper- or lowercase letter, OR if one of the literal characters *A^$0-9* is the last character on the line.
8. **grep** **-v** *'[0-9]' practice*
9. **grep** **-w** *'is' ~/*
10. **grep** *'[[^\?Mt]' file*

COMMAND SUMMARY

-f The file option alerts **egrep** and **fgrep** to the presence of a reference file, the name of which immediately follows the option on the command line. This file contains the target(s) that will be searched for in the input. Regular **grep** does not recognize this option.

-v The reverse option instructs **grep** to print all lines that do *not* match the pattern.

-c The count option requests a count of the number of lines in the searched file(s) that contain a match.

-l The list option displays a list of filenames that contain a match; matched lines themselves are not displayed.

-n The number option displays the line number for lines in searched file(s) that contain a match.

-w Option instructing **grep**, **egrep**, or **fgrep** to match words, not strings that are part of words.

-i Instruction to ignore the case of letters in string when matching.

-r Option that instructs GNU **grep** and **egrep** to examine files in the directory listed as an argument, then to recursively examine files in all subdirectories of the directory.

-x Select lines if the whole line is an exact match to the target.

-e Option that instructs **grep** to consider the next argument as the target even if it includes a - for the first character.

-F Option to GNU **grep** to behave like **fgrep**.

-E   Option to GNU **grep** to behave like **egrep**.

^   Match beginning of line.

$ Match end of line.

.   Match any single character.

*   Match any number of occurrences (including 0) of previous character.

+   Match at least one of the previous object.

?   Match if there are zero or one of the previous object.

{*n*}   Match if there are *n* of the previous object.

{*n*,}   Match if there are *n* or more of the previous object.

{*n*, *m*}   Match if there are between *n* and *m* of the previous object.

[ ]   Match any one character (or one from a set of characters) enclosed within brackets.

-   Indicates a range, as in *a-z*, which represents any character from *a* through *z*.

[^]   Match any character not included within the brackets, after the caret.

\<   Match beginning of a word.

\>   Match end of a word.

****   Remove "magic" of special characters; interpret them literally.

Editing the Data Stream with sed

O B J E C T I V E S

After completing this chapter, you will be able to

- Use **sed** commands to substitute text, add text, and edit input from a file or utility
- Use files containing **sed** commands to execute several editing changes at one time
- Quit editing after reaching a specified line or location
- Control the output of **sed**
- Employ regular expressions to select lines and text for editing

Most editing sessions are conducted interactively. A file is read into an editor's memory buffer and its contents are displayed on the screen. We enter a command to make a change, the results are observed, and the next command is issued. After all changes are completed, the editor's buffer copy is written back to disk and the editor exits. This interactivity is essential in many editing situations, but it takes up both time and resources. For example, both the modification of every instance of a date and the deletion of all blank lines in a file entail reading the whole file into memory, making the needed changes individually or globally, and then writing the file. If the file is large, it consumes even more memory and time.

With **sed**, the stream **ed**itor, the whole file is *not* read into memory for editing. Rather, one line is read into a buffer, edits are made to that line, the line is written to output, the next line is read and edited, and so on, until the last line of the whole file is edited. The **sed** utility interprets a set of routine editing commands that make use of regular expressions for matching lines. Thus, **sed** can be used to effectively edit large file(s) from the shell command line or a command file.

This chapter guides you through a complete set of **sed** editing commands. We explore making global substitutions, specific line changes, and deletions; we address lines by context and by number, and use meta-characters for matching. The last section examines how **sed** edits input and writes output.

16.1 Creating Example Files for sed Exercises

In this chapter, you use **sed** to make editing changes to example files. For ease of access in your account, we suggest you place the example files in a *Power-utilities* directory.

1. If you do not have a directory named *Power-utilities*, create it now with:
   mkdir *Power-utilities*
2. Make *Power-utilities* your current directory by entering:
   cd *Power-utilities*

   The exercises in this chapter employ two example files to explore how **sed** works.
3. Create a short file named *sed-test* with the following contents:

> **NOTE:** For the exercises in this chapter to work properly, the lines of the example file must be entered exactly as they are presented here.

```
one
a2
3
4abc abc abc
5d d d d d d aa
6a a a a a a
7dog DOG
dog eight a m a
cat Nine cat cat cat cat
azz10
11
12DOG
thirteen
```

4. Create a file called *gdbase* containing the following lines:

> **NOTE:** As with all example files, this file must be created exactly as shown. For instance, the *v* in line 1 must be lowercase. When typing the lines of this file, you need only use one space or tab between fields.

```
Carrots     veg       1.39   1   n
Milk        Dairy     1.89   2   n
Magazine    Sundry    3.50   1   y
Cheese      Dairy     4.39   1   n
Sandwich    Deli      3.89   2   y
Onions      Veg        .89   6   n
Chicken     Meat      4.89   2   n
Newspaper   Sundry    1.00   1   y
Fish        Meat      3.79   3   n
Floorwax    Hshld     4.65   1   y
Melon       Fruit     1.98   3   n
Celery      Veg       1.79   1   n
Napkins     Hshld     1.49   6   y
```

16.2 Quitting sed After Matching Specific Text or Line Number

The **sed** editor reads lines into a memory buffer and then takes whatever actions you request. One of the many actions is to simply quit when the first matched line is encountered.

Quitting After a Line with a Specified Number

Lines in a file have line numbers (*addresses*) that can be used as editing reference points. The first line is line 1, the second is line 2, and so on. We can instruct **sed** to exit at a line specified by its line number.

1. Enter:

   sed '3 **q**' *sed-test*

   Buffers are temporary storage areas for data. When **sed** processes input, it reads a line into buffer and then performs specified matching and other actions. In this case, the first line is read into the memory buffer (or *pattern space*), and **sed** determines that the line is not line 3. **sed** prints the contents of memory to output, reads in the next line, and concludes that it is not line 3. **sed** writes the line to output and then reads in the third line. After deciding that this is line 3, **sed** takes the action called for at line 3. Namely, it writes the line to output and **quits**.

2. Enter:

   sed '7 **q**' *sed-test*
   sed '7 **q**' *gdbase*

   The first 7 lines of each file are read and output; **sed** quits after processing line 7 lines.

Because many of the commands used to give instruction to **sed** also have special meaning to the shell, many programmers simply enclose **sed** command instructions in single quotes to ensure that the command is passed to **sed** without the shell interpreting any special characters.

Creating a Script to Read First Lines of Files

We can construct a shell script that instructs **sed** to display the first ten lines of any file given as an argument. This is especially useful if your system does not have the **head** utility.

1. Create a file named *topp* containing this one line:

   sed '*10* **q**' *$1*

2. Make the file executable:

   chmod *700* *topp*

3. Examine the first ten lines of files by entering:

   topp */etc/passwd*
   topp *gdbase*

The shell interprets the *$1* in the **sed** command line inside the script as a variable to be replaced with the first argument from the command line (*/etc/passwd* in the first command and *gdbase* in the second). As a result, **sed** is given two arguments: the '*10* **q**' and the filename. When **sed** reaches the tenth line of whatever file it is reading, it quits.

Quitting After the First Line Containing a Matched Pattern

Lines can be matched by content as well as line number.

1. Enter:

   sed '*/aa/* **q**' *sed-test*

   The contextual address, *aa*, initiates **sed**'s editing action. The output consists of lines from the *sed-test* file, from the first line through the line that contains the contextual address, *aa*. As soon as a line matches the search string, **sed** quits.

2. Enter:

   sed '*/Onions/* **q**' *gdbase*

Each line is read into memory and examined to determine if a matching string is present. When a line matches, **sed** outputs the line and quits. Lines after the line containing *Onions* are not displayed because **sed** is instructed to quit after processing the first *Onions* line. A **sed** contextual address is placed within slashes.

Using Regular Expressions to Quit

We can instruct **sed** to quit at a specified line number, specific text, or a line that matches a regular expression.

1. Enter:

   sed '/[0-9]/ **q**' *sed-test*

The first line that contains any one of the target characters (digits in the range *0* through *9* anywhere on the line) is a matching line. **sed** prints all lines from the first line to the first line with a match, and then **sed** quits.

2. Enter:

   sed '/^[0-9]/ **q**' *sed-test*

All lines are printed, including the first line that has a digit between *0* and *9* at the beginning of the line, and then **sed** quits processing.

3. Enter:

   sed '/^[0-9].*[A-Z]$/ **q**' *sed-test*

This argument contains a regular expression instructing **sed** to locate the first line that matches the following criteria:

COMMAND	INTERPRETATION
^	Beginning of line
[0-9]	Followed by a digit, *0* to *9*
.*	Followed by any number of any characters
[A-Z]	Followed by an uppercase letter
$	Followed by the end of the line

sed reads in a line, checks for match, writes the line to output, and reads in another line until a line matches these criteria. Then **sed** is instructed to:

q	Quit

sed writes out the matching line and quits.

16.3 Deleting Lines from a Copy of a File

One common editing action is to delete lines. We can identify lines to delete by line number, by matching specific content, or by using a regular expression.

Deleting Lines by Number

1. Instruct **sed** to act on the second line of *gdbase* by entering:

   sed '2 d' *gdbase*

This command is instruction to read each line from the file *gdbase* and output it, with one exception. If the line has a line number of 2, **sed** is to delete it.

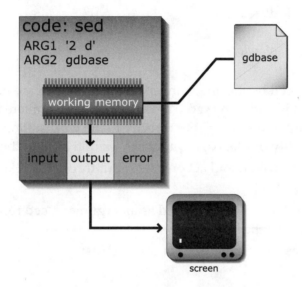

The number 2 in this command instructs **sed** to execute the specified command on line 2 of its input. The **d** is the **sed** instruction to delete the specified line. Hence, line 2 is deleted and is not output. The **sed** utility performs the specified operation, and the resulting output goes, by default, to the screen.

2. Examine the original file:

   more *gdbase*

The original files are not affected. Line 2 is still present in the file.

Deleting Lines by Specifying a Range

In addition to deleting specific lines, we can instruct **sed** to not output a series of lines by identifying the beginning and ending lines.

1. Enter the command:

   sed '3,6 **d'** *sed-test*

   Output consists of a copy of the *sed-test* file, with lines 3 through 6, inclusive, deleted. In this command, the range of lines is defined by the comma separating the line numbers 3 and 6.

2. Examine the following:

   cat *sed-test*
   sed '5,11 **d'** *sed-test*
   cat *gdbase*
   sed '1,10 **d'** *gdbase*
   cat *gdbase*

   Lines specified by the line numbers in the argument are deleted in the copy of the file that is output by **sed**. The original file is not altered. The file is read by **sed** as input, but output goes directly to the workstation or is redirected to another utility or file. No changes are written back to the input file.

   Instruct **sed** to read and act on user input through the keyboard:

   sed '3,7 **d'**

   Because no filename is specified as an argument, **sed** reads from input that is connected to the keyboard.

3. Enter at least nine short lines of test such as:

   ```
   line1
   line2
   line3
   line4
   line5
   line6
   line7
   line8
   line9
   ```

   End the input by entering:

   CTRL-D

As you enter a line, it is displayed on the screen. Once you press the ENTER key, the line is read by **sed** and placed in its memory pattern space. No action is specified for line 1, so it is simply written out to the screen, appearing below the line you entered. Likewise for line 2. The command **3,7** tells **sed** that it should act on lines 3, 4, 5, 6, and 7. The specified action is to delete those lines from the pattern space. The result is that **sed** outputs lines 1 and 2, deletes lines 3 through 7, and then outputs lines 8 and 9.

Deleting Lines with Content That Matches

Just as we can instruct **sed** to quit at a specific line number or content, we can also delete lines that match a specific line number or content.

1. Enter:

     sed '/*Dairy*/ **d'** *gdbase*

   Every line in the *gdbase* file that contains the string of characters *Dairy* is not included in the output.

2. Enter:

     sed '/*a*/ **d'** *sed-test*

   If there is a letter *a* on a line, that line is deleted, not printed on the screen.

3. Enter:

     sed '/[0-9]/ **d'** *sed-test*

   All lines with any digit anywhere on the line are deleted.

4. Enter:

     sed '3,/*cat*/ **d'** *sed-test*

   This **sed** command is instruction to delete lines starting at line number 3, through the first line that matches the string *cat* somewhere on the line.

Using a Regular Expression to Delete Lines

In addition to literal patterns, regular expressions can be used in addresses for **sed** commands. As examined before, ^$ is a regular expression that matches blank lines; locate lines that have a beginning followed by zero additional characters and then the end of the line. The very definition of a blank line.

1. Edit the file *gdbase* and place a blank line between lines 11 and 12, and another before the last line in the file.
2. From the shell, enter this command:

     sed '/^$/ **d'** *gdbase*

The output consists of a copy of the entire file *gdbase*, but the blank lines are not included in the output. The regular expression **^$** combines the beginning-of-line symbol (**^**) with the end-of-line symbol (**$**) to logically define a line that begins and ends but contains nothing.

The file *gdbase* was only read as input by **sed**. It did not actually remove the blank lines from the file. The blank lines that you inserted in the file remain until you explicitly remove them.

3. Enter:

> **sed** '/^[0-9]/ **d'** *sed-test*

Lines that have a digit at the beginning of the line are deleted and not output.

4. Enter:

> **sed** '/^[a-z]/ **d'** *sed-test*

Lines that start with a lowercase letter match and are deleted.

16.4 Making Basic Substitutions for Specific Text

If it is 2003, about to be 2004, how can we quickly change the year scattered through the text of several files of often used form letters? With **grep**, we can locate the lines. Suppose we need to make substitutions textually. We need **sed**.

Substituting for the First Instance of a Pattern on All Lines

With **sed** we can replace a specified pattern of text on a line with replacement text.

1. Enter the following command:

> sed 's/a/AAA/' *sed-test*

This command outputs all lines from *sed-test*, with the first instance of the character *a* on a line replaced with *AAA* in all uppercase. No address (line number) is specified in this command. When **sed** receives no explicit addresses, all lines of input are examined. In this case, because the command is to substitute one pattern for another pattern, only the first instance on each line that contains the specified pattern is changed. All lines are examined and output, but just the first match on each line is changed.

2. Enter:

    sed **'s/***Dairy***/DAIRY/'** *gdbase*

The full contents of the file *gdbase* are output, and the first instance of *Dairy* on each line is changed to uppercase.

The components of this command are as follows:

COMMAND	INTERPRETATION
sed	Instruction to the shell to run the **sed** utility.
' '	The single quotes tell the shell to pass all enclosed characters to **sed** without interpretation.
s/*Dairy***/DAIRY/**	Editing command; tells **sed** to make a **s**ubstitution. Search for the first instance of the pattern *Dairy* on a line and replace it with the string *DAIRY*.

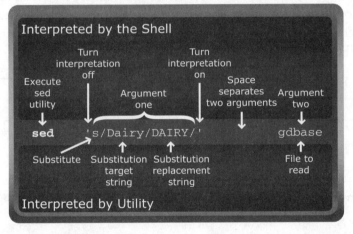

Because target patterns can be composed of any string of characters including digits, we can also substitute new patterns for numbers.

3. Enter the following:

    sed **'s/***3***/4/'** *gdbase*

By instructing **sed** to search for the pattern *3* and substitute *4*, we are able to change the prices for Magazine, Cheese, Sandwich, and Fish from $3 and change, to $4 and change. As expected, the **sed** utility interprets

s/target/replacement/ as instruction to replace only the first instance of
the target pattern on a line. It examines and changes all lines, but makes
a substitution for just the first instance of a target on each line.

4. Enter:

    sed 's/^$/*BLANK LINE/***'** *gdbase*

Every line consisting of just a beginning and an end (blank lines) is replaced
with the string *BLANK LINE* throughout the output.

Substituting for Multiple Instances of a Pattern

To substitute for *all* matches of a pattern on a line, we must include the global flag
in the **sed** command.

1. To change all instances of *a* to *AAA*, enter:

    sed 's/*a/AAA***/g'** *sed-test*

In this example, **sed** examines all lines and changes all instances of the target
string to the replacement. The **g**lobal flag at the end of the substitution
argument instructs **sed** to look for multiple targets on the line and change
them all to the replacement string.

UTILITY	ADDRESS	COMMAND	FLAG	FILE
sed		s/*a*/AAAA/	g	*gdbase*

2. Enter the following:

    sed 's/*1/2***/g'** *gdbase*

Notice in the output that if a line includes more than one instance of the
character *1*, all those instances are replaced with the character *2*. The global flag
in the command is instruction to target all matched patterns on the line.

16.5 Printing Selected Lines

We can control the output from **sed** to display all lines, display only those lines
that match a contextual address, or display those with a particular line number.

Summarizing the Basic sed Operating Procedure

When **sed** is processing input lines, it does the following:

- **sed** copies a line from input to the memory or pattern space.
- **sed** examines the line in the pattern space to determine if it matches either the command's contextual or line address.
- If the line matches, **sed** makes whatever editing change we requested to the current line in the pattern space.
- Unless the editing change was to delete the line, **sed** then writes the contents of the pattern space to output. This automatic write of the current line in the pattern space after processing takes place whether or not the line was modified.
- **sed** reads a new line from input into the pattern space and begins again.

Because **sed** prints the pattern space line to output even if no changes were made to the line, both modified and unmodified lines from a file or input are displayed on the screen.

Printing Line Numbers

Because **sed** maintains a record of each line number as it processes lines, we can request that **sed** output the number for any line matching a criteria.

1. Enter the following:

    sed -n '/N/ =' *sed-test*
    sed -n '/ab/ =' *sed-test*

The line number for the first line containing the target anywhere on the line is displayed.

Using Line Numbers to Print Lines

Among the actions **sed** can execute on a line while it is in the memory pattern space is to explicitly print the line.

1. Enter:

    sed '3,5 p' *sed-test*

The output consists of one copy of every line from *sed-test* and two copies of lines 3, 4, and 5.

sed reads the first line and puts it in the buffer pattern space. No action for line *1* is specified. With processing completed, the pattern space line is automatically written to output. The second line is read into the buffer. No action for line 2 is called for. With processing completed, the pattern space line is automatically written to output. Line *3* is read into the pattern space. The command *3,5* **p** specifies an action on line 3, namely to **p**rint the line. Thus, **sed** prints this line (3) to output. With processing completed, the pattern space line is automatically written to output. (The second time this line is output.) **sed** reads in the next line, line *4*. Lines *4* and *5* are each printed once because of the **p** command, and a second time because of the automatic print following completion of processing of the line. Lines *6* and beyond are printed just one time because of the automatic printing of the line after processing in the pattern space.

Suppressing Automatic Printing

We can tell **sed** to turn off the automatic printing of each processed line.

1. Enter:

   sed -n '3,5 p' *sed-test*

   The output includes only the lines explicitly mentioned in the command, lines *3*, *4*, and *5*. The **-n** option to **sed** is instruction not to perform the automatic printing of the pattern space after processing each line. Only those lines that we explicitly request should be printed.

2. Enter:

   sed -n '8 p' *gdbase*

   Only line *8* is output.

Printing Lines Not Matched

The basic operation of **sed** is to match lines, take action, and print. We can instruct **sed** to print all lines that do *not* match the target.

1. Enter:

   sed -n '/[a-z]/ !p' *sed-test*

   Lines with any lowercase letter are matched. **sed** prints all lines that do not match the target. The automatic printing of the pattern space line is turned off.

2. Enter:

> **sed -n '/^$/ !p'** *gdbase*

Empty lines match, so the output is all lines that are not empty.

Printing Lines with Substitutions

We can make changes to lines and print all lines or just those modified.

1. Enter:

> **sed 's/***Dairy***/***DAIRY***/ p'** *gdbase*

In this case, **sed** reads each line of *gdbase* into memory and scans each line for a match with the contextual address *Dairy*. When a match is made, the specified substitution from *Dairy* to *DAIRY* is performed, and then the resulting line is **printed**. This explicit **print** command is a separate function from the default write-the-buffer-to-output that **sed** performs on all the lines in the buffer. The line on which the substitution is performed is written to output twice—once by **print** and again by **sed**'s default output of the buffer. Other lines in *gdbase* are not **printed** from the buffer by **p** because no address match is made.

2. Enter:

> **sed 's/***Dairy***/***DAIRY***/'** *gdbase*

Here, no explicit call to **print** is made in the edit script. The specified substitution is performed, and the modified line is written to standard output along with all other lines of *gdbase* that were unmodified. No duplication takes place as it did in step 1, because of the absence of the **print** flag in the editing command.

Suppressing sed's Default Output with Substitutions

As examined with line number printing, the **-n** option to **sed** instructs **sed** not to perform the automatic print when each line is processed.

1. Enter:

> **sed -n '1,5 s/***veg***/***Tuber***/ p'** *gdbase*

This time, output consists only of the one line of *gdbase* that is modified by the substitution. All other lines are **n**ot printed.

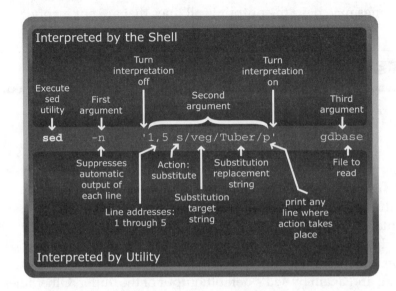

The **-n** option instructs **sed** not to perform its default write-to-output of every line. Only lines of input where a substitution takes place are printed to output. The **print** command copies the buffer contents to standard output, and because the usual writing of the buffer at the end is suppressed, only the modified lines are output.

Printing Lines at Intervals

If you are using a Linux or GNU version of **sed**, you can print a line, skip a given number of lines, print another, and so forth.

1. Enter:

   sed -n '1~2 p' *sed-test*

   Starting with line *1*, every other line is output.

2. Enter:

   sed -n '2~3 p' *sed-test*

   Lines *2, 5, 8,* and *11* are output. **sed** starts with line 2 and outputs every third line from there.

Printing Lines Selected by Content

We have explored using the **p** flag to print selected lines. We have explored the **-n** option that suppresses automatic printing and allows us to output only the matching lines specified in the **sed** command. We can use this to examine the effects of commands very carefully.

1. Enter:

    sed '/*aa***/ p'** *sed-test*

    Lines that include *aa* somewhere on the line are output twice, all other lines just once.

2. Enter:

    sed -n '/*aa***/ p'** *sed-test*

    All lines that match the target (contain at least one set of *aa* characters on the line) are output; all other lines are not output. This form of the **sed** command tells it to act like **grep**.

3. Enter:

    sed -n '/^[*0-9***]/ p'** *sed-test*

    The regular expression matches lines that begin with a digit. Only matching lines are output. Again, **sed** is wearing its **grep** hat.

4. Enter:

    sed -n '/[*A-Z***]/ p'** *sed-test*

    Only lines that contain at least one uppercase letter are output.

5. Enter:

    sed -n '/^[^*a-z***]/ p'** *sed-test*

    Lines that begin with a character other than *a* through *z* are selected and printed.

16.6 Performing Complex Substitutions and Printing

We often want to make an editing change in many places throughout a file. Sometimes we want the whole file output with changes, sometimes we need just the changed lines. This section examines complex substitutions with **sed** using the **p**rint flag and **-n** option to output only the modified lines.

Printing Only Lines with Substitutions

In earlier exercises, we made basic substitutions to the lines from files. The output was all lines with some lines modified. By controlling the printing, we can examine only those lines which match and are affected by the command given **sed**.

1. To make substitutions and print changed lines twice, enter:

     sed 's/*aa***/AA/ p'** *sed-test*

   Each line is brought into the pattern memory space and examined for the string *aa*. If *aa* is located, it is replaced with *AA* and printed. After processing each line, whether modified or not, **sed** automatically output the line.

2. To output only the modified lines, enter:

     sed -n 's/*aa***/AA/ p'** *sed-test*

   The lines that contain the target *aa* are selected and the required substitution to *AA* is made. The modified lines are output because of the **print** flag. All lines with no match are not output because the **-n** option turned off the automatic print.

3. To change the first target on lines, enter:

     sed -n 's/*a***/AAAA/ p'** *sed-test*

   A substitution is made for the first instance of *a* on each line containing the target. Only the modified lines are output.

4. To substitute for all of the target strings, enter:

     sed -n 's/*a***/AAAA/g p'** *sed-test*

   Every instance of the character *a* is replaced with *AAAA* and output.

5. Enter:

     sed -n 's/^[*a-z***]/:/ p'** *sed-test*

   Lines with a lowercase letter at the beginning of the line are selected. The first character is replaced with a : and output. Only the modified lines are printed.

Making Substitutions on a Range of Lines

In previous examples, we selected lines based on content. All lines in the input that match were selected, modified, and output. We can narrow the field by instructing **sed** to examine only a portion of the input.

1. Enter:

   sed '*1,5 s/a/AAAA/*g' *sed-test*

   This instruction tells **sed** to examine only lines *1* through *5*, making appropriate substitutions only in those lines. All five lines are output even if no substitution is made.

2. Enter:

   sed -n '*1,5 s/a/AAAA/*g **p**' *sed-test*

   The same modifications to the first five lines are completed, but only the changed lines are output.

Using Contextual Addresses in Substitutions

Contextual addresses can be used to specify a line for any action.

1. Enter the following:

   sed -n '*/c/ s/a/AAAA/*g **p**' *sed-test*

   Lines are selected for substitution only if they contain a character *c* somewhere on the line. If the line matches, then the character *a* is replaced with *AAAA*, globally, and the modified lines are printed.

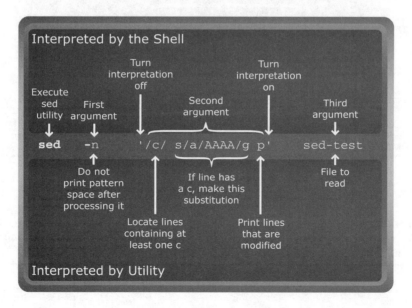

2. Enter:

   sed -n '*/[1-5]/* **s/***a***/***AAAA***/g p'** *sed-test*

   The line target is the digits *1* through *5*. Lines containing one of the line target characters are selected for further processing, namely locating each *a*, substituting it with *AAAA*, and then printing the line.

3. Enter:

   sed '*/Cheese/* **s/***Dairy***/***DAIRY***/g'** *gdbase*

   Each line is scanned for the contextual address, *Cheese*. When that address is matched, any instance of *Dairy* in the line is replaced with *DAIRY*. No substitution is executed on the line containing *Milk*, even though the word *Dairy* also appears in that line. This line is not matched by the contextual address, and therefore no substitution takes place. The following table shows the components of the preceding command line.

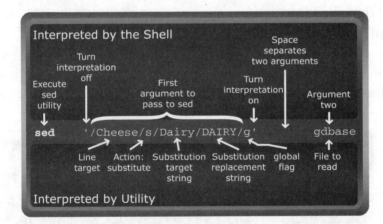

COMMAND	INTERPRETATION
sed	Instruction to the shell to execute the **sed** utility.
/Cheese/	The contextual address, enclosed within slashes. Used by **sed** to select lines for editing.
s/*Dairy***/***DAIRY***/**	The internal command (**s**ubstitute) and its arguments *Dairy* and *DAIRY*. Both the target, *Dairy*, and the replacement, *DAIRY*, are identified by enclosure in slashes.

COMMAND	INTERPRETATION
' '	Instructs shell not to interpret any special characters but pass the enclosed command as is to **sed**.
gdbase	The input file that is read and processed by **sed**.

> **SUMMARY:** This command line uses the contextual address /*Cheese*/ to instruct sed to execute the specified substitution command only on lines containing the pattern *Cheese*. A line number address always matches only the specified line(s), but a contextual address examines the whole file and matches from zero to all lines of input, depending on the number of matches.

Using a Combined Numerical/Contextual Address

An address range can consist of two line numbers, two contextuals, or a combination of addresses.

1. Enter a combination address command:

    sed '7,/*Fish*/ s/*Meat*/*Animal*/' *gdbase*

Here, two address types are combined to form the address range for this command. *Meat* is replaced with the pattern *Animal* on lines starting at line 7 and ending, inclusively, with the first line containing the pattern *Fish*. Notice that *Fish*, although separated by a comma from **7**, is still enclosed by slashes. The following table explains the elements of the preceding command line:

UTILITY	*Address1*	ADDRESS 2	COMMAND	FILE(S)
sed	7	/Fish/	**s**/Meat/Animal/	gdbase

> **NOTE:** When a range is passed as the address, the elements of the range, contextual or otherwise, must be separated by a comma (for example, 7,30 or 10,/Fish/ or /Milk/,/Fish/).

The substitute command is one of the most powerful commands available to the **sed** user. This single, relatively simple command can quickly affect a large file of data.

16.7 Reading and Writing Files from sed

With the **sed** editor, we can modify text in files, read the contents of one file into another file at whatever location we choose, and write parts of a file into a new file.

Reading In a File at a Specified Address

1. Create a read-in file named *comment.file* containing the following three lines:

```
**********************************************************
J + J is our new Fish supplier, as of 12/19/2003
**********************************************************
```

2. Enter the following commands:

> **sed** '/Fish/ **r** *comment.file*' gdbase
> **who** | **sed** "/*$USER*/ **r** *comment.file*"
> **sed** '5 **r** *comment.file*' *sed-test*

The entire contents of *comment.file* are added:

- After every line containing the contextual address *Fish* in *gdbase*
- After the entry with your login in the output of **who**
- After line *5* in the *sed-test* file

> **SUMMARY:** The **r**ead command is most useful when you need to add text in several places to a file. As is true for most other **sed** commands, read can be used with either line numbers or contextual addresses, and requires an argument specifying the name of the file to be read.

Writing Lines to Another File

We can instruct **sed** to examine a file and write target lines to another file.

1. Enter the following command:

   sed '1,6 w *wfile***'** *gdbase*
   more *wfile*

   As the **sed** utility runs, it outputs all lines to your screen. At the same time, as a result of the **write** command, lines *1* through *6* are written to the file *wfile*.

   Examine the contents of the file *wfile*. The command in step 1 instructed **sed** to apply the **write** command to lines *1* through *6* of the file *gdbase*. Like the **read** command, the **write** command takes a single argument—the filename to which output should be written. In this case, lines *1* through *6* are in the buffer, and the contents are written to the new file because of the edit action specified, *1,6* **w**. In each case, the buffer is written to your screen in the usual way.

2. Enter:

   sed '/*ab***/,/***zz***/ w** *ab-out***'** *sed-test*
   more *ab-out*

   When **sed** encounters the first line containing the string *ab,* it writes the matching line to output and all other lines it encounters until it locates a line with *zz* somewhere on the line. It concludes its writing with the *zz* line.

3. Write out matching lines:

   sed '/*a$***/ w** *a-end***'** *sed-test*
   more *a-end*

   Lines with an *a* located at the end are written to the *a-end* file.

16.8 Passing Multiple Instructions to sed

More than one action can be performed by **sed** on each line it reads as input. Multiple instructions can be passed from the command line or from a command file similar to those used with **grep**. Examples of both methods are examined in this section.

Entering Multiple Instructions on the Command Line

1. Enter this command:

   sed -e 's/*Veg***/VEG/' -e 's/***Meat***/MEAT/'** *gdbase*

The file *gdbase* is displayed, with both specified strings shifted to uppercase. The -e option preceding each instruction set on the command line informs **sed** that more than one set of editing instructions is included. This option is used when two or more sets of instructions are passed to **sed** in the same command line. It is not needed, of course, when only one instruction is specified.

2. Enter:

   sed -e -n '/^[*a-z*]**/ p' -e 's/**[*0-9*]**/XXX/g p'** *sed-test*

   A line is brought into the memory pattern space. If there is a lowercase letter at the beginning of the line, the line is printed. Without changing the contents of the pattern space, **sed** executes the second command. If there is a digit on the line, it is replaced with *XXX*, globally, and the modified line is output. Both actions take place on each line, then the next line is brought in for processing.

3. Enter:

   head *-5 sed-test* | **sed -n -e 's/**a*/Q/g p' -e 's/Q/ZZ/ p'**

   The **head** utility passes only the first five lines from *sed-test* to **sed**. The first instruction to **sed** globally changes all *a* characters on the line to *Q*'s and prints the line. With *Q*'s in place, the line appears on the screen. The second instruction tells **sed** to change every *Q* to *ZZ* and print the line. The line appears on the screen with *ZZ* wherever the *Q* previously resided. In fact, there are no *Q* characters in the original file. The only way the *ZZ*'s can replace *Q*'s is if the second instruction acts on the line after the first changed *a*'s to *Q*'s. All instructions are completed on each line before it is replaced with the next.

Putting Multiple Instructions in a Command File

The -e option is convenient for passing multiple edit instructions to **sed** from the command line, but it's not the best choice for more complex **sed** scripts. Some scripts may contain many more additional instructions. When this is the case, it's more reasonable to use a file containing the commands.

1. Create a command file called *modify.rec* that contains the following lines:

   s/*Magazine/Sunpaper*/**g**
   /*Sandwich*/ **d**

2. Have **sed** read the command file *modify.rec* for instructions and read the input file *gdbase* by entering:

   sed -f *modify.rec gdbase*

   In the output resulting from this command, all instances of the word *Magazine* are changed to *Sunpaper,* and all lines containing *Sandwich* are deleted. The **-f** option instructs **sed** to open the file that follows the **-f** flag and to take its instructions from that file.

3. Enter the following:

   head *-20* **/etc/passwd** | **sed** **'s//bin/bash/**/bin/tcsh**/g'**

   An error message is received because **sed** cannot determine which slashes separate the target and replacement portions of the command line.

4. Tell **sed** not to interpret the slashes that are part of **/bin/bash** and **/bin/tcsh** with:

   head *-20* **/etc/passwd** | **sed** **'s/\\/bin\\/bash/\\/bin\\/tcsh/g'**

5. Create another file called *sed-pw-cmds* containing the following:

   s/root/ROOT/**g**
   s/*/bin**/bash/**/bin**/tcsh/***g**

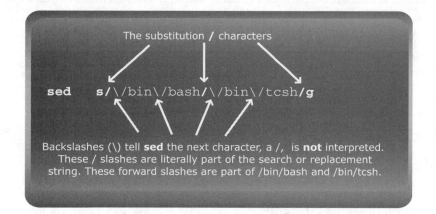

6. Enter:

   head *-20* **/etc/passwd** | **sed -f** *sed-pw-cmds*

   Every instance of the string *root* is changed to *ROOT* and **/bin/bash** is to be changed to **/bin/tcsh** in the output. The backslashes are critical, because the **/** at the beginning of **/bin** could be interpreted as a slash separating the parts of the substitution command. This command line includes backslashes in front of the slashes in **/bin/bash** to tell **sed** to interpret the slashes as literal parts of the search and replacement strings.

Appending Text with sed in a Command File

1. Create another command file named *add-item* that contains the following lines:

   /Fish/a
   Waxpaper Hshld 1.48 1 y
   /Napkins/a
   Rice Veg .79 1 n

2. Enter the following command:

   sed -f *add-item gdbase* **>** *gdbase-rev2*

   The components of the command line in step 2 are listed in the following table:

COMMAND	INTERPRETATION
sed	Execute the **sed** utility.
-f	Option passed to **sed** informing **sed** that a file, listed as the next option, is to be read for instructions.
add-item	The filename containing **sed** commands.
gdbase	The input filename.
>	Redirect output from **sed** to the filename that follows.
gdbase-rev2	The name of the file that receives the redirected output of **sed**.

3. Examine the file *gdbase-rev2:*

   more *gdbase-rev2*

   Its contents reflect the edits specified by the script in *add_item*. At the two contextual addresses, *Fish* and *Napkins*, **sed** is instructed to append new text as the following lines. The backslash is included after the *a* to instruct the shell not to interpret the ENTER. The new *Waxpaper* entry is placed after the line containing *Fish*. The *Rice* entry is placed after the line containing *Napkins*.

4. To have the new line added before and after *Fish*, modify the *add-item* file to read as follows:

/*Fish/a*
Waxpaper Hshld 1.48 1 y
/*Fish/i*
Waxpaper Hshld 1.48 1 y

5. Rerun the command:

sed -f *add-item gdbase* **>** *gdbase-rev3*
more *gdbase-rev3*

The *i* in /*Fish/i* is instruction to **sed** to insert the new text before the current line. Because we still have the *a* in /*Fish/a*, **sed** also inserts the new text after the current line.

16.9 Examining the Workings of the sed Utility

The **sed** utility is a complex stream editor that often produces unexpected results. This section is an examination of how **sed** works. With knowledge of **sed**'s operation, writing proper commands is easier.

Multiple Command Execution

A simple test demonstrates how **sed** operates on multiple commands—either applied line by line to each line of input, or one command at a time to all lines.

1. Create a file *explorer* to contain only the following three lines:

s/*Veg*/*Vgtbl*/**g**
s/*Milk*/*Got Milk*/**g**
s/*Vgtbl*/*VEGTBL*/**g**
3q

Let's consider what will happen with this script:

If the first instruction in the script is applied to all input lines before the second instruction is applied, then all input lines will be displayed with *Veg* replaced by *Vgtbl*. Likewise, *Milk* will be replaced throughout the input with *Got Milk* and the string *Vgbtbl* will be changed to *VEGTBL* on all lines of the file before **sed** quits.

- Conversely, if the entire script is applied to one input line in the pattern space at a time, then **sed** quits after processing the third line of input.

2. Enter this command:

    sed -f *explorer gdbase*

    Output consists of only the first three lines of *gdbase*.

    The first line of *gdbase* is buffered, read, and the substitution commands executed if there is a match. The *Veg* and *Milk* substitution lines are executed, and then at the third line, the **quit** command is executed, terminating **sed**. The resulting output is only three lines because only three lines are read into the buffer and acted upon.

    The **sed** utility is called a **stream editor** because it edits input, line by line, in a stream. It executes all edits (commands) on each line of input before reading the next line. When **sed** operates on input, it:

    - Reads a single line from the input stream into its buffer (pattern space)
    - Executes all specified commands on that line
    - Writes out the pattern space
    - Reads the next line

3. As another example, create a command file named *sed-cmds* with the following text:

    s/*a*/*A*/**p**
    s/*a*/*A*/**gp**
    s/*A*/*B*/**p**
    s/*A*/*B*/**gp**
    4q

4. Enter:

    sed -f -n *sed-cmds sed-test*

All commands are applied to each line of input. The first line is read in, lowercase *a* characters are replaced with uppercase *a* characters, and the line is printed. With the line still in the pattern space, the second command changes the first *A* on the line to a *B* and prints the pattern space. The third command line from the command file globally changes all other instances of *A* to *B* on the line. This line is not number 4, so **sed** does not quit. The procedure continues until line 4 when **sed** quits.

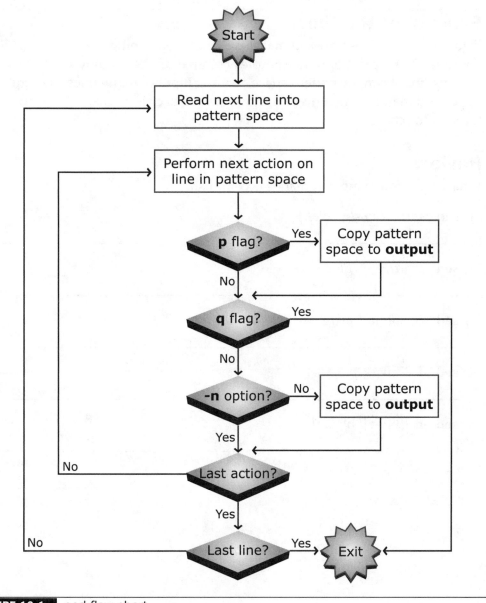

FIGURE 16-1 sed flow chart

Examining the Flow

Figure 16-1 examines how **sed** makes decisions concerning the **p**rint flag, the **q**uit flag, and the **n**o print option. Complex commands can employ multiple actions: printing lines from the pattern space, reading input of many lines, and quitting at a specified match. **sed** follows this flow chart of decisions. Start at the top and go through the chart.

■ Review

What do the following commands accomplish?

1. **sed** **'s/***fries/chips***/g'** *file1*

_____

2. **sed** **'/***start/***,$** **d'** *file2*

_____

3. **sed** **-e** **'s/***food/drink***/g'** **-e** **'/^$/** **d'** *file3*

_____

4. **sed** **-f** *changes* *projectA*

_____

5. **sed** **-n** **'/^[***a-z***]/** **p'** *file1*

_____

■ Answers to Review

1. Looks in *file1* for all instances of *fries* and replaces them with *chips*.
2. Looks in *file2*, the first instance of the string *start*, and deletes that line and all others to the end of the file.
3. Looks in *file3*, replaces all instances of *food* with *drinks*, and deletes all the blank lines.
4. Looks in the file *changes* to find **sed** commands to apply to file *projectA*.
5. Looks in *file1* and outputs lines that begin with lowercase *a–z*. The **-n** tells **sed** not to perform the automatic printing of the pattern space after processing each line.

■ Conclusion

The **sed** utility is a powerful **stream ed**itor that permits editing large files with precision. By employing regular expressions to identify the exact content to be altered with **sed**'s substitution commands, we can modify part or all of a file, write out modified lines, all lines, read in a file, and read from a command line instruction using command files.

COMMAND SUMMARY

Summary of sed Commands

s   Instruction to substitute in the pattern space; must be followed by a target regular expression and a replacement pattern separated by slashes.

g   If used as a flag for the substitute command, executes substitutions on all occurrences of the pattern in the target address, not just the first instance.

p   Instruction to print pattern space.

d   Instruction to delete pattern space.

i   Instruction to insert a line before the pattern space.

a   Instruction to add a line after the pattern space.

{ }   Instruction to group the commands included in the curly braces.

w *filename*   Instruction to write the pattern space to the following *filename*.

r *filename*   Instruction to read into the pattern space from the following *filename*.

Summary of sed Options

-n   Instruction to not print pattern space.

-e   Indicates that more than one instruction per command line is passed; must precede each instruction.

-f *filename*   Alerts **sed** to the presence of a command *filename*.

Summary of sed-Specific Meta-Characters

!   Matches all lines not covered in the address.

\(Marks beginning of a pattern.

\)   Marks end of a pattern.

Data Manipulation with awk

17

Before beginning this chapter, you should be able to

- Manipulate data with basic utilities
- Edit files with the **vi** editor
- Issue complex shell commands
- Use regular expressions
- Globally search and print using regular expressions with **grep**
- Change location in the file system

O B J E C T I V E S

After completing this chapter, you will be able to use **awk** to

- Display and manipulate lines of input that match a pattern
- Access, display, and manipulate specified parts of input lines
- Perform arithmetic and Boolean operations on input lines
- Operate with both command-line and command-file instructions
- Employ regular expressions in pattern matching

One of the most powerful data manipulation utilities is **awk**, a program that incorporates a wide range of data matching, modifying, and programming features. The name **awk** is the first letters of the last names of its three developers, Aho, Weinberger, and Kernighan. The **awk** utility, like **grep**, is a pattern-matching tool, but with the added ability to perform specified, often complex, operations on records or on specific fields in records after a pattern is matched. In addition, **awk** is fully programmable—capable of supporting the loops, conditional statements, and variables expected in a programming language.

This chapter introduces the powerful and comprehensive **awk** utility. We examine command files, enhance **awk** program readability, perform arithmetic operations, format output, and explore other related advanced topics.

17.1 Selecting Records with awk

The **awk** utility reads data files or input that is the output of another utility. In this section, several introductory forms of the **awk** utility are used to manipulate data read from files.

Running Example awk Commands

In the chapter on **sed**, you created the file *gdbase* in the *Power-utilities* directory. This file is also used extensively for data with exercises in this chapter.

1. Change directories to *Power-utilities* and use the editor to examine the *gdbase*:
   cd *~/Power-utilities*
   vi *gdbase*

2. Confirm that the contents of *gdbase* match the following lines. If the file is missing or contains different information, create it or modify it as shown. You need to use only one space or tab between fields. There is a lowercase *v* in the first record.

```
Carrots    veg       1.39   1   n
Milk       Dairy     1.89   2   n
Magazine   Sundry    3.50   1   y
```

```
Cheese      Dairy      4.39   1   n
Sandwich    Deli       3.89   2   y
Onions      Veg         .89   6   n
Chicken     Meat       4.89   2   n
Newspaper   Sundry     1.00   1   y
Fish        Meat       3.79   3   n
Floorwax    Hshld      4.65   1   y
Melon       Fruit      1.98   3   n
Celery      Veg        1.79   1   n
Napkins     Hshld      1.49   6   y
```

For the exercises in this chapter to work properly, the lines must be entered as they are presented here.

Carefully examine the placement of all special characters in the following command.

3. Enter:

> **awk** **'/***Fish***/ {print}'** *gdbase*

All lines in *gdbase* containing the *pattern* (string of characters) *Fish* are selected by **awk** and displayed. The output from **awk** appears on the screen. The original file is not affected.

The following figure describes the elements of the preceding **awk** command:

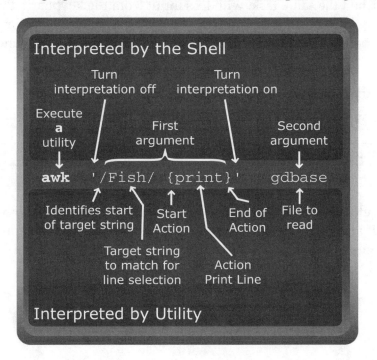

COMMAND	INTERPRETATION
awk	Instructs the shell to execute the **awk** utility.
' '	Single quotes instruct the shell to not interpret the enclosed pattern-action statement, ensuring that **awk** receives this information intact.
/Fish/	The *target string*, or *pattern*, delimited by slashes, is the object of the search in the records of the specified database. All lines containing the target are selected for whatever action follows.
{print}	The action statement of the command, enclosed in braces, instructs **awk** to output the selected records. The print statement is one of many actions supported by **awk**. Unless otherwise instructed, **print** outputs each entire record containing the target.
gdbase	The input filename. **awk** reads this file and applies the specified pattern-action statements to its lines.

The search-and-print action you just demonstrated is an example of **awk**'s basic functionality. After extracting records from the specified input, **awk** outputs (prints) the selected lines. The output of **awk** is routed either to the workstation or to another specified destination.

This basic command closely emulates the process of **grep**, which could have accomplished the same task, with less input from the keyboard. But when **grep** finds a target and prints the line, it is working essentially at its limit. **awk**, on the other hand, is performing only an elementary part of its functionality.

The awk Command Syntax

The basic syntax for an **awk** command is as follows:

COMMAND	OPTION	PATTERN	ACTION	FILENAME
awk		/Fish/	{print}	gdbase

The **awk** utility examines each line in the input file for a match with the specified pattern. If a match is found, the designated action is performed on that line. After processing a line, each succeeding line is examined until the file has been completely traversed.

Not Specifying an Action

In the preceding example, both the target and the action were specified in the command line. You need not, however, explicitly state the action in **awk**, as long as a pattern is specified.

1. Enter:

   awk '/*Meat*/ *gdbase*

   All lines in *gdbase* that contain the target *Meat* are displayed.

   ```
   Chicken  Meat  4.89  2  n
   Fish     Meat  3.79  3  n
   ```

   The default action of **awk** is to print (output) the whole of any record that meets the selection criteria.

Not Specifying a Pattern

In the previous example, a selection or matching criterion was specified, but no action was requested. We can also specify an action without providing pattern-matching criteria.

1. Enter the command line:

   awk '{print}' *gdbase*

   Every record of the entire file *gdbase* is printed.

   When no pattern (target) is specified, all records read from input are considered as matching the selection specification. Whatever action is specified in the **awk** statement is performed upon every record (line) that is read.

17.2 Using a Database with awk

As you have seen in previous examples, both **awk** and **grep** can be used to select records containing specified patterns. One of the most important differences between **awk** and **grep** is **awk**'s ability to select records on the basis of the *location* of values within a record. In addition, **awk** can select pieces of a record for processing. This can only be accomplished when the data is organized in a structured manner, as in a database.

Organizing the Components of the Database

A database is essentially a file that contains data. The raw content of a database tends to be in a rather elementary form that is not usually meant to be read directly. Every database is built around a central, unifying concept or definition. For example, items in the file *gdbase* pertain to the inventory of a typical grocery; that is, its unifying data concept.

In database jargon, information that describes a single item or object is called a *record*. Database records are usually arranged in horizontal lines, or *rows.* The first line, or row, of *gdbase,* shown next, is its first record.

```
Carrots  veg  1.39  1  n
```

The preceding record is divided into five interrelated segments called *fields*. Each field contributes its own piece to the overall data picture.

The following chart lists the name of each field in *gdbase* and relates these field names to the first record in the database:

NAME	TYPE	UNIT PRICE	QUANTITY	TAX STATUS
Carrots	veg	1.39	1	n

Printing a Field Element from a Database

Displaying a particular field contained in a record is one of **awk**'s most useful roles.

1. Enter the command:

   awk '{print $1}' *gdbase*

The first field of each record in *gdbase* is displayed.

```
Carrots
Milk
Magazine
Cheese
Sandwich
Onions
Chicken
Newspaper
Fish
Floorwax
Melon
Celery
Napkins
```

Because no pattern for record selection is specified, **awk** takes action on all records in the file. The **print** action statement, which includes the predefined variable **$1**, instructs **awk** to print the first field of each record.

COMMAND	PATTERN	ACTION	FILENAME
awk		{print $1}	gdbase

Using Predefined awk Variables

In the preceding example, we instructed **awk** to display the first field of all the records read from the file *gdbase* by specifying **$1**, a variable **awk** interprets as the value of each record's first field.

A *variable* is an expression that can be assigned a value other than its own literal name. Variables are often defined by users or programmers when they write **awk** scripts. Additionally, some variables like **$1** are predefined in **awk**'s program code. The **awk** field variable consists of a dollar sign followed by a number and is often seen in **awk** commands. The **$** is the *field operator*, and the **1** is the *literal number component*. In this case, **$1** is interpreted as the value of a record's first field. The actual content (value) of the first field of a record usually changes from record to record and from database to database. However, to **awk**, whatever is in the first field of the currently examined record is the value of **$1**, because this variable relationship has been predefined to **awk**.

Displaying Multiple Fields

In addition to displaying just one field or all fields, **awk** can be used to display multiple fields. Fields can be output in any order.

1. Enter the command:

    awk '{print $3 $1 $2}' *gdbase*

The third field, followed by the first field, followed by the second field of all records in *gdbase* are displayed without spaces between the fields.

```
1.39Carrotsveg
1.89MilkDairy
3.50MagazineSundry
4.39CheeseDairy
3.89SandwichDeli
```

```
.89OnionsVeg
4.89ChickenMeat
1.00NewspaperSundry
3.79FishMeat
4.65FloorwaxHshld
1.98MelonFruit
1.79CeleryVeg
1.49NapkinsHshld
```

The output is jammed together. There are no spaces separating the fields in the output, because we included no instruction telling **awk** to put spaces between the fields. Stay tuned, more at 11:00.

Including Spaces in awk's Output

For more readable output, we must request that **awk** separate the fields in its output with spaces.

1. Enter:

   awk '{print $3, $1, $2}' *gdbase*

   The commas separating the specified fields in the print action statement instruct **awk** to insert spaces after the third field and after the first field in the output.

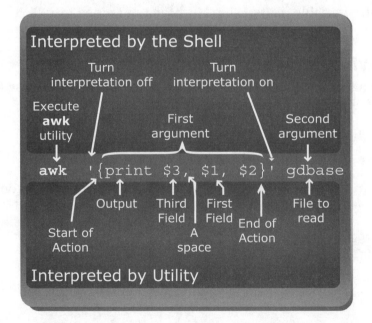

Selecting All Fields

The **awk** utility provides variables that have values equal to one or all fields of a record.

1. Enter:

> **awk '{print $1}'** *gdbase*

The first field of all records is output.

2. Now enter:

> **awk '{print $0}'** *gdbase*

The output from **awk** is all fields from all records.

The predefined variable *$0* has a value of the whole record—that is, the entire line. The all-fields variable is used to define or match the attributes of an entire record.

Identifying Variables and Strings of Characters

The *$1* is a variable. **awk** interprets every variable as instruction to replace it with its value. We can create variables and use them with **awk**.

1. Enter:

> **awk -v** *item*='Grocery Item' **'{print** *item*, **$1}'** *gdbase*

COMMAND	INTERPRETATION
awk	Run the **awk** utility.
-v	First argument passed to **awk** tells **awk** that a variable definition follows.
item	Name of new variable.
=	Assignment operator. Value on right is assigned to variable to left.
'Grocery Item**'**	Value assigned to variable. Quotes instruct shell to pass as is.
{print *item*, **$1}**	Action to be taken. Output the value of the variable *item* followed by a space, then the value of the first field.

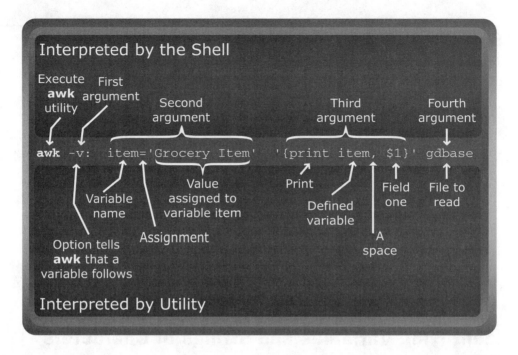

To **awk** the alpha characters *item* are seen as a variable.

2. Try the following:

    awk '{print *item*, $1}' *gdbase*

We did not define the variable. **awk** interprets the string *item* as a variable, cannot find it, and ignores it. The comma is still interpreted, and a space is output at the beginning of the line.

We can also tell **awk** that an object is just a string of characters with no special meaning.

3. Enter:

    awk '{print "*Item:*", $1, "*Price:*", $3}' *gdbase*

For each record, the output consists of the literal string of characters *Item:* followed by a space, then the value in field 1, then a space, followed by the string *Price:*, then another space, and the value in field 3. The double quotes instruct **awk** that the alpha characters enclosed are just characters; they have no special meaning.

In earlier examples, we matched lines that had strings somewhere on the line.

4. Enter:

> **awk** '/*Fruit*/ {**print $0**}' *gdbase*

The character string *Fruit* is seen as a string, not a variable, because it is inside the slash search characters. If a character or string is seen by **awk** outside double quotes or outside slash characters, the string is seen as a variable. Inside double quotes, the string is just a string. Inside slashes, it is a regular expression character string for matching.

Employing Numbers

To **awk**, a character or string is a variable unless it is quoted or inside slashes. What about digits?

1. Enter:

> **awk** '{**print** *12345*, **$1**}' *gdbase*

The output consists of the number *12345* followed by the value of the variable **$1**, the contents of field 1. Numbers are not interpreted as variables and are not quoted.

Identifying Field and Record Delimiters

For database information to be organized and accessible, it must be structured in a logical manner. Fields and records provide the basic structural elements for a database.

1. Enter:

> **head** *-15* /*etc*/*passwd*

The first *15* lines of the file /*etc*/*passwd* are output. Each line is a record. Each record is divided into fields. Fields are characters separated, or *delimited,* from other fields in a record. This delimiting is accomplished by inserting a special character between the fields. The character—called the *field separator*—is chosen by the database creator. In the case of the password file, the field separator is the colon character. The advantage of this approach is that among records, the number of characters in a specific field can vary. With a field separator in use, it is not necessary to specify a given field's length. The field separators tell whatever utility is reading the data record exactly where one field ends and another begins.

Fields are often delimited by white space (one or more spaces or tabs), which adds a degree of readability for the user. The default field delimiter for **awk** is one or more spaces or tabs. The current example (the *gdbase* file) uses multiple spaces to align fields for clarity, but a single space or tab is sufficient.

Records, which are groups of fields, are usually delimited with a newline character. Using a newline character is advantageous because each line in the file is a record.

Changing the Field Separator Using an Option

Some files have fields that are separated by delimiters other than spaces or tabs. For example, the fields of the file */etc/passwd* are delimited by colons. When alternative delimiters are used, **awk** must be informed.

1. Attempt to print the first field of the records in the */etc/passwd* file by entering:

    awk '/root/ {print $1}' /etc/passwd

    The entire record for *root* is displayed. (If your *root* record includes a space somewhere on the line, your output will be only the portion of the record to the left of the first space.) In the command just entered, the colon field delimiter in */etc/passwd* is not recognized by **awk**. There is no field-separating white space (spaces or tabs) between the fields in the file, and consequently, **awk** is not able to identify the correct fields in the record. Examine some fields from your own password file record. Enter the following, which specifies the new field separator:

    awk -F: '/root/ {print $1, $4, $7}' /etc/passwd

    The output from **awk** is three fields from every record in the password file that contains the string *root*. Each record's field 1, the login ID; field 4, the group id; and field 7, the start-up program, are output. The **-F:** tells **awk** that the fields are separated by colons in the input file.

    Likewise, if we were to use **-F'*'**, the * would be interpreted as the field separator.

2. As another example, enter:

    awk -F: '{print $1, $3, $4}' /etc/passwd | head -20

or

> ypcat *passwd* | head *-20* | awk **–F:** ' {print **$1, $3, $4**}'

Fields 1, 3, and 4 of the first 20 lines in the password file are output, with spaces between the fields. The **–F:** option informs **awk** that as it reads input, it should consider the colon (:) as the field separator. The output field separator is still a space, even though we changed the input field separator.

17.3 Selecting Records with Regular Expressions

The power available in using regular expressions to make matches used with **grep** and **sed** is also available with **awk**.

Making Selections Ignoring Letter Case

In this first example of using regular expressions in **awk**, we instruct **awk** to select one of two possible letters in the pattern-matching process.

1. Enter:

> awk '/[Vv]eg/ {print $0}' *gdbase*

The following output is displayed:

```
Carrots   veg   1.39   1   n
Onions    Veg   .89    6   n
Celery    Veg   1.79   1   n
```

The pattern /[Vv]eg/ matches either *V* or *v* followed by *eg*, allowing lines containing either *Veg* or *veg* to be matched.

Specifying the Beginning of Lines

We can use the full complement of regular expressions.

1. Enter:

> awk **-F:** '/^r/ {print **$2, $1**}' */etc/passwd*

All lines in the password file that start with a character *r* are selected.

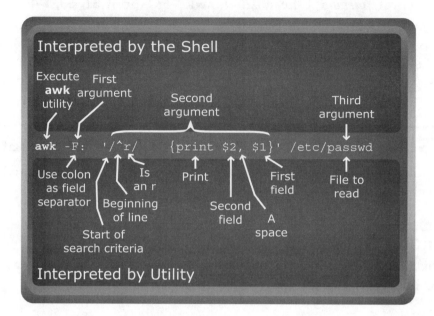

2. As a more complex example, enter:

awk -F: '/^[^*a-m*]/ {**print** "*Login:*", **$1**}' */etc/passwd*

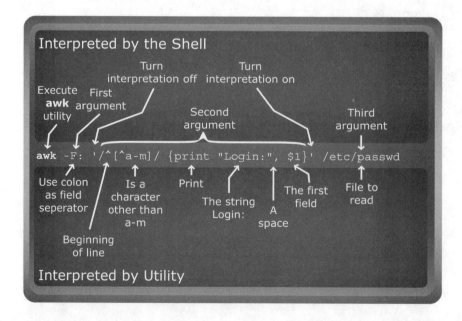

All lines beginning with a character other than characters *a* through *m* are chosen. The action portion of the command line instructs **awk** to output the string *Login* followed by a space and then the value in field 1.

Explicitly Defining the Search Using Regular Expressions

We can tell **awk** exactly what should match.

1. Enter:

    awk -F: '/^[a-m][a-z]*:/ {print $1, $7}' */etc/passwd*

Lines beginning with a character that is a lowercase *a* through *m*, followed by zero or more *a* to *z* characters, and then followed by a colon are selected. Because the first field is the user name and is always at the beginning of a record in the password file, this regular expression matches lines where the user's name begins with characters *a* through *m*, but the remainder of the name must consist of lowercase letters—no uppercase, no digits, no punctuation in the user name.

The full power of regular expressions is available in **awk** to matches in lines or fields.

17.4 Selecting Records by Specific Database Components

The advantage of **awk** over the basic pattern-matching process of **grep** becomes evident when **awk** is applied to very specific components of a database.

Selecting Lines by Field Value

A database may have many records, with each record containing a "first field," a "second field," and so forth. You can select one or more records based upon the contents of one or more specified fields with **awk**.

1. Enter the following:

    awk '$5 == "y" {print $0}' *gdbase*

    If the value in the fifth field is exactly one character, *y*, the line is chosen. There are many lines with a *y* in other fields that are not chosen.

2. Enter:

    awk '/y/ {print $0}' *gdbase*

If a *y* is anywhere on a line, the line is chosen.

3. Enter:

   awk '$3 == *3.79*' *gdbase*

   This command instructs **awk** to print all records for which the numeric value of the third field is exactly *3.79*. The == is the relational operator EQUAL TO and enforces absolute equality between the specified field on the left, field *3*, and the value of the number on the right, *3.79*.

   The output of **who** consists of several fields. We can ask for an exact match and output added text, using strings.

4. Use your *login-name* as you enter:

   who | **awk** '$1 == "*login-name*" { **print** "*login*" , *$1*, "*tty*" , $2}'

   The output consists of the string *login* followed by your login name, and then the string *tty* followed by the tty second field in the output of **who**. Character strings are enclosed by double quotes and can be used in output print statements or for field matching.

5. Relative values can also be specified as an **awk** parameter. Enter the following:

   awk '$3 < *3.79*' *gdbase*

   The output is a display of all records having a third-field numeric value less than *3.79*. The < is the relational LESS THAN operator.

Matching If Two Conditions Are Met

Relational operators such as EQUAL TO and LESS THAN define a relationship between two quantities. The logical operator AND is supported by **awk**, allowing us to require that two relationships match, thereby extending the scope of pattern searches.

1. Enter:

   awk '$3 < *4.00* *&&* $3 > *2.00*' *gdbase*

   The output from this command displays all lines in *gdbase* having third-field values less than *4.00* and greater than *2.00*. Here, two relationships are connected by the logical AND operator **&&**. In this case, *both* relationships have to match before **awk** will select a line.

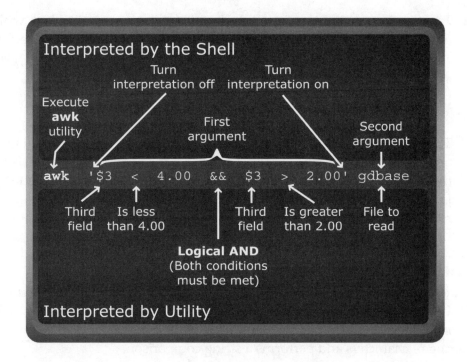

Matching If One of Two Conditions Is Met

The logical operator OR is also a part of **awk**. We can select lines if either one of two specified conditions matches.

Records can be selected if they contain any one of a number of patterns by using the metacharacter for OR.

1. Enter:

   awk '/*Dairy*/ | |/*Meat*/ {**print**}' *gdbase*

   The following is displayed:

   ```
   Milk      Dairy   1.89  2  n
   Cheese    Dairy   4.39  1  n
   Chicken   Meat    4.89  2  n
   Fish      Meat    3.79  3  n
   ```

   The pattern /*Dairy*/ | |/*Meat*/ is considered matched when a line has a match of either string—*Dairy* or *Meat*. If a line contains either string anywhere on the line, it is displayed.

2. Try it with more than two patterns in this format, separating each with two pipes. Any successful match will select the line and the action is performed. The last examples told **awk** to select lines if any of several values were anywhere on the line. We can use the OR logic more broadly.

3. Enter:

> **awk '$2 == "***Meat***" | | $5 == "***y***"'** *gdbase*

The relationships in this command are connected by the | | logical OR operator. Any input line is selected if either the second field consists of the exact character string *Meat* or if the fifth field consists of the letter *y*. Logical OR selects the record provided that at least *one* of two stated relationships matches.

Carefully Using Numbers

In the prior examples, numbers to be compared have been presented without double quotes, as in *2.00*, but character strings are inside double quotes, as in "*Meat*". When we enclose an item in double quotes, **awk** regards the item as a string of characters and performs a string comparison.

1. Compare the following:

> **awk '$3 == "***1***" {print $0}'** *gdbase*
> **awk '$3 == "***1.0***" {print $0}'** *gdbase*
> **awk '$3 == "***1.00***" {print $0}'** *gdbase*

When we put a series of digits inside double quotes, we are instructing **awk** to interpret them as a string of characters. In the third line just shown, we must have the exact match to the contents of the file, *1.00*, to match.

2. Remove the double quotes:

> **awk '$3 ==** *1* **{print $0}'** *gdbase*
> **awk '$3 ==** *1.0* **{print $0}'** *gdbase*
> **awk '$3 ==** *1.00000* **{print $0}'** *gdbase*

If we do not quote a series of digits, **awk** interprets the digits as a number with a numerical value. Numerically, 1 is equal to 1.0 is equal to 1.00 is equal to 1.00000, so the match is made.

Finding Records by Searching Fields Using Expressions

Real expressions can be employed to specify fields for matching strings.

1. Enter:

    awk **'$3 ==** *.89'* *gdbase*

    All records having a third field string value of *.89* are displayed.

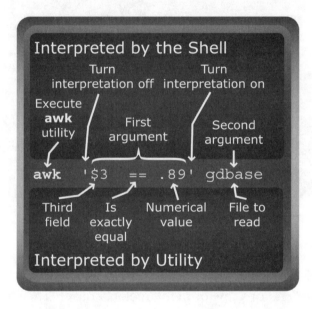

2. Now enter:

    awk **'$3 ~** */\\.89/'* *gdbase*

    The use of the ~ operator tells **awk** to search the third field of the records and select the record if the string *.89* is anywhere in the field. Pattern matching is not confined to the explicit string consisting of only the three *.89* characters. Records with *1.89* or *2.89* (and so on) are selected. The backslash is included to indicate that the period is just a period—not a regular expression special *metacharacter*.

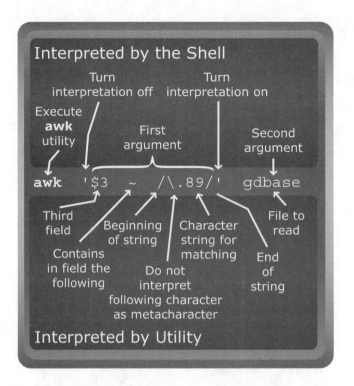

3. Enter:

> **awk '$2 ~ /ry$/'** *gdbase*

The **$** is the "end of a line or field" metacharacter. The string is now limited to a field containing an *ry* at the end of field 2.

Using Logical Negation

In **awk** commands, relationships can be logically excluded as well as included.

1. Enter:

> **awk '! ($2 == "Meat")'** *gdbase*

The output from this command is all lines having a second field value that is *not* the word *Meat*. The negation operator (**!**) reverses the sense of the selection. Without the **!**, lines with *Meat* would be selected; with the **!**, the lines with *Meat* are rejected and all others chosen.

You can use the negation operator to identify any records in a database file that have too few or too many fields. For example, confirm that each entry of *gdbase* contains exactly five fields by entering the following command:

awk '! (*NF* == *5)'* gdbase**
awk '! (*NF* == *6)'* gdbase**

The variable *NF* in this command line is predefined in **awk** as **Number of Fields** and is set to the number of fields in the current line. No lines from *gdbase* are displayed when we ask for records that have other than five fields. All lines are selected when we ask for lines that have other than six fields.

2. Enter:

awk '$2 *!~ /Meat/* {print}' gdbase**

In this case, the negation operator is used to search for records that have a specified field that does not contain a particular character string.

17.5 Creating and Using awk Command Files

Many **awk** commands can be entered quite effectively from the command line, but when commands grow into more complex scripts that take full advantage of this utility's power, the command line alone becomes a less efficient means of putting **awk** to work. Entering complex **awk** commands is tedious, time-consuming, and a perfect environment for input errors—especially when the command must be used more than once. When you place these complex **awk** statements in their own files and then associate these files to **awk** on the command line, you reduce both complexity and the potential for errors.

The following examples show you how to create a command file and then instruct **awk** to read the file for instructions. The examples are basic, yet still apply to more complicated commands.

Creating a Basic Command File

1. Create a file called *print.dairy* that contains the following line:

/*Dairy*/ {print $1, $3}

The command line in *print.dairy* breaks down as follows:

COMMAND	PATTERN	ACTION	FILENAME
None	*/Dairy/*	{print $*1*, $*3*}	None

Command files such as *print.dairy* are not executable files, but merely text files that are specifically written for and read by **awk**. The shell is not starting a child process. The files are not executable. As long as **awk** can read the file, it can follow the instructions.

Instructing awk to Read a Command File

1. Enter:

   awk -f *print.dairy gdbase*

   The resulting output is the first and third fields of all records in *gdbase* that contain the string *Dairy*. This is the same result that would be obtained if the following had been entered:

   awk '*/Dairy/* **{print $1, $3}**' *gdbase*

   The components of the complete command that is ultimately executed are as follows:

COMMAND	INTERPRETATION
awk -f	This **awk** command instructs the shell to run the **awk** utility and pass the **-f** option. To **awk**, the **-f** is instruction to open the file named as the next argument for instructions.
print.dairy	This argument, the command filename, immediately follows the **-f** option; it specifies the name of the command file to read.
gdbase	The file **awk** reads as input. **awk** applies the pattern-action instructions located in the command file to this data.

The file *print.dairy* contains an **awk** pattern-action statement. Neither an actual command (**awk**) nor an input file is present. Special character protection in the form of single quotes is absent as well. This is permissible because the shell never sees the contents of the command file, so there's no need to tell the shell not to interpret its special characters. The shell merely passes the unopened reference filename to **awk**, which then opens the file and reads its contents for instructions. Because it is not a script, just a file for **awk** to read, we do not change the permissions to execute. Read is enough.

Selecting Lines by Record Number

Records can be selected based on field value or content. They can also be selected based on the record number.

1. Create a new command file named *findNR* containing the following **awk** statement:

    NR == 6 {**print**}

2. Enter:

    awk -f *findNR gdbase*

The following output is displayed:

```
Onions  Veg  .89  6  n
```

Examine the file *gdbase*. This output is the sixth record (line) of that file. The output is determined by the contents of the command file *findNR* that you just created; specifically, by the statement *NR* == 6. The element *NR* is another predefined **awk** variable, denoting **N**umber of the **R**ecord. Here, if the value of *NR* is 6, the line is selected.

After **awk** reads in the contents of *findNR*, the overall command to the utility becomes, "If the current record is the sixth record, then perform the specified action (in this case, print)."

Specifying the Input Field Separator in a Command File

We know from experience that the fields in the */etc/passwd* file are separated by colons. We have to tell **awk** every time we use it.

1. Enter:

    awk -F: '{**print** $1, $4, $3, $7}' */etc/passwd*

Even though the records in the password file consist of one long string of characters, the output is just specific fields, selected by **awk** using the colon as the input field separator. We can also pass the same field separator information in an **awk** command file.

2. Create a file named *awk-cmdA* containing the following lines:

```
BEGIN {
FS=":"
}
{
print $1, $4, $3, $7
}
```

3. From the shell, instruct the shell to read the instructions in the file:

awk -f *awk-cmdA* */etc/passwd* | **more**

The output is the same. Using the **-F** command line argument or the internal input **Field Separator** variable **FS,** we can inform **awk** which character was used in the input to separate fields.

The **FS** variable value must be specified in the BEGIN code block.
The output consists of the fields separated by spaces, not colons.

Specifying the Output Field Separator

Regardless of the input field separator, by default, **awk** separates fields in output with spaces. We can specify another character or characters to be used as the output field separator.

1. Create a new file called *awk-cmdB* containing the following lines:

```
BEGIN {
FS=":"
OFS="+"
}
{
print "Login " $1, "GID " $4, $7
}
```

2. Run **awk** employing the commands in the *awk-cmdB* file:

awk -f *awk-cmdB* */etc/passwd* | **more**

Instead of the spaces separating the fields in output, the fields are separated by + characters. The variable *OFS* is used to specify the **Output Field Separator.** Each field is identified with colons in each record at input and a plus sign in the output.

Identifying the Output Record Separator

By default, **awk** outputs one record to a line. In the previous examples, the selected fields from each record were output on separate lines because **awk** uses the new line as its default output record separator. Of course, we can change it.

1. Create a short file, called *great-tchrs*, consisting of grade school teachers. (If you use your own teachers, carefully follow the format: *name* : *grade* : *school*.)

   > *Miss Selquist:1:Baxter*
   > *Miss Cox:2:Baxter*
   > *Miss Dahinden:3:Baxter*
   > *Miss Conrad:4:Baxter*
   > *Miss Casey:5:Baxter*
   > *Mrs Helfrick:5:Gibbs*
   > *Mr Jones:6:Whipple*
   > *Mr Sponseller:7:Whipple*
   > *Mr Hall:8:Whipple*

2. Create an **awk** command file named *awk-cmdC* consisting of the following lines:

   ```
   BEGIN {
   FS=":"
   OFS="+"
   ORS="--------"
   }
   {
   print "NR is " NR, $1, $2
   }
   ```

3. With the data file and command file completed, have **awk** follow the instructions:

   > **awk -f** *awk-cmdC great-tchrs*

   The output is not one record to a line, but many records to a line separated by a series of dashes. If we do not specify an Output Record Separator, **awk** employs a new line. Unfortunately, the **F** and **R** characters are not very distinct, but **OFS** determines the output separator for Fields, and **ORS** controls the output separator for Records.

4. As a more complex example, create another command file *awk-cmdD* consisting of:

```
BEGIN {
FS=":"
OFS="+"
ORS="|"
}
{
print "NR is " NR, $1, $4, $7
}
```

5. Enter:

awk -f *awk-cmdD* **/etc/passwd | more**

The output displays:

- Output fields are separated by + characters: **OFS="+"**
- Records are separated by a | character: **ORS="|"**
- The input fields are separated (password file) with colons: **FS=":"**

Employing a Different Input Record Separator

In all the examples played with so far, the input records consisted of a line. Each line contained fields, but it is the line that is the record.

1. Create a new file named *manyrecords* with the following content:

Kenny : Joyce$ Bob : Koettel$Harry : Reed$Danny : Colon$ Gene : Calhoun

2. Create another **awk** command file called *awk-cmdD* containing:

```
BEGIN {
RS="$"
FS=":"
}
{
print "NR is " NR, $1, $2
}
```

3. Enter:

awk -f *awk-cmdD* *manyrecords*

The fields at input are separated by : and records are separated by the **$** character. The fields at output are separated by spaces and records by new lines.

■ Review 1

1. What command do you enter to print the third field of *file1*?

   _____

2. What command will print the third field, followed by a space, followed by the second field of *file2*?

   _____

3. Using **awk**, write a command line that functions like the following **grep** command:

   grep *pattern file3*

   _____

4. What would you enter to print any lines of *file4* that do not contain four fields?

   _____

5. Which option of **awk** allows **awk** to read from a command file?

   _____

6. What internal variable can be used to set each of the following:
   a. Input record separator?

   _____

   b. Output record separator?

   _____

   c. Input field separator?

   _____

   d. Output field separator?

   _____

7. Where must internal record and field separator variables be set?

   _____

17.6 Making awk Programs Easier to Read

To some degree, the syntax of **awk** itself enforces the formatting of its command files. For example, action statements must always be enclosed by braces. As long as its basic syntax is not violated, **awk** permits a reasonable freedom in formatting to enhance readability for users and programmers.

Formatting awk Command Files

Following is an example of **awk** code written in a linear, command-line style:

> */Dairy/*{**print $1,$3**}

It is possible to write the identical code in an expanded style that is much easier to interpret visually, without violating the command syntax—like this:

> */Dairy/* {
> **print $1, $3**
> }

1. Reformat the *print.dairy* file exactly as just shown.

   This new version of *print.dairy* provides identical results. In this second version, however, the intent of the command file is more immediately apparent. The **awk** utility can use a command file in which multiple spaces and tabs are equivalent to one space, and newline characters are often ignored, thus allowing the second format to work. Each action associated with a given pattern is placed on a line by itself, with action statements indented with multiple spaces for clarity. You can see that, in a more complex command file, this simplification is a valuable aid.

   Notice that the pattern */Dairy/* is followed by an opening brace on the same line. This is done to connect the indicated action(s) on the next line with the line containing the pattern */Dairy/*.

   Verify that the reformatted file performs identically to the original version.

2. Enter:

>   **awk -f** *print.dairy gdbase*

and examine the output.

Improving Readability with Variables

Several predefined **awk** variables have been used in this chapter so far. *User-defined variables* are also supported by **awk**, and they work well when you are trying to improve code readability.

1. Copy the file *print.dairy* to a new file named *print.dairy2.*

>   **cp** *print.dairy printdairy2*

2. Modify the new file by deleting the old action and inserting three new lines, as follows:

>   */Dairy/* {
>   *name* = **$1**
>   *price* = **$3**
>   **print** *name, price*
>   }

3. Enter the following command:

>   **awk -f** *print.dairy2 gdbase*

and examine the output.

Some new syntax has been included in this example of **awk** command file formatting. You've seen how the **==** provides a test for equality. In this case, the single **=** symbol is the *assignment* operator. Here, the variable *name* is assigned the value of the first field, **$1**. The variable *price* is assigned the value of the third field, **$3**. *Assignment* is, essentially, the process of storing the value of an expression in a variable; the value is *assigned*. Assignment proceeds from right to left. With the assignments in the preceding command, the **print** statement displays the variable's values, not the literals *name* and *price.*

Assignments can be made from predefined expressions, such as the field specifiers in this example, as well as from constants, user-defined expressions, and arithmetic statements.

4. Compare the new code:

>   */Dairy/* {
>   *name* = **$1**

```
    price = $3
    print name, price
}
```

with the original version:

```
/Dairy/ {print $1, $3}
```

Both versions of the code produce the same output. Although the original version is more compact, it is somewhat harder to understand. Using variable names that imply the role of the variable in the code, as *name* and *price* do, is always good practice and is permitted by **awk**. In this example, storing the values of predefined expressions such as *$1* in word-based variables makes the intent of the code more understandable. Assigning the value of *$1* to a variable called *x* would also be permitted, but would hardly improve readability.

Including Literal Words in awk Print Statements

The **print** statements have displayed output—numbers, the values of variables, and so on. More complex output, such as phrases or sentences, can also be passed to **print** in combination with variables and code-generated values. Doing this can greatly clarify the operation of an **awk** program, as well as make its output more friendly.

1. Create a file called *quoting* that contains the following lines:

```
{
price = $3
print cost is price
}
```

2. Enter:

```
awk -f quoting gdbase
```

Output from this command is limited to the third field value of *gdbase*.

The words *cost is* did not display because of the way **awk** interprets its code. Unless otherwise specified, any string passed to **print** in **awk** code is taken as a *variable* to be evaluated. Thus, **awk** attempted to find the current value of the three variables *cost is price* and to display their values. Because *price* was the only variable with an assigned value, that value was the only output for each record of *gdbase*.

3. Quotation marks are the key to defining a string of characters as literals. To display the phrase *cost is*, you'll need to modify the file *quoting* as follows:

```
{
price = $3
print "cost is " price
}
```

For readability, a space is inserted within the quoted section, at the end of the phrase *cost is*. The output is

```
cost is  1.39
instead of
cost  is1.39
```

Rather than entering a space after the word *is*, you could use a comma:

print "cost is", price

4. Enter:

awk -f *quoting gdbase*

Now for each selected line, **print** displays *cost is* and the value of the variable *price* (**$3**).

Using Variable Names as Words

In **awk**, literals are always enclosed in quotation marks, as demonstrated in the preceding exercise. Variables, on the other hand, are not quoted. To illustrate this fact, a string can be passed both literally and as a variable in the same command.

1. Enter:

awk '{*item* = **$1**; **print** *item, item*}' *gdbase*

Notice the output of this command. After the variable *item* is assigned the first field value of *gdbase* for each record, the resulting value in each record is printed twice per line.

2. Now enter the following:

awk '{*item* = **$1**; **print** "*item*", *item*}' *gdbase*

Here, the first argument to **print** is enclosed in quotes, forcing a literal interpretation. Accordingly, each line of output contains one literal instance of the word *item* followed by a space and then the value of *item* as a variable.

■ Review 2

1. What is an **awk** command file?

   _____

2. When is an **awk** command file useful?

   _____

3. What is the advantage of using variable names over field names?

   _____

4. Why would you want to avoid naming a variable something like *x* or *int*?

   _____

5. Why is it important to properly format an **awk** command file?

   _____

6. What does the following command line accomplish?
      awk '{print *"Name"*, **$3,** *"Phone"*, **$1}'** *fowl.db*

   _____

17.7 Performing Arithmetic Operations in awk

In addition to manipulating character strings, the **awk** utility can apply arithmetic operations to variables and data.

Subtracting a Constant from a Numeric Field

1. Create a new command file called *change* containing the following program:

   ```
   {
   print $1, $2, $3 - .10, $4, $5
   }
   ```

   Notice that the number *.10* is not enclosed in quotes. Numerical arguments are considered by **awk** to be variables having values equal to their inherent numeric values.

2. Have **awk** read the new command file by entering:

> **awk -f** *change gdbase*

The - used in the *change* command file is **awk**'s *subtraction operator*. Here, this operator instructs **awk** to subtract a constant from the value of a field in each record output by the **print** statement. Output is all of *gdbase*, but with its original third field values reduced by *.10*, as follows:

```
Carrots   veg   1.29   1   n
Milk   Dairy   1.79   2   n
Magazine   Sundry   3.40   1   y
Cheese   Dairy   4.29   1   n
Sandwich   Deli   3.79   2   y
Onions   Veg   0.79   6   n
Chicken   Meat   4.79   2   n
```

> etc...

3. Create another **awk** command file to reduce prices by 35 cents.

Apply the file to *gdbase* and examine the output.

Adding a Constant to a Variable

Employing user-defined variables can make the command file *change* easier to read. Once defined, they can be used in arithmetic operations.

1. Modify *change* to read as follows:

> {
> *name* = **$1**
> *type* = **$2**
> *price* = **$3**
> *quantity* = **$4**
> *taxable* = **$5**
> **print** *name, type, price* + *.10, quantity, taxable*
> }

2. Enter the following command to instruct **awk** to read commands from *change* and data from *gdbase*:

> **awk -f** *change gdbase*

You have assigned the values of all five fields of *gdbase* to variables, which are ultimately passed to **print**. Focus here is on the third field variable, *price*, which has its value increased by the constant *.10* before printing. Although it seems that **awk** has added a number to a word, remember that the word *price* is the name of a variable (a character string storing the value of the third field of *gdbase*, which is a number).

Multiplying One Variable by Another

Assigning code elements to user-defined variables is good general practice. The intent and operation of code is almost always clarified by the presence of variables. Although constants tend to be concise and compact by nature, their functions can be clarified by assignment to a variable. Once this is done, for example, in the *change* file, variables can be used in an arithmetic operation.

1. Modify the *change* file as follows:

   ```
   {
   name = $1
   type = $2
   price = $3
   quantity = $4
   taxable = $5
   change = .50
   print name, type, price * change, quantity, taxable
   }
   ```

2. Enter:

   awk -f *change gdbase*

   The third field of the output is a new price of one half the old price. In this version of the commands in the *change* file, a new user-defined variable, *change*, is defined and assigned the value *.50*. The value of the variable *price* is multiplied by the value of the variable *change*, and the result becomes the third output field for all records of *gdbase*.

Using Variable Division Outside the print Statement

The clarity already afforded the program by variables can be further enhanced by performing arithmetic operations on their own lines, assigning the results to a third variable, and then passing it to **print**.

1. Modify *change* as follows:

```
{
name = $1
type = $2
price = $3
quantity = $4
taxable = $5
change = 3
saleprice = price / change
print name, type, price, saleprice, quantity, taxable
}
```

2. Apply the newly modified file to *gdbase,* with the following command:

   awk -f *change gdbase*

   In this example, each record's *price* is divided by the value of the *change* variable *3* and the result assigned to the variable *saleprice.* The **print** line outputs the value of the new variable *saleprice* as the fourth field.

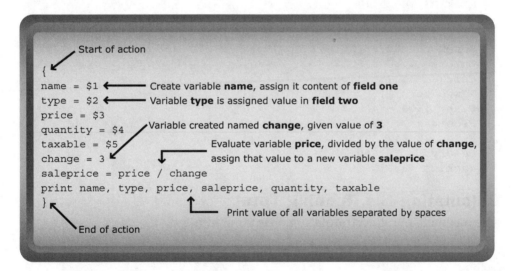

Maintaining a Running Total

The way in which **awk** creates and initializes (that is, assigns initial value to) variables can be used to maintain an updated or "running" total on items in a database.

1. Copy *change* to a file called *running* and modify it to contain the following lines:

```
{
name = $1
price = $3
quantity = $4
total = price * quantity
running = running + total
print name, total, running
}
```

2. Have **awk** read the commands from the *running* file and use *gdbase* as the input:

```
awk -f running gdbase
```

The output includes one line for each item, showing the item's name, total cost (price multiplied by quantity purchased), and the current running total.

```
Carrots  1.39  1.39
Milk   3.78   5.17
Magazine  3.50  8.67
Cheese  4.39  13.06
Sandwich  7.78  20.84
Onions  5.34  26.18
Chicken  9.78  35.96
Newspaper  1.00  36.96
Fish  11.37  48.33
Floorwax  4.65  52.98
Melon  5.94  58.92
Celery  1.79  60.71
Napkins  8.94  69.65
```

Calculating the Running Total

The mechanism for accumulating a running total is:

running = *running* + *total*

This line generates the running total, which seems to appear "out of nowhere," without the definitions and assignments that usually accompany a new variable.

The variable *running* is actually created when **awk** processes the first record of *gdbase*. In **awk**, a new variable has a value of zero *at the time of its creation*, and this line of code tells **awk** to literally "Create a new variable, and assign to it the sum of zero plus the current value of *total*."

By the time the next record is processed, the variable *running* has a nonzero value, and the statement translates as follows: "Assign to the variable *running* the sum of its present value plus the value of *total*." This process continues until all records in the file are processed. The value of *running* increases as each *total* is added.

Combining the Addition Operation and Variable Assignment

An addition operation and the assignment of its result can be combined with a single operator.

1. Open the file *running* and locate this line:

   running = running + total

2. Change this line to read as follows:

   running += total

3. Apply the modified *running* file to *gdbase*:

   awk -f *running gdbase*

The code has been condensed by the combining operator +=, which instructs **awk** to set the value of *running* to its current value plus the value of *total*. The result is the same as before.

The operator += takes the value held by the variable to the left of the operator, adds to it the value specified on the right of the operator, and assigns the result of the sum back to the variable on the left of the operator. For example, *a += 1* is equivalent to *a = a + 1*. If *a* is *b*, then *a+=1* is *7*.

SUMMARY: The arithmetic operations addition, subtraction, multiplication, and division are supported in **awk**. These operations can be performed with either constants or variables. They can be performed in a **print** statement or in conjunction with variable assignment. They are floating-point operations. The operate-and-assign operators (+=, – =, *=, and /=) are also supported. A variable to the left is operated on (+, –, *, /) by an element to the right. The result is then assigned back to the variable to the left.

17.8 Using the printf Function to Format Output

The **awk** utility borrows some of its notation and functions from the C programming language, in which the utility is written. Maybe Kernighan, who was an author of both, had something to do with it. The C function, **printf**, is commonly used in **awk** code to provide additional formatting capabilities over basic **print**.

Printing Strings

Create a new command file called *taxes* that contains the following lines:

```
$5 == "y" {
price = $3;
taxedprice = price + price * .065;
printf "%s %s\n", $1, taxedprice
}
```

1. Apply this tax-calculating file to *gdbase* by entering:

   awk -f *taxes gdbase*

   This application selects all records having *y* in the fifth field, indicating that the associated item is taxable. The *taxes* program then calculates a *taxedprice* equal to *price* plus 6.5 percent of *price.* The output is as follows:

   ```
   Magazine   3.7275
   Sandwich   4.14285
   Newspaper  1.065
   Floorwax   4.95225
   Napkins    1.58685
   ```

   The **printf** statement introduced in this example contains the following elements:

   printf "%s %s\n", $1, *taxedprice*

COMMAND	INTERPRETATION
printf	The formatting statement begins with the **printf** function itself.
"%s %s\n",	The *control string*, also called the *format string*, has symbols enclosed in double quotes that specify how **printf** will ultimately format its output. The **%** is a placeholder for a value that is named later in the **printf** call. The **s** specifies the type of value to be inserted; here, a **s**tring of characters. The **\n** at the end of the control string tells **printf** to print a new line at that position. Unlike **print**, **printf** must be explicitly instructed to print new lines.
$1, *taxedprice*	The arguments to the **printf** call. The values of these two variables (strings of characters) will be the formatted output.

Left- and Right-Justifying the Output

The arguments **$1** and *taxedprice* in the previous example could also have been displayed by regular **print**. When more complex demands are made on the format, however, **printf** is the stronger function.

1. Reopen the file *taxes*. Modify the **printf** statement as follows:

   printf "%-20s %10s\n", $1, *taxedprice*

2. Run the *taxes* application again. The output resembles the following:

```
Magazine    3.7275
Sandwich    4.14285
Newspaper    1.065
Floorwax    4.95225
Napkins    1.58685
```

The newly added format specifiers *-20* and *10* have altered the appearance of the output. They also provide insight into how **printf** handles format and variable arguments. Formatting specifiers and the values to which they refer must appear in the same order in their respective locations in the overall **printf** line. Here, the specifier **%-20s** refers to the value in variable **$1**, and **%10s** applies to *taxedprice*. These numerical specifiers create minimum field widths of 20 and 10 characters. Their respective variables are left- and right-justified against the boundaries of each field width.

Aligning the Decimal and Truncating Numbers

Although the output produced by the command in the preceding section shows some improvement in formatting over the **print** command used in the "Printing Strings" exercise earlier in this section, it could still be made better. For instance, all decimal points in the output should be aligned, and the monetary values held to two decimal places.

1. Reopen the command file *taxes*. In the **printf** statement, change the *s* in *%10s* to *.2f*, as shown here:

   printf "%-20s %10.2f\n", $1, *taxedprice changed line*

2. Enter:

   awk -f *taxes gdbase*

   and you'll get the following output:

```
Magazine    3.73
Sandwich    4.14
```

```
Newspaper  1.06
Floorwax   4.95
Napkins    1.59
```

This modification instructed **printf** to express the variable *taxedprice* as a floating-point number held to a precision of two decimal places rather than a string. This results in an improved alignment.

> **NOTE:** For a quick reference of the **printf** commands used in this chapter, refer to the command summary at the end of this chapter.

17.9 Using the BEGIN and END Patterns

The basic **awk** process consists of receiving input, operating on that input in some specified manner until it has been completely processed, and then terminating. This entire sequence of **awk** operation is also called the *main loop*. When it becomes necessary for **awk** to perform other tasks before or after its main loop is executed, the **BEGIN** and **END** statements can be used to embed these additional routines in the code.

Using BEGIN in a Command File

1. Reopen the file *running*. Modify it as follows:

```
BEGIN {
print "The running totals are: "
}
{
name = $1
price = $3
quantity = $4
total = price * quantity
running += total
print name, total, running
}
```

> **N O T E :** Correct syntax requires that the word **BEGIN** be followed by an opening brace **{** on the same line.

2. Run **awk** with the new command by entering:

   awk -f *running gdbase*

The **BEGIN** statement instructs **awk** to execute the associated instructions before any processing whatsoever of the input file *gdbase*. Here, only after printing the quoted phrase "The running totals are:" does **awk** enter its main loop.

Using END in a Command File

This next exercise modifies the last two lines of the file and adds an **END** section.

1. Reopen the file *running* and modify it as follows:

   BEGIN {
   print *"The name and price for each of your items is: "*
   }
   {
   name = $1
   price = $3
   quantity = $4
   *total = price * quantity*
   sum += total
   print *name, total*
   }
   END {
   print *"the total cost of all items is: "* *sum*
   }

> **N O T E :** As is the case with **BEGIN**, the word **END** must be followed by an opening brace **{** in the same line.

2. Enter:

   awk -f *running gdbase*

Here, the **END** statement is used to clarify the final output of this application. This application of *running* is identical to the preceding version except that the running total is not printed as each line is processed. Instead, it is printed after *all* records are processed. Because no pattern is initially specified with the action that accumulates the running total *sum += total*, this action is performed as every line is processed. After all lines have been processed, the **END** statement is executed, and its associated action—printing the running total—is performed.

■ Review 3

1. How would you create a variable named *animals* and assign it the value of the second field of a record multiplied by the fourth field?

_____

2. What will be the result of the following lines?

```
fowl    =  $0
duck    =  $1
geese   =  $2
swans   =  $3
subtotal  =   duck  +  geese  +  swans
print  fowl  subtotal
```

_____

3. What advantages do the **BEGIN** and **END** statements give you?

_____

4. The statement **duck** += *1* is equivalent to what?

_____

5. What **awk print** statement will multiply the contents of the third field times the fifth field and then print the results after first printing all the original fields?

_____

Conclusion

This chapter examined the pattern-matching and data-processing utility **awk**, including database structure, basic **awk** syntax, and a variety of advanced features. You extracted specific fields from a database, employed command files to pass pattern-action statements, improved the readability of **awk** code, used arithmetic operators in **awk** commands, and used the **printf** function to create formatted output. Using the **BEGIN** and **END** statements, you employed arithmetic operators in the context of a database application.

Answers to Review 1

1. awk '{print $3}' *file1*
2. awk '{print $3, $2}' *file2*
3. awk '/*pattern*/ {print}' *file3*
   or
   awk '/*pattern*/ {print $0}' *file3*
4. awk '! (*NF* == 4)' *file4*
5. -f
6. The answers are as follows:
   a. **RS**
   b. **ORS**
   c. **FS**
   d. **OFS**
7. In the **BEGIN** section

Answers to Review 2

1. A file containing **awk** instructions
2. When you have lots of long, complicated **awk** instructions; or when you are going to use the same instructions over and over; or when you wish to keep a record of what you are doing

3. Using variable names rather than field names makes their contents easier to identify and therefore easier to work with.

4. Variable names such as *x* or *int* have little specific meaning and thus are no better than field names for helping a programmer read code and identify variables.

5. A poorly formatted program is also difficult to read and understand. This can cause problems when you are debugging or modifying the program at a later date.

6. For all records, the word *Name*, a space, third field, a space, the word *Phone*, a space, and the first field are output from the file *fowl.db*.

■ Answers to Review 3

1. **animals = $2 * $4**

2. Add the fields **$1**, **$2**, and **$3** together and print the result after printing the entire record.

3. The **BEGIN** and **END** statements allow you to have actions performed either before the database file is processed or after all records have been processed.

4. **duck = duck + 1**

5. **{print $0, $3 * $5}**

COMMAND SUMMARY

-F*character*   The field separator flag. When used on the command line, the **-F** flag informs **awk** to use the specified *character* as the field separator.

–v *variablename=value*   Assign the value *val* to the variable *var* before execution of the program begins. Such variable values are available to the BEGIN block of an **awk** program.

-f *filename*   The command file flag. When used on the **awk** command line, the **-f** flag instructs **awk** to reference a *filename* containing commands.

'   '   Shell quotation marks used on the command line to protect **awk** pattern-action statements from unwanted interpretation by the shell.

/pattern/   The *pattern* to be matched and then operated on by **awk**. Practically any pattern recognized by **sed** or **grep** can be matched by **awk**.

{   Begins a block of actions.

}   Ends a block of actions.

;   Separates actions in a block.

print "*string***"**   Prints the characters enclosed by the double quotes, followed by a new line.

print *variable1,variable2*   Prints *variable1* and *variable2*, separated by a blank space (for example, *price quantity*) and followed by a new line.

BEGIN   Instructs **awk** to perform the following block of actions before processing the database.

END   Instructs **awk** to perform the following block of actions after processing the database.

Summary of awk Operators

TYPE OF OPERATOR	OPERATORS	FUNCTION
Logical	*a* **ll** *b*	Evaluates to true if either *a* or *b* is true.
	a **&&** *b*	Evaluates to true if both *a* and *b* are true.
	!a	Evaluates to true if *a* is not true.

TYPE OF OPERATOR	OPERATORS	FUNCTION
Assignment	a = b	Assigns the value of b to a.
	a += b	Assigns to a the value that results from adding the value of b to the value of a.
Arithmetic	+	Addition operator.
	-	Subtraction operator.
	*	Multiplication operator.
	/	Division operator.
Relations	a == b	Evaluates to true if a matches b.
	a < b	Evaluates to true if a is less than b.
	a > b	Evaluates to true if a is larger than b.
	a ~ b	Evaluates to true if field a contains the string b.

Summary of awk Predefined Variables

$#**   The value of **$# is the content of the #th field in the current record.

$0   The value of **$0** is the content of all the fields in the current record.

NF   The value of **NF** is the **N**umber of **F**ields in the current record.

NR   The value of **NR** is the **R**ecord **N**umber of the current record.

FS   The value of **FS** is the value of the **F**ield **S**eparator. Default separators (delimiters) are one or more spaces, or a tab.

OFS   The output field separator, a space by default.

RS   The value of **RS** is the value of the **R**ecord **S**eparator; the default separator is a newline character.

ORS   The output record separator, by default a newline.

Summary of awk Printing Commands

printf *"string "*   Prints the *string* enclosed by the double quotes.

printf *" \tstring\n"*   Prints the *string* enclosed by the double quotes, preceded by a tab and followed by a new line.

printf *"string %s\n",* *variable*   Prints the *string* enclosed by the double quotes; replacing % with the value held by *variable,* and starting a new line.

printf *"%ns",* *variable*   Prints the value held by *variable*, right-justified to *n* number of spaces.

printf *"%-ns",* *variable*   Prints the value held by *variable*, left-justified to *n* number of spaces.

printf *"%nf",* *variable*   Prints the value of *variable* as a floating-point number, right-justified against the end space of a field *n* characters wide.

printf *"%n.nf",* *variable*   Prints the value of *variable* as a floating-point number, rounded to the *n*th decimal point, right-justified to the *n*th space.

Programming with the Shell

18

O B J E C T I V E S

After completing this chapter, you will be able to

- Access variables from within a script
- Write shell scripts that obtain input from and write output to users
- Utilize looping and branching control structures within a script
- Provide error checking in scripts
- Manage error messages
- Properly lay out code in a script
- Provide for branching as a result of user input
- Exit with appropriate status messages
- Employ functions to modularize code
- Handle command-line options within scripts

In previous chapters, we employed UNIX utilities and basic control statements in command lines entered at the shell prompt and in shell scripts. In this chapter, we explore more integrated, complex shell scripts that employ extensive program control statements and advanced utilities to perform repetitive and complex tasks. New shell features are introduced—both interactively at the prompt and within scripts.

In this chapter and the one that follows, we focus on how to program in the **sh**, **bash**, and **ksh** shells. Most shell scripts on UNIX systems are written in one of the **sh** family shells. At least one is available on all versions of UNIX. The C shell programming language is very similar to **sh** family shell programming, but has important differences. Most scripts written for the **csh** family of shells are not correctly interpreted on an **sh** shell, and scripts written for an **sh** family shell fail in a **csh** type shell.

This chapter guides you through development of several complete shell scripts, including an interactive menu program that allows the user to select programs to be run, several utility scripts that perform complex tasks, a script that employs functions to modularize the code, and an examination of how to employ command-line options as arguments to scripts.

18.1 Interactively Choosing Options from a Menu

A common use of interactive scripts is to present menu-like interfaces for users so that they need not directly face the hazards of communicating with the shell. A shell running a menu script prompts the user for input and then performs some action based on the user's response. In this exercise, you create a script that presents a short menu interface.

Displaying Lines on the Screen

We can use **cat** to output lines from a script to the terminal.

1. At the command line, enter the following line:

    cat << *xxx*

    After you press ENTER, there is no shell prompt.

2. Enter some lines:

This is text
I am entering
When does it stop
After a line contains only xxx
xxx

After you enter *xxx*, every line of text that you previously entered is displayed, except for the *xxx* line. The command **cat** << *xxx* is unusual. We know the following:

cat > *xxx*	Output of **cat** is redirected to file *xxx*
cat >> *xxx*	Output of **cat** is appended to file *xxx*
cat < *xxx*	File *xxx* is connected to input of **cat**

What does **cat** << *xxx* mean?

It cannot be instruction to connect the file *xxx* to the input of **cat** and start reading from the end of the file. There is nothing there; that would make no sense.

The *xxx* is a *TAG line* that can be any string. This command is instruction to the shell to read every line following this one in the file and write it to the input to **cat** until encountering a line consisting of only the *TAG* string. Upon reading a line that matches the *TAG*, the shell stops providing input to **cat**, which outputs all lines that it read and exits.

 N O T E : In the scripts we will create in this chapter, use either **USER** or **LOGNAME** as appropriate. Also, the first line of each script requests that the shell start a child **bash** shell to execute the script. If you do not have access to the **bash** shell and are using the Korn or Bourne shell, change the line to read **#!/bin/ksh** or **#!/bin/sh** instead.

3. Create a new script named *menu1* containing the following lines:

#!/bin/bash
cat <<++
MAIN MENU
1)   *Print current working directory*
2)   *List all files in current directory*

3)   *Print today's date and time*
++
echo *Please enter your selection* **$USER**:

 N O T E : Make sure that there are no spaces before or after ++ in line 2 or line 7.

4. Make the file executable and then run it by entering:

chmod *755 menu1*

menu1

This displays the menu on your screen. No functionality is included yet. However, if there is a problem with permissions, the path, or this section of the code, the problem can be identified and more easily remedied. It's a good idea to review your script for typos and the like before adding another section of code.

Examining the Code

Following are the elements of the present version of the *menu* script:

COMMAND	INTERPRETATION
#!/bin/bash	Specifically requests that the script be interpreted by whatever shell you specified. This serves two purposes: reminding the programmer what shell is used and ensuring that the required shell is the one actually doing the interpreting. When you tell your interactive shell to run this script, the shell reads the first line and then starts the appropriate child shell to interpret the script.
cat <<++	Instruction to read the lines following this command line in the script as input to **cat**. Each line of the file is given to **cat** until a line is reached that consists of only the ++ characters located at the beginning of the line. The output from **cat** is the terminal display.
++	The ++ is the *tag* indicating the end of the lines in the file to be read as input to **cat**.

The code between the << and the *TAG* is called a *here document*, because the shell reads from right "here." The closing TAG is included on a line by itself. The ++ that serves as the tag in this example is discretionary; you can use any string of characters. The two occurrences of the tags must match exactly, and the closing tag must appear alone at the beginning of a line, with no characters, including spaces or tabs, before or after it. Often programmers use the string *EOH* as a tag, signifying **End Of Here** document.

Using **cat** in a *here document* such as this, instead of using multiple **echo** statements, is more efficient and permits greater flexibility because you can arrange the display text as desired.

1. Edit the script file again, and add the following lines to the end of the script:

    read *selection*
    echo *Your selection was $selection*

2. Run the script:

    menu1

3. When you are prompted for input, type a *1*, *2*, or *3*, and then press ENTER.

After the program confirms the selection you typed, it exits, and the shell prompts you for your next command.

Debugging a Script

When creating scripts, there is little room for error. The shell expects exact syntax to be followed. Fortunately, we can have the shell run in a debugging mode that informs us of the actions it is taking.

1. Enter one of the following commands:

    ksh -x *menu1*
    bash -x *menu1*
    sh -x *menu1*

These commands explicitly start a shell with two arguments: the **-x** option and the script name. Because the *menu* file is included as an argument, the commands in *menu* are executed. This is just one of the many ways to run a shell script—starting a child shell and giving it two arguments, the **-x** option and the script file, to execute.

Deciphering the -x Output

The output of the command you've just entered is initially confusing: commands are listed and output is, in general, a jumble.

Normally, when the shell interprets a script, the shell reads each line, starts the needed child processes, interprets each aspect of the line (performs variable substitution, expands filenames, and so forth), and then has the process execute the specified code. When you run a script with the **-x** option, however, the shell:

- Reads each line and processes the line
- Displays the results of its processing of the command line
- Executes the specified commands

Each interpreted command line is displayed on the screen preceded by a plus sign. You will notice the following output line:

```
+ cat
```

What follows on your screen is the remainder of the **cat** *here document*.

Next comes the *result* of running **cat**: the menu is displayed on your screen.

The next command is an **echo** statement, again preceded by a plus sign. What follows is the result of that command: the variable *name* replaced with your login name.

Finally, you see another plus sign followed by a **read** statement. The shell is waiting for you to enter input from the keyboard.

1. Enter a response and conclude the script.

When running a shell with the **-x** option, the shell displays each utility and its interpreted arguments just before execution.

```
+ line 1 code, variable substituted
line 1 output
+ line 2 code, variable substituted
line 2 output
```

Debugging an Error

One of the most instructive exercises you can do to learn how the shell works is to enter into a working script and to intentionally include an error to see how the shell identifies it.

1. Make a copy of the *menu1* script, and name it *menu-err*:

   cp *menu1 menu-err*
2. Call up the *menu-err* file, and remove the closing **++** tag after the menu display.
3. Run the script in debug mode by entering:

   bash -x *menu-err*   (or **ksh**)

The **cat** utility reads the remainder of the file, code and all, and the script quits. There is no *TAG* indicating when to stop reading input.

4. Fix the problem, and run the script again to make sure it works.

5. Make another error in **menu-err**, such as deleting the variable *selection* after the **read**.

6. Practice bugging and debugging until you are comfortable with the process.

As you complete the exercises in this chapter, use the **-x** debug option to locate errors you may make accidentally, and also use **-x** on working scripts to see how they function.

Handling Multiple Choices with the case Statement

The parts of a programming language used to control what a program does based on some criteria are called *control structures*. To accomplish tasks using the menu, we need to be able to control which of several possible actions the menu will take.

1. Copy the *menu1* script to a new file *menu2*:

   cp *menu1 menu2*

2. Replace the line:

   echo *Your selection was $selection*

   with the following lines:

   case *$selection* **in**
   1) **pwd ;;**
   2) **ls -l ;;**
   3) **date ;;**
   esac

3. When you have added these lines, run the script again:

   menu2

4. When prompted, enter one of the three choices: *1, 2,* or *3*.

5. Run the program again making a different choice.

   The action specified in the code in the script's **case** code block that matches your selection is executed.

6. Run the script in debug mode by entering:

   ksh -x *menu2*

As the shell executes a line of code from the program, it is displayed with a + preceding it.

The Components of the case Statement

The **case** control structure determines which one of several actions is taken based on the value of its first argument. The **case** control structure and others like it are often referred to as *branching* structures.

The following table contains a somewhat stilted English-language translation of the **case** structure used in the *menu* script. In the lines of code preceding the **case** structure, the value of the variable *selection* was determined by the number entered by the user at the **read** command. The **case** structure takes action based on the value of *selection*.

COMMAND	INTERPRETATION
case $*selection* **in**	The shell evaluates the variable *selection* and passes its value as the first argument to **case**.
1)	If the first argument to **case** has the value *1*, this block of code is executed.
pwd	—Run **pwd** to print working directory.
;;	—End of this branch of the **case**, go to the **esac**.
2)	In the case where *selection*, and therefore the first argument to **case**, is *2*:
ls -l	—Run **ls -l** to list the files in this directory.
;;	—End of this course of action, go to **esac**.
3)	In the case where the first argument to **case** is *3*:
date	—Run **date** to print the date and time.
;;	—End of this course of action.
esac	End of this **case** control structure, go to **esac**.

A complete **case** control structure always includes the following major components:

- The **case** statement itself indicates the beginning of the control structure. Its first argument, often a *variable* to be evaluated, determines which branch the **case** will follow.

- The *condition segment* begins with a character followed by a right (closing) parenthesis. This is the string of letters and/or numbers to be compared to the value of the first argument to **case**. If the **case** first argument value matches the string preceding the **)**, the commands specified between the **)** and the **;;** are executed.

- Each branch is terminated with two semicolons (;;). The **esac** segment indicates the end of the **case** structure. Yes, **esac** is **case** spelled backward.

Identifying Errors in case Code

1. Call up the *menu2* script, remove the **esac**, write the file, and debug with

    ksh -x *menu2*

2. Correct the previous error.
3. Remove the **;;** after option *1* and write the file.
4. Run the script:

    ksh –x *menu2*

    Choose option *1*.
5. Repair and return the script.

> **T I P :** It's a good idea, once a script is working, to make intentional errors and observe how the shell communicates its findings to you. Reading the shell's error messages is most instructive when we already know the error we introduced. By running through that exercise several times, the shell's error messages become familiar.

Making a Script Loop Continually by Using while

As it stands now, the *menu* script quits after you make one choice. Usually, a menu script should perform the desired action and then present the menu display again to continue until we choose to exit. The process of repeating actions within a program, called *looping,* is accomplished in several ways, including the **while** structure examined in Chapter 13, "Employing Shell Special Characters and Programming Structures."

If we are going to make the menu loop, we also need to provide a choice for users to select when they wish to exit.

1. Copy *menu2* to *menu3.*
2. Edit the *menu3* script file, making the following changes:
    - Add three lines before **cat.**
    - Add a new *x* option in the menu.
    - Add the *x)* option in the **case.**
    - Add two lines at the end.

> **N O T E :** Be sure to enter all five spaces in the **while** statement; they are critical.

```
#!/bin/ksh
leave=no                          #new line
while [ $leave = no ]             #new line
do                                #new line
cat <<++
                  MAIN MENU
1)   Print current working directory
2)   List all files in current directory
3)   Print today's date and time
x)   Exit                         #new line
++
    echo Please enter your selection $USER:
    read selection
    case $selection in
        1) pwd  ;;
        2) ls -l  ;;
        3) date  ;;
        x) leave=yes  ;;          #new line
    esac
    done                          #new line
    exit 0                        #new line
```

3. Once your modifications to *menu3* are complete, run the script again. Make a few selections and observe the results.

4. When you are ready, indicate your wish to exit by typing **x** when prompted.

5. Once the script works, introduce an error into the code, run the script in **-x** mode, examine error messages, and repair the code.

Interpreting the while Loop Code

The **while** loop is a major control structure. Call up your *menu3* script again to examine the code.

In general, the form of the **while** loop is:

```
while [ expression ]
do
```

statement 1
statement 2
.
.
.
done

The **while** loop structure causes the shell to continue executing the code between the **do** and its closing line **done**, as long as the command after the **while** enters an exit value of *0*, true. (And no, *done* is not *do* spelled backward.)

while [$*leave* = *no*]

The command [$*leave* = *no*] is executed first. This is a form of the **test** command, which evaluates the *truth* of its contents and issues an exit code of *0* or *1*, *true* or *false*. The variable *leave* has the value *no*, therefore, *no* = *no* is *true*, and **test** returns a *0* to **while**. Because **while** is given a *0*, the code between the **do** and the **done** is executed. After each loop through the **do**...**done**, the test is evaluated again. As long as *leave* is equal to *no*, the loop continues to run.

The new condition section in the *menu* script, for the *x* option on the menu, changes the value of the variable *leave* from *no* to *yes*. Once this happens, the bracket test command evaluates its contents *no* = *yes* as *false,* so the **while** loop does not run the **do**...**done** code. Program control proceeds on to the statements following the **done** statement. In this example, the only command following the **done** statement is **exit**. So, choosing selection *x* ends the whole loop and exits the program.

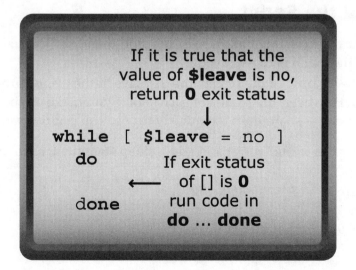

> **N O T E :** The **exit** statement in this menu does not accomplish much, because every program has an automatic, implicit **exit** at the end of the file, anyway. If your code lets the interpreting shell reach the bottom of the file, it exits automatically. It's better programming practice, however, to call **exit** explicitly, with an argument of **0**. This is a way to indicate specifically how the shell script ended. The UNIX convention for exiting is that **0** means "everything was okay." Any other number means something went wrong.

Clearing the Screen

You may have noticed that the screen would be easier to read and work with if it were cleared before each display of the menu.

1. Call up your *menu3* script, and add a **clear** statement, like this:

   ```
   #!/bin/ksh
   leave=no
   while [ $leave = no ]
   do
   clear                    #new line
   cat <<++
   ```

2. Save your file.

Pausing the Script

1. Run the menu again, make a selection, and then exit. The screen clears before the menu is redisplayed.

   With the clearing of the screen, the displays in the *menu3* program are easier to read. However, the results of each choice you make on the menu go by very quickly—sometimes too quickly to see. You can fix that, too.

2. Change your *menu3* script and add a **sleep** statement, as follows:

   ```
   esac
   sleep 2                  #new line
   done
   exit 0
   ```

3. Run the script again and make a few selections. Notice how the **sleep** command pauses the program for two seconds.

The **sleep** program when started waits the number of seconds given to it as an argument, then exits.

Waiting for User Response

The **sleep** statement forces a prescribed wait, but the wait may not be long enough when there's a lot of output. It may be too long in other situations. A better solution is to wait until the user indicates a readiness to continue.

1. Copy *menu3* to *menu4*.
2. Modify the *menu4* file, replacing the **sleep** statement with two new statements. For historical reasons, one or both of the following will work:

> **esac**
> **echo** *"Press Enter to continue \c"*   *#new line*
> **read** *hold*   *#new line*
> **done**
> **exit 0**

   or:

> **esac**
> **echo -n** *"Press Enter to continue"*   *#new line*
> **read** *hold*   *#new line*
> **done**
> **exit 0**

3. Run the script again to check your modifications:

   menu4

4. Make two or three selections. After each selection, you must press ENTER to get back to the menu.

The **\c** (originally from Bell Labs' version) or the **-n** option (in Berkeley versions) portion of the **echo** statement instructs the shell to eliminate the newline at the end of the output line, which allows the cursor to park at the end of the line until a selection is made. Having the cursor remain on the prompt line makes the menu easier to use. The **read** statement causes the shell to wait for input to assign to the variable *hold*. The new variable *hold* is created, but its value is never accessed. We don't need the variable, we just want the shell to pause until the user presses ENTER, and the **read** statement is a good way to accomplish that.

This version of the menu is a little easier to work with because the user can move as quickly or slowly as desired.

Handling the Selection of an Invalid Option

So far, the menu performs actions based on four possible entries. What happens if the user enters some other value?

1. Run your script and, in response to the prompt, type:

   8

   You are prompted to press ENTER to continue, and the menu is simply redrawn, with no action taken. The shell cannot locate an option *8* after the **case** before it reaches **esac**. It would be better if some more explicit action occurred, such as an error message.

2. Exit from the *menu4* script by choosing option:

   x

Creating a Branch for Invalid Choices

When the user enters an option that is unacceptable, we can have the program display an appropriate error message instead of just ignoring it.

1. Copy the *menu4* script to *menu5*.
2. Use the editor to add a new condition after the *x) condition*, as follows:

   ```
   x)   leave=yes  ;;
   *)   echo "Invalid choice. Try again."  ;;          #new line
   esac
   ```

3. Run the script again.
4. Enter a value other than *1, 2, 3,* or *x*.

   The script provides you with the error message concerning incorrect input.

The **)* condition contains statements that are performed if the shell encounters any value at all. The ***** is the wildcard matching character. If this branch were placed as the first branch in the **case** code, it would match anything the user enters. It is placed in the code as the last branch. The branches corresponding to selections *1, 2, 3,* and *x* are coded before this wildcard branch. If a user enters one of the coded options such as *3,* the correct **case** branch is followed. If a user enters a selection *other* than those already designated in previous condition statements, the code in this branch is executed. By placing this last, we capture only those responses not dealt with in previous branches.

Including Multiple Values in a case Segment

As it stands now, your script terminates when a lowercase *x* is entered by the user.

1. Run your *menu5* script again, and see what happens when you type a capital as the selection:

   X

   The *X* is seen as an invalid choice.

2. Exit the script by typing *x* and pressing ENTER.

   There are two ways to modify the script so that the user can exit by typing either an uppercase *X* or lowercase *x*. One way is to have two separate **case** segments that perform the same thing; one matches *X,* the other *x.* There is an easier way.

3. Using the editor, modify the exit segment of the **case** so that it reads:

   q|Q|e|E|x|X)   leave=yes **;;**

4. Run the script, and exit by typing an uppercase *X.*

5. Run the script again, and exit with a lowercase *q.*

   Any one of the upper- and lowercase *Q, E,* and *X* letters is seen as a match for this branch.

   When you wish to have the same set of instructions followed in a **case** statement when the user enters any of several values, use the pipe | between the accepted values. This character is interpreted in **case** code as the OR statement. It indicates that the **case** statements following it should be executed if the argument to **case** contains one of the listed values. You are not limited to two possibilities, but instead may include many values, each separated from the others with a pipe.

   The **case** statement has the following format. Note the indentation for readability.

   ```
   case $variable in
       string|string2)
           code statement(s)
       ;;
   ```

```
        string3)
              code statement(s)
              ;;
        *)
              code statement(s)
        ;;
esac
```

Adding a Condition to Display a File

This exercise adds a new item to the menu and the appropriate code in the **case**.

1. Copy *menu5* to *menu6*.

2. In *menu6*, change the menu display to include the new option:
   1) *Print current working directory*
   2) *List all files in current directory*
   3) *Print today's date and time*
   4) *Display contents of a file*   #*new line*
   x) *Exit*

3. Add a new **case** branch after 3) **date** **;;** to display a chosen file:

       4)   #*new line*
         echo "*Enter a filename*"   #*new line*
         read *fname*   #*new line*
         more *$fname*   #*new line*
       ;;   #*new line*

   Run your modified script and select the new option.

4. When prompted, type the name of an existing file.

5. Select option *4* again, but this time enter a fictitious filename.

   You get an error message from the **more** utility indicating that the requested file does not exist.

Avoiding Errors with the if Statement

You can modify the script to make the shell check and see if a file exists before running **more**.

1. Start editing the *menu6* file, and change the lines for the new option 4 to look like this:

   4)
   echo *"Enter a filename"*
   read *fname*
   if [**-r** *$fname*]   #*new line*
   then   #*new line*
      more *$fname*
   else   #*new line*
      echo *"menu: Cannot access file $fname"*   #*new line*
   fi   #*new line*
   ;;

2. Run this version of the script, again selecting the option to see a file.

3. Enter the name of a fictitious file.

This time, there is no error message from **more**; rather, the error message comes from the menu program.

Examining the Code

The **if** statement is another example of a branching structure. It is more general than **case** because it can use expressions to test for many other conditions beyond simple string comparisons. The construct can be translated as follows:

COMMAND	INTERPRETATION
if [**-r** *$fname*]	If the value of the variable *fname* is the name of a readable file (**-r**), the test brackets return a *0* exit code; otherwise, a *1* exit status code is returned. If the exit status is *1*, the code following **then** is executed; otherwise, the code following the **else** is executed.
then **more** *$fname*	If bracket test returns a *true, 0*, the **more** utility is executed.
else **echo** *"menu: Cannot ...."*	If bracket test returns *false, 1*, the **echo** is run.
fi	End of **if**.

A form of the **if** control structure is:

   if [*expression*]
   then

> *statement(s)*
> **else**
> *other statement(s)*
> **fi**

This form makes a provision for what should be done whether the **if** statement is evaluated as true or false: **if** true, **then**... **if** not true (**else**)... All possibilities are covered.

Repeating an Action on Multiple Objects

So far, you have used one looping control structure, **while**. The **while** structure is used to repeat a sequence of actions as long as some condition remains true. As you explored in an earlier chapter, the **for** loop repeats a sequence of actions on all of a specified list of objects, such as filenames or variables.

 N O T E : Make sure you are in a **bash** or **ksh** shell for the following exercises.

1. Make backup copies of two of the files in your current directory:

    for *fn* **in** *menu1 menu2*

    When you press ENTER, you are greeted by the shell's secondary prompt, usually > unless you changed the value of the variable *PS2*. Because you entered **for** and have not provided a **do done** segment of code, the shell prints a secondary prompt to let you know that it is expecting more instructions.

2. Give the shell what it is waiting for. Type the following lines in response to the prompts you receive:

    do
    wc $*fn*
    cp $*fn* $*fn.bak*
    done

    The **for** command you entered in step 1 instructs the shell to create a new variable *fn* and to give it values listed after the **in**. It also specifies that the statements between **do** and **done** are to be repeated **for** each value of the variable *fn*. The statements here tell the shell to run two utilities: **wc** to count the elements in the file and **cp** to create a copy of the file, giving it the same name as the original with the added extension *.bak*.

3. Examine the list of filenames in your current directory:

   ls

Included in the list should be two new files with the *.bak* extension, created when you issued the **for** command.

Examining the Code

COMMAND	INTERPRETATION
for *fn* **in** *menu1 menu2*	The **for** command takes as its first argument a variable name followed by **in** and a *list* of words that are used as different values for the variable. For each variable value, it performs the same set of *statement(s)* in the list between the **do done** segment. The value of the named variable (in this case, *fn*) is set to the first word in the word list (*menu1* in this case). Then, the statements between the **do** and **done** are executed. Next, the value of the variable is set to the second word in the list, and the statements are executed again. This process is repeated until the end of the word list is reached.
do	The word **do** alone on a line starts the body of the loop, which is ended with **done**, which is also alone on a line. Within the body of the loop, you may specify as many statements as you wish. For clarity, they should all be indented when used in a script.
wc $fn	Execute **wc** giving it the current value of the variable *fn* as an argument.
cp $**fn **$fn.bak	This command instructs the shell to evaluate the current value of the variable *fn*, making a copy of the file, naming it *fn.back*.

The general syntax of the **for** command is as follows:

for *variable* **in** *list*
do
    statement(s)
done

The command must begin with the word **for** followed by a variable name, then the word **in**, and then a word list.

1. Remove the files now (unless you find them useful) by typing:

   rm *.bak*

Using a for Loop in the Menu Script

You just used a **for** loop at the command line. You can use the same structure in a script.

1. Copy *menu6* to *menu7*.
2. Use the editor to modify the script *menu7*, adding a fifth option:

   1) *Print current working directory*
   2) *List all files in current directory*
   3) *Print today's date and time*
   4) *Display contents of a file*
   5) *Create backup file copies*   *#new line*
   x) *Exit*

3. Add the following new **case** branch statement after branch 4 and before *x*:

   5)
   echo *Enter filenames*
   read *fnames*
   for *fn* **in** *$fnames*
   do
         if [**-r** *$fn*]
            then
            cp *$fn* *$fn.bak*
            else
            echo "*menu: Cannot access file $fn*"
            fi
      done
      ;;

4. Run a test of this version of the script, creating two or three backup file copies.

Examining the Code

The code included in the *menu* is described as follows:

COMMAND	INTERPRETATION
echo *Enter filenames*	Once the user has chosen option *5*, the message requesting *filenames* is displayed.
read *fnames*	A new variable is created containing the name(s) of file(s) entered by the user in response to the previous **echo** request.
for *fn* **in** $*fnames*	The value of a new variable *fn* is used to cycle through all names listed in the variable *fnames* and for each value in the following **do** loop.

do
  if [-r $*fn* **]**
   then cp $*fn* $*fn.bak*
   else echo *"menu: Cannot...."*
  fi
	The code in the **do** loop is executed for each value of *fn*. First, the bracket test program evaluates whether it is true that the current value of *fn* is a readable file. If it is, the file is copied into a new file with the same filename and a *.bak* extension. If the file is not readable, the code following the **else** is run.

Eliminating Newlines from the echo Statements

The script is now a fully functional menu. In this section, we make modifications to the code that make the menu easier to use. When you used an **echo** command in this menu, the cursor was placed on the line that followed (with one exception). In menus, it is helpful to have the cursor remain on the prompt line until the user enters a response and presses ENTER.

1. Use the editor to modify the **echo** commands in the *menu7* script. Use either:

   echo *"prompt string:* \c*"*

   or

   echo -n *"prompt string:* "

   Whenever **echo** outputs a line, it includes a newline character at the end, which puts the cursor on the next line in the screen display. The **-n** and \c are instructions to **echo** to output the line without including a newline character at the end. The quotes allow you to use a blank space between the end of the prompt and the cursor.

2. Modify the **echo** line in the code outside the *Here* document after line ++:

   4) Display contents of a file
   5) Create backup file copies
   x) Exit

++
        echo "Please enter your selection $USER: \c"   *#modified line*

3. Save the file and return to the shell.

4. Run *menu7* and make a few selections.

5. Exit the menu.

Using an Alternative Exit

Currently, the script starts by testing whether it is true that the value of the variable *leave* is equal to *no*. It is, and the **do** to **done** code is executed, and then the evaluation takes place again. After each loop, the question of whether *leave* is equal to *no* must be evaluated to decide whether to loop again.

   Another method of exiting uses a loop with no exit condition (an *infinite loop*) and then uses an explicit call to the shell **exit** code to end the program.

1. Copy *menu7* to *menu8*.

2. Use the editor to modify the *menu8* script.

3. Delete the following line:

        leave=no

4. Replace the third line, which is:

        while [*$leave* = *no*]

   with the following line that includes a space:

        while :

5. Replace the code in the last **case** selection:

        q | Q | e | Ex | X)
           leave=yes

           ;;

   with:

        q | Q | e | Ex | X)
        exit 0

           ;;

6. Delete the last line, **exit 0**.

7. After completing the modifications, run the script to confirm that all is in working order.

The **while** loop continues to recycle the **do**...**done** code as long as **while** evaluates its argument as true. In the previous version, a [ ] was evaluated. As long as the test evaluated as true, the **while** loop continued. In the shell, two arguments to **while** are *always* evaluated as true (the word *true* and the colon). Once the **while** loop is started with one of those two arguments, it continues indefinitely. Some other mechanism has to be used to end the program.

The **exit 0** in the **case** statement causes the current shell that is running the script to terminate when that option is selected. We do not ever reach a condition where the **while** evaluates to false; we just tell the process that is running the script to exit. Suppose we start a car. The radio's *on-off* knob breaks as we turn it on. We cannot turn the radio off. Even though we cannot turn it *off*, we can stop the car, which stops the radio.

Examining Errors

1. With *menu* working, go back into the code and change it to reflect a common error, such as leaving out a space in one of the [ ] test commands.
2. Run the script, watching for the error message.
3. Fix that error and make another, and so forth.

The shell's error messages are a function of how the syntax breaks its flow. For instance, it does not tell us that we cannot put a space between a variable name and the equal sign in a variable assignment; (*aa* = *12*) fails from the shell's view because there is no **aa** utility, not because it doesn't know what to do with a space.

Making the Finished Product Easier to Read

Now that the menu works, it's important for the script that runs the menu to be easily readable. No program is ever really complete, and someday, someone (quite possibly you) will need to change the program. Modifying a program is considerably easier when you can read what is already there and can decipher what each line of code does and what each variable contains. To ensure that the program is readable, now and in the future, you should always complete the following finishing touches. Each of these practices is discussed further in the paragraphs that follow.

- Verify that each variable has a name that describes its content.

- Check your line indentation and use of blank lines between sections.
- Add comment lines—including a header comment at the beginning of the program—that explain how the program works.

The listing of the code for this program at the end of the chapter includes comments for your inspection.

1. Copy *menu8* to *menu*.
2. Add comments, check indents, and so forth, as you read this section:

    vi *menu*

Selecting Names for Variables

Notice that the variable names we have employed so far are words or derivatives of words. They describe the data contained in the variable, which is good programming practice. For example, when you're thinking of a name for a variable that will contain a filename, call it *filename* or *fname* or *filnme*, but not *x*.

Employing Line Indentation

Review the indentation of lines in the scripts examined thus far. Consistent indentation is very important for maintaining the readability of code. Here are some guidelines to follow:

- In general, the components of a control structure should be located in the same column. The body of the structure should be indented one level. For example, the associated **if**, **then**, **else**, and **fi** statements should all start in the same column. So should a **while** with its associated **do** and **done**.
- Do not indent unnecessarily; indent only within statements that suggest a need for it.
- Use the same indentation distance for all levels. Use one, two, and three TABs, for instance; or four, eight, and twelve spaces. Be consistent.

Providing Comments for Future Users

A professional programmer includes comments attached to and inside programs; these comments explain how the code works. When the shell finds a pound sign (#) on a line, the shell does not interpret the remainder of the line. Thus, helpful comments can be added to a script without affecting how the script works—provided that a # precedes the comments on the line, and the comments are not inside structures.

Comments should be used to explain the parts of the code that will likely be less understandable to other people (or even to you, after some time has passed). In addition, a comment header at the beginning of the program should specify the name of the program, its author, date of creation, and its function.

Explicitly Calling the Shell to Interpret a Script

There is one exception to the rule about comment lines beginning with the # character. Notice that the first line of the scripts in this section begins with a # followed by an exclamation mark (!), or "bang." The #! indicates that the script should be interpreted by whatever command interpreter is named following the bang—in this case, */bin/bash*. A line that begins with #! is *not* a comment line. This line is instruction to your interactive shell to have a particular kind of child shell interpret the script. This explicit call avoids the possibility of having the wrong shell interpret the script.

18.2 Constructing a Backup Script

The *menu* program that you just completed provides the user with a general menu to accomplish specific tasks. This next program is not a menu, but a utility that accomplishes a specific set of tasks.

Backing Up Files to a Directory

One of the options to the previous menu program makes a backup copy of a file in the current directory. When working on projects, we often need to create deliberate backup copies of several files in a specific directory for one of several reasons.

1. Create a backup 1 file named *bu1* and add the following:

```
#!/bin/bash
for xx in $*
  do
    cp $xx ~/BACKUPS/$xx
    ls -l ~/BACKUPS/$xx
  done
echo
```

> **echo** *"bu: Backups Completed"*
> **echo**

2. Create a directory to hold backups:

   mkdir *~/BACKUPS*

3. Make the script executable, and then run it using some files as arguments:

   chmod *755 bu1*
   bu1 menu menu7

4. Examine the contents of the target directory:

   ls *~/BACKUPS*

   Copies were made of each file to the directory.

Making Certain a File Is Readable

1. If we provide a filename that does not exist, we get an error message from **cp**. Instead, we can have *bu* check as we did in the *menu*.

2. Copy *bu1* to *bu2*.

3. Modify the code in *bu2* to match the following:

   #!/bin/bash
   for *xx* **in $***
   do
     if [-f $xx **]**   *#line added*
       then   *#line added*
       cp $*xx* *~/BACKUPS/$xx*
       ls -l *~/BACKUPS/$xx*
     else   *#line added*
       echo *"---"*   *#line added*
       echo *"bu: Cannot find file $xx"*   *#line added*
       echo   *#line added*
     fi   *#line added*
   done
   echo
   echo *"bu: Backups Completed"*
   echo

4. Run the script using names of files that exist and that do not exist. The **if** test that determines if the file is readable is included inside the **for** loop so the script tests each filename before attempting to copy it.

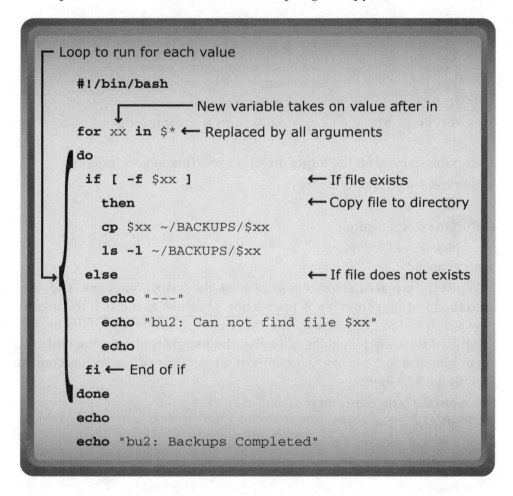

```
Loop to run for each value

    #!/bin/bash
                        New variable takes on value after in
    for xx in $*  ← Replaced by all arguments
    do
      if [ -f $xx ]                    ← If file exists
        then                           ← Copy file to directory
        cp $xx ~/BACKUPS/$xx
        ls -l ~/BACKUPS/$xx
      else                             ← If file does not exists
        echo "---"
        echo "bu2: Can not find file $xx"
        echo
      fi  ← End of if
    done
    echo
    echo "bu2: Backups Completed"
```

Determining if a Target Directory Exists

1. Copy the file *bu2* to *bu3*, and change *bu3* to add the following **if** construct to the beginning, before the **for** loop:

   #!/bin/bash
   if [**-d** *~/BACKUPS*]   *#Start of addition*
   then

```
        echo
        echo "bu: Making Backups"
     else
        echo
        echo "bu: **Cannot find ~/BACKUPS directory"
        echo "Create it and try again."
        echo
        exit 1
     fi                          #End of addition
     for xx in $*                #First lines of existing script
     do
```

2. Run the script with the target directory residing in your home.

3. Remove the backup directory:

      rm -r ~/BACKUPS

4. Run the script again:

      bu3 menu3 menu7

      echo $?

   When the target directory does not exist, the script complains. The **-d** option to the **[** testing command is instruction to return a *true*, *0*, if the directory exists. If it does, the **echo** is run, the **if** ends, and the rest of the program runs. If the directory does not exist, the user is told, and the child shell running the script is instructed to **exit** with a code of *1*, which is confirmed with the **$?** value.

5. Create the target directory:

      mkdir ~/BACKUPS

6. Run the script with a **-x** option to the shell:

      bu3 menu3 menu7

      bash -x

   As each step of the program is executed, the command line is displayed on the screen.

18.3 Using Options with Scripts

We constantly use arguments that are options or flags when we execute utilities. The **-w** option to **wc** is interpreted by **wc** to be an instruction to output the word count. To **wc**, the following arguments produce the same result:

```
wc -c -l
wc -l -c
wc -cl
wc -lc
```

We pass arguments to scripts using the **$1**, which is interpreted as the first argument. There is no reasonable way to use **$1** and to accomplish the flexibility of having options in one or several arguments as we just examined with **wc**.

Executing All Lines in a Script

1. Create a script named *run1* containing the following lines:

   ```
   date
   cal
   ls
   who | wc -l
   ```

2. Make the script executable and have the shell run it:

   chmod *755 run1*

   run1

   All lines in the script are executed, one after another.

Although we have created scripts like this many times, doing so again accomplishes several things. It confirms that the script works without errors, that the path is correct, and that all permissions are in order.

Selecting Code Using Command-Line Options

To facilitate employing command-line options, we need to modify the code and use a feature of the **sh** family of shells, **getopts**.

1. Copy *run1* to *run2* and modify the copy to match the following:

   #!/bin/bash   #*(or ksh, if that is your shell)*

   while getopts *dclw* *option*

   do

     case *$option* **in**

       d) **date ;;**

       c) **cal ;;**

     l) **ls ;;**
     w) **who | wc -l ;;**
    esac
   done

Because the script is a copy of a previous script that was executable, *run2* is already executable.

2. Enter:

   run2 -c
   run2 -w
   run2 -dc
   run2 -l -c
   run2 -X

Each option argument is interpreted as instruction to execute one block of code in the **case** structure. If we include a *-w* option argument, the number of users logged on is displayed. The argument *-dc* is interpreted as two options, *d* and *c*; the output is both the date and calendar. If the option is not defined, **getopts** complains.

The **getopts** function requires two arguments:

- A list of all options that the script is to handle when the script is executed with arguments
- A variable name

The **getopts** function examines the full set of arguments for options following a dash in the argument list. It then assigns the first option that matches its list of acceptable options to the variable *option* and runs the **do** loop.

The **case** runs the code appropriate for the first option. When completed, **getopts** changes the value of *option* to the second option in the argument list that matches one of the acceptable options and runs the **do** loop. Again, **case** locates the branch that matches and then runs the correct code.

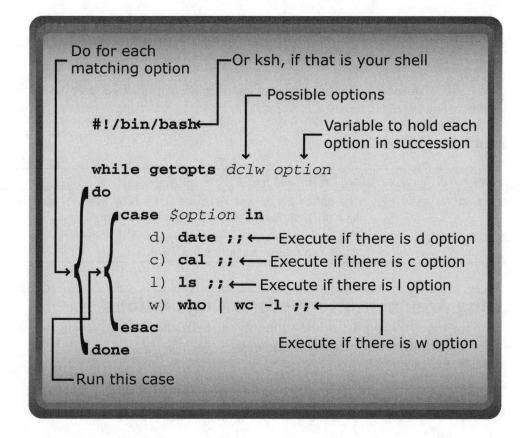

Including an Argument to an Option

When passing an option to a script, we often want to include data as an argument to the option. If there are several printers, we issue **lpr** **-P** *printername*. The printer name makes sense only if the **-P** option is present.

1. Copy *run2* to *run3* and modify the copy to match the following:

   while getopts *dc:lw option*   #note the colon after the c
   do
   case $*option* **in**
   d) **date** *;;*
   c) **cal $OPTARG** *;;*   #argument added
   l) **ls** *;;*
   w) **who** | **wc -l** *;;*

2. Save the file and run it with:

run3 -c 1752 | **more**

run3 -c 2004 | **more**

To instruct **getopts** to include an argument to an option, two parts of the code must be present.

Examining the Code

COMMAND	INTERPRETATION
getopts *dc:lw option*	The option *c* must be designated as having itself an argument by including a colon after it in the **getopts** argument.
cal *$OPTARG* ;;	The option's argument is employed in the command line using the predefined variable *OPTARG*.

Using Arguments to Perform Calculations

Using the **getopts** program in the **sh** family of shells allows us to create customized utilities that employ arguments.

1. First, create a script named *calc1*, and insert the following contents:

```
#!/bin/bash        #(or ksh)
echo "square of $1 is \c"      #or use -n option and delete \c
echo "$1 * $1" | bc
echo "cube of $1 is \c "
echo "$1 * $1 * $1" | bc
echo "raising 2 to power of $1 is \c "
echo "2 ^ $1" | bc
```

Make the script executable and run it with an argument:

chmod *755 calc1*

calc1 2

calc1 7

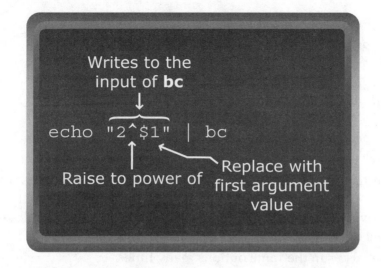

Using getopts to Select Functionality

1. Copy *calc1* to *calc2* and integrate it into a **getopts**:

```
#!/bin/bash       #(or ksh, if that is your shell)
while getopts s:c:p: option
do
  case $option in
s)
        echo "square of $OPTARG is \c "................#edited line
        echo "$OPTARG * $OPTARG" | bc................#edited line
        ;;
c)
        echo "cube of $OPTARG is \c " ................#edited line
        echo "$OPTARG * $OPTARG * $OPTARG" | bc......#edited line
;;
p)
        echo "raising 2 to power of $OPTARG is \c "............#edited line
        echo "2 ^ $OPTARG" | bc................#edited line
        ;;
  esac
done
```

2. Make it executable and run it:

calc2 -s 5
calc2 -c 5
calc2 -p 5
calc2 -s 5 -p 12
calc2 -c 5 -p 12 -s 15
calc2 -c 5 -p 12 -s 15 -X
calc2 -c -p 12 -s 15

Depending on the option specified, the *calc2* script produces the square, cube, or calculates the result of 2 raised to the power given. If an option is not provided when it is expected, or if an option not defined is employed, **getopts** complains.

We can also run the same options many times.

3. Try:

calc2 –p *5* **–p** *10* **–p** *12*

18.4 Using Functions with a bash or ksh Shell

The **bash** and **ksh** shells accept function definitions, which were explored with aliases in an earlier chapter.

1. Switch to a **bash** or **ksh** shell if you are not in one.

2. At the prompt, enter:

power()
{
echo "2 ^ $1" | bc
}

The function is now in the memory of the shell.

3. Enter:

power 16
power 32

Functions employ the usual interpretation of **$1** as the first argument.

Employing Functions in Scripts

We can define and employ functions in scripts as well as at the command line. This exercise defines the calculations from *calc2* as functions and calls them from the **getopts** structure.

1. Copy *calc2* to *calc3* and make it conform to the following:

```
#!/bin/bash        #(or ksh, if that is your shell)
#Function Definitions
square()
   {
   echo "square of $1 is  \c "
   echo "$1 * $1" | bc
   }
############### You can visually separate functions using #'s.
cube()
   {
   echo "cube of $1 is  \c "
   echo "$1 * $1 * $1" | bc
   }
##############
power()
   {
   echo "raising 2 to the power of $1 is  \c "
   echo "2 ^ $1" | bc
   }
#Body of Program
while getopts s:c:p: option
do
case $option in
   s) square $OPTARG ;;
   c) cube $OPTARG ;;
   p) power $OPTARG ;;
   esac
done
```

2. Run *calc3* with several options and arguments:

  calc3 -p 5
  calc3 -s 5 -p 12
  calc3 -c 5 -p 12 -s 15
  calc3 -c 5 -p 12 -s 15 -X

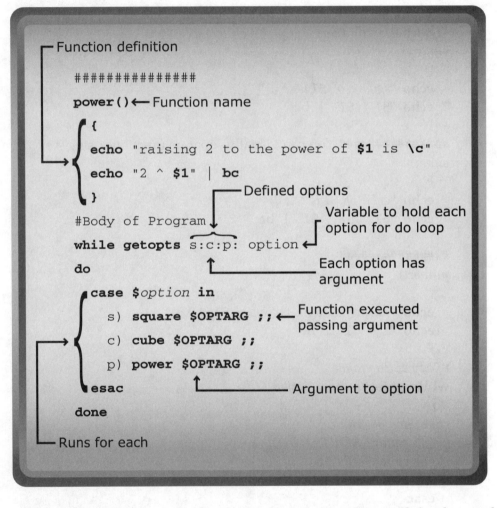

The functionality is the same, however, the code is now in modules that can be used in other program; likewise, additional functions are easily defined and called.

■ Review

1. What are the three major components of the shell's **case** structure?

   _____

2. To write a shell script that performs a series of actions as long as some condition is true, what control structure would you use?

   _____

3. What is the best way to have a script pause so that users have time to read what is on the screen?

   _____

4. What is the * (splat) used for within **case** structures?

   _____

5. How can you get **case** to accept several alternatives as acceptable conditions for the same set of actions?

   _____

6. What is the closing part of an **if** structure in the shell?

   _____

7. What closes a **do** code segment?

   _____

8. What is wrong with the following code segment?
   ```
   3)
   echo "Enter a filename"
      read $fname
      if [ -f fname]
         echo The contents of fname:
         more fname
      else
         echo < No such file
      ;
   ```

   _____

9. What code line tells the shell to expect *m* and *x* options, each with arguments?

   _____

■ Conclusion

Shells in the **sh** family provide a wide collection of features that make creating powerful programs reasonably easy. The shells allow us to make decisions with **if then else**, work in **for** and **while** loops, process options with **getopts**, and build code in modular functions. Additionally, debugging code is facilitated using the **-x** option to the shell.

■ Answers to Review

1. **case**, a condition statement, and **esac**

2. **while**

3. Use **echo** to prompt them to press a key to continue and **read** to wait for their input.

4. To signify the default condition

5. Separate each alternative with a | pipe.

6. **fi**

7. **done**

8. The code should be:

```
3)
echo "Enter a filename"
read fname
if [ -f $fname ]
then
echo The contents of $fname
more $fname
else
echo No such file $fname
fi
;;
```

9. while **getopts** *m:x: option*

COMMAND SUMMARY

#!/bin/bash or #!/usr/bin/bash Requests that the following script be interpreted and executed in the specified shell.

while [*expression* **]**

> **do**
> > *command-list*
> **done**

As long as the expression evaluates true, the command-list continues to be executed.

y|Y|yes|YES) *command-list* **;;** The pipe (|) is seen as OR. If the argument to **case** contains one of the listed values y, Y, yes, YES, the command-list following it should be executed.

if [-r $*filename* **]**

> **then**
> > *command-list 1*
> **else**
> > *command-list 2*
> **fi**

If the value of the variable *filename* is the name of a readable file, the test bracket returns a zero exit code, and *command-list 1* following is executed. Otherwise, *command-list 2* following **else** is executed.

for *variable-name* **in** *word-list*

> **do**
> > *command-list*
> **done**

The value of *variable-name* is set to the first word of *word-list.* Then the *command-list* is executed. The same procedure is repeated for each of the remaining words in *word-list.*

while

>   **do**
>   *command-list*
>   **done**

The **while** loop executes *command-list* unless it is terminated by force or exit command.

getopts *option-string var*   The *option-string* contains the option characters to be recognized. If a character is followed by a colon, the option is expected to have an argument, which should be separated by white space. Each time **getopts** is invoked, it places the option in the shell variable *var*. When an option requires an argument, the argument is placed into the variable OPTARG.

function-name $OPTARG   The argument to an option from the command line is passed to the function *function-name*. The value passed can be referenced using the argument descriptor $1. If multiple values are passed to the function *function-name*, each of the arguments can be referenced using $1, $2, $3, and so forth.

if-then

>   **if** [*expression*]
>   *then*
>   *command-list*
>   *fi*

if-then-else

>   **if** [*expression*]
>   *then*
>   *command-list*
>   *else*
>   *command-list*
>   *fi*

case

>   **case** *variable-list* **in**
>   *string)*

```
      command-list
      ;;
    string)
      command-list
      ;;
   * )
      command-list
      ;;
  esac
```

while loop

```
   while [ expression ]
   do
     command-list
   done
```

for loop

```
   for varname in word-list
   do
     command-list
   done
```

Control Structures

cat <<TAG   Instructs **cat** to read from file to *TAG*.

clear   Clears the screen.

echo -n   Does not add a new line at end of **echo** output.

echo " \c"   Does not add a new line at end of echo output.

exit #   Exits the program giving the shell **#** exit status.

read *var*   Assigns a new variable *var* to whatever the user types from keyboard until the ENTER is pressed.

menu Program

```ksh
#!/bin/ksh
#  Program  name:  menu
#  Written  by:  your  name  here
#  Date:  current  date  here
#  Description:
#       This program prints a menu and executes choice.
#       Then it reprints the menu for another selection.
#       This goes on until the user enters the exit option.
#       Choices are:
#            1)    Print  current  working  directory
#            2)    List  all  files  in  current  directory
#            3)    Print  today's  date  and  |time
#            4)    Display  contents  of  file
#            5)    Create  backup  copies  of  files
#            x)    Exit  back  to  the  shell

# start infinite loop .. exit is in case x
while :
do
clear

# print menu display
cat <<++
                MAIN MENU
        1) Print current working directory
        2) List all files in current directory
        3) Print today's date and time
        4) Display contents of a file
        5) Create backup file copies
        x) Exit
++

# prompt for user input
echo  "Please enter your selection $USER: \c"

# set variable named selection to value of user input
read selection

# start case based on variable selection
case  $selection in
```

```
# selection 1 ... print working directory
    1)
        pwd
        ;;

# selection 2 ... list files
    2)
        ls -l
        ;;

# selection 3 ... display today's day and time
    3)
        date
        ;;

# selection 4 ... view a file
    4)
        echo -n "Enter a filename: "
        read fname
# or
# echo "Enter a filename: \c"
        if [ -r $fname ]
        then
            echo "The contents of $fname: "
            more $fname
        else
            echo "menu: Cannot access file $fname"
        fi
        ;;

# selection 5 ... make backup copies of a list of
# user entered files
    5)
        echo -n "Enter filenames: "
        read fnames
        for fn in $fnames
        do
            if [ -r $fn ]
            then
                cp $fn $fn.bak
            else
                echo "menu: Cannot access file $fn"
        done
        ;;
```

```
# selection x ... exit
   q|Q|e|E|x|X)
      exit 0
      ;;

# default case
   *)
      echo "Invalid choice. Try again. "
      ;;

# end the case
esac

# pause before redisplaying menu
echo -n "Press Enter to continue "
read hold

# end the while
done
```

Shell Programming with Multiple Utilities

19

Many of the exercises in this text guided your creation of basic to rather complex shell scripts. The last chapter explored several scripts that employed many features of the **sh** shells. In this chapter, we explore more integrated, complex shell scripts that employ multiple advanced utilities to manipulate data.

In this chapter and the one that precedes it, we program in the **sh**, **bash**, and **ksh** shells.

This chapter guides you through development of three powerful shell scripts, including a telephone database program, a complex utility that locates users in a group and currently logged on, and a project task-management script.

19.1 Creating a Phone Search Script

One useful shell script task is to search a phone list file for a desired number. The shell script that follows can be used to search a phone list file by name or phone number.

Searching the Phone Database

To explore this series of scripts, we need a database of people and phone numbers.

1. With the editor, create a new file called *phone.list* that contains the following lines. (Add other people as you wish.)

```
Phil Barnhart 321-4567
Walter Mitchell 234-1029
Kenny Joyce 882-7200
Walter Mitchell 543-9681
Lillian Frank 567-4823
Mabel Joyce 123-4567
```

2. From the command line, enter:

   grep *walter phone.list*

   No matches are found.

3. Enter:

   grep -i *walter phone.list*

The entries in the phone database may be in varying states of capitalization. Employing the **-i** option to **grep** instructs it to **i**gnore case.

4. Look for a whole name:

    grep -i *walter mitchell phone.list*

The shell passes four arguments to the **grep** child process: an option, **-i**, and three non-option arguments: *walter*, *mitchell*, and *phone.list*. To **grep**, the first non-option argument *walter* is the search string target; all other arguments are interpreted as names of files to open and search. "I looked," says **grep**, "but the file *walter* does not exist."

5. Enter just two arguments after the option:

    grep -i *'walter mitchell' phone.list*

The first non-option argument is *walter mitchell*, which **grep** interprets as the target; and the last argument is interpreted as a filename.

All is in order, except we are limited to one search at a time. We cannot, for example, look for both *walter* and *mabel* in the same search.

6. Enter:

    grep -i *walter mabel phone.list*

Again, *mabel* is seen as a file, not a target.

Creating a Search Script

Of course, we can accomplish locating specific lines and a lot more with a shell script.

1. Create a file called *phon*, and enter the following lines:

    #!/bin/bash   *#or*   *#!/bin/ksh*
    grep -i *$* phone.list*

2. Make the script executable and run the script by entering

    chmod 755 *phon*
    phon Mabel
    phon 45

Lines containing the target strings are selected and output.

Examining the Code

COMMAND	INTERPRETATION
#!/bin/bash (or #!/bin/ksh)	The shell starts a child shell of the type specified in the first line and passes all arguments on the command line (*Mabel*).
grep -i $* *phone.list*	The shell replaces the argument marker **$*** with all arguments it receives (*Mabel*), then starts a child process, passing it three arguments, **-i**, *Mabel*, and *phone.list*. Finally, the shell instructs the child process to execute the **grep** code.

The lines are selected and output because **grep** displays all lines from the file *phone.list* that contain the target string.

Interpreting Multiple-Word Arguments

As it stands now, the *phon* script is mildly useful. It saves having to type the **grep** command line; however, to get a specific person's number, we will want to enter the first and last names as the first argument to the *phon* script.

1. Enter the following:

    phon Walter Mitchell

    We are told the usual:

    ```
    grep: Mitchell: No such file or directory
    phone.list:Walter Mitchell 234-1029
    phone.list:Walter Mitchell 543-9681
    ```

2. Pass *Walter Mitchell* as only one argument:

    phon 'Walter Mitchell'

    Doesn't help.

Interpreting the Code

When we enter the command line *phon* '*Walter Mitchell*', the current shell starts a child shell to execute the command lines in the *phon* script. The interactive shell passes the child shell the one argument from the command line, *Walter Mitchell*, a 15-character string that has a space as one of its characters.

The child process interprets the commands in the *phon* script. It reads the script command line:

```
grep -i $* phone.list
```

The child shell processes this line according to the shell's rules. The variable **$*** is evaluated and replaced on the command line with its value, the single argument *Walter Mitchell*. Once the variable substitution is completed, the command line becomes:

```
grep -i Walter Mitchell phone.list
```

The shell interpreting the script starts a child process and passes it four (not three) arguments. The process then executes the **grep** code.

To the **grep** utility, the four arguments are interpreted in the usual way:

- I	IGNORE CASE
Walter	The pattern to search for
Mitchell	The first file to search
phone.list	The second file to search

When **grep** searches through more than one file for a pattern, **grep** prefaces each line of its output with the name of the file where the match was found. Hence, the output contains the name of the *phone.list* file. The first file, *Mitchell,* does not exist, so **grep** reports the error message.

Interpreting Spaces...Not

The *phon* script would be a more useful utility if it did not have this behavior for arguments that contain embedded blanks, such as *Walter Mitchell*. The script should treat the value of an argument as a single word. We can quote *within* the script to accomplish this.

1. Change the **grep** line of the *phon* script to quote the variables:

   grep -i "$*" *phone.list*

2. Try the script again, using the same argument from the last example. Enter:

   phon 'Walter Mitchell'

   This time, there is no error message indicating that the file *Mitchell* cannot be located. Putting the variable **$*** within double quotes fixes the problem.

Examining the Code

When the shell interprets the **"$*"**, it encounters the first double quote and turns off interpretation of all characters except the dollar sign, backquote, and backslash. In this situation it interprets the $, but not special characters like spaces. The shell replaces $* with its value, producing the intermediate command line:

```
grep -i "Walter Mitchell" phone.list
```

Spaces are not interpreted inside double quotes. The string *WalterspaceMitchell* is now a single argument.

If a variable is inside double quotes, the shell interprets the dollar sign and characters that follow as a variable identifier and replaces the string with the variable's value. However, if the value includes special characters like spaces, they are not interpreted because they are inside double quotes.

So far, so good.

Performing Multiple Searches

We often want the numbers of several committee members at the same time.

1. Search for more than one person's number by entering:

   phon *walter mabel*
   phon *'walter mabel'*

   Houston, we have a problem.

   There is no line with the string *walter mabel*.

2. Modify the **phon** script to include the following **for** statement:

   #!/*bin*/*bash*   #*or*   #!/*bin*/*ksh*
   for *name* **in** $*
   do
       grep -i "*$name*" *phone.list*
   done

3. Try the modified *phon* script by entering:

   phon Walter Mabel

   You get output consisting of lines that match either target:

   ```
   Walter Mitchell 234-1029
   Walter Mitchell 543-9681
   Mabel Joyce 123-4567
   ```

Examining the Code

Two arguments are entered following *phon* on the command line.

COMMAND	INTERPRETATION
#!/bin/bash (or #!/bin/ksh)	Start a child **bash** shell to execute the script code.
for *name* in $*	Shell replaces **$*** with all arguments: *Walter Mabel*. A new variable called *name* is created and initially given the value of *Walter*.
do	Beginning of loop that is traversed for each value given to *name*.
grep -i "$name" *phone.list*	Code is executed in each loop; **grep** locates all lines containing target string in file *phone.list*.
done	End of loop. Control goes back to top, where *name* takes on next value in list following **in**, and the commands in the loop are executed again.

Each time **grep** runs, the output is displayed on the screen.

Passing Distinct Arguments

The program works well, but let's explore further…

1. Enter:

     phon frank mitchell

     The output consists of the lines containing the string *frank* or containing *mitchell*. There is no line with the name *frank mitchell*.

2. Look for a person who does not exist in the database by insisting on one argument:

     phon 'frank mitchell'

     Again, the output is the result of **grep**'s searching for each name as separate arguments.

3. Go back into the script, and put double quotes around the $* in the **for** code:

     ```
     #!/bin/bash              #or   #!/bin/ksh
     for name in "$*"
       do
       grep -i "$name" phone.list
       done
     ```

4. Run the script by entering:

> *phon* '*walter mitchell*'
>
> *phon* '*frank mitchell*'

The data on *Walter Mitchell* is selected and output. There is no entry for *frank mitchell*, so nothing is output.

5. Try:

> *phon* *walt phil mabel*

No lines are selected.

Examining the Code

The double quotes in the "**$***" instruct the shell to replace the variable **$*** with all arguments such as *walter mitchell* or *walt phil mabel*. These values are still inside double quotes. Spaces are not interpreted. Each collection of arguments is sent as the search string, argument *1*, to **grep**.

Because of the double quotes, the multiple arguments to *phon* that the user enters are passed as one argument to **grep**. No problem when the search is for *walter mitchell*; that string exists in the file. Agreed, there is no entry for *frank mitchell*, and it should not produce matches for *frank* and *mitchell* separately. However, we want the data for each of *walt, phil*, and *mabel*. Because the spaces are not interpreted, the string *walt phil mabel* is passed as one argument, and **grep** finds no matching lines.

The solution is to use the default action of the **for** function.

1. Modify the script by deleting the **in** "**$***" characters in the **for** line:

```
#!/bin/bash                 #or    #!/bin/ksh
for name                #modified line
  do
grep -i "$name" phone.list
  done
```

2. Run the script by entering:

> *phon* '*walter mitchell*'
>
> *phon* '*frank mitchell*'
>
> *phon* *walt phil joyce*
>
> *phon* *walt phil* '*mabel joyce*'

When no list of objects is supplied following the **in** of a **for** loop, the shell reads the objects in the variables **$1**, **$2**, **$3**, and so forth. If we do not supply a list of names after the **in**, the shell reads the argument list. The advantage of this form is that when we specify an object as one argument (*'mabel joyce'*), it is treated as one argument in the **for** loop as well.

Removing Duplicate Output Lines

The *phon* script is more useful now because it accepts multiple search patterns. These patterns do not have to be names; any characters will do. Many of the commands issued thus far produced duplicate output.

1. For example, type:

   phon *Walter Mitchell*

   The **grep** in the **for** loop looked for lines containing *Walter*; then on the next loop, it looked for lines containing *Mitchell*.

   The output appears cluttered if several entries are repeated. Because **grep** runs multiple times, the output may be haphazard and unsorted.

2. Enter the following:

   phon *Walter Mabel*

   The output is:

   ```
   Walter Mitchell 234-1029
   Walter Mitchell 543-9681
   Mabel Joyce 123-4567
   ```

   The lines are not in alphabetical order, even though the source file, *phone.list*, is sorted. The output results from two runs of the **grep** utility: the first, using the argument *Walter*, selects the first two lines of output; the second run, using the argument *Mabel*, selects the remaining line. The pattern arguments *Walter* and *Mabel* are not in alphabetical order, so the output is not alphabetized either.

   You can fix both problems—duplicate output and unsorted output—with a minor addition to the *phon* script.

3. Change the **done** line of the *phon* script to the following:

   done | sort -u

4. Try the new version of *phon* on the two earlier examples:

   phon *Walter Mitchell 102*
   phon *Mabel Joyce Walter Mitchell*
   phon *'Mabel Joyce' Walter Mitchell*

   All commands now produce sorted output with no duplicates.

This illustrates an important property of loop constructs in modern **sh** shells: the output can be redirected. In this case, the **for** block of code—that is, everything from the keyword **for** through the keyword **done**—is a single program function. Its output is the output that previously was displayed on your screen. The modified line now takes the output of the **for** loop and pipes that output directly to the **sort** utility. The **-u** option to the **sort** utility instructs **sort** to produce **u**nique output lines—duplicates are eliminated.

This version of the *phon* script is considerably more useful than the first one we created, yet it remains simple. It uses a few features of the shell programming language to significantly increase its capabilities.

19.2 Creating a Complex Group Member Script

This section guides you through development of a complex script that determines which members of your UNIX group are currently logged on.

The single-line record for each user account on the system is kept in one of two places. On most installations, the local file *letc/passwd* contains the data about each user. Some systems are part of a larger network that uses one computer to handle all password requests for all the networked systems, called a Network Information Service (NIS). When an NIS is serving passwords, it maintains a database that can only be accessed through special commands.

In either case, the record for each user consists of fields separated by colons, like this:

```
cassy:CsTg7.KnyE/xhG:376: 200:Catherine Thamzin:/mla/cassy:/bin/tcsh
```

As explored before, the fields in each record are:

```
loginid:password:userid:groupid:info:home directory:start program
```

Searching for the Login String Anywhere in the File

First, here's a quick survey of details of commands used in earlier chapters.

The **grep** utility searches each line in a file looking for a match to a string of characters. When it finds a match anywhere on a line, **grep** outputs the whole line.

1. To search for your own record in *letc/passwd*, enter the following command. (Use *$LOGNAME* if appropriate.)

    grep *$USER* *letc/passwd*

Or, if you are on an NIS network, enter:

ypcat *passwd* | **grep** *$USER*

The shell interprets the **$** as indicating a variable and locates the value of the *USER* variable (the user's login ID). The shell substitutes the value for the string **$USER** in the command line, passing it as the first argument to **grep**. When the child process executes the **grep** code, the user's login ID first argument is interpreted as the search string.

The **grep** utility opens the */etc/passwd* file to read. If you are using NIS, there is no filename argument, so **grep** reads from input where the output of **ypcat** is connected. Either way, **grep** has access to the contents of the password information records and searches through all lines, selecting only those lines that have the user's login character string *anywhere* in the line. If a person's login were *student1*, then **grep** would locate *student1*, as well as *student10, student11,* and so on. Likewise, if the string *student1* were included in any other field of a record in the password file, the line would be selected.

Searching for Matches in a Specific Field

When searching the password file, we usually want just the record for a specific user. If the target exactly matches the first field of the record, then we want to select the line.

In the following script file, substitute your own *login ID* for the string *yourlogin*.

1. Create a script file called *mylogin* and enter:

   echo *Your entry in the password file is:*
   awk -F: **'$1 == "***yourlogin***" {print $0}'** */etc/passwd*

   Or, if you are using NIS on a network, enter:

   ypcat *passwd* | **awk -F**: **'$1 == "***yourlogin***" {print $0}'**

2. Make the script *mylogin* executable and run it:

   chmod 755 *mylogin*
   mylogin

   The output is the argument to **echo** telling you what is coming, followed by the */etc/passwd* entry for your login.

Examining the Code

The **awk** command line instructs the **awk** utility to locate all lines in */etc/passwd* that have a first field that matches your login ID exactly, and then to output all fields of each selected line. The elements of the **awk** command line are as follows:

COMMAND	INTERPRETATION
awk	Instructs the shell to execute the **awk** utility.
-F:	This argument is passed by the shell to **awk** and instructs **awk** to use the colon as the **F**ield separator.
' '	Instruction to the shell to pass enclosed characters to **awk** without interpreting any characters.
$1 == "yourlogin**" {print $0}**	This entire string of characters, enclosed by single quotes, is passed uninterpreted by the shell to **awk**. The **awk** utility receives and then interprets this code, as described next.
/etc/passwd	This argument, passed to **awk**, is interpreted by **awk** as the file to open and read for input.

The code between the single quotes, which is received and interpreted by **awk**, instructs **awk** to examine the first field of each record and select all records where the first field is a character string exactly matching the value of *yourlogin*. The **awk** utility *requires* that any character string must be enclosed by double quotes. This allows spaces between characters to be identified as part of a target string. Within this code, the command elements are as follows:

COMMAND	INTERPRETATION
$1	Instructs **awk** to examine the first field of each record, looking for matches.
== " *yourlogin* "	The double equal signs are an absolute equality operator instructing **awk** that an *exact* match to field **1** is needed. Only the record from */etc/passwd* with *yourlogin* in the first field is matched.
{print $0}	The code **{print $0}** is the action to be taken on selected lines. It instructs **awk** to print all fields of each selected record.

Therefore, all fields in the */etc/passwd* entry for *yourlogin* become the output of this instance of **awk**.

Locating Group IDs

Each user on the system has a group identification number (group ID) that permits the sharing of files and programs among group members. The group ID is the fourth field in the */etc/passwd* file.

Obtaining a Specific User's Group ID

With **awk**, records can be selected according to a specific criterion. From these records, specific fields can then be output.

1. Modify both lines of the script *mylogin* to match the following:

    echo *Your login and groupid are:*
    awk -F: **'$1** == "*yourlogin*" {**print $1, $4**}' */etc/passwd*

    Or, if you are using NIS:

    echo *Your login and groupid are:*
    ypcat passwd | awk -F: **'$1** == "*yourlogin*" {**print $1, $4**}'

2. Run the script. The output is the login ID and group ID of the specific login that is hard-coded into the script as *yourlogin*.

3. Modify the *mylogin* script to process information about another user by changing *yourlogin* to their *login*.

4. Run the script again.

    Fields 1 and 4, the login name and group ID, are output.

Quoting Special Characters

When the shell encounters a command line, it scans the elements of the line for any special characters that might be present. The shell then expands special characters or makes necessary substitutions where indicated. Then the shell executes the utilities called in the command and passes the remaining arguments to the utilities. This section reviews special characters and how the shell interprets them.

Evaluating Variables and File-Expansion Characters

The **echo** utility has a simple task: it reads whatever arguments it receives and writes them to standard output.

The output is connected to the screen unless it is redirected to a file or another utility.

1. For instance, enter the following:

    echo *Preparing the shell is quite fun*

Six arguments, separated by spaces, are passed to **echo** and subsequently written by **echo** to standard output. In this case, standard output is not redirected, and the output of **echo** is displayed on the screen.

2. The shell completes interpretation of all special characters on the command line before the arguments are passed to **echo**. For example, enter the following:

    echo *$USER* has a home directory of *$HOME*

In the preceding line, the variables *USER* and *HOME* are evaluated by the shell before the seven resulting arguments are passed to **echo**.

3. Enter the following:

    touch *my myfiles lye2 llye2 synth*
    echo [mls]y*

Files are listed that have names beginning with *m*, *l*, or *s* followed by a *y* and then zero or more other characters. The brackets have special filename-expansion meaning to the shell.

Double quotes instruct the shell not to interpret most characters, including brackets and the asterisk.

4. Enter the following:

    echo "[mls]y*"

The brackets and asterisk are not interpreted.

5. Enter:

    echo "[My login is *$USER*]"

In this case, the double quotes instruct the shell to pass the brackets without interpretation. On the other hand, the *$USER* variable *is* evaluated, although it is enclosed by double quotes. The shell evaluates variables even when enclosed in double quotes.

6. Contrast the effect of single quotes. Enter the following:

    echo '[My login is *$USER*]'

In this case, the variable *$USER* is not evaluated, but is displayed as a literal string.

Turning Interpretation Off and On

When the shell reads a command line and encounters a single quote, it turns off interpretation of all special characters until it encounters the next matching quote.

1. Demonstrate the "on-off" nature of shell interpretation by entering:

a=*Hello*

echo ' $a ' $a ' $a ' $a

The first and third instance of $*a* in this command are echoed literally, because both instances are enclosed by single quotes. The second and fourth instances are not quoted and, therefore, are evaluated by the shell.

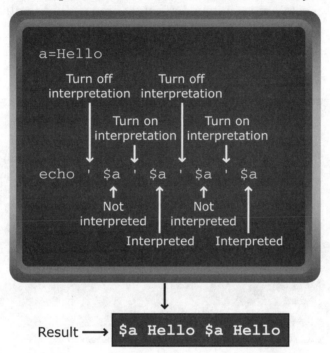

Result ⟶ `$a Hello $a Hello`

The shell always begins command-line processing at the left with interpretation switched on. The process moves from left to right. When the first single quote is encountered, interpretation is switched off. In the previous command, the first instance of $*a* is not interpreted and is passed literally to **echo**. When the second single quote is encountered, shell interpretation is reactivated. The second instance of **$a** is then read. Because interpretation is back on, the variable is evaluated and replaced by its value. The third instance of $*a* is enclosed in quotes like the first and not interpreted. With interpretation turned back on by the fourth single quote, the last $*a* is interpreted. The information passed as arguments to **echo** is:

```
$a   Hello   $a   Hello
```

echo reads its arguments and writes them to output, the screen.

2. The use of single quotes instructs the shell to not interpret double quotes. Enter the following:

   echo '"$USER"'

   When the shell encounters the first single quote, it turns interpretation off until it reaches the next matching quote, at the far end of the command line. Because the double quotes in this command are encountered by the shell when interpretation is switched off, they are passed literally to **echo**.

3. For a more complex and ultimately very useful example of turning interpretation on and off, enter the following:

   echo 'My login is '"$USER"' on this machine**'

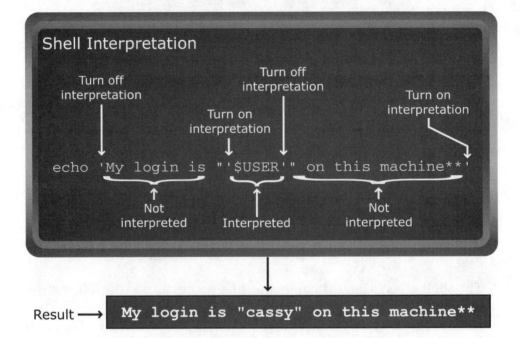

At first glance, **$USER** appears to be well inside single and double quotes, but it is not quoted at all. The first single quote turns interpretation off. The string *My login is* " is inside the single-quoted section, surrounded by single quotes, and hence, is safe from shell interpretation. Included in this uninterpreted section is a double quote. The first single quote on the command line turned off interpretation. The second single quote, just to the left of **$USER**, reactivates shell interpretation. Hence, **$USER** is not quoted and therefore is evaluated as a variable. The single quote immediately following *$USER* switches off shell interpretation again, allowing the string *" on this machine*** to be passed literally to **echo**. The final output of **echo** in this case is

```
My login is "yourlogin" on this machine**
```

The double quotes in this command are passed *uninterpreted*, because the shell encountered both when interpretation was off. The evaluation of *$USER* is therefore displayed in the output of **echo** with double quotes on each side.

Obtaining Group ID of User Executing the Script

The use of quotes in command lines has an especially practical implementation in shell scripts. In the current version of the script *mylogin*, the output of the login ID and group ID from the password file is determined by the login that is hard-coded in the **awk** line of the script. To obtain information about a different user, you must explicitly change *login* in the script.

1. Edit the *mylogin* script, replacing your login name with the variable in the **awk** part of the script:

   awk -F: '$1 == "$USER" {print $1, $4}' /etc/passwd

   or

   ypcat *passwd* **| awk -F***:* **'$1 == "$USER" {print $1, $4}'**

2. Run the script:

   mylogin

   Nothing is returned. The variable **$USER** is inside the single quotes that surround the line and is not interpreted. **awk** was not successful in locating any lines in the password records that contained the literal string *$USER*.

3. To make the script determine information about the user who runs the script, modify the **awk** portion of the script as follows, taking care as you enter the single and double quotes:

   awk -F: '$1 == "'$USER'" {print $1, $4}' /etc/passwd

   or

   ypcat *passwd* **| awk -F***:* **'$1 == "'$USER'" {print $1, $4}'**

4. Run the script.

The **echo** line is displayed, as are the login ID and group ID of the user.

The single quotes in this version of the **awk** line are essential to its correct function, because the double quotes are essential to **awk** and must be passed uninterpreted to **awk**, while variable *$USER* must be interpreted by the shell.

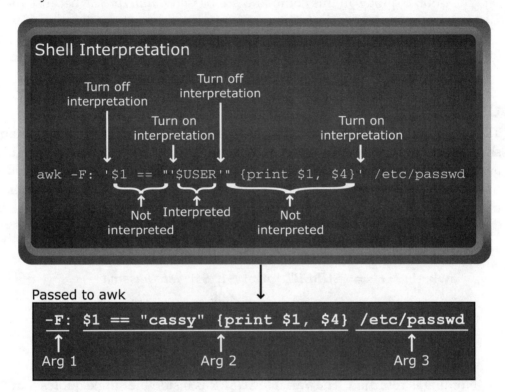

Examining the Code

COMMAND	INTERPRETATION
`'$1 == "'`	*The string $1 == "* is enclosed by single quotes and is not interpreted by the shell. The unevaluated **$**, all alphanumeric characters, special characters (double quotes), and spaces are passed to **awk** as-is, not interpreted by the shell.

COMMAND	INTERPRETATION
$USER	When the shell encounters the $ in front of *USER*, it is after the second single quote. Interpretation is back on and the shell evaluates this variable as the login of the user who executes the script.
'" {print $1, $4}'	Shell interpretation is switched off again by the first of another pair of single quotes, and the characters **" {print $1, $4}** are passed to **awk** uninterpreted. Again, the double quote is not interpreted because it is inside single quotes, which is good, because **awk** needs it.

Interpretation by awk

After shell interpretation has finished, the three arguments shown next are finally passed to **awk**. Now **awk**, and not the shell, handles the remaining processing of the command.

> -**F**:
> **$1** == "*yourlogin*" {print $1, $4}
> /etc/passwd

The following table describes how **awk** interprets the elements of this code:

COMMAND	INTERPRETATION
-**F**:	This option to **awk** tells it to consider the colon as the field separator as it reads the input.
$1 == "*yourlogin*"	Specifies the selection criteria. All records where the value of the first field is an exact match to the string that is *yourlogin* are selected for action. Because *yourlogin* is a character string, not a numeric value, **awk** requires it to be enclosed by double quotes. You had the needed double quotes passed by the shell to **awk** as part of the quoted sections earlier.
{print $1, $4}	This string directs **awk** to take action on all selected lines. The first and fourth fields of the selected record(s) are printed (output).
/etc/passwd	Interpreted by **awk** as a file to open and read for input. Remember that in an NIS environment **awk** reads from input, where the output of **ypcat** is connected.

Passing User-Defined Data into a Script

The ability of the shell to transfer command-line arguments into scripts can be used to make scripts adaptive to user input. Even with the presence of the variable *$USER*, which lets the script automatically conform to the current user, the script is still unnecessarily restrictive. With the following modifications, the user can specify any login ID as an argument on the command line, and the script will locate information pertaining to that user.

1. Create a new script file called *groupon1* containing the following lines:

   #!*/bin/bash*   #or   #!*/bin/ksh*
   echo The user group id for the login $1 is:
   awk -F: **'$1 == "'$1'" {print $1, $4}'** */etc/passwd*

   Or, if you are in NIS:

   ypcat *passwd* | **awk -F**: **'$1 == "'$1'" {print $1, $4}'**

2. Make the script executable.
3. Run the *groupon1* script by entering the following command:

   groupon1 $USER

   The output is your login ID and your group ID.
4. Make a note of your group ID: **gid** is: _____
5. Try the script again, using as argument a login ID other than your own.

Examining the Code

The critical element of the script **groupon1** is the variable **$1**, which replaces **$USER**. This variable is evaluated by the shell as the first argument entered by the user after **groupon1** on the command line. If a user enters **groupon1** *bob*, the shell would place the string *bob* in the script replacing the **$1** variable. With *bob* in the search-pattern quotes, **awk** would have extracted and printed the specified data about this user.

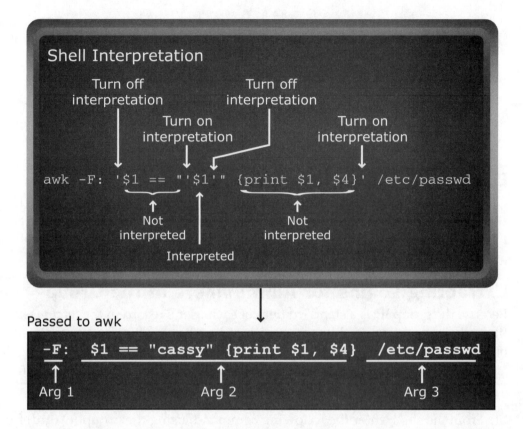

The script *groupon1* illustrates an interesting aspect of variable evaluation. Two instances of *$1* reside on the **awk** line. The instance of *$1* outside the single quotes, in the middle of the command line, is interpreted by the shell as the first argument on the command line. The other instances are inside single quotes, so the shell passes them uninterpreted to **awk**. To **awk**, they are interpreted as the first field in the specified records. The same variable notation, *$1*, because of command-line quoting, is evaluated by the shell as having one meaning, or is passed to a different program where it has a very different meaning.

> **S U M M A R Y :** Information can be passed to a utility inside a script in three ways. You can
> —Hard-code the exact information in the script
> —Set the value of a variable that the shell can read
> —Pass the value as an argument to the script on the command line

Determining Group Membership

On a UNIX/Linux system, many users may be members of the same group. They share the same group ID, which is a number assigned by the system administrator. Like login IDs, group IDs can be matched and extracted from the password database.

Extracting Logins for All Members of the Group

Because the group ID is a standard field of each user's record in the */etc/passwd* file and always occupies the same position in each record, it can be readily obtained.

The **awk** utility can be used to extract records that have an exact match in a specific field.

1. From the shell, enter the following command, using the group ID (**gid**) for your account, which you obtained earlier, in the command line for *gid-num*:

   awk -F: **'$4** == *gid-num* **{print $1}'** */etc/passwd* **|** **more**

   Or, if your data is available through NIS:

   ypcat *passwd* **|** **awk -F**: **'$4** == *gid-num* **{print $1}'** **|** **more**

   The list of all user login names on the system that share your **gid** is displayed. In essence, this **awk** line is instruction to locate all records that have your login in field 4, and then to output field 1, the login names.

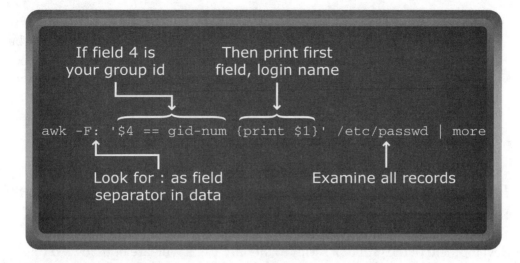

Examining the Code

COMMAND	INTERPRETATION
**$4 == ** *gid-num*	Instructs **awk** to select only lines where the fourth field matches the number you supplied (*gid-num*). There are no double quotes around the match string; **awk** does not employ double quotes around *numbers*— only around *character strings*.

Obtaining a Group ID with Command Substitution

The **awk** utility can also be used to explicitly select the group ID.

1. From a **bash** or **ksh** shell, enter the following command:

   echo *my Gid is* **$(awk -F**: **'$1 ==** ″**'$USER'**″ **{print $4}'** */etc/passwd*)

   Or, in an NIS environment:

   echo *my Gid is* **$(ypcat** *passwd* **|** **awk -F**: **'$1 ==** ″**'$USER'**″ **{print $4}'**)

   The output is:

   ```
   my Gid is ###
   ```

   where ### is your group ID number.

The command substitution instruction **$(awk -F: '$1 == "'$USER'" {print $4}')** tells the shell that all characters within it constitute a command to be executed by a subshell, and that the output of this command is to replace the **$(**) on the command line. Here, the output of the command is placed on the **echo** command line, where it becomes an argument to **echo**. For a user whose group ID is *300*, **echo** receives and displays these arguments:

```
my Gid is 300
```

Identifying All Group Members Who Are Logged On

Users on larger networks often look at the output of **who** to determine if any of their colleagues are logged on. This section of the chapter continues the development of the *groupon* script to identify users who are both logged on *and* members of a particular group.

Selecting Group ID and Group Members from Login

Command substitution can be used in a script to set the value of a variable to the results of a command.

1. Copy the script:

    cp *groupon1 groupon2*

2. Modify the script *groupon2* as follows:

    #!/bin/bash or #!/bin/ksh
    grpnum=$(awk -F: '$1 == "'$1'" {print $4}' /etc/passwd)
    awk -F: '$4 == '$grpnum' {print $1}' */etc/passwd*

    Or, if you are using NIS:

    grpnum=$(ypcat passwd | awk -F: '$1 == "'$1'" {print $4}')
    ypcat *passwd* | **awk -F: '$4 == '$grpnum' {print $1}'**

3. Execute the script by entering the following command line:

    groupon2 $USER | **more**

    The output is a sorted list of all login IDs who are members of the same group as the user whose login is entered as an argument to *groupon2*.

4. Try the script again, using another login ID instead of your own, to see which accounts are in the same group as that user.

Examining the Code

There are two code lines in this script. The first sets the value of a new variable *grpnum* equal to the output of the command substitution **awk** command line. This **awk** command outputs the fourth field (group number) for the user whose login was included as the first argument on the command line (**$1**). Hence, *grpnum* is set equal to the group ID of the specified user.

The second **awk** command line outputs the first field (login ID) for all records in the password file that have a fourth field equal to the value of the variable *grpnum*. Because *grpnum* is a variable with a numerical value, it is not inside double quotes for **awk**.

The following table describes the elements of *groupon2*.

COMMAND	INTERPRETATION
grpnum=**$(** *awk command*)	First, the shell executes the **awk** command that is inside the **$( )** and then replaces **$(***awk command***)** with the resulting group ID for the specified user. The variable *grpnum* is then assigned the resulting value that was the output of the **awk** command.
awk -F*:* **'$4 == '$***grpnum***'**	The variable **$***grpnum* is placed in the middle of the argument, outside the single quotes. Hence, the **$***grpnum* is interpreted by the shell, and its value is passed as part of the argument to **awk**.
{print $1}' **/etc/passwd**	If the value of *grpnum* is equal to the value in the fourth field in a password record, the first field, login ID, is output.

The first line creates a variable named *grpnum* and assigns it the value of the group ID of the specified user. The second line instructs **awk** to select all lines where the fourth field is equal to the value of *grpnum* and to then print the login name, field 1. The output is the login names of all users who have the same group ID as the user supplied as an argument to the command.

Creating Files of Logged On and Group Members

As it now stands, the *groupon* script identifies the group ID for a chosen user and then locates all users who have the same group ID. The following changes to the script enable it to determine not only the login ID of each user who is a user member of the chosen group, but also those who are logged on at the time the script is run.

1. Copy *groupon2* to *groupon3*.
2. Change *groupon3* to match the following:

    #!/bin/bash   or **#!/bin/ksh**
    set +o *noclobber*
    grpnum=$(awk **-F:** **'$1** == **"'$1'"** {**print $4}'** */etc/passwd*)
    awk -F: **'$4** == **'$***grpnum***' {print $1}'** */etc/passwd* \
    | **sort** > *grplist*   *#added this line and* \ *to above*
    who | **awk '{print $1}'** | **sort** > *loglist*   *#added line*

    Or, in NIS:

    set +o *noclobber*
    grpnum=$(**ypcat passwd** | **awk -F:** **'$1** == **"'$1'"** {**print $4}'**)
    ypcat *passwd* | **awk -F:** **'$4** == **'$***grpnum***' {print $1}'** \
    | **sort** > *grplist*   *#added this line and* \ *to above line*
    who | **awk '{print $1}'** | **sort** > *loglist*   *#added line*

3. Run the script, having the shell pass your user name as an argument:

    groupon3 **$USER**

4. List the files in your current directory that have the name *list* in them:

    ls **list**

    The two new files *loglist* and *grplist* are included.

5. Examine each file:

    more *loglist*
    more *grplist*

The *loglist* file contains the names of all users currently logged on. The *grplist* file contains login names for all users who belong to your group or the group of *$USER*.

Examining the Code

Following is an analysis of this new version, ***groupon3***.

COMMAND	INTERPRETATION
set +o *noclobber*	Instructs shell to overwrite existing files if output is redirected to them. If you run the script a second time, the files are updated.

COMMAND	INTERPRETATION
\	The \ at the end of the fourth line tells the shell not to interpret the newline character that follows. The shell accepts this line and the next line from the script as one command line, from **awk** through *grplist*.
sort > *grplist*	The output of **awk** is piped to **sort** and its output placed in a file. This output consists of all system users who are members of the same group. From **sort**, the output is redirected to a new file *grplist*.

A new line follows:

> **who** | **awk** '{print $1}' | *sort* > *loglist*

The components of this line are:

COMMAND	INTERPRETATION
**who	awk**	The output of **who** is passed (piped) to **awk**.
{print $1}	Instruction to **awk** to select only the first field (login).
	sort > *loglist*	The output, consisting of a list of logins of users currently logged on, is sorted and placed in the temporary file, *loglist*.

Locating Group Members Who Are Logged On

The file *loglist* contains a sorted list of all users currently logged on. The file *grplist* contains a sorted list of all users in the same group as the user. With **comm**, we can identify all users logged on and in the selected group.

1. Enter:

> **comm** -12 *grplist loglist* | **more**

The output is all user names that are listed in both files: users who are both logged on and in your group.

COMMAND	INTERPRETATION
comm -12 *grplist loglist*	The **comm** utility compares the two temporary files just created. Entries common to both files (-12) are selected, producing a list of users who are both in the selected group and currently logged on.

We can add this functionality to the script.

2. Copy *groupon3* to *groupon4*.

3. Add the following lines to *groupon4*:

comm -12 *grplist loglist*
rm *grplist loglist*

4. Run the script:

groupon4 $USER | **more**

Using Standard Input
One temporary file can be eliminated by properly reading standard input.

1. Modify the last three lines of *groupon4* to read as follows:

who | **awk** **'{print $1}'** | **sort** \
| **comm** *−12 − grplist*
rm *grplist*

2. Run the script:

groupon4 $USER

3. Run the script with a different login ID argument.

Examining the Code
The change in this version is the addition of a minus sign as an argument to **comm**. The **comm** utility always compares two files. The command previously used was in this form:

```
comm   file1   file2
```

In the *groupon4* command line, no second filename is listed as an argument to **comm**; instead, a minus sign is the first argument, and the second argument is *grplist*. The minus sign is interpreted by **comm** to mean "Read from standard input," which in this case is the output of **sort**. The minus sign included as an argument to **comm** tells **comm** to retrieve information from standard input *as though it were the name of a file located at this place in the command line*. Given this, **comm** compares the following: (1) data supplied from standard input (the output of **sort**) and (2) the data from the filename supplied as an argument on the command line, *grplist*.

Developing a Script That Handles Errors

Some error-checking capability is beneficial to any shell script. Users will regularly make typing errors or enter the wrong data. A script should inform its users when this has occurred and assist them to use it properly.

Modifying the groupon Script

This final version of *groupon* contains three sections inserted at the beginning of the script. The new sections handle error checking and the creation of the correct value for a variable *person* (the login ID to be used for searching). The new variable, *person*, is defined in the error-checking section and passed into the main script, which is the only change to that part of the script.

1. Copy *groupon4* to *groupon5*.
2. Modify the *groupon5* script to include the following:

    #!/bin/bash   *or*   **#!/bin/ksh**
    ############## User enters 2 or more arguments ##############
    if ["$2"]
    then
        cat <<*EOH-A*
           You entered more than one argument. Please enter:
              groupon   *or*   *groupon loginid*
    EOH-A
        exit *1*
    ##############User enters 1 argument ##############
    elif ["*$1*"]
    then
        person=$1
    ##############User enters 0 arguments ##############
    else
        person=$USER
    fi
    ############## Main Program ##############
    echo
    set +o noclobber
    echo *Members of the same group as $person logged on are:*

```
grpnum=$(awk -F: '$1 == "'$person'" {print $4}' /etc/passwd)  #changed
awk -F: '$4 == '$grpnum' {print $1}' /etc/passwd \
| sort > grplist
who | awk '{print $1}' | sort \
| comm -12 - grplist
rm grplist
```

3. Run the program without any arguments.

4. Run the program with your login ID as an argument.

5. Run the program with a different login ID as an argument.

6. Run the program giving two legal login IDs as arguments.

Examining Multiple- and Single-Argument Code

The first section added is:

```
##############User enters 2 or more arguments #############
if [ "$2" ]
then
    cat <<EOH-A
        You entered more than one argument. Please enter:
            groupon    or  groupon loginid
EOH-A
    exit 1
```

As the comment line indicates, this section of the script responds to an incorrect number of inputs. The script is designed to accept only one argument or no arguments, and if two or more are entered, the script displays an error message, as well as examples of correct input. If a user enters three arguments, this error code captures the error. (If a person enters three arguments, it is also true that they entered two.)

COMMAND	INTERPRETATION
if ["$2"]	If there is a second command-line argument, the variable $2 is set equal to that argument. If the variable 2 exists, the **test** statement enclosed in brackets ["$2"] evaluates as true and indicates the existence of an illegal second argument.

COMMAND	INTERPRETATION
cat<<EOH-A	Marks the beginning of the *here document* that contains the error message and correcting prompts. This message is displayed if the preceding line evaluates as true.
EOH-A	The *EOH-A* that follows the message text is *not* indented because it marks the end of the *here document*.
exit *1*	Exits the script with the status set to the value 1. Recall that **0** is a successful exit status. Setting the exit status to **1** specifies that the script processed an error.

Setting the Variable for Login ID to the User

The next section of code is:

```
############## User enters 0 arguments ##############
else
    person=$USER
fi
```

This section runs when the script is given no arguments on the command line. No error checking is needed in this case because the current user's login ID is always available as a default argument. Accordingly, the variable *person* is set to the user's login ID.

Checking for Invalid Login Name

What happens when a login name for a user is entered, and the name is not valid?

1. Try executing the script by providing an illegal login name like *sickbird* (a user that does not exist).

    groupon5 *sickbird*

2. Copy *groupon5* to *groupon*:

    cp *groupon5 groupon*

3. Modify the code for error checking of one argument as follows:

    ```
    ################## User enters 1 argument ######
    elif [ "$1" ]
    then
    ```

```
              person=$1
              grep "^$person": /etc/passwd >> /dev/null
              if [ $? -ne 0 ]
              then
                  cat <<EOH-B
                The login id you requested does not exist.
                Please use a valid id.
      EOH-B
                  exit 2
          fi
```

4. Run the script with real and fictitious user names.

Examining the Code

When the user inputs a single argument (the correct number), but the input is not a legal login ID, this code processes the error by displaying the appropriate message. The correct input for this script has a very specific attribute, and this error section looks for that attribute.

COMMAND	INTERPRETATION
grep "^$person": /etc/passwd	The shell interprets the variable *person* replacing $*person* with its value. The argument passed to **grep** is like the ^*cassy:* string. To **grep** this is instruction to output lines containing the variable's value only when it is at the beginning of a line and is followed immediately by a colon in password data. All logins in the password data are at the beginning of a line and followed by a colon. If the string the user entered is not found at the beginning of a line, it is not a login ID. The colon makes the match exact.
>> /dev/null	Because **grep** is used here only to test for correct input, its output need not be displayed or stored in a readable file. Given this, the file named **/dev/null** becomes the destination of **grep** output. This special file serves as a system wastebasket and incinerator. Output sent there is never seen again. The **>>** is instruction to add to an existing file, in case you have **noclobber** set.

COMMAND	INTERPRETATION
if [$? -ne 0]	This **if** statement checks the exit status of the previous **grep**. The **?** is a shell variable set to the exit status of the previous command that was run. If **grep** finds matching lines, it exits with a status of **0**. Otherwise, it exits with nonzero, indicating an error condition. If the login entered is not a valid name, an error message is printed. If the status is zero, then the login is valid, and the related error section that follows is skipped.
cat <<_EOH-B_	The _here document_ is used to print the error message if it is true that the exit code from **grep** is not equal to **0**.
exit 2	Instructs the shell running the script to exit the script with the status of **2**. Because the script did not finish successfully, the status it reports to your interactive shell is not **0**.

The Main Section of groupon

If the user enters two or more arguments, the error section of the code (prior to the main section) displays an error message. If the user enters one argument, the variable _person_ is set to the value of the argument and tested. If the user enters no argument, the variable _person_ is set to the user's login ID. In the latter two cases, the main section of the program is given a value for _person_. It instructs **awk** to look for password records that have the first field matching the value of the variable _person_. The main program now completes the processing, searching for the group ID number, other members of the group, users currently logged on, and ultimately the set of members of the selected group who are currently logged on. A complete copy of the script is listed at the end of the chapter.

19.3 Creating a Complex Script for Project Management

This last program is developed in the usual incremental fashion, leading to a script that reads a file and outputs a report on the status of projects.

Managing Work with a Staff

When a group of people work on a project together, each takes on responsibilities. Success is often determined by how well someone keeps track of the tasks, the people, and whether tasks are completed. The script developed in this section outputs a list of unfinished tasks and updates a file with tasks completed or still under way.

Creating Data Files

The following two files consist of minimal data about the staff members working on a book and a series of tasks that are under way. When developing an application, the data files should be just large enough to demonstrate the functionality of the program and short enough to not overwhelm. After the application is completed, more data can be added.

1. With **vi**, create a file named *staff* with the following content. The fields are separated by a colon.

   File: *staff*

   ```
   +ID:  First   and   Last
   ic:Isaac   Chellin
   jm:John   Muster
   nh:Nate   Hinerman
   ```

   This file consists of two fields of data separated by a colon: the two-character unique ID for each staff member and their name.

2. Create a file named *tasks* with the following contents. The fields are separated by a colon.

   File: *tasks*

   ```
   +ID: Tasks to do  : completed
   jm:plan   chapter layout:x
   ic:complete   illustrations   util2:
   nh:convert   old   format   to   new:x
   nh:integrate   edits   1:
   jm:edit   version1:
   ic:devise   illustration   format:x
   jm:complete   integration   of   graphics:x
   nh:fine   detail   edit:
   ```

   This file consists of three fields (one might be empty) separated by colons: the staff member ID, the project description, and an *x* if the project is completed.

Planning the Script Development

The goal is to write a script that tells us what tasks are assigned to each person and what tasks are not finished. To accomplish that goal, we need to prepare the data for **join**, join the files, and modify the resulting joined data to produce the desired output.

The way to attack a problem like this is through planning and incremental development. If we try to accomplish the whole thing at one time, it leads to frustration and hours of debugging.

The Plan:

1. Sort each file on its join field and join the two sorted files.
2. Output only needed fields from **join**.
3. **Sort** the output from **join** on the last name.
4. Format the output.
5. Use **tee** to output one version to file and the other to screen.

Creating an Initial Script That Sorts and Joins Data

1. With the visual editor, create a script named *work1* with the following contents:

   ```
   echo
   sort staff > staff.s
   sort tasks > tasks.s
   echo FILE: staff.s
   cat staff.s
   echo
   echo FILE: tasks.s
   cat tasks.s
   echo
   echo JOINED:
   join -t: staff.s tasks.s
   rm tasks.s staff.s
   ```

2. Make the file executable:

   ```
   chmod +x work1
   ```

3. Enter the following:

   ```
   locale
   ```

4. If your standard is not POSIX, do the following:

    export LC_ALL="POSIX"

5. Execute the script:

    work1 **|** **more**

Each file is displayed and the results of **join** follow. The records are joined on the sorted first field, the ID of the staff member.

Examining the Code

COMMAND	INTERPRETATION
echo	A blank line is sent to output, the screen.
sort *staff* **>** *staff.s*	This line instructs the shell to pass one argument to **sort** and to connect its output to the file *staff.s*. If we add new employees, we can add them anywhere in the file because the file's lines will be sorted every time the script is run.
sort *tasks* **>** *tasks.s*	The data from the file *tasks* is sorted and written to a new, temporary *tasks.s* file.
echo *FILE: staff.s*	The arguments *FILE:* and *staff.s* are passed to **echo**, which writes them to output, the screen.
cat *staff.s*	The **cat** utility reads the sorted *staff.s* file and writes it to output.
echo *FILE: tasks.s*	Dsplays *FILE: tasks.s*.
cat *tasks.s*	The *tasks.s* file is read and written to the screen by **cat**.
echo *JOINED:*	Output the string *JOINED*.
join -t: *staff.s tasks.s*	In this line, **join** is given three arguments.
-t:	Instruction to **join** to use the colon as the field separator when it reads the input files.
staff.s	File to read for input data.
tasks.s	Second file to read.
	Thus, **join** reads the data from the two files, *staff.s* and *tasks.s*, interpreting the colon as the field separator. If the value in the first field (staff member ID) of a record from the file *staff.s* matches the value in the first field of a record in the second file *tasks.s*, **join** outputs both lines together as one line.
rm *tasks.s staff.s*	After the joined, sorted files are displayed, the temporary files are removed. The output is the names, IDs, tasks, and completion status for each staff member.

Selecting Specific Fields to Output

1. Copy *work1* to *work2* and modify the **join** line to be:

   join -t: -o *1.2 2.2 2.3 staff.s tasks.s*

   Because you copied *work1* to *work2*, the permissions on *work2* should include execute.

2. Run the script:

   work2 | more

   The join line is modified to instruct **join** to just output three fields.

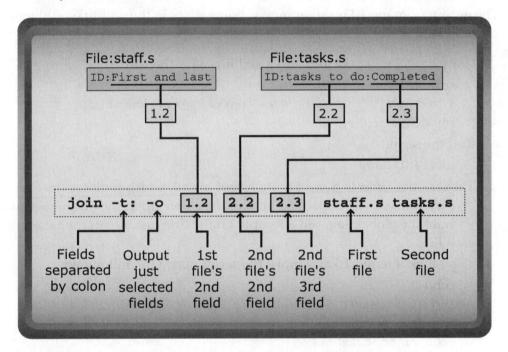

Sorting by Last Name and Completed Fields

Although the data is properly joined, the output is not sorted in a useful way.

1. Copy *work2* to *work3* and remove the last three lines of *work3*. Then, add the following four lines to the end of *work3*:

   echo *SORTED joined:*
   join -t: -o *1.2 2.2 2.3 staff.s tasks.s* \
   | **sort -t: +0 -1 +2 -3**
   rm *tasks.s staff.s*

2. Run the script:

work3 | more

The output of **sort** is displayed on the screen last, and the data is sorted based on staff members' names and then status of completion. When **join** outputs the joined data, it only outputs three fields: Name, Task, and Status. The arguments to **sort** instruct it to sort on the first field of its input, *Name*, and then on completion status, field 3.

Formatting the Output

The output from *work3* is rather messy. Some space in the output would make it easier to read.

1. Copy *work3* to *work4* and add a **sed** line after the **sort**:

```
sort -t: +0 -1 +2 -3 \
| sed 's/:/     /'          # <--- this is 5 spaces   line added
rm  tasks.s  staff.s
```

2. Run the script:

work4 | more

The output of **sort** is passed to the input of **sed**, which replaces the first : on each line with five spaces. There is one colon left in the output because without the global flag, **sed** acts only on the first instance of the target on each line.

3. Copy *work4* to *work5* and make the script match the following:

```
echo
sort  staff  >  staff.s
sort  tasks  >  tasks.s
echo  FILE: staff.s
cat  staff.s
echo  FILE: tasks.s
cat  tasks.s
echo
echo  JOINED:
join -t: -o 1.2 2.2 2.3  staff.s  tasks.s \
| sort -t: +0 -1 +2 -3 \          #This slash is new#
```

```
| sed 's/:/    /' \
| sed 's/:x/    **COMPLETED**/'    #<--- 3 spaces in replacement string
rm tasks.s staff.s
```

4. Run the script:

```
work5 | more
```

This version passes the output from **sed** to another process running **sed**, which replaces the string *:x* with three spaces and ***COMPLETED*** on the line. When this **sed** receives input, only one colon is on each line. If there is an *x* following the colon, the task is completed. If not, there is more work to be done. Only completed tasks are labeled.

Writing Output to a File and the Screen

In the last version, the output is displayed, but is not saved in a file. The intermediate versions are cluttering up the output.

1. Copy *work5* to *work6* and make the script match the following:

```
echo
sort staff > staff.s
sort tasks > tasks.s
join -t: -o 1.2 2.2 2.3 staff.s tasks.s \
| sort -t: +0 -1 +2 -3 \
| sed 's/:/    /' \
| sed 's/:x/    **COMPLETED**/' \ #modified
| tee all.tasks | grep -v '**CO' #added
rm tasks.s staff.s
```

2. Run the script:

```
work6 | more
more all.tasks
```

The list of tasks not completed is displayed on the screen; a complete list is written to the file *all.tasks* in the current directory. The **tee** utility reads all lines of output from **sed**, writes each to output, and saves a copy of each in a memory buffer. The output of **tee** is redirected to **grep**, and the buffer copy is written to the new *all.tasks* file. The arguments to **grep** instruct it to look for lines containing the target ***CO*, and then to output all lines that do not match, namely the uncompleted tasks.

Adding Data to the Files

The application works with limited data, which demonstrates its functionality. To examine its power, add more data.

1. Add more staff members to the *staff* file:

   ```
   jk:June  Kim
   jl:Jay  Lee
   km:Kevin  McKay
   mc:Marcelo  Carvalho
   ms:Marcelo  Santiago
   yg:Yvan  Go
   nm:Nathan  Moy
   sk:Sunggak  Kim
   jh:Johan Hadiwijaya
   ```

2. Add yourself and a friend to our staff.

3. Add the following to the *tasks* file:

   ```
   jm:plan  chapterlayout:x
   ic:complete  illustrations  util2:x
   nh:convert  old  format  to  new:x
   nh:integrate  edits  1:x
   nh:integrate  edits  2:
   jm:write  new  materials:x
   yg:review ch20:x
   jm:edit  version1:
   jk:check  error  list:
   ms:establish  net  between  nh and  jm:x
   nm:revise  questions:x
   mc:review all  chapter  errors:
   ic:devise  illustration  format:x
   jm:complete  integration  of  graphics:x
   nh:fine  detail  edit:
   sk:devise  new  reviews  utils2:
   sk:create  ascii  table:x
   nh:convert  graphics  listings:
   jh:check awk:x
   ```

4. Give yourself and your friend some tasks.

5. Run the script using the complete data:

   > *work6* | **more**
   > **more** *all.tasks*

   When the script is executed, it outputs a list of tasks still under way and updates the master file of all tasks.

Creating Scripts by Planning and Incremental Development

In these examples, we did most of the planning and then guided your development of the scripts in an incremental fashion. When you made an error, it was fairly easy to locate because the error had to be related to the new code you entered.

There are distinct advantages to this approach. First, making an initial plan, even though it is modified during execution, forces us to identify the essential tasks. Second, by building an essential component as one of the first steps, we are successful and moving in the right direction. Once a short fundamental program is working, better ideas concerning how to proceed present themselves, and the quality of the resulting code is higher. Conversely, attempting to develop a complex script or program all at once leads to massive debugging problems, poor design, and frustration. We can't keep that much in our heads at one time.

■ Review

Describe the actions of the following lines in a script:

1. *#!/bin/ksh*

2. *datetime=`date`*

In a Korn shell:
    datetime=$(date)

3. **if ["$3"]**
then
    echo *Three arguments or more*
fi

4. **cat * > /dev/null**

■ Conclusion

This chapter illustrates the development of several practical shell scripts. These programs might be installed on a system to allow users to identify other users of specific groups who are currently logged on, to access phone numbers, and to maintain at least basic information concerning a project. As the scripts were developed through the exercises of the chapter, you observed the addition of features that gave the scripts added flexibility and scope. Alternative methods of accomplishing the tasks were presented. You also employed error-checking routines to verify the correct user input. The major programming features of the **sh** family of shells were examined in this chapter.

   To explore shell programming further, write scripts and read the **man** pages. As you do your work, watch for opportunities to create a basic script that will save time and effort. Start by writing a small part of it. Make this simple part work, and then grow it to accomplish more. The more you ride the bicycle, the better you become. The **man** pages for **bash** and **ksh** contain careful explanations of all features of the shells. Although they are not teaching documents, they are very useful for expanding your knowledge. Having successfully worked through this text to this point, you are more than prepared to attack the manual pages. We suggest you read the **bash** and **ksh** pages carefully. Most important, think of shell programming as Tinkertoys for adults. Have fun.

■ Answers to Review

1. Instruct the current shell to run the current script using a Korn shell.
2. The variable *datetime* is assigned the value from the output of **date**.
3. If the user enters three or more arguments for the script, the string *Three arguments or more* is **echo**ed to the screen.
4. No output. A copy of each file in the current directory is sent to */dev/null*, never to be seen again.

COMMAND SUMMARY

cat << tag   Instructs **cat** to read from file to *tag*.

clear   Clears the screen.

echo -n   Does not add a new line at the end of **echo** output.

echo " \c"   Does not add a new line at the end of echo output.

exit #   Exits the program, giving the shell # exit status.

read *var*   Assigns a new variable *var* to whatever the user enters from keyboard.

Listing for groupon Program

```
#!/bin/bash  or  #!/bin/ksh
############## User enters 2 or more arguments #######
if [ "$2" ]
then
    cat << EOH-A
     You entered more than one argument.
     Please enter:
      groupon
     or
      groupon login_id
EOH-A
  exit 1
############## User enters 1 argument ###############
elif [ "$1" ]
then
  person=$1
```

```
grep  "^$person": /etc/passwd  >>  /dev/null
if [  $?  -ne  0  ]
then
 cat  <<  EOH-B
```
The login id you requested does not exist.
Please use a valid id.
EOH-B

```
    exit 2
    fi
```

############## *User enters 0 argument* ###############
else

```
    person=$USER
fi
```

############## *Main Program* ######
echo
set +o noclobber

echo Members of the same group as $person logged on are:

grpnum=$(awk -F: '$1 == "'$person'" {print $4}' /etc/passwd)

```
awk -F: '$4 ==  '$grpnum' {print $1}'  /etc/passwd  \
 |  sort  >  grplist
```

```
who | awk  '{print $1}' | sort  \
 |  comm  -12  -  grplist
```

rm grplist

Modifying the User Environment

20

U NIX and its grandchild, Linux, were created to provide us with a powerful, very stable, computing environment of great flexibility. The more we explore, the more we realize that the designers, from the beginning, took the approach of making as few *carved in stone* decisions as possible. Rather, they provide tools and structures that permit us to tailor the system and the environment to meet our needs.

The same operating system is driving an order tracking application in an auto parts store and passing web pages to your browser. UNIX/Linux underlies the amazing systems that create special effects in films, transfer money, and handle telephone switching. UNIX/Linux presents engineers with a workspace to write code one minute, then watch an animation, and later access data that appears to be on the same system, but is actually on a server in another building—or another country. Each of these changes takes place by starting a new program or modifying the contents of a file.

By varying the *startup* program in the last field of the *letc/passwd* file, one user is presented with a shell prompt at login, another is connected to a data entry program for a large database application, and another is dropped into a 3-D modeling environment.

As users, we choose from a large variety of options that affect how our environment behaves: Do we want to start an X Window? If so, what GUI? We decide how programs behave: Do we want the editor to include numbers on the screen when editing? Do we want the shell to clobber files? What aliases for command lines would be useful? We simply make requests. When interacting with a program, we can, on the fly, request a modification in the way it works.

Additionally, as many programs are executed, they read startup control files located both in system directories and in home directories. Each of us can put instructions in our control files in our home directories that instruct the various programs to function in specific ways. We can tailor our environment to our needs. Each control file is read by one or more specific programs. To further customize the environment, we can also create personal housekeeping files and request that the shell read them. This chapter explores how we can use files to tailor our environment.

The features you are able to control depend on the shell and version of UNIX you are using, as well as the changes added by the administrator of your system when your account was established. The Korn, Bourne, Bash, and C shells have different capabilities, and there are further differences among shells as they have developed over time. How you employ the initialization files is largely determined by what you want to have happen—what features you want running.

This chapter first guides you through customizing your account. Specific commands and utilities for all shells are examined, with recommendations for where they could be employed. Keyboard customizing concludes the chapter.

20.1 Employing Control Files with the Shells

The following summary of control-file shell process interaction should be viewed as a guide, not a statement of absolute fact. Distributors, authors, and system administrators play with this functionality to achieve their particular goals. We have to explore and react.

System files vary greatly. Because of these variations, you should examine how to customize your login shell first. Each shell has its own functionality, and customizing all the shells at once could prove quite confusing.

Getting the Latest Start-up Files

Because this subject is in flux, we maintain additional information and exercises on this topic at our web site **www.muster.com** in the section on UNIX Made Easy materials.

Customizing the Bourne Shell

The Bourne shell, written by Steve, is the first shell developed for UNIX. When you log in with an **sh**, it reads:

- Login shell reads:
    /etc/profile
    .profile
- Child shells reads:
    None

A child **sh** reads no startup files. The PATH and other important aspects of the shell are passed to child processes through environmental variables from their parent shells.

1. If your login shell is an **sh**, edit the startup file:

    vi *~/.profile*

    Modify or enter:

    PS1='sh $ '
    PS2='-2-sh $ '

2. Modify the *PATH* variable to include the current directory:

    If the *PATH* variable is defined in the file, add a **:.** to the end of it.

    If *PATH* is not defined, request it be modified:

    PATH=$PATH:.

3. After editing, have the **sh** source the *.profile* file to make certain no errors are present:

    . ./.profile

4. Log out and back in.

The *.profile* file is accessed by the **sh** at login. If you want information read by an **sh** login shell to be passed to its child shells, you must establish variables with the values, then export the variables to make them environmental.

Modifying How the ksh Behaves

The Korn shell is one of the improved versions of the Bourne shell. When you start a **ksh**, what it reads to set up the user's environment depends on how it is set up. In its basic form:

- Login shell reads:
    /etc/profile
    ~/.profile
- Child shells reads:
    None

The *.kshrc* is not read unless we instruct the **ksh** to read it.

1. See if a variable named *ENV* is defined in the memory of your **ksh**. Enter:

    echo $ENV

2. If it is not set, add the following to the ~/.*profile* file:

    ENV=~/.kshrc

Now, with the *ENV* variable set to a file, every time a **ksh** is started, it reads the file.

3. Log out and back into the **ksh**.

4. Start a child **ksh**.

The files read by a **ksh** are:

- Login shell with *ENV* set reads:
  /etc/profile
  ~/.profile
  *~/.***kshrc**

- Child shells with *ENV* set reads:
  ~/.**kshrc**

5. Make additional changes to the .*kshrc* file such as:

    set -o *vi*
    set -o *noclobber*
    set -o *ignoreeof*
    PS1='$PWD $ '
    PS2='-2-ksh $ '   *#makes secondary prompt more obvious*
    PATH=$PATH:~/bin:. *#adds bin in home to path*
    . ~/aliases-ksh   *#has shell read aliases file in home directory*

6. Source the .*kshrc* to be certain there are no errors:

    . ./.kshrc

7. Log out and then log back in.

The .*kshrc* specifications take effect.

Customizing the bash Shell

The **bash** shell is a modern **sh** family shell that incorporates many features of both the C and Korn shells. To set up the user's environment, the **bash** shell reads:

- Login shell reads:
  /etc/profile
  /etc/bashrc

~/.*bash_profile* (Usually, if this file does not exist, **bash** reads ~/.*profile*.)
~/.*bashrc*

- Child shells read:

/etc/bashrc
~/.*bashrc*

The login **bash** shells read the system and then the home *profile* and *bashrc* files. Child shells only read the *bashrc* files. Some versions of the **bash** shell read the ~/.*bashrc* file only if the variable *BASH_ENV* is set equal to ~/.*bashrc* as an environmental variable.

1. Add some lines to the ~/.*bashrc* such as:

   set -o *vi*
   set -o *noclobber*
   set -o *ignoreeof*
   PS1='$PWD $ '   #*or any of the other features examined earlier*
   PS2='-2-bash $ '   #*makes secondary prompt more obvious*
   PATH=$PATH:~/bin:.   #*adds bin in home to path*
   . ~/aliases-ksh   #*has shell read aliases file in home directory*

2. Start a **bash** shell and have it source the *.bashrc* file:

   bash
   . ./.bashrc

   Correct any errors.

3. If your login shell is a bash, log out and log back in.

   The new specifications are now in effect.

Tailoring the csh

When a C shell is started, it usually reads the startup files in the following order:

- Login shell reads:

/etc/csh.cshrc
~/.*cshrc*
~/.*login*

- Child shell reads:

  /etc/csh.cshrc

  ~/.cshrc

After reading the system files, the C shell locates the *.cshrc* file in the user's home directory. The *.cshrc* file is read each time a **csh** is started. The *.login* file is only read once when the user logs on, and it is read after the *.cshrc*, allowing us to tailor the login shell differently than the child shells.

1. Edit the *.cshrc* file and add or change the following:

   set *prompt=*'csh % '

   setenv *ENV ~/.kshrc*   *#when you start a child ksh from a csh, it gets ENV*

   source *~/aliases-csh*   *#reads aliases file*

2. If the *path* variable does not include your home directory or a *bin* directory in your home, add them:

   path=($*path ~/bin* .)

3. Edit the *.login* file and add:

   set *prompt=*'login-csh % '

   set *noclobber*

   set *ignoreeof*

4. In a **csh**, source the files to make certain they have no errors:

   source *.cshrc*

   source *.login*

5. Start a child **csh** shell.

   A child shell reads the *.cshrc* file only, so the prompt is set as it is specified in that file. The login shell follows the *.cshrc* by reading the *.login* where the prompt is reset. Each kind of **csh** shell has its own prompt.

6. If the csh is your login shell, log out and back in.

Tailoring the tcsh Shell

The **tcsh** is a C shell with added features. It usually reads the following files:

- Login shell reads:

  /etc/csh.cshrc

  ~/.tcshrc (If this file does not exist, the *.cshrc* is read.)

  ~/.login

- Child shell reads:

    /etc/csh.cshrc (If this file does not exist, the */etc/tcshrc* is read.)

    ~/. tcshrc (If this file does not exist, the *.cshrc* is read.)

Essentially, anything you would do in the *.cshrc* file you can do in the *.tcshrc* file. Additionally, several features of the **tcsh** can be specified:

1. If you have a *.tcshrc* file, add the lines listed earlier for the *.cshrc* file.
2. Add:

    bindkey *-v*   *#instructs shell to use vi commands for editing history list*

20.2 Properly Using the Control Files

The control files facilitate tailoring our environments to a high degree. We must decide what to put in each file to reach your desired goals.

All the shells use shell environmental variables. In the C shell, we must use the **setenv** command. In the **sh** shells, we must create the variable and then use the **export** command to make the variable environmental. Once created, the variables are then available to all child processes including subshells of any type (C, Bourne, Korn, and so on). Keep in mind, though, that some variables, like *CDPATH* in the Korn shell, can be exported to a child C shell and not work. The C shell uses the local variable *cdpath* to provide the directory finding feature.

All the shells use local variables, the value of which are not passed to a subshell. However, by including commands to create local variables in the *.cshrc* or *.kshrc* files, you can ensure that frequently used local variables contain the values you want and will be available to child shells.

Deciding When to Use Each Control File

The way files are read by the shells affects what happens. If you want all C shells to act in a specific way, put the command or set the variable in the *.cshrc* file because it is read by all C shells when they are started.

Users often want the login shell to have information that is not passed on to child shells. Sometimes variables are set to make it easy to change directories to an often-used directory. You can give instruction to a login shell by entering the information as a local variable in the *.profile* file for the Korn shell and the

.login file for the C shell. Because child shells do not read those files, they are not given the information. If you do want the information passed to the child shells, you can put it in the *.cshrc* or *.kshrc* or *.bashrc* files, or use environmental variables in the *.login* or *.profile* files.

The order of reading of the startup files has consequences for users of the shells.

Reading a File of Aliases

We suggest you create two files for aliases and put aliases in each, then include a line like the next one in the startup files:

```
.  ~/.aliases-ksh
```

and

```
.aliases-csh
```

This line in the *.kshrc* and *.bashrc* files is instruction to the shells to read the file *.aliases-ksh* in the home directory. When a **ksh** shell starts, it reads the *.kshrc* file, finding the instruction to also read the *aliases-ksh* file. Likewise, a **bash** shell reads the same *.aliases-ksh* file.

If the following line is in the *.cshrc* file, a **csh** or **tcsh** reads the alias file:

> **source** ~/.aliases-csh

Identifying Other Files Read at Login

One other factor may affect how the shells behave at startup. Your administrator may have included **source** or dot commands in startup files telling the shell to read other files located on your system.

1. Use **more** or **pg** to read through the control files in your home directory, and locate any **source** or dot commands.

On some systems, the C shell has been modified to read a systemwide initialization file, such as *letclcsh.login*. If you have such a file, examine it.

20.3 Tailoring How the Shell Interacts with You

In the previous exercises, we examined which control files are read at startup and which are read when you create child shells. This section examines a variety of commands that you can include in one of the control files to modify how your shell functions.

Using Environmental and Local Shell Variables

Many of the C shell variables mentioned in the following pages will be local variables (lowercase). Because the C shell program reads the *.cshrc* file each time it is started, those local variables set in *.cshrc* are read by child shells. This means that they function virtually as environmental variables. Consequently, the C shell uses these in its operation.

However, the C shell also maintains a number of environmental shell variables (uppercase) of the same name. Since they are environmental variables, they are passed to child Bourne or Korn shells. Additionally, Bourne and Korn shells must have certain variables defined explicitly as environmental variables if they are to be used.

When creating C shell environmental variables, you must use the C shell command **setenv**. However, the format of the value of the variable to be passed must be acceptable to the Bourne or Korn shells (for example, *ENV=~/.kshrc*).

Customizing C Shell History

The C and Korn shells maintain a history list of commands you have issued. Two aspects of the history mechanism are determined by variables that you can set in the run-control files.

We must tell the C shell to record our commands:

1. Include the following in the *~/.cshrc* file:

    set *history=50*

2. We can also request that the shell keep its history record after log off and make it available when we log on. The command is:

    set *savehist=50*

    Setting the *savehist* variable to *50* instructs the shell to save the last *50* commands you used in a file named *.history* when you log off. When you next initiate a C shell, the contents of the *.history* file are included at the beginning of your history list. The *.history* file resides in your home directory. This option is not available on all systems.

Customizing ksh and bash History

Unlike in the C shell, we do not need to set any history variable for the **ksh** and **bash** shells to provide the history facility. The history mechanism is preset to save commands. We can change the number of saved commands by entering a command like the following, from either the command line or in the *.profile* file:

HISTSIZE=50
export HISTSIZE

Requesting Notification When C Shell Jobs Are Completed

We can request the shell to notify us immediately when a background job is completed, rather than waiting until it issues a new prompt. Include the following in a C shell run-control file:

set *notify*

Including File Completion

If the file completion feature of the shells is useful, include the appropriate instruction in the control files.

In the C shell (*.cshrc*):

set *filec*

In the Korn shell (*.profile* or *.kshrc*):

set -o *vi-tabcomplete*

Including a Personalized Prompt

The C shell allows us to have different prompts for login versus all other shells. The Korn shell has a primary prompt and a different secondary prompt for requesting additional information.

Enabling the umask Built-in Command

The value for **umask** masks the owner, group, and other permission fields for each file or directory as you create it. To select a suitable **umask**, refer to Chapter 9, "Setting File and Directory Permissions." The command is the same for both the C and Korn shells and can be included in control files.

20.4 Creating Variables for Shortcuts

The modifications made to the run-control files thus far have changed the ways the shells and utilities work. We can also create entries that are very specific to our needs.

Creating Shell Variables to Save Work

We can create variables that contain pathnames that we frequently use, and then use the variables instead of long pathnames. For instance, if an environmental variable *PSC* is set to *~/Projects/Secret/Code/*, we can enter **cd $PSC**, and we are changed to the targeted directory.

Calling Other Files to Assist

We can create a *.logout* file that is read whenever we log out of the system.
    The C shell automatically looks for a *.logout* file in the home directory when we log out.

   1. Create a *.logout* file in your home directory and put in some useful information that you should see at logout.

Accessing a Reminder File at Login

We can create a file that contains reminders for the day and is automatically displayed when we log on. Have the file read by the shell when it processes either *.login* or *.profile* by including:

   source *~/.reminder_file*

or

   . *~/.reminder_file*

20.5 Using stty to Set Input and Output Options on a Terminal

You often modify the terminal display using keys such as BACKSPACE, or signal a program interrupt with CTRL-C. These and other keystroke bindings can be changed through the use of the **stty** utility. This feature of UNIX is particularly useful in situations where you are familiar with one keyboard configuration, but must work on another.

Setting Terminal Control Characters

You can examine the current terminal settings by typing:

> **stty --all**

or

> **stty -a**

The output of this command contains lines similar to the following:

```
erase kill werase rprnt flush lnext susp  intr quit stop  eof
^H    ^U   ^W     ^R    ^O    ^V    ^Z/^Y ^C   ^\   ^S/^Q ^D
```

or

```
speed 1200 baud; line = 1; intr=DEL; quit = ^|; erase = ^h;
kill = @; eof = ^d; eol = ^'; swtch = ^'
```

Depending on your system, you will see a number of special commands to the terminal and the characters that are bound to those commands. It is possible to remap the commands to any key that you wish. In the following exercises, you will rebind keys in some rather strange ways, but when you log out and log back on, the original bindings take effect.

One of the commands is the *erase* command. This **^h** or **^H** (case insensitive) command erases the character to the left of the cursor and is usually mapped to the BACKSPACE key on your keyboard.

1. The next three commands set the keys using the **stty** command:
    > **stty** *erase* CTRL-H
    > **stty** *intr* CTRL-C
    > **stty** *eof* CTRL-D

2. If you modify normal terminal command keys to rather unusual settings, set them back to more normal keystrokes by either logging off and back on again, or on some systems, typing:
    > **stty** *sane*

The **stty** program gives us control over fundamental aspects of the keyboard. If you are on a computer using another operating system and accessing UNIX or Linux across the Net, you may have to modify how the keyboard functions because some other systems trap signals that are essential to UNIX.

■ Review

1. You set *filec* in your *.login* file. You unset it in your *.cshrc* file. Is it on in your login shell? Is it on in your child C shells?

    _____

2. What do you put in your *.profile* file so that your *.kshrc* file is read each time you start a Korn shell?

    _____

3. In which file would you place all assignments of (a) environmental variables and (b) local variables in the C shell? In the Korn shell?

    _____

    _____

4. In the C shell, what command would you use to have the shell reread the *.login* file immediately? What command would you use to have the Korn shell read *.profile* immediately?

    _____

5. What do you enter to enable the file completion feature in the C shell? The Korn shell?

    _____

■ Conclusion

In this chapter, you have been customizing many aspects of your user environment. You created or modified several initialization files (*.login*, *.profile*, *.cshrc*, *.kshrc*), which makes it possible to customize how the shells and the keyboard work.

One of the strong points of UNIX is the flexibility that users have in setting up their customized environment. Additional information about shell variables can be found in the **man** pages for **sh**, **csh**, and **ksh**.

■ Answers to Review

1. Yes, it is on in your login shell because the login file is read after *.cshrc* during login. No, because only *.cshrc* is read when a child shell is started.

2. ENV ~/.kshrc
   export ENV

3. In the C shell:

   a. *.login*

   b. *.cshrc*

   In the Korn shell:

   a. *.profile*

   b. **.kshrc** *or whatever* **ENV** *is set to*

4. **source** *.login*
   . *.profile*

5. **set** *filec*
   set *-o vi-tabcomplete*

COMMAND SUMMARY

Environmental Shell Variables

PATH Path searched when looking for command issued by user.

SHELL The path and filename of the user login shell.

HISTFILE Korn shell: Sets name for history file used for saving history list when shell exits.

ENV Has the value that is the name of a file where local variables are set and tells shell to read that file each time a Korn shell is started.

PS1 Bourne shell family: Sets prompt variable.

Local Shell Variables

filec C shell: Turns on file completion.

savehist C shell: Instructs shell to store history list when shell exits.

set -o vi Korn shell: Sets type of command-line editor.

set -o vi-tabcomplete Korn shell: File completion.

stty –all Displays various terminal information, for example, baud rate and the characters to be used to perform actions such as deleting characters (BSD).

stty -a Similar to **stty** *--all*.

stty action character Changes the character used to perform various actions, such as deleting a character.

Index

INTERNATIONAL CONTACT INFORMATION

AUSTRALIA
McGraw-Hill Book Company Australia Pty. Ltd.
TEL +61-2-9417-9899
FAX +61-2-9417-5687
http://www.mcgraw-hill.com.au
books-it_sydney@mcgraw-hill.com

CANADA
McGraw-Hill Ryerson Ltd.
TEL +905-430-5000
FAX +905-430-5020
http://www.mcgrawhill.ca

**GREECE, MIDDLE EAST,
NORTHERN AFRICA**
McGraw-Hill Hellas
TEL +30-1-656-0990-3-4
FAX +30-1-654-5525

MEXICO (Also serving Latin America)
McGraw-Hill Interamericana Editores S.A. de C.V.
TEL +525-117-1583
FAX +525-117-1589
http://www.mcgraw-hill.com.mx
fernando_castellanos@mcgraw-hill.com

SINGAPORE (Serving Asia)
McGraw-Hill Book Company
TEL +65-863-1580
FAX +65-862-3354
http://www.mcgraw-hill.com.sg
mghasia@mcgraw-hill.com

SOUTH AFRICA
McGraw-Hill South Africa
TEL +27-11-622-7512
FAX +27-11-622-9045
robyn_swanepoel@mcgraw-hill.com

**UNITED KINGDOM & EUROPE
(Excluding Southern Europe)**
McGraw-Hill Education Europe
TEL +44-1-628-502500
FAX +44-1-628-770224
http://www.mcgraw-hill.co.uk
computing_neurope@mcgraw-hill.com

ALL OTHER INQUIRIES Contact:
Osborne/McGraw-Hill
TEL +1-510-549-6600
FAX +1-510-883-7600
http://www.osborne.com
omg_international@mcgraw-hill.com

Dad Teaching by Cassy Muster, age 10
dryerase marker on whiteboard

Thank You...

...for teaching yourself Linux/UNIX using the guides and discussions in this text.
Comments and suggestions are welcome and appreciated.

—John Muster
Berkeley, CA

Visit www.muster.com

- Additional Problems and Resources
- Media Demonstrations
- Downloadable Files Used in Exercises in This Book
- Instructor Resources
- Consulting and Teaching Availability
- Links to Useful Sites for Linux/UNIX Professionals

MLA
Box 10164
Berkeley, CA 94709